Essays in International
Litigation and the
Conflict of Laws

Essays in International Litigation and the Conflict of Laws

LAWRENCE COLLINS LL.D. (Cantab.),
LL.M. (Columbia Univ.), F.B.A

*Solicitor, London; Fellow, Wolfson College, Cambridge;
Visiting Professor, Queen Mary and Westfield College, London;
Member, Institut de Droit International*

CLARENDON PRESS · OXFORD

Oxford University Press, Great Clarendon Street, Oxford OX2 6DP

Oxford New York

Athens Auckland Bangkok Bogota Bombay
Buenos Aires Calcutta Cape Town Dar es Salaam
Delhi Florence Hong Kong Istanbul Karachi
Kuala Lumpur Madras Madrid Melbourne
Mexico City Nairobi Paris Singapore
Taipei Tokyo Toronto
and associated companies in
Berlin Ibadan

Oxford is a trade mark of Oxford University Press

Published in the United States
by Oxford University Press Inc., New York

© *Lawrence Collins 1994*

First published 1994
First issued in paperback with corrections 1996

British Library Cataloguing in Publication Data
Data available

Library of Congress Cataloging in Publication Data
Collins, Lawrence (Lawrence Antony)
Essays in international litigation and the conflict of laws/
Lawrence Collins.
p. cm.
1. Civil procedure (International law) 2. Arbitration and award.
International. 3. Conflict of laws. I. Title.
KF7615.6.C65 1993
341.5'5—dc20 93–15686
ISBN 0–19–825732–5
ISBN 0–19–826566–2 (Pbk)

Printed in Great Britain on acid-free paper by
Bookcraft (Bath) Ltd, Midsomer Norton, Avon

CONTENTS

PREFACE

The differentiation between international litigation and the conflict of laws in the title of this collection is intended to convey the point that the majority (in size and number) of the pieces included deal with topics of great practical importance which have not traditionally been treated fully in the texts on the conflict of laws or private international law. This is particularly so in relation to the contributions on provisional and protective measures (including that on the extra-territorial reach of *Mareva* injunctions), to those on forum selection, *forum non conveniens* and actions for negative declarations, and to those on the obtaining of evidence abroad (including the problem of blocking statutes intended to prevent evidence being obtained). Even the contributions on choice of law deal with issues which are (or were when they were written) comparatively neglected, and which remain of contemporary relevance.

Not only has international (or transnational) litigation increased enormously in practice, but in recent years it has attracted more scholarly interest than it did when this author first began to write on the subject. The pieces collected in this volume were written over twenty five years, most of which have been spent in the practice of litigation with an international element. Inevitably, interest in some of these topics was sparked, or increased, by professional involvement in cases. It has not been possible, or desirable, altogether to exclude consideration of decisions in cases in which I have been professionally involved, but the temptation, which is sometimes great, to enter into detailed criticism of such decisions has been avoided. To praise those which were won would be unseemly trumpet blowing, and to criticise those which were lost would smack of sour grapes. The contributions are re-printed substantially as originally published, and an introductory note has been added to each of them, in order to report on more recent developments. The pace of change in the subject is such that this is so even in relation to the pieces which were published in recent years.

I have benefited much over the years from contact with scholars, practitioners and judges, but there are three late colleagues whom I should especially acknowledge. The first is Profesor Clive Parry, of Downing College, Cambridge, who taught me between 1960 and 1964 and who, with his extraordinary imagination and originality, gave me an interest in international law which I have not lost. The second is Dr. F. A. Mann, to whose firm I was introduced by Clive Parry (a firm in which I have been a partner since 1971), who showed me how it is possible to be both a practitioner and a scholar without compromise in either capacity, and with whom I had a close personal and professional relationship, from the day in 1966 (my first day as an articled clerk at Herbert Smith & Co.) in which he introduced me to the *Barcelona Traction* case team until his death in 1991. The third is Dr. J. H. C. Morris, who wrote to me in 1975 inviting me to meet him in Oxford for 'more than a friendly chat', thus beginning an immensely stimulating and rewarding involvement in Dicey and Morris on *The Conflict of Laws*.

Acknowledgement is gratefully given, for permission to re-publish contributions, to the Curatorium of the Hague Academy of International Law, and to the editors of the Law Quarterly Review, the International and Comparative Law Quarterly, and the Journal of Business Law. Thanks are also due to Gillian Spiers for assistance with proof-reading.

This collection is dedicated to my wife, Sara, and my children, Hannah and Aaron, and to the memory of my parents, Phoebe and Sol Collins, of Cricklewood.

Lawrence Collins
July 1, 1993

TABLE OF CASES

Page numbers in bold type refer to where the case is mentioned in the text, page numbers in normal type refer to where the case is mentioned in the footnotes.

United Nations Tribunal in Libya

United States

TABLE OF CONVENTIONS
AND TREATIES

Page numbers in bold type refer to where the case is mentioned in the text, page numbers in normal type refer to where the case is mentioned in the footnotes.

TABLE OF LEGISLATION

Page numbers in bold type refer to where a law is mentioned in the text, page numbers in normal type refer to where a law is mentioned in the footnotes.

I

Provisional and Protective Measures in International Litigation

1

Provisional and Protective Measures in International Litigation

This is the text of a series of lectures delivered at the Hague Academy of International Law in 1991. The lectures were delivered in that part of the programme of the Academy which is primarily devoted to private international law. But the lectures are not limited to that field, particularly because research into related problems in public international law and European law revealed some interesting parallels.

The lectures developed some ideas first discussed in an article entitled 'Provisional Measures, the Conflict of Laws and the Brussels Convention' in (1981) 1 Yb. Eur. L. 249. Today the subject is of even greater importance. The enormous cost of litigation has made trials of disputes often prohibitively expensive. Pre-emptive remedies frequently have a decisive effect on the outcome of litigation, and that is one of the reasons for a shift in focus from final trials to interlocutory proceedings. But these developments have received little systematic attention. Considerable attention has in the past been devoted to two topics (the availability of provisional remedies in the courts in aid of arbitration; and interim measures in the International Court of Justice), and this contribution was intended to be a first step to a more comprehensive and comparative treatment of a very important subject.

The topical importance of the subject is underlined by the fact that there have been several significant developments since these lectures were revised in 1992 for publication in the *Recueil des cours* of the Hague Academy of International Law.

Section III (pp. 30–34) is critical of the decision of the House of Lords in *The Siskina* [1979] AC 210 that the English court did not have jurisdiction to grant a *Mareva* injunction in relation to assets in England if the substance of the dispute was to be tried abroad; and Section V (pp. 66–67) is critical of the suggestions in the Court of Appeal in the *Nissan* and *Channel Tunnel* cases that it follows from *The Siskina* that the English court has no jurisdiction (or should in its discretion not exercise its jurisdiction) to grant an interlocutory injunction against a defendant subject to the *in personam* jurisdiction in a case where the parties have agreed to arbitration outside England.

In January 1993 the House of Lords affirmed the decision of the Court of Appeal in the *Channel Tunnel* case, but in reasoning which is likely to be a major step in the destruction of *The Siskina* as an authoritative decision: *Channel Tunnel Group Ltd.* v. *Balfour Beatty Construction Ltd.* [1993] 2 WLR 262 (HL). Lord Mustill delivered the leading speech. He did not wish to reconsider the correctness of *The Siskina*, but held that it was not a bar to the grant of an injunction against a defendant who was subject to the *in personam* jurisdiction of the court merely because the parties had agreed to arbitration abroad. The court therefore had jurisdiction to grant an injunction in such a case, but it would not be granted in the circumstances: this was so particularly because the relief sought would pre-empt the decision of the arbitration tribunal and because the courts in Belgium (where the arbitration was to be held) were the natural forum for interim relief. But Lord Browne-Wilkinson (with whom Lord Keith and Lord Goff of Chieveley agreed) went considerably further in casting doubt on *The Siskina*. Not only did he agree that *The Siskina* did not preclude relief where the defendant was subject to the *in personam* jurisdiction merely because the parties had agreed to arbitration abroad, he also added his agreement to the view expressed by Lord Goff of Chieveley (with whom Lord Mackay of Clashfern agreed) in *South Carolina Insurance Co.* v. *Assurantie Maatschappij 'de Zeven Provincien' NV* [1987] AC 24, 44, that the power of the court to grant injunctions is not restricted to certain exclusive categories. It is, therefore, suggested that the authority of *The Siskina* is seriously weakened by this decision. In *The Veracruz I* [1992] 1 Lloyd's Rep. 353 (CA) (followed in *The P.* [1992] 1 Lloyd's Rep. 470 and in *Zucker* v. *Tyndall Holdings plc* [1992] 1 WLR 112 (CA)) it was held that the court had no jurisdiction to grant a *Mareva* injunction in favour of a buyer against the seller of a ship which was about to be delivered (but had not been delivered) in a state which was not in conformity with the contract of sale. This decision was based on the view that *The Siskina* was authority for the proposition that an injunction could only be granted in aid of a *pre-existing* cause of action (see Collins, 'The Legacy of The Siskina' (1992) 108 LQR 175) and, it is suggested, it should not survive scrutiny if the House of Lords is called on to review it.

A second major development relates to the criticism in Section III (pp. 38–39) of the extended interpretation, adopted especially by the French courts, of the meaning of provisional or protective measures for the purposes of Article 24 of the Brussels Convention. The French courts have held that they are entitled to award provisional damages even if the substance of the dispute belongs to the courts of another country, and it is suggested in Section III that the expression should not be interpreted by the *lex fori* or the *lex causae* but according to an autonomous Convention interpretation. In Case C-261/90 *Reichert* v. *Dresdner Bank (No. 2)* [1992] IL Pr. 404 the European Court confirmed that Article 24 is to be given an autonomous interpretation: 'provisional or protective measures' are to be understood as meaning measures which are 'intended to maintain a legal or factual situation in order to safeguard rights an application for the recognition of which has been made to the court with jurisdiction as to the substance of the matter' (p. 426). It should follow from this decision that orders for interim payments are not within the scope of Article 24.

Thirdly, the House of Lords has, in *Kirklees Metropolitan Borough Council* v. *Wickes Building Supplies Ltd.* [1992] 3 WLR 170, reversed the decision of the Court of Appeal criticised, *post*, pp. 167–168. The House of Lords held that where a public authority (including a local authority) brings a law enforcement action, in which an interlocutory injunction is sought, the court has a discretion not to require a cross-undertaking in damages. The local authority was exercising a law enforcement function, and it was under a duty to enforce the law under the Shops Act 1950. Proceedings for an injunction were in practice the only proceedings by which the law could effectively be enforced, and the judge was therefore entitled to dispense with the cross-undertakings in damages. The mere fact that the store might have a Community law defence based on Article 30 of the EEC Treaty did not compel the court to require an undertaking in damages, because if the European Court were to hold that United Kingdom law were in conflict with Article 30 of the EEC Treaty, the United Kingdom Government would be under an obligation to compensate any damage caused to private parties. In so holding, Lord Goff of Chieveley doubted (in the light of subsequent developments in the European Court) the majority decision of the Court of Appeal in *Bourgoin SA* v. *Ministry of Agriculture, Fisheries and Food* [1986] QB 716 that a breach of Article 30 would not give rise to a right to damages. The actions of the local authorities were subsequently vindicated when the European Court held that the restrictive effects on trade of national rules prohibiting shops from opening on Sundays were not excessive or disproportionate: Case C-169/91 *Stoke-on-Trent Council* v. *B & Q plc* [1993] 2 WLR 730.

It should also be noted that in the *1971 Montreal Convention Cases* (*Libya* v. *UK*; *Libya* v. *US*) 1992 ICJ Rep., 3, 114 the International Court of Justice refused to order interim measures to enjoin the United Kingdom and the United States from taking action to force Libya to surrender the individuals suspected of complicity in the bombing of the Pan American jumbo which crashed at Lockerbie. The International Court held, by a majority, that Libya's rights under the Montreal Convention to try its own nationals and to arbitrate any disputes thereunder were not appropriate for protection by the indication of interim measures. The reason was that on 31 March 1992 (three days after the close of the hearing) the Security

Council had decided that the Libyan Government was under a duty to comply with a previous Security Council resolution to provide a full and effective response to requests for the surrender of the individuals; the March 1992 resolution called upon all States to act strictly in accordance with it, notwithstanding the existence of any rights or obligations conferred or imposed by any international agreement. In those circumstances any rights granted by the Montreal Convention were superseded, and indeed an indication of the measures requested by Libya would be likely to impair the rights which appeared prima facie to be enjoyed by the respondent States under the Security Council resolution.

I

Provisional and Protective Measures

I. INTRODUCTION

It was only recently that Advocate General Tesauro reminded the European Court of Justice that 'the purpose of interim protection is to achieve that fundamental objective of every legal system, the effectiveness of judicial protection.'[1]

Interim protection [he continued] is intended to prevent so far as possible the damage occasioned by the fact that the establishment and the existence of the right are not fully contemporaneous from prejudicing the effectiveness and the very purpose of establishing the right . . . ,

and he referred to the statement of the German/Polish Mixed Arbitral Tribunal of 1924 that

Par les mesures conservatoires les Tribunaux cherchent à remédier aux lenteurs de la justice, de manière qu'autant que possible l'issue du procès soit la même que s'il pouvait se terminer en un jour.[2]

The purpose of these lectures is to draw attention to some of the most important and topical problems presented by the use and abuse of provisional and protective measures in international litigation. They will draw on private and public international law, on national and comparative law, and on European Community law and administrative law; and on the practice of national courts, and of international and supranational courts and tribunals.

The writer is not aware of any previous study of the subject dealing with this range of material.[3] In the field of private international law in particular, little attention has been given on a systematic basis to the problems discussed in this paper.[4] Since the classic work of Dumbauld in

From *Recueil des cours*, 234 (1992–III), 9.

[1] Case C-213/89 *R* v. *Secretary of State for Transport, ex parte Factortame Ltd.* (*No. 2*) [1991] 1 AC 603, 360.
[2] *Ellermann* v. *État Polonais* (1924) 5 TAM 457, 459.
[3] It is for this reason that he is especially grateful to those friends who generously agreed to read parts of the manuscript: Hazel Fox, Ian Gosling, Horatia Muir Watt and Philippe Trosset.
[4] Some (but by no means all) of the general issues are raised in Collins, 'Provisional Measures, the Conflict of Laws and the Brussels Convention', (1981) 1 Yb. Eur. L. 249; Delaporte, 'Les mesures provisoires et conservatoires en droit international privé', in

1932,[5] the power of the Permanent Court of International Justice and of the International Court of Justice to indicate provisional measures has been the subject of close examination, especially in the last 20 years.[6] This author would not be the first to deprecate a rigid division between the disciplines of private international law and public international law, and research for this paper has revealed some fascinating parallels. For example, it is now well known to those who are familiar with the operation of the Brussels Convention on jurisdiction and the enforcement of judgments of 1968 that Article 24 of the Brussels Convention allows a court which has no jurisdiction over the substance of the case to order provisional and protective measures pending the decision of the court which does have jurisdiction over the substance. It is equally well known that there is a controversy whether an order for an interim payment of damages (*référé-provision*) is a provisional or protective measure within the meaning of Article 24.[7]

What will almost certainly be unknown to most of those private international lawyers is that a very similar question was considered by the Permanent Court of International Justice in the *Chorzów Factory* case in 1927. In its judgment of 1926, the Permanent Court had decided that Poland had acted in breach of the German–Polish Geneva Convention of 1922 concerning Upper Silesia by (*inter alia*) the expropriation of the Chorzów factory.[8] Negotiations for reparations failed, and the German Government brought a new case against Poland claiming compensation for the expropriation. Poland objected that the Permanent Court had no jurisdiction in the second case on the ground that disputes over reparation were not differences relating to the application of the Geneva Convention. The Permanent Court rejected this objection in a passage of which the first sentence will be familiar to all public international lawyers:

It is a principle of international law that the breach of an engagement involves an obligation to make reparation in an adequate form. Reparation therefore is the indispensable complement of a failure to apply a convention and there is no necessity for this to be stated in the convention itself. Differences relating to

Travaux du comité français de droit international privé, 1987–1988, p. 147; Schlosser, 'Co-ordinated Transnational Interaction in Civil Litigation and Arbitration', (1990) 12 *Mich. J. Int. L.* 150. See also Reichert, 'Provisional Remedies in International Litigation: A Comprehensive Bibliography', (1985) *19 Int. L.* 1429, who deals mainly with the public international law material.

[5] Dumbauld, *Interim Measures of Protection in International Controversies* (1932). See also Guggenheim, 'Les mesures conservatoires dans la procédure arbitrale et judiciaire', (1932) *Collected Courses*, Vol. 40, p. 645; Niemeyer, *Einstweilige Verfügungen des Weltgerichtshofs* (1932).

[6] See especially Sztucki, *Interim Measures in the Hague Court* (1983), and other literature cited in Section XIV, *infra*.   [7] See *infra*, Section III.

[8] *Series A, No. 7*, 25 May 1926.

reparations, which may be due by reason of failure to apply a convention, are consequently differences relating to its application.[9]

Germany then made an application for interim measures of protection. It argued that Poland's obligation to make reparation had been established, and that only the upper limits of quantum were in issue. Accordingly it asked the Permanent Court to indicate to Poland a sum to be paid immediately as a provisional measure pending final judgment. Germany made it clear that if the final judgment were less than the amount sought by way of interim protection (30 million Reichsmarks) it would refund the difference. It is possible (if not probable) that the German Government had in mind that the German/Polish Mixed Arbitral Tribunal had decided only three years before that it had power to grant an interim payment as a protective measure.[10]

The Permanent Court refused the request on the ground that its power to indicate measures of interim protection was not a proper basis for the German application. In words which would be just as relevant to the question raised by Article 24 of the Brussels Convention, it said:[11]

. . . the request of the German Government cannot be regarded as relating to the indication of measures of interim protection, but as designed to obtain an interim judgment in favour of a part of the claim . . .

Nor, perhaps, is it widely known among those lawyers who practise in national courts that the European Court of Human Rights in Strasbourg has the power to consider whether judicial measures of interim protection conform to the principles of the European Convention on Human Rights;[12] or that the European Court of Justice in Luxembourg has decided that national courts may in certain circumstances have a duty to provide interim measures of protection.[13]

As these lectures were being delivered, oral argument was being heard in the Peace Palace on Finland's application for interim measures in its action against Denmark in respect of a dispute concerning the passage of oil rigs through one of the straits linking the Baltic to the Kattegat and thence to the North Sea. Finland claimed that the construction of a bridge by Denmark would deny its right of passage, and asked the International Court of Justice to indicate that Denmark should, pending the decision by the International Court on the merits, refrain from continuing with the construction of a bridge over one of the straits and from any other action

---

[9] *Series A, No. 8*, at 21.

[10] *Ellermann* v. *État Polonais* (1924) 5 TAM 457, 459.

[11] *Series A, No. 12*, at 10.

[12] *Chappell* v. *United Kingdom*, 1989, Ser. A, Vol. 152, Section XII, *infra*.

[13] Case C-213/89 *R* v. *Secretary of State for Transport, ex parte Factortame Ltd.* (*No. 2*) [1991] 1 AC 603. See *infra*, Section XIII.

which might prejudice the outcome of the proceedings. The decision on this application is discussed below in Section XIV. In the course of oral argument Denmark argued that it was a general principle of law that a party who obtained interim protection from a court should compensate the other party if it subsequently turned out that the interim protection should never have been granted, and in support of this argument Denmark relied on the procedural law of several countries. The International Court denied the request for interim measures of protection, and therefore did not decide this question. But it is likely that the parties and the Court were not aware that a related question had been considered in a decision of the United States Supreme Court rendered only three weeks before. In *Connecticut* v. *Doehr*[14] four members of the Supreme Court (Justices White, Marshall, Stevens and O'Connor) thought that the due process clause of the United States Constitution required a plaintiff to post a bond or other security to protect the defendant whose property was subject to prejudgment attachment.

2. A GENERAL PRINCIPLE OF LAW?

The interim protection of rights is no doubt one of those general principles of law common to all legal systems, and therefore, to use the language of Article 38 (1) (c) of the Statute of the International Court of Justice (now offensive to some), 'the general principles of law recognized by civilized nations'.[15] As President Jiménez de Aréchaga put it in the *Aegean Sea Continental Shelf* case (*Greece* v. *Turkey*):[16]

The essential object of provisional measures is to ensure that the execution of a future judgment on the merits shall not be frustrated by the actions of one party *pendente lite* . . . According to general principles of law recognized in municipal systems, and to the well-established jurisprudence of this Court, the essential justification for the impatience of a tribunal in granting relief before it has reached a final decision . . . is that the action of one party '*pendente lite*' causes or threatens a damage to the rights of the other, of such a nature that it would not be possible fully to restore those rights, or remedy the infringement thereof, simply by a judgment in its favour.

For present purposes, it is not necessary to do more than outline the types of measure which are available to achieve these objects in every developed legal system. In the modern law the primary function of provisional and protective measures is to preserve the integrity of the final judgment, but there are historical grounds for seeing their origin in the

---

[14] 111 S. Ct. 2105 (1991).   [15] See Dumbauld, *supra* footnote 5, p. 180.
[16] *ICJ Reports 1976*, 3, at 15–16. Cf. the reliance by the UN Tribunal in Libya, in its decision of 18 February 1952, on Italian law: 12 *UNRIAA* 359 at 361.

desire of those administering the law to prevent violent self-help, as in some of the interdicts of Roman law,[17] and the sequestration of the Middle Ages; and this idea survives in such modern codes as the German Code of Civil Procedure, Article 940 of which provides that an application for an injunction may be made in an urgent matter in connection with a disputed legal relationship, if the injunction is necessary 'in order to prevent the use of force or for other reasons'.[18]

There have been attempts to categorize or systematize the range of measures which may be described as provisional or protective,[19] and it will be seen that for certain purposes it is sometimes necessary for a court or arbitral tribunal to determine whether a particular remedy is provisional or protective. Some modern examples of the remedies will be sufficient. There are two types of remedy which are of particular practical importance. First, and perhaps most important, are those remedies which ensure that, pending final determination of a dispute, the status quo will be maintained. In England, this is achieved by the interlocutory injunction, which can be granted by a judge *ex parte*: the equivalent in the United States is the temporary restraining order, followed by the preliminary injunction. The same function is fulfilled in France by the *ordonnance de référé*, which may be made *ex parte* in urgent cases (*sur requête*); in Germany by the *Einstweilige Verfügung*; and in Italy by the *provvedimenti d'urgenza*.[20]

Similar remedies are available in supra-national or international tribunals. Thus the European Court of Justice is empowered to prescribe interim measures on an interlocutory basis,[21] and it has already been seen that the International Court of Justice has, by Article 41 of its Statute, the power to indicate any provisional measures which ought to be taken to preserve the respective rights of either party.

3. THE EXERCISE OF DISCRETION

There is no doubt that the exercise of the power to grant interim protection, whether in a national court or an international or supra-national tribunal, requires a delicate appreciation. The denial of the remedy may prejudice the plaintiff, but its grant may prejudice the defendant. As Hoffmann J. has recently said:[22]

[17] On which see Buckland and McNair, *Roman Law and Common Law* (2nd ed. rev., 1965), pp. 420–423.

[18] See also Elkind, *Interim Protection: A Functional Analysis* (1981), pp. 30–31.

[19] See Knoepfler and Schweizer, 'Les mesures provisoires et l'arbitrage', in *Swiss Essays on International Arbitration* (ed. Reymond and Boucher, 1984), p. 221, at 223–226.

[20] See generally Tarzia (ed.), *Les mesures provisoires en procédure civile* (1985).

[21] EEC Treaty, Arts. 185–186; EEC Statute, Art. 36; Rules of Procedure, Arts. 83 *et seq.*

[22] *Films Rover International Ltd.* v. *Cannon Film Sales Ltd.* [1987] 1 WLR 670, 680.

The principal dilemma about the grant of interlocutory injunctions . . . is that there is by definition a risk that the court may make the 'wrong' decision, in the sense of granting an injunction to a party who fails to establish his right at the trial (or would fail if there was a trial) or alternatively, in failing to grant an injunction to a party who succeeds (or would succeed) at trial. A fundamental principle is therefore that the court should take whichever course appears to carry the lower risk of injustice if it should turn out to have been 'wrong' in the sense I have described. The guidelines for the grant of . . . interlocutory injunctions are derived from this principle.

A second, and very important, function of protective measures is to secure the ultimate judgment of the court by preventing the defendant from disposing of assets pending final determination of the proceedings. This function is closely related to the first when the assets are themselves the subject-matter of the proceedings, but it is not necessary for there to be such a connection.[23] Securing the effectiveness of the ultimate judgment is the function of the *saisie* in France, *arrest* in Germany, *sequestro* in Italy, and the *Mareva* injunction in England.

In France the *saisie conservatoire* is available in support of all civil claims for a money judgment (whether liquidated or not). By Article 48 of the Code of Civil Procedure (ancien):

En cas d'urgence et si le recouvrement de la créance semble en péril, le président du tribunal de grande instance ou le juge d'instance du domicile du débiteur ou dans le ressort duquel sont situés les biens à saisir pourra autoriser tout créancier, justifiant d'une créance paraissant fondée en principe, à saisir conservatoirement les meubles appartenant à son débiteur.

The *saisie-arrêt* is a protective attachment of a third party's debt to the defendant (usually a bank). By Article 557 of the Code of Civil Procedure (ancien):

Tout créancier peut, en vertu de titres authentiques ou privés, saisir-arrêter entre les mains d'un tiers les sommes et effets appartenant à son débiteur, qui ne sont pas des immeubles par nature, ou s'opposer à leur remise.[24]

From 1992 these provisions will be replaced by a new law on *saisie et mesures conservatoires*, which will apply to movable property, tangible or intangible, belonging to a debtor.[25]

When Professor Schlosser, in his report on the 1978 Accession

---

[23] In Italy *sequestro giudiziario* is attachment to ensure that judgment can be satisfied; *sequestro conservativo* is a protective attachment to preserve property in dispute.

[24] Other remedies include *saisie-revendication* (attachment of goods which are subject of action and in hands of third party); *saisie-maritime* (provisional arrest of ship in a maritime action); the protective registration of a charge over the debtor's business (*inscription de nantissement de fonds de commerce*) or real property (*inscription provisoire d'hypothèque judiciaire*).   [25] Law No. 91-650, 9 July, 1991.

Convention to the 1968 Brussels Convention on jurisdiction and the enforcement of judgments in civil or commercial matters, referred to the wide variety of provisional measures available in the United Kingdom,[26] he probably had in mind the great judicial developments in English procedural law since 1975 which have led to three major changes in the English law of protective remedies.

The first was the decision in *American Cyanamid Co. v. Ethicon.*[27] In that case the House of Lords put an end to the practice which had developed of requiring a plaintiff who sought an interim injunction to show that he had a probability of ultimate success at trial, or at any rate a strong prima facie case. The House of Lords decided that the court must merely be satisfied that the claim is not frivolous or vexatious, i.e. that there is a serious question to be tried. Lord Diplock, delivering the only speech, clearly deprecated the practice which had arisen of undertaking a preliminary trial of an action at the stage of proceedings for an interim injunction. The present practice is, at least in theory, that the court does not consider the underlying merits of the action at the stage of the application for an interim injunction, but (once satisfied that there is a serious question to be tried between the parties) concentrates on the issues whether the plaintiff would be adequately compensated by damages after trial (and therefore would not be justified in obtaining an injunction), and, if he would not, whether the balance of convenience requires that an injunction be granted. Where, however, the grant or refusal of the injunction would effectively dispose of the whole action finally in favour of whichever party was successful, then the strength of the plaintiff's case on the merits must be taken into account.[28]

The relevance of the underlying merits at the interlocutory stage is not purely theoretical. Most cases are settled before trial, and a provisional view by the court on the merits expressed at an early stage will usually lead to a settlement.[29] In Germany the merits of the case are taken into account on an application for interim measures. The more credible the case on the merits, the more likely will be the plaintiff to show that interim relief is necessary to preserve the status quo or to prevent significant prejudice (Arts. 935, 940, Code of Civil Procedure). In France the plaintiff has to show a prima facie case, although in cases involving freedom of expression (e.g. privacy cases or actions to prevent publication) a higher test may be required. The regrettable result of Lord Diplock's intervention is that in England the opportunity for the court to ensure a settlement has been lost

---

[26] OJ 1979, C59, para. 183.   [27] [1975] AC 396.

[28] *NWL Ltd. v. Woods* [1979] 1 WLR 1924, 1306 (HL); *Cayne v. Global Natural Resources plc* [1984] 1 WLR 225 (CA); *Lawrence David Ltd. v. Ashton* [1989] ICR 123 (CA); *Lansing Linde Ltd. v. Kerr* [1991] 1 WLR 251 (CA).

[29] *Fellowes & Son v. Fisher* [1976] QB 122, 133 (CA), *per* Lord Denning MR.

in many cases, by departing from the plain and common-sense view that

in considering whether to grant an interlocutory injunction, the right course for a judge is to look at the whole case. He must have regard not only to the strength of the claim but also to the strength of the defence, and then decide what is best to be done.[30]

Or, as it has been put in the United States:[31]

The critical element in determining the test to be applied is the relative hardship to the parties. If the balance of harm tips decidedly toward the plaintiff, then the plaintiff need not show as robust a likelihood of success on the merits as when the balance tips less decidedly.

The second development in England was the form of injunction which has become known as the Anton Piller order, after *Anton Piller KG* v. *Manufacturing Processes Ltd.*[32] This is most frequently made in cases of copyright infringement or passing-off. The order is made by a judge *ex parte* authorizing entry and inspection of the defendant's premises. In the words of Lord Justice Bridge,

to give effective relief to the copyright owners seeking to enforce their legal remedies against the pirates the courts have found it necessary to devise a form of order for what may be called instant discovery granted on ex parte application.[33]

The order does not give authority to the plaintiff or his lawyer to enter the defendant's premises. But the court order requires the defendant to give permission to the plaintiff's lawyers to enter his premises to search for evidence and remove it for safekeeping. The *Anton Piller* order has been a very useful tool in the fight against video-piracy and other forms of copyright infringement, but the abuse of the order has led to much criticism. As Scott J. recently said:[34]

. . . I come back to consider Anton Piller orders and their nature. They stand, as has been said on many occasions, at the extremity of the court's jurisdiction. Some may think that they go beyond it. They involve the court in the hypocrisy of pretending that the entry and search are carried on because the owners of the premises have consented to it. They impose on plaintiffs' solicitors the almost impossible task of describing fairly to non-lawyers the true effect and nature of the orders. They present respondents with orders of great complexity and jurisprudential sophistication and give little time for decisions to be taken as to the response to be made to them. They vest the plaintiffs, one side in what is usually

---

[30] *Hubbard* v. *Vosper* [1972] 2 QB 84, 96, *per* Lord Denning MR.

[31] *Benda* v. *Grand Lodge of International Ass'n of Machinists and Aerospace Workers*, 584 F. 2d 308, 315 (9th Cir. 1978), cert. dismissed 441 US 937 (1979), applied in *Republic of the Philippines* v. *Marcos*, 862 F. 2d 1355, 1372 (9th Cir.), cert. den. 490 US 1035 (1988).

[32] [1976] Ch. 55 (CA): see Denning, *The Due Process of Law* (1980), pp. 123–130.

[33] *Rank Film Distributors* v. *Video Information Centre* [1982] AC 380.

[34] *Bhimji* v. *Chatwani* [1991] 1 All ER 705, 712.

highly contentious litigation, with the trappings of apparent administrative authority to carry out the search. The usual presence of a policeman adds to this illusion.

Indeed, as it will appear below, the nature of the procedure has come under the scrutiny of the European Court of Human Rights.[35]

The third development, and one with major implications for international commerce, is the creation of what has become known as the *Mareva* injunction.[36] The late development of this remedy in effect filled a gap in the English law of procedure caused by the absence of the effective pre-trial attachment of assets found in civil law systems, and also in the United States until its scope was curtailed by the Supreme Court.[37] Lord Donaldson MR recently summarized it:

> ... the Mareva injunction was introduced in the 1970s because the courts held that they must necessarily have jurisdiction and did have jurisdiction to prevent parties to actions frustrating their orders by moving assets out of the jurisdiction, or dissipating assets in one way or another, with a view to making themselves proof against a future judgment.[38]

The *Mareva* injunction is an interlocutory injunction restraining a defendant from removing his assets out of the jurisdiction pending trial. In order to obtain the order, the plaintiff has to show that he has a good arguable case on the merits, that there is real risk that ultimate judgment will be unsatisfied by reason of the disposal of the assets unless the defendant is restrained from disposing of them.[39] The utility of these injunctions has been increased by the granting of ancillary orders for discovery and interrogatories to find out where the assets are.[40]

4. OUTLINE

It is the purpose of these lectures to explore some of the problems which arise in international litigation in connection with these provisional or

---

[35] Section XII, *infra*.

[36] After *Mareva Compania Naviera SA* v. *International Bulkcarriers SA* [1975] 2 Lloyd's Rep. 509: see Dicey and Morris, *Conflict of Laws* (11th ed., 1987), 192–194; Gee, *Mareva Injunctions* (2nd ed., 1990). See further *infra*, Section VIII. 3 and 4. For the position in the United States cf. *Ebsco Industries Inc.* v. *Lilly,* 840 F. 2d 333 (6th Cir.), cert. den. 488 US 825 (1988) (injunctive remedy available in fraud claim).

[37] *Shaffer* v. *Heitner,* 433 US 186 (1977), Section II, *infra*.

[38] *Jet West Ltd.* v. *Haddican* [1992] 2 All ER 545, 547 (CA).

[39] *Third Chandris Shipping Corp.* v. *Unimarine SA* [1979] 1 QB 645 (CA); *Ninemia Maritime Corp.* v. *Trave (The Niedersachsen)* [1983] 1 WLR 1412 (CA); *Derby & Co. Ltd.* v. *Weldon (No. 1)* [1990] Ch. 48 (CA).

[40] *A.* v. *C.* [1981] QB 956; *Bekhor Ltd.* v. *Bilton* [1981] QB 923 (CA); *Derby & Co. Ltd.* v. *Weldon (Nos. 3 & 4)* [1990] Ch. 65 (CA).

protective measures. It is not possible to give an exhaustive account of the possible problems that may arise in international litigation, but this paper will endeavour to consider the following matters:

(a) The relationship between jurisdiction to grant provisional or protective measures and jurisdiction to determine the substantive merits of the dispute between the parties.

(b) Whether it is possible or appropriate to grant these measures, when the proceedings on the substance are continuing in another country.

(c) Whether the jurisdiction to grant these measures is affected by the fact that the parties have agreed to some other method of dispute resolution as the exclusive method, such as a submission to the exclusive jurisdiction of the courts of another country, or the submission of disputes to international arbitration.

(d) Some particular problems which are raised by international arbitration, including the power of courts in the country of arbitration to grant protective measures, the effect of orders of courts in other countries, the power of the arbitrators themselves to order provisional measures, and some special problems which are raised by arbitration under the World Bank Convention, the International Centre for the Settlement of Investment Disputes.

(e) The territorial reach of protective measures, and, in particular, whether they can extend to assets outside the country granting them.

(f) The recognition and enforcement of foreign provisional and protective orders.

(g) The international implications of injunctions to restrain proceedings in other countries, and the implications of these measures in the context of international securities and fraud cases.

(h) The attachment by foreign States of property in the hands of former officials, and the attachment of State property by private plaintiffs.

(i) Human rights and protective measures; especially the limits on the powers of national courts, and the binding character of measures taken by the European Commission on Human Rights.

(j) Protective measures in European Community law, and in particular the powers of the European Court, and the power of national courts to issue interim measures against Community acts; the role of interim measures in references to the European Court under Article 177 of the EEC Treaty, the duty of national courts to provide interim remedies in domestic cases in order to give effect to directly effective, or potentially directly effective, Community law.

(k) Interim measures in international tribunals, particularly in the International Court of Justice.

2

The Relationship between Provisional and Protective Measures and Jurisdiction to Determine the Merits

I. *FORUM ARRESTI* AND *FORUM PATRIMONII*

It has already been seen that the assertion of jurisdiction to attach property is one of the most valuable protective measures. Two important questions arise on the exercise of this jurisdiction. The first is the extent to which the assertion of jurisdiction to attach property itself alone gives jurisdiction to the attaching court to determine the merits of the dispute; and the second question is whether the forum may exercise that jurisdiction even if it recognizes that the substance of the dispute will be determined in another country.

The first question relates to the assumption of jurisdiction over foreigners by the attachment of their property, with (sometimes) the assumption of jurisdiction being limited to the value of the property attached. That is generally described as the *forum arresti*. The expression *forum patrimonii* is used for those systems where the presence of assets is sufficient to justify the assumption of jurisdiction to an unlimited extent.[41] But because the purpose of attachment is frequently to obtain pre-judgment protection for a creditor against a defaulting debtor, there is an overlap between attachment of these kinds and purely provisional or protective measures.

In the United States the *forum arresti* was introduced when the American colonies adopted the process of foreign attachment from England, where its origin was said to be the 'custom of London, under which a creditor might attach money or goods of the defendant either in plaintiff's own hands or in the custody of a third person, by proceedings in the mayor's court or in the sheriff's court': *Ownbey* v. *Morgan*,[42] in which the Supreme Court quoted *Drake on Attachment* (s. 3):

This custom, notwithstanding its local and limited character, was doubtless known to our ancestors, when they sought a new home on the Western continent, and its

---

[41] See Nadelmann, *Conflict of Laws: International and Interstate* (1972), pp. 226–228, 248–249.　　　　　　　　　　　　　　　　　　　[42] 256 US 94, 104 (1921).

essential principle, brought hither by them, has, in varied forms, become incorporated into the legal systems of all our states; . . . Our circumstances as a nation have tended peculiarly to give importance to a remedy of this character. The division of our extended domain into many different states, each limitedly sovereign within its territory, inhabited by a people enjoying unrestrained privilege of transit from place to place in each state, and from state to state; taken in connection with the universal and unexampled expansion of credit, and the prevalent abolishment of imprisonment for debt; would naturally, and of necessity, lead to the establishment, and, as experience has demonstrated, the enlargement and extension, of remedies acting upon the property of debtors.

In *Ownbey* v. *Morgan* the Supreme Court (speaking through Justice Pitney—Justices Holmes and Brandeis, probably the two most distinguished judges in the history of the Supreme Court, were also members of the majority) held that the Delaware rule in foreign attachment cases which conditioned the defendant's right to appear and contest the merits upon his first giving special bail or undertaking, and which had been in force since colonial days and had originated in the custom of London and its counterparts in other states, was not arbitrary and unreasonable and in violation of the due process clause of the United States Constitution. The custom of foreign attachment in the City of London was sometimes said to have been a continuation of the custom in the Roman courts when London was under Roman occupation, but this 'may be dismissed as something out of the realm of legend'.[43] But it is found in England no later than the end of the fifteenth century.[44] It became obsolete when the House of Lords held in 1881 that the process of foreign attachment did not apply where the garnishee was a corporation.[45]

2. UNITED STATES PRACTICE

In 1977 the United States Supreme Court held that the *quasi in rem* procedure was capable of being tested against the 'minimum contacts' approach under the due process clause of the constitution: *Shaffer* v. *Heitner*.[46] The effect of the decision was to remove the mere presence of

---

[43] Millar, *Civil Procedure of the Trial Court in Historical Perspective* (1952), p. 482.

[44] See *Mayor and Aldermen of the City of London* v. *Cox* (1867) LR 2 HL 239, 243; cf. *London Joint Stock Bank* v. *Mayor and Aldermen of the City of London* (1875) 1 CPD 1, 13, affd. (1879–1880) 5 CPD 494; (1881) 6 App. Cas. 393. See Millar, *op. cit., supra* footnote 43, pp. 482–483.

[45] *Mayor and Aldermen of the City of London* v. *London Joint Stock Bank* (1881) 6 App. Cas. 393. But a similar problem in the United States was overcome by legislation: see 256 US at 106. See also Beale, 'The Exercise of Jurisdiction in Rem to Compel Payment of a Debt', (1913) 27 Harv. L. Rev. 107, 112. Cf. Bridge LJ (dissenting) in *The Siskina* [1979] AC 210, 240 (CA).

[46] 433 US 186 (1977). On this decision see Lowenfeld, 'In Search of the Intangible: A Comment on *Shaffer* v. *Heitner*', (1978) 53 NYUL Rev. 102; Symposium (Vernon, Reese,

property as a basis for the assumption of jurisdiction where the property was unrelated to the cause of action. *Shaffer* v. *Heitner* was not a case involving an international dispute, but an inter-state case. It was a shareholders' derivative suit in Delaware in relation to the affairs of Greyhound Corporation, which was incorporated in Delaware but had its principal place of business in Arizona. The action was against Greyhound Corporation and its subsidiary and 28 officers or former officers of the companies. The plaintiff alleged that the defendants had violated their duties to Greyhound Corporation by causing it and its subsidiary to engage in actions that resulted in the corporations being held liable for substantial damages in an anti-trust action and a large fine in criminal contempt action. All of the activities which led to these penalties took place in yet another state of the American Union, Oregon. The plaintiff asserted jurisdiction over the individual defendants (who were all non-residents of Delaware) by attaching the Delaware property of the defendants, which consisted of their shares, or options to purchase shares in the Greyhound Corporation. Under Delaware law (in common with the laws of many countries) the shares were deemed to be situate in Delaware (even though the certificates were not in Delaware). The defendants argued that the *ex parte* attachment was in violation of the United States Constitution, because it did not accord them due process of law and they did not have sufficient contacts with Delaware to sustain the jurisdiction of that state's courts.

The basis of jurisdiction asserted by the Delaware courts was the attachment or seizure of property present in the jurisdiction, not the fact that the defendants were in breach of their duty to a Delaware corporation. In 1878 the United States Supreme Court held in *Pennoyer* v. *Neff*[47] that

the State, through its tribunals, may subject property situated within its limits owned by non-residents to the payment of the demand of its own citizens against them; and the exercise of this jurisdiction in no way infringes upon the sovereignty of the State where the owners are domiciled. Every State owes protection to its own citizens; and, when non-residents deal with them, it is a legitimate and just exercise of authority to hold and appropriate any property owned by such non-residents to satisfy the claims of its citizens. It is in virtue of the State's jurisdiction over the property of the non-resident situated within its limits that its tribunals can inquire into that non-resident's obligations to its own citizens, and the inquiry can then be carried only to the extent necessary to control the disposition of the property. If the non-resident have no property in the State, there is nothing upon which the tribunals can adjudicate.

Sedler), 63 Iowa L. Rev. 991 (1978); Riesenfeld, 30 Hastings LJ 1183 (1978). For a recent discussion of the constitutionality of State attachment statutes see *Connecticut* v. *Doehr*, 111 S. Ct. 2105 (1991).   [47] 95 US 714, 723 (1878).

Attachment in the United States was plainly a form of *forum arresti*. Indeed, as early as 1828 Mr Justice Story said:

Where a party is within a territory, he may justly be subjected to its process, and bound personally by the judgment pronounced on such process against him. Where he is not within such territory, and is not personally subject to its laws, if, on account of his supposed or actual property being within the territory, process by the local laws may, by attachment, go to compel his appearance, and for his default to appear judgment may be pronounced against him, such a judgment must, upon general principles, be deemed only to bind him to the extent of such property, and cannot have the effect of a conclusive judgment in personam, for the plain reason that, except so far as the property is concerned, it is a judgment *coram non judice*.[48]

But, by the middle of the twentieth century, the United States Supreme Court was prepared to apply the due process standard of the Fourteenth Amendment to the exercise of judicial jurisdiction by state courts. In the famous case of *International Shoe Co.* v. *Washington*,[49] the Supreme Court confirmed that, in order to subject a defendant to jurisdiction, if he was not present within the territory of the forum, he must have 'certain minimum contacts with it such that the maintenance of the suit does not offend "traditional notions of fair play and substantial justice" '. In *Shaffer* v. *Heitner* the Supreme Court applied this principle to the exercise of what had come to be called *quasi in rem* jurisdiction, and held that the case for applying to jurisdiction *in rem* the same test of 'fair play and substantial justice' as governed assertions of jurisdiction *in personam* was simple and straightforward. In order to justify an exercise of jurisdiction *in rem*, the basis for jurisdiction must be sufficient to justify exercising jurisdiction over the interests of persons in a thing. The standard for determining whether an exercise of jurisdiction over the interests of persons was consistent with the due process clause was the minimum contacts standard elucidated in *International Shoe Co.* v. *Washington*. The Supreme Court recognized, however, that the presence of property might bear on the existence of jurisdiction by providing contacts among the forum State, the defendant, and the litigation. For example, when claims to the property itself were the source of the underlying controversy between the plaintiff and the defendant, it would be unusual for the state where the property was located not to have jurisdiction, and in such cases, the defendant's claim to property located in the state would normally indicate that he expected to benefit from the state's protection of his interest. Nevertheless

the fiction that an assertion of jurisdiction over property is anything but an assertion of jurisdiction over the owner of the property supports an ancient form

---

[48] *Picquet* v. *Swan,* 5 Mason 35 (1828).   [49] 326 US 310, 316 (1945).

without substantial modern justification. Its continued acceptance would serve only to allow state court jurisdiction that is fundamentally unfair to the defendant.[50]

But the Court did note that the presence of property

suggests that a State in which property is located should have jurisdiction to attach that property, by use of proper procedures, as security for a judgment being sought in a forum where the litigation can be maintained consistently with *International Shoe*.[51]

In fact the assumption of jurisdiction on the facts of the case in *Shaffer* v. *Heitner* seems to have been eminently reasonable. Why should it not have been possible to sue the officers of a Delaware corporation in Delaware for wrongs allegedly done to the corporation and its shareholders? It is true that vast numbers of corporations whose business and administration have nothing to do with Delaware are organized under the corporation law of that state because for reasons of tax and corporate law it is convenient to do so. It was also true, as the majority pointed out, that Delaware law had introduced no jurisdictional rule over non-residents specifically claiming jurisdiction in relation to the operation of the affairs of Delaware corporations. But more convincing than the view of the majority is that of the only dissentient voice in the Supreme Court, Brennan J., who thought that Delaware, as the state of incorporation, had:

an unusually powerful interest in ensuring the availability of a convenient forum for litigating claims involving a possible multiplicity of defendant fiduciaries and for vindicating the state's substantive policies regarding the management of its domestic corporations . . . [The directors] elected to assume powers and to undertake responsibilities wholly derived from that state's rules and regulations, and to become eligible for those benefits that Delaware law makes available to its corporations' officials.[52]

The decision in *Shaffer* v. *Heitner* does not mean, of course, that attachment of property is no longer possible in the United States. In particular, a court in the United States may exercise attachment jurisdiction if the defendant or the cause of action have links with the state in which the court sits such that the exercise of jurisdiction is consistent with due

---

[50] 433 US at 212.
[51] At 210, citing Von Mehren and Trautman, 'Jurisdiction to Adjudicate: A Suggested Analysis', (1966) 79 Harv. L. Rev. 1121, at 1178 who say:

Ultimately, all that should remain of *Pennoyer* v. *Neff, Harris* v. *Balk*, and their progeny is specific jurisdiction to secure assets against dissipation and concealment while a controversy is being litigated in an appropriate forum.

See also Hazard, 'A General Theory of State Court Jurisdiction', (1965) Sup. Ct. Rev. 241, 248–249; Beale, *supra*, footnote 45 at 123–124.
[52] 433 US at 222, 228.

process.[53] As the *Restatement (Second), Judgments* (1982) and *Conflict of Laws* (1988 revisions) recognize, a court may exercise attachment jurisdiction in an action concerning a claim against the owner of the property if (*a*) the court may properly exercise jurisdiction to adjudicate the claim under other heads of jurisdiction, in personam, or *in rem*; (*b*) the action is to enforce a judgment against the owner of the property; (*c*) the action is properly in aid of other proceedings concerning the claim; or (*d*) the exercise of such jurisdiction is otherwise reasonable.[54]

An example of the application of this principle in international litigation is *Papendick* v. *Bosch GmbH*,[55] in which *quasi in rem* jurisdiction was exercised over shares in a Delaware subsidiary of a West German company. The incorporation of the subsidiary was directly connected with the action, and the underlying cause of action was related to the property. In New York at first the spirit of the decision of the Supreme Court was not followed. *Feder* v. *Turkish Airlines*[56] surely abused the *Shaffer* decision by allowing *quasi in rem* jurisdiction over a Turkish airline in relation to an air crash near Istanbul. The Turkish airline was not carrying on business in New York, but it had a bank account at Chase Manhattan in New York, with deposits of approximately $100,000, which it had opened to facilitate the purchase of spare parts.

3. PRACTICE IN EUROPE

The *forum patrimonii* type of jurisdiction is exemplified by Article 23 of the German Code of Civil Procedure, which allows an action *in personam*, not limited in any way by the value of the property, against a defendant without a German domicile in a district where he has assets. This type of jurisdiction is found in several other countries.[57] This jurisdiction, it must

---

[53] *Intermeat Inc.* v. *American Poultry Inc.*, 575 F. 2d 1017 (2d Cir. 1978). The decision of the Supreme Court does not affect maritime attachment: *Amoco Overseas Oil Co.* v. *Compagnie nationale algérienne de navigation*, 605 F. 2d 648 (2d Cir. 1979); *Trans-Asiatic Oil Co. Ltd.* v. *Apex Oil Co.*, 743 F. 2d 956 (1st Cir. 1984); *Schiffahartgesellschaft Leonhardt* v. *Bottachi*, 773 F. 2d 1528 (11th Cir. 1985).

[54] *Judgments*, s. 8; *Conflict of Laws*, s. 66.

[55] 410 A. 2d 148 (Del. 1979), cert. den. 446 US 909 (1980).

[56] 441 F. Supp. 1273 (SDNY 1977). Contrast *Majique Fashions Ltd.* v. *Warwick & Sons*, 414 NYS 2d 916 (NY App. Div. 1979) (bank account connected with agency dispute: jurisdiction upheld); *Banco Ambrosiano SA* v. *Artoc Bank & Trust Ltd.*, 464 NE 2d 432 (NYCA 1984) (correspondent bank relationship was closely related to the plaintiffs' claim on its loan: attachment upheld).

[57] See Nadelmann, *op. cit., supra*, footnote 41, at pp. 230–232. In Switzerland also an attachment is allowed where a plaintiff shows a prima facie case that the defendant is indebted to him, that the assets attached belong to the defendant, and that the defendant is not domiciled in Switzerland. Article 4 of the Swiss Private International Law Act of 1987 provides that an action to validate an attachment may be brought at the place where the

be emphasized, is a jurisdiction *in personam*, unlimited by the value of the asset. The asset may even be a claim by the defendant against the plaintiff.[58]

Nadelmann[59] and others have repeated the old and famous example of the Russian who left his galoshes in an hotel in Berlin and consequently could be sued in Berlin for a debt of 100,000 marks. But even in the nineteenth century it was recognized in Germany that:

such a jurisdiction . . . rests upon an actual exercise of power at the moment of detention, and ultimately therefore must be referred to a complete distrust of the judicial system of other States, and to an endeavour to claim for our own jurisdiction, in a onesided and partial fashion, as many suits as possible in which subjects of this country are concerned, and to wrest them from the court which ought naturally . . . to have the right of decision. It seems right, therefore, to refuse international recognition to such a jurisdiction.[60]

Consequently, it was generally recognized that this jurisdiction was exorbitant and not entitled to recognition in other countries. Even before the historic decision of the German Federal Supreme Court in 1991, it had been branded as exorbitant by Article 3 of the Brussels Convention on jurisdiction and the enforcement of judgments of 1968. The effect of the Convention is that exorbitant rules of jurisdiction may no longer be relied on as against defendants domiciled within Contracting States, although they continue to be available as against persons who are not domiciled in the Contracting States.

Until 1991 the German rule applied, therefore, where the defendant was not domiciled in a Contracting State. But in July 1991 the German Federal Supreme Court decided that the jurisdiction under Article 23 of the Code of Civil Procedure could be exercised only if the dispute had a sufficient link with Germany. The facts of the case arose out of the same facts as the English decision in *Muduroglu Ltd.* v. *T C Ziraat Bankasi*.[61] The plaintiffs were a construction company incorporated in Northern Cyprus, and controlled from England. They had carried out work on a harbour construction contract in Libya, and had given a bank guarantee to a Libyan Government agency to secure the return of advance payments made to the plaintiffs. The bank guarantee was backed by a counter-guarantee from the defendants, a Turkish bank. When the Libyan Government called on the guarantees, the Turkish bank paid and recouped itself from security

---

debtor's property is attached. This ground of jurisdiction is branded as exorbitant by the Lugano Convention as regards defendants domiciled in Convention countries.
[58] See Drobnig, *American–German Private International Law* (2nd ed., 1972), pp. 322–323.   [59] pp. 230–231.
[60] Von Bar, *Theory and Practice of Private International Law* (2nd ed., 1892, trans. Gillespie), p. 912.   [61] [1986] QB 1225 (CA).

provided by the plaintiffs. The plaintiffs sued in England, claiming that the bank should not have paid the Libyan Government and therefore had no right to recoup itself from the plaintiffs' money. The case had nothing to do with England, except that the controlling shareholders and directors of the plaintiffs were resident there and the Turkish bank had a branch in London, and accordingly the English action was stayed on the bank's application because Turkey was the *forum conveniens*.

Subsequently the plaintiff company assigned part of its claim to its managing director, who brought an action against the Turkish bank in Germany, by attaching assets there. The Federal Supreme Court held that there was not a sufficient link with Germany to justify the exercise of jurisdiction. Although the plaintiff had given an address in Germany, there was no proof of actual residence; and there was no evidence that the plaintiff would be left without a remedy in Turkey or Northern Cyprus. The court did not give definitive guidance as to what type of links with Germany are necessary to support the jurisdiction under Article 23.

The Accession Convention of 1978 also brands as exorbitant the Scottish rule based on the seizure of property in Scotland. In *Alexander Ward & Co. Ltd.* v. *Samyang Navigation Co. Ltd.*, Lord Hailsham regarded it as anomalous:

This brings me to the . . . very interesting argument advanced on the part of the appellants which relates to the peculiarly Scottish procedure known as arrestment *ad fundandum jurisdictionem* or *jurisdictionis fundandae causa*. Both counsel for the appellants and the learned Dean of Faculty for the respondents initiated us with zeal, thoroughness and learning into the mysteries of this procedure which has, for three hundred years at least, formed part of the Scottish law. We are informed that it was originally an importation from Holland, providing an exception for reasons of 'expediency and the encouragement of trade' to the general principle—'*Actor sequitur forum rei*'. The appellants argued with great force that there was serious authority for the proposition that this means of securing jurisdiction was anomalous and should not be extended. I fully concur in this opinion which in any event seems well established.[62]

A Scots court took jurisdiction in a commercial claim against the United States Government on the sole ground that the United States Government had property in Scotland, and (remarkably) the relevant property was its

---

[62] 1975 SLT 126, 129. See also *Stenhouse London Ltd.* v. *Allwright*, 1972 SLT 255, 258; *Leggatt Bros.* v. *Gray*, 1908 SC 67, 72, where the history is discussed; Anton, *Private International Law* (2nd ed., 1990), pp. 188–194, with references to the literature; also Report of the Scottish Committee on Jurisdiction and Enforcement (the Maxwell Report, 1980), para. 13.164. The 1978 Accession Convention also added the provisions of Danish law which give jurisdiction over foreigners on the basis of (*inter alia*) the ownership of property: s. 246 (2) (formerly s. 248 (2)) Administration of Justice Act. Cf. South Africa: Forsyth, *Private International Law* (1981), pp. 174–175.

Consulate-General in Edinburgh.[63] The jurisdiction in this case was not based on the attachment of the property, but on its presence, and it will be suggested in Section XI that if the jurisdiction had been based on attachment it would have been the clearest invasion of consular immunity.

In France, an attachment can be effected in the place where the property is, and finally confirmed at the court of residence (domicile) of the defendant debtor or, if the defendant is not resident in France, at the residence of the third party who is the debtor of, or in possession of a property of, the defendant.[64] In this way the French courts may order the attachment in France of the French property of a foreign defendant. Traditionally French courts have allowed the attachment to stand while the plaintiff proceeded to prove the underlying claim in a foreign court and have accordingly stayed proceedings brought in France to confirm the attachment.[65] But the Cour de Cassation has held that the French courts are not bound to stay the proceedings to confirm the attachment, and accordingly it held that the French courts could exercise their jurisdiction to determine the merits of a case where a Lebanese man resident in Lausanne was sued by his (Lebanese) wife, who attached movable (a bank account in Nice) and immovable property belonging to the husband and situate in France: *Nassibian* v. *Nassibian*.[66]

This comes close to a *forum arresti*. As Professor Mayer has said:[67]

La Cour de cassation . . . a admis que les difficultés éventuelles relatives à *l'existence de la créance* peuvent être tranchées par le juge français compétent pour statuer sur l'action en validité, même si le fond du litige relève normalement de la compétence d'un ordre juridictionnel étranger (par exemple celui du domicile du débiteur). Par ce biais est introduite la possibilité de donner compétence au fond au juge français chaque fois que le débiteur possède en France des biens susceptibles de faire l'objet d'une saisie-arrêt, d'une saisie conservatoire ou d'une saisie-revendication, ou encore de l'inscription d'une hypothèque conservatoire. Cette compétence, cependant, est *facultative* pour le juge.

It is not a *forum patrimonii*, because the proprietary nature of the attachment ensures that the jurisdiction is limited to the value of the assets seized. But the *Nassibian* case does not require the French court to rule on the validity of the underlying claim. Previous practice in such cases as the

---

[63] *Forth Tugs Ltd.* v. *Wilmington Trust Co.*, 1987 SLT 153, *infra*, Section XI. 5.

[64] See Art. 557 *et seq.* CPC (ancien); *Juris classeur de droit international*, Fasc. 581-B, paras. 90–101 (Huet); Bauer, *Compétence judiciaire internationale des tribunaux civils français et allemands* (1965), pp. 66–67.

[65] See, e.g., *Soc. Intrabank* v. *Veuve Beidas*, Trib. gr. inst. Paris, 14.1.1970, 1970 *Rev. crit.* 714, note P.L.; Droz, *Compétence judiciaire et effets des jugements dans le marché commun* (1972), pp. 200–202; Herzog, *Civil Procedure in France* (1967), pp. 200–201.

[66] Cass. civ. I, 6.11.1979, 1980 *Clunet* 95, rapp. Ponsard, 1980 *Rev. crit.* 588, note Couchez.

[67] *Droit international privé* (4th ed., 1990), p. 191.

Intrabank case[68] showed that if the case had no connection with France other than the presence of property, then the French court could refuse to exercise its jurisdiction on the substance of the claim, and leave the merits to be decided by the foreign court.[69] So also will it refuse to exercise jurisdiction on the merits if the courts of another country have exclusive jurisdiction.[70]

Most recently, in *Fahim* v. *Saudi Investment Bank*,[71] a Saudi bank had lent Fahim (a Saudi national) 7.5 million Saudi rials, and when default was made the Saudi bank attached funds held by him at the Banque Nationale de Paris, and obtained a charging order (*hypothèque judiciaire provisoire*) over property in Paris belonging to him. Mr Fahim had already sued the bank in Saudi Arabia, and he sought to lift the attachments on the basis that the French court had no power to determine the validity of the bank's claim. The Cour de Cassation held that the French court had jurisdiction to attach the bank accounts in France and to grant a charging order over French immovable property belonging to a foreign debtor and were competent

pour, dans cette phase conservatoire, apprécier provisoirement à cette occasion le principe de la créance invoquée, alors même que cette dernière question ferait l'objet d'une instance en cours devant une juridiction étrangère.

It is possible that these lines of authority may diverge; but they may perhaps be reconciled on the basis that the French court will have jurisdiction in any event to consider the merits in an application to set aside the attachment; but it will not *confirm* an attachment order if there are already proceedings pending abroad. In effect, where there are no foreign proceedings in progress, the French court may rule on the substance of the case; but if there are proceedings abroad, the French court will only rule on the substance to the extent necessary to ensure that the attachment is maintained.

---

[68] *Supra*, footnote 65.

[69] See Lagarde, (1986) *Collected Courses*, Vol. 196, 1, at pp. 136–137.

[70] *Banque camerounaise de développement* v. *Soc. des établissements Rolber*, Cass. civ. I, 18.11.1986, 1987 *Rev. crit.* 773, note Muir Watt, where the Cour de Cassation confirmed that the rule in *Nassibian* applied to a case where the defendant bank (a Cameroon State-owned bank) had bank accounts which were attached in an action by a Liechtenstein corporation on bills of exchange in a case with no apparent connection with France.

[71] Cass. civ. I, 6.12.1989, 1990 *Rev. crit.* 545, note Couchez.

3

Protective Measures in Aid of Proceedings in Foreign Countries

I. CIVIL LAW COUNTRIES

Developments in the second half of the twentieth century have, as has been seen, confirmed Bar's view that the presence of assets belonging to a defendant is not a sufficient basis of jurisdiction to determine the merits, and that if such a jurisdiction is exercised, it is exorbitant, or contrary to comity, or unreasonable. But equally these developments have confirmed his view that it is absolutely necessary to distinguish between, on the one hand, jurisdiction based on attachment or arrestment, and, on the other hand, the use of provisional measures which

> ... are adopted *ex necessitate* to meet emergencies, and not unfrequently are dictated by the voice of humanity, e.g. arrestment to prevent an unscrupulous debtor from making away with the property . . .[72]

In language which speaks equally well for the conditions of today, he concluded that 'every State is competent to pronounce such temporary orders if the facts necessary to justify them are found in existence within its territory'. But, he warned, 'an application for an interim order must be refused, as a matter that properly belongs to the court in which the main action is pending, if the applicant has sufficient time to apply to that court'.[73]

Bar thought (probably wrongly) that the prevailing view in France was that the French courts were not competent to confirm attachments if they had no jurisdiction over the claim; the view in Italy was different. Bar concluded: 'I should incline to hold the Italian doctrine sound and practical.' Today that doctrine is now widely, but not universally, accepted. The courts of most countries will in appropriate cases order provisional or protective measures in aid of proceedings in other countries, and this power is expressly recognized in Article 24 of the Brussels and Lugano Conventions on jurisdiction and the enforcement of judgments in civil and commercial matters:

> Application may be made to the courts of the Contracting State for such provisional, including protective, measures as may be available under the law of

---

[72] *Theory and Practice of Private International law* (2nd ed., 1892, trans. Gillespie), p. 913.
[73] *Ibid.*

that State, even if, under this Convention, the courts of another Contracting State have jurisdiction as to the substance of the matter.

It seems to have been accepted in France since 1850 that an attachment may be made of property in France even if a foreign court has jurisdiction over the substance of the case, and that the French attachment proceedings will be stayed to await the outcome of the decision of the foreign court.[74] Indeed, as long ago as 1913 Joseph Beale criticized the Anglo-American *forum arresti* and submitted that the 'French method of dealing with the problem is far preferable to our own'.[75] He went so far as to include in his case-book on the conflict of laws a translation of a decision of the Civil Tribunal of the Seine in 1890, in which the plaintiff, an Austrian resident in Vienna, made an attachment in Paris of a debt due from a Parisian banker to the defendant, a German, who was resident in London. The court decided that it was not competent to determine the substance of the plaintiff's claim, but it continued the attachment for a period sufficient for the plaintiff to sue the defendant before a court of competent jurisdiction.[76]

It has been seen in Section II that in the *Nassibian* case the Cour de Cassation derived from the power of the French courts to attach property in France the competence to rule on the merits of the claim. But in principle

Les procédures conservatoires et d'exécution relèvent des lois de compétence de l'État où ces procédures sont diligentées même si d'autres juridictions sont internationalement compétentes pour statuer sur le fond.[77]

A frequently cited modern example is *Soc. Intrabank* v. *Beidas*,[78] where it was held that the French court had jurisdiction to rule on the validity of the *saisie-arrêt* (but not on the existence of the debt) while the creditor, a Lebanese Bank, pursued foreign proceedings with a view to ultimate execution in France. In cases of urgency the juge des référés has jurisdiction to order 'toutes mesures de sauvegarde', even where there is a valid contractual provision conferring exclusive jurisdiction on the courts of another country.[79] Similarly, provisional measures were ordered in relation to the assets of a Vietnamese company in France notwithstanding

---

[74] See Francescakis, 1958 *Rev. crit.* at 134–135.

[75] 'Jurisdiction in Rem To Compel Payment of A Debt', (1913) 27 Harv. L. Rev. 107, at 123.

[76] *Todesco* v. *Dumont*, Trib. civ. Seine, 8.3.1890, 1891 *Clunet* 559, in Beale, *Cases on the Conflict of Laws*, Vol. 1 (2nd ed., 1927), p. 339.

[77] *Soc. Varonas Investment Corp.* v. *Électricité de France*, Cass. civ. II, 29.2.1984, 1985 *Rev. crit.* 545, note Sinay-Cytermann.

[78] Trib. gr. inst., Paris, 14.1.1970, 1970 *Rev. crit.* 714, note P. L.

[79] *Cie de signaux et d'entreprises électriques* v. *Soc. Sorelac*, Cass. civ. I, 17.12.1985, 1986 *Rev. crit.* 537, note Gaudemet-Tallon. But in that case the court recognized that some matters in which the juge des référés might have jurisdiction (e.g., as in that case, the appointment of an expert) might be excluded by the terms of the jurisdiction agreement.

a provision in its statutes providing for the exclusive jurisdiction of the Vietnamese courts.[80]

In Italy, the court may grant provisional remedies which are to be enforced in Italy or which concern relationships which are subject to the jurisdiction of the Italian courts.[81] As a result a party to a foreign proceeding may apply to the Italian court for sequestration of property in Italy, irrespective of the residence of the defendant and irrespective of whether the underlying debt has any connection with Italy.[82]

2. UNITED STATES AND ENGLAND

In its 1977 decision in *Shaffer* v. *Heitner*[83] the United States Supreme Court held that the assertion by the States of the Union of *quasi in rem* jurisdiction through the process of foreign attachment was unconstitutional: the *mere* presence of property was not a sufficient basis of jurisdiction, and was inconsistent with the due process limitation on state power. The Due Process Clause of the Fourteenth Amendment to the United States Constitution did not contemplate that a state might make a binding judgment against a defendant with whom the state had no relevant connection.[84] *Shaffer* v. *Heitner* decided that the mere presence of the property of the defendant in the state was not a relevant connection for that purpose. But when it struck down the exercise of jurisdiction based purely on the presence of assets, it accepted the view (put forward by von Mehren and Trautman, by Beale and by Hazard)[85] that the presence of assets might justify the grant of *protective* measures. It indicated that the presence of property within the jurisdiction

at most, . . . suggests that a State in which property is located should have jurisdiction to attach that property . . . as security for a judgment being sought in a forum where the litigation can be maintained consistently

with the due process requirements of minimum contacts.[86]

---

[80] *Lafitte* v. *Soc. les Transitaires Réunis et Ortoli*, Paris, 8.10.1964, 1965 *Clunet* 901.

[81] Art. 4 (3), Code of Civil Procedure.

[82] See Cappelletti and Perillo, in *Civil Procedure in Italy* (1965), pp. 411–412. See, e.g., *Gagliardi* v. *Larocca*, 8.6.1985, No. 3464, *Riv. dir. int. proc.*, 1987, p. 79: a case of *sequestro giudiziario* of property in Italy and abroad. Provisional measures may be ordered even if jurisdiction on the merits is doubtful: Art. 4 (3), Code of Civil Procedure, confirmed by law of 26.11.90 (No. 353).

[83] 433 US 186 (1977).

[84] *International Shoe Co.* v. *Washington*, 326 US 310, 319 (1945).

[85] Von Mehren and Trautman, 'Jurisdiction to Adjudicate: A Suggested Analysis', (1966) 79 Harv. L. Rev. 1121, at 1178; Beale, *op. cit., supra* footnote 75, at 123–124; Hazard, 'A General Theory of State Court Jurisdiction', (1965) Sup. Ct. Rev. 241, at 284–285.

[86] 433 US at 210.

In *Barclays Bank SA* v. *Tsakos*[87] the plaintiff was the French subsidiary of an English bank, which had claims against the defendants, Greeks living in France. The bank attached their apartment in the Watergate complex in Washington, in proceedings to enforce a guarantee given by the defendants on behalf of their son for US $1.4 million. The bank brought actions in France and Switzerland, as well as in the District of Columbia. The bank obtained attachments in France and Switzerland, but it was too late, since the defendants had taken steps to remove their assets. The District of Columbia Court of Appeals applied the dictum in *Shaffer* that the court might have power to attach property 'as security for a judgment being sought in a forum where the litigation can be maintained' consistently with due process. In the present case, the bank:

is willing to forbear adjudication here of the underlying claim against the Tsakos, which can await the outcome of the litigation in Europe. What the Bank seeks at bottom is simply to preserve the status quo of the attachment lien pending that outcome. We do not deal here with just a barebones attachment to secure jurisdiction. An allegation is made of intended effective removal of the property by way of sale and non-availability of assets elsewhere.[88]

In England, the question of the relationship between jurisidiction to order provisional measures and jurisdiction to hear the merits arose in a very simple form in a case involving a *Mareva* injunction: *The Siskina*.[89] The *Siskina* was carrying marble slabs originating in Italy and destined for Saudi Arabia. The *Siskina* was owned by a one-ship Panamanian company, but managed by Greeks in Piraeus. The shipowners, when the ship was near the entrance to the Suez Canal, alleged that the charterers had not paid the full freight due under the charter party, and ordered the master to turn back and go to Cyprus and unload the cargo, where the shipowners issued a writ in rem against the cargo. After discharge of the cargo (worth US $5 million) the vessel left Cyprus and sank on the way to Greece. The shipowners made a claim on London underwriters, and were likely to receive US $750,000 in insurance. The cargo owners were anxious about this money, since the shipowners had no other assets: in particular the cargo owners were anxious that the money should not be paid to the shipowners, because they would then be beyond reach of their claim for compensation for the storage charges and additional expenses caused by what they said was the wrongful arrest of their cargo in Cyprus.

The cargo owners sought to have the insurance money retained in England until their claim for damages was settled. The bills of lading

---

[87] 543 A. 2d 802 (DC App. 1988). See also *Carolina Power & Light Co.* v. *Uranex*, 451 F. Supp. 1044 (ND Cal. 1977).   [88] 543 A. 2d at 805.

[89] [1979] AC 210 (Kerr J.; CA; HL). See Kerr J. (1978) 41 MLR 1, 11–15: Lipstein [1978] CLJ 241.

contained a clause giving exclusive jurisdiction to the courts of Genoa. The only connection which the case had with England was the location of the insurance money. If the plaintiffs were to have any hope of satisfying judgment it was essential for them to have the money frozen. The issue was a very simple one. Could the cargo owners obtain an order from the court to ensure that the money did not leave London? If they could obtain such an order pending the outcome of a claim in Genoa, then at least to the extent of the $750,000 in London a judgment obtained in Genoa might be effective. If they could not obtain such an order, then the money would disappear through a 'black hole' to a foreign bank account of the Panamanian company.

The case arose before the accession of the United Kingdom to the Brussels Convention of 1968, and Article 24 of that Convention was not directly concerned, although (as it will be seen) it was invoked in the judgments, particularly in the Court of Appeal. It has already been seen that (except in cases of arrest of ships) English law has no procedure for pre-trial attachment of property, but that a similar result can, in many cases, be achieved by a *Mareva* injunction, which is an *in personam* order restraining the defendant from disposing of property. Once a bank, or other third party, has notice of the order, it will be in contempt of court (and liable to penalties) if it allows the property to be disposed of. The *Mareva* injunction is therefore extremely effective if the property (usually money) is in England, if it is in the hands of a bank, and if the plaintiff knows with which bank the money is held and gives notice of the order to the bank.

But in *The Siskina* the problem was that the defendant was abroad. If the *Mareva* jurisdiction were *in rem* that would not have presented a problem, because the *res*, the money representing the insurance proceeds, was in London. But the jurisdiction is *in personam*, and accordingly the plaintiff had to show that the English court had jurisdiction *in personam*. The defendant, however, was abroad, and the case had no connection with England whatsoever, except for the location of the money. As Kerr J. (the judge at first instance—a distinguished commercial judge and later a member of the Court of Appeal) put it, the basic contention of the plaintiffs was that the *Mareva* jurisdiction could be extended to provide a general power of attachment even in cases in which English courts had no other basis of jurisdiction against the defendants.[90] But he held that the court did not have such a power. The legal issue, from first instance to the Court of Appeal and then in the House of Lords, was the scope of application of the provision in Order 11 of the Rules of the Supreme Court that the English court had jurisdiction if in the action 'an injunction is

[90] [1979] AC at 215.

sought ordering the defendant to do or refrain from doing anything within the jurisdiction'.[91] On their face the words plainly allow a *Mareva* injunction even if the case has no other connection with England, but the obstacle was a consistent series of cases in English law, not in their inception involving a foreign element, which decided that the court had no power to grant an interlocutory injunction except in protection or assertion of a legal or equitable right.[92] The central issue in *The Siskina* was whether it was also necessary for the English court to have jurisdiction in relation to the merits of that legal or equitable right.

The Court of Appeal held, by a majority (Lord Denning MR and Lawton LJ, with Bridge LJ dissenting), that the court did have the power to grant the injunction. The view of the majority was that the *Mareva* injunction was an injunction which was 'sought ordering the defendant to do or refrain from doing anything within the jurisdiction' within the meaning of Order 11 of the Rules of the Supreme Court. Lord Denning MR invoked Community law in support of his view that the injunction should be granted. He said:[93]

comity in this case is all in favour of granting an injunction seeing that it is a close parallel to 'saisie conservatoire' with which other countries are very familiar. I go further. Now that we are in the common market it is our duty to do our part in harmonising the laws of the countries of the nine . . . Now under article 220 it is the duty of the member states to seek to secure the 'reciprocal recognition' of the 'judgments of courts'. To do so in this case means that we should regard a determination by the Italian courts—one of the countries of the common market— with the same respect as a determination of the English courts; and that we should give our aid to the enforcement of it to the same extent as we would our own. In particular, we should take protective measures to see that the moneys here are not spirited away pending the decision of the Italian courts.

He then went on to refer to the Brussels Convention of 1968 (to which the United Kingdom had not then acceded) and said:

. . . meanwhile the creditor can apply to the courts of his own (the creditor's) country for protective measures to be taken against the assets of the debtor—when those assets are situate in the creditor's country—so as to prevent the debtor disposing of them before the creditor obtained the judgment in the substantive case: see article 24 . . . In order to harmonise the laws of the common market countries, it is therefore appropriate that we should apply protective measures here so as to prevent these insurance moneys being disposed of before judgment.

Bridge LJ, dissenting, noted that negotiations for the accession of the United Kingdom were then in progress, and doubted that the Convention

---

[91] RSC Order 11, Rule 1 (1) (i) (now Rule 1 (1) (*b*)).
[92] *North London Railway Co.* v. *Great Northern Railway Co.* (1883) 11 QBD 30 (CA).
[93] [1979] AC at 233–423.

gave any basis of jurisdiction to order provisional measures in such cases. On this aspect he was, of course, wrong, although on the English law of jurisdiction his view (and that of Kerr J.) was upheld by the House of Lords in a decision which Lord Denning has described as the most disappointing reversal in his career.[94]

The decision of the House of Lords was that the injunction provision of what is now Order 11, r. 1 (1) (c) could only be used if the injunction was in connection with an underlying dispute subject to the jurisdiction of the English court. Lord Diplock was highly critical of Lord Denning's appeal to Community law. He said:[95]

With regard to the alternative suggestion that the High Court should have jurisdiction to order the attachment of assets of a foreign defendant notwithstanding that it had no jurisdiction to adjudicate upon the merits of the claim, it is the fact that article 24 of the Convention of 1968 expressly preserves the jurisdiction of courts of member states in which the national law provides for this, to make orders of a protective or provisional character on the application of a claimant, notwithstanding that under the Convention jurisdiction to adjudicate on the merits of the claim in aid of which the protective or provisional orders are requested is vested in the courts of some other member state. It is also the fact that the codes of civil procedure of several of the original member states which provide for the provisional attachment (*saisie conservatoire*) of the assets of an alleged debtor within the territorial jurisdiction of the court do extend this general power to the attachment of assets of a non-resident defendant pending adjudication of the merits of a claim against him in an action brought in some foreign court; but as article 24 of the Convention indicates, this is a field of law in which it has not been considered necessary by member states or by the Council or Commission to embark upon a policy of harmonisation . . . [T]here may be merits in Lord Denning M.R.'s alternative proposals for extending the jurisdiction of the High Court over foreign defendants but they cannot, in my view, be supported by considerations of comity or by the Common Market treaties.

The Siskina was followed by the Supreme Court of Ireland in *Serge Caudron* v. *Air Zaire*,[96] where (in a case having no connection with Ireland) employees of Air Zaire sought unsuccessfully to restrain the disposal of a Boeing 737 held in Dublin and belonging to Air Zaire. The

---

[94] *Due Process of Law* (1980), at p. 141.

[95] [1979] AC at 259–260. See also Lord Hailsham, at 262–263. Cf. *Perry* v. *Zissis* [1979] 1 Lloyd's Rep. 607 (CA). Contrast *Securities and Investment Board* v. *Pantell SA* [1990] Ch. 426; *Finers* v. *Miro* [1991] 1 All ER 182 (CA). See also *Suncorp Realty Inc.* v. *PLN Investments, Inc.* (1985) 23 DLR (4th) 83. In *House of Spring Gardens Ltd.* v. *Waite* [1984] FSR 277, 283 it was accepted that where proceedings on the substance of the case were pending both in England and in a foreign jurisdiction, a *Mareva* injunction could be granted in the English proceedings, pending the outcome of the foreign proceedings and while the English proceedings on the merits were left 'to go to sleep'.

[96] (1986) 6 ILRM 10.

Supreme Court of Ireland had been asked by the plaintiffs to prefer the approach of Lord Denning MR to that of Lord Diplock. But Chief Justice Finlay, while recognizing the hardship faced by the plaintiffs in having to litigate exclusively in Zaire without prospect of any judgment being satisfied, and while accepting that the policy considerations behind Lord Denning's approach were attractive, nevertheless agreed with Lord Diplock that the implementation of such a policy was for the legislature, and not for the judiciary.[97] This decision is in striking contrast to the decision of the Court of Appeal of Paris in which an attachment over the same airline's aircraft at Paris was allowed in a similar action by employees of Air Zaire.[98]

It was regrettable that the English courts, having accepted in principle a remedy of (indirect) attachment by means of the *Mareva* injunction, were constrained by history from developing the remedy to prevent an obvious injustice. The courts had been prepared, in the development of the *Mareva* injunction, to depart from the nineteenth-century principle that, 'You cannot get an injunction to restrain a man who is alleged to be a debtor from parting with his property'.[99] But they were not prepared to take the extra step necessary to prevent injustice.

3. THE BRUSSELS AND LUGANO CONVENTIONS

The position has now been remedied (but so far only in part) following the accession by the United Kingdom to the Brussels Convention of 1968 (and, subsequently, the Lugano Convention). Section 25 of the Civil Jurisdiction and Judgments Act 1982 provides that the court is to have power to grant interim relief where (*a*) proceedings have been or are to be commenced in a Contracting State other than the United Kingdom or in a part of the United Kingdom other than that in which the court in question exercises jurisdiction; and (*b*) they are or will be proceedings whose subject-matter is within the scope of the 1968 Convention. It is also provided that on an application for interim relief under that section the court may refuse to grant that relief if, in the opinion of the court, the fact that the court has no jurisdiction (apart from the section) in relation to the subject-matter of the proceedings in question makes it inexpedient for the court to grant it. Consequently, if the facts of *The Siskina* were to recur, the injunction might be granted if the plaintiffs were contemplating litigation in Italy

---

[97] See also Kerr J. (1978) 41 MLR 1, at 15.

[98] *Air Zaire* v. *Gauthier* (1984) 77 Int. LR 510.

[99] *Lister & Co.* v. *Stubbs* (1890) 45 Ch. D. 1, 14, *per* Cotton LJ. See also *Mills* v. *Northern Railway of Buenos Ayres Co.* (1870) LR 5 Ch. App. 621; *Robinson* v. *Pickering* (1881) 16 Ch. D. 660; *Newton* v. *Newton* (1885) 11 PD 11.

under the jurisdiction clause in the bill of lading.[100] The 1982 Act also provides that similar powers may be exercised in relation to proceedings which are to be commenced in States which are not Contracting States, but this part of the Act has not yet been brought into force.[101]

Since the relevant provisions of the Civil Jurisdiction and Judgments Act 1982 came into force in 1987, there have been two important decisions on the application of Article 24 in English proceedings, both of which involved cases where the substantive proceedings on the merits were pending in France. In *Republic of Haiti* v. *Duvalier*[102] the Republic of Haiti had commenced proceedings in Grasse against the former President of the Republic of Haiti and various members of his family, claiming they were responsible for embezzling sums totalling $120 million from the Republic of Haiti during the presidency of Baby Doc Duvalier, between 1971 and 1986. The Duvalier family denied liability, and claimed that it had been a tradition in Haiti for over 180 years for a new government to take legal proceedings against those who were in charge under the previous regime. There was evidence that the members of the Duvalier family had been attempting to conceal their assets. They passed large amounts of money through a French lawyer who was an expert on the concealment of funds within the Swiss banking system, and used lawyers as intermediaries in order to take advantage of legal professional privilege or confidentiality.

The Republic of Haiti obtained orders in England restraining the defendants from removing money from England and they were ordered to disclose to the plaintiffs the nature, location and value of their assets (wherever situate). Since the Duvalier family were not in England, the order would not have been effective but for the fact that they had English solicitors who administered some of their assets outside England, and the order was that the Duvalier family 'were ordered acting by Messrs. [name of solicitors], to disclose to the plaintiffs' solicitors . . . information known to [the solicitors] as to the nature, location and value of those defendants' assets'. It was also ordered that the solicitors should not disclose the making of the order until they had complied with it on the defendants' behalf.

The point of general importance in *Republic of Haiti* v. *Duvalier* was that it was held that, even where the proceedings were pending abroad and the application was made on the basis of section 25 of the 1982 Act giving effect to Article 24, nevertheless the order could relate to assets outside England. In view of earlier decisions of the Court of Appeal, it was not argued that the court had no power to grant an order in relation to assets

---

[100] In *The Siskina* cargo owners other than the plaintiffs had commenced proceedings in Cyprus.　　　　　　　　　　　　　　　　　　　　　　　　　　[101] S. 25 (3).
[102] [1990] 1 QB 202. For subsequent proceedings in France see Section XI, *infra*.

abroad,[103] but it was argued that because the English courts had no jurisdiction on the merits, and none of the Duvalier family was resident in England, and the assets concerned were mainly, if not wholly, outside England, the proper court to make the orders was either the court at Grasse or the courts where the assets were located. The Court of Appeal accepted that this argument was supported by the judgment of the European Court in *Denilauler* v. *Couchet Frères*[104] where it was said:

The courts of the place or, in any event, of the Contracting State, where the assets subject to the measures sought are located, are those best able to assess the circumstances which may lead to the grant or refusal of the measures sought . . .

But the Court of Appeal recognized that the plaintiffs, when they started the English proceedings, did not know where the assets were located, and one of their objects was to find out. The proceedings were started in England because it was in England that the information was available, and the remedy could be exercised even if the defendants were outside England. The order was made because of the

plain and admitted intention of the defendants to move their assets out of the reach of the courts of law, coupled with the resources they have obtained and the skill they have hitherto shown in doing that, and the vast amount of money involved. This case demands international co-operation between all nations . . . [I]f ever there was a case for the exercise of the court's powers, this must be it . . . If the Duvalier family have a defence to the substantive claim, and feel that they are being persecuted, then their remedy . . . is to co-operate in securing an early trial of the dispute. It is not to secrete their assets where even the most just decision in the world cannot reach them.[105]

Similarly, in *X* v. *Y*[106] proceedings were pending in Paris and an injunction was granted to restrain the defendant from dealing with any sums of money held with the London branch of the National Bank of Detroit. There was evidence that the defendant was taking every step available to him to avoid paying an undisputed debt of about US $8 million due to a French bank, so as to put pressure on the bank to settle a dispute with him relating to the ownership of shares. There was

an irresistible inference to be drawn that, if he were free to do so, the defendant would remove his assets out of the jurisdiction so that they would not be available to satisfy a judgment of the French court. If, as seems likely, those assets were removed to Saudi Arabia, they would clearly not be available to satisfy a judgment

---

[103] As to which see Section VIII, *infra*.
[104] Case 125/729 [1980] ECR 1553, at 1570.
[105] [1990] 1 QB 202, 217.
[106] [1990] 1 QB 220. See also *Alltrans Inc.* v. *Interdom Holdings Ltd.* [1991] 4 All ER 458 (CA).

of the French court. For there is agreed evidence . . . that any judgment of a French court against a defendant would not be enforceable in Saudi Arabia.[107]

In other Contracting States there has been extensive use of the power to order provisional measures notwithstanding the lack of jurisdiction over the merits. Article 24 is not itself the source of the power. It is merely permissive. National law may (not must) supply the remedy. In *Republic of Haiti* v. *Duvalier*[108] the English Court of Appeal suggested that the effect of Article 24 is that:

the Convention *requires* each contracting state to make available, in aid of the court of another contracting state, such provisional and protective measures as its own domestic law would afford if its courts were trying the substantive action.

This conclusion is almost certainly wrong as a matter of law, but nevertheless in practice the courts of the Contracting States do make their remedies available in aid of proceedings in other Contracting States. In Germany, after some initial hesitation, a number of courts have made use of Article 917 (2) of the Code of Civil Procedure to order attachment as security for claims being pursued in foreign courts.[109]

A serious issue has arisen, not yet resolved by the European Court, as to the meaning of provisional or protective measures within the meaning of Article 24. The obvious case is the attachment of assets. Less obvious cases include orders to preserve evidence.[110] In the Netherlands the provisional examination of witnesses has been held to be within Article 24, so that the Dutch court held that it could order witnesses to be examined in support of proceedings which had to be taken in Belgium because of an exclusive jurisdiction clause.[111] In Belgium and France (and the Netherlands) it has been held that an order for the designation of an expert is a protective measure.[112]

The critical issue, however, has been whether a court which has no jurisdiction on the substance of a case may nevertheless make an interim payment order. A power to order an interim payment exists in many systems of law, and it has already been seen that in international adjudication the power to order such interim payments as a protective measure was accepted by the German–Polish Mixed Arbitral Tribunal and rejected by the Permanent Court of International Justice.[113] Most

---

[107] At 231–232.

[108] [1990] 1 QB 202, 212. Cf. *X* v. *Y* [1990] 1 QB 220, 228.

[109] See Court of Justice of European Communities, *Digest of Case-Law relating to the European Communities*, D Series, cases at I-24.

[110] *Soc. Eli Lilly*, Cr. d'App., Brussels, 11.2.1977, *Digest*, I-24-83.

[111] *Peter van Tiel BV* v. *Korenman*, not yet reported. This seems a very questionable use of Article 24.

[112] Huet, 1989 *Clunet* 96 at 99. See, e.g., *Stadtwerke Essen A.G.* v. *Soc. Trailigaz*, Paris, 19.3.1987 [1988] Eur. Comm. Cas. 291.   [113] Section I, *supra*.

developed national systems of law provide a similar remedy. Thus in English law it is possible (although by no means easy) for a plaintiff to obtain an order for an interim payment in respect of damages if the court is satisfied that the plaintiff would, if the action proceeded to trial, obtain judgment for substantial damages.[114] It is clear that in such a case the court must, in advance of the trial of the action, be *satisfied* that the plaintiff will succeed. It does not have to decide the case on the merits, but there can be no doubt that it is dealing in advance with the very question which will be decided at the trial. So too in the case of the *référé-provision* in French law. Thus by Article 809 (2) of the Code of Civil Procedure the President of the Tribunal de Grande Instance can order a *provision* if the existence of the debt is not 'sérieusement contestable'. It is not necessary for the plaintiff to show urgency, and the onus is on the defendant to show that he has a defence on the merits.

In France it has been decided on several occasions that a French court may, on the basis of Article 24 of the Brussels Convention, order a *provision* even if a foreign court has, under the Convention, sole jurisdiction over the merits. In a series of cases the French courts have decided that they can make an award of provisional damages to a French employee against his Belgian employer;[115] and that they can award provisional damages to French plaintiffs injured in road accidents in Germany[116] and Scotland.[117] But, as has been pointed out in France,[118] it does not follow from the fact that a measure is characterized in French law (or any other national law) as a provisional or protective measure that it is to be characterized in the same way for the purposes of the Brussels Convention. The European Court has generally adopted a method of interpretation by which terms in the Convention are to be given a Convention interpretation, and are not to be characterized by the *lex fori* or the *lex causae*. There is no reason to believe that Article 24 should be an exception. It is hard to resist the conclusion that interim payments are not

---

[114] Ord. 29, r. 11; on which see, e.g., *British and Commonwealth Holdings plc* v. *Quadrex Holdings Inc.* [1989] QB 842 (CA).

[115] *Soc Verkor* v. *Tron*, Versailles, 27.6.1979, 1980 *Clunet* 894, note Holleaux; see also 1979 *Rev. crit.* 128, note Mezger.

[116] *Diehm* v. *Sicre*, Aix, 4.5.1981, 1983 *Rev. crit.* 110, note Couchez. But the Aix Court of Appeal, however, expressed doubts whether an interlocutory order for provisional payment in respect of a tort claim fell within the scope of Article 24, and reduced the amount to be paid to 1,000 francs, with the rest to be left in court, and the question of principle to be decided by the full court. In its final judgment in 1982 the Court of Appeal upheld the order, but that was after a German court had held the defendant liable.

[117] *Soc. Nordstern* v. *Eon*, Rennes, 20.5.1980, *Digest*, I-24-B11, note. See also *Sahm* v. *Maechler*, Colmar, 5.3.1982, *ibid.* (interim payment in commercial case).

[118] See especially Holleaux, 1980 *Clunet* 894, and Huet, 1982 *Clunet* 942 at 946–947. See also Gothot and Holleaux, *La Convention de Bruxelles du 27.9.1968* (1985), pp. 115–117.

provisional or protective measures for the purposes of the Convention.[119]

There are signs that the French courts are resiling from the tendency to allow Article 24 to be used to subvert the Convention system.[120] In *Menegatti* v. *Soc. Mettalurgica Nava Stefano e Giuseppina*,[121] the plaintiff was an Italian living in France who was the exclusive commercial agent in France of an Italian company. After his agency was terminated, he asked the President of the Tribunal de Commerce of Paris for an interim payment of 380,000 francs and the appointment of an expert to take an account between the parties. Since the agency agreement contained an exclusive submission to the courts of Como he relied on Article 24 as the basis of jurisdiction. The Paris Court of Appeal seems to have accepted that in principle these remedies would have been provisional measures within the meaning of Article 24, but it decided that the Italian judge was better placed to rule on these provisional measures, that is, the Italian court was the more appropriate forum.

In another, but not wholly different, context the French courts have decided that an application to the court for *provision* may be incompatible with an agreement to arbitrate. Thus under Article 8 (5) of the arbitration rules of the International Chamber of Commerce the parties may in certain circumstances apply to national courts for 'interim or conservatory measures'. It is now well established that for this purpose *référé-provision* is not an interim or conservatory measure, and accordingly the French court cannot allow a plaintiff, in breach of an agreement to arbitrate, to apply for a *provision*, at any rate if the arbitration is in progress.[122]

---

[119] See also Collins, *Civil Jurisdiction and Judgments Act 1982* (1983), p. 99. In the Netherlands it has been doubted whether an order for interim damages is within Article 24: *Kosmo Foam BV* v. *Sullhofer*. Dist. Ct. Hague, 31.5.1988, [1991] IL Pr. 356.

[120] In *Soc. Tag-Group* v. *Halbardier*, Cass. soc., 17.12.1986, 1988 *Rev. crit.* 92, 96–97, obs. P. L., it was held that a *provision* could not be ordered where the Luxembourg court had jurisdiction; but the claim for a *provision* was not made on the basis of Article 24.

[121] Paris, 17.11.1987, 1989 *Clunet* 96, note Huet.

[122] See *République islamique d'Iran* v. *Eurodif*, Cass. civ. I, 14.3.1984, 1984 *Rev. crit.* 644, note Bischoff, 1984 *Clunet* 598, note Oppetit; *Soc. ESW* v. *Soc. TAI*, Rouen, 7.5.1986, and *SIAPE* v. *Soc. IEC*, Paris, 14.5.1986, 1986 *Rev. arb.* 565, note Couchez. See also *Maeght* v. *Soc. Galerie Maeght-Lelong*, Trib. gr. inst. Paris, 21.2.1986, 1986 *Rev. arb.* 565, note Couchez; *Soc. Estram* v. *Soc. Ipitrade International*, Cass. Civ. I, 20.3.1989, 1989 *Rev. arb.* 494, note Couchez; Couchez, 'Référé et arbitrage', 1986 *Rev. arb.* 155; Huet, 1989 *Clunet* 96, at 97–98. See also *infra*, Section V.

4

Jurisdiction Clauses

The importance of jurisdiction clauses in international commercial contracts can hardly be exaggerated. They are an everyday feature of international financial and commercial life. When parties agree on a jurisdiction clause conferring exclusive[123] jurisdiction on the courts of a country, they not only confer jurisdiction on those courts, but they also purport to exclude the jurisdiction of other courts which but for the clause would have had jurisdiction. Such clauses have been enforced in England since the end of the eighteenth century,[124] and in varying degrees in most other countries, including France, Germany and the United States. It is true that many countries will not give effect to a derogation from their jurisdiction if it is contained in a standard form contract and deprives the weaker party of the protection of the local courts. It is also true that in common law jurisdictions the traditional rule has been that although in principle such clauses must be given effect, the court retains a discretion to override the jurisdiction clause where justice requires it.[125]

In the United States a marked hostility to jurisdiction clauses ended with the famous decision of the Supreme Court in *M/S Bremen* v. *Zapata Offshore Co.*[126] In that case there was a contract for the towage by deep sea tug of an oil rig from Louisiana to Italy. The oil rig was owned by a United States company, and the tug was owned by a German company. The contract provided that any dispute should be decided by the English courts. The rig was damaged in a storm in the Gulf of Mexico. When the

---

[123] So-called 'non-exclusive' jurisdiction clauses confer jurisdiction on the courts of more than one country: see *Evans Marshall & Co. Ltd* v. *Bertola SA* [1973] 1 WLR 349, at 360; *Commercial Bank of the Near East plc* v. *A.* [1989] 2 Lloyd's Rep. 319, 321; *Kurz* v. *Stella Musical Veranstaltungs GmbH* [1992] Ch. 196.

[124] *Gienar* v. *Meyer* (1796) 2 H. Bl. 603.

[125] See, for England, *The El Amria* [1981] 2 Lloyd's Rep. 119, 123 (CA), and other cases cited at Dicey and Morris, *Conflict of Laws* (11th ed., 1987), pp. 412–413. For France, see J.-Cl. dr. int. Fasc. 581-C, paras. 4 *et seq.* (Huet).

[126] 407 US 1 (1972), on which see Collins, 'Forum Selection and an Anglo-American Conflict—the Sad Case of the Chaparral', (1971) 20 *ICLQ* 530, 'Choice of Forum and the Exercise of Judicial Discretion—the Resolution of an Anglo-American Conflict', (1973) 22 *ICLQ* 329 (post, p. 253). See also *Carnival Cruise Lines Inc.* v. *Shute*, 111 S. Ct. 1522 (1991) (an inter-state case).

United States company sued the German tug owners in Florida, the latter relied on the English jurisdiction clause. A majority of the Court of Appeals for the Fifth Circuit held that it was contrary to United States public policy for the plaintiffs to be deprived of their right of action—there was evidence that the English court (but not the United States court) would give effect to exculpatory clauses in the contract. But the Supreme Court held that jurisdiction clauses are prima facie valid and should be enforced unless the party seeking to resile from such a clause can show enforcement is unreasonable, and that a 'freely negotiated private international agreement, unaffected by fraud, undue influence, or overweening bargaining power . . . should be given full effect'.[127]

Article 17 of the Brussels Convention of 1968 provides (in broad terms) that where parties, one or more of whom is domiciled in a Contracting State, have agreed in writing that the courts of a Contracting State shall have jurisdiction to settle any disputes, then those courts shall have exclusive jurisdiction. The provision has been somewhat liberalized by the 1978 Accession Convention, the Spanish-Portuguese Accession Convention, and the Lugano Convention. Once these are fully in force, the general result will, in EEC and EFTA countries, be to give effect to a jurisdiction agreement which is either (*a*) in writing or evidenced in writing or (*b*) in a form which accords with practices which the parties have established between themselves or (*c*) in international trade or commerce, in a form which accords with the usage with which the parties are, or ought to have been, aware and which in such trade or commerce is widely known to, and regularly observed by, parties to contracts of the type involved in the particular trade or commerce concerned.

2. MEASURES IN A COURT OTHER THAN THE CHOSEN FORUM

It is, however, well established in many jurisdictions that the forum may grant provisional or protective measures even though the parties have agreed to the exclusive jurisdiction of the courts of another country. Thus there can be no doubt that under the Brussels Convention, where jurisdiction clauses are given full effect subject to certain limitations of form, Article 24 allows courts in Contracting States other than the chosen forum to order such measures.

This raises again the question of the extent to which orders such as provisional orders for interim payments should properly be regarded as provisional orders within the meaning of Article 24. In *Menegatti* v. *Soc.*

---

[127] 407 US at 12–13.

Metallurgica Nova Stefano e Giuseppina[128] the Court of Appeal of Paris refused to accede to a claim for 380,000 francs (and for the appointment of an expert to take an account) in a claim by a commercial agent (an Italian living in France) against his Italian principals under a contract giving jurisdiction to the courts of Como. But it was refused, not on the ground that a *référé-provision* was outside the scope of Article 24, but on the ground that the Italian judge would be in a better position to rule on such a claim. This approach is close to *forum non conveniens*.[129]

When the Convention does not apply, French courts have concluded that they have jurisdiction to grant provisional measures, even where the parties have agreed to the jurisdiction of a foreign court on the substance of the litigation, at any rate if the parties have not reserved that power to a chosen court: *Cie de Signaux et d'entreprises électriques* v. *Soc. Sorelec*,[130] where an expertise was refused because the contract was regarded as reserving such matters for the chosen court in Libya. But in cases of urgency, a remedy not involving consideration of the merits may be sought in France. Thus in *Lafitte* v. *Soc. les Transitaires réunis*,[131] it was held that the French court had jurisdiction to appoint a provisional administrator over property situate in France belonging to a foreign company, even though there was an exclusive jurisdiction clause in the statutes of the Vietnamese company providing for the jurisdiction of the courts of Vietnam.

In some maritime cases the English court has refused to give effect to a *foreign* jurisdiction clause, on the ground that to do so would (*inter alia*) deprive the plaintiffs of the security which they had obtained by arresting a ship.[132] But it has also been held in such a case that the jurisdiction clause may be enforced, and the security released, but only on condition that the defendant provides other equivalent security to satisfy the judgment of the foreign court.[133] But it was also settled (in the context of arbitration clauses) that the court did have jurisdiction to allow the continuance of the arrest of the ship pending the outcome of foreign proceedings; that jurisdiction was to be exercised, not in order to provide security for the foreign action, but only (which may not in practice be different) as security for the English action *in rem*, which was stayed, but which might be re-activated if the defendant did not satisfy the foreign judgment.[134] Now, by section 26 of the Civil Jurisdiction and Judgments Act 1982, where the

---

[128] Paris 17.11.1987, 1989 *Clunet* 96, note Huet, who cites other cases in France and Belgium in which provisional measures were granted notwithstanding a jurisdiction clause.
[129] See Section III, *supra*.
[130] Cass. civ. I, 17.12.1985, 1986 *Rev. crit.* 537, note Gaudemet-Tallon.
[131] Paris, 8.10.1964, 1965 *Clunet* 901, note Sialelli.
[132] See *The Athenée* (1922) 11 Ll. LR 6 (CA); *The Fehmarn* [1957] 1 WLR 815 (CA).
[133] *The Eleftheria* [1970] P. 94.
[134] *The Rena K.* [1979] QB 377; *The Tuyuti* [1984] QB 838 (CA). See Section V. *infra*.

court stays or dismisses Admiralty proceedings on the ground that the dispute should be submitted to the determination of a foreign court, the English court may, if a ship has been arrested, either order that the property arrested be retained as security for the satisfaction of the foreign judgment or order that the stay or dismissal of the English proceedings be conditional on the provision of equivalent security for the satisfaction of any judgment.

In England, the court is prepared to grant interim measures, even though the parties have agreed to the jurisdiction of a foreign court, provided that the court has jurisdiction to grant the measures, either *in personam* or *in rem*. In *Law* v. *Garrett*,[135] an early case on exclusive jurisdiction agreements, the parties were all British subjects, who had entered into an agreement to carry on business in partnership as engineers and merchants in St Petersburg. The agreement provided that 'all disputes, no matter how or where they shall arise, shall be referred to the St. Petersburg Commercial Court'. The Court of Appeal held that there was a prima facie duty on the English court to act on the agreement to refer disputes to the St Petersburg court, but it also held that the English court had jurisdiction to appoint a receiver over partnership assets in England if it were shown (which it was not) that no adequate relief could be obtained in Russia.

In *The Siskina*,[136] however, the bill of lading provided for the exclusive jurisdiction of the courts of Genoa. The English court held that it had no jurisdiction to order protective measures, not because of the exclusive jurisdiction clause, but because there was no head of *in personam* jurisdiction under Order 11 of the Rules of the Supreme Court which justified the assumption of jurisdiction to order protective measures. But where the defendant is subject to the *in personam* jurisdiction of the English court, or where the defendant's ship is arrested in England, then the existence of a foreign jurisdiction clause should not, of itself, be a bar to the grant of protective measures.[137]

In the United States there is no reason in principle why provisional measures should not be granted in an appropriate case even if the parties have agreed to the jurisdiction of a foreign tribunal and are litigating the substance of their dispute abroad. It is true, as will be seen in the next section, that several United States courts have refused to order provisional measures if the parties had agreed to arbitration governed by the New York Convention. It will be suggested that these decisions are incorrectly

---

[135] (1878) 8 Ch. D. 26 (CA).   [136] [1979] AC 210.

[137] In *WAC Ltd.* v. *Whillock,* 1990 SLT 213, 219 the Scots court held that it had jurisdiction to interdict a threatened wrong in Scotland even if the parties had agreed to the exclusive jurisdiction of the Northern Ireland courts. See infra, Section V, for a contrary argument in the context of arbitration.

decided, and that the law is correctly represented by several decisions to the opposite effect. But there is no reason to suppose that these decisions apply to foreign jurisdiction clauses, as distinct from arbitration clauses. The only case, however, which seems to deal specifically with the question in the context of jurisdiction clauses is in a contrary sense: *Sanko Steamship* v. *Newfoundland Refining Co. Ltd.*[138] In that case the plaintiffs, shipowners, sued for breach of a time charter and sought a pre-judgment attachment in New York. The charter provided for the jurisdiction of the English courts (with an option for either party to elect for arbitration in London). The court held that the effect of the decision of the Supreme Court in *M/S Bremen* v. *Zapata Off-Shore Co.* was that the defendants were entitled to a dismissal of the action, and with the dismissal, the lifting of the attachment. But in the *Bremen* case the ability of the court to order security was not an issue because the parties had agreed that a bond should be posted which was to be available both in England and in the United States. The *Sanko Steamship* decision is of little authority, and it is suggested that it is wrong.

In the *Sanko Steamship* case the consequence of the holding that the United States court did not have power to retain security while the substance of the case was being determined in the chosen court meant that the plaintiff was left with no effective remedy. In the earlier English cases a similar doubt about the power to retain security led to the opposite conclusion, namely that it would be unjust to stay the English proceedings in favour of the courts of Marseilles in the one case,[139] and of the Soviet Union in the other.[140]

3. OVERRIDING A FORUM SELECTION

It has already been seen[141] that the English court (in cases where Article 24 of the Brussels Convention does not apply) does not have an effective method of providing interim relief against a foreign defendant who is not subject to the *in personam* jurisdiction of the English court.[142] But the need for effective interim relief may require the English court to override the choice of a foreign court. This need lay behind the decision in *Evans Marshall & Co. Ltd.* v. *Bertola.*[143] In that case Evans Marshall were wholesale wine merchants, who were the distributors in England and Scotland of a Spanish sherry called Bertola. They had been the distributors for over 20 years, when the Spanish company was taken over by a new

---

[138] 411 F. Supp. 285 (SDNY 1976), affd. 538 F. 2d 313 (2d Cir. 1976), cert. den. 429 US 858.   [139] *The Athenée, supra.*   [140] *The Fehmarn, supra.*
[141] Section III, *supra.*   [142] *The Siskina* [1979] AC 210.
[143] [1973] 1 WLR 349 (CA).

owner, Sr. Ruiz-Mateos, who owned other sherry interests, including Williams and Humbert, and who decided to take over distribution themselves in breach of contract. They appointed new distributors, an English company closely associated with the Spanish producers. The distribution agreement contained the clause: 'If any law claim arises between the two parties it will be submitted to the Barcelona Court of Justice.'

Evans Marshall sued Bertola and the new distributors in England, and sought an injunction restraining Bertola and the new distributors from distributing or selling Bertola sherry, otherwise than through Evans Marshall. Bertola applied to set aside the English proceedings on the basis that it was a foreign company and that the parties had agreed to the exclusive jurisdiction of the Spanish courts. It was held that this was an appropriate case for the jurisdiction clause to be overridden,[144] because the essence of the case was exclusively concerned with England and Scotland, because it was 'a battle about the proper marketing of sherry in the United Kingdom'. All the essential witnesses were in England, and all the issues essentially related to the marketing conditions of sherry in England and nowhere else. This was because Bertola had purported to terminate the contract on the ground Evans Marshall had not made proper efforts to market and develop the sherry, which had become the second best selling sherry in Scotland, but was not a market leader in England. Another reason was that the plaintiffs were also suing the new distributors, who were in England, and the proceedings would have to go on against them in England in any event. In addition, the fact that interlocutory relief was necessary to preserve the status quo was 'an additional and very cogent reason' for disregarding the jurisdiction clause.

That was a case where the jurisdiction clause would, if it had been given effect, have *deprived* the English court of jurisdiction. It was therefore a case in which the *forum* was confronted with a *foreign* jurisdiction clause, and yet was asked to grant protective measures. What of the case where the forum is the jurisdiction to which the parties have agreed and on which they have *conferred* jurisdiction? What is the attitude of that court where one party seeks protective measures abroad? That was the situation in *The Lisboa*.[145] In that case a bill of lading provided that all proceedings should be brought in London. The plaintiffs' vessel *Lisboa* was on a voyage from Buenos Aires in Argentina to Chioggia in Italy, with a cargo of wheat owned by the defendant cargo owners. During the voyage the vessel had engine trouble and had to reduce her speed and stop on several occasions.

---

[144] Article 17 of the Brussels Convention had no application. The case was decided before the accession to the Brussels Convention by the United Kingdom (1987) or Spain (1991).

[145] [1980] 2 Lloyd's Rep. 546 (CA).

She broke down off Tunisia. The vessel was eventually towed to Chioggia, and the cargo owners claimed a large sum of money for towage expenses. The cargo owners issued legal proceedings in Venice (in breach of the jurisdiction clause in the bill of lading) and the President of the Court of Venice authorized the arrest of the vessel. The owners then sued in England for damages for the unlawful arrest of the vessel in breach of the exclusive jurisdiction clause, and then the cargo owners issued proceedings in England on the substance of the case claiming that the vessel was unseaworthy. The owners then applied for an injunction to restrain the cargo owners from proceeding with the arrest of the ship.

The three members of the Court of Appeal were unanimous in deciding that no injunction should be granted. Lord Denning MR thought that the phrase in the bill of lading 'any and all legal proceedings against the carrier' did not prevent proceedings against the 'ship' and any other interpretation would deprive the cargo owner of the only effective remedy against a one ship company. Lord Justices Waller and Dunn were less convinced, but thought the point was at least arguable. Lord Denning MR also thought that for the purposes of the clause 'legal proceedings' meant only proceedings to establish liability and did not extend to proceedings to obtain security.

He went on:

Suppose, however, that the interpretation was wrong: and that [the clause] does prohibit the cargo-owner from arresting the vessel in any other jurisdiction than England. Suppose then that in breach of that prohibition, the cargo-owner does go to another jurisdiction—such as the Court of Venice—and gets the ship arrested there. Will the English Court grant an injunction to stop the arrest? In the present case we are concerned with a clause giving exclusive jurisdiction to the Courts of *this country*. It is similar to an arbitration clause providing for arbitration in London. If one of the parties breaks that clause and brings proceedings in the Courts of a foreign country, then the Courts of this country have jurisdiction to restrain him from continuing those proceedings—. . . This jurisdiction is, however, to be exercised with great caution so as to avoid even the appearance of undue interference with another Court . . . I am clearly of the opinion that we should not grant an injunction so as to compel the release of this vessel. I can conceive of some cases where an injunction might be granted. For instance, if the cargo-owners had no ground whatever for making any claim against the owners—and nevertheless arrested the ship—this Court might grant an injunction to prevent the continuance of the arrest . . . but when the arrest is made in good faith—for the purpose of obtaining security for a just demand—then I am of opinion that the English Courts should not restrain it by an injunction, even though it is said to be in breach of an exclusive jurisdiction clause . . . nor should they award damages for the breach of such a clause. It seems to me that, by the maritime law of the world, the power of arrest should be, and is, available to a creditor—exercising it in good faith in respect of a maritime claim—wherever the ship is found—even though the merits of the dispute have to be decided by a Court in another country or by an arbitration in another country . . .[146]

Lord Justices Waller and Dunn agreed that in any event no injunction should be granted, for otherwise the cargo owners would be deprived of their security, but Lord Justice Dunn seems to have accepted that at trial it might be decided that the vessel had been wrongfully arrested and the owners might therefore be entitled to damages. This is a subject to which it will be necessary to return in Section VI.

[146] At 549–550.

5

Arbitration

It is not difficult to understand why a party which has agreed to contract to submit disputes to arbitration may wish to enlist the assistance of courts in order to obtain interim protection. Sometimes, of course, the purpose is to avoid arbitration altogether, and consequently consideration of the question whether a party to an arbitration may nevertheless apply to judicial tribunals for interim protection cannot be entirely separated from the issue of the enforceability of arbitration clauses in general. But for present purposes the legal enforceability of the arbitration agreement itself, whether under the New York Convention or otherwise, will be assumed. Nevertheless, even a party who is in principle prepared to submit the substance of a dispute to arbitration will have to take account of the fact that the arbitral tribunal may take considerable time to be constituted, and the claimant may suspect the respondent of wishing to dissipate, or secrete, its assets. Even if the tribunal has been constituted, arbitrators simply do not have the range of remedies, and sanctions, available to them in order to enforce the status quo or otherwise protect the positions of the parties.

The authority of arbitrators to make interim protection orders may derive either from the procedural law governing the arbitration, usually the law of the place where the arbitration takes place, or from the arbitration agreement itself. Thus, under Article 183 of the Swiss Private International Law Statute of 1987:

1. Unless the parties have otherwise agreed, the arbitral tribunal may, on motion of one party, order provisional or conservatory measures.

2. If the party concerned does not voluntarily comply with these measures, the arbitral tribunal may request the assistance of a competent state judge; the judge shall apply his own law.

3. The arbitral tribunal or the state judge may make granting the provisional or conservatory measures subject to appropriate sureties.

In English law the arbitrators are not given a specific statutory authority, although the Arbitration Act 1950 provides that nothing in its provisions concerning the powers of the court shall prejudice any powers the arbitrators may have.[147] There are certain types of orders which are

---

[147] S. 12 (6), proviso.

beyond the scope of the powers of an arbitrator in any event, whatever the arbitration agreement may say. For example, there is no basis in English law for the grant of an injunction or for the appointment of a receiver by an arbitrator. Subject to that, in order to ascertain whether the arbitrator has the power to grant interim relief it is necessary to construe the arbitration agreement, particularly in the light of section 12 (1) of the Arbitration Act 1950, which creates an implication that, in the absence of express agreement to the contrary, the parties shall do 'all . . . things which during the proceedings or reference the arbitrator or umpire may require'.[148]

Further, by agreeing to arbitration under rules such as the UNCITRAL Arbitration Rules, the parties may by contract confer jurisdiction on the arbitrators to order protective measures. Thus Article 26 of the UNCITRAL Rules gives the tribunal power to 'take any interim measures it deems necessary in respect of the subject-matter of the dispute, including measures for the conservation of the goods forming the subject-matter in dispute . . .'.

There is little available material on the exercise of interim powers by arbitrators, because such decisions are normally given in private and are not usually published. But all practitioners will have had experience of them, and some of them have been published, or referred to in published decisions. Thus a New York federal court confirmed an award made in the course of an arbitration requiring funds represented by a letter of credit to be placed in escrow pending the outcome of the arbitration.[149] Another example comes from a very distinguished panel (MM Lalive, Robert, and Goldman) in *Framatome* v. *Atomic Energy Organisation of Iran*.[150] In that case the Iranian Government organization instructed an Iranian bank to make a call under a performance guarantee given by a banking syndicate pursuant to the contractual obligation of the French construction company. The construction company sought interim relief in the form of a declaration that the bank guarantees were unenforceable and that the call was fraudulent and unjustified, and asked for an order that the Iranian Government organization suspend any call until a decision was reached on the merits. Motivated, no doubt, by the fact that one of the parties was a State entity, the tribunal seems to have been influenced by the practice in the International Court of Justice[151] in its decision. First, it referred to the general principle of international arbitration that the parties must refrain from any acts which might have a prejudicial effect on the execution of the ultimate award, and from any acts which might aggravate or extend the

---

[148] See Mustill and Boyd, *Commercial Arbitration* (2nd ed., 1989), p. 328.
[149] *Sperry International Trade Inc.* v. *Government of Israel,* 532 F. Supp. 901 (SDNY 1982).
[150] 1983 *Clunet* 914; (1985) 10 *Yb. Comm. Arb.* 47.
[151] *Infra*, Section XIV.

dispute.[152] This is one of the bases upon which the International Court of Justice (like its predecessor, the Permanent Court of International Justice) indicates interim measures of protection. Secondly, the tribunal did not make an order as such, but 'proposed' that the claimant should withdraw its allegation of fraud and the defendant should renounce its call under the guarantee, until the arbitral proceedings were concluded. This is also an echo of the practice of the International Court of Justice, which has power only to 'indicate' interim measures, and perhaps of the ICSID tribunal, which may only 'recommend' them.

In 1990 the International Chamber of Commerce introduced Rules for a Pre-arbitral Reference Procedure, under which parties may by contract agree to a procedure involving the appointment of a person who will have the power to make certain orders prior to an arbitral tribunal (or a national court) being seised of the dispute. The powers of the Referee will include the power to order not only conservatory measures, but also mandatory orders for payment or for a party to take any step which ought to be taken according to the contract. Unless the parties otherwise agree in writing, a Referee appointed under these Rules is not to act as an arbitrator in subsequent proceedings.[153]

2. RESORT TO THE COURTS

It is clearly not always possible, and it is sometimes not desirable, to apply to arbitrators for provisional or protective measures. First, they may not yet have been appointed, or their appointment may not have been confirmed. Second, they may not have the requisite powers, or the exercise of the powers may not be effective. Thus in Italy interim measures are an essential and unrenounceable part of judicial protection, and they are available from the court even where there is an arbitration agreement. Interim measures are exclusively reserved to the ordinary courts and arbitrators cannot issue them.[154]

---

[152] This formula is derived from the *Electricity Company of Sofia and Bulgaria* case, *PCIJ Ser. A/B, No. 79*, at 199. See Section XIV, *infra*. For the power of arbitrators in ICSID arbitral proceedings to grant interim measures, see Section VII, *infra*, and cf., in particular, *Amco Asia* v. *Indonesia* (1985) 24 ILM 365, 368 (where M. Goldman was also one of the arbitrators).

[153] See Smit, 'Provisional Relief in International Arbitration: The ICC and Other Proposed Rules', (1991) 1 Am. Rev. Int. Arb. 388.

[154] See Code of Civil Procedure, Art. 818; Vigoriti, 'International Arbitration in Italy', (1990) 1 Am. Rev. Int. Arb., Vol. 1, 77 at 86–87. For other countries see Rubino-Sammartano, *International Arbitration Law* (1989), pp. 347–348. For other literature on provisional measures and arbitration see Ramos-Mendez, 'Arbitrage international et mesures conservatoires', 1985 *Rev. arb.* 51; Knoepfler and Schweizer, 'Les mesures provisoires et l'arbitrage', in *Swiss Essays on International Arbitration* (ed. Reymond and Boucher, 1984), p. 221; Ouakrat, 'L'arbitrage commercial international et les mesures provisoires: étude générale', (1988) 14 DPCI 239; Varady, 'The Taking of Provisional Measures in Arbitration', *Hague-Zagreb-Ghent Colloquium*, Session VIII-1989.

To which court should the parties resort? This is by no means as easy a question as it may seem. The natural answer should be that they should resort to the country where the arbitration is being conducted, because the courts of that country are the most natural to deal with matters ancillary to an arbitration. But it may be in some other country that the relevant assets are situate, or the parties are present, and the court where the arbitration is being conducted may not be in the best position to supervise provisional measures.

There is no doubt, of course, that the court of the place where the arbitration is being conducted will have jurisdiction to grant provisional measures. Thus, under section 12 (6) of the Arbitration Act 1950 the English court has in relation to an English arbitration the power to make orders in respect of the preservation, interim custody or sale of any goods which are the subject-matter of the reference; the detention, preservation or inspection of any property which is the subject of the reference; and interim injunctions or the appointment of a receiver. Under the Swiss Private International Law Statute of 1987 the State judge may assist an arbitral tribunal in execution of provisional or conservatory measures (Art. 183), and the State judge at the seat of the arbitral tribunal has jurisdiction in relation to judicial assistance generally (Art. 185). Under the Swiss Concordat, now applicable only in domestic arbitration, 'the ordinary judicial authorities alone have jurisdiction to make provisional orders' unless the parties voluntarily submit to a provisional order proposed by the arbitral tribunal (Art. 26).

There can be little doubt that a request for interim measures from a court is not to be regarded as a waiver of the right to arbitrate. The Geneva Convention of 1961 provides:

A request for interim measures or measures of conservation addressed to a judicial authority shall not be deemed incompatible with the arbitration agreement or regarded as a submission of the substance of the case to the court. (Art. 6 (4).)

and Article 9 of the UNCITRAL Model Law is to the same effect. Under Article 8 (5) of the Rules of Arbitration of the International Chamber of Commerce:

Before the file is transmitted to the arbitrator, and in exceptional circumstances even thereafter, the parties shall be at liberty to apply to any competent judicial authority for interim or conservatory measures, and they shall not by so doing be held to infringe the agreement to arbitrate or to affect the relevant powers reserved to the arbitrator.[155]

In France it has been held that, as a result of this provision, a party to an ICC arbitration could nevertheless obtain a *saisie conservatoire* under

---

[155] Cf. Rules of the London Court of International Arbitration, Art. 15.4; UNCITRAL Model Law, Art. 9.

Article 48 of the Code of Civil Procedure (ancien), because it does not involve an examination of the merits of the litigation: *République Islamique d'Iran* v. *Framatome*.[156] Iran argued that the only conservatory measures which could be ordered in the course of an arbitration were those which in no way involved a consideration of the merits of the litigation, and that the judge ordering a *saisie conservatoire* had to consider the merits. But the Cour de Cassation decided that all the judge had to do in such a case was decide on 'apparence de bon droit', and that did not involve a consideration of the merits, which was reserved to the arbitrators.

This case involved a French arbitration, and a more difficult and controversial question is whether the courts in one country may grant provisional measures when the parties have agreed to international arbitration in another country. It is not likely that Article 8 (5) of the ICC Rules is of much assistance in answering that question. Plainly it primarily relates to the courts where the seat of the arbitration is situated or is to be situated.[157] But it cannot relate exclusively to those courts, because Article 8 (5) may apply, in cases where the parties have not chosen the seat of arbitration, to situations prior to the establishment of the seat.

It is clear from the decision in *Guinea* v. *Atlantic Triton Company*[158] that in principle provisional measures in the form of an attachment can be obtained in France in aid of a foreign arbitration. That case concerned an ICSID arbitration, and will be considered in more detail in Section VII. But the Cour de Cassation accepted that recourse to a court for conservatory measures designed to guarantee the execution of an anticipated award was permissible, and held that the power of national courts to order conservatory measures could only be excluded by express provision of the parties or by an implied agreement resulting from the adoption of arbitral rules which barred such recourse. In its decision of 28 June 1989, the Cour de Cassation considered the validity of a *saisie-arrêt* under Article 558 of the Code of Civil Procedure (ancien) which had been obtained by Iran against Eurodif: *Eurodif* v. *République Islamique d'Iran*.[159] In this case the Cour de Cassation set aside the *saisie-arrêt* obtained by Iran against Eurodif. The basis of the decision appears to be that the steps taken by Iran against Eurodif were not conservatory in nature (because there was no urgency and there was no suggestion that

---

[156] Cass. Civ. I, 20.3.1989, 1990 *Clunet* 1004, note Ouakrat. Cf. also *Eurodif* v. *République Islamique d'Iran*, Cass. civ. I, 14.3.1984, 1984 *Rev. crit.* 644, note Bischoff, 1984 *Clunet* 598, note Oppetit, where it does not seem to have been doubted that (subject to questions of immunity) attachment was available even though an international arbitration was in progress.

[157] Cf. *Channel Tunnel Group Ltd.* v. *Balfour Beatty Construction Ltd.* [1992] 2 WLR 741, 757 (CA), discussed *infra*, Section V.5.

[158] Cass. civ. I, 18.11.1986, 1987 *Rev. crit.* 760, note Audit; 1987 *Clunet* 125, note Gaillard; (1987) 26 ILM 373.

[159] Cass. civ. I, 28.6.1989, 1990 *Clunet* 1004, note Ouakrat.

Eurodif was insolvent or trying to make itself judgment-proof), but in effect designed to obtain execution in advance of judgment. That was not permitted where there was a binding arbitration agreement, and an arbitration in progress.

It has already been seen[160] that, in the practice of the Permanent Court of International Justice, and in decisions on the scope of Article 24 of the Brussels Convention of 1968, there is a question whether an order for interim payment is a provisional or protective measure. The Permanent Court has held that it is not, and it has been submitted that, despite several French decisions to the contrary, it is not a provisional or protective measure for the purpose of Article 24 of the Brussels Convention. What of arbitration? Can a party to an arbitration nevertheless resort to a court for an order for an interim payment?[161] The French courts have answered firmly in the negative, at any rate if an arbitration is proceeding. Under Article 8 (5) of the ICC Rules of Arbitration the parties are permitted to apply to a competent judicial authority for interim or conservatory measures. In France it has been decided that a request for a *référé-provision* or interim payment from a court is not the kind of protective measure which is available from a court when the parties have agreed to arbitrate, at any rate if the arbitration has been commenced. In *République Islamique d'Iran* v. *C.E.A.*[162] the Cour de Cassation decided that a request for a *provision* could not be assimilated to a simple provisional conservatory measure within the meaning of the ICC Rules; and subsequently it has been held more generally that *référé-provision* is incompatible with an agreement to arbitrate.[163] The essence of the reasoning is that a judge who is asked to order a *provision* may only do so if the debt is not seriously contestable, and that is the very question which is reserved to the arbitral tribunal.

In Italy attachments have been allowed pending arbitration in Switzerland[164] and in London.[165] The rationale of these decisions is that conservatory attachment can only be ordered by the courts of the place where the attachment is to be executed, and that proceedings to confirm

---

[160] Section III, *supra*.

[161] The question whether they can apply to the *arbitrators* for an interim payment raises a different question. In principle arbitrators should have power to make an interim or partial *award*, but that is not the same as an order for a provisional payment: cf. award in (1982) 7 *Yb. Comm. Arb.* 124.

[162] Cass. civ. I, 14.3.1984, 1984 *Rev. crit.* 655, note Bischoff.

[163] *Soc. Buzzichelli* v. *Sarl SERMI*, Cass. civ. II, 18.6.1986, 1986 *Rev. arb.* 565, note Couchez. See in the same sense *Maeght* v. *Soc. Galerie Maeght-Lelong*, Trib. gr. inst. Paris, 21.2.1986, *ibid*; and, for other cases on Article 8 (5) of the ICC Rules see *Soc. ESW* v. *Soc. TAI*, Rouen, 7.5.1986; *SIAPE* v. *IEC*, Paris, 14.5.1986, *ibid*. See also Couchez, 'Référé et arbitrage', 1986 *Rev. arb.* 155, 163–164.

[164] *Scherk Enterprises AG* v. *Soc. des Grandes Marques*, 12.5.1977, 4 *Yb. Comm. Arb.* 286.   [165] *Bos e Figli* v. *Occon*, 2.11.1987, 14 *Yb. Comm. Arb.* 677.

the attachment are under the exclusive jurisdiction of the Italian court. It has also been decided that an interim injunction may be granted pending arbitration.[166]

There is therefore little room for doubt that in principle the grant of protective measures by a judicial tribunal is not incompatible with an agreement to arbitrate, and that, in particular, pre-award attachment is not precluded by the New York Convention.[167] But, as will be seen in the succeeding subdivisions of this section, international practice is not uniform.

3. UNITED STATES PRACTICE

It is notorious that, in many cases in the United States, federal and state courts have refused to grant attachments in cases where the parties have agreed to arbitrate, either on the ground that resort to attachment procedure is inconsistent with an agreement to arbitrate, in general, or inconsistent with the obligations of the United States under the New York Convention, in particular.[168]

Long before the New York Convention and the development of international commercial arbitration as it is now known, the great Judge Learned Hand said:[169]

. . . is it clear that to deny [the plaintiff] provisional remedies, will promote resort to arbitration? We should assume not. The most common reason for arbitration is to substitute the speedy decision of specialists in the field for that of juries and judges; and that is entirely consistent with a desire to make as effective as possible recovery upon awards, after they have been made, which is what provisional remedies do.

No one would now say in the context of international commercial arbitration that a 'speedy decision' was usually attainable, but the rest of what Judge Learned Hand said is as valid today as it was in 1944. Yet his decision was dismissed as obsolete and inconsistent with a subsequent Supreme Court decision,[170] on a different point, by the leading case denying the remedy in federal courts: *McCreary Tire and Rubber Co.* v.

---

[166] But it was not granted on the facts: *Pama Industrie SA* v. *Schultz Steel Co.*, Verona, 22.4.1985, 12 *Yb. Comm. Arb.* 494.

[167] Van den Berg, *The New York Arbitration Convention of* 1958 (1981), pp. 139–144.

[168] See, especially, Brower and Tupman, 'Court Ordered Provisional Measures under the New York Convention', (1986) 80 AJIL 24; Becker, 'Attachments in Aid of Arbitration—the American Position' (1985) 1 Arb. Int. 40; McDonnell, 'Availability of Provisional Relief in International Commercial Arbitration', (1984) 22 Col. J. Trans. L. 273; Report of IBA Sub-Committee, 'Interim Court Remedies in Support of Arbitration', (1984) 3 Int. Bus. L. 101.

[169] *Murray Oil Products Inc.* v. *Mitsui & Co. Ltd.*, 146 F. 2d 381 (2d Cir. 1944).

[170] *Bernhardt* v. *Polygraphic Company of America, Inc.*, 350 US 198 (1956).

CEAT SpA.[171] In that case McCreary was the exclusive distributor of tyres manufactured by CEAT under a contract governed by Italian law, which provided for arbitration under ICC Rules in Belgium. McCreary brought an action for breach of the agreement in the United States and attempted to attach debts owed to CEAT there. CEAT obtained a mandatory stay of the proceedings because of the arbitration clause, both Italy and the United States being parties to the New York Convention. The attachment was also discharged. The court recognized that although attachment might ultimately be available for the enforcement of an arbitration award, the complaint sought to 'bypass the agreed upon method of settling disputes',[172] which was prohibited by the New York Convention. The New York Convention forbade the courts of a Contracting State from entertaining a suit which violated an agreement to arbitrate. The decision assumed, without any supporting reasoning, that resort to attachment was in itself a breach of the arbitration agreement, and that to allow attachment would be inconsistent with the New York Convention. It must be borne in mind that this was not a case where the plaintiff genuinely desired arbitration, and was *bona fide* seeking protective remedies from a judicial tribunal. McCreary had brought an action in Massachusetts which was stayed after CEAT had relied on the arbitration clause, and then sought an attachment in Pennsylvania. Consequently the merits were all in the direction of CEAT, and there seems to have been no evidence that McCreary would have been prejudiced by the lifting of the attachment.

In *Metropolitan World Tanker Corp.* v. *TN Pertambangan*[173] the *McCreary* case was followed, and an attachment was vacated, on the basis that there was no indication in the New York Convention that pre-arbitration attachment was warranted under the Convention:

Indeed, the very purpose behind the convention is to bring about the settlement of appropriate disputes solely through arbitration proceedings, and to allow a resort to attachment before such proceedings would seem to put an unnecessary and counter-productive pressure on a situation which could otherwise be settled expeditiously and knowledgeably in an arbitration context.[174]

But this also was a case in which the plaintiffs were attempting to bypass arbitration[175] and the suggestion that attachment would unnecessarily exacerbate a dispute which would otherwise be settled expeditiously and knowledgeably in arbitration is unrealistic and naive.

---

[171] 501 F. 2d 1032 (3d Cir. 1974).   [172] At 1038.

[173] 427 F. Supp. 2 (SDNY 1975).

[174] At 4. Contrast *Coastal States Trading Inc.* v. *Zenith Navigation SA*, 446 F. Supp. 330 (SDNY 1977).

[175] As was *ITAD Associates* v. *Podar Bros.*, 636 F. 2d 75 (4th Cir. 1981). See also *Cordoba Shipping Co.* v. *Maro Shipping Ltd.*, 494 F. Supp. 183, 188 (D. Conn. 1980).

The New York Court of Appeals, by a bare majority of 4 to 3, followed *McCreary* in *Cooper* v. *Ateliers de la Motobecane*.[176] In that case there was a contract between the parties to establish a new corporation in the United States to distribute a French defendant's products, with disputes over valuation of shares to be resolved by arbitration in Switzerland. When disputes arose the defendant demanded arbitration, but the plaintiff commenced an action for a money judgment and obtained an *ex parte* attachment on a debt owed by a New York corporation to the defendant. The New York Court of Appeals held that the attachment should not stand, pending arbitration. The majority reasoned as follows: the provisional remedy of attachment was, in part, a device to secure the payment of a money judgment; it was open to dispute whether attachment was necessary in the arbitration context, since 'arbitration, as part of the contracting process, is subject to the same implicit assumptions of good faith and honesty that permeates the entire relationship'; there would be uncertainty if attachments were permitted and the foreign business entity would be subject to United States laws with which it was unfamiliar. The majority said:

Whenever a matter of foreign relations is involved, one must consider the mirror image of a particular situation. Is it desirable to subject American property overseas to whatever rules of attachment and other judicial process may apply in some foreign country when our citizen has agreed to arbitrate a dispute? It can be assumed that American business entities engaging in international trade would not encourage such a result. Permitting this type of attachment to stand would expose American business to that risk in other countries. The essence of arbitration is resolving disputes without the interference of judicial process and its strictures. When international trade is involved, this essence is enhanced by the desire to avoid unfamiliar foreign law. The UN Convention has considered the problems and created a solution, one that does not contemplate significant judicial intervention until *after* an arbitral award is made. The purpose and policy of the UN Convention will be best carried out by restricting pre-arbitration judicial action to determine whether arbitration should be compelled.[177]

The reasoning is wrong. Attachment is often necessary to preserve the efficacy of arbitration, and whilst in theory arbitration is intended to be dispute settlement without court intervention, the intervention of courts is often desirable, and sometimes necessary, to preserve the integrity of arbitration. There is nothing in the New York Convention which prevents pre-award provisional or protective measures. Consequently, there is nothing in the point that an opposite result would subject United States

---

[176] 456 NYS 2d 728, 57 NY 2d 408, 442 NE 2d 1239 (1982).

[177] 456 NYS 2d at 732. For a change in the New York procedural rules to allow attachment, see Becker, (1985) 2 *Arb. Int.* 365, who points out it is of little practical effect, since *Cooper* is based on an (erroneous) interpretation of *federal* law, which governs.

businesses to attachment in foreign countries. As has been seen above, they are already liable to such attachment even if they have agreed to arbitration.

As in the Federal cases from *McCreary* onwards, in the *Cooper* decision and some at least of those which follow it,[178] the plaintiff was not *bona fide* seeking provisional relief pending arbitration, but rather avoiding arbitration by suing in United States, and attaching property either to obtain jurisdiction or (perhaps) embarrass the defendant. Only in *Drexel Burnham Lambert Inc.* v. *Ruebsamen*[179] did the plaintiff apparently seek to retain an attachment in New York (pending arbitration against Germans in Germany) for the genuine purpose of obtaining security for the award. Indeed the Appellate Division expressly recognized that, but for the New York Convention, the plaintiffs would ordinarily have been entitled to an order of attachment in aid of arbitration under the facts of the case. The Appellate Division noted the plaintiffs' argument that the *Cooper* decision was internally contradictory in that (*a*) it did not refute or distinguish the maritime cases[180] which held that pre-arbitration attachments were permissible under the New York Convention and (*b*) the New York Convention made no distinction between maritime and other types of arbitration. In answer, the court merely held that it was constrained and bound by the *Cooper* decision.

Apart from maritime cases, the federal cases which allow attachment pending arbitration are at first instance. The best known is *Carolina Power and Light Company* v. *Uranex*.[181] In this case a uranium buyer brought an action against the seller, a French company, for breach of contract which provided for arbitration in New York. The plaintiff proceeded *ex parte* in the federal court in California to attach an $85 million debt owed to Uranex by a San Francisco corporation which marketed uranium throughout the United States, and simultaneously sought arbitration in New York. The money was due to Uranex pursuant to a uranium supply contract and had no relationship to the litigation, and but for the attachment the funds would have been transferred out of the country in the ordinary course of business. It was treated as a case governed by the New York Convention, because both France and the United States were parties to it. The court thought the contacts of Uranex with California were not an adequate basis under the *International Shoe* decision to support an assumption of *in personam* jurisdiction.[182] But the plaintiffs relied on the passage in *Shaffer* v. *Heitner*[183] which suggested that a state in which property was located

---

[178] See especially *Fabergé International Inc.* v. *Di Pino*, 491 NYS 2d 345 (NY App. Div. 1985); *Shah* v. *Eastern Silk Industries Ltd.*, 493 NYS 2d 150 (NY App. Div. 1985).
[179] 531 NYS 2d 547 (NY App. Div. 1988).
[180] Relied on by the dissenting judge in *Cooper*, and discussed *infra*.
[181] 451 F. Supp. 1044 (ND Cal. 1977). [182] *Supra*, Section II.
[183] 433 US 196, 209 (1977), *supra* Section II.

should have jurisdiction to attach the property, by use of proper procedures, as security for a judgment being sought in a forum where the litigation could be maintained consistently with *International Shoe*. The court concluded that in the circumstances of the case a fair reading of the opinion of the Supreme Court in *Shaffer* v. *Heitner* required that the application of notions of 'fair play and substantial justice' included consideration of both the jeopardy to the plaintiffs' ultimate recovery and the limited nature of the jurisdiction sought, that is, jurisdiction merely to order the attachment and not to adjudicate the underlying merits of the controversy. Uranex had no other assets within the United States and its business appeared unlikely to bring such assets into the country in the future. The court maintained the attachment, so that the plaintiff could file an action directed to the underlying merits in a jurisdiction that had *in personam* jurisdiction over *Uranex* (presumably France). Accordingly, the decision is not strictly a case of attachment in aid of arbitration. But the court expressly refused to follow *McCreary*. Its reasons were essentially these: nothing in the text of the New York Convention, or in its policies, precluded pre-judgment attachment; and in domestic arbitrations pre-judgment attachments were permitted, and there was no significant difference in the scheme for domestic arbitrations and those governed by the New York Convention.

This decision was applied in *Compania de Navegacion y Financiera Bosnia SA* v. *National Unity Maritime Salvage Corp.*[184] In this case the court did not require an action to be commenced in another jurisdiction against the defendant. It was held that the court had power to order provisional relief pending a foreign arbitration, particularly where the defendants were allegedly participating in a scheme to secrete assets.[185]

There is, in addition, a consistent line of maritime cases in which it has been held that the specific provisions of United States federal law allow arrest or attachment in maritime cases. In *Andros Cia Maritima SA* v. *Andre et Cie*[186] there were charter parties for the carriage of wheat from the United States to Iraq, containing an arbitration clause providing for arbitration in London. Claiming sums due under the charter party, Andros commenced an action in the United States and effected a maritime attachment on all funds, credits or other properties owned by Andre and held within New York by Garnac Grain Co. Section 8 of the Federal Arbitration Act allowed, in Admiralty cases, the party claiming to be aggrieved to bring a proceeding by seizure of the vessel, and the court would then have jurisdiction to direct the parties to proceed with the arbitration and would retain jurisdiction to enter its decree upon the

---

[184] 457 F. Supp. 1013 (SDNY 1978).
[185] Cf. *Tampimex Oil Ltd.* v. *Latina Trading Corp.*, 558 F. Supp. 1201 (SDNY 1983).
[186] 430 F. Supp. 88 (SDNY 1977).

award. Those provisions are still in force except to the extent that they were 'in conflict' with the provisions of the Arbitration Act designed to give effect to the New York Convention. The court concluded that section 8 was no more inimical to the Convention's design to encourage submissions of international commercial disputes to arbitration proceedings, than it had been to the long-standing federal policy reflected in the Arbitration Act as a whole, favouring resort to arbitration of disputes. Congress had plainly and emphatically declared that although the parties had agreed to arbitrate, the traditional Admiralty procedure with its concomitant security should be available to the aggrieved party without in any way lessening its obligation to arbitrate its grievance rather than litigate the merits in the Court. The retention of jurisdiction pending arbitration was not inconsistent with the Convention, nor did it discourage resort to arbitration:

True enough, an attachment may, in some manner and degree, further embarrass already unsettled relations between the parties; nonetheless, the arbitration process—by contrast to settlement negotiations, for example—hardly draws its strength from the parties' mutual good will.[187]

This was the forerunner of many cases allowing attachment in maritime cases.[188] More recently, in *EAST Inc.* v. *M/V Alaia*,[189] a charter party provided for arbitration in London. The charterers rejected the ship as unseaworthy and filed an *in rem* action under the Federal Arbitration Act to compel arbitration under the charter party and to obtain security for the arbitration award through the arrest of the vessel. The court held that the case was governed by the New York Convention, but that the arrest of a vessel prior to arbitration was not inconsistent with the Convention. *McCreary* had been criticized, especially in the Admiralty context, and the court distinguished *McCreary* on the basis that the plaintiff there had sought actively to avoid arbitration, initiating state court proceedings by attaching the property of the defendant. Conversely, section 8 of the Federal Arbitration Act had expressly reserved the right of an aggrieved party in an Admiralty case to employ traditional Admiralty law procedures to obtain security for arbitration. Clearly relief in the complaint was to

---

[187] At 92.
[188] See also *Drys Shipping Corp.* v. *Freights, Sub-Freights etc.*, 558 F. 2d 1050 (2d Cir. 1977); *Atlas Chartering Services* v. *World Trade Corp.*, 453 F. Supp. 861 (SDNY 1978); *Paramount Carriers Corp.* v. *Cook Industries, Inc.* 456 F. Supp. 599 (SDNY 1979); *Construction Exporting Enterprise* v. *Nikki Maritime Ltd.*, 558 F. Supp. 1372 (SDNY 1983); *Cordoba Shipping Co. Ltd.* v. *Maro Shipping Ltd.*, 494 F. Supp. 183 (D. Conn. 1983); *Irinikos Shipping Corp.* v. *Tosco Corp.*, not yet reported (D. Mass. 1984); *Sembawang Shipyard Ltd.* v. *M/V Charger*, 15 Yb. Comm. Arb. 600 (ED La. 1989); *Castelan* v. *M/V Mercantil Parati*, not yet reported (DNJ 1991).
[189] 876 F. 2d 1168 (5th Cir. 1989).

compel arbitration, and the court concluded that pre-judgment attachment under section 8 as an aid to arbitration was manifestly not inconsistent with the aims of the New York Convention.

4. INJUNCTIONS AND ARBITRATION

All of these cases involved pre-judgment attachments. What of other provisional remedies? Sometimes a plaintiff may need injunctive relief of a kind related to the merits, for example to prevent continuing breach of contract. There is again no reason in principle why he should not. The United States decisions support this conclusion.

In *Rogers Burgun, Shahine and Deschler, Inc.* v. *Dongsan Construction Co. Ltd.*,[190] the plaintiffs ('RBSD') were sub-contractors in a hospital project in Saudi Arabia, and Dongsan were the main contractors. Under the sub-contract, to secure an advance payment from the main contractors, the sub-contractors provided a letter of guarantee from a Saudi bank in the full amount of an advance payment. The sub-contract provided for arbitration in France under ICC Rules. A dispute arose with regard to RBSD's performance, and RBSD commenced proceedings in New York alleging breach of contract and seeking sums owed, and an injunction enjoining Dongsan from calling the letter of guarantee. Dongsan filed a motion to dismiss or stay pending arbitration. The motion to stay the proceedings was granted, but it was held that the fact that the dispute was to be arbitrated did not deprive the court of its authority to provide provisional remedies, namely, an injunction to restrain calling upon the guarantee. The court recognized that a preliminary injunction would issue only upon the showing of irreparable harm and either likelihood of success on the merits or sufficiently serious questions going to the merits to make them a fair ground for litigation and a balance of hardship tipping decidedly towards the party requesting the preliminary relief. The relief sought was minimal since the plaintiffs sought only to preserve the status quo with respect to the letter of guarantee. The contract dispute involved a million dollars and Dongsan was a Korean corporation with no fixed assets in the United States. Although it had assets in bank accounts in New York and New Jersey, they were liquid and could easily be depleted or removed from the United States. Any arbitral award obtained in Paris would, as a result, be frustrated. With respect to the letter of guarantee, the potential frustration of recovery was doubled. The money securing the letter was currently in RBSD's possession, and if Dongsan was permitted to call the letter, those assets would be transferred essentially from RBSD to

---

[190] 598 F. Supp. 754 (SDNY 1984).

Dongsan. Any arbitral determination that the plaintiffs were entitled to recover or that Dongsan was not entitled to call the letter would be meaningless if Dongsan were to transfer its liquid assets, increased by the moneys securing the letter, out of the reach of the court. Since there would then be no adequate remedy at law, the court found that there could be irreparable harm if Dongsan was not enjoined from calling the letter.

In *Borden Inc.* v. *Meiji Milk Products Co. Ltd.*,[191] Borden commenced an action seeking a preliminary injunction in aid of arbitration. Borden was a manufacturer and distributor of food and dairy products in the United States, and Meiji manufactured milk and milk products in Japan and other parts of the world. They entered into a trademark licence and technical assistance agreement, pursuant to which Borden licensed the use of its name to Meiji to be used on a variety of margarine products manufactured and sold in Japan. Following expiry of the agreement, Borden contended that the use of certain packaging by Meiji in Japan was a violation of the agreement. All disputes were to be settled by arbitration in Japan. Borden filed a demand for arbitration in the New York court. The situs of the arbitration, which would either be New York or Japan, had not been determined. The court held that entertaining an application for a preliminary injunction in aid of arbitration was consistent with the powers of the court. *McCreary* was distinguished on the basis that the plaintiffs in *McCreary* sought to bypass arbitration altogether. Entertaining such an application for provisional remedies in connection with an arbitral controversy was not precluded by the Convention but was, on the contrary, consistent with its provisions and spirit.[192]

But an injunction was refused in *Pilkington Bros. plc* v. *AFG Industries Inc.*,[193] where an arbitration was pending between Pilkington and AFG in connection with a dispute over failure of AFG to make royalty reports and payments, followed by a further arbitration about a sale by AFG of glass technology allegedly in breach of licence agreements. The English Commercial Court made an *ex parte* order restraining AFG from disclosing certain information. Pilkington sought in the United States a preliminary injunction in similar terms to that of the interim injunction issued by the English court. It did not ask the court to decide the merits of its underlying trade secret and contract dispute, but simply to duplicate the English court order under principles of international comity, because it feared that the English order afforded it inadequate protection in the United States. The court had denied its request for a temporary restraining order, because it

---

[191] 919 F. 2d 822 (2nd Cir. 1990).
[192] Cf. *Tennessee Imports Inc.* v. *Filippi*, 745 F. Supp. 1314 (MD Tenn. 1990); and for injunctive relief by courts in cases of non-international arbitration, see *Teradyne Inc.* v. *Mostek Corp.*, 797 F. 2d 43 (1st Cir. 1986); *Ortho Pharmaceutical Corp.* v. *Amgen Inc.*, 882 F. 2d 806 (3d Cir. 1989).   [193] 581 F. Supp. 1039 (D. Del. 1984).

had failed to demonstrate irreparable injury. It was held that principles of international comity did not require, and militated against, the issuance of a duplicative order which would interject the United States court into the arbitration dispute before the English courts and the English arbitrators. The court said:[194]

By issuing an identically worded injunction while arbitration is still proceeding under the watchful jurisdiction of the English High Court, this Court would offend, rather than promote, principles of international comity. For were this Court to issue Pilkington's requested relief, it would interfere unnecessarily in those foreign proceedings—proceedings in which Pilkington agreed by contract to participate.

5. THE PRACTICE IN ENGLAND

The practice in England deserves a separate section because of the importance of London as a centre of international commercial arbitration. But it has to be said that in England the scope of the power of the courts to grant interim protection in aid of international commercial arbitration is still a matter of some difficulty. It has already been seen that in the United States the decision in *McCreary*, and the federal and state court decisions which follow it, rest on the assumption that resort to judicial attachment procedures is inconsistent with the agreement to arbitrate. If they were not, those decisions would have no basis. Among the reasons for supposing that these decisions are wrong is that normally the subject-matter of arbitration clauses is the determination of *disputes*, and not the place where security is to be obtained.

In England it seems to be accepted that a '*Scott* v. *Avery* clause' (whereby the parties agree that the award of an arbitrator is to be a condition precedent to the enforcement of rights under a contract) may have the effect of preventing a claim in the courts for interim relief, such as an injunction, or other steps to secure the claim.[195]

Research has not revealed a case in which injunctive relief or security was refused by an English court on the ground that the effect of the arbitration clause was to prevent it, but the question has been the subject of discussion in the context of resort to *foreign* courts to obtain attachments, notwithstanding an arbitration clause providing for arbitration in London. In *Marezura Navegacion SA* v. *Oceanus Mutual Underwriting Assn.*[196] an arbitration clause in the rules of a Protection and Indemnity Club provided for arbitration in London, and that 'such Arbitration shall be a condition precedent to the commencement of action at law'. When the

---

[194] At 1046.
[195] Mustill and Boyd, *Commercial Arbitration* (2d ed., 1989), pp. 162–163, 338.
[196] [1977] 1 Lloyd's Rep. 283.

P&I club arrested the plaintiffs' ship in the Netherlands Antilles in connection with a claim for calls (i.e., premiums) the plaintiffs sought an injunction in England to restrain the action in the Netherlands Antilles. Robert Goff J. refused the injunction on the ground (*inter alia*) that the arbitration agreement did not expressly or impliedly prevent any party from taking proceedings abroad for the purpose only of obtaining security and pursuing those proceedings to the stage necessary to obtain security and no further. This was so even if it was necessary in the foreign proceedings to assert the underlying claim in order to obtain the security.

That decision is consistent with the subsequent decision of the Court of Appeal in *The Lisboa*,[197] which concerned a clause submitting disputes to an *English* court, and where one of the parties had arrested the other's ship in proceedings in Italy. It has already been seen[198] that the Court of Appeal refused an injunction to restrain the proceedings in Italy, and that one of the grounds (*per* Lord Denning MR) was that the jurisdiction clause extended only to proceedings to establish liability, and not to proceedings to obtain security for the ultimate enforcement of judgment.

But in *Mantovani* v. *Carapelli SpA*,[199] another decision of the Court of Appeal, it was decided that an arbitration clause providing for arbitration in London did have the effect of prohibiting an action in Italy to obtain security. That case will be considered more fully in Section VI on the right to obtain damages for wrongful attachment, but for present purposes it is necessary to point out that the arbitration clause provided that 'the obtaining of an award shall be a condition precedent to the rights of either party . . . to bring any action or other legal proceedings against the other of them in respect of any such dispute'. The Court of Appeal decided that the correct interpretation of that clause was that any form of application for ancillary relief was within the arbitration clause and prohibited resort to judicial procedures for such relief. It is suggested that the views of Robert Goff J. in *Marezura* and of Lord Denning MR in *The Lisboa* are far preferable to the views of the Court of Appeal in *Mantovani*, both as a matter of interpretation and of policy. As for interpretation, it should have been held that the proceedings in Italy were not 'in respect of any such dispute' since, to adopt Lord Denning's formulation, they were not designed to establish liability. As regards policy, it is plainly just that in principle parties should have the ability to seek security from a party who may not be able or willing to satisfy an award.

But these were cases of *foreign* proceedings in alleged breach of an arbitration agreement providing for arbitration (or judical proceedings in *The Lisboa*) in London. What of proceedings in England to obtain

---

[197] [1980] 2 Lloyd's Rep. 546.   [198] Section IV, *supra*.
[199] [1980] 1 Lloyd's Rep. 375.

injunctive relief or security in the face of an arbitration clause providing for international arbitration (whether in England or abroad)? The issue has most frequently arisen in maritime cases in connection with the power of arrest. In a series of cases it was decided that (*a*) the court had *jurisdiction* to arrest a ship for the purposes of providing security for an arbitration;[200] (*b*) but that jurisdiction should not be *exercised* for the purpose of providing security;[201] (*c*) nevertheless, even if the court was bound to stay an action under section 1 of the Arbitration Act 1975 (which gives effect to the New York Convention) the court could maintain the arrest of a ship if the stay might not be final.[202] These distinctions (without differences) have been obsolete since section 26 of the Civil Jurisdiction and Judgments Act 1982 came into force in 1987. This section provides that where the court stays Admiralty proceedings on the ground that the dispute in question should be submitted to arbitration, the court may (if property has been arrested or bail given to prevent or obtain release from arrest) order that the property arrested be retained as security for the satisfaction of any arbitration award, or order that the stay be made conditional on the provision of equivalent security for the satisfaction of the award.[203] It is likely that the discretion to order security will only be exercised (as it was under the previous law) if it is shown that the defendant might not satisfy the award.[204]

If there is an English arbitration, the court has a power to make an order 'securing the amount in dispute in the reference'.[205] Although there have been suggestions that this power may only be exercised in relation to a specific fund in dispute,[206] it has been held that where there is provision for arbitration in England this power, in conjunction with the power to order interim injunctions,[207] permits the grant of *Mareva* injunctions by the courts in support of English arbitrations. In the *Rena K*[208] cargo owners sued shipowners, and claimed damages for breach of contract in relation to the carriage of a cargo of sugar from Mauritius to Liverpool in a Greek ship. The bill of lading incorporated charter party provisions providing for arbitration in London. The cargo owners commenced an action *in rem* against the ship and *in personam* against its owners. Brandon J. held that

---

[200] *The Andria* [1984] QB 477 (CA); *The Tuyuti* [1984] QB 838 (CA).

[201] *The Rena K* [1979] QB 377; *The Andria, supra; The Tuyuti, supra.*

[202] *Ibid.*

[203] It is possible that such a condition may not be imposed if the action is subject to a mandatory stay under the Arbitration Act 1975, s. 1: see Mustill and Boyd, *Commercial Arbitration* (2nd ed. 1989), p. 341.   [204] Mustill and Boyd, p. 340.

[205] Arbitration Act 1950, s. 12 (6) (*f*).

[206] Mustill and Boyd, p. 332. Cf. *The Tuyuti* [1984] QB 838, 844 (CA); *The Rena K* [1979] QB 377, 408. Contrast *Mantovani* v. *Carapelli SpA* [1980] 2 Lloyd's Rep. 375, 382, *per* Browne LJ.   [207] Arbitration Act 1950, s. 12 (6) (*h*).

[208] [1979] QB 377.

the court had power to grant, by way of alternative security, a *Mareva* injunction in respect of the ship. There was no reason in principle why it should not be available where the action was stayed pending arbitration. Indeed, 'it is now settled law that *Mareva* injunctions may issue in aid of arbitrations'.[209]

Although it is well settled that there is jurisdiction under the Arbitration Act 1950 to grant injunctive relief in relation to an English arbitration, the position with regard to foreign arbitrations is not so clear. The view has been expressed by the present writer[210] that, provided that the English court has *in personam* jurisdiction over the defendant, a *Mareva* injunction or other interlocutory relief may be granted in aid of a foreign arbitration. Thus in Australia an injunction was granted in favour of a Japanese shipping company against an Australian defendant restraining it from disposing of property in Australia, pending the outcome of arbitration proceedings in London.[211] This view is indirectly supported by the reasoning in *Roussel-Uclaf* v. *G. D. Searle & Co. Ltd.*[212] where the French drug company, Roussel, brought an action in England against the United States drug company Searle, and sought an injunction restraining the sale of a heart drug which Roussel claimed was a patent infringement. There was a licence agreement between Roussel and Searle providing for ICC arbitration. Searle had commenced an arbitration, which was proceeding with its seat in Sweden. It was ultimately held that the English subsidiary of Searle was entitled to obtain a stay of the English proceedings because of the arbitration clause. The injunction was refused at an earlier stage, not because it was suggested that the arbitration clause prevented the grant of an injunction, but because the public interest might be affected if heart patients were deprived of the drug.

But whether an injunction may be granted in aid of a foreign arbitration is not free from doubt because of the lingering effect of the unfortunate decision of the House of Lords in *The Siskina*,[213] where Lord Diplock said that a *Mareva* injunction could only be granted in order to preserve 'the *status quo* pending the ascertainment by the court of the rights of the parties and the grant to the plaintiff of the relief to which his cause of action entitles him'.[214] This decision has been criticized above,[215] but it was concerned with a case where the court (on the House of Lord's interpretation of the Rules of the Supreme Court) had no *in personam* jurisdiction over the defendant.

---

[209] *Bank Mellat* v. *Helliniki Techniki SA* [1984] QB 291, 302, *per* Kerr LJ.
[210] In Dicey and Morris, *Conflict of Laws* (11th ed., 1987), p. 558; Collins, *Civil Jurisdiction and Judgments Act 1982* (1983), pp. 138–139.
[211] *Sanko Steamship Co. Ltd.* v. *DC Commodities (A'asia) Pty. Ltd.* [1980] WAR 51.
[212] [1978] 1 Lloyd's Rep. 225.   [213] [1979] AC 210.
[214] At 256.   [215] Section III, *supra*.

In *Channel Tunnel Group Ltd.* v. *Balfour Beatty Construction Ltd.*[216] the plaintiffs were Eurotunnel, the consortium developing the Channel Tunnel, and the defendants were a consortium who had contracted to build the tunnel. The contract provided for arbitration in Brussels before three arbitrators under ICC Rules. A dispute arose as to the proper price to be paid to Eurotunnel for the cooling system, and the contractors threatened to suspend work. Eurotunnel sought an injunction in England. It was held that the express power in the Arbitration Act 1950, section 12, for injunctions to be granted in aid of arbitration did not apply to foreign arbitrations: the 1950 Act was concerned with arbitrations whose seat was England.

Nor could the injunction be granted under the inherent jurisdiction of the court. There were two specific statutory powers to grant injunctions in aid of arbitrations, and these did not apply: first, the power under the Arbitration Act 1950 did not apply because the seat of the arbitration was in England; second, the power under section 25 of the Civil Jurisdiction and Judgments Act 1982 to grant interim relief in relation to arbitration proceedings abroad had not been brought into force. Consequently, the Court of Appeal took the view that where the specific powers most appropriate were not available, it would not be right to grant relief under the general power in the Supreme Court Act 1981, section 37, to grant injunctions.

Moreover, the Court of Appeal drew attention to suggestions in the unreported decision in *Nissan (UK) Ltd.* v. *Nissan Motor Co. Ltd.*[217] that the decision in *The Siskina* precluded the grant of an injunction if the defendants were entitled to a mandatory stay of the English proceedings. The present writer has expressed the view that this suggestion is wrong.[218] When Lord Diplock said in *The Siskina* that an injunction could only be granted where the underlying claim was justiciable or where the court had jurisdiction to enforce it by final judgment, he was speaking in the context of a foreign defendant outside the jurisdiction. It would be a wholly unnecessary (and retrograde) extension of an already unfortunate decision to extend it to the case of defendants who are in England and subject to the *in personam* jurisdiction of the English court.

The position could (and should) be put beyond doubt if section 25 (3) of the Civil Jurisdiction and Judgments Act 1982 were brought into force. It provides that the court may grant interim relief in relation to any arbitration proceedings. There is no requirement that the court should have *in personam* jurisdiction over the defendant, but section 25 (2)

---

[216] [1992] 2 WLR 741 (CA).
[217] Unreported: see [1992] 2 WLR at 758–759.
[218] Collins, 'The Legacy of The Siskina', (1992) 108 *LQR* 175, 181.

provides that the court may refuse interim relief if, in the opinion of the court, the fact that the court has no jurisdiction apart from section 25 in relation to the subject-matter of the proceedings makes it inexpedient for the court to grant interim relief.

6

Remedies for Measures Taken in the 'Wrong' Jurisdiction

I. INTRODUCTION

This section will consider the consequences of provisional measures taken in the 'wrong' forum, i.e. in a court which is not the court chosen as the jurisdiction in which disputes are to be determined, or, in the case where there is an arbitration agreement, in a court which is not a court sitting in the country which is the seat of the arbitration. It will also consider the remedy available in the 'right' forum, i.e. the forum of the chosen court or the seat of the arbitration. The remedy in the 'wrong' forum primarily would be the stay of the local proceedings, or the discharge of the injunction or attachment. But what if the 'wrong' forum considers (as it often will) that the attachment or injunction in aid of the foreign proceedings is justifiable? Can the defendant resort to the 'right' forum to prevent the continuance of the foreign proceedings or to obtain damages for any loss caused by the relief?

This question has been considered in three English decisions but has received little attention elsewhere. The French courts, it seems, will not rule on the validity of an attachment abroad or award damages in respect of it.[219] In the United States Professor Reese[220] has suggested that the violation of a choice of forum clause may give rise to damages for its breach, and the point has been raised, but not decided, in two decisions.[221]

In the first of the English decisions, there was a London arbitration

---

[219] Cf. Batiffol and Lagarde, *Droit international privé*, 7th ed., Vol. 2, para. 681 (2) (but in these cases the French court had jurisdiction under Article 14 or 15 of the Civil Code, and they were not cases of breach of arbitration or jurisdiction clauses). The question has also arisen in an ICSID arbitration, where arbitrators refused damages claimed in respect of allegedly wrongful attachment proceedings in French courts: *Guinea* v. *Atlantic Triton*, 1988 *Clunet* 181, note Gaillard; 1987 *Rev. crit.* 760, note Audit, *infra*, Section VII.

[220] 'The Contractual Forum: Situation in the United States', (1964) 13 Am. J. Comp. L. 187.

[221] *Nute* v. *Hamilton Mutual Insurance Co.*, 72 Mass. (6 Gray) 174, 181 (1856) and *Copperweld Steel Co.* v. *Demag-Mannesmann-Bohler*, 578 F. 2d 953 (3d Cir. 1978) (where the point arose in the United States court, and the German defendant counterclaimed for damages caused by the United States court having taken jurisdiction despite a German jurisdiction clause: this was a hopeless claim).

clause; one of the parties effected an arrest of the other's vessel in the Netherlands Antilles: *Marazura Navegacion SA* v. *Oceanus Mutual Underwriting Assn.*[222] In the second decision, there was a London arbitration clause in the contract of sale: the sellers obtained an Italian court order detaining some of the buyer's goods; the buyer claimed damages in the arbitration for loss suffered as a result of the Italian proceedings: *Mantovani* v. *Carapelli SA.*[223] In the third case, a bill of lading provided for the exclusive jurisdiction of the English court; cargo owners arrested the owners' ship in Italy; the shipowners issued proceedings in England for damages caused by the arrest in Italy and for an injunction requiring the cargo owners to have the ship released: *The Lisboa.*[224]

2. REMEDIES IN THE 'RIGHT' FORUM

It has already been seen in Section V that the approach of the English courts in such cases is to consider whether on its correct interpretation the arbitration or jurisdiction clause is intended to prohibit the parties from seeking provisional or protective measures outside the chosen forum. In *Marazura Navegacion SA* v. *Oceanus Mutual Underwriting Assn.*[225] a P&I club (a mutual marine insurance club) arrested a ship in the Netherlands Antilles, in the course of a dispute about the shipowners' liability to pay calls (the equivalent of premiums). Relying on a London arbitration clause in the rules of the club, the plaintiff shipowners sought an injunction in the English court to restrain the club from continuing with the proceedings in the Netherlands Antilles, but the injunction was refused. Robert Goff J. said that the effect of the arbitration clause was to provide that the English arbitration tribunal was the only tribunal which could 'adjudicate upon any difference or dispute' within the meaning of the clause, but it was

difficult to see why such agreement expressly or impliedly precludes any party from taking proceedings abroad for the purpose only of obtaining security and pursuing such proceedings to the stage necessary to obtain security and no further, even if such proceedings involve the assertion before the tribunal of a claim, which is the subject of a dispute within the clause.[226]

It was not necessary for the purposes of that decision to express a final view on this issue, because he refused an injunction on the ground of the balance of convenience: damages were an adequate remedy for the shipowners and they could not give an effective undertaking in damages

---

[222] [1977] 1 Lloyd's Rep. 283.
[224] [1980] 2 Lloyd's Rep. 546 (CA).
[226] [1977] 1 Lloyd's Rep. at 288–289.

[223] [1980] 1 Lloyd's Rep. 375 (CA).
[225] [1977] 1 Lloyd's Rep. 283.

(that they would compensate the P&I club if it were subsequently held that the injunction should not have been granted).

Mantovani v. *Carapelli SpA*[227] concerned the sale of a large consignment of soya bean meal under a contract incorporating the standard terms and conditions of contract 119 of the Grain and Feed Trade Association (GAFTA 119) which provided as follows:

Neither party hereto . . . shall bring any action or other legal proceedings against the other of them in respect of any such dispute until such dispute shall first have been heard and determined by the arbitrators . . . and it is expressly agreed and declared that the obtaining of an award . . . shall be a condition precedent to the rights of either party thereto . . . to bring any action or other legal proceedings against the other of them in respect of any such dispute.

The dispute which arose was whether the buyers were entitled to refuse to take the goods on the ground that weighing and sampling facilities had been refused. The sellers sent an invoice to the buyers' bank, but the buyers refused to take up and pay for the documents, and the dispute was referred to arbitration. Both parties were Italian. The sellers won the arbitration (and the arbitrators' decision was eventually upheld), but for present purposes the interest of the decision lies in the consequences of the proceedings for security taken by the sellers in the Italian courts. Shortly after the arbitration proceedings were commenced, the sellers started legal proceedings in Italy in an attempt to obtain security in respect of the claim for damages submitted to arbitration in London. An order was obtained from the Italian court for the detention of some of the buyers' goods; the order was later discharged because the sellers had not provided any bank guarantee as required under Italian procedure. After the arbitration award had been issued, further proceedings were commenced in Italy by the sellers against the defendants in Verona, when the buyers' bank accounts were sequestrated. Subsequently a quantity of wheat in store was substituted as security, and an attachment order on certain land owned by the buyers was issued instead.

The buyers complained in the arbitration that those proceedings in Italy were in breach of the arbitration clause and that as a result of the breach they suffered considerable financial loss. Under the then prevailing procedure in England, the arbitrators asked the court to rule whether the sellers were in breach of contract in starting legal proceedings in Italy, and, if so, whether the buyers were entitled to damages. It was submitted on behalf of the seller that (*a*) what happened in Italy was not, on the proper construction of the arbitration clause, a breach of it and (*b*) that, in any event, in the modern law the proper remedy for such a breach was not to claim damages, but to seek some form of equitable relief, either by an

[227] [1980] 1 Lloyd's Rep. 375 (CA).

application for a stay or by an injunction. The sellers argued that the object of the arbitration clause was to ensure that the dispute which had arisen between the parties should be dealt with under the arbitration clause and not by any other form of proceedings; that all that had happened in Italy was that the sellers had tried to protect themselves against a possible disappearance of the buyers' assets, and that had nothing to do with the dispute, being an ancillary precaution taken to safeguard the subject-matter of the dispute; it was, therefore, not a proceeding 'in respect of' the dispute. Such a procedure would have been possible in England by way of a *Mareva* injunction, but as the buyers had no assets in England, the sellers had gone to the jurisdiction where the buyers had got some assets, Italy.

The Court of Appeal held that the arbitration clause prohibited 'other legal proceedings' which were 'in respect of' the dispute and that, consequently, any form of application for ancillary relief, and in particular that sought in Italy, was a breach of the arbitration clause. The court thought that the need to resort to foreign courts to seek ancillary relief had to be balanced against the possibility that proceedings outside the jurisdiction might be oppressive to one of the parties to an arbitration. The consequence was that, although the buyers were ordered to pay the sellers approximately US $1.8 million with interest on the sellers' claim in relation to the sale of goods dispute, the buyers were successful in their counterclaim of approximately £50,000 against the sellers.

That case should be contrasted with the decision in *The Lisboa*.[228] The Court of Appeal held that the shipowners were not entitled to an injunction restraining the arrest of a ship in Italy, notwithstanding that the bill of lading provided for the exclusive jurisdiction of the English courts. Lord Denning MR based the decision on the wider ground (*inter alia*) that the expression 'any and all legal proceedings' should be construed as relating only to proceedings to establish liability, and did not extend to proceedings to enforce a judgment or award or to obtain security, since any other interpretation would deprive a cargo owner of his only effective remedy against a one ship company. But he also said:

. . . when the arrest is made in good faith—for the purpose of obtaining security for a first demand—then I am of opinion that the English Courts should not restrain it by injunction, even though it is said to be in breach of an exclusive jurisdiction clause . . . nor should they award damages for the breach of such a clause. It seems to me that, by the maritime law of the world, the power of arrest should be, and is, available to a creditor—exercising it in good faith in respect of a maritime claim—wherever the ship is found—even though the merits of the dispute have to be decided by a Court in another country or by an arbitration in another country.[229]

---

[228] [1980] 2 Lloyd's Rep. 546 (CA). [229] [1980] 2 Lloyd's Rep. at 549–550.

The other members of the Court of Appeal expressed no view on this aspect, except that Dunn LJ indicated that, if it were held at trial that the vessel had been wrongfully arrested, the *Mantovani* case showed that the plaintiffs would have a remedy in damages.

Although damages as a remedy for breach of an arbitration clause has a respectable history[230] and there are historical links between arbitration clauses and exclusive jurisdiction clauses,[231] the philosophy behind the decisions in *Mantovani* v. *Carapelli* and *The Lisboa* is quite different. The remedy sought in *The Lisboa*, the injunction, has a more modern feel, as has the limitation put on the scope of the jurisdiction clause by Lord Denning. The decision in *Mantovani* v. *Carapelli* leads to an unnecessary distinction between protective measures taken in England and those taken abroad. It has been seen in Section V that if the seat of the arbitration is England, the English court has jurisdiction to grant protective measures under section 12 (6) of the Arbitration Act 1950, if the arbitration is in progress. If arbitration is contemplated (but not yet commenced) the plaintiff may bring an action in the courts, and the court may stay the proceedings while allowing provisional and protective measures to stay in place.[232]

As Megaw LJ pointed out in *Mantovani* v. *Carapelli*,[233] if measures are taken in England, and the defendant alleges that they are in breach of an arbitration agreement, then the appropriate remedy is for the defendant to seek a stay. If he succeeds, and if the injunction was wrongly granted, he may seek an enquiry as to damages on the cross-undertaking. If the same has occurred abroad, then he will usually have equivalent remedies in the foreign court. But a successful resort to provisional measures in England will not give rise to a right to damages, and there is no reason why the same should not be so if the remedy has been obtained in a foreign court.

As regards proceedings for provisional or protective measures in breach of jurisdiction agreements, Article 24 of the Brussels Convention of 1968 provides for the grant of such measures by the court of one Contracting State even if courts of another Contracting State have jurisdiction. It surely must be inconsistent with the Convention for the English court to seek to enjoin a party from obtaining an attachment in France (or to award damages) on the ground that the parties had agreed to the jurisdiction of the English court.

---

[230] *Doleman* v. *Ossett Corporation* [1912] 3 KB 257; Mustill and Boyd, *Commercial Arbitration*, (2nd ed., 1989), pp. 461, 524.

[231] See Kahn-Freund, 'Jurisdiction Agreements: Some Reflections', (1977) 26 *ICLQ* 825, 833.   [232] *The Rena K* [1979] QB 377.

[233] [1980] 1 Lloyd's Rep. at 384.

7

ICSID Arbitration

The propriety of provisional measures in national courts in the context of arbitration under the World Bank Convention on the Settlement of Investment Disputes between States and Nationals of Other States deserves a separate heading. It has been suggested in Section V that there is no inherent inconsistency between an agreement to refer disputes to arbitration, on the one hand, and resort to national courts for provisional or protective relief, on the other. Accordingly, it was also suggested that there is nothing in the New York Convention of 1958 which requires Contracting States to ensure that their courts do not assume jurisdiction to give such relief.

The position with regard to the World Bank Convention is somewhat different. The Convention established the International Centre for Settlement of Investment Disputes ('ICSID') against the background (as the preamble to the Convention puts it) that disputes between Contracting States and nationals of other States in connection with private investment 'would usually be subject to national legal processes' and that 'international methods of settlement may be appropriate in certain cases'. Accordingly, Article 26 of the Convention provides:

Consent of the parties to arbitration under this Convention shall, unless otherwise stated, be deemed consent to such arbitration to the exclusion of any other remedy . . .

The World Bank Convention, which came into force in 1966, set up an autonomous arbitration system under public international law. Two important issues have arisen on provisional measures and their relationship with the ICSID arbitration: the first is the scope of the power of ICSID tribunals to recommend provisional measures; the second is the propriety of the grant of provisional measures by national courts. These issues are linked in two ways: first, it may be said that the fact that an ICSID tribunal has power only to 'recommend' provisional measures suggests that the Contracting States did not intend to deprive national courts of the power to prescribe provisional measures.[234] Secondly, in the majority of the cases in which an ICSID tribunal was asked to recommend provisional measures,

---

[234] See, especially, Gaillard, 1985 *Clunet* at 942–944; 1987 *Clunet* 125, at 128.

the purpose of the applicant (in two cases out of three, the Respondent State) was to prevent the other party from seeking relief in national courts.

2. PROVISIONAL MEASURES AND ICSID TRIBUNALS

Article 47 of the convention provides:

Except as the parties otherwise agree, the Tribunal may, if it considers the circumstances so require, recommend any provisional measures which should be taken to preserve the respective rights of either party.

The word 'recommend' was deliberately preferred to the word 'prescribe',[235] and consequently it is likely that a recommendation under Article 47 is not binding. A similar issue arises in relation to the power of the International Court of Justice (and its predecessor, the Permanent Court of International Justice) to 'indicate' provisional measures. Except for the substitution of the word 'recommend' for the word 'indicate' the relevant parts of Article 47 of the World Bank Convention and of Article 41 of the Statute of the International Court of Justice are identical. It will be seen below[236] that the prevailing (but not unanimous) view is that an 'indication' of interim measures of protection by the International Court of Justice is not legally binding. It is only necessary to mention that the view that it might be binding (and the same must apply to a 'recommendation' by an ICSID tribunal) is based on the thought that the parties are under an implied obligation to do nothing to frustrate their agreement to arbitrate and that an indication by the International Court of Justice (and also a recommendation by an ICSID tribunal) would be declaratory of an already existing obligation. Normally, of course, a party will have a strong interest in complying with a 'recommendation' by an ICSID tribunal, to whose jurisdiction it has submitted and whose awards will be enforceable. The position with regard to the International Court is very different. But such considerations did not prevent the Republic of the Congo from failing to comply with a recommendation from an ICSID tribunal in *AGIP* v. *Congo* that it would preserve (and produce) the claimant's documents in its custody.[237]

---

[235] ICSID, *History of the Convention*, Vol. 1, p. 206, where the Working Paper and Preliminary and First Drafts use the word 'prescribe'. See also Vol. 2, Pt. 2, pp. 812–815. See Brower and Goodman, 'Provisional Measures and the Protection of ICSID Jurisdictional Exclusivity against Municipal Proceedings', (1991) 6 ICSID Review—FILJ 431, at 440–443, on the history of Article 47 and at 451–460, on the extent to which the jurisdiction of the Tribunal must be established before it recommends provisional measures.

[236] Section XIV, *infra*.

[237] See Delaume, 'ICSID Tribunals and Provisional Measures—A Review of the Cases' (1986) 1 ICSID Review—FILJ 392, at 393.

Other parallels with practice in the International Court are worthy of mention. In *Amco Asia Corp.* v. *Indonesia*[238] the Republic of Indonesia requested from the tribunal an order that the claimants should take no action which might aggravate or extend the dispute. They complained that the plaintiffs had published propaganda in Hong Kong newspapers calculated to discourage foreign investment in Indonesia. The tribunal decided that the article could not have done any actual harm or aggravated or exacerbated the dispute; it was necessary for the party which asked for a provisional measure to specify the rights that the measure would be intended to preserve, and those rights were the rights in dispute, and no such right could be threatened by the publication of the articles.

The argument of the applicant and the decision of the tribunal reflect two important principles of international adjudication. The first is that the parties are under an obligation (in the words of the Permanent Court of International Justice in the *Electricity Company of Sofia and Bulgaria* case[239])

to abstain from any measure capable of exercising a prejudicial effect in regard to the execution of the decision to be given and, in general, not to allow any step of any kind to be taken which might aggravate or extend the dispute.

The application by Indonesia was a direct and literal invocation of this principle. The second is that provisional measures are designed to protect rights in issue, and not other rights. This too is a principle which has been accepted by the International Court, most recently when Guinea-Bissau unsuccessfully sought an indication from the International Court that Senegal should cease activities in a disputed maritime boundary area. Since the case involved the validity of an arbitral award delimiting the maritime area, and not the rights of the parties to the maritime area itself, the application failed.[240]

3. PROVISIONAL MEASURES AND NATIONAL COURTS

In view of the provision in Article 26 of the Convention that consent to ICSID arbitration is consent to such arbitration 'to the exclusion of any other remedy' it is not surprising that it was held in Belgium and Switzerland that the effect of Article 26 was that it was not possible for a private party to obtain an attachment in those countries in aid of an arbitration brought, or to be brought, before an ICSID tribunal in proceedings against a Contracting State. Both cases arose out of a dispute

---

[238] (1985) 24 ILM 365.
[239] *PCIJ* Ser. A/B, No. 79, at 199. See *infra*, Section XIV.
[240] See *Arbitral Award of 31 July 1989* case, *ICJ Reports*, 1990, 64.

between the Republic of Guinea and Maritime International Nominees Establishment ('MINE'), concerning an agreement for the equipment and management of ships to transport bauxite from Guinea. MINE had obtained an arbitration award by default under American Arbitration Association Rules, in the sum of $25 million. Subsequently the award was set aside.[241] MINE then commenced an ICSID arbitration, as it should always have done, but then sought attachments in Belgium and Switzerland.[242] In Belgium, the Antwerp court decided that it was not competent to grant an attachment because an attachment was a 'remedy' within the meaning of Article 26 of the Convention, which was excluded by that provision. A remedy, the court thought, was the means by which a right was enforced, or the violation of a right was prevented, redressed or compensated.[243] In Switzerland an attachment was first obtained by MINE on the basis of the United States default award which it had wrongly obtained, but in the course of those proceedings the Swiss Federal Tribunal indicated that an attachment in support of an ICSID proceeding would not have been possible.[244] Subsequently the Geneva court decided that:

recourse to ICSID arbitration should be considered as an implied waiver of all other means of settlement (Art. 26)—when a State agrees to submit a dispute to ICSID arbitration and to thereby give an investor access to an international forum, this State should not be exposed also to other means of pressure or to other remedies.[245]

It is not surprising that this view has been advanced in applications to ICSID tribunals for recommendations under Article 47 that national proceedings should be halted on the ground that they are inconsistent with ICSID arbitration. In the first ICSID arbitration, *Holiday Inns* v. *Morocco*,[246] Holiday Inns had contracted to construct hotels in Morocco, but ceased construction in the course of a dispute with Morocco, which they submitted to ICSID arbitration. Subsequently, the Moroccan Government obtained orders from the Moroccan courts authorizing it to complete the hotels at Holiday Inns' expense, and appointing a judicial administrator. On Holiday Inns' application for a recommendation of provisional measures, the Moroccan Government argued (*inter alia*) that the court orders were properly made to protect the rights of the parties *pendente lite*. The tribunal did not directly address the issue of the relationship between

---

[241] See *MINE* v. *Guinea*, 693 F. 2d 1094 (DC Cir. 1982), cert. den. 104 S. Ct. 71 (1983).

[242] See Marchais, 'ICSID Tribunals and Provisional Measures—Introductory Note to Decisions of Antwerp and Geneva in *MINE* v. *Guinea*', (1986) 1 ICSID Review—FILJ 372.

[243] (1985) 25 *ILM* 1639.   [244] See 1 *Int. Arb. Rep.* 257.

[245] (1986) 1 ICSID Review—*FILJ* 383, at 390. See also decision of Office de poursuites (1987) 27 *ILM* 382.

[246] Lalive, 'The First "World Bank" Arbitration (*Holiday Inns* v. *Morocco*)—Some Legal Problems', (1980) 51 BYIL 123.

ICSID arbitration and provisional measures in national courts, but instead ruled that the parties should abstain from any measures incompatible with the upholding of the contract.[247]

It has already been seen that in proceedings against Guinea, MINE had attempted to secure attachments in Belgium and Switzerland. The Republic of Guinea sought and obtained from the ICSID tribunal the following recommendations:[248]

... that MINE immediately withdraw and permanently discontinue all pending litigation in national courts, and commence no new action ... that MINE dissolve every existing provisional measure in national courts (including attachment, garnishment, sequestration, or seizure of the property of Guinea, by whatever term designated and by whatever means performed) and seek no new provisional remedy in a national court.

When the Republic of Guinea sought a recommendation in another ICSID arbitration (*Atlantic Triton*) that Atlantic Triton should desist from attachments in the French courts (to be discussed below), the application was dismissed as moot, because at that stage the Court of Appeal of Rennes had lifted the attachment. In 1986 the tribunal refused to grant damages in favour of the Republic of Guinea for the unlawful attachment because it was wrong to reproach Atlantic Triton for having adopted the commonly recognized view that there was no inconsistency between agreeing to international arbitration, on the one hand, and seeking provisional remedies in national courts, on the other, and because the question whether the World Bank Convention and the ICSID Rules were exceptions to other arbitration rules was 'very delicate'.[249] Nor was Atlantic Triton liable in quasi-delict because its resort to the French court was not an abuse of right.

In *Guinea and Soguipeche* v. *Atlantic Triton Co.*[250] Atlantic Triton was a Norwegian company which had agreed to undertake the conversion, equipping and operation of three vessels acquired by Guinea with a view to establishing a fishing industry designed to meet the food needs of the urban population. The Government of Guinea requested technical assistance from the Food and Agriculture Organization to improve the poor results obtained by the National Fishing Company. The study showed that the ships were unsuitable for fishing in Guinea, that the Norwegian nets were unsuitable and the ships had not been properly maintained. Subsequently,

---

[247] Lalive, at 136–137.   [248] (1986) 1 ICSID Review—FILJ at 386.

[249] (1987) 12 *Yb. Comm. Arb.* 183. A fuller version is at 1988 *Clunet* 181, note Gaillard, Cf. Van den Berg (who was one of the arbitrators), 'Some Recent Problems in the Practice of Enforcement under the New York and ICSID Conventions', (1987) 2 ICSID Review—FILJ 439, at 453–455.

[250] Cass. civ. I. 18.11.1986, 1987 *Rev. crit.* 760, note Audit; 1987 *Clunet* 125, note Gaillard, (1987) 26 *ILM* 373; (1984–1986) 82 ILR 76.

Guinea refused to pay Atlantic Triton, which cancelled the agreement. Atlantic Triton obtained an order from the President of the Commercial Court at Quimper authorizing attachment of the three ships as security for its claim, and subsequently requested arbitration under ICSID.

The Court of Appeal of Rennes[251] decided that the lower court lacked jurisdiction to grant the conservatory order requested, because of Article 26 of the ICSID Convention. But the Cour de Cassation[252] decided that Article 26 was not intended to prevent recourse to a judge for conservatory measures designed to secure the execution of an award. The power of national courts to order conservatory measures could only be excluded by express consent of the parties, or by implied agreement resulting from the adoption of arbitral rules which required such waiver. The ICSID Convention and Rules did not amount to such a waiver.

The decision of the Cour de Cassation has been the subject of considerable criticism. M. Delaume, formerly the Senior Legal Adviser to the World Bank, has suggested that it was 'dispensed in total disregard for the official views of the ICSID community'.[253] As he points out, France endorsed the exclusive character of ICSID proceedings in the submissions of the Procureur-Général before the Rennes court, and also was among those (more than 80) Contracting States represented on the Administrative Council of ICSID who unanimously adopted a resolution in 1984, in which revised ICSID Arbitration Rules were introduced. Rule 39 (5), under the heading of 'Provisional Measures', provides that nothing:

shall prevent the parties, provided that they have so stipulated in the agreement recording their consent, from requesting any judicial or other authority to order provisional measures, prior to the institution of proceeding, or during the proceeding, for the preservation of their respective rights and interests.

This provision applies to consent to ICSID arbitrations given after 26 September 1984, and does not in any way affect or amend the Convention itself.

It remains to be seen whether the change in the Rules will have the intended effect of only allowing national court attachments if the parties have specifically consented. It is possible that the new Article 39 (5) may be

---

[251] (1985) 24 *ILM* 340, on which see Gaillard, 1985 *Clunet* 925; Flécheux, 1985 *Rev. arb.* 439.

[252] No doubt much influenced by the views of Gaillard, *op. cit.*, who relies on the *travaux préparatoires* relating to Art. 26 and 47 as suggesting that recourse to national courts was not intended to be excluded. It is suggested, however, that the passages he cites are of no assistance.

[253] Delaume, 'Judicial Decisions Related to Sovereign Immunity and Transnational Arbitration', (1987) 2 ICSID Review—FILJ 403, at 421. See also Friedland, 'ICSID and Court-Ordered Provisional Remedies: An Update', (1988) 4 Arb. Int. 161; Friedland, 'Provisional Measures in ICSID Arbitration', (1986) 2 Arb. Int. 335, 350–356; Marchais, 'Mesures provisoires et autonomie du système d'arbitrage C.I.R.D.I.', (1988) 14 *DPCI* 275.

outside the scope of the rule-making power in Article 44 of the Convention, and that some national courts will on grounds of public policy regard the agreement to oust their jurisdiction as ineffective. But the Cour de Cassation itself expressly recognized that the right to resort to national courts for interim measures could be excluded by means of an express agreement of the parties or by an implicit agreement resulting from the adoption of arbitration rules which contain a renunciation of the right. The new rule 39 (5) will result in such an implicit agreement, and therefore it is extremely unlikely that the fundamental issue will arise again in France.

8

Extraterritorial Provisional Measures

I. INTRODUCTION

When the Court of Appeals for the Ninth Circuit held that the United States court had jurisdiction to grant a preliminary injunction restraining former President Marcos and Mrs Marcos from disposing of their assets, it also ruled that the injunction against the Marcoses could apply to their assets abroad:

The injunction is directed against individuals, not against property; it enjoins the Marcoses and their associates from transferring certain assets wherever they are located. Because the injunction operates *in personam*, not *in rem*, there is no reason to be concerned about its territorial reach . . . A court has the power to prevent a defendant from dissipating assets in order to preserve the possibility of equitable remedies . . . The injunction here enjoins the defendants from secreting those assets necessary to preserve the possibility of equitable relief.[254]

Many countries exercise jurisdiction to order provisional measures in relation to acts or things abroad. In Italy the fact that an order may take effect abroad does not constitute a limitation on the power to order provisional measures. Thus, in *Gagliardi* v. *Larocca*[255] the dispute concerned the succession to the estate of an Italian citizen who had left property in Italy and other countries, particularly in Switzerland and Venezuela. An illegitimate son claimed his share of the inheritance and obtained *sequestro giudiziario* under Article 670 of the Code of Civil Procedure in relation to the properties left by the deceased. The Court of Cassation considered the *sequestro* lawful in relation to the foreign property. It was irrelevant that it might be difficult to enforce the measures abroad. That was left to foreign judges and would be solved by them on the basis of their procedural rules, including the relevant international conventions. Similarly, it is apparent from the order of the Italian court which was the subject of German enforcement proceedings in *Brennero SAS* v. *Wendel GmbH*[256] that the Italian court was able, in *inter partes* proceedings, to make a provisional protective order which purported to affect assets in Germany.

---

[254] *Republic of the Philippines* v. *Marcos*, 862 F. 2d 1355, 1363–1364 (9th Cir.), cert. den. 490 US 1035 (1988).

[255] Cass. No. 3464 of 8 June 1985, 1987 *Riv. dir. int. priv. proc.* 79.

[256] Case 258/83 [1984] ECR 3971.

In France the remedy of *saisie-conservatoire* is primarily territorial, and according to some authors *exclusively* territorial.[257] There is no doubt that the French court has jurisdiction to order a *saisie-conservatoire* if the debtor has property in France, whether or not the debtor is domiciled abroad, and even if a foreign tribunal has exclusive jurisdiction.[258] So also can the French court order a *saisie-arrêt* if the third party debtor (i.e. the person who owes money to the defendant) is domiciled in France, irrespective of the domicile of the debtor; in such a case France is the location of the property, because a debt is situate at the place where the debtor resides.[259] So also can the French court make an order in respect of tangible movables situate in France held by a third party abroad for the benefit of the defendant, for in that case too the property is situate in France.[260] Professor Huet also puts forward the view[261] that if the defendant is domiciled in France, the French court ought to be able to authorize a *saisie* even if the property is abroad. But he recognizes that the French court may not be able to rule on the *validity* of such a *saisie*, which it can only do if the property is situate in France.[262] Conversely, the French court cannot rule on the validity of an attachment made in a foreign country, whatever the domicile or nationality of the plaintiff or defendant.[263]

Two decisions of the European Court of Justice concerned the enforceability in Germany of French court orders (both of a protective nature) which purported to affect assets situate in Germany: *De Cavel* v. *De Cavel (No. 1)*;[264] *Denilauler* v. *Couchet Frères*.[265] In *De Cavel* a French family court made an order in the course of French divorce proceedings, which purported to freeze furniture and other property in the couple's flat in Frankfurt, and also the contents of a safe hired by the wife in a Frankfurt bank, and the wife's account in a bank in Frankfurt. In *Denilauler*, in the course of proceedings in France by a French company against a German company for the purchase price of goods, the president of the court made an *ex parte* order authorizing the freezing of the German company's accounts at the Société Générale Alsacienne de Banque at Frankfurt. For

---

[257] See Loussouarn and Bourel, 3rd ed., 1988, para. 448; Batiffol, 1986 *Rev. crit.* at 332, citing *Soc. Cyprien Fabre* v. *Banque privée*, Cass. Civ. 12.5. 1931, 1932 *Clunet* 387, note Perroud; *Allouche* v. *Soc. union commerciale africaine*, Cass. civ. I, 4.5.1976, 1977 *Rev. crit.* 352, note D. Mayer.

[258] *Soc. Varonas Investment Corp.* v. *Électricité de France*, Cass. civ. II, 29.2.1984, 1985 *Rev. crit.* 545, note Sinay-Cytermann.

[259] *Fayad* v. *Nasrallah*, Trib. gr. inst. Nice, 25.7.1980, 1982 *Clunet* 160, note Huet.

[260] Huet, 1982 *Clunet* at 163.

[261] At 164–165; see also J.-Cl. dr. int. Fasc. 581-B, paras. 90–101 (Huet).

[262] See the *Nassibian* and *Intrabank* cases discussed in Section II, *supra*.

[263] *Allouche* v. *Soc. union commerciale africaine*, *supra*, 1977 *Rev. crit.* 352, note D. Mayer.

[264] Case 143/78 [1979] ECR 1055.   [265] Case 125/79 [1980] ECR 1553.

reasons developed by the author elsewhere,[266] it is likely that the French court had no jurisdiction under French law to make an attachment of property in Germany. The enforceability of such orders is considered below.[267]

2. THE TERRITORIAL SCOPE OF *IN PERSONAM* ORDERS

In England, as has been seen, the custom of London provided for the process of foreign attachment, which fell into disuse in the nineteenth century after it had been held that it did not apply if the third party who owed money to the debtor was a corporation, but before then it was clear that it applied only to the attachment of debts which were situate within the jurisdiction:

it is quite obvious . . . that the custom of foreign attachment cannot in reason apply to debtors or garnishees out of the jurisdiction; and it is so settled by authority.[268]

But it has also long been established that, where the defendant is subject to the personal jurisdiction of the English court, there is no reason in principle why an English injunction should not be granted in relation to acts abroad. Thus, in *Kerr on Injunctions*[269] it was said:

As a consequence of the rule, that in granting an injunction the Court operates *in personam*, the Court may exercise jurisdiction independently of the locality of the act to be done, provided the person against whom relief is sought is within the reach and amenable to the process of the Court. That jurisdiction is not founded upon any pretension to the exercise of judicial or administrative rights abroad, but on the circumstance of the person to whom the order is addressed being within the reach of the Court.

A recent, and colourful, example, is the case of Mr Barker, who was an employee of the Queen (in what capacity is not known) and who proposed to publish a book called *Courting Disaster*, in which he was going to reveal information about matters which he had learned in the course of his employment in the royal household. This would have been in breach of the express terms of his contract of employment. Mr Barker had given serialization rights to various magazines abroad, including *Paris Match*. Mr Barker disputed the right of the court to make an order having effect

---

[266] Collins (1989) 105 LQR 262, 290–294 (post, pp. 216–220).

[267] *Infra*, Section IX.

[268] Willes, J. in *Mayor etc. of the City of London* v. *Cox* (1867) 2 LR HL 239, 266; the same was so in the United States: see Beale, 'Jurisdiction in Rem to Compel Payment of Debt', (1914) 27 Harv. L. Rev. 107, 116–117.

[269] 6th ed. Paterson, 1927, p. 11.

outside England. The Court of Appeal had no hesitation in affirming the injunction, and dismissing the argument that it would be contrary to the European Convention on Human Rights for foreigners to be deprived of the information and the suggestion that it was not 'for the English courts to decide whether the democratic rights of foreigners would be infringed by disclosure of information received in confidence'. Lord Donaldson MR said:[270]

. . . I would have thought that much more relevant was the question of whether a man's word is his bond and whether contractual obligations freely entered into shall be maintained. It is not a question of what foreigners are entitled to read, but what somebody subject to the jurisdiction of this Court is entitled to publish, and it is an incidental result that, if he cannot publish, foreigners cannot read. I am bound to say, having read this book, I do not think they will miss anything at all, but that is merely a personal view.

The covenant of confidentiality which Mr Barker gave when he was employed in the Royal Household was not limited territorially, and the English court had jurisdiction to enforce the covenant by ordering Mr Barker not to break his obligation of confidentiality anywhere in the world. Nourse LJ added that it was true that foreign courts might not enforce the agreement if it were sued on there, but

that has nothing at all to do with the question whether it is or is not right for the English court to grant an injunction to restrain a breach of a worldwide undertaking entered into in an English contract between persons who are amenable to the jurisdiction of the English court.[271]

The passage from the judgment of the United States Court of Appeals for the Ninth Circuit with which this section opened shows that the law in the United States is similar. In *United States* v. *First National City Bank*[272] the Supreme Court decided that the United States court had jurisdiction to enjoin a New York bank from transferring any property of its customer held by the bank at a branch in Uruguay. The bank had actual and practical control over its branches, and accordingly

the branch bank's affairs are, therefore, as much within the reach of the *in personam* order . . . as are those of the home office. Once personal jurisdiction of a party is obtained, the District Court has authority to order it to 'freeze' property under its control, whether the property be within or without the United States.[273]

---

[270] *Att. Gen.* v. *Barker* [1990] 3 All ER 257, 261.
[271] At 262. See also *Acrow (Automation) Limited* v. *Rex Chainbelt Inc.* [1971] 3 All ER 1175 (CA).   [272] 379 US 378 (1965).
[273] At 384. See also, e.g., *Fleming* v. *Gray Manufacturing Co.*, 352 F. Supp. 724 (D. Conn. 1973); *Restatement Second, Conflict of Laws*, s. 53.

In the United States the primary remedy for a plaintiff who seeks to secure himself pending judgment is attachment of assets, and it has already been seen that that remedy is limited territorially to assets within the jurisdiction of the court which orders the attachment. It has not therefore been necessary for United States courts to develop a form of injunction akin to the English *Mareva* injunction. Indeed it was once said by the Supreme Court:[274]

Every suitor who resorts to chancery for any sort of relief by injunction may, on a mere statement of belief that the defendant can easily make away with or transport his money or goods, impose an injunction on him to use so much of his funds or property as the court deems necessary for security or compliance with its possible decree. And, if so, it is difficult to see why a plaintiff in any action for a personal judgment in tort or contract may not, also, apply to the chancellor for a so-called injunction sequestering his opponent's assets pending recovery and satisfaction of a judgment in such law action. No relief of this character has been thought justified in the long history of equity jurisprudence.

But today there seems to be a greater readiness to provide a remedy by way of injunction, at any rate if there is no adequate attachment remedy. Thus in *Re Feit & Drexler, Inc.*[275] the Court of Appeals for the Second Circuit referred to the general rule that a party may not obtain injunctive relief where it is claiming a loss which can be adequately remedied by an award of money damages. But the court also accepted that, even where the ultimate relief sought is money damages, federal courts had jurisdiction to grant preliminary injunctions where it was shown that the defendant intended to frustrate any judgment on the merits by transferring its assets out of the jurisdiction.

No doubt this power is more readily exercised when the defendant is, at any rate prima facie, guilty of fraud. In such a case, also, the courts are no doubt more readily disposed to extend the injunction so as to apply to assets outside the jurisdiction. In *Ebsco Industries Inc.* v. *Lilly*[276] a purchaser of a company brought an action against the seller for fraud. The defendant took steps to conceal assets and had refused to disclose what assets he had or where they were. In these circumstances an injunction was granted, which, like the injunction in the *Marcos* case, extended to assets outside the jurisdiction (which was Ohio). In the *Marcos* case[277] the

---

[274] *DeBeers Consolidated Mines* v. *United States*, 325 US 212, 222–223 (1945).

[275] 760 F. 2d 406 (2d Cir. 1985). See also *USACO Coal Co.* v. *Carbomin Energy*, 689 F. 2d 94 (6th Cir. 1982).

[276] 840 F. 2d 333 (6th Cir. 1988), cert. den. 488 US 825 (1988).

[277] *Republic of the Philippines* v. *Marcos*, 862 F. 2d 1355 (9th Cir.), cert. den. 490 US 1035 (1988).

allegation of fraud led the court to find that the preliminary injunction was necessary to preserve the possibility of equitable relief. It was not therefore a case strictly comparable to the English *Mareva* injunction.

3. *MAREVA* INJUNCTIONS

It has already been seen in Section I that the *Mareva* injunction was developed in England from 1975 in order to fill a serious gap in the English law of remedies, namely the absence of the remedy of attachment pending judgment. In two cases[278] in that year the Court of Appeal, in each case with Lord Denning MR presiding, decided that such an injunction could be granted to restrain a foreign defendant from removing its assets from the jurisdiction. The injunction, as subsequently developed and extended, is now known as the *Mareva* injunction, after the second of the cases. The practice has since been followed in Canada,[279] Australia[280] and New Zealand.[281] In 1981 the practice was given statutory authority by section 37 (3) of the Supreme Court Act 1981, which confirmed that a *Mareva* injunction may be granted whether or not the defendant is domiciled, resident or present within the jurisdiction.[282] The *Mareva* injunction now extends not only to the removal of assets, but also to their dissipation.[283]

The description of an injunction as a *Mareva* injunction is a convenient label to describe an injunction restraining the removal or dissipation of assets in which the plaintiff claims no proprietary interest, and strictly it should be distinguished from cases in which the plaintiff seeks to trace assets. Thus in the case of the ordinary *Mareva* injunction, where the plaintiff does not claim a proprietary interest in bank accounts, the defendant is entitled to use them for normal business purposes, or to pay legal fees. But where the plaintiff claims that the money in the bank is really the plaintiff's property, 'there is, in general, no reason why a

---

[278] *Nippon Yusen Kaisha* v. *Karageorgis* [1975] 1 WLR 1093 (CA); *Mareva Compania Naviera SA* v. *International Bulkcarriers SA* [1975] 2 Lloyd's Rep. 509 (CA).

[279] *Chitel* v. *Rothbart* (1982) 141 DLR (3d) 268 (Ont. CA); and other cases referred to by Rogers and Hately, (1982) 60 Can. B. Rev. 1, 33–35. For the special problems of the practice in a federal system see *Aetna Financial Services Ltd.* v. *Feigelmann* [1985] 1 SCR 2.

[280] See, e.g., *Riley McKay Pty. Ltd.* v. *McKay* [1982] 1 NSWLR 264; *Hiero Pty. Ltd.* v. *Somers* (1983) 47 ALR 605; *Devlin* v. *Collins* (1984) 37 SASR 98; *Perth Mint* v. *Mickelberg (No. 2)* [1985] WAR 117; *Pearce* v. *Waterhouse* [1986] VR 603; *Jackson* v. *Sterling Industries Ltd.* (1987) 71 ALR 457.

[281] *Hunt* v. *BP Exploration (Libya) Ltd.* [1980] 1 NZLR 104.

[282] This removed doubts which had been expressed in some of the early cases. See also *Bekhor & Co. Ltd.* v. *Bilton* [1981] QB 923, 936 (CA); *The Siskina* v. *Distos Compania Naviera SA* [1979] AC 210, 261.

[283] Since *Rahman (Prince Abdul) bin Turki al Sudairy* v. *Abu-Taha* [1980] 1 WLR 1268 (CA).

defendant should be permitted to use money belonging to another in order to pay his legal costs or other expenses'.[284] That there is a distinction between the two forms of remedy is clear,[285] but it is not always drawn in practice.

In order to obtain a *Mareva* injunction the plaintiff must show that he has at least a good arguable case on the merits,[286] and that there is a real risk that a judgment in favour of the plaintiff would be unsatisfied if the injunction were not granted.[287] The fundamental principle underlying the jurisdiction is that, within the limits of its powers, no court should permit a defendant to take action designed to ensure that subsequent orders of the court are rendered less effective than would otherwise be the case.[288]

Although Lord Denning MR expressed the view that a *Mareva* injunction operated *in rem*,[289] it does not operate as an attachment on property as such, but is relief *in personam*, restraining the owner of the assets from dealing with them. Accordingly, it does not achieve priority over the security interests of third parties,[290] nor does it give the plaintiff security rights in priority to other creditors.[291] Consequently, a defendant will normally be allowed to make payments to his creditors in the normal course of business.[292] The injunction must not be used so as to amount to an instrument of oppression which would bring about the cessation of ordinary trading and the court must look at all the circumstances of the case in deciding whether, and to what extent, the injunction should be varied in order to allow the defendant to make payments.[293]

---

[284] *Polly Peck International plc* v. *Nadir* [1992] 2 Lloyd's Rep. 238 (CA).

[285] See *A.* v. *C.* [1981] QB 956n; *PCW (Underwriting Agencies) Ltd.* v. *Dixon* [1983] 2 Lloyd's Rep. 197; *Aetna Financial Services Ltd.* v. *Feigelmann* [1985] 1 SCR 2, 13; cf. *Bankers Trust Co.* v. *Shapira* [1980] 1 WLR 1274 (CA); *Republic of Haiti* v. *Duvalier* [1990] 1 QB 202, 214 (CA).

[286] *Rasu Maritima SA* v. *Pertamina* [1978] QB 644 (CA); *Ninemia Corp.* v. *Trave GmbH* [1983] 1 WLR 1412 (CA); *Derby & Co. Ltd.* v. *Weldon* [1990] Ch. 48, 57–58 (CA).

[287] *Third Chandris Shipping Corp.* v. *Unimarine SA* [1979] QB 654 (CA); *Ninemia Corp.* v. *Trave GmbH* [1983] 1 WLR 1412 (CA); *Patterson* v. *BTR Engineering (Aust) Ltd.* (1989) 18 NSWLR 319.

[288] *Derby & Co. Ltd.* v. *Weldon (Nos. 3 & 4)* [1990] Ch. 65, 76, *per* Lord Donaldson MR; *The Coral Rose* [1991] 1 Lloyd's Rep. 563, 568 (CA); *Atlas Maritime Co. SA* v. *Avalon Maritime Ltd. (No. 3)* [1991] 1 WLR 917, 920–921 (CA).

[289] *Z Ltd.* v. *A-Z* [1982] QB 558, 573 (CA), said to have been *per incuriam* in *Att.-Gen.* v. *Times Newspapers Ltd.* [1991] 2 WLR 994, 1011, *per* Lord Ackner.

[290] *Cretanor Maritime Co. Ltd.* v. *Irish Marine Management Ltd.* [1978] 1 WLR 966 (CA).

[291] *Iraqi Ministry of Defence* v. *Arcepey Shipping Co. SA (The Angel Bell)* [1981] QB 65; *Bekhor & Co. Ltd.* v. *Bilton* [1981] QB 923, 942 (CA); *Derby & Co. Ltd.* v. *Weldon* [1990] Ch. 65, 76 (CA); *Aetna Financial Services Ltd.* v. *Feigelmann* [1985] 1 SCR 2, 26; *Jackson* v. *Sterling Industries Ltd.* (1987) 71 ALR 457, 461, 462 (High Ct. of Australia).

[292] The '*Angel Bell* variation', established in *Iraqi Ministry of Defence* v. *Arcepey Shipping Co. SA* [1981] QB 65. See also *Admiral Shipping* v. *Portlink Ferries Ltd.* [1984] 2 Lloyd's Rep. 166 (CA); *Avant Petroleum Inc.* v. *Gatoil Overseas Inc.* [1986] 2 Lloyd's Rep. 236 (CA).

[293] *The Coral Rose* [1991] 1 Lloyd's Rep. 563 (CA); *Atlas Maritime Co. SA* v. *Avalon Maritime Ltd. (No. 3)* [1991] 1 WLR 917 (CA).

There are two important ways in which the jurisdiction is made effective. First, the court may make ancillary orders in aid of *Mareva* relief to enable the plaintiff to obtain disclosure of documents or information from a defendant concerning his assets,[294] and even an ancillary order restraining a defendant from leaving the jurisdiction and requiring him to deliver up his passport.[295] Second, a third party such as a bank with which the defendant has an account, is guilty of contempt of court if it knowingly assists in a breach of the order, i.e. if knowing the terms of the injunction it wilfully assists the defendant to disobey.[296] This is so whether or not the defendant has been served with or knows of the order, because the third party would be guilty of conduct which knowingly interferes with the administration of justice by causing the order of the court to be disobeyed.[297]

4. WORLDWIDE *MAREVA* INJUNCTIONS

The *Mareva* injunction was developed in order to prevent the removal of assets from the jurisdiction, and it was assumed by Parliament[298] and held by the Court of Appeal[299] that the exercise of the *Mareva* jurisdiction was limited to assets within the jurisdiction. In several Commonwealth jurisdictions, however, this limitation on the scope of *Mareva* injunctions was not accepted.[300] But in a series of decisions of the Court of Appeal in

---

[294] See, e.g., *A. v. C.* [1981] QB 956; *Bekhor & Co. Ltd. v. Bilton* [1981] QB 923 (CA); *House of Spring Gardens Ltd. v. Waite* [1985] FSR 173 (CA); *Bank of Crete SA v. Koskotas*, [1991] 2 Lloyd's Rep. 587 (CA).

[295] *Bayer AG v. Winter* [1986] 1 WLR 497 (CA), applied in *Re Oriental Credit* [1988] Ch. 204. For the remedy of an order for the issue of a writ prohibiting a debtor from leaving the realm (*ne exeat regno*), where his absence will materially prejudice the plaintiff in the prosecution of the action, see *Felton v. Callis* [1969] 1 QB 200; *Lipkin Gorman v. Cass, The Times*, 29 May, 1985. It has been held that this writ may issue in aid of a *Mareva* injunction (*Al Nakhel for Contracting & Trading Ltd. v. Lowe* [1986] QB 235; cf. *Thaya v. Thaya* [1987] 2 FLR 142) but the better view is that it may not be issued solely for the purpose of enforcing a *Mareva* injunction, and that in such a case the appropriate remedy is an injunction to restrain the defendant from leaving the jurisdiction: *Allied Arab Bank v. Hajjar* [1988] QB 787.

[296] *Z Ltd. v. A–Z* [1982] QB 558 (CA).

[297] *Ibid.* at 578, *per* Eveleigh LJ, approved in *Att.-Gen. v. Times Newspapers Ltd.* [1992] 1 A.C. 191.

[298] Supreme Court Act 1981, s. 37 (3).

[299] *Ashtiani v. Kashi* [1987] QB 888 (CA). See also *The Bhoja Trader* [1981] 2 Lloyd's Rep. 256 (CA); cf. *Allied Arab Bank v. Hajjar* [1988] QB 787, 796; *Reilly v. Fryer* [1988] 2 FTLR 69 (CA). Contrast *Re A Company* [1985] BCLC 333 (CA); *Bayer AG v. Winter* [1986] 2 FTLR 111, 112.

[300] *Ballabil Holdings Pty. Ltd. v. Hospital Products Ltd.* (1985) 1 NSWLR 155; *Coombs & Barei Construction Pty. Ltd. v. Dynasty Pty. Ltd.* (1986) 42 SASR 413; *Yandil Holdings Pty. Ltd. v. Insurance Co. of North America* (1987) 7 NSWLR 571; *National Australia Bank v. Dessau* [1988] VR 521 (but contrast *Brereton v. Milstein* [1988] VR 508); *Banco Ambrosiano*

1988 it was held, reversing previous practice, that *Mareva* injunctions and ancillary disclosure orders could be granted in relation to assets abroad. First, in *Babanaft International Co. SA* v. *Bassatne*[301] an injunction was granted, after judgment in a fraud action, restraining the judgment debtors from disposing of any of their assets worldwide. Second, in *Republic of Haiti* v. *Duvalier*[302] an injunction was granted (in aid of proceedings pending in France[303]) restraining the defendants from dealing with their assets wherever situated and requiring the defendants to disclose information relating to their assets worldwide. Third, in two decisions in *Derby & Co. Ltd.* v. *Weldon*[304] it was held that a pre-judgment *Mareva* injunction and ancillary disclosure could be granted in relation to assets worldwide in the course of litigation pending in England, irrespective of whether the defendant had assets in England.[305] These decisions have been the subject of a full survey by the present author,[306] and it is not necessary for present purposes to do more than summarize the general principles and draw attention to more recent developments.

The basis for the development of the worldwide Mareva injunction was the recognition that the *Mareva* injunction operates *in personam*, and that where the defendant is personally subject to the jurisdiction of the court, an injunction may be granted in appropriate circumstances to control his activities abroad.[307] Although exceptional or special circumstances must be present to justify a worldwide *Mareva*, that does not mean more than that the court should go no further than necessity dictates, and that in the first instance it should look to assets within the jurisdiction.[308] The jurisdiction will be exercised more readily after final judgment has been obtained against the defendant, or if the claim is a proprietary claim.[309] It may be

---

Holdings SA v. *Dunkeld Ranching Ltd.* (1987) 85 Alta. R. 278 (CA) (but contrast *Zellers Inc.* v. *Doobay* [1989] 3 WWR 497 (BC)); *Asean Resources Ltd.* v. *Ka Wah International Merchant Finance Ltd.* [1987] LRC (Comm.) 835.

[301] [1990] Ch. 13 (CA).   [302] [1990] 1 QB 202 (CA).

[303] See Civil Jurisdiction and Judgments Act 1982, s. 25 (1), and Sched. 1, Art. 24.

[304] [1990] Ch. 48 (CA); (*Nos. 3 & 4*) [1990] Ch. 65 (CA).

[305] Before these cases it was often said that a plaintiff who sought *Mareva* relief must give grounds for a belief that the defendant had assets within the jurisdiction. That this was the normal case did not mean that it was a necessary pre-condition: [1990] Ch. at 77–80.

[306] Collins, 'The Territorial Reach of Mareva Injunctions', (1989) 105 *LQR* 640 (post, p. 189).

[307] *Babanaft International Co. SA* v. *Bassatne* [1990] Ch. 13, at 38, 41 (CA); *Derby & Co. Ltd.* v. *Weldon (No. 6)* [1990] 1 WLR 1139, 1149 (CA). For the territorial scope of *Anton Piller* orders (the 'search and seizure' orders sanctioned by *Anton Piller KG* v. *Manufacturing Processes Ltd.* [1976] Ch. 55 (CA) discussed *infra*, Section XII) cf. *Cook Industries* v. *Galliher* [1979] Ch. 439; and contrast *Protector Alarms Ltd.* v. *Maxim Alarms Ltd.* [1978] FSR 442; *Altertext Inc.* v. *Advanced Data Communications Ltd.* [1985] 1 WLR 457.

[308] *Derby & Co. Ltd.* v. *Weldon (Nos. 3 & 4)* [1990] Ch. 65, 79 (CA).

[309] See, e.g., *Republic of Haiti* v. *Duvalier* [1990] 1 QB 202, at 213–214, *per* Staughton LJ (CA). After judgment, a disclosure order relating to assets worldwide may be made: *Interpool Ltd.* v. *Galani* [1988] QB 738 (CA); cf. *Maclaine Watson & Co. Ltd.* v. *International*

appropriate to make an order even if it will not be recognized by the courts of the country where the assets are situated, since the English court may still make its order effective by striking out the defence if the defendant disobeys the order.[310] But the English court will not normally grant a worldwide injunction in connection with proceedings in England to enforce a foreign judgment or foreign arbitration award.[311]

In one of the many decisions in the *Derby & Co. Ltd.* v. *Weldon* litigation[312] the Court of Appeal decided that the jurisdiction could be exercised to order the transfer of assets from one jurisdiction to another, or to restrain the transfer of assets from one foreign jurisdiction to another, or to order the return to England of assets from a foreign jurisdiction. In that case the first and second defendants were English residents, who controlled a Panamanian company and a Luxembourg company. The English court granted worldwide *Mareva* injunctions against the defendants and several companies controlled by them, and also ordered the appointment of a receiver of the assets of the corporate defendants. By agreement between the receiver and the lawyers for the Luxembourg company, the assets of the Luxembourg company (£29 million) were transferred into a Swiss account in the joint names of the receiver and the Swiss lawyer for the Luxembourg corporation. The receiver subsequently came to have joint control, with the Swiss lawyers for one of the trustees of some Liechtenstein trusts, of assets of £72 million, which were held in a joint account in Switzerland and included £47 million deposited with banks outside Switzerland by the Swiss banks holding the joint account in order to obtain higher interest rates.

The question arose whether the money held outside Switzerland should be returned to Switzerland on the maturity of the deposit, and whether the receivership assets in Switzerland should be transferred out of Switzerland. The Court of Appeal held that the money held outside Switzerland should not be returned there, because there was evidence that the Swiss courts might not recognize the English orders, but the court refused to order the transfer of assets held in Switzerland to another country, because any such order would be ineffective without the voluntary concurrence of those defendants who were joint holders with the receiver.

The practice in relation to worldwide *Mareva* injunctions is subject to two important limitations. First, in order to prevent harassment of the defendant and unnecessary multiplicity of actions, the plaintiff must normally undertake not to make use of information disclosed under the

---

Tin Council (No. 2) [1989] Ch. 286 (CA); *Yandil Holdings Pty. Ltd.* v. *Insurance Co. of North America* (1987) 7 NSWLR 571.

[310] *Derby & Co. Ltd.* v. *Weldon (Nos. 3 & 4)* [1990] Ch. at 81.

[311] *Rosseel NV* v. *Oriental Commercial Shipping (UK) Ltd.* [1990] 1 WLR 1387 (CA).

[312] *(No. 6)* [1990] 1 WLR 1139 (CA).

order in foreign proceedings without the leave of the court.[313] Secondly, what has become known as 'the *Babanaft* proviso' has been inserted in such orders in order to make it clear that the English court is not purporting to make third parties abroad subject to the contempt powers of the English court. The basis of this proviso requires some explanation.

It has already been seen that it is well established in English law that a third party who, knowing of an injunction, acts in such a way as to frustrate its effect, is guilty of contempt of court. The most recent example of a case of this kind is *Attorney-General* v. *Times Newspapers Ltd.*,[314] where it was held that the *Sunday Times* newspaper was guilty of contempt of court because, knowing of injunctions granted against the *Observer* and the *Guardian* newspapers restraining the publication of extracts from the *Spycatcher* book, it nevertheless, itself, published extracts from the book. In so doing, the House of Lords approved the decision in *Z Ltd.* v. *A-Z*,[315] in which the Court of Appeal had decided that a bank, which knowing of a *Mareva* injunction against a defendant, nevertheless allows the defendant to move his money in breach of the order, is itself guilty of contempt of court.

It was suggested by this author[316] that there can be no contempt of court by a third party, such as a bank, which is wholly abroad and which acts wholly abroad, even if it knows of the injunction. Lord Donaldson MR in *Derby & Co. Ltd.* v. *Weldon (Nos. 3 & 4)*[317] said that where a person was wholly outside the jurisdiction, and assisted in breach of the order, either it would not be a contempt, or it would involve an excess of jurisdiction to seek to punish it. But the *Babanaft* proviso does give rise to some difficulties, and the principal difficulty arises from its effect on banks in London (whether they are English or foreign) with branches (or, perhaps, subsidiaries) abroad. The form of the *Babanaft* proviso approved in *Derby & Co. Ltd.* v. *Weldon (Nos. 3 & 4)* (and since applied with some variations in many orders) was this:

Provided that, in so far as this order purports to have any extraterritorial effect, no person shall be affected thereby or concerned with the terms thereof until it shall be declared enforceable or be enforced by a foreign court and then it shall only affect them to the extent of such declaration or enforcement unless they are: (*a*) a person to whom this order is addressed or an officer of or an agent appointed by a power of attorney of such a person or (*b*) persons who are subject to the jurisdiction of this court and (i) have been given written notice of this order at their residence or place

---

[313] *Babanaft International Co. SA* v. *Bassatne* [1990] Ch. at 41, 47; *Republic of Haiti* v. *Duvalier* [1990] 1 QB at 217; *Derby & Co. Ltd.* v. *Weldon* [1990] Ch. at 55–56, 60; *Tate Access Floors Inc.* v. *Boswell* [1991] 2 WLR 304, 313.

[314] [1991] 2 WLR 994 (HL).   [315] [1982] QB 558 (CA).

[316] (1989) 105 LQR at 283.   [317] [1990] Ch. 65, at 82.

of business within the jurisdiction, and (ii) are able to prevent acts or omissions outside the jurisdiction of this court which assist in the breach of the terms of this order.[318]

The effect of this proviso is that in principle acts by third parties (i.e. persons who are not themselves parties to the action) abroad do not give rise to a contempt of court by them unless and until a foreign court enforces or recognizes the English order. But that principle is displaced where the third party is 'subject to the jurisdiction' of the English court, and has been given notice at a residence or place of business in England and is 'able to prevent acts or omissions outside the jurisdiction of this court which assist in the breach of the terms' of the order.

The proviso is primarily (but not exclusively) directed at banks, for it is banks who are most likely to be the relevant third parties in a case in which a *Mareva* injunction has been granted. The banks which for this purpose are 'subject to the jurisdiction' of the English court are primarily those (1) which are registered in England under the Companies Act 1985, or registered in Scotland but with a place of business in England and (2) which are incorporated outside Great Britain but which have established a place of business in Great Britain. In the latter case the bank will normally[319] have filed with the Registrar of Companies the name and address of a person resident in Great Britain authorized to accept process on behalf of the company. It is also theoretically possible for a foreign bank to be resident in England without having a place of business there, if its central control and management is exercised in England, but not from a fixed place of business, but this would be an exceptionally rare case, and can be discounted for present purposes.

Accordingly the exception to the proviso is primarily directed at English banks or foreign banks with branches in England (usually London). The major English banks have branches all over the world, and the effect of the exception is that an English bank which allows the defendant to make withdrawals from a foreign branch will be guilty of contempt. In *Securities and Investments Board v. Pantell SA*[320] it was held that where the defendants had already transferred money from Barclays Bank in London to its branch in Guernsey:

if the branch of Barclays Bank in Guernsey is holding moneys belonging to either of the defendants, the bank (being a bank locally resident in England) will, after service of the order, be required not to part with such moneys from the accounts held with the bank with their Guernsey branch.

---

[318] [1990] Ch. at 84.
[319] See Dicey and Morris, *Conflict of Laws* (11th ed., 1987), pp. 294–296.
[320] [1990] Ch. 426, 433.

Where the bank is a foreign bank with a branch in London, it will only be in exceptional cases (e.g., where the account abroad is under its control) in which it will be 'able to prevent acts or omissions outside the jurisdiction'. The mere fact that a foreign bank with a branch in London is part of one juridical entity should not mean, for this purpose, that the foreign bank is in contempt because of the acts of one of its branches outside England.

9

Enforcement Abroad

I. INTRODUCTION

The effect of provisional measures granted in one country in the territory of another country is a subject which appears to have received no full treatment in the literature. The reasons are not hard to find. In the first place, despite the richness of material on provisional measures affecting assets or actions abroad discussed in the preceding section, in the normal case provisional measures are taken in the place where they are most likely to be effective, i.e. the place where the assets are or where the defendant is, and it is not normally necessary to seek to enforce them abroad. As the European Court put it in *Denilauler* v. *Couchet Frères*:[321]

> The courts of the place . . . where the assets subject to the measures sought are located, are those best able to assess the circumstances which may lead to the grant or refusal of the measures sought or to the laying down of procedures and conditions which the plaintiff must observe in order to guarantee the provisional and protective character of the measures ordered.

In the second place, the recognition and enforcement of judgments has traditionally been limited to judgments which are final, in the sense of determining matters finally between the parties, and provisional or protective measures do not fall into this category. Thirdly, the enforcement of judgments (as distinct from their recognition) has traditionally been limited to the enforcement of judgments awarding a sum of money as debt or damages, and provisional or protective measures rarely,[322] if ever, award a sum of money. It is true that section 102 of the *Restatement Second, Conflict of Laws*, contemplates that 'a valid judgment that orders the doing of an act other than the payment of money, or that enjoins the doing of an act, may be enforced, or may be the subject of remedies, in other states'. But the *Restatement* itself recognizes that the application of this principle to judgments of foreign States (as distinct from the judgments of sister states of the American Union) is controversial.[323]

Consequently, until recently at least, the desirability of enforcing provisional or protective measures abroad has not been apparent, and

---

[321] Case 125/79 [1980] ECR 1553, 1570.
[322] This reservation is necessary because of the controversy whether orders for interim payments are provisional or protective in the sense discussed in this paper: see, *supra*, Sections I and II.　　　　　　　　　　　　　　　　　　　　　[323] Comment *g*.

where (for a variety of reasons) it has been thought helpful to seek to enforce them abroad, there has been resistance from the court in which recognition or enforcement is sought. This reluctance of the foreign court to recognize or enforce the orders of the court in which the measures are taken may lead the court in which the measures are sought to a greater caution. Thus, concerned at the consequences for third parties abroad, the English courts have narrowed the effect of *Mareva* injunctions on them, especially foreign banks, by the *Babanaft* proviso discussed earlier.[324] On the other hand, where there is evidence that the foreign court would not recognize the English orders, the English courts have widened the scope of the *Mareva* injunction against the defendants in order to avoid the consequences of the foreign court's unwillingness to recognize the English order. Thus in *Derby & Co. Ltd.* v. *Weldon (No. 6)*[325] the defendants controlled substantial funds in Swiss bank accounts. Some of those funds had been placed by the Swiss banks (as is commonly the case) on deposit outside Switzerland. These so-called 'fiduciary deposits' (because they are made by the Swiss banks on behalf of their customers) are placed outside Switzerland because substantially higher interest rates can be obtained in this way. There was evidence of Swiss law before the English court (but, it should be noted, no final finding of Swiss law) that the Swiss court would not enforce or recognize the interlocutory English court order which had appointed a receiver over the funds. Indeed, it was suggested that Article 271 of the Swiss Penal Code made it a criminal offence for the receiver to exercise any powers in Switzerland. There was also evidence that the Swiss court would not recognize the final judgment of the English court in so far as it related to foreign defendants who had not submitted to the jurisdiction of the English courts. For these reasons the Court of Appeal ordered the defendants not to allow the repatriation to Switzerland of the fiduciary deposits held outside Switzerland.

It follows from the generally (but not exclusively) territorial nature of provisional measures that they do not generally come under the scrutiny of foreign courts. But developments in modern technology, travel and communication have led to a perception that there is an increasing need for extraterritorial measures. Correspondingly, foreign courts have had to define and refine their reaction to such measures.

2. THE TRADITIONAL VIEW

The next section will consider the extraordinary course of the litigation in the United States and England between the liquidator of Laker Airways

---

[324] *Supra*, Section VIII.   [325] [1990] 1 WLR 1139 (CA).

and those international airlines which Sir Freddie Laker alleged had conspired to drive him out of business. In that litigation the English courts granted injunctions restraining the liquidator from suing British Airways and other airlines in the United States courts. When the United States Court of Appeals for the District of Columbia Circuit confirmed that those defendants who had not already obtained 'anti-suit' injunctions in the English courts should be enjoined from seeking them, it also decided that the injunctions granted by the English court restraining the pursuit of the American anti-trust actions were not entitled to recognition, or 'comity' as the Court of Appeals put it. The reason was that:

... the action before the United Kingdom courts is specifically intended to interfere with and terminate Laker's United States antitrust suit. The District Court's antisuit injunction was purely *defensive*—it seeks only to preserve the district court's ability to arrive at a final judgment adjudicating Laker's claims under United States law ... In contrast, the English injunction is purely *offensive*—it is not designed to protect English jurisdiction, or to allow English courts to proceed to a judgment on the defendant's potential liability under English anticompetitive law free of foreign interference. Rather, the English injunction seeks only to quash the practical power of the United States courts to adjudicate claims under United States law against defendants admittedly subject to the courts' adjudicatory jurisdiction.[326]

In *Pilkington Brothers* v. *AFG Industries Inc.* [327] arbitration proceedings (of great length and complexity) were pending in England between Pilkington, an English corporation, and AFG, a Delaware corporation, about technology in glass. Pilkington obtained an order in the English Commercial Court restraining AFG from disclosing the technology. Pilkington sought an equivalent injunction in Delaware. But it did not ask the Delaware court to decide the merits of its trade secret and contract dispute with AFG or to form its own judgment based on that dispute, but rather, relying solely on principles of international comity, it requested the American court to duplicate the English order because the plaintiff feared that the English order afforded it inadequate protection.

The District Court was invited to reject the application on the ground that the English order was not 'final'. It refused, however, to fashion a rule that prevented recognition and enforcement of foreign interim injunctions. Instead, it ruled that 'general principles of comity' would be offended if the English order were duplicated:

By issuing an identically worded injunction while arbitration is still proceeding under the watchful jurisdiction of the English High Court, this Court would defeat,

---

[326] *Laker Airways Ltd.* v. *Sabena Belgian World Airlines*, 731 F. 2d 909, 938 (DC Cir. 1984).   [327] 581 F. Supp. 1039 (D. Del. 1984).

rather than promote, principles of international comity. For were this Court to issue Pilkington's requested relief, it would interfere unnecessarily in those foreign proceedings . . . For example, upon a future application to this Court for a sanction against violations of its order, this Court would be compelled to interpret and apply an injunction which was drafted by the English High Court in furtherance of the High Court's special role under the English Arbitration Act. This might lead to inconsistent interpretations and inconsistent enforcement. Any interpretation of the High Court's order should be made by that court, not a United States district court . . . Finally, modifications of an injunction in one jurisdiction could lead to confusion and procedural tangles in the other jurisdiction. It is far simpler to have one court receive all applications for modifications.[328]

None of these reasons could be said to be compelling, and it may be that what the court was really doing was disguising its reluctance to make a similar order without an investigation of the merits by purporting to defer to the jurisdiction of the English court. But the contrast with the *Laker Airways* case is striking. In *Laker Airways* comity precluded recognition of the English order because the United States court perceived that the English court was interfering with the United States judicial process. In *Pilkington* comity precluded recognition or enforcement because the United States court thought (or said it thought) that recognition or enforcement might interfere with the English judicial process.

In a case to be discussed in the next section, a federal court in New York ordered a bank carrying on business in Hong Kong to return to New York money alleged to be the fruits of illegal insider trading by the defendant. The order was obtained in New York by the United States Securities and Exchange Commission, and when the defendant in the New York proceedings sued the bank in Hong Kong to recover his deposits, the Hong Kong court held that for the Hong Kong court to recognize or enforce the New York court's order would be contrary to the principle that the court would not enforce a foreign public law. In fact, the question of enforcement did not arise. The only issue was whether the bank's duty to repay a Hong Kong deposit could be affected by the New York order. Under the applicable principles of the conflict of laws, the New York order could not be the subject of recognition because on no view was it final. The true issue was whether the bank's liability to pay the plaintiff was affected under the law governing the deposit, or under the law where the deposit had to be paid. These issues were not addressed, but instead the court refused to order payment on a ground not involving the conflict of laws, namely that, on the facts, to force the bank to pay might result in it being a constructive trustee by knowingly assisting its customer: the bank argued that it had good reason to believe that the customer had made profits by

---

[328] At 1046.

the misuse of confidential information, and that some of those profits might have found their way into the accounts.[329]

3. THE BRUSSELS AND LUGANO CONVENTIONS

Neither of these cases turned on the question whether the provisional measures ordered by the foreign court were final or whether they made an order which was not for the payment of money. If there can be said to be a trend on this question, then it is that the trend is towards the international recognition of such measures. The most notable examples are the Brussels and Lugano Conventions. The provisions of those Conventions which deal with the recognition and enforcement of judgments are not limited either to money judgments or (which is more unusual) to final judgments.[330] In *De Cavel* v. *De Cavel (No. 1)*[331] the European Court held that in principle 'provisional protective measures relating to property—such as . . . the freezing of assets' are included within the scope of the 1968 Convention, and that: 'in relation to the matters covered by the Convention, no legal basis is to be found therein for drawing a distinction between provisional and definitive measures.' In *Denilauler* v. *Couchet Frères*[332] the European Court confirmed that provisional and protective measures ordered in one Contracting State could be the subject of recognition and enforcement under the Convention in another State.

It has already been seen[333] that both of these cases involved orders of the French courts which were provisional or protective, and which purported to affect property in Germany. In *De Cavel* a French family court made an order in the course of French divorce proceedings, which purported to freeze furniture and other property in the couple's flat in Frankfurt, and also the contents of a safe hired by the wife in a Frankfurt bank, and the wife's account in a bank in Frankfurt. In *Denilauler*, in the course of proceedings in France by a French company against a German company for the purchase price of goods, the French court made an *ex parte* order authorizing the freezing of the German company's accounts at the Frankfurt branch of a French bank. This author has suggested that the legal basis under French law for the latter order was doubtful.[334] Without considering the implications of the extraterritorial nature of the French orders, the European Court held in each of these cases that the French

---

[329] *Nanus Asia Co. Inc.* v. *Standard Chartered Bank* [1990] 1 HKLR 396.
[330] See Jenard Report, paras. 186–187.
[331] Case 143/78 [1979] ECR 1055, 1066–1067.
[332] Case 125/79 [1980] ECR 1553, 1571.   [333] *Supra*, Section VIII.
[334] See Collins, 'The Territorial Reach of Mareva Injunctions', (1989) 105 LQR 262, 290–292 (post, pp. 216–218).

order was not enforceable in Germany, on grounds wholly unconnected with the fact that the French orders purported to reach assets in Germany. In *De Cavel* the Court held that, because the 1968 Convention did not apply to questions of status and matrimonial rights in property, it equally did not apply to orders authorizing provisional measures in the course of divorce proceedings. In *Denilauler* the Court held that the recognition and enforcement provisions of the Convention did not apply to *ex parte* orders which were intended to be enforced without prior service.[335]

Brennero SAS v. *Wendel GmbH*[336] is a third case in the European Court in which protective measures affecting property abroad were sought to be enforced in the foreign State where the property was situate. The case involved a dispute between two shoe manufacturers, one Italian and one German. The Italian company sued the German company in an Italian court, and obtained what was described as a protective seizure order. The order purported to seize the German company's assets up to an amount of 700 million lire. But the German company had no assets in Italy, and a German court made an order for enforcement under the 1968 Convention. The decision of the European Court was concerned only with the appeal aspects of the procedure for enforcement in Germany. Advocate General Slynn recorded that because the Italian order was made *inter partes* it was not disputed that it was in principle enforceable in Germany.

In none of these cases was the fundamental question addressed, namely the extent to which orders made in one State affecting property in another State are enforceable in the latter. Involving as it does the relationship between Article 24 of the Convention[337] and the provisions for recognition and enforcement, it was worthy at least of consideration. But there is now a consistent jurisprudence that provisional and protective orders affecting assets abroad (such as worldwide *Mareva* injunctions)[338] are entitled to recognition and enforcement, at any rate if the action in which they are made falls within the scope of the relevant Convention, and if they are made *inter partes*.

---

[335] Applied on this aspect in *EMI Records Ltd.* v. *Modern Music Karl-Ulrich Walterbach GmbH* [1991] 3 WLR 663.   [336] Case 258/83 [1984] ECR 3971.

[337] Discussed *supra*, Section III.

[338] See *Babanaft International Co. SA* v. *Bassatne* [1990] Ch. 13, 31–32 (CA).

10

Public International Law and Extraterritorial Orders

It should not be necessary nowadays to demonstrate that the exercise of civil jurisdiction by national courts is subject to the constraints of public international law. It is true that the terminology sometimes disguises the public international law element. When *Kerr on Injunctions* stated that the jurisdiction to order acts abroad is 'not founded upon any pretension to the exercise of judicial or administrative acts abroad',[339] or when Lord Justice Kerr said that there was no reason of international comity preventing worldwide *Mareva* injunctions from being granted,[340] they were saying that no breach of foreign sovereignty would be involved. Sometimes the reference to public international law is more explicit, as when Lord Donaldson MR confirmed that the *Mareva* injunction should not conflict with 'the ordinary principles of international law' and that, in particular, 'considerations of comity require the courts of this country to refrain from making orders which infringe the exclusive jurisdiction of the courts of other countries'.[341]

This author has suggested[342] that the extension of the *Mareva* jurisdiction to assets abroad is justifiable in terms of international law and comity provided that the case has some appropriate connection with England, that the court does not affect title to property abroad, and that the court does not seek to control the activities abroad of foreigners who are not subject to the personal jurisdiction of the English court. In *Derby & Co. Ltd.* v. *Weldon (No. 6)*[343] Staughton LJ warned that the effect of the extension of the extraterritorial *Mareva* jurisdiction was 'an increasing interference with transactions and property abroad', and he went on:

This should not in my view be regarded lightly. If it ever became common practice for English courts not merely to assume jurisdiction over defendants abroad under

---

[339] 6th ed. Paterson, 1927, p. 11, a reference to *Lord Portarlington* v. *Soulby* (1834) 3 My & K. 104, 108.

[340] *Babanaft International Co. SA* v. *Bassatne* [1990] Ch. 13, 32 (CA).

[341] *Derby & Co. Ltd.* v. *Weldon (Nos. 3 & 4)* [1990] Ch. 65, 82 (CA).

[342] (1989) 105 LQR at 299 (post, p. 225).

[343] [1990] 1 WLR 1139, 1153 (CA).

R.S.C., Order 11, but also to order them to transfer assets here so that eventual judgment could be more readily enforced, that would in my view justifiably be regarded as unacceptable chauvinism by the international community.

In that case the Court of Appeal ordered the defendants not to allow the return to Switzerland of funds deposited outside Switzerland by Swiss banks, one of the reasons was that there was evidence (but certainly no finding) that it would have been an offence punishable with imprisonment for the receiver appointed by the English court to do any act in Switzerland in that capacity. The order not to allow the return of the assets to Switzerland therefore prevented a conflict of jurisdiction.

Nor is there any doubt that the '*Babanaft* proviso' is intended to prevent an excess of international jurisdiction. In the *Babanaft* case Kerr LJ thought that the proviso was the 'internationally appropriate course',[344] and in *Derby & Co. Ltd.* v. *Weldon (Nos. 3 & 4)*[345] Lord Donaldson MR said that it might be 'an excess of jurisdiction' to seek to punish a third party, who was wholly outside the jurisdiction, for assisting in the breach of an English court order, and that the *Babanaft* proviso was necessary because foreign banks had taken offence at being 'ordered about' by the English courts.

The effect of the *Babanaft* proviso is to limit the risk of an interference with foreign sovereignty by restricting the effect of the injunction to persons subject to the jurisdiction of the English court. But that risk is not entirely eliminated, for the mere fact that the injunction affects only persons subject to the jurisdiction does not mean that no breach of international law or comity is involved. In *Mackinnon* v. *Donaldson, Lufkin & Jenrette Corp.*[346] Hoffmann J. accepted Dr F. A. Mann's view[347] to that effect. That case concerned the question whether the court should order the London branch of a United States bank to produce documents held at its head office in New York which were unrelated to the business of its London branch. Hoffmann J. said:[348]

It does not follow from the fact that a person is within the jurisdiction and liable to be served with process that there is no territorial limit to the matters upon which the court may properly apply its own rules or the things which it can order such a person to do . . . In principle and on authority it seems to me that the court should not, save in exceptional circumstances, impose such a requirement upon a foreigner, and, in particular, upon a foreign bank. The principle is that a state should refrain from demanding obedience to its sovereign authority by foreigners in respect of their conduct outside the jurisdiction. It is perhaps ironic that the most frequent insistence upon this principle by Her Majesty's Government has been as a result of its violation by the courts and government agencies of the United States.

---

[344] [1990] Ch. at 37.   [345] [1990] Ch. at 82–83.   [346] [1986] Ch. 482.
[347] 'The Doctrine of Jurisdiction in International Law' (1964) *Collected Courses*, Vol III, p. 146.   [348] [1986] Ch. at 493.

That an injunction granted in one country in relation to acts in another country can give rise to serious questions of sovereignty is illustrated by two incidents involving conflicts between the United States and the United Kingdom. The first relates to international securities legislation; the second relates to international civil aviation. In each case injunctions granted against private parties gave rise to serious inter-governmental disputes. This author was professionally involved in those cases, and the reader must make his or her judgment on the correctness of the positions taken by the Governments. The first example is the affair of the Standard Chartered Bank and the action by the United States Securities and Exchange Commission against Wang and Lee; the second is the litigation arising out of the collapse of Laker Airways.

2. SECURITIES LAW

It would be wholly outside the scope of this paper to discuss in detail the territorial scope of securities legislation, and the permissible limits of jurisdiction in an increasingly worldwide securities market. It is sufficient for present purposes to say that the United States Securities and Exchange Commission and the United States federal courts have reacted to these problems by exercising jurisdiction over violations of securities laws (especially insider trading and fraud) when relevant acts or omissions have taken place in the United States or when relevant acts or omissions abroad have had substantial effects in the United States.[349]

A recent example will indicate the breadth of this jurisdiction. In *Consolidated Gold Fields plc* v. *Minorco SA*[350] actions in the United States courts by the target of a hostile takeover bid in England were able to frustrate the bid, notwithstanding that the United Kingdom Monopolies and Mergers Commission had cleared a takeover, and notwithstanding that the Takeover Panel (a non-statutory body which regulates takeovers on the London Stock Exchange) had ordered the target company (Consolidated Gold Fields) to discontinue the United States proceedings unless the directors obtained the approval of the shareholders in general meeting—the Takeover Panel considered that the majority view of the shareholders as to the future of their company should be respected, and that their view should not be pre-empted by the action of the directors in pursuing the United States proceedings. In addition to a claim in the United States court that the proposed acquisition would be in breach of the United States antitrust laws, Consolidated Gold Fields alleged that Minorco had violated the anti-fraud provisions of the securities laws by making false and

---

[349] See *Restatement Third, Foreign Relations Law*, s. 416.
[350] 871 F. 2d 252 (2d Cir.), cert. dismissed 492 US 939 (1989).

misleading statements about the extent to which Minorco was controlled by South African corporations and individuals. The Court of Appeals for the Second Circuit held that the lower court had jurisdiction to grant a preliminary injunction in favour of Consolidated Gold Fields, even though only 2.5 per cent of its shares were held by United States residents, and the overwhelming majority of those shares were held in the names of nominee accounts in the United Kingdom.

In its offer documents, Minorco stated that the offer

is not being made directly or indirectly, or by use of the mails or by any means or instrumentality of interstate or foreign commerce or of any facilities of a national securities exchange of, the United States of America, its possessions or territories or any area subject to its jurisdiction or any political sub-division thereof.

Minorco sent the offer documents to the United Kingdom nominees for United States resident shareholders. Minorco did not post offer documents to the United States resident shareholders who owned shares directly, but the documents stated that Minorco would accept tenders from United States residents as long as the acceptance form was sent to Minorco from outside the United States.

The Court of Appeals held that the lower court should have asserted jurisdiction once it noted that Minorco knew that the British nominees were required by law to forward the tender offer documents to the target's shareholders and ADR depository banks in the United States. This 'effect' (the transmittal of the documents by the nominees) was said to be a direct and foreseeable result of the conduct outside the territory of the United States.

The Securities and Exchange Commission, mindful of the very small United States shareholding, filed a brief as *amicus curiae* supporting subject-matter jurisdiction over the fraud claims, but urged that the court should abstain from granting a remedy for reasons of international comity. The Court of Appeals accepted that it was a settled principle of international and domestic law that a court may abstain from exercising enforcement jurisdiction when the extraterritorial effect of a particular remedy is so disproportionate to harm within the United States as to offend principles of comity. The lower court was directed to conduct additional fact-finding to determine whether an appropriate remedy, consistent with comity principles, might be fashioned in this case. The bid ultimately failed because of the delays caused by the United States proceedings.

Securities and Exchange Commission v. *Wang & Lee*

In June 1988 the Securities and Exchange Commission filed a complaint in the District Court for the Southern District of New York alleging that the defendants Lee and Wang had violated the Securities Exchange Act of 1934 by defrauding purchasers and sellers of securities on United States exchanges. It was alleged that Lee, a national of Taiwan and a resident of Hong Kong, had dealt in numerous securities on the basis of material, non-public information obtained by Wang during the course of his employment as financial analyst with the well-known investment bankers, Morgan Stanley & Co. On the same day the District Court issued a series of *ex parte* orders including a temporary restraining order and an order freezing assets. The order freezing assets applied to the Standard Chartered Bank, an English bank with branches in New York (and, as will be seen, in Hong Kong) as well as to Lee and numerous other persons or entities alleged by the SEC to hold funds for the benefit of Lee or under his control.

Lee admitted that he had been guilty of insider trading, but he then commenced efforts to transfer money from his United States brokerage accounts into a bank account which he maintained in Hong Kong. He delivered instructions to Morgan Stanley, directing the transfer of almost $5 million from his accounts there through Standard Chartered Bank's branch in New York for credit to an account held by a company which he controlled at a branch in Hong Kong. A few weeks later Lee, through his Hong Kong lawyers, demanded payment of accounts maintained at the Hong Kong branch of Standard Chartered Bank by Lee and companies he controlled. Standard Chartered Bank refused to honour his demand, relying on the temporary restraining order granted by the New York court. When the SEC became aware of these developments, it obtained from the district court in New York, an *ex parte* 'anti-suit injunction', restraining Lee and his associates

from commencing or maintaining any action, suit or other proceeding whether within or without the United States of America with respect to any of the assets subject to the aforesaid temporary restraining order, other than in the United States District Court for the Southern District of New York.

A preliminary injunction was subsequently issued when Lee failed to appear.

Lee then renewed his demand on Standard Chartered Bank for payment in Hong Kong on two corporate accounts that he controlled, and the New York court again ordered Lee's Hong Kong lawyers immediately to withdraw all demands made on behalf of Lee. The two corporations instituted an action against the bank in Hong Kong, seeking the funds in the accounts. The next month, August 1988, the SEC applied to the District Court in New York for an order directing the Standard Chartered Bank, New York branch, to pay into the court registry all assets controlled by Lee. The bank deposited under protest US $12.5 million into the registry.

The Hong Kong court in *Nanus Asia Co. Inc.* v. *Standard Chartered Bank*[351] held that the order of the United States District Court had no direct, or indirect, effect in Hong Kong. For Hong Kong to recognize or enforce the New York order would be contrary to the rule that the court had no jurisdiction to entertain an action for the enforcement, either directly or indirectly, of a penal, revenue or other public law. It did not have extraterritorial effect in Hong Kong, and the anti-suit injunction would not be recognized. The contract between the plaintiffs and the bank was governed by Hong Kong law, and the New York order was not a defence because it was an indirect enforcement of foreign public law for a private party to raise a defence based on foreign law, to vindicate or assert the right of a foreign State. The disgorgement proceedings amounted to the enforcement of a sanction, power or right at the instance of the State in its sovereign capacity, and were, therefore, part of its public law. But the court did not grant judgment in favour of Lee and his companies. It held that the bank was on notice given by the SEC that the funds could be proceeds of insider trading and subject to a constructive trust in favour of allegedly defrauded investors as beneficiaries. Wang, in disclosing the confidential information, was in breach of the trust obligation to Morgan Stanley and to its customers. Lee, as a 'tippee' of Wang, assumed a duty of confidentiality and was under an obligation to abstain from trading with insider information. If he traded while in possession of the confidential information, he held the resulting profits as constructive trustee. A bank would be liable to the innocent beneficial owners of funds if it gave knowing assistance to a fraudulent scheme. The bank had knowledge of Wang's breach of duty and when Lee knowingly traded with the advantage of the confidential information, he assumed the same duty and was in breach of trust. The rights of investors to the funds held by the receiver were susceptible of being severed from the SEC's prior exercise of its public statutory rights to secure disgorgement. Investor claims, even if statutory, would not be made in the direct or indirect exercise of penal or public law rights. The court held:

... the Bank had knowledge of the fact that a constructive trust could arise in respect of the profits made by Lee, in breach of the duty he assumed from Wang which was owed to Morgan Stanley and its corporate customers. The Bank further had knowledge of the fact that the profits were subject to a constructive trust in favour of the defrauded investors entitled to claim against the Receiver. In my view, knowledge of the existence of either constructive trust, created the exceptional situation where the Bank ceased to be under its contractual duty to comply with its plaintiff customer's instructions. In fact the Bank had knowledge of both.[352]

---

[351] [1990] 1 HKLR 396.   [352] At 419.

The court's recognition of the constructive trust did not amount to a direct, or indirect, enforcement of United States penal or other public law. The court concluded:

. . . this Court will always take whatever effective steps are legally available to it under Hong Kong law, to deal with illegal or morally reprehensible commercial conduct. The only limits on the court's power are those imposed by Hong Kong law and at times by the sufficiency of the evidence adduced. Where a conflict of laws situation does arise, in this area as in others, the dispute should be approached in a spirit of judicial comity, rather than judicial competitiveness.

Subsequently, the District Court in New York entered final judgment against Lee in default, and ordered an enquiry to determine the amount of profits from the insider trading; declared that those profits be disgorged into the registry and that they were impressed with a constructive trust for the benefit of defrauded investors; and provided for a receiver to receive the disgorged funds for later distribution.

Standard Chartered Bank then appealed to the United States Court of Appeals for the Second Circuit, contending that the lower court had no jurisdiction to make an order requiring it to return funds which in good faith it had transferred to Hong Kong on the instructions of its customer. In essence it claimed that it was put in double jeopardy: on the one hand, it would have to pay the money into a court in New York if the District Court's order stood; on the other hand, it might be required by the Hong Kong court to repay the same money to its customer. It was strongly supported by the British Government.

The British Government took the view that if the District Court's final judgment contemplated that the $12.5 million paid by the bank into the registry should be transferred to a receiver for distribution to allegedly defrauded investors, without requiring proceedings binding in Hong Kong on all parties, including Lee and his companies, establishing the constructive trust claimed, the bank would continue to be exposed to the possibility of double liability in Hong Kong by virtue of the orders. The appellant would continue to be exposed to liability in Hong Kong until there had been a proper enquiry as contemplated by the Hong Kong court, a due exercise of the tracing rights of the beneficiaries and a determination of the final ownership of the balance.

The British Government claimed that the District Court in New York violated widely accepted principles of jurisdiction under international law and ignored the requirements of international comity by its orders and exceeded its proper authority in issuing the anti-suit injunctions. It should have sought to avoid a conflict of jurisdictions by utilising existing multilateral agreements concerning judicial co-operation to communicate with the Hong Kong court or by directing the SEC to make use of all procedures available to it in Hong Kong under Hong Kong law to recover from Lee, instead of seizing funds of the bank, an uninvolved third party, for the benefit of unidentified allegedly defrauded investors. It also claimed that personal jurisdiction over a foreign entity by reason of trading, or even the establishment of a branch within the State, did not give the State general jurisdiction over the actions of that entity and its assets and activities anywhere in the world, particularly when the exercise of the jurisdiction was inconsistent with the law of the other State where the affected assets were located. The determination of title to such choses in action as banking debts was within the jurisdiction of the courts of the state where the debt had its situs, unless the account document specified otherwise. This was a recognized rule of private international law, which rested upon the rule of territorial sovereignty existing in public international law. The order involved not the mere freezing of assets to preserve the status quo, but the removal of assets from Hong Kong and the potential distribution in the United States, which were significantly more intrusive on British sovereignty. The bank would be unfairly penalized if it were made to violate the laws of a foreign sovereign. The New York court had failed to consider the effect of its assertion of extraterritorial jurisdiction on the international banking system, since it ran contrary to the general legal principle that the law of the situs of an account governed the banking relationship, unless the account documents provided otherwise.

The British Government also maintained that the anti-suit injunctions violated jurisdictional principles of international comity. They applied not only to Lee, Wang and their nominees and agents, but were extended specifically to include their attorneys in Hong Kong and other foreign jurisdictions. The District Court failed to establish that it had personal jurisdiction over those it enjoined, particularly Lee's Hong Kong lawyers. International law did not justify jurisdictional assertions of such sweeping scope. Principles of international law and comity required that anti-suit injunctions be issued only in exceptional circumstances, having regard to competing interests.

In a Diplomatic Note annexed to the United Kingdom Government brief to the Court of Appeals of the Second Circuit, and therefore a public document, the British Government said that it was 'vigorously opposed to insider dealing' but it was seriously concerned about the order in question. It said:

> . . . the actions of the United States Court in the present case are equally unacceptable under international law because of their extraterritorial aspects. These actions seek to regulate, by means of a purported mandatory judicial order, relations between a banking company, not of United States nationality, namely the Standard Chartered Bank, and a customer of that Bank in respect of a sum of money held in accounts in a branch of that Bank in Hong Kong. The presence of

another branch of the same Bank in the United States is immaterial. The interference of banking activities outside the United States in this case is not only inconsistent with international law, but it is disruptive of normal international relations in the financial field. The actions of the court in this case also have serious implications for the international banking practices of foreign banks operating in the United States . . . if this extraterritorial claim is upheld, it will add complexity and uncertainty to international banking transactions that involve the United States.

The SEC maintained in its brief that the order had precisely the intended effect, since the Hong Kong court, after noting that the federal court proceedings in Hong Kong had put the bank on notice of a constructive trust, relieved the bank, at least temporarily, of its obligation to pay Lee the money. Unlike a garnishment or attachment, the SEC had obtained no line against the money, nor had the District Court affected title to that money. Possible double liability was not an issue, since the District Court expressly stated that it would leave it open for the bank to apply for the return of the money if matters changed. In addition, the Hong Kong court should, and probably would, give recognition to a final United States judgment against Lee, thus discharging the bank's debt to Lee.

The case was settled before the Court of Appeals for the Second Circuit had an opportunity to rule on the appeal and before the Hong Kong court definitively decided whether the Bank was under an obligation to repay. As a result this case, and the diplomatic incident which surrounded it, leaves unanswered a number of significant questions in the field of the international enforcement of securities law and the application of interim remedies in a complex international situation. Among those questions are these: (1) Did the New York court have jurisdiction to order the return of the funds from Hong Kong? (2) Would it be relevant whether the bank was in good faith in transferring the funds from New York to Hong Kong? (3) Should the New York court have been influenced by the possibility that the Bank might have to pay twice? (4) Was the Hong Kong court right in determining that the SEC was asserting a public law right?

3. THE ANTI-SUIT INJUNCTION: LAKER AIRWAYS AND THE AIRLINES

It has already been seen that in the case of *SEC* v. *Wang and Lee* the United States court granted an injunction restraining Lee (and his Hong Kong lawyers) from prosecuting an action in Hong Kong against the bank. That injunction was not effective because neither Lee nor his lawyers were in New York, and therefore could not be fined or imprisoned for contempt.

The jurisdiction exercised in common law countries to restrain by injunction the institution or continuance of proceedings in foreign courts goes back to the end of the eighteenth century.[353] As long ago as 1834 it was said:[354]

In truth, nothing can be more unfounded than the doubts of the jurisdiction. That is grounded, like all other jurisdiction of the court, not upon any pretension to the exercise of judical and administrative rights abroad, but on the circumstance of the person of the party on whom this order is made being within the power of the court. If the court can command him to bring home goods from abroad, or to assign chattel interests, or to convey real property locally situate abroad;—if, for instance, as in *Penn* v. *Lord Baltimore* (1750) 1 Ves. Sen. 444, it can decree the performance of an agreement touching the boundary of a province in North America; . . . in precisely the like manner it can restrain the party being within the limits of its jurisdiction from . . . the instituting or prosecution of an action in a foreign court.

In modern times the circumstances in which the remedy of an injunction can be made available to restrain foreign proceedings have been a matter of some controversy and development. The traditional view (expressed in the case in which a party sought unsuccessfully to restrain proceedings in France) was this:

. . . the court has jurisdiction to restrain the prosecution of proceedings before the foreign court, because it is a jurisdiction which applies *in personam* against a party and does not involve conflict between the tribunals of the two countries. But it is only exercised very rarely, with great caution, to avoid even the appearance of interfering with the foreign court, and if the foreign action is vexatious and useless.[355]

More recently, it has been held by the House of Lords that an injunction may be granted when an action has been brought in a foreign court which is not the *forum conveniens* (or appropriate forum) for the conduct of the proceedings,[356] but this view has been doubted by the Privy Council (which consisted in that case of four law lords and a retired Lord Justice of Appeal). Speaking through Lord Goff in the *Aérospatiale* case, the Privy Council criticised the formulation of principle in *Castanho* v. *Brown & Root (UK) Ltd.*:[357]

In practice, however, the principle so stated would have the effect that, where the parties are in dispute on the point whether the action should proceed in an English or a foreign court, the English court would be prepared, not merely to decline to

---

[353] See *Wharton* v. *May* (1799) 5 Ves. Jr. 27, 71 and other cases cited in Dicey and Morris, *Conflict of Laws*, (11th ed., 1987), p. 389.
[354] *Lord Portarlington* v. *Soulby* (1834) 3 My & K. 104, 108, *per* Lord Brougham LC.
[355] *Settlement Corp.* v. *Hochschild* [1966] Ch. 10, 15, *per* Ungoed-Thomas J.
[356] *Castanho* v. *Brown & Root (UK) Ltd.* [1981] AC 557, 575, *per* Lord Scarman; *South Carolina Insurance Co.* v. *'De Zeven Provincien NV'* [1987] AC 24, 40, *per* Lord Brandon.
[357] *Soc. Nat. Industrielle Aérospatiale* v. *Lee Kui Jak* [1987] AC 871, 895–896 (PC).

adjudicate by granting a stay of proceedings on the ground that the English court was forum non conveniens, but, if it concluded that England was the natural forum, to restrain a party from proceeding in the foreign court *on that ground alone*. Their Lordships cannot think that this is right . . . [It] leads to the conclusion that, in a case where there is simply a difference of view between the English court and the foreign court as to which is the natural forum, the English court can arrogate to itself, by the grant of an injunction, the power to resolve that dispute . . . But, with all respect, such a conclusion appears . . . to be inconsistent with comity, and indeed to disregard the fundamental requirement that an injunction will only be granted where the ends of justice so require . . .

It is clear, therefore, that what is the *forum conveniens* is only one of the factors to be taken into account when the grant of an injunction is in issue. In these cases the plaintiff asserts an unusual right, the right not to be sued in the foreign court. In general, the exercise of this jurisdiction may be justified (at least where the foreign action is vexatious or oppressive) on the principle that the equitable jurisdiction to grant injunctions may be exercised where the defendant (who is the plaintiff in the foreign proceedings) has behaved, or threatens to behave, in a manner which is unconscionable.[358] Such injunctions are normally sought by parties 'who are not seeking to assert any independent court of action but simply a right not to be sued in a foreign court'.[359]

It is remarkable that almost all of the modern decisions in England on the exercise of this power concern proceedings in the United States.[360] It is not hard to find the reasons why litigation is brought in the United States, where (at least to the foreign eye) the appropriate forum is a court outside the United States: among them are the availability to plaintiffs of contingency fees in the United States (compared with the great expense of lawyers' fees in complex actions in other countries); the availability of extensive oral and documentary discovery in United States procedure (compared with limited documentary discovery in some countries, and no discovery at all, in other countries); the availability of jury trials in civil actions (almost unknown elsewhere); the presence of strict liability principles in some tort cases, and much higher levels of damages awards, including punitive damages; and the availability of causes of action unknown in other countries. The theory has always been that the exercise

---

[358] *South Carolina* case [1987] AC at 40.

[359] *Associated Newspapers plc* v. *Insert Media Ltd.* [1988] 1 WLR 509, 514, *per* Hoffmann J.

[360] In addition to the cases cited in footnotes 356 and 357, *supra*, and the *Laker Airways* litigation discussed *infra*, see *Smith Kline & French Laboratories Ltd.* v. *Bloch (No. 1)* [1983] 1 WLR 730 (CA); *(No. 2)*, *The Times*, 13 November 1984 (CA); *Metall und Rohstoff AG* v. *ACLI Metals Ltd.* [1984] 1 Lloyd's Rep. 598 (CA); *Bank of Tokyo Ltd.* v. *Karoon* [1987] AC 45n (CA); *E. I. du Pont de Nemours* v. *Agnew (No. 2)* [1988] 2 Lloyd's Rep. 240 (CA); *Pan American World Airways Inc.* v. *Andrews*, *The Times*, 29 October 1991. Cf. *National Mutual Holdings Pty. Ltd.* v. *Sentry Corp.* (1989) 87 ALR 539.

of this power does not involve interference with the jurisdiction of the foreign court, because it is an injunction directed, not to the foreign court, but *in personam* to the defendant (or plaintiff in the foreign court). It is now, however, recognised that one of the reasons for the caution with which the jurisdiction must be exercised is that 'it involves interference with the process of the foreign court concerned.'[361] There could be no clearer illustration of this than the Laker Airways litigation.

Laker Airways was founded as a charter airline in 1966, and by 1977 had obtained the necessary authorizations from the United States and British Governments to inaugurate a low-cost transatlantic airline service between London and New York. Its fares were approximately one-third of competing fares offered by other transatlantic carriers. But in 1981 its financial conditions rapidly deteriorated because a large amount of its revenue was in pounds, but most of its debts, such as those on its United States financed fleet of DC-10 aircraft, and expenses, were in dollars. Several airlines allegedly conspired to set predatory prices (i.e. uneconomic prices designed to drive Laker Airways out of business) and in October 1981 Pan American, TWA and British Airways dropped their fares for the full service flights to equal those charged by Laker Airways for its 'no frills' services. Other airlines allegedly pressured Laker's lenders to withhold financing which had previously been promised. Laker Airways went into liquidation in February 1982.

In November 1982 Laker Airways, a Jersey company in liquidation, brought an anti-trust action in the United States District Court for the District of Columbia against two American airlines, Pan American and TWA, and four foreign airlines, British Airways, British Caledonian Airways, Lufthansa and Swissair, alleging that the defendants conspired and agreed on a predatory pricing scheme to destroy Laker Airways' transatlantic service. In February 1983 separate proceedings were brought by Laker Airways against Sabena and KLM, based on essentially the same allegations. In September 1983 similar proceedings were commenced against UTA and SAS.

In January 1983 British Airways, British Caledonian, Lufthansa and Swissair brought actions in the English Court seeking declarations of non-liability to Laker Airways and orders enjoining Laker Airways from continuing its actions against them in the United States. They were granted at the outset an *ex parte* injunction by a series of additional restraining orders.

In its turn, in March 1983, Laker Airways obtained a preliminary injunction in the United States District Court restraining those defendants who had not yet taken action in England from taking any action abroad

---

[361] *South Carolina* case [1987] AC 14, 40.

that would impair or interfere with the United States District Court's jurisdiction, or Laker Airways' freedom to prosecute the action. This decision was affirmed by the United States Court of Appeals for the District of Columbia.[362]

In May 1983 Parker J., a judge of the Commercial Court in England, discharged the injunction on the basis that the jurisdiction was properly in the United States District Court.[363] After this judgment the British Government invoked its powers under the Protection of Trading Interests Act 1980 to determine that measures taken in the United States threatened to damage the trading interests of the United Kingdom, with the exception of American air carriers, from complying with United States anti-trust measures in the District Court arising out of any agreement or arrangement, or any act done by a UK designated airline relating to the provision of air carriage under various treaty arrangements. The Court of Appeal reinstated the injunctions in July 1983.[364] In October 1983 in proceedings commenced by Lufthansa and Swissair, the English court issued an injunction, following the decision of the Court of Appeal, restraining Laker from taking any further steps in the United States District Court action, or commencing any further proceedings against Lufthansa or Swissair (except discovery).

In an opinion issued in November 1983, the United States District Court reviewed the proceedings to date and appointed an *amicus curriae* to assist the court to determine what action by the court was required or appropriate in light of the decisions of the British courts and the resulting incapacity of Laker.[365]

In July 1984 the House of Lords reversed the decision of the Court of Appeal and discharged the injunctions.[366] Following the decision of the House of Lords, Laker Airways sought and obtained from the District Court in Washington injunctions against British Airways and British Caledonian restraining them from taking any further proceedings abroad to interfere with the United States actions.[367] Subsequently the litigation was settled by a payment by the airlines to the liquidator.

This bare outline of the litigation does not do justice to its importance, or to the seriousness of the dispute between the United States and the United Kingdom (and other countries involved). Many of the issues are outside the scope of this paper, especially the territorial scope of the United States anti-trust laws, and the relationship between national law and the international agreements governing civil aviation. But at least two

---

[362] *Laker Airways Ltd.* v. *Pan American Airways*, 559 F. Supp. 1124 (DDC 1983), affd. *sub. nom Laker Airways Ltd.* v. *Sabena Belgian World Airways*, 731 F. 2d 909 (DC Cir. 1984). [363] [1984] QB 142.
[364] [1984] QB 142 (CA). [365] 577 F. Supp. 348 (DCC 1983).
[366] [1985] AC 58. [367] 604 F. Supp. 280 (DCC 1984).

aspects of the affair are directly relevant to the issue of the territorial scope of provisional measures. Both relate to the underlying question whether it is true, as the older authorities indicate, that the exercise of the jurisdiction does not interfere with the process of the foreign court but is directed *in personam* at a party, normally the plaintiff in the foreign proceedings.

From the time the English High Court granted *ex parte* injunctions until the time the House of Lords held that they should be discharged, the liquidator of Laker Airways was unable to prosecute the proceedings in the United States against British Airways, British Caledonian, Lufthansa and Swissair. Although Parker J. held that no injunction ought to be granted, the injunctions were maintained pending appeal. After the Court of Appeal held that the injunctions ought to be imposed, they remained in force until the decision of the House of Lords.

The two leading judgments in the United States courts concerned the propriety of corresponding injunctions in the United States against Pan American, TWA, Sabena and KLM restraining them from taking action in England to interfere with the United States proceedings. These injunctions were sought by Laker Airways before those airlines had taken any action in England similar to that of British Airways and the other airlines who had acted to obtain *ex parte* injunctions in the English courts. The United States courts were, therefore, in these decisions, not directly concerned with the actions of British Airways and those airlines which had taken action in England, but, to put it at its lowest, they certainly took them into account when deciding to prevent Pan American and other airlines from taking similar action.

The judgment of Judge Harold Greene in the District Court for the District of Columbia shows clearly the exasperation and anger of a judge who believed that his jurisdiction was being invaded by a foreign court. To the extent that the English court was under the impression that its injunctions operated only on the plaintiff and not on the United States court, he said:

. . . as the Supreme Court held over a century ago, there is no difference between addressing an injunction to the parties and addressing it to the foreign court itself. *Peck v. Jennes*, 48 U.S. (7 How.) 612, 624–625 . . . Mr. Justice Parker has also stated . . . that the type of injunction he issued 'does not represent an interference by one court with the proceedings of another'. With utmost respect, this Court must differ. It can hardly be said that an order which, for example, directs a party not to file further papers in this Court, as did the order of the British court . . . is anything other than a direct interference with the proceedings in this Court.[368]

When the injunctions were obtained in England, the airlines argued (*inter alia*) that the United States courts were an inappropriate forum

---

[368] 559 F. Supp. at 1128.

because of procedural differences (especially the availability of more extensive discovery, in the United States) between England and the United States. Judge Green retorted:

. . . it is hardly the proper province of a foreign court to prohibit the conduct of litigation here because it does not agree with the way in which the United States Congress and the American courts, including the Supreme Court, have dealt with this particular procedural problem.[369]

He referred to the 'denigration of American law by British courts', in particular to the statement of Lord Denning MR in *Smith Kline & French Laboratories Ltd.* v. *Bloch*:

As a moth is drawn to light, so is a litigant drawn to the United States. If he can only get his case into their courts, he stands to win a fortune.[370]

Judge Greene concluded:

. . . The Court exceedingly regrets that it must issue an injunction in this case. However, it is worth emphasizing that this Court had no part in precipitating the current dispute. The lawsuit pending before it was proceeding in its normal course, when the British court, without appropriate regard to principles of comity, proceeded to interfere with that action. At that juncture, this Court's options were severely limited. It could either issue its own injunction to prevent at least the remaining defendants—those from the United States and some of those from the European continent—from seeking shelter from United States law in a British court, or it could acquiesce in silence in the effort to have a foreign tribunal decide on this Court's jurisdiction and to see the plaintiff's Sherman Act rights dissipated. With regret, the Court has no choice but to follow the former course.[371]

It was in direct response to this judgment that Lord Donaldson MR, giving the judgment of the English Court of Appeal, in which the injunctions were confirmed, said:

Whatever the ultimate conclusion in this litigation—and it seems likely that the unsuccessful party or parties will wish to take the matter to the House of Lords—we and all other English judges would deeply regret any misunderstanding on the part of our brethren in the United States of what exactly we are doing and why we are doing it . . . First, let it be said, and said loud and clear, that no one has ever suggested that the United States District Court is without jurisdiction to try Lakers' complaint . . . Second, let it be said at no less volume and with no less clarity that no submission has been made to this court that the civil procedures of the United States courts and, in particular, the system of pre-trial discovery by the taking of depositions, the administration of interrogatories and the disclosure of documents, the limited circumstances in which a successful defendant would be awarded costs and the conduct of litigation upon the basis of contingency fees are in any way to be criticised . . . Third, let it be said no less loudly and clearly that neither the English

---

[369] At 1133.   [370] [1983] 1 WLR 730, 733 (CA).   [371] At 1136, 1138–1139.

courts nor the English judges entertain any feelings of hostility towards the American antitrust laws or would ever wish to denigrate that or any other American law. Judicial comity is shorthand for good neighbourliness, common courtesy and mutual respect between those who labour in adjoining judicial vineyards. In the context of the United Kingdom and the United States, this comes naturally and, so far as we are concerned, effortlessly.[372]

Judge Greene was not satisfied by these conciliatory remarks. A few months later he issued a decision appointing an *amicus curiae* to assist the United States court 'in the restoration of the integrity of the litigation process', who was requested to assist the court in determining what action was required in the light of the incapacity of Laker Airways which had been imposed by the order of the English Court of Appeal. In his decision he described the English injunctions as being 'as broad and intrusive as are unprecedented', and as 'premature and therefore improper even on their own terms', and concluded:[373]

. . . in these unusual circumstances where substantial legal interests are at stake but one of the parties is prevented from asserting its position as a consequence of the intrusion of foreign courts and foreign executive officials into the United States judicial process on bases that, at least *prima facie*, do not appear legitimate it should not simply sit by and permit these interests to be dissipated by default. . . . [T]he Court has concluded that the time has come to end the paralysis and to proceed with these lawsuits.

The United States Court of Appeals for the District of Columbia affirmed Judge Greene's judgment imposing the injunctions, but in more restrained language. But the Court of Appeals recognized that the case represented a 'head-on collision' between opposing antitrust policies, and that problems posed by the case were exacerbated by the fact that it involved 'antisuit injunctions designed to preempt the parties' access to the courts of foreign jurisdictions'. Their solution required the court to minimize 'the interference with the judicial processes of other nations that our courts will permit'.[374]

The majority opinion (Judge Starr dissented on the ground that the injunction was too wide) was written by Judge Wilkey. The essence of the decision was that both the United States and Great Britain shared concurrent prescriptive jurisdiction over the transactions giving rise to

---

[372] [1984] QB at 185–186.

[373] *Laker Airways Ltd.* v. *Pan American World Airways*, 577 F. Supp. 348, 354–355 (DDC 1983). A report was filed by the *amicus curiae* but in view of the House of Lords decision in 1985, discharging the injunctions, no action was taken on it: see 604 F. Supp. at 284. See also *Laker Airways Ltd.* v. *Pan American World Airways*, 604 F. Supp. 280, 284 (DDC 1984); *Laker Airways Ltd.* v. *Pan American World Airways*, 103 FRD 42 (DDC 1984).

[374] *Laker Airways Ltd.* v. *Sabena Belgian World Airlines*, 731 F. 2d 909, 916 (DC Dir. 1984).

Laker Airways' claim. The application of United States antitrust law to the alleged conspiracies between KLM, Sabena and the other defendants was founded upon the harmful effects occurring within the territory of the United States as a direct result of the alleged wrong-doing. That aspect of territorial jurisdiction was entirely consistent with nationally and internationally recognized limits of sovereign authority. Although most of the conspiratorial acts took place in other countries, the economic consequences of the alleged actions gravely impaired significant American interests. In addition to the protection of American consumers' and creditors' interests, the United States had a substantial interest in regulating the conduct of business within the United States. Foreign airlines flew to the United States on the basis that they would obey United States law.

As regards anti-suit injunctions, Judge Wilkey said:

It is well settled that English and American courts have power to control the conduct of persons subject to their jurisdiction to the extent of forbidding them from suing in foreign jurisdictions. However, the fundamental corollary to concurrent jurisdiction must ordinarily be respected: parallel proceedings on the same *in personam* claim should ordinarily be allowed to proceed simultaneously, at least until a judgment is reached in which one can be pled as *res judicata* in the other . . . Courts have a duty to protect their legitimately conferred jurisdiction to the extent necessary to provide full justice to litigants. Thus, when the action of a litigant in another forum threatens to paralyze the jurisdiction of the court, the court may consider the effectiveness and propriety of issuing an injunction against the litigant's participation in the foreign proceedings.[375]

But this was not a situation where two courts were proceeding to separate judgment simultaneously under one cause of action. Rather, the sole purpose of the English proceeding was to *terminate* the American action.

The dispute was defused when the House of Lords held that the English Court of Appeal had been wrong to grant the injunctions. The essence of the decision was that where (as in this case) there was only one forum in which Laker Airways could bring its antitrust actions, namely the United States, an injunction restraining the United States proceedings would only be granted if British Airways and British Caledonian could show that it was 'unconscionable' for Laker Airways to sue them in the United States. Lord Diplock said that the British airline accepted, by operating scheduled routes to and from the United States, that they would become subject to the American antitrust laws. It was therefore:

impossible to argue plausibly either that Laker by submitting itself to such a regime precluded itself from relying on any cause of action against [British Airways] and

---

[375] 731 F. 2d at 926–927.

[British Caledonian] that might accrue to it under American antitrust laws as a result of what these airlines subsequently did within the territorial jurisdiction of the United States; or that there was anything so unconscionable or unjust in Laker's conduct in pursuing such cause of action in a U.S. court that an English judge, in the proper exercise of a judicial discretion, would be entitled to grant an injunction to prevent Laker from doing so.[376]

Lord Scarman added that particular caution was needed before an injunction restraining foreign proceedings would be granted because it was, 'however disguised and indirect, an interference with the process of justice' in the foreign court.[377]

After the House of Lords discharged the injunctions, Laker Airways applied to the District Court in Washington for an extension of the injunctions to British Airways and British Caledonian. Judge Greene imposed the injunctions, and referred to the airlines' attempts, which had been successful for one and a half years, 'to frustrate the jurisdiction of this Court and to interfere with Laker's right to free access to the courts of this nation'.[378]

The Midland Bank proceedings

The only effective injunction granted and maintained by the English courts was that in favour of the Midland Bank. The liquidator of Laker Airways had warned Midland Bank that he intended to join it to the United States proceedings on the basis that it had withdrawn financial support from Laker Airways in circumstances from which a United States court might infer a conspiracy with the airlines and the aircraft manufacturers McDonnell Douglas to put Laker Airways out of business. Midland Bank contended that its dealings with Laker Airways had been in the ordinary course of its banking business in England, and that for some months, at the request of the Bank of England, it had tried to organize financial help for Laker Airways and had extended its own and its subsidiaries' commitments to help Laker Airways; it was only after it had received information about Laker Airways' trading figures from the Civil Aviation Authority and had consulted with them and with the Bank of England, that it decided to tell Sir Freddie Laker that unless he could get financial help elsewhere and quickly, it would have to appoint a receiver. Midland Bank issued proceedings in England claiming a declaration that it was not liable and seeking an injunction restraining the liquidator from instituting or continuing an antitrust suit against it in the United States.

---

[376] *British Airways Board* v. *Laker Airways Ltd.* [1985] AC 58, 84.
[377] At 95.
[378] *Laker Airways Ltd.* v. *Pan American World Airways*, 604 F. Supp. 280, 284.

The Court of Appeal held that (notwithstanding the decision of the House of Lords) the Midland Bank and its subsidiary were in a wholly different situation from British Airways and British Caledonian.[379] Although the three members of the Court of Appeal accepted that the primary test was whether it would be unconscionable or unjust to allow Laker Airways to institute proceedings in the United States there was some difference of emphasis. But what is clear is that in substance the court upheld the injunction because Laker Airways' conduct in threatening to join Midland Bank to the American proceedings was unconscionable and unjust in that the exercise of jurisdiction by the United States court over Midland Bank would, in the circumstances of the case, be contrary to public international law. Dillon LJ emphasized the extraterritorial nature of United States antitrust jurisdiction, and the lack of connection of the bank's relevant activities with the United States. He said:[380]

. . . the United States courts claim that any person in any part of the world who, with knowledge of the primary conspiracy, takes steps in his own country in defence of his own legitimate interests may be held to have made himself a party to the conspiracy and to be liable to an antitrust suit before a United States jury in a United States court even though what he did subjected him to no civil or criminal liability by the law of his own country . . . Prima facie, therefore, in view of the oppressive nature, to English minds, of the United States procedures, it is unconscionable and unjust for a person who is subject to the jurisdiction of the English courts to seek to invoke the United States jurisdiction under these United States Acts against an English company or individual who is not subject to United States jurisdiction . . . It seems to me all the more important . . . to insist on keeping the United States statutory provision of the Sherman and Clayton Acts within the territorial jurisdiction of the United States in accordance with accepted standards of international law.

Without specific reference to international law, Lawton LJ made essentially the same point. The connection of the banks with Laker Airways:

arose from banking transactions in England which were governed by English law and were intended to be so governed . . . They did nothing in the United States which would have been governed by the United States antitrust legislation. At the material time, save on the international inter-bank market, they themselves had no banking business in the United States. Midland Bank's subsidiary bank in California, which had a separate legal existence and over which they had no managerial control, had no connection of any kind with the airlines involved in the liquidator's antitrust suit . . . [I]t cannot be said that the plaintiff banks have submitted themselves to the United States antitrust legislation in the way that British Airways and British Caledonian Airways have done.[381]

---

[379] *Midland Bank plc* v. *Laker Airways Ltd.* [1986] QB 689 (CA).
[380] [1986] QB at 704, 711.   [381] At 699–700.

11

The Property of Foreign States

No doubt the title of this section will convey the impression that it is concerned primarily with sovereign immunity, and it is certainly true that there has been much discussion of that subject in the context of the attachment of State property. But it is easy to overlook the fact that States are frequently plaintiffs in foreign courts, as well as defendants. Accordingly, this section will deal not only with issues of sovereign immunity, but also with provisional and protective measures in the context of claims by foreign States for the return of their property.

I. CLAIMS BY FOREIGN STATES AGAINST THEIR FORMER OFFICIALS

There have been two striking examples in recent years of attempts by Governments to use foreign courts to assist them in recovering property allegedly stolen from the State by former rulers: the first example is the claims brought by the Republic of Haiti in the French and English courts against Baby Doc Duvalier and his family in connection with allegations that they had looted the Treasury of the Republic; the second example is the claims brought by the Republic of the Philippines against former President Marcos and Mrs Marcos for the recovery of State property.

These cases are directly relevant to the theme of these lectures because they demonstrate that claims by foreign States against their former officials are especially likely to involve questions of protective or provisional measures: very often vast sums of money are involved, the officials have access to sophisticated methods of movement of money, and speed of response is invariably necessary if the assets are not to disappear through accounts in Panama or the Cayman Islands or Luxembourg. But these cases require separate treatment because claims by foreign States are likely to raise delicate questions involving foreign relations and the justiciability of the claims.

As early as 1810 the United States recognized the right of the King of Spain to resort to its courts.[382] In 1826 it was held in England that 'a foreign state is as well entitled, as any individual, to the aid of this court in the assertion of its rights'.[383] In 1871 the United States Supreme Court said:

---

[382] *King of Spain* v. *Oliver*, 2 Washington's Circuit Court, 841 (1810).
[383] *Colombian Government* v. *Rothschild* (1826) 1 Sim. 94, 104.

A foreign sovereign, as well as any other foreign person, who has a demand of a civil nature against any person here, may prosecute it in our courts. To deny him this privilege would manifest a want of comity and friendly feeling.[384]

It is significant that the Supreme Court emphasized that the claim should be of 'a civil nature'. Ten years earlier in *Emperor of Austria* v. *Day and Kossuth*[385] the Lord Chancellor, Lord Campbell, accepted that a foreign sovereign could not sue in England 'merely to support his political power and prerogatives' and Turner LJ agreed that the court could not and should not 'interfere in aid of the prerogatives of a foreign sovereign'.[386] But in that case the Emperor of Austria sued in England to prevent the circulation of spurious Hungarian banknotes produced by Day & Sons, 'the well known lithographers', on the instructions of Louis Kossuth, the famous Hungarian revolutionary who claimed to be the lawfully appointed Governor President of Hungary. The action for delivery up of the spurious banknotes, and an injunction to restrain their circulation, was allowed because the claim involved 'rights of property quite sufficient to found jurisdiction in this court'.[387]

Accordingly, it was accepted by the middle of the nineteenth century in England and the United States that a foreign State could sue in respect of a claim of 'a civil nature' and also in respect of 'rights of property'. Thus in one of several cases following the American Civil War in which English courts allowed the United States Government to sue for property in England held for the defeated Confederate Government it was said:

The right of a foreign state which has been recognised by Her Majesty, whether it be a monarchy or a republic, to sue in the courts of this country for public property belonging to the state, has not been, and cannot be, denied.[388]

2. EMBEZZLEMENT OF STATE PROPERTY

In 1849 Frederick Kuepper, an official of the post office in Prussia, who had allegedly embezzled the equivalent of some 5,000 United States dollars, absconded to the United States. He went to St Louis, Missouri, where he died later that year. Frederick William IV, the King of Prussia, sued Kuepper's administrator. It was held that the King of Prussia could sue in the state court in Missouri:[389]

---

[384] *The Sapphire* v. *Napoleon III*, 78 US (11 Wallace) 164 (1871).

[385] (1861) 3 De GF and J. 217, 238.

[386] At 251.   [387] At 253–254.

[388] *United States of America* v. *Wagner* (1867) LR 2 Ch. App. 582, 591, *per* Turner LJ. Cf. *Banco de Bilbao* v. *Sancha and Rey* [1938] 2 KB 176 (CA); *Banco de España* v. *Federal Reserve Bank of New York*, 114 F. 2d 438 (2d Cir. 1940).

[389] *King of Prussia* v. *Kuepper's Administrator*, 22 Mo. 550 (1856), in 5 *Am. Int. LC* 428, at 431.

If the subjects of foreign governments will contract obligations or affect themselves with liabilities to their kings or princes, and afterwards migrate to the United States, there is nothing in the nature of our institutions which shields them from their just responsibilities. While our government grants the rights and privileges of citizenship to all foreigners who are naturalized under our laws, there is neither policy nor justice in screening them from the civil liabilities which they have contracted with the government to which they were once subject. Our tribunals afford no assistance in the enforcement of the penal codes of foreign nations, nor would they aid despotic rulers, in the exercise of an arbitrary power, in making special and retrospective laws affecting foreigners residing here, who were once their subjects. But when laws have been made abroad, and debts have been contracted under those laws, there is no reason for refusing our assistance in their collection.

There was therefore no reason in principle why a foreign Government should not sue an official in the post office for the return of funds stolen from the post office.

Five thousand dollars, even in 1849 values, is a small sum compared to the amounts claimed by the Republic of Haiti from Baby Doc Duvalier, and by the Republic of the Philippines from Ferdinand and Imelda Marcos. It is now necessary to give an account of these cases before reverting to the fundamental question whether the former President of a country, who is alleged to have looted the Treasury, is in the same legal position as the Prussian postmaster who has taken money from the post office and fled to the United States.

Republic of Haiti v. *Duvalier*[390]

The Republic of Haiti commenced proceedings in the Tribunal de Grande Instance at Grasse, France, in July 1986. The proceedings were against various members of the Duvalier family, including Jean-Claude ('Baby Doc') Duvalier, his wife, and his mother (the widow of 'Papa Doc' Duvalier, who was the President from 1957 until his death in 1971). In the French proceedings it was claimed that the family was responsible for embezzling sums totalling more than $120 million from the Republic during the presidency of Baby Doc Duvalier, between 1971 and 1986, and it was suggested that this was only the tip of the iceberg and that very much larger sums were involved.

The English Court of Appeal[391] granted a worldwide *Mareva* injunction in aid of the French proceedings under Article 24 of the Brussels

---

[390] In England: [1990] 1 QB 202; in France, Aix, 25.4.1988, 1988 *Clunet* 779; Cass. civ. I, 29.5.1990, 1991 *Clunet* 137; Dehaussy, 'Le statut de l'État étranger demandeur sur le for français: droit international coutumier et droit interne', 1991 *Clunet* 109.

[391] *Supra*, Sections III and VIII.

Convention. The decision of the Court of Appeal recited that there was evidence that the Duvalier family had been attempting to conceal their assets; and that they had been advised by a French lawyer, who had written a book which dealt with the concealment of funds within the Swiss banking system, including the advantage of using a fiduciary as the legal owner of the assets to be concealed, rather than the beneficial owner himself, and the added advantage of choosing a lawyer as a fiduciary, since professional secrecy would protect the identity of the client. For this reason the Duvalier family used an English firm of solicitors which held 11 accounts in their name in various jurisdictions.

The Duvalier family were ordered not to deal with assets, wherever situated, which represented the proceeds of the sums claimed in the French proceedings, and were ordered to permit 'by' the English solicitors[392] inspection of documents and to disclose information relating to their worldwide assets. The Duvalier family had argued that an order should not be made in relation to assets abroad because the English court had no jurisdiction on the merits, the Duvalier family were not resident in England, there was no judgment against them, the assets concerned were mainly, if not wholly, outside the jurisdiction, and the proper court to make such orders was either the French court at Grasse or the courts having jurisdiction where the assets were located. But the Court of Appeal affirmed the injunction because of

the plain and admitted intention of the defendants to move their assets out of the reach of the courts of law, coupled with the resources they have obtained and the skill which they have hitherto shown in doing that, and the vast amount of money involved. This case demands international co-operation between all nations.[393]

In the French proceedings the Duvalier family claimed that the French courts could not exercise jurisdiction in order to enforce claims of foreign States based on their public law. The Court of Appeal of Aix held that the claim was maintainable because the real claim of Haiti was not for the enforcement of its public law, but for the restitution of funds which had been misappropriated by the defendants. But ultimately the proceedings failed when the French Cour de Cassation decided that the claims by the Republic of Haiti were founded upon public law, in the sense that their purpose was related to the exercise of governmental power. Litigation relating to relations between a State and its officers, whatever the nature of the wrongs committed by them, were necessarily related to the exercise of public power and could only be governed by the principles of public law. The reasoning was based on the 1977 Resolution of the Institut de droit

---

[392] The order was not made against the solicitors, but the effect of it was that they, as agents of the Duvalier family, had to give the information to the plaintiffs.
[393] [1990] 1 QB at 217.

international, by which it was resolved that public law claims should be considered inadmissible in so far as they were related to the exercise of governmental power, unless the subject-matter of the claim, the needs of international co-operation or the interests of the States concerned required a different result.[394]

Republic of Philippines v. *Marcos*[395]

A wholly different result was reached in very similar circumstances in the United States in the *Marcos* affair. The political background will be familiar. After some 20 years as President of the Philippines, Ferdinand Marcos left the Philippines with his wife Imelda Marcos. His successor, President Aquino, was recognized by the United States. Mr and Mrs Marcos arrived in Hawaii, accompanied by numerous crates filled with jewels and precious metals, and including 22 crates full of Philippine currency. The crates were impounded by United States customs.[396]

The Republic of the Philippines began litigation in the United States and Switzerland to recover or freeze assets which it claimed were the property of the Republic improperly possessed or controlled by Mr and Mrs Marcos. The Republic alleged that President Marcos had engaged in (*inter alia*) widespread and systematic theft of State property.

In Switzerland, the Federal Tribunal upheld an attachment made (at the request of the Philippines Government under the Swiss law on international mutual assistance in criminal matters) against property in the custody of Marcos, and rejected the suggestion that he was entitled to immunity as a former head of State.[397] In New York the Republic sought to recover five substantial properties, including a 71-storey office building on Wall Street, which were held through companies incorporated in Panama, the Netherlands Antilles and the British Virgin Islands, which were alleged to be creatures of the Marcoses. In the New York proceedings the court of Appeals for the Second Circuit confirmed a preliminary injunction restraining the transfer of the properties pending trial.[398] In an action in California the Republic claimed that Marcos had used his position of power and authority to convert to his use property belonging to the Philippines and its people, and alleged claims (*inter alia*) for conversion,

---

[394] *Annuaire*, Vol. II (1977), p. 328.

[395] 806 F. 2d 344 (2d Cir. 1986); 818 F. 2d 1473 (9th Cir. 1987), on rehearing 862 F. 2d 1355 (9th Cir.), cert. den. 490 US 1035 (1988). Cf. *Islamic Republic of Iran* v. *Pahlavi*, 467 NE 2d 245 (NY Ct. App. 1984) (claim against Shah and Empress for recovery of 35 billion dollars allegedly misappropriated; dismissed on *forum non conveniens* grounds even though no remedy elsewhere).

[396] See *Azurin* v. *Von Raab*, 803 F. 2d 993 (9th Cir. 1986).

[397] 82 ILR 53; (1988) 44 *Ann. suisse de droit international*, p. 226.

[398] 806 F. 2d 344 (2d Cir. 1986).

fraud and constructive trust. The Court of Appeals for the Ninth Circuit, by a majority, in 1987, refused an injunction restraining the transfer of property held anywhere in the world by or on behalf of the Marcoses. The ground for the refusal was that the Republic had not shown a sufficient likelihood that it would ultimately prevail on the merits of the case: this was because adjudication of many of the Republic's claims would be barred by the act of State doctrine and/or by the political question doctrine.[399] But the Court of Appeals reheard the case *en banc*, and, again by a majority, decided that the act of State doctrine and political question doctrine would not be barriers to the action, and granted worldwide injunctions.[400]

Thus the Court of Appeals for both the Second Circuit and the Ninth Circuit rejected arguments which, in a somewhat different form, the French Cour de Cassation accepted. In the United States there is no developed rule that the courts will not enforce claims based on foreign public law[401] or the exercise of foreign governmental power. Instead, the Marcoses relied on the act of State doctrine and the political question doctrine. Discussion of the controversial scope of these concepts is outside the scope of this paper. It is sufficient to note that the act of State doctrine may be summarized (at the risk of oversimplification) by saying that the United States courts will not enquire into the validity of an act of an official of a foreign State under the law of that State.[402] The doctrine is based essentially on the perceived need for the separation of powers between the United States Government and its judiciary, so that the judiciary does not embarass the executive by deciding questions which impact on the conduct of relations with foreign States. The political question doctrine is also based on the separation of powers, and in this context it represents a judicial unwillingness to be involved in the adjudication of a dispute where there are no 'judicially discoverable and manageable standards for resolving it'.[403]

The Second Circuit held that the act of State doctrine would be inapplicable to the extent that the acts of Marcos were private acts, as distinct from acts as head of State; in any event the Marcos government was no longer in power, and the danger of interference with the Executive's conduct of foreign policy was much less than in the typical case where the act of State was that of the current foreign government. The act of State doctrine reflected respect for foreign states, so that when a State

---

[399] 818 F. 2d 1473 (9th Cir. 1987).
[400] 862 F. 2d 1355 (9th Cir. 1988), cert. den. 490 US 1035.
[401] See *Banco Nacional de Cuba* v. *Sabbatino*, 376 US 398, 414 (1964).
[402] The cases are cited in *Restatement Third, Foreign Relations Law*, s. 443.
[403] *Baker* v. *Carr*, 369 US 186, 217 (1962). See *Restatement Third, Foreign Relations Law*, s. 1, Rep. Note 4.

came into the courts of the United States and asked that the courts scrutinize its actions, the justification for application of the doctrine might well be significantly weaker:

As a practical tool for keeping the judicial branch out of the conduct of foreign affairs, the classification of 'act of state' is not a promise to the ruler of any foreign country that his conduct, if challenged by his own country after his fall, may not become the subject of scrutiny in our courts. No estoppel exists insulating a deposed dictator from accounting. No guarantee has been granted that immunity may be acquired by an ex-chief magistrate invoking the magic words 'act of state' to cover his or her past performance. The classification might, it may be supposed, be used to prevent judicial challenge in our courts to many deeds of a dictator in power, at least when it is apparent that sustaining such challenge would bring our country into a hostile confrontation with the dictator. Once deposed, the dictator will find it difficult to deploy the defense successfuly. *A fortiori*, when a ruler's former domain has turned against him and seeks the recovery of what it claims he has stolen, the classification has little or no applicability.[404]

As for the 'political question' doctrine:

Bribetaking, theft, embezzlement, extortion, fraud, and conspiracy to do these things are all acts susceptible of concrete proofs that need not involve political questions. The court, it is true, may have to determine questions of Philippine law in determining whether a given act was legal or illegal. But questions of foreign law are not beyond the capacity of our courts . . . The court will be examining the acts of the president of a country whose immediate political heritage is from our own. Although sometimes criticized as a ruler and at times invested with extraordinary powers, Ferdinand Marcos does not appear to have had the authority of an absolute autocrat. He was not the state, but the head of the state, bound by the laws that applied to him. Our courts have had no difficulty in distinguishing the legal acts of a deposed ruler from his acts for personal profit that lack a basis in law.[405]

A worldwide injunction was imposed. The Court of Appeals agreed with the District Court that the Republic had at least a fair chance of prevailing on the merits, including on the merits of its constructive trust claim. It had presented evidence that in February 1986 the Marcoses had transported from the Philippines to Hawaii $8.2 million worth of cash, negotiable instruments, jewellery and other property, allegedly derived from their wrongdoing in the Philippines. The Republic also presented evidence that, since at least 1968, the Marcoses had bank accounts in the United States which were used to transfer money to accounts in the name of aliases under which Ferdinand Marcos and Imelda Marcos acted, which was then transferred to a Liechtenstein trust, with which the Marcoses communicated by code. The injunction was directed against individuals, not against

---

[404] 862 F. 2d at 1360–1361.   [405] At 1361.

property, and enjoined the Marcoses and their associates from transferring certain assets wherever they were located. As has been seen in Section VIII, because the injunction operated *in personam*, not *in rem*, there was no reason to be concerned about its territorial reach.

3. THE ROLE OF PUBLIC POLICY

It is well established that a foreign State cannot sue abroad to recover assets belonging to a former monarch whose property has been confiscated by his Republican successors.[406] But what if the President of the Republic has looted the Treasury and fled abroad? Is he in the same position as the official from the Prussian post office who has embezzled money which should have been delivered? It is, of course, superficially tempting to conclude that there is no relevant difference between the Prussian postmaster, on the one hand, and Baby Doc Duvalier and Ferdinand Marcos, on the other. Why should former officials, of low rank or high rank, be above the ordinary law of theft and embezzlement?

But there are significant differences. The action may have a purely political purpose; the law which applies will be that of the plaintiff State; and the officials who direct the action may themselves be no better than the defendant. In May 1992, at the time of the Presidential election in the Philippines, an article in *The Times* said:

Recent history has exposed the iniquitous lifestyles of this ruling class: Ferdinand Marcos and his cronies . . . are said to have drained the country of US$5 billion. The masses should have learnt not to invest their hopes in these types. When Corazon Aquino led the people's power revolution in 1986 she embodied the hopes of millions of Filipinos for renewal and an equitable redistribution of wealth. Their hopes have been dashed, for her administration appears to be as riddled with chicanery as the last.[407]

When the Court of Appeal confirmed the worldwide *Mareva* injunction against Baby Doc Duvalier, Staughton LJ noted that Baby Doc Duvalier and his co-defendants:

observe that it has been a tradition in Haiti for over 180 years for a new government to take legal proceedings against those who were in charge under the previous regime. One is reminded of the Roman historian who noticed that it was the practice of the later emperors to bring to justice the murderers of the previous emperor but one.[408]

---

[406] See *Banco de Vizcaya* v. *Don Alfonso* [1935] 1 KB 140; *Republic of Iraq* v. *First National City Bank*, 353 F. 2d 47 (2d Cir. 1965), cert. den. 382 US 1027 (1966).
[407] *The Times*, 11 May, 1992. [408] [1990] 1 QB at 206.

Indeed, in the course of that litigation there were governmental changes in Haiti which brought to power persons who were more sympathetic to the Duvalier family.

When the French Cour de Cassation held that the claim by the Republic of Haiti could not be pursued in France, in essence it held that the Republic was not pursuing proprietary rights, but was attempting to exercise public powers. One is reminded of the terms in which the High Court of Australia dismissed the British Government's attempt to prevent publication of *Spycatcher*.[409] Peter Wright was a member of the British Security Services between September 1955 and January 1976. After his retirement he went to live in Australia, and while living there he wrote a book called *Spycatcher* about the activities of MI5 on which he had been engaged. It dealt with methods of electronic surveillance and of interception, and operations concerning surveillance and interception involving breaches of civil and international law, investigations into Soviet penetration of the Service before 1971, including allegations of a plot by members of MI5 to destabilize the 1974–1976 government of Harold Wilson, the planned assassination of President Nasser of Egypt by MI6, the bugging of embassies of friendly States by MI5, in particular the French embassy during the period of Britain's application to join the Common Market, and an allegation that Sir Roger Hollis, formerly Director-General of MI5, had been a Soviet spy. This led to litigation by the British Government in Australia against Peter Wright, in England against newspapers which had published extracts from the book, in Australia against the publishers, and in Hong Kong and New Zealand against newspapers. The ultimate result of the cases was that the British Government failed to obtain an injunction in Australia against Peter Wright, and that it was partially successful (until the book became widely available through imports from countries where it had been lawfully published) in preventing the press from printing details of it in England and elsewhere. The English decisions involved questions primarily of domestic law, namely, whether in view of Peter Wright's duty of confidentiality to the Crown, it was right to grant injunctions against various newspapers. In November 1991 the European Court of Human Rights decided unanimously that there had been no violation of the newspapers' right of freedom of expression caused by the injunction in the period before the confidentiality of the book's contents had been destroyed by its publication in the United States; but (by a majority of 14 to 10) that there had been a violation in the period thereafter. Other applications to

---

[409] See 'The Spycatcher Cases', ed. Fysh, 1989, in [1989] 2 *Fleet Street Reports*, which is a collection of decisions in England (five sets of proceedings), Australia, Hong Kong and New Zealand. For subsequent cases see *Att.-Gen.* v. *Times Newspapers Ltd.* [1991] 2 WLR 994 (HL); *Sunday Times* v. *United Kingdom, Observer and Guardian* v. *United Kingdom*, ECHR, 26 November 1991.

the European Commission on Human Rights arising out of the affair are still pending.[410]

In the first House of Lords decision[411] it was held, by a 3 to 2 majority, that an interlocutory injunction against the *Guardian* and the *Observer* newspapers should stand, even though *Spycatcher* had by then become available in the United Kingdom as a result of imports from the United States where it was on public sale. The majority thought that the Attorney-General had an arguable case for the protection of an important public interest by permanent injunction, and that it would be unjust to discharge the injunction to deprive him irrevocably of the opportunity of having the case properly adjudicated at full trial on appropriate evidence. Damages were a worthless remedy, and there was a substantial public interest in maintaining the efficiency of the Security Service. But following a full trial on the case in the Chancery Division before Scott J., the House of Lords affirmed the decisions of the lower courts and refused an injunction because the Crown had not shown that the disclosure was likely to damage, or had damaged, the public interest. The worldwide publication of *Spycatcher* had destroyed any secrecy as to its contents, and copies were readily available to anyone who wished to obtain them.[412]

In the High Court of Australia the United Kingdom Attorney-General's action against the publishers and Peter Wright failed because the Attorney-General's case was founded on the relationship between Peter Wright and the British Government in his capacity as a member of the British Security Service engaged in counter-espionage activities. The result was unanimous but there were significant differences in the reasoning. The majority held that there was a rule, founded on international law, whereby a claim to enforce the governmental interests of a foreign state was unenforceable. Mason CJ, speaking for the majority, said:

. . . the action is neither fully nor accurately described as an action to enforce private rights or private interests of a foreign State. It is in truth an action in which the United Kingdom Government seeks to protect the efficiency of its Security Service as 'part of the defence forces of the country'. The claim for relief . . . arises out of, and is secured by, an exercise of a prerogative of the Crown, that exercise being the maintenance of the national security. Therefore, the right or interest asserted in the proceedings is to be classified as a governmental interest. As such, the action falls within the rule of international law which renders the claim unenforceable.[413]

---

[410] Especially arising out of the finding that the *Sunday Times* was guilty of contempt in publishing extracts even though it was not named in any injunction, and had not assisted any other party to breach it: *Att.-Gen.* v. *Times Newspapers Ltd.* [1991] 2 WLR 994 (HL).

[411] *Att.-Gen.* v. *Guardian Newspapers Ltd.* [1987] 1 WLR 1248 (HL).

[412] *Att.-Gen.* v. *Guardian Newspapers Ltd.* (*No. 2*) [1990] 1 AC 109.

[413] *Att.-Gen.* (*UK*) v. *Heinemann Publishers Australia Pty.* (1988) 78 ALR 449, 460. For criticism see Mann, (1988) 104 *LQR* 497; Collier, [1989] *CLJ* 33. For New Zealand see *Att. Gen.* (*UK*) v. *Wellington Newspapers Ltd.* [1988] 1 NZLR 129.

That formulation has some similarity with the rule accepted by the French Cour de Cassation in the *Duvalier* case, but in language reminiscent of the American 'political question' doctrine Mason CJ went on:

> It is perhaps tempting to suggest that, because of the close relationship between the United Kingdom and Australia, an exception should be made to enable the United Kingdom to enforce in our courts an obligation of the kind now in question. But what if a less friendly or a hostile State were to resort to our courts for a similar purpose? Our courts are not competent to assess the degree of friendliness or unfriendliness of a foreign State. There are no manageable standards by which courts can resolve such an issue and its determination would inevitably present a risk of embarrassment in Australia's relations with other countries . . . In any event the principle of law renders unenforceable actions of a particular kind. Those actions are actions to enforce the governmental interest of a foreign State. There is nothing in the statement of the principle, nor in the underlying considerations on which it rests, that could justify the making of an exception or qualification for actions by a friendly State. The friendliness or hostility of the foreign State seeking to enforce its claims in the court of the forum has no relevant connection with the principle.

What the *Duvalier* case in France and the *Spycatcher* case in Australia have in common is that in each case what appeared to be involved was a private law claim: in *Duvalier* the Republic of Haiti contended that it was asserting a proprietary right; in *Spycatcher* the British Government claimed it was enforcing a private law duty of confidence.

In each case the courts refused to allow a foreign State to assert its right as a Government: in effect they abstained from deciding a political controversy. Private international law is essentially concerned with the vindication and recognition of *private* rights. The issue for the courts in cases of this kind is to determine whether, as in the case of the Prussian postmaster, the claim is essentially one based on private law, or, as in the case of *Spycatcher*, is really designed to assert the security interests and enforce the secrecy laws of the foreign State. The *Duvalier/Marcos* type of case is much more difficult. In every country theft and embezzlement is not only a crime, but gives the true owner a right to recover the stolen assets. There is no reason in principle why the State should not recover property which has been stolen and taken abroad, even if the thief is a former head of Government or head of State. But the court in which the action is brought must be astute to ensure that its process is not being abused for purely political ends. In the *Spycatcher* case Brennan J., while agreeing with the result, decided it on the ground that it was contrary to public policy to enforce an obligation of confidence owed by a foreign Government. One answer to the question whether claims of the *Duvalier/ Marcos* type should be allowed is that they should be enforced unless application of the foreign law, or vindication of the proprietary interest, would be contrary to public policy in the circumstances of each case. But the only way in which public policy could be used on a case by case basis would be by questioning the *bona fides* of the plaintiff Government. Consequently the choice appears to be stark: to allow such claims in accordance with the spirit of the *Marcos* case; or to disallow them under the theory espoused by the Cour de Cassation. To allow such claims might allow foreign courts to be turned into political instruments; to disallow them would be to allow stolen property on an enormous scale to stay in the hands of thieves. In principle, it is suggested that (subject to the safety valve of public policy) the result in the *Marcos* case is the right one. This does not mean that every purported proprietary right will be protected. The Australian court would not protect the right of confidence in the *Spycatcher* case, and no doubt no English or American court would have protected the alleged right of the Soviet Union to prevent the publication abroad of books by its greatest author.[414]

4. SOVEREIGN IMMUNITY AND PRE-JUDGMENT ATTACHMENT

It has already been seen[415] that pre-judgment attachment is capable of fulfilling two, inter-related, functions. The first function is to secure the jurisdiction of the court, and the second is to give a measure of security to a creditor who is concerned that the debtor will make himself judgment-proof. It has also been seen that attachment to obtain jurisdiction, *ad fundandam jurisdictionem*, is (except for the power of arrest in maritime cases) increasingly out of favour: not only is it branded as an exorbitant basis of jurisdiction in the Brussels and Lugano Conventions, but also the highest courts of the United States and Germany have held it to be out of keeping with modern ideas of fairness in the exercise of civil jurisdiction.[416]

A full survey of the law and practice relating to sovereign immunity is not only outside the scope of this work, but is also the subject of considerable recent literature.[417] This section will consider some of the specific problems which have arisen in relation to provisional and protective measures. The obvious starting point is that today there can be no doubt that States are not entitled to immunity from suit in the courts of

---

[414] Cf. *Bodley Head Ltd.* v. *Flegon* [1972] 1 WLR 680.

[415] Section II, *supra*.

[416] *Shaffer* v. *Heitner*, 433 US 186 (1977); BGH, 2 July, 1991, NJW 1991, 3092.

[417] See, e.g., Schreuer, *State Immunity: Some Recent Developments* (1988); Trooboff, 'Foreign State Immunity: Emerging Consensus on Principles', (1986) *Collected Courses*, Vol. 200, p. 235; Crawford, 'Execution of Judgments and Foreign State Immunity', (1981) 75 AJIL 820. (1979) 10 *Netherlands Yb. Int. L.* contains a number of articles on execution against State property: see especially Higgins, p. 35; Seidl-Hohenveldern, p. 55; J. F. Lalive, p. 153.

foreign countries in relation to their commercial activities, and that they are not entitled under public international law to immunity from execution in relation to property which is used for commercial purposes, or (to put it slightly differently) which is not dedicated to use for governmental purposes.

But it does not follow that jurisdiction may be exercised over a State merely because it has commercial property in the forum State. It is true that Admiralty jurisdiction *in rem* is now universally regarded as being available against State-owned ships in commercial use. This jurisdiction was confirmed by the 1926 Brussels Convention for the Unification of Rules concerning the Immunity of State-owned Ships, and re-affirmed by the 1952 Brussels Convention relating to the Arrest of Sea-going Ships. This early exception to the rule of absolute immunity gained only late acceptance in England[418] and the United States.[419]

But outside the field of Admiralty actions *in rem*, there is a widely held view that the mere presence of the property of the State is insufficient to found jurisdiction, even if it is commercial property. In his 7th Report to the International Law Commission,[420] Mr Sucharitkul, the Special Rapporteur, concluded that a State was immune from seizure of its property *ad fundandam jurisdictionem*, especially if the property was devoted to public services. The United States Foreign State Immunities Act 1976 does not permit attachment whose purpose is 'to obtain jurisdiction'.[421] But this is by no means the unanimous view.

In Germany, it had been held that neither the requirement of an explicit waiver (nor, probably, the prohibition on attachment to found jurisdiction) was required by international law. In 1983 in the *National Iranian Oil Co.* case[422] the Federal Constitutional Court held that the United States legislation was not evidence of general public international law: it had been passed for reasons of political expediency. In that case British and American plaintiffs used NIOC in Frankfurt, and NIOC claimed its oil revenues were held in trust for the Government of Iran. The Constitutional Court held that the attachment did not violate international law, since there was no general rule of international law that an account of a foreign government agency with separate personality should be treated as property of the foreign State. In any event, even if the revenues were the property of the foreign State, they would only be immune if the property was intended to be used for internationally protected governmental purposes.

---

[418] The 1926 Convention was not ratified by the United Kingdom until 1979; but in 1975 the Privy Council accepted the restrictive theory of immunity in Admiralty actions: *The Philippine Admiral* [1977] AC 373. See also *The I Congreso del Partido* [1983] 1 AC 244.

[419] Foreign State Immunities Act 1976, s. 1605 (*b*).

[420] *ILC Yb.*, 1985, Vol. II, Pt. 1, p. 29.

[421] S. 1610 (*d*) (i) (2).

[422] 65 ILR 215.

Both in that case and in the *Central Bank of Nigeria* case[423] jurisdiction was based on Article 23 of the Code of Civil Procedure, and in neither case was there any substantial connection with Germany. It must be doubtful whether attachments of this kind would now be possible after the 1991 ruling of the Federal Supreme Court on Article 23 (in general, and not with reference to the property of a foreign State) that there must be, in addition to the presence of property in Germany, a sufficient link with Germany.[424]

In other countries jurisdiction has been assumed against States on the basis of presence of property, but in cases where there was in fact (although not required by law) a real connection of the claim with the forum. Thus in South Africa an attachment to found jurisdiction was made against property of the Republic of Mozambique, in a case where it was alleged that the Republic had succeeded to obligations under a contract for survey and planning work in Mozambique. Some of the services under the contract were to be provided in South Africa, and all payments were to be made there.[425] In the remarkable case of *Forth Tugs Ltd.* v. *Wilmington Trust Co.*[426] the Scots court held that it had jurisdiction in a claim against the United States Government on the basis of the presence in Scotland of property belonging to it. The claim arose out of salvage services rendered in the Firth of Forth to an oil tanker which belonged to the United States. The remarkable feature of the case was that the relevant property owned by the United States Government in Scotland was its Consulate-General in Edinburgh. In Scots law the mere *presence* of real property is a basis of jurisdiction, and attachment is not required. This decision is therefore consistent with international law only because the asssumption of jurisdiction involved the *presence* of the property in Scotland, and not its attachment. For it is impossible to view the attachment of consular property as anything other than the clearest possible violation of international law.

In Switzerland the attachment of property is a basis of jurisdiction in relation to defendants who are not domiciled in Switzerland or in a Lugano Convention country, but the courts have required, where a foreign State is the defendant, a connection between Switzerland and the underlying claim. The leading modern judgments of the Swiss Federal Tribunal were rendered in 1956 and 1960 in *Kingdom of Greece* v. *Julius Baer & Co.*[427] and *United Arab Republic* v. *X.*[428] In these cases the Federal Tribunal ruled that even where the claim arises out of a commercial activity, the Swiss court cannot exercise jurisdiction to attach assets, even of a commercial nature, unless the legal relationship to which the foreign State

---

[423] 65 ILR 131 (Frankfurt, 1976).   [424] *Supra*, n. 416.

[425] *Inter-Science Research & Development Services (Pty.) Ltd.* v. *Republica de Moçambique* 1980 (2) SA 111.   [426] 1987 SLT 153.

[427] 23 ILR 195.   [428] 65 ILR 385.

is a party is connected with Switzerland, in the sense that it has its origin in Switzerland, or falls to be performed in Switzerland, or the foreign State has taken some relevant steps in Switzerland. So in the case of *Kingdom of Greece* v. *Julius Baer & Co.* the attachments were set aside: Julius Baer, the well-known Swiss bank, was a plaintiff, but it was suing on bonds issued by the Greek State to a Swedish company, which Julius Baer had subsequently acquired. It was not necessary to decide whether public loans were acts *jure gestionis*. The attachments were vacated because the loan was raised in Sweden from a Swedish company; the sum loaned was paid to Greece by an English bank; Greece had not performed any act which would have made Switzerland a place of performance; and it did not undertake to repay the bonds in Switzerland, since repayment was to be made in London, New York or Athens. But in *United Arab Republic* v. *X*, and also in *Banque Centrale de Turquie* v. *Weston*,[429] there was a sufficient connection: in the former case because, in a claim arising out of a lease of premises in Vienna, the rent was payable in Switzerland and the agreement provided for the jurisdiction of the Zurich courts. In the latter case, Lloyds Bank International had made a time deposit with a Turkish bank. It was held that a Swiss assignee of the deposit could attach funds belonging to the Turkish Central Bank: the deposit was repayable in Swiss francs at a Swiss bank. But the mere fact that the assignee was Swiss would not have provided the necessary connection.[430]

In view of the international developments relating to the attachment of property as a basis for jurisdiction, particularly as reflected in the practice in the United States and in Germany, and in the Brussels and Lugano Conventions, it is an obvious conclusion that attachment against State property should only be allowed as a basis for the assumption of jurisdiction if there is a connection between the forum and the claim against the foreign State.

But there is no reason in principle why there should be a connection between the attached *property* and the *claim*. Nevertheless this view has commended itself to the French Cour de Cassation and the International Law Commission. In *Eurodif Corp.* v. *Islamic Republic of Iran*,[431] the Iranian Organisation for Economic and Technical Investment and Assistance (OIAETI) and the French Atomic Energy Commision (CEA) agreed to establish a corporation under French law, SOFIDIF, 40 per cent of whose capital was held by the former and 60 per cent by the latter, and through a

---

[429] 65 ILR 417.

[430] See *Italian Republic* v. *Beta Holding SA* (1966) 65 ILR 394. See also *Arab Republic of Egypt* v. *Cinetelevision International* (1979) 65 ILR 425.

[431] Cass. civ. I, 14.3.1984, 1984 *Rev. crit.* 644, note Bischoff; 1984 *Clunet* 598, note Oppetit; 77 ILR 513. See also Synvet, 'Quelques réflexions sur l'immunité d'exécution de l'État étranger', 1985 *Clunet* 865.

transfer of shares SOFIDIF became a member of Eurodif, with Iranian holdings representing 10 per cent of the latter's capital. Eurodif was to provide uranium to SOFIDIF. The Iranian Government undertook a 10 per cent participation on a loan to CEA. The agreements contained an ICC arbitration clause. Subsequently, as a consequence of the Iranian Revolution, the new leaders discontinued the nuclear development programme initiated by the former régime, and failed to pay its share of the operating costs of Eurodif. The CEA, Eurodif and SOFIDIF invoked the arbitration clause to enforce payment. At the same time Eurodif and SOFIDIF petitioned the president of the Commercial Tribunal in Paris to authorize attachments for an amount provisionally estimated at 9 billion francs, corresponding to the damage sustained by Eurodif by virtue of the Iranian termination of its right to take delivery and of its obligation to make shareholder advances. The Court of Appeal of Paris set aside the attachment, on the basis that funds attached were purely public funds. The Cour de Cassation held that in general foreign States were entitled to immunity from execution. But there were exceptional cases where it did not apply, and one of them was where the assets attached had been allocated for an economic or commercial activity of a private law nature which had given rise to the claim at issue. In this case, the debt attached was owed to the Iranian State and had its origin in the very funds which had been allocated for the nuclear programme. The Court of Appeal of Paris should have considered whether the activity was of a commercial nature. It was subsequently held that the claimant had shown that the assets were commercial assets.[432]

In 1991 the International Law Commission presented to the General Assembly draft articles on the jurisdictional immunities of States and their property. Article 18 (1) of that text provides:

No measures of constraint, such as attachment, arrest and execution, against property of a State may be taken in connection with a proceeding before a court of another State unless and except to the extent that:

   (*a*) the State has expressly consented to the taking of such measures as indicated:

      (i) by international agreement;

---

[432] See Delaume, 'Recent French Cases on Sovereign Immunity and Economic Development Activities', (1987) 2 ICSID Review–FILJ 152. See also *Banque camerounaise de développement* v. *Rolber*, Cass. civ. I, 18.11.1986, 1987 Rev. crit. 773, note Muir Watt, 77 ILR 532; *République islamique d'Iran* v. *Framatome*, Cass. civ. I, 20.3.1989, 1990 *Clunet* 1004, note Ouakrat; 1990 *Rev. crit.* 347. For Italy see *Socialist People's Libyan Arab Jamahiriya* v. *Rossbeton*, Corte di Cassazione, 25.5.1989; noted Radicati di Brozolo, (1990) 84 AJIL 573, where a pre-judgment attachment against aircraft owned by the Libyan State airline was upheld. But the attachment is only allowed if there is Ministerial authorization; and the practice is not to grant it. Therefore the judgment is of little practical effect. See also Condorelli and Sbolci, 'Measures of Execution against the Property of Foreign States: The Law and Practice in Italy', (1979) 10 *Netherlands Yb. Int. L.* 197.

(ii) by an arbitration agreement or in a written contract; or

(iii) by a declaration before the court or by a written communication after a dispute between the parties has arisen;

(*b*) the State has allocated or earmarked property for the satisfaction of the claim which is the object of that proceeding; or

(*c*) the property is specifically in use or intended for use by the State for other than government non-commercial purposes and is in the territory of the State of the forum and has a connection with the claim which is the object of the proceeding or with the agency or instrumentality against which the proceeding was directed.

Accordingly, except in the case of waiver and the (inevitably rare[433]) case of the earmarking of funds for satisfaction of judgment, attachment is allowed only if the property 'has a connection with the claim which is the object of the proceeding or with the agency or instrumentality against which the proceeding was directed'. Where, therefore, the claim is against an agency or instrumentality of the State it is not necessary that there be a connection between the property and the claim. It is sufficient that the property be owned by the agency or instrumentality against which the proceeding was directed. But where the property is owned by the State, the draft continues to insist that there be a connection between the property and the claim. There is simply no sense in this requirement. If the plaintiff has a good arguable claim in relation to a commercial contract there is no reason why the plaintiff should not be able to take effective action to obtain a form of security for judgment (or to execute judgment) against commercial property whatever its origin and whether or not it is linked to the claim.

5. WAIVER OF IMMUNITY

International practice is unanimous that immunity from attachment or execution may be the subject of waiver, and it has been seen in the preceding section that the International Law Commission draft Articles conform to that practice. In the United States the Foreign Sovereign Immunities Act of 1976 prohibits attachment as the basis of jurisdiction, and only permits pre-jugdgment attachment if the foreign State has 'explicitly waived its immunity from attachment prior to judgment'.[434] In addition the Act of 1976 also provides that the property of a foreign central bank is immune from attachment, unless the bank has explicitly waived its immunity from attachment in aid of execution. It is probable that this

---

[433] See *Benvenuti et Bonfant SARL* v. *Congo*, Paris, 26.6.1981, 65 ILR 88.

[434] ss. 1610 (*d*) (i).

means that there is complete immunity from pre-judgment attachment of the property of a central bank, irrespective of its consent.[435]

In *Libra Bank Ltd. v. Banco Nacional de Costa Rica*[436] the Court of Appeals for the Second Circuit decided that the expression that

the borrower hereby irrevocably and unconditionally waives any right or immunity from legal proceedings including suit, judgment and execution on grounds of sovereignty which it or its property may now and hereafter enjoy

was an explicit waiver of pre-judgment attachment, since pre-judgment attachment was a form of 'legal proceedings'. In that case the opinion was written by Judge Timbers, who also wrote the opinion in the leading case, among several in which it was held that a waiver in a treaty provision in relation to 'suit or execution of judgment or other liability' was not an explicit waiver of immunity from prejudgment attachment under the 1976 Act. In *S. & S. Machinery Co. v. Masinexportimport*[437] the same court held that a foreign state did not have to use the precise words 'pre-judgment attachment' but

a waiver from pre-judgment attachment must be explicit in the common sense meaning of that term: the asserted waiver must demonstrate unambiguously the foreign state's intention to waive its immunity from prejudgment attachment in this country. We do not take lightly the congressional demand for explicitness. It would be improper for a court to subvert this directive by substituting a judicially reconstituted gloss on a facially unclear document for an unequivocal waiver by the foreign state.

Accordingly a provision of the United States–Romanian Agreement on Trade Relations was not regarded as an explicit waiver of pre-judgment attachment, since the provision in question provided only that neither Government would 'claim or enjoy immunities from suit or execution of judgment or other liability' for commercial or financial transactions. The *Libra Bank* decision was distinguished on the basis that the language of the agreement in that case was virtually 'all inclusive'.

These decisions led to moves by the American Bar Association and others for the amendment of the 1976 Act to permit pre-judgment

---

[435] See *Banque Compafina v. Banco de Guatemala*, 583 F. Supp. 320 (SDNY 1984).

[436] 676 F. 2d 47 (2d Cir. 1982).

[437] 706 F. 2d 411, 416 (2d Cir. 1983), cert. den. 104 S. Ct. 161 (1983), applied in *O'Connell Machinery Co. v. MV Americana*, 734 F. 2d 115 (2d Cir. 1984). See also on the US–Iran Treaty *New England etc. v. Iran Power*, 502 F. Supp. 120 (SDNY 1980) (not a waiver; but Presidential blocking order had the effect of suspending immunity); *Reading & Bates Corp. v. NIOC*, 478 F. Supp. 724 (SDNY 1979) (no waiver); *E-Systems Inc. v. Islamic Republic of Iran*, 491 F. Supp. 1294 (ND Tex. 1980) (not a waiver; Presidential order and Treasury regulations did not have the effect of suspending immunity); *Behring International v. Imperial Iranian Air Force*, 475 F. Supp. 383 (DNJ 1979) (no waiver, but previous Treaty had the effect of removing immunity).

attachment of the property of a foreign State's agencies or instrumentalities which were engaged in commercial activities, provided that the property would be subject to execution after judgment. But these efforts were unsuccessful, because the State Department took the view that pre-judgment attachment could be particularly disruptive when applied to agencies or instrumentalities which were engaged in both governmental and commercial activities; in the State Department's view there was no demonstrated need for permitting pre-judgment attachments for mixed function agencies or instrumentalities.[438]

6. INJUNCTIONS AND IMMUNITY

In England, it has already been seen, there is no remedy of attachment in claims *in personam*. The equivalent remedy is a *Mareva* injunction. In the United States a preliminary injunction to keep a letter of credit open was regarded as equivalent to a pre-judgment attachment: *Atwood Turnkey Drilling Inc.* v. *Petroleo Brasileiro SA*.[439] In that case it was held that the national oil company of Brazil waived immunity from pre-judgment attachment through a waiver provision in a letter of credit ('from any execution or attachment in aid of execution prior to judgment or otherwise'). The court said:

. . . the parties do not dispute that the purpose of the injunction is to secure the payment of a judgment which may be rendered in the litigation. Accordingly, Petrobras's property in the United States used for commercial purposes is subject to pre-judgment attachment, whether by means of an injunction or more traditional methods of attachment.[440]

In the United Kingdom, as in the United States, the availability of remedies of this nature is now regulated by statute. In *Trendtex Trading Corp.* v. *Central Bank of Nigeria*,[441] which was decided before the State Immunity Act 1978 was enacted, it was held by the Court of Appeal (following early indications to the same effect by the Privy Council in *The Philippine Admiral*[442]) that the restrictive theory of sovereign immunity should be adopted in England. The decision was mainly concerned with immunity from suit, but the Court of Appeal also granted a *Mareva* injunction. It was argued by the Central Bank that the money standing to its credit in the books of the Midland Bank in London was money

---

[438] (1985) 79 AJIL 770

[439] 875 F. 2d 1174 (5th Cir. 1989). Cf. *American International Group Inc.* v. *Islamic Republic of Iran*, 493 F. Supp. 522 (DDC 1980) (post-judgment preliminary injunction restraining transfer of property from the United States).   [440] At 1177.

[441] [1977] QB 529 (CA).   [442] [1977] AC 373.

belonging to the Federation of Nigeria, and that it was not subject to seizure or to an injunction. Lord Denning MR said that whether a *Mareva* injunction could be granted depended on precisely the same grounds as immunity from suit. If the Central Bank of Nigeria was entitled to immunity from being sued, so also could the funds be immune from being seized, but otherwise not.[443]

By section 13 (2) of the State Immunity Act 1978[444] relief is not to be given against a State by way of injunction or order for specific performance, and the property of a State is not to be subject to any process for the enforcement of a judgment or arbitral award, but such relief or process may be given

with the written consent of the State concerned, and any such consent (which may be contained in a prior agreement) may be expressed so as to apply to a limited extent or generally; but a provision merely submitting to the jurisdiction of the courts is not to be regarded as a consent . . .

But these provisions do not prevent the issue of any process in respect of property 'which is for the time being in use or intended for use for commercial purposes'.

The 1978 Act does not, in general, confer immunity on a 'separate entity' belonging to a State, i.e. an entity which is distinct from the executive organs of the government of the State, and is capable of suing or being sued. A separate entity only has immunity if the proceedings relate to anything done by it in the exercise of sovereign authority, and the circumstances are such that a State would have been immune.[445] But although for these purposes a central bank may be a separate entity, it is also provided that in such a case it is entitled to immunity from injunctive relief as if it were a State.[446] Further the property of a central bank is not to be regarded as in use or intended for use for commercial purposes.

As in the case of the United States legislation of 1976, there were political and commercial implications in the State Immunity Act 1978. On the one hand, the United Kingdom Government was concerned that, without specific statutory authority for the restrictive view of sovereign immunity, loans to foreign Governments would increasingly be made from New York, rather than London, by banks who were apprehensive that the courts might eventually not uphold (or fully uphold) the decision in *Trendtex*. On the other hand, the Government was anxious to ensure that foreign central banks would continue to hold substantial deposits in

---

[443] [1977] QB at 561. See also *Hispano Americana Mercantil SA* v. *Central Bank of Nigeria* [1979] 2 Lloyd's Rep. 277 (CA).

[444] Cf. Foreign States Immunities Act 1985 (Australia), ss. 29–31, 34 and Australian Law Reform Commission, Report No. 24, *Foreign State Immunity* (1984), pp. 83–84.

[445] S. 14 (1)–(2).   [446] S. 14 (4).

London without fear of interference. The 1978 Act therefore provided that commercial property should be subject to process of execution, but not (unless there had been a written waiver) central bank deposits.

It has already been seen that the 1978 Act specifically provided that injunctions could not be granted against a State (or a central bank) without its written consent. In the debate on the State Immunity Bill, the United Kingdom Government expressed the view that injunctions were not appropriate remedies against States. The ultimate sanction for such orders lay in contempt, and the processes of punishing contempt could not be used against a foreign State. Despite the urgings of Lord Wilberforce and Lord Denning, the Government refused to amend the Bill to allow *Mareva* injunctions.

In *A Company Limited* v. *Republic of X*[447] the issue (as in some of the United States cases) concerned the interpretation of a contractual waiver of immunity. The plaintiffs sued a foreign Government for failure to pay for rice delivered, and obtained leave to issue proceedings against them outside the jurisdiction. They also obtained *ex parte* a *Mareva* injunction. The agreement between the parties provided that the Government 'hereby waives whatever defence it may have of sovereign immunity for itself or its property (present or subsequently acquired)'. The State suggested that this was not a written consent to the *Mareva* injunction, because it referred only to a waiver of defences, and even if it applied to enforcement, it did not cover relief by way of injunction or orders for specific performance. Saville J. held that, read in the context of what was undoubtedly a commercial agreement, the intent and purpose of the provision was quite clear, namely, to put the State on the same footing as a private individual so that neither in respect of the State nor its property would any question of sovereign immunity arise in connection with the State's obligations to the plaintiffs under the agreement. It was argued that the court should adopt a restrictive interpretation of such clauses, since one of the parties was a sovereign State. The judge disagreed:

The present case is concerned with an ordinary commercial transaction and I can see no good reason why the clause in question should not be construed in like manner to the rest of the contract in accordance with the ordinary principles of construction for commercial contracts, by looking at the bargain as a whole in its context and giving the words used, if capable of bearing them, a construction which accords with commercial common sense . . . If [the clause] does amount to the consent of the State to the enforcement of judgments and awards against its property, then why, in the absence of express provision, should the words used not apply to prejudgment attachment in the form of *Mareva* injunctive relief . . . ?[448]

---

[447] [1990] 2 Lloyd's Rep. 520.

[448] At 523. It was also held that the waiver did not extend to diplomatic property because in such a case the consent had to be given to the court at the time when the court was asked to

In his 7th Report to the International Law Commission, Mr Sucharitkul concluded:[449]

Precautionary or pre-judgment attachment is not permissible and should be discouraged. There is no necessity to over-protect creditors *vis à vis* a State debtor. Compulsion of whatever form cannot afford an ideal solution to any difference with a foreign State. The existence of a final judgment is enough ground in support of diplomatic negotiations.

It is likely, however, that international law does not require immunity from precautionary or pre-judgment attachment, and to allow it, in cases where the State's liability is not seriously contested, cannot reasonably be said to over-protect creditors. What is clear, however, is that some countries (especially the United States and the United Kingdom) have regarded it as politically and financially expedient to allow foreign States to keep assets within their jurisdiction free of the fear of attachment, except where they have waived immunity. It is suggested that international law does not require them to protect sovereign assets (irrespective of whether the assets have a connection with the claim) provided that the claim has a genuine link with the forum.

give judgment. It was not sufficient for it to be given in a prior agreement. This aspect of the decision is very doubtful.

[449] *ILC Yb.*, 1985, Vol. II, Pt. 1, p. 38.

12

Human Rights

This section will pick up two themes for consideration. The first is the need for judicial procedures for the grant of provisional and protective measures to be in conformity with fundamental rights. The second is the grant of interim measures in the system of the European Convention on Human Rights. What these have in common is the role of the European Court of Human Rights in the consideration of interim measures: in the first category, it has had to consider whether measures ordered by the English courts were in conformity with the Convention; and in the second it has had to consider whether interim measures indicated by the Commission were binding on the State concerned.

I. THE EUROPEAN CONVENTION AND ORDERS OF NATIONAL COURTS

The newspapers which had been prevented by interlocutory injunctions from printing extracts from *Spycatcher* complained to the European Commission on Human Rights that the injunctions were in breach of (*inter alia*) Article 10 of the European Convention, in that they constituted an unjustified interference with their freedom of expression. In two decisions of the European Court on Human Rights in 1991[450] it was held that the interference was justified as being 'necessary in a democratic society' (Article 10 (2)) in the period before the book became widely available, but not thereafter. The cases turned on wider considerations of freedom of expression, and not on the compatibility of protective measures, such as interlocutory injunctions, with the Convention. But it is worthy of note that in the *Guardian/Observer* case it was suggested that the grant of the interlocutory injunction was not 'prescribed by law' in accordance with the requirement of Article 10 (2). In the first *Sunday Times* case[451] it had been held that two of the requirements which flowed from the expression were, first, that the law must be adequately accessible; the citizen must be able to have an indication that is adequate in the circumstances of the legal rules applicable to a given case. Second, a norm could not be regarded as a 'law' unless it was formulated with sufficient precision to enable the citizen to

---

[450] *Observer and Guardian* v. *UK, Sunday Times* v. *UK (No. 2)*, Ser. A., Vols. 216 and 217, 1991. On the *Spycatcher* case generally, see Section XI, *supra*.

[451] Series A, No. 30, p. 31 (1979).

regulate his conduct: he must be able—if need be with appropriate advice—to foresee, to a degree that is reasonable in the circumstances, the consequences which a given action may entail.

The point arose in the *Guardian/Observer* in the context of the application of the rules in English law for the grant of interlocutory injunctions, principally those emerging from the case of *American Cyanamid Co. v. Ethicon Ltd.*[452] The European Court of Human Rights held that the rules were accessible, in that they had been enunciated by the House of Lords in 1975; the fact that the rules had to be adapted to novel situations did not mean that the second condition was not fulfilled. It concluded that there was no doubt that the rules were formulated with a sufficient degree of precision, that the newspapers must have been able to foresee, to an extent that was reasonable in the circumstances, a risk that the interlocutory injunctions would be imposed.

Anton Piller orders and the Human Rights Convention

The English *Anton Piller* order[453] is a drastic form of injunction requiring a defendant to give the plaintiff entry to the defendant's premises for the purpose of discovering material which, for example, infringes copyright or is a breach of confidence. There can be no doubt that the *ex parte Anton Piller* order has been a most valuable weapon against the dishonest misappropriation of intellectual property, and particularly against dishonest copyright infringement ('video pirates') and the dishonest abuse of trade secrets by ex-employees. But there is also little doubt that the exercise of the jurisdiction gives rise to serious misgivings about the propriety of granting drastic and oppressive orders against defendants who are neither notified nor heard, and who must obey the order before they may have an opportunity to apply to the court to have it discharged.[454]

Although it has sometimes been called a 'civil search warrant'[455] there is a legal fiction that the defendant consents to entry of the plaintiffs' representatives to his premises: but in fact the defendant consents because

---

[452] [1975] AC 396. At the risk of over-simplification, the case decided that in an application for an interlocutory injunction the plaintiff must show there is a serious case to be tried: the grant or refusal of the injunction then is a matter for the court's discretion on the balance of convenience.

[453] After *Anton Piller KG v. Manufacturing Processes Ltd.* [1976] Ch. 55 (CA). This section is based on Collins, '*Anton Piller* Orders and Fundamental Rights', (1990) 106 *LQR* 173. See also Dockray and Laddie, 'Piller Problems', (1990) 106 *LQR* 601.

[454] See *Wardle Fabrics Ltd. v. G. Myristis Ltd.* [1984] FSR 263; *Columbia Picture Industries v. Robinson* [1987] Ch. 38; *Bhimji v. Chatwani* [1991] 1 WLR 989; but cf. *WEA Records v. Visions Channel 4* [1983] 1 WLR 721 (CA).

[455] See Oliver '*Anton Piller*. The Civil Search Warrant', in *Cambridge Lectures 1983*, ed. Baldwin, p. 68.

he is ordered to, and if he refuses he faces fine or imprisonment. In *Universal Thermosensors Ltd.* v. *Hibben*,[456]

Mrs Hibben was alone in her house, with her children in bed. She was brought to the door in her house, with her children in bed. She was brought to the door in her night attire at 7.15 a.m., and told by a stranger knocking on the door that he had a court order requiring her to permit him to enter, that she could take legal advice forthwith, but otherwise she was not permitted to speak to anyone else at all. But how could she get legal advice at that time in the morning? She rang her solicitor's office but, predictably, there was no response.

Scott J., a persistent critic of the procedure, said in a recent case:[457]

Anton Piller orders . . . stand, as has been said on many occasions, at the extremity of the court's jurisdiction. Some may think that they go beyond it. They involve the court in the hypocrisy of pretending that the entry and search are carried on because the owners of the premises have consented to it. They impose on plaintiffs' solicitors the almost impossible task of describing fairly to non-lawyers the true effect and nature of the orders. They present respondents with orders of great complexity and jurisprudential sophistication and give little time for decisions to be taken as to the response to be made to them. They vest the plaintiffs, one side in what is usually highly contentious litigation, with the trappings of apparent administrative authority to carry out the search. The usual presence of a policeman adds to this illusion.

In *Columbia Picture Industries* v. *Robinson*[458] (a video pirate case) the same judge expressed the view that the practice of the court had allowed the balance to swing too much in favour of plaintiffs and that *Anton Piller* orders had been too readily granted and with insufficient safeguards for defendants. He said:[459]

It is a fundamental principle of civil jurisprudence in this country that citizens are not to be deprived of their property by judicial or quasi-judicial order without a fair hearing. *Audi alteram partem* is one of the principles of natural justice and contemplates a hearing at which the defendant can, if so advised, be represented and heard. What is to be said of the *Anton Piller* procedure which, on a regular and institutionalised basis, is depriving citizens of their property and closing down their business by orders made *ex parte*, on applications of which they know nothing and at which they cannot be heard, by orders which they are forced, on pain of committal, to obey, even if wrongly made?

Lock plc v. *Beswick*[460] was a case where employers were proceeding against former employees who had set up a rival business allegedly using business secrets belonging to their former employers. Hoffmann J. endorsed the view of Scott J. and drew attention to the use of *Anton Piller* orders in such cases as a 'pre-emptive strike to crush the unhatched

---

[456] 5 February 1992, not yet reported.
[457] *Bhimji* v. *Chatwani* [1991] 1 WLR 989, 1001–1002.　　　　　[458] [1987] Ch. 38.
[459] At 73–74.　　　　　[460] [1989] 1 WLR 1268.

competition in the egg by causing severe stress on the financial and management resources of the defendants or even of their financial support'. He thought that many employers regarded competition from former employees as presumptive evidence of dishonesty and could not understand the distinction between genuine trade secrets on the one hand and skill and knowledge on the other. Judges dealing with *ex parte* applications could have difficulty in dealing with alleged abuse of confidential information described in technical language: 'It may look like magic but turn out merely to embody a principle discovered by Faraday or Ampère.'[461]

At 10.45 a.m. on 2 March 1981, some 16 or 17 persons arrived, without prior notice, at the premises of the Video Exchange Club in Bath. Five of them were solicitors to, or employees of, film companies or organizations for the protection of film producers and distributors, and the other 11 or 12 were police officers. The Video Exchange Club was run by Mr Chappell, who also had his home on the premises. The film companies were convinced he was a video pirate. The police were satisfied that he was also engaged in the unlawful distribution of pornographic videos. The police had a search warrant and the representatives of the film companies were armed with an order made by Whitford J. The order was in the usual *Anton Piller* form requiring Mr Chappell to (*inter alia*) permit the plaintiffs, with their solicitors, to enter his premises for the purpose of searching for and removing any unlicensed copies of films, and documents relating thereto. The order also contained the usual undertaking by the plaintiffs' solicitors to explain the meaning of the order to the person served, and to inform him that he had the right to obtain legal advice before complying with the order, provided it was obtained forthwith.

After the order had been executed, Mr Chappell applied to have it set aside on the grounds that the plaintiffs had not made full disclosure to Whitford J. about the role of the police in the affair, and that the order had been executed in an oppressive manner (in particular, because the *Anton Piller* order and the search warrant had been executed simultaneously by some 17 persons). The Court of Appeal (in an unreported judgment) held that Whitford J. had not been adequately informed about the plan to execute the *Anton Piller* order and the search warrant simultaneously and what had happened was 'unfortunate and regrettable', but that the original order should not be set aside.

Mr Chappell complained to the European Commission on Human Rights that the *Anton Piller* order was in breach of his rights under the Human Rights Convention. The Commission held his complaint under Article 8 of the Convention was admissible, but by a bare majority

---

[461] At 1281.

expressed the opinion there had been no violation. The European Court of Human Rights unanimously upheld the view of the Commission.[462] By Article 8 of the Convention:

1. Everyone has the right to respect for his private and family life, his home and his correspondence.

2. There shall be no interference by a public authority with the exercise of this right except such as is in accordance with the law and is necessary in a democratic society . . . for the protection of the rights . . . of others.

The United Kingdom Government accepted that the *Anton Piller* order had involved an interference with the exercise of Mr Chappell's rights to respect for his private life and home, and Mr Chappell conceded that the interference had the aim of protecting 'the rights of others', i.e. the copyright holders. The contested issues were whether the order had been made 'in accordance with the law' and whether it had been 'necessary in a democratic society'. The European Court of Human Rights agreed with the Court of Appeal that the circumstances of execution of the order had been 'disturbing' and 'unfortunate and regrettable', but held that the order was in 'accordance with the law', as interpreted in previous decisions of the European Court because (*a*) whether or not the *Anton Piller* jurisdiction was based on statute (Supreme Court Act 1981, s. 37) or on the inherent jurisdiction of the Court, 'law' included unwritten or common law; (*b*) the basis of the exercise of the *Anton Piller* jurisdiction was both 'accessible', in the sense that the case-law was published, and 'foreseeable' in the sense that the discretionary factors in the exercise of the jurisdiction were well established, and not so amorphous as not to constitute 'law'.

Because the *Anton Piller* order is granted *ex parte* without the defendant being notified or heard, the Court thought it was 'essential this measure should be accompanied by adequate and effective safeguards against arbitrary interference and abuse'. But the safeguards were adequate and (in particular) it was sufficient that the execution of the order was conducted by the plaintiffs' solicitor (who is also an officer of the court in the sense of being answerable to the Court for any default). The shortcomings in the execution of the order were not so serious that its execution must be regarded as disproportionate to the legitimate aim.

The effect of the judgment is that no criticism of the *Anton Piller* order can be made merely because it is made *ex parte* and not in open court, provided it is accompanied by adequate and effective safeguards to prevent arbitrary interference and abuse, and that the execution of the Order is proportionate to the legitimate aim. But it is likely that the *Anton Piller* jurisdiction (a technique which is unknown—even in the United States—

---

[462] Ser. A, Vol. 152 (1989).

outside the United Kingdom and the Commonwealth) has, like the *Mareva* jurisdiction, been abused in many cases.

Two further points should be made before leaving the *Chappell* case. The first is that in a different, but related context, the powers of investigation by the European Commission in competition cases, the European Court of Justice in Luxembourg confirmed that the fundamental right to the inviolability of the home

must be recognized in the Community legal order as a principle common to the laws of the Member States in regard to the private dwellings of natural persons.

But that right did not apply to business undertakings' premises, because the protective scope of Article 8 (1) of the European Convention on Human Rights (the principles of which have been regarded by the Luxembourg court as an integral part of the European Community Law) was concerned with 'the development of man's personal freedom' and should not therefore be extended to business premises. Although this conclusion is questionable, it may not make any practical difference, since the Court held:[463]

. . . in all the legal systems of the Member States, any intervention by the public authorities in the sphere of private activities of any person, whether natural or legal, must have a legal basis and be justified on the grounds laid down by law, and, consequently, those systems provide, albeit in different forms, protection against arbitrary or disproportionate intervention. The need for such protection must be recognized as a general principle of Community Law.

The second point is that it should not be thought that the *Anton Piller* order is the only provisional order in civil proceedings which may violate fundamental rights. Many systems of law provide for *ex parte* orders, i.e. orders which are made by the court without notice to the party to whom they are addressed. But it is 'a basic principle of justice that an order should not be made against a party without giving him an opportunity to be heard', but that was subject to an exception where

giving such an opportunity appeared likely to cause the applicant injustice, by reason either of delay or action which it appeared likely the respondent . . . would take before the order was made.[464]

No doubt there are orders in all legal systems which deserve scrutiny, but it is sufficient to mention here two orders in English law which may sometimes overstep the limits. First, the effect of an *ex parte Mareva* injunction may be to paralyse the business and personal activities of a

---

[463] Cases 46/87 and 227/88 *Hoechst AG* v. *Commission* [1989] ECR 2859, 2924; see also Case 85/87 *Dow Benelux NV* v. *Commission* [1989] ECR 3137, 3157; Cases 97–99/87 *Dow Chemical Iberia* v. *Commission* [1989] ECR 3165, 3185–3186.

[464] *Re First Express Ltd.*, *The Times*, 10 October 1991, *per* Hoffmann J.

defendant, who may ultimately be under no liability to a plaintiff, who has merely to show a good arguable case to obtain the injunction. As Staughton LJ said in *Derby & Co. Ltd.* v. *Weldon (No. 6)*, one of the consequences of the development of the *Mareva* injunction is

the restraints that are placed on defendants in the conduct of their affairs before there has been any determination of liability against them; they may, after all, eventually be found to owe nothing.[465]

Secondly, in some cases the English court will grant an injunction restraining a defendant from leaving the United Kingdom, or a special order to that effect called a writ *ne exeat regno*. The extreme and excessive way in which this jurisdiction has sometimes been exercised is illustrated by this extract from the judgment of Leggatt J. in *Allied Arab Bank* v. *Hajjar*:[466]

At 9 p.m. on 13 January 1987 there was served on the first defendant, who is a Jordanian citizen then temporarily resident within the jurisdiction, a writ *ne exeat regno*. It had been issued earlier that day by leave of Hirst, J., and was duly marked with the sum by way of bail or security which the first defendant must find if he was to avoid arrest. He was unable, or in the words of the writ, he refused, to pay the required sum. So he was forthwith arrested and taken to Kingston jail when he spent one of the most distressing and humiliating nights of his life. The sum with which the writ was marked was $36,000,000. On the next day the first defendant was brought before Hirst J. Undertakings were exacted from him as the price of release from prison. They were to comply, subject to minor variations, with the discovery orders which the judge had made under specified paragraphs of his order relating to the first defendant's own assets, to the assets of the other defendants, and to inter-company dealings between the various defendant companies. There were also undertakings not to leave the jurisdiction without the consent of the court or the plaintiffs' solicitors; forthwith to deliver up his passport; to swear an affidavit that he had no other passport; not to apply during the currency of the undertaking as to discovery for any other travel documents . . .

The court held that the writ *ne exeat regno* should never have been issued (because the conditions specified in the Debtors Act 1869 had not been fulfilled) and the defendant was entitled to damages for the injury he had suffered through it having been wrongfully issued.

2. INTERIM MEASURES AND THE EUROPEAN COMMISSION ON HUMAN RIGHTS

The European Commission on Human Rights exercises in urgent cases,

---

[465] [1990] 1 WLR 1139, 1153 (CA).   [466] [1988] QB 787, at 789.

like other analogous bodies,[467] powers which are designed to secure interim protection pending final determination of a complaint. By Rule 36 of its Rules of Procedure:

The Commission, or where it is not in session, the President may indicate to the parties any interim measure the adoption of which seems desirable in the interest of the parties or the proper conduct of the proceedings before it.

The European Court of Human Rights does not itself exercise a similar power, unlike (for example) the Inter-American Court of Human Rights, which has the express power under the American Convention on Human Rights.[468]

In the *Cruz Varas* case[469] the main applicant was Cruz Varas, who was a Chilean who (with his wife and son) sought political asylum in Sweden in 1987. In the following year the Swedish National Immigration Board decided that Cruz Varas had not invoked sufficiently strong reasons for asylum and decided to expel the applicants. An appeal to the Swedish Government was rejected, and following further investigations by the police authorities, the National Immigration Board adhered to its previous decision.

Cruz Varas and his wife and son made an application to the European Commission on Human Rights alleging violations of various provisions of the Convention. The application was made on 5 October 1989. On the following day the Commission, at 9.00 a.m., indicated interim measures under Rule 36 of its Rules of Procedure as follows:

The Commission . . . decided . . . to indicate to the Government of Sweden . . . that it was desirable in the interest of the parties and the proper conduct of the proceedings before the Commission not to deport the applicants to Chile until the Commission had had an opportunity to examine the application during its forthcoming session from 6 to 10 November 1989.

The Agent for Sweden was notified of the Commission's decision at 9.10 a.m., and the decision was confirmed by telefax at 12.00 noon, and the

---

[467] The practice of the United Nations Human Rights Committee is particularly interesting. By Rule 86 of its Rules of Procedure,

The Committee may, prior to forwarding its final views on the communication to the State party concerned, inform the State of its views whether interim measures may be desirable to avoid irreparable damage to the victim of the alleged violation. In doing so, the Committee shall inform the State party concerned that such expression of its views on interim measures does not imply a determination on the merits of the communication.

This communication of views is not, of course, binding, but it has been used effectively to prevent death sentences being carried out, even before a decision on admissibility had been taken: see McGoldrick, *The Human Rights Committee: Its Role in the Development of the International Covenant on Civil and Political Rights* (1991), pp. 131–132.

[468] Art. 63 (2). See also Rules of Procedure, Art. 23; *Velásquez Rodríguez* case (1988) in (1989) 28 *ILM* 291, 300–303.   [469] Ser. A, Vol. 201 (1991).

Swedish Minister of Labour was informed by 12.45. Cruz Varas was deported to Chile at 16.40 on the same day, and his wife and son went into hiding in Sweden. The following month the Commission made a further decision under Rule 36:

in respect of Mr. Cruz Varas the Commission, given the failure of the Government to comply with its earlier indication not to deport him to Chile, now indicates that it is desirable in the interest of the parties and the proper conduct of the proceedings before the Commission, that the Government take measures which will enable this applicant's return to Sweden as soon as possible.

But later that year and in 1990 the National Immigration Board rejected requests for Cruz Varas to return to Sweden.

The Commission decided by a majority that there had been no violation of Article 3 (prohibition on torture) because, in view of the improvement in the political situation in Chile, there was not a real risk that Cruz Varas would again be exposed to treatment contrary to Article 3 in Chile; or of Article 8 (respect for family life) because the splitting up of the family was the result of their failure to comply with lawful orders. But it found (by 12 votes to 1) that Sweden was in breach of its obligation under Article 25 of the Convention 'not to hinder in any way the effective exercise' of the right of individual petition, by not complying with the Rule 36 indication of interim measures. The Commission decided that the decision to deport the applicant in the face of the interim decision had frustrated the application, and was incompatible with the effective exercise of the right of petition.

But the European Court of Human Rights held by a bare majority (10 votes to 9) that the failure to comply with the indication from the European Commission did not amount to a violation of Sweden's obligation under Article 25 (1). It decided that, by contrast with the systems prevailing in the International Court of Justice, in the European Communities, and in the Inter-American Convention on Human Rights, the European Convention on Human Rights did not contain a specific provision empowering the Convention organs to order interim measures. The *travaux préparatoires* were silent on the question.

In the absence of a specific Convention provision providing for the power to order interim measures, the Court decided that a Rule 36 indication could not give rise to a binding obligation. It thought that it would strain the language of Article 25 to infer an obligation to comply with a Rule 36 indication. The practice of States revealed almost total compliance with Rule 36 indications. Subsequent practice could be taken as establishing the agreement of States regarding the interpretation of a Convention provision, but could not create new rights and obligations which were not included in the Convention at the outset. The practice was based on good faith co-operation with the Commission, as reflected in the recommendations of the Council of Europe bodies. No assistance could be derived from the general principles of international law where no uniform legal rule existed. Accordingly, the power to order binding interim measures could not be inferred from Article 25 (1) or from other sources. The Court concluded that

> no assistance can be derived from general principles of international law since, as observed by the Commission, the question whether interim measures indicated by international tribunals are binding is a controversial one and no uniform legal rule exists.

This conclusion is the same as that of Mann J. in *R. v. Home Secretary, ex p. Kirkwood*.[470] That was a case in which the United States Government sought the extradition of Kirkwood, an alleged murderer. Kirkwood applied to the Commission claiming that his extradition would be contrary to Article 3 of the Convention, in that inordinate delay in carrying out the penalty in California amounted to inhuman and degrading treatment and punishment.[471] The Commission indicated to the United Kingdom that extradition should not take place for a specified period. During that period the United Kingdom Government took no action to extradite Kirkwood. Mann J. had evidence from the Home Secretary that it was the practice of the United Kingdom to comply with Rule 36 indications, and went on: 'That is a practice. It cannot be more, because the indication is a mere indication and gives rise to no obligation in the field of public international law.'[472] Mann J.'s assumption was not necessary for that decision, and it is plain that this issue was not the subject of detailed examination.

What is striking about the decision of the European Court of Human Rights is not that it was wrong—for it was probably right in deciding that the use of the expression 'indicate' shows that there is no obligation on the State to comply—but the absence of reference to the very considerable material on whether interim measures 'indicated' by the International Court of Justice and its predecessor, the Permanent Court of International Justice, are binding. The nine dissenting judges concluded that there is an implication under the Convention scheme that measures under Article 36 bind the State concerned. They thought that was the only means to protect the applicant against a possible violation of his or her rights causing irreparable harm; it was implicit in the Convention that the Convention organs had the power to require the parties to abstain from a measure which might not only give rise to serious harm but which might also nullify the result of the entire procedure under the Convention.

The European Court of Human Rights was almost certainly not

---

[470] [1984] 1 WLR 913.
[471] On this aspect see now *Soering* v. *United Kingdom*, Ser. A, Vol. 161 (1989).
[472] [1984] 1 WLR 913, at 919.

provided by the applicant, the Commission, or the Governments with the relevant material on the practice of the International Court of Justice. There is a considerable body of opinion (but not the preponderant one) that measures 'indicated' by the International Court *are* binding. That is a topic which will be taken up again in Section XIV. Thus Judge Hudson said of the expression 'indicate':

It may have been due to a certain timidity of the draftsmen. Yet it is not less definite than the term *order* would have been, and it would seem to have as much effect. The use of the term does not attenuate the obligation of a party within whose power the matter lies to carry out the measures 'which ought to be taken'. An indication by the Court . . . is equivalent to a declaration of obligation contained in a judgment, and it ought to be regarded as carrying the same force and effect.[473]

Is it not possible—or perhaps probable—that if this material had been before the European Court of Human Rights, then at least one of the majority would have been with those who ultimately became the minority?

---

[473] Hudson, *The Permanent Court of International Justice 1920–1942* (1943), pp. 425–426.

13

European Community Law
and Interim Measures

It has been seen in the previous section how the European Court of Justice decided in the *Hoechst* case[474] that the search and seizure powers of the Commission officials in competition investigations were subject to the fundamental right of freedom from arbitrary and disproportionate intervention by public authorities. These search and seizure powers are not provisional or protective measures within the meaning of this paper; they are conferred on an administrative body, and although their main function is the preservation of evidence (like the *Anton Piller* order in English law discussed in the previous section) they are not exercised in the course of civil proceedings, and the true analogy is probably the power of search and seizure in criminal proceedings.

Nor will this section be concerned with the power of the Commission itself to take protective measures. In *Camera Care Ltd. v. Commission*[475] the European Court held that in competition investigations the Commission had the implied power to take protective measures in order to avoid their power of decision in such cases being rendered 'ineffectual or even illusory' because of the action of the target of the investigation. In that case the proprietor of Camera Care, a small business engaged in the supply and repair of cameras, complained to the Commission that Hasselblad, the well-known Swedish camera manufacturers, were abusing their dominant position by cutting off supplies to him after he had engaged in price-cutting and parallel importing. The Commission refused to take interim measures on the ground that it had no power to do so. The European Court held that the Commission had the implied power to take interim measures but emphasized that they should only be taken in urgent cases to avoid serious and irreparable damage or to avoid a situation which was intolerable to the public interest. After the decision of the European Court, the Commission did not in fact impose interim measures.[476]

This section will therefore be concerned with the grant of interim measures by *courts*. It will primarily be concerned with interim measures in

---

[474] Cases 46 and 227/88 *Hoechst AG v. Commission* [1989] ECR 2859.
[475] Case 792/79R [1980] ECR 119.
[476] For subsequent proceedings see Case 86/82 *Hasselblad v. Commission* [1984] ECR 883.

national courts, but will begin with some observations on the practice of
the European Court. There are two areas of particular interest: the first is
interim measures in the context of proceedings by the Commission against
Member States under Article 169 of the EEC Treaty; the second is interim
measures in proceedings brought under Article 173 for the annulment of
acts of the Community.

Article 169 gives the Commission power to bring before the European
Court a complaint that a Member State has failed to fulfil its obligations
under the Treaty. Once a judgment under Article 169 has been given, the
legislative authorities of the Member State concerned must amend its
legislative provisions so as to make its law conform with Community law,
and its courts are under a duty to secure compliance with the relevant
Community law in actions involving individuals.[477] The judgment of the
European Court under Article 169 is declaratory only and it has no
jurisdiction to order the Member State to take steps to comply with its
obligations, for example by implementing a directive or removing import
restrictions. Nevertheless, the European Court has held that it has power
to order interim measures in Article 169 cases, the effect of which is that in
interim proceedings it can grant more effective orders than it can at the
final hearing. The power was first asserted in 1977 when the United
Kingdom was ordered to desist from paying subsidies to pig producers.[478]

After France had failed to comply with the judgment of the Court
condemning its ban on imports of British mutton and lamb[479] the
Commission brought new proceedings complaining that France was in
breach of its obligation under Article 171 'to take the necessary measures
to comply with the judgment' of the European Court. But the European
Court refused to grant interim measures requiring France to comply with
the earlier judgment. The reason given by the Court was that France was
already under an obligation to comply with the judgment as a result of
Article 171.[480]

A good example of the exercise of the power to order interim measures
in Article 169 cases is the *Dundalk Water Supply* case.[481] In that case an
Irish local authority invited tenders for a new water supply scheme, which
required compliance with an Irish technical standard. Only one firm was
authorized to apply that standard, and that firm was Irish. Following
complaints of unlawful discrimination made by a Spanish firm, the

---

[477] See Cases 314 to 316/81 and 83/82 *Procureur de la République* v. *Waterkeyn* [1982] ECR
4337, on the consequences of Case 152/78 *Commission* v. *France* [1980] ECR 2299.
[478] Cases 31 and 53/77R *Commission* v. *United Kingdom* [1977] ECR 921.
[479] Case 232/78 *Commission* v. *France* [1979] ECR 2729.
[480] Cases 24/80R and 97/80R *Commission* v. *France* [1980] ECR 1319. The dispute was
settled by the adoption in 1980 of a regulation setting up a common organization of the
market in mutton and lamb.
[481] Case 45/87R *Commission* v. *Ireland* [1987] ECR 783 and 1369.

Commission instituted proceedings under Article 169 against Ireland, and obtained an emergency *ex parte* interim order from the President of the European Court, that, pending the *inter partes* application for interim measures, no award of the contract for the water supply scheme be made. But a month later the President was persuaded on the *inter partes* hearing that, although there was a prima facie case (later upheld by the European Court on the hearing of the merits), it would not be right to make the interim order because, among other reasons, there was evidence that the existing water shortage created a fire risk, and even a risk to the health of the inhabitants of Dundalk.

By Article 185 of the EEC Treaty the European Court has power to suspend the application of a contested act, and by Article 186 it may prescribe interim measures in any case before it. Provision is made in the Statute and the Rules of the European Court for the President of the Court to order interim measures on an interlocutory basis.[482] It is not necessary, or desirable, to give a detailed account of the practice of the European Court in these cases, which are fully treated in the literature.[483] But the following points are worthy of emphasis. The request must be genuinely urgent (and since 1982 the practice has been to grant *ex parte* orders in cases of great urgency) and the applicant will normally have to show that it has a prima facie case on the merits and that irreparable harm would occur unless interim measures were granted. In principle, the admissibility of the main application is not examined on the application for interim measures, but where the defendant institution contends that the main application is manifestly inadmissible, then the President must consider whether there are any grounds for concluding prima facie that it is admissible. For example, an application directed at a decision addressed to a Member State was dismissed because it was not of individual concern[484] and an application for interim suspension of a directive was dismissed because prima facie the directive was a measure of general application.[485]

In deciding whether interim measures should be granted, the European Court balances the interests of the applicant against the damage which would be caused if the order were made. In anti-dumping cases the Court will consider not only the interests of manufacturers and exporters who claim that duty should not be imposed, but also the interests of the community industry to which damage is being caused by the continuance of dumping.[486] The applicant must show that the damage suffered by it as a

---

[482] EEC Statute, Art. 36, and Rules of Procedure, Arts. 83 ff. European Court of First Instance, Rules, Arts. 104 ff.

[483] See, especially, Lasok, *The European Court of Justice: Practice and Procedure* (1984), Chap. 8.   [484] Case 82/87R *Autexpo Spa* v. *Commission* [1987] ECR 2131.

[485] Case 160/88R *FEDESA* v. *Commission* [1988] ECR 4121.

[486] Case 273/85R *Silver Seiko Limited* v. *Council* [1985] ECR 3475.

result of the anti-dumping duty is special to it, and it is not inherent in the imposition of duties, such as a rise in its prices and a consequent diminution of market share; the applicant must also show that the balance of interests is in its favour in the sense that grant of the measures would not cause appreciable injury to community industry.[487]

2. THE POWER OF NATIONAL COURTS TO ORDER INTERIM MEASURES

A number of issues of general importance arise in relation to the grant of interim measures by national courts in the context of Community law. They include the following: the extent to which references to the European Court may be made under Article 177 of the EEC Treaty in the course of interlocutory proceedings which may not involve a final determination of the merits of the case; whether, if such references *may* be made, they *must* be made by national courts from which no appeal may be taken; and, perhaps most important, whether the ordinary processes of national litigation may, directly or indirectly, interfere with the implementation of Community law.

Under the Community law system national courts have no power to declare acts of the Community institutions invalid.[488] The European Court has exclusive power to rule on the validity of such acts, usually in the context of direct proceedings against Community institutions under Article 173 of the EEC Treaty, or in preliminary rulings given to national courts under Article 177 of the Treaty. Article 177 confers jurisdiction on the European Court to give preliminary rulings on (*inter alia*) the interpretation of the Treaty and on the validity and interpretation of acts of the institutions of the Community. Lower courts have a discretion to request preliminary rulings, but

where any such question is raised in a case pending before a court or tribunal of a member state, against whose decisions there is no judicial remedy under national law, that court or tribunal *shall* bring the matter before the Court of Justice (Art. 177 (3), emphasis added).

An important reason for the reluctance of national courts to refer under Article 177 at the stage of application for interim relief is that interlocutory proceedings have two characteristics which militate against the desirability of references to the European Court being made in the course of them. In the first place, they do not usually involve final decisions on any disputed points of law, in the sense that at the trial of the action the judge will have

---

[487] Case 77/87R *Technointorg* v. *Council* [1987] ECR 1793.
[488] See Case 314/85 *Firma Foto-Frost* v. *Hauptzollamt Lübeck-Ost* [1987] ECR 4199.

to take a further view on some matters on which only a provisional view was necessary at the interlocutory stage. In the second place, they often take place in a context that requires speedy and informal determination. For example, in the normal case in England, an injunction may be granted at a very early stage, either on an *ex parte* application by the plaintiff, or at a hearing *inter partes* but before the defendants have had an opportunity to file evidence in reply. If either party raises a question of European Community law and requests the national court to refer it to the European Court under Article 177 a substantial delay will be unavoidable. In any event, whatever decision is given on the hearing for an injunction will not be a final one, and the national court will not have made any relevant factual findings.

A recent example of the inter-relationship between injunctions and Community law is the 'sex-shop' case, *Portsmouth City Council* v. *Richards*,[489] where a local authority sought an interim injunction to restrain the operation of an unlicensed sex shop. The defendants had persuaded several courts in criminal proceedings, or proceedings for judicial review involving other local authorities, to refer questions to the European Court, the ultimate object of which was to determine whether the licensing provisions of the local government legislation were compatible with the prohibition on restriction of imports under Article 30 of the EEC Treaty. The defendants had been convicted of more than 30 offences in various parts of the country, and had brought 45 applications for judicial review against licence refusals, most of which had been unsuccessful. But a number of courts had been persuaded to make references to the European Court on the compatibility of the legislation with Community law.

In the *Portsmouth* case the defendants resisted the application for an injunction on the ground of the pending applications to the European Court. Kerr LJ pointed out that by seeking to rely on Article 30 the defendants had succeeded in neutralizing the effect of the criminal law. The Court of Appeal held that the local authority was entitled to the exceptional remedy of an interim civil injunction to restrain criminal offences because the activities of the defendants had effectively nullified the criminal law. The fact that references were pending to the European Court did not prevent an injunction being granted. Kerr LJ said:[490]

It must also be borne in mind that in order to decide whether or not to grant an interim injunction, a reference under Article 177 can only be 'necessary to enable [the court] to give judgment' . . . since the grant or refusal of an injunction is not a final judgment. Accordingly, there is no necessary correlation . . . between the circumstances that there is a pending reference or that one may be granted on the one hand, and the mandatory refusal of an interlocutory injunction on the other. The two things are not interdependent.

[489] [1989] 1 CMLR 673.   [490] At 704.

In *Polydor* v. *Harlequin Record Shops Ltd*[491] the defendants imported into the United Kingdom from Portugal records which were lawfully made in Portugal with the consent of the Portuguese copyright holders, but without the consent of Polydor, the United Kingdom copyright holders. Polydor sought an interlocutory injunction and were granted one by the judge at first instance, Megarry VC. The defendants argued that the EEC–Portuguese Free Trade Agreement had the effect of prohibiting the use of copyright law to prevent parallel imports, but the Vice-Chancellor refused to make a reference because the facts were not found or agreed, and it could not be said that a ruling from the European Court was necessary to enable the trial court to give judgment. This decision was reversed by the Court of Appeal, which refused to allow the interim injunction to stand, and made a reference to the European Court, because if the view of the Court of Appeal as to the effect of the Portuguese Agreement was right (which it was found by the European Court not to be) the action by Polydor was dead, and in the words of Templeman LJ:

What I am not prepared to do is to allow the plaintiffs to have an injunction which to my mind would be a complete breach of Community law on the view I have formed, unless and until the European Court has ruled that some other interpretation is to be placed [on the Agreement].[492]

These were both decisions of the English Court of Appeal. But it must not be thought that the relationship between national interlocutory proceedings and Community law is primarily a question of national law. Indeed, on the contrary, it is plain that it is primarily a question of Community law. In 1977 the European Court decided in *Hoffmann-La Roche* v. *Centrafarm*[493] that a national court *could* make a reference under Article 177 in proceedings for an interim injunction but that even a court of last resort was not under an obligation to do so in such proceedings, provided that at a subsequent stage of the proceedings on the substance of the case the question of Community law might be re-examined and be the subject of a reference under Article 177. In that case the Roche group, relying on its trade mark rights, obtained an interlocutory injunction from the German court restraining parallel imports of the drug Valium. The defendants resisted the action on the ground (*inter alia*) that Roche's conduct was an abuse of its dominant position (Art. 86 of the EEC Treaty) and an unlawful restriction of imports (Art. 30). In agreeing with the opinion of Advocate General Capotorti (which contains an interesting comparative survey of interim injunctions) the European Court accepted that

---

[491] [1980] 2 CMLR 413.   [492] At 426.

[493] Case 107/76 [1977] ECR 957. See also Collins, 'Art. 177 of the EEC Treaty and English Interlocutory Proceedings', (1974) 23 ICLQ 840; Collins, *European Community Law in the United Kingdom* (4th ed., 1990), pp. 189–194.

it often happens, especially in matters concerning the protection of industrial and commercial property, that the decision adopted in the interlocutory proceedings is accepted as the solution to the dispute;[494]

but the fact that the substance might be reviewed in the main action achieved the main object of Article 177, which is to ensure that Community law is interpreted and applied in a uniform manner in all the Member States.

That was not a case involving the validity of Community law. What was at issue was the compatibility of Roche's conduct with Community law. If, of course, the conduct was in breach of Community law, and Centrafarm had a valid defence, then the effect of the injunction would be to permit commercial activity in breach of Community law. But it is now clear that the *Hoffmann-La Roche* case must be read subject to two subsequent decisions. These decisions show that, where the validity of Community rules are in issue even in interlocutory proceedings, a national court cannot in effect rule that they are prima facie invalid by granting an interim injunction restraining their implementation, without at the same time making a reference to the European Court for a preliminary ruling as to their validity.

In the *Foto-Frost* case[495] the plaintiffs sought an order in the German courts directing the tax authorities to disapply a tax levied on binoculars imported from Carl Zeiss Jena in East Germany. Under the applicable Community regulation, the Commission had the power to decide whether the taxes should be waived, and in a Commission decision addressed to the German Government, it had refused to allow them to be waived. The plaintiffs claimed that the decision was invalid. Advocate General Mancini thought that the *Hoffmann-La Roche* case applied in such a case, and that there was no obligation to make a reference in interlocutory proceedings even if there were an issue of the validity of an act of a Community institution: the purpose was to prevent the time taken up by the proceedings for a preliminary ruling from frustrating the interim protection sought by the plaintiff. That was said in the context of the rule in Germany (and many other countries) that an applicant for an interim injunction must show prima facie evidence, in the sense of material which demonstrates that the plaintiffs' case is probably right. But the Court rejected that conclusion: national courts

may consider the validity of a Community act and, if they consider that the grounds put forward before them by the parties in support of invalidity are unfounded, they may reject them, concluding that the measure is completely valid. By taking that

---

[494] [1977] ECR 957, at 972.
[495] Case 314/85 *Firma Foto-Frost* v. *Hauptzollamt Lübeck-Ost* [1987] ECR 4199.

action they are not calling into question the existence of the Community measure. On the other hand, those courts do not have the power to declare acts of the Community institutions invalid . . . [T]he main purpose of the powers accorded to the Court by Article 177 is to ensure that Community law is applied uniformly by national courts. That requirement of uniformity is particularly imperative when the validity of a community act is in question. Divergences between courts in the Member States as to the validity of Community acts would be liable to place in jeopardy the very unity of the Community legal order and detract from the fundamental requirement of legal certainty . . . Since Article 173 gives the Court exclusive jurisdiction to declare void an act of a Community institution, the coherence of the system requires that where the validity of a Community act is challenged before a national court the power to declare the act invalid must also be reserved to the Court of Justice.[496]

But the Court added that the rule that national courts may not themselves declare Community acts invalid might have to be qualified in certain circumstances in the case of proceedings relating to an application for interim measures.

In the *Zuckerfabrik* case[497] in 1991 the European Court decided that in interlocutory proceedings national courts were not prevented by Community law from suspending the operation of an administrative measure based on a Community regulation. But the suspension of such a measure may be granted by a national court only if it has serious doubts as to the validity of the Community measure and refers the question of the validity of the contested measure to the Court of Justice, if that has not already been done; and if the matter is urgent, there is a risk to the applicant of serious and irreparable harm and the national court takes due account of the Community's interests.

That case involved proceedings in Germany in which the plaintiffs contested levies imposed by the German customer authorities pursuant to a Council regulation, which the plaintiffs claimed was invalid. The European Court held, first, that the national court had the power to grant interim orders suspending the imposition of the levies: the reason was that when national authorities were responsible for the administrative implementation of Community regulations, the right to judicial review guaranteed by Community law included the right of individuals to contest the legality of such regulations indirectly before a national court and to require that court to refer questions to the European Court for a preliminary ruling. That right, and with it the effectiveness of Article 177 of the EEC Treaty, would be jeopardized if, pending the decision of the European Court, which had sole jurisdiction to declare a Community regulation invalid, an individual could not, when certain conditions were fulfilled, obtain an order suspending the operation of an administrative measure based on a

---

[496] At 4230–4231.   [497] Cases C-143/88 and C-92/89, 21 February 1991.

Community regulation whose validity was contested. Nor could the provisional protection afforded by Community law to parties before national courts depend on whether they were challenging the compatibility of provisions of national law with Community law or the validity of secondary Community legislation, since in both cases the challenge was based on Community law.

But the national court was subject to two important limitations. First, an interim order suspending the operation of the Community act could be justified only if the facts and legal arguments submitted by the applicants convinced the national court that there was serious doubt as to the validity of the Community regulation on which the contested administrative measure was based. Second, the suspension of the operation of the instrument must remain a provisional measure. In proceedings for interim relief, therefore, a national court could order suspension only until such time as the European Court ruled on the question of validity. If a ruling had not yet been sought from the Court, therefore, it was the responsibility of the national court to seek such a ruling itself. Third, national courts should only make such an order in the circumstances applicable to actions for interim relief before the European Court, that is to say if the matter was urgent, if there was a risk to the applicant of serious and irreparable harm and if due account was taken of the Community's interests.

3. THE DUTY OF NATIONAL COURTS TO GRANT INTERIM PROTECTION

Many, perhaps most, countries with developed and democratic constitutions allow the courts to review the legality or constitutionality not only of delegated legislation, but also of primary legislation. Most of these countries also allow the courts, in appropriate cases, to grant interim orders suspending the operation of laws alleged to be unconstitutional until their legality is determined. Thus in Germany, the Federal Constitutional Court may provisionally suspend the application of primary legislation; and so may the ordinary courts, provided that they refer the case to the Constitutional Court. The Constitutional Court will suspend the operation of legislation if it is urgently necessary to avoid severe disadvantage: like all courts in this situation it has to consider the consequences if the law is suspended, and yet is ultimately held to be lawful, and the consequences if the law is not suspended, and yet is ultimately held to be unlawful: an interim order is more likely to be made if the freedom or economic existence of a private party is at stake, but mere economic disadvantage is not sufficient.[498] In the United States a preliminary injunction restraining

---

[498] See, e.g., *BVerfGE* 18, 34/36; 12, 276/80.

the implementation of legislation alleged to be unconstitutional may be granted if the plaintiff has the requisite *locus standi*. Thus a number of doctors, a professional organization, members of the clergy, and an individual whose health insurance provided abortion coverage, were granted a temporary injunction restraining the implementation of the Pennsylvania Abortion Control Act.[499]

In the celebrated *Simmenthal* case[500] in 1978 the European Court held that:

any national court must, in a case within its jurisdiction, apply Community law in its entirety and protect rights which the latter confers on individuals and must accordingly set aside any provision of national law which may conflict with it, whether prior to or subsequent to the Community rule.[501]

When the Irish Government urged the Supreme Court of Ireland not to enjoin it from prosecuting Spanish fishermen, it argued that the court should never grant an interlocutory injunction which in effect prohibited, even for a short period, the exercise of the power contained in a statute, or, alternatively, that it should do so only if the statutory provision were clearly unconstitutional. The Supreme Court answered:[502]

It is . . . the duty of the courts to protect persons against the invasion of their constitutional rights or against unconstitutional action. It would seem wholly inconsistent with that duty if the Court were to be without power in an appropriate case to restrain by injunction an action against a person which found its authority in a statutory provision which might eventually be held to be invalid having regard to the Constitution.

Spanish fishing interests were also at stake in the *Factortame* litigation, which gave rise to some of the most significant decisions of the House of Lords and the European Court in recent years. The United Kingdom Merchant Shipping Act 1988 provided for the establishment of a new register of all British fishing vessels. The effect of the legislation was to make fishing vessels eligible for registration if (*a*) the vessel was British-owned; (*b*) the vessel was managed, and its operations were directed and controlled, from within the United Kingdom; and (*c*) any charterer, manager or operator of the vessel was a qualified person or company. The definition of British-owned in the Act involved 75 per cent beneficial ownership by individuals who were British citizens resident and domiciled in the United Kingdom, or by companies which are ultimately 75 per cent

---

[499] *American College of Obstetricians* v. *Thornburgh*, 737 F. 2d 283 (3d Cir 1984), affd. 476 US 747 (1986).

[500] Case 106/77 *Amministrazione delle Finanze dello Stato* v. *Simmenthal SpA* [1978] ECR 629. [501] At 644.

[502] *Pesca Valentia Ltd.* v. *Minister for Fisheries* [1985] IR 193. See also Case 223/86 *Pesca Valentia Ltd.* v. *Minister for Fisheries* [1988] ECR 83; Case C-93/89 *Commission* v. *Ireland* [1991] 3 CMLR 697.

owned by such citizens and at least 75 per cent of whose directors were such British citizens.

The effect of these provisions was to exclude from fishing Spanish-owned vessels which were on the register before 1 April 1989 (and to prevent new Spanish-owned vessels from registering). The consequence was that many of the Spanish-owned vessels could not fish, or only outside EEC waters, and several had tried without success to sell their vessels, and faced bankruptcy. They claimed that the British nationality and residence requirements were contrary to Community law. Ultimately the European Court held in a series of decisions that (*a*) when exercising the power granted to Member States to define rules for the utilization of their quotas, the Member States may determine which vessels in their fishing fleets may fish against their national quotas; and that, in particular, a Member State may lay down conditions designed to ensure that the vessel has a real economic link with the State;[503] (*b*) but that the United Kingdom legislation contravened Article 52 (freedom of establishment) of the EEC Treaty in so far as it required British ownership of the vessels, although it was not contrary to Article 52 to require that the vessel must be managed and its operations directed and controlled from within the United Kingdom.[504]

For present purposes the importance of the case is in the decisions of the House of Lords and the European Court on whether the Spanish fishing interests were entitled to interim relief, pending the final decision of the English courts on the merits of the litigation brought in England to challenge the legislation and the final decision of the European Court in the proceedings brought by the Commission against the United Kingdom Government. In England the principal problems arose because of (*a*) the doctrine of the sovereignty of parliament, and the inability of the courts to set aside primary legislation, and (*b*) the traditional immunity of the Crown from the grant of injunctions. In summary, this part of the litigation followed the following course:

(1) In December 1988 certain Spanish fishing interests commenced applications in England for judicial review of the decision of the Secretary of State for Transport to remove Spanish-owned vessels from the register and to render them ineligible for registration.

(2) In March 1989 the Divisional Court requested a preliminary ruling on the merits of the case from the European Court, and granted an interim injunction restraining the Secretary of State from enforcing

---

[503] Case 3/87 *R.* v. *Minister of Agriculture, ex p. Agegate Ltd.* [1989] ECR 4459; Case 216/87 *R.* v. *Minister of Agriculture, ex p. Jaderow Ltd.* [1989] ECR 4509.

[504] Case 221/89 *R.* v. *Secretary of State for Transport, ex p. Factortame Ltd.* (*No. 2*) [1991] 3 CMLR 589; Case C-246/89 *Commission* v. *United Kingdom* [1991] 3 CMLR 706.

the legislation against the applicants, but in the same month the Court of Appeal set aside the interim relief.[505]

(3) In April 1989 the House of Lords refused the applicants an interim injunction to restrain the application of the Merchant Shipping Act 1988, because the court had no power to make an order postponing the operation of a statute pending a reference to the European Court, and had no power to grant an interim injunction against the Crown. But the House of Lords referred to the European Court the question whether under Community law a national court was under an obligation to provide an effective interlocutory remedy to protect rights which were directly effective.[506]

(4) In August 1989 the European Commission brought proceedings under Article 169 of the EEC Treaty against the United Kingdom for a declaration that, by imposing the nationality requirements, the United Kingdom was in breach of the EEC Treaty, and by an Order in October 1989 the President of the Court (Judge Due) granted an interim measures order requiring the United Kingdom to suspend the nationality requirements as regards fishing vessels which were until 31 March, 1989, fishing under the British flag and under a British fishing licence.[507]

(5) In June 1990 the European Court decided that in a case concerning Community law in which an application was made for interim relief, if a national court considered that the only obstacle which precluded it from granting such relief was a rule of national law, it had to set aside that rule.[508]

(6) In October 1990 the House of Lords held that an interim injunction ought to be granted, especially in view of the fact that the applicants' case was prima facie a strong one, and that the detriment of the public interest which would occur if they eventually failed in their challenge did not outweigh the damage which would be caused to the applicants if interim relief were not granted and they were ultimately successful.[509]

It is of course a commonplace that the United Kingdom has no written constitution. One of the many consequences is that it is accepted that the legislative supremacy of Parliament means that the court cannot question the validity of an Act of Parliament.[510] It follows that in the normal case the question of interim protection against the application of a United

---

[505] [1989] 2 CMLR 353. [506] [1990] 2 AC 85.

[507] Case 246/89R *Commission* v. *United Kingdom* [1989] ECR 3125.

[508] Case C-213/89 *R.* v. *Secretary of State for Transport, ex p. Factortame Ltd.* [1990] 3 CMLR 1. [509] [1991] 1 AC 603.

[510] See, e.g., *Manuel* v. *Att. Gen.* [1983] Ch. 77.

Kingdom statute cannot arise. Community law takes precedence over national law, and the legislative technique in the United Kingdom legislation to achieve this precedence is provided by section 2 of the European Communities Act 1972, which provides, in effect, that directly effective Community law rights are to take effect in the law of the United Kingdom, and that statutes passed after 1972 are to be construed and take effect subject to directly enforceable Community rights.

After the ruling of the European Court that provisions of national law restricting the exercise of directly effective Community rights must be set aside, there was much comment in the United Kingdom (especially in the press) that the European Court had usurped the sovereignty of Parliament. In the second *Factortame* decision Lord Bridge answered this criticism:[511]

Some public comments on the decision of the European Court of Justice, affirming the jurisdiction of the courts of member states to override national legislation if necessary to enable interim relief to be granted in protection of rights under Community law, have suggested that this was a novel and dangerous invasion by a Community institution of the sovereignty of the United Kingdom Parliament. But such comments are based on a misconception. If the supremacy within the European Community of Community law over the national law of member states was not always inherent in the E.E.C. Treaty . . . it was certainly well established in the jurisprudence of the European Court of Justice long before the United Kingdom joined the Community. Thus, whatever limitation of its sovereignty Parliament accepted when it enacted the European Communities Act 1972 was entirely voluntary. Under the terms of the Act of 1972 it has always been clear that it was the duty of a United Kingdom court, when delivering final judgment, to override any rule of national law found to be in conflict with any directly enforceable rule of Community law. Similarly, when decisions of the European Court of Justice have exposed areas of United Kingdom statute law which failed to implement Council directives, Parliament has always loyally accepted the obligation to make appropriate and prompt amendments. Thus there is nothing in any way novel in according supremacy to rules of Community law in those areas to which they apply and to insist that, in the protection of rights under Community law, national courts must not be inhibited by rules of national law from granting interim relief in appropriate cases is no more than a logical recognition of that supremacy.

Thus in United Kingdom constitutional theory, the Merchant Shipping Act 1988 was not void to the extent that it conflicted with EEC law, but it was to be read as if it contained a provision which enacted that the registration rules were to be 'without prejudice to the directly enforceable Community rights of nationals of any member state of the E.E.C.'[512]

The case was seen, therefore, by the House of Lords as one involving a dispute as to the interpretation of the Merchant Shipping Act 1988, rather

---

[511] [1991] 1 AC at 658–659. [512] [1990] 2 AC at 140, *per* Lord Bridge.

than its validity. As Lord Bridge pointed out, interim relief is not normally necessary in such cases because the court can immediately decide the question of interpretation.[513] But in the *Factortame* case the question of interpretation could not be decided immediately because it was accepted that it might take two years for the European Court to give a ruling on the content of the relevant European law—in fact the European Court gave judgment on the substance of the case 26 months after the first judgment of the House of Lords. It followed that if the interim order were given in favour of the applicants, it would irreversibly determine in their favour for two years rights which were necessarily uncertain.

Consequently the House of Lords held that, as a matter of United Kingdom constitutional law, the court had no power to grant interim relief which would have the effect of conferring rights which were prima facie 'directly contrary to Parliament's sovereign will'.[514] But the House of Lords made a reference to the European Court under Article 177 of the EEC Treaty for a ruling on whether EEC law empowered or obliged the English court to provide interim protection of disputed rights in Community law before their existence was established. As is by now well known, the European Court ruled that the supremacy of Community law entailed that;

. . . any provision of a national legal system and any legislative, administrative or judicial practice which might impair the effectiveness of Community law by withholding from the national court having jurisdiction to apply such law the power to do everything necessary at the moment of its application to set aside national legislative provisions which might prevent, even temporarily, Community rules from having full force and effect are incompatible with those requirements, which are the very essence of Community law . . . [T]he full effectiveness of Community law would be just as much impaired if a rule of national law could prevent a court seized of a dispute governed by Community law from granting interim relief in order to ensure the full effectiveness of the judgment to be given on the existence of the rights claimed under Community law. It follows that a court which in those circumstances would grant interim relief, if it were not for a rule of national law, is obliged to set aside that rule.[515]

The decision of the European Court did not oblige the English court to grant interim protection. Its effect was to prevent the English court from relying on special rules of English law—such as the presumption of legislative validity or Crown immunity from injunctive relief—to deny protection. Therefore when the case went back to the House of Lords, the main issue was whether the injunction should be granted in the circumstances of the case. In the normal case involving private rights, the

---

[513] [1990] 2 AC at 140, *per* Lord Bridge.

[514] At 143. The House of Lords also held that the traditional immunity of the Crown from injunctive relief had been preserved by the Crown Proceedings Act 1947.

[515] Case C-213/89 [1991] 1 AC 603, 644.

court had to be satisfied that there was a serious question to be tried, and, if so, where the balance of convenience lay. An important issue arose, therefore, whether the ordinary principles relating to interlocutory injunctions in cases involving private rights applied in a case where the public interest was involved.

This issue was considered and decided by the Supreme Court of Canada in 1987 in a decision which was, apparently, not cited in the House of Lords: *Manitoba (Att. Gen.)* v. *Metropolitan Stores Ltd.*[516] In that case an employer sought an interlocutory injunction restraining the Manitoba Labour Board from exercising its powers under legislation which the employer claimed was contrary to the Canadian Charter of Rights and Freedoms. The Supreme Court of Canada noted that[517]

Whether or not they are ultimately held to be constitutional, the laws which litigants seek to suspend . . . by way of interlocutory injunctive relief have been enacted by democratically-elected legislatures and are generally passed for the common good, for instance: . . . the protection of public health, natural resources and the environment . . . It seems axiomatic that the granting of interlocutory injunctive relief . . . is susceptible temporarily to frustrate the pursuit of the common good. While respect for the Constitution must remain paramount, the question then arises whether it is equitable and just to deprive the public, or important sectors thereof, from the protection and advantages of impugned legislation, unless the public interest is taken into consideration in the balance of convenience and is given the weight it deserves.

The court concluded[518] that

in a case where the authority of a law enforcement agency is constitutionally challenged, no interlocutory injunction or stay should issue to restrain that authority from performing its duties to the public unless, in the balance of convenience, the public interest is taken into consideration and given the weight it should carry. Such is the rule where the case against the authority of the law enforcement agency is serious, for if it were not, the question of granting interlocutory relief should not even arise. But that is the rule also even where there is a prima facie case against the enforcement agency . . .

The House of Lords in the *Factortame* case approached the question in a similar way. It held that test of 'a serious question to be tried' did not apply. There was a presumption that an Act of Parliament was compatible with Community law, and the Government had a right and a duty to enforce the law. Accordingly, in such a case the applicants had to show not only that the balance of convenience was in their favour, but also that they had a strong prima facie case that the relevant provisions of the Merchant Shipping Act 1988 were incompatible with Community law. It was held

[516] [1987] 1 SCR 110.   [517] At 135.   [518] At 149.

that they had shown such a prima facie case in the light of the decisions of the European Court in related litigation.[519]

Similarly, the President of the European Court had held in the interim measures phase of the Commission's case against the United Kingdom that the freedom of establishment provisions of the EEC Treaty prima facie included the right to incorporate and manage a company whose object was to operate a fishing vessel registered in the State of establishment under the same conditions as a company controlled by nationals of the State. Accordingly, there was a *prima facie* case, and the European Court was able to consider the urgency of the application for interim measures in relation to the necessity for an order to prevent serious and irreparable damage. The European Court balanced the United Kingdom's interest in settling the problems of the 'Anglo-Spanish' vessels against the damage caused to those vessels which had been deprived of their registration, and concluded that the interim measures would not jeopardize the objective of the British legislation, which was to establish a genuine link between the vessels fished against the British quotas and the British fishing industry.

The approach of the House of Lords was similar. Lord Goff pointed out that, where a party is a public authority performing duties to the public, the balance of convenience must be looked at more broadly:

. . . particular stress should be placed upon the importance of upholding the law of the land, in the public interest, bearing in mind the need for stability in our society, and the duty placed on certain authorities to enforce the law in the public interest . . . So if a public authority seeks to enforce what is, on its face, the law of the land, and the person against whom such action is taken challenges the validity of that law, matters of considerable weight have to be put into the balance to outweigh the desirability of enforcing, in the public interest, what is on its face the law, and so to justify the refusal of an interim injunction in favour of the authority, or to render it just or convenient to restrain the authority for the time being from enforcing the law.[520]

That was why the strength of the applicants' case was such an important factor. Once it had been shown that the applicants had strong grounds for challenging the validity of the provisions relating to residence and domicile, it was clear that there was obvious and immediate damage which would continue to be caused if no interim relief were granted. Those factors were not outweighed by the evidence of potential losses to British fishing interests.

The effect of this series of decisions was to grant effective interim relief in a case where it was ultimately held that the applicants were right.

---

[519] Case 246/89R *Commission* v. *United Kingdom* [1989] ECR 3125; Case 3/87 *R.* v. *Minister of Agriculture, ex p. Agegate Ltd.* [1989] ECR 4459; Case 216/87 *R.* v. *Minister of Agriculture, ex p. Jaderow Ltd.* [1989] ECR 4509.   [520] [1991] 1 AC at 673.

Consequently, the risk which the court took was justified. But Community law did not require that risk to be taken. All it required was that the court should be free to consider whether to take it. A more questionable use of the European Court's ruling led to a situation in England in the winter of 1991/1992, in which a number of large stores were able to flout the restrictions on the opening of shops on Sundays.

The background to *Kirklees Borough Council* v. *Wickes Building Supplies Ltd.*[521] was that retailers in England were prevented by the Shops Act 1950 from selling on Sundays a large range of goods, including (as in that case) building and decorating materials for domestic use by home owners ('Do-it-yourself' or DIY shops). Because the legislation provided for fines which the retailers were prepared to pay, the local authorities who had the responsibility of enforcing the law sought and obtained injunctions in the civil courts to restrain Sunday trading. The retailers contended that the Shops Act 1950 was in breach of Article 30 of the EEC Treaty in that it had the effect of unlawfully restricting imports. In the *Torfaen* case[522] the European Court held that Sunday trading restrictions were not in breach of Article 30 if the restrictions did not exceed the effects intrinsic to them, and that it was a question of fact whether specific national rules were within the permissible limits. But in *Stoke-on-Trent Council* v. *B & Q plc*[523] the House of Lords referred to the European Court a series of questions on the effect of two decisions[524] subsequent to the *Torfaen* case, and in particular whether they had the effect of making it a question of law rather than a question of fact whether Sunday trading laws were in breach of Article 30 of the EEC Treaty.

While the reference by the House of Lords was still pending, and while the law was therefore in an uncertain state, the Kirklees Borough Council sought an interim injunction against the retailers. The local authority was not prepared to give a cross-undertaking in damages, which is normally required of an applicant for an interim injunction. This undertaking fulfils the same function as the bond or security given in other systems of law: if it is ultimately decided that the injunction should not have been granted, then the applicant has to pay damages to the defendant for any loss caused by the imposition of the injunction. In *Hoffmann-La Roche & Co.* v. *Secretary of State for Trade and Industry*[525] it was held that the Crown, i.e.

---

[521] [1991] 3 WLR 985 (CA).

[522] Case 145/88 *Torfaen BC* v. *B. & Q. plc* [1990] 2 QB 19.

[523] [1991] Ch. 48.

[524] Case C-332/89 *Ministère public* v. *Marchandise* and Case C-312/89 *Union Départmentale des Syndicats CGT de l'Aisne* v. *Soc. int. de distribution d'équipements familiaux* (*Conforama*), 28 February 1991, not yet reported.

[525] [1975] AC 295.

the United Kingdom central government, was not required to give a cross-undertaking when it sought to enforce what was prima facie the law of the land. The Court of Appeal held that the local authority would be required to give a cross-undertaking as a condition of the grant of an interim injunction, for two reasons: first, the rule in *Hoffmann-La Roche* did not apply to local authorities, as distinct from the Crown or central government; secondly, the consequence of the European Court's ruling in *Factortame* was that, if the retailers were correct in their argument, that the Shops Act 1950 was incompatible with EEC law, the national court had the duty to protect their right to open their stores. As Mann LJ put it:

If the right is established, then it must be established with unrestricted retrospective effect . . . To grant an interim injunction without the protection . . . of an undertaking in damages would preclude effective retrospective effect if the right is ultimately established for there would be no recompense for the period of inhibition.[526]

The judgment rests on a misreading of *Factortame*. The European Court did not say that the national court must in every case protect disputed Community rights: what it said is that there must be no rule of national law which prevents those rights being frustrated. To give the court a power to dispense with a cross-undertaking where the alleged Community law right is doubtful is in no way inconsistent with the decision of the European Court.

[526] [1991] 3 WLR at 999–1000.

14

Interim Measures
in International Tribunals

I. A GENERAL PRINCIPLE OF LAW

The wealth of the literature on interim measures in the practice of the International Court of Justice and its predecessor makes it unnecessary to attempt a full survey here.[527] Indeed, a cynic may think that the volume of this literature is in inverse proportion to the effectiveness of the remedy and to the respect shown by respondent States to the orders of the Court. Consequently, this section will be confined to some observations on the practice in international tribunals.

First, it should not be in doubt that the principle underlying interim protection is a general principle of law within the meaning of Article 38 (1) (c) of the Statute of the International Court.[528] In one of its final acts the Permanent Court of International Justice said that the provision in its Statute and Rules for interim measures of protection

. . . applies the principle universally accepted by international tribunals . . . to the effect that the parties to a case must abstain from any measure capable of exercising a prejudicial effect in regard to the execution of the decision to be given and, in general, not to allow any step of any kind to be taken which might aggravate or extend the dispute . . .[529]

The universality of the remedy and the conditions for the grant of interim protection lead inescapably to that conclusion. This is not to say that the rules relating to interim measures are the same in all countries or that all tribunals have found the same answers to the problems. In international tribunals, in particular, the power to order or indicate interim measures is an integral part of the process of the peaceful settlement of

---

[527] See especially Dumbauld, *Interim Measures of Protection in International Controversies* (1932); Dumbauld, *Relief Pendente Lite in the Permanent Court of International Justice*, (1945) 39 AJIL 371; Mendelson, 'Interim Measures of Protection in Cases of Contested Jurisdiction', (1972–1973) 46 BYIL 259; Elkind, *Interim Protection: A Functional Approach* (1981); Sztucki, *Interim Measures in The Hague Court* (1983).

[528] See Dumbauld, pp. 177–178.

[529] *Electricity Company of Sofia and Bulgaria* case, PCIJ, Ser. A/B, No. 79, 194, at 199. But in the *Aegean Sea Continental Shelf* case, *ICJ Reports 1976* 3, at 13, the International Court left open the question whether Article 41 of the Statute conferred upon it the power to indicate interim measures of protection for the sole purpose of preventing the aggravation or extension of a dispute.

disputes, and this is the reason why the Permanent Court and the International Court have emphasized the duty of the parties not to exacerbate the dispute. This is a constant theme in international practice. As early as 1907, the Convention for the establishment of a Central American Court of Justice gave the court power (Art. 18) to 'fix the situation in which the contending parties must remain, to the end that the difficulty shall not be aggravated and that things shall be conserved in *status quo* pending a final decision'. In municipal tribunals, the maintenance or restoration of the *status quo* is also the primary purpose of interim measures, and it has been seen in Section I that the preservation of the peace was also a purpose of the injunction in civil law. Today the overriding reason for such measures is to ensure that the final judgment of the court will not be prejudiced by the actions of the parties.

It is possible, but not certain, that the universality of the principle leads to the conclusion that an international tribunal has an inherent power to grant interim measures even if the instrument under which it is established does not expressly give it that power.[530] Thus, in his separate opinion in the *Northern Cameroons case (Preliminary Objections)*[531] Judge Sir Gerald Fitzmaurice referred (*inter alia*) to interim measures of protection, and said:

Although much . . . of this incidental jurisdiction is specifically provided for in the Court's Statute, or in Rules of Court which the Statute empowers the Court to make, it is really an inherent jurisdiction, the power to exercise which is a necessary condition of the Court—or of any court of law—being able to function at all.

In *E-Systems, Inc.* v. *Iran*[532] the United States–Iran Claims Tribunal asserted that it had an 'inherent power' to issue such orders as might be necessary to conserve the respective rights of the parties and to ensure that the Tribunal's jurisdiction and authority were made fully effective. Accordingly, it 'requested' Iran to apply for a stay of parallel proceedings in Iran. But it is doubtful whether this was truly an exercise of an inherent power. The Claims Settlement Declaration of 19 January 1981 under which the Tribunal was established provided that the procedure of the Tribunal was to be governed by the arbitration rules of the United Nations Commission on International Trade Law (UNCITRAL) except to the extent modified by the Governments or by the Tribunal. The provisional rules in force when that award was rendered (and the definitive rules subsequently adopted[533]) incorporated, in an unmodified form, Article 26 of the UNCITRAL Rules, which provides for interim measures 'in respect of the subject-matter of the dispute', which include (but only *include*) measures for the conservation of goods forming the subject-matter in

---

[530] See, e.g., *The Gramophone case*, British–German Mixed Arbitral Tribunal (1922) 1 TAM 857.   [531] 1963 *ICJ Reports 1963* 15, 103.
[532] (1983) 2 CTR 51, 57.   [533] 2 CTR 405.

dispute. There can be little doubt that this provision gave the Tribunal the necessary authority, as Messrs Holtzmann and Mosk (concurring) thought, and as the Iranian members (who also concurred in the result) denied. Subsequently, the Tribunal relied both on its inherent power and the power expressly granted by the UNCITRAL Rules (under which it was expressly directed to function) when granting interim protection.[534]

2. THE BINDING CHARACTER OF INTERIM MEASURES

It is doubtful, however, whether the general character of the principle sheds any light on the controversial question whether interim measures indicated by the International Court are binding. Article 41 of the Statute of the International Court (and the virtually identical provision in the Statute of its predecessor) provides that the Court has 'the power to indicate, if it considers that circumstances so require, any provisional measures which ought to be taken to preserve the respective rights of either party'. It is clear that when the Statute of the Permanent Court was being drafted and negotiated the word 'indicate' was chosen deliberately and the word 'order' avoided with equal deliberation.[535] So also was it deliberately provided that notice of the measures 'suggested' should forthwith be given to the Council of the League of Nations (or to the Security Council under the present Statute).

If, of course, the indication of interim measures by the Court is nothing more than a declaration by the Court of the parties' pre-existing obligation to abstain from acts which might prejudice the outcome of the case or otherwise aggravate or extend the dispute (in the expression of the Permanent Court in the *Electricity Company of Sofia and Bulgaria* case), then that might provide support for a view that indications of interim measures are legally binding. This view was put forward in 1929 by Elihu Root, who said:

The parties to a case, when they submitted their controversy to the Court, might be regarded as having come under an obligation not to destroy the subject matter of their controversy or in any way to anticipate the judgment of the Court by action of their own. Such an obligation was implied in their acceptance of the jurisdiction of the Court. Under Article 41 of the Statute, the Court would merely indicate what

---

[534] *Behring International, Inc.* v. *Iranian Air Force* (1985) 8 CTR 238, at 275, but this was a case dealing with preservation of property, for which Article 26 of the UNCITRAL Rules specifically provides, as was *United Technologies International, Inc.* v. *Iran* (1986) 13 CTR 254. See also *Iran* v. *US* (1984) 5 CTR 112; *Bendone-Derossi International* v. *Iran* (1984) 6 CTR 130. See generally Caron, 'Interim Measures of Protection: Theory and Practice in Light of the Iran–United States Claims Tribunal', 46 *Zeitschrift für Auslandisches Offentliches Recht und Völkerrecht* 465 (1986). [535] See Sztucki, p. 264.

the duty of the parties required and what action was necessary if the parties conformed with the obligations involved by their submission to the Court.[536]

It is true that the International Court, when it indicates interim measures, routinely includes an indication in its formal Order that the parties 'should each ensure that no action is taken which might prejudice the rights of the other Party in respect of the carrying out of any decision on the merits which the Court may subsequently render' or 'which might aggravate or extend the dispute submitted to the Court'.[537]

In an unpublished paper (shortly to be included in a volume of his collected works) Sir Hersch Lauterpacht, who had an enormous influence on the development of the law of interim measures in the International Court, did not accept the view that measures indicated under Article 41 are binding on the basis that Article 41 embodies a general principle of law that the parties are under an obligation not to conduct themselves so as to render the eventual judgment of the Court impossible of execution. His view was that the legal consequences of liability in public international law are generally limited to the obligation to pay damages, and therefore there is no such occurrence in the international sphere as irreparable damage. He expressed a more cautious view in his great published work[538] on the International Court:

> While the Statute, in using studiously restrained language on the subject, seems to negative the notion of a binding effect of conservatory measures as a matter of legal obligation, the caution with which the Court administers this Article of the Statute suggests that outright denial of any binding effect of conservatory measures may be misleading. It cannot be lightly assumed that the Statute of the Court or a legal instrument contains provisions relating to any merely moral obligations of States and that the Court weighs minutely the circumstances which permit it to issue what is no more than an appeal to the moral sense of the parties . . . Whatever may be the answer—and none is here ventured—to this question, it ought to be clear that a party acts at its peril and that the Order must be regarded at least as a warning estopping a party from denying knowledge of any probable consequences of its action.

Sir Gerald Fitzmaurice as a judge of the International Court was thought by many to have erred on the side of caution, if not of reaction, but writing

---

[536] Quoted in Sztucki, p. 79; for a similar view see Dumbauld, p. 169.

[537] *Anglo-Iranian Oil Co.* case (*Request for the Indication of Interim Measures of Protection*), *ICJ Reports 1951* 89, at p. 93. See also *Fisheries Jurisdiction* cases, *ICJ Reports 1972* 12, at 17; 30, at 35; *Nuclear Tests* cases, *ICJ Reports 1973* 99, at 106; 135, at 142; *Diplomatic and Consular Staff* case, *ICJ Reports 1979* 7, at 21 (only the second part of the formula); *Military and Paramilitary Activities* case, *ICJ Reports 1984* 169, at 187; *Frontier Dispute* case, *ICJ Reports 1986* 3, at 11–12.

[538] *Development of International Law by the International Court* (1958), pp. 253–254.

at a time before he became a member of the Court, he expressed a view which, it is suggested, makes much sense:

The whole logic of the jurisdiction to indicate interim measures entails that, when indicated, they are binding—for this jurisdiction is based on the absolute necessity, when the circumstances call for it, of being able to preserve, and to avoid prejudice to, the rights of any parties, as determined by the final judgment of the Court. To indicate special measures for that purpose, if the measures, when indicated, are not even binding (let alone enforceable), lacks all point, except in so far as the parties may be expected to give a voluntary compliance to the Order of the Court.[539]

There can be little doubt, however, that the preponderant view is that an indication of interim measures is not binding.[540]

This controversy may perhaps be of a somewhat esoteric character in view of the abysmal record of respect for, and compliance with, measures of protection indicated by the International Court. In the majority of the cases since the Second World War in which interim measures were requested, the Respondent State did not appear in the proceedings.[541] In most of the cases in which interim measures were granted the Respondent State ignored them.[542]

There is of course an explanation for the disparity between the numbers of applications for interim measures by Claimant States, on the one hand, and, on the other hand, the lack of respect shown for the Court and its orders by Respondent States. A Claimant, well knowing that the order may be ineffective, nevertheless desires a judicial forum for its grievances, and a political forum in which to complain of the Respondent's disregard of

---

[539] *Law and Procedure of the International Court of Justice* (1986), pp. 548–549, first published in (1958) 34 BYIL 1. Cf. Rosenne, *Law and Practice of the International Court* (2nd rev. ed., 1985), p. 427. See also Hambro, 'The Binding Character of the Provisional Measures Indicated by the International Court of Justice', in *Wehberg Festschrift*, p. 164.

[540] See for many references Sztucki, pp. 262–293. Cf. World Bank Convention on the Settlement of Investment Disputes between States and Nationals of Other States, Art. 47: an ICSID tribunal may only 'recommend' provisional measures. The *travaux préparatoires* show that the expression 'recommend' was deliberately preferred to the word 'prescribe'. See *supra*, Section VII.

[541] See *Anglo-Iranian Oil Co.* case, *ICJ Reports 1951* 89; *Fisheries Jurisdiction* cases, *ICJ Reports 1972* 12 and 30; *Nuclear Tests* cases, *ICJ Reports 1973* 99 and 135; *Pakistani Prisoners of War* case, *ICJ Reports 1973* 328; *Aegean Sea Continental Shelf* case, *ICJ Reports 1976* 3; *Diplomatic and Consular Staff* case, *ICJ Reports 1979* 7.

[542] *Anglo-Iranian Oil Co.* case; *Fisheries Jurisdiction* cases; *Nuclear Tests* cases; *Diplomatic and Consular Staff* case; but no complaint was made of non-compliance with the order in the *Nicaragua* case; and in the *Frontier Dispute* case both parties had requested provisional measures. See Oxman, 'Jurisdiction and the Power to Indicate Provisional Measures', in *The International Court of Justice at a Crossroad* (ed. Damrosch, 1987), pp. 323–354, who also points out (p. 344), that one result of the orders was the withdrawal of acceptance of compulsory jurisdiction by Iran and France following, respectively, the *Diplomatic and Consular Staff* and *Nuclear Tests* cases. But their failure to appear showed the value of their acceptance.

the Court's judgment. The most obvious modern examples are the cases concerning the *Diplomatic and Consular Staff in Tehran* and the *Nuclear Tests* in the Pacific. Conversely, the Respondent State, in an effort to weaken the legal and political effect of the Court's judgment, and to avoid even the appearances of a submission to its jurisdiction (although an opposition to interim measures or an objection to jurisdiction can in no way be regarded in law as a submission) will not take a direct part in the proceedings and will flout the Court's authority.

3. JURISDICTION ON THE MERITS

Against this background the very well documented question of the extent to which the Court must satisfy itself that it has jurisdiction on the merits before it indicates provisional measures may seem arid. This question has been the subject of an exhaustive literature,[543] and it is not necessary for present purposes to do more than indicate that the International Court has adopted an approach that it has jurisdiction to grant interim remedies if the absence of jurisdiction is not manifest and if the instrument said by the claimant to confer jurisdiction on the Court prima facie does so. This approach was ultimately derived from Sir Hersch Lauterpacht, particularly his contribution to the argument of Sir Frank Soskice for the United Kingdom in the *Anglo-Iranian Oil Co.* case,[544] and his separate opinion in the *Interhandel* case.[545]

More stringent tests have been asserted in several separate and dissenting opinions, particularly in the *Anglo-Iranian Oil Co.* case, the *Nuclear Test* case and *Aegean Sea Continental Shelf* case. There are those who appear to be unhappy with a mere 'prima facie' condition of jurisdiction over the merits, such as Judges Jiménez de Aréchaga[546] and Nagendra Singh,[547] but who do not, however, put forward an alternative and workable test. On the other hand, there are several dissenting opinions in cases where interim measures were indicated which assert that the Court must be *satisfied* that it has jurisdiction over the merits before it indicates interim measures. The most eloquent proponent of this view has been

---

[543] Among which particular reference must be made to Mendelson, 'Interim Measures of Protection in Cases of Contested Jurisdiction', (1972–1973) 46 BYIL 259; Merrills, 'Interim Measures of Protection and the Substantive Jurisdiction of the International Court', [1977] *CLJ* 86, and to Sztucki, pp. 221–259.

[544] *ICJ Pleadings*, p. 401; see Mendelson, p. 269.

[545] *ICJ Reports 1957* at 118.

[546] *Nuclear Tests* cases, *ICJ Reports 1973* 99, at 107; 135, at 143; *Aegean Sea Continental Shelf* case, *ICJ Reports 1976* 3, at 16.

[547] *Aegean Sea Continental Shelf* case, at 118; contrast *Nuclear Tests* cases, at 108, 145. Cf. also *Aegean Sea Continental Shelf* case, at 20 (Judge Lachs), 32 (Judge Tarazi).

Judge Gros in the *Nuclear Tests* case.[548] An intermediate view was expressed in the well-known joint dissenting opinion of Judges Winiarski and Badawi Pasha in the *Anglo-Iranian Oil Co.* case, to the effect that:

the Court ought not to indicate interim measures of protection unless its competence, in the event of this being challenged, appears to the Court to be nevertheless reasonably probable.[549]

Nevertheless, the now prevailing opinion is the prima facie test first expressed by the majority in that case. The formulations vary, but the essence is that the Court will not act if its lack of jurisdiction is manifest,[550] but that

on a request for provisional measures the Court need not, before deciding whether or not to indicate them, finally satisfy itself that it has jurisdiction on the merits of the case, or as the case may be, that an objection taken to jurisdiction is well-founded yet it ought not to indicate such measures unless the provisions invoked by the Applicant appear, prima facie, to afford a basis on which the jurisdiction of the Court might be founded.[551]

As Judge Schwebel has pointed out, in this context whether 'might' means 'possibly might' or 'might well' or 'might probably' is a question of some controversy.[552]

The essential point, as Judges Winiarski and Badawi Pasha pointed out 40 years ago, is that *ex hypothesi* the Court is asked to indicate interim measures before it has decided whether it has jurisdiction over the merits. Moreover, and most important, if ultimately the Court decides it has no jurisdiction there will be no other international (or any) tribunal in which the dispute may be decided. Consequently, since the jurisdiction over States remains (however regrettably) only with their consent, if the Court has indicated interim measures in a case where it has no jurisdiction over the merits it will have acted without the Respondent State's consent.

In the municipal sphere this does not present a serious problem. Most parties to litigation are private persons or corporations, and when a State is a party it is usually (although not necessarily) the local sovereign. There is therefore not usually an impediment to a grant of provisional measures pending a final determination of jurisdiction. Thus in England section 24 of the Civil Jurisdiction and Judgments Act 1982 provides that a court may

---

[548] *ICJ Reports 1973* 99, at 119–123; 135, at 153–158. See also Judges Forster (111–112), Petren (125, 160); *Pakistani Prisoners of War* case *ICJ Reports 1973* 328, at 334 (Judge Petren). [549] *ICJ Reports 1951* 89, at p. 97.

[550] *Fisheries Jurisdiction* cases, *ICJ Reports 1972* 12, at 15; 30 at 33.

[551] *Military and Paramilitary Activities in and against Nicaragua* case, *ICJ Reports 1984* 169, at 179. See also *Nuclear Tests* cases, *ICJ Reports 1973* at 101, 139; *Diplomatic and Consular Staff* case, *ICJ Reports 1979* 7, at 13; *Arbitral Award of 31 July 1989* case, *ICJ Reports 1990* 64, at 69; *Passage through the Great Belt* case, *ICJ Reports 1991* 12, at 15.

[552] *ICJ Reports 1984* at 207.

grant interim relief even if the jurisdiction of the court is doubtful and remains to be decided. Again, in municipal law, if the court finds that it has no jurisdiction, there will usually (but not necessarily) be a court in another country which does have jurisdiction. This consequence is almost invariably absent in disputes between States, where also it may take several years for the jurisdictional issues in the International Court to be decided. Thus in the notorious *Barcelona Traction* case[553] (where, however, interim measures were not sought) it took eight years for the issues of jurisdiction to be decided against Belgium, which it could have, and should have, decided, in its judgment on preliminary objections in 1964,[554] some two years after the action had been commenced.

4. THE BALANCE OF CONVENIENCE

Judges Winiarski and Badawi Pasha in the *Anglo-Iranian Oil Co.* case rightly pointed out the differences between practice in the International Court and practice in national tribunals. But what of similarities? Two cases in which interim measures were refused use reasoning which must be an almost everyday experience of national tribunals. Thus in the *Aegean Sea Continental Shelf* case[555] Greece sought an order (*inter alia*) that both Greece and Turkey should, unless with the consent of each other and pending the final judgment of the Court, refrain from all exploration activity or any scientific research, with respect to the continental shelf areas within which Turkey had granted licences, or which were otherwise in dispute. The Court held that an indication of interim measures was not appropriate because Greece had not shown that irreparable prejudice would be caused to rights which were the subject of dispute. The seismic exploration undertaken by Turkey was carried out by a vessel traversing the surface of the seas and causing small explosions to occur at intervals under water, and the purpose of those explosions was to send sound waves through the sea bed so as to obtain information regarding the geophysical structure of the earth beneath; but no complaint had been made that this form of seismic exploration involved any risk of physical damage to the sea bed or sub-soil, or to their natural resources; it did not involve the establishment of installations on or above the sea bed of the continental shelf; and no suggestion had been made that Turkey had embarked upon any operations involving the actual appropriation or other use of the natural resources of the areas of the continental shelf which were in dispute. The alleged breach by Turkey of the exclusivity of the right claimed by Greece to acquire information concerning the natural resources

---

[553] *ICJ Reports 1970* 3.   [554] *ICJ Reports 1964* 6.   [555] *ICJ Reports 1976* 3.

of areas of continental shelf, if it were established, was one that might be capable of reparation by appropriate means.[556]

More recently, Finland has brought to the International Court a dispute between Finland and Denmark relating to Denmark's project to construct a bridge (road and rail) across the strait of the Great Belt, which connects the Baltic with the Kattegatt. Finland claims that the construction of the bridge will permanently close the Baltic for drill ships and oil rigs which require more than 65 metres' clearance. It sought interim measures to the effect that Denmark should, pending the decision by the Court on the merits of the case, refrain from continuing or otherwise proceeding with such construction works as will impede the passage of ships, including drill ships and oil rigs, to and from Finnish ports and shipyards.

In its Order of 29 July 1991 the International Court refused interim measures in reasoning which will be just as familiar to municipal lawyers as to international lawyers. Denmark had given assurances that no physical obstruction would occur before the end of 1994, and in the normal course the proceedings before the Court would have concluded by that time. There was no evidence that Finland was actually suffering economic loss as a result of the continuation of the project. As a result there was no need for interim measures. But it is particularly interesting that the Court did not accede to Denmark's argument based on the availability of a remedy in damages. Denmark had argued that Finland would not ultimately be entitled to an order that the project be discontinued, or modified, or dismantled, but only to an order for damages, since restitution in kind would be excessively onerous. The Court said, however, that the prospect of such an order could not be excluded, and Denmark would have to consider itself to what extent it should delay or modify the project.[557] It would, therefore, be at Denmark's risk. By contrast, therefore, with the *Aegean Sea Continental Shelf* case, the case was decided not on grounds that damages would be an adequate remedy, but on the ground that there was no requisite degree of urgency. But by its warning the Court made it clear to Denmark that, at any rate as regards actions taken after the pronouncement of the Court, it would not be able to rely on the hardship caused by a finding that it would have to abandon or modify the project.

5. THE MERITS OF THE CLAIM

Discussion of that decision leads naturally to consideration of another issue which is common to the grant of interim protection in both municipal law

---

[556] To put it in terms of English law, damages were an adequate remedy.

[557] *Passage through the Great Belt* case, *ICJ Reports 1991* 12. See also Judge Oda, at 25–26.

and international law, namely the relevance of the merits of the underlying claim. It has already been seen[558] that all municipal systems have had to find a solution to this question, and that the solution ranges from the current English test that there merely be a serious question to be tried on the merits to the more stringent test in civil law countries that there must be a probable, or prima facie, prospect of success on the merits.

In proceedings before the International Court the question is one of particular importance for these reasons: the first is the paramountcy of the consensual basis of jurisdiction, coupled with the fact that in so many of the modern cases in which interim measures have been sought not only have Respondent States contested the jurisdiction of the International Court, but they have also not appeared before the Court to state their objections, and have usually confined themselves to extra-forensic objections, principally correspondence. In such cases for the Court to express a view on the merits, even a provisional or prima facie view, is to tread on delicate, if not dangerous, ground. On the other hand, the consequences of an indication of interim measures (if one makes, as one must, the inevitably false assumption that the indication is likely to be complied with) are such that it would be wholly wrong to place the Respondent State under the duty to comply with the indication (whether it is legal, political or moral) unless the Applicant State has, at least, a serious case. This is particularly so because (in a genuinely contested case) the length of time between the indication of interim measures of protection and the final judgment on the merits is likely to be several years.

There is no doubt that the general practice of the International Court is to treat the underlying merits as, in theory, wholly irrelevant on the application for interim measures. It is necessary to add 'in theory' because it is wholly unrealistic to suppose that the apparent merits of the case have no influence on the outcome of the application for interim measures of protection. In the *Passage through the Great Belt* case[559] Judge Shahabuddeen referred to 'the general pattern of advocacy' whereby counsel have sought, on applications for interim measures, to prove or disprove the possibility of the existence of the right claimed. In fact this is surely a pattern common to all legal systems. In England, however much in theory the only duty of the plaintiff who seeks an interlocutory injunction is to show a seriously arguable case, nevertheless he will invariably seek to show that he has a very *strong* case on the merits, if not a conclusive one, and the defendant will seek to show (as he must, if he challenges the contention that the plaintiff has an arguable case) that the plaintiff has *no* case on the merits.

Writing in 1932, Dumbauld thought:[560]

---

[558] Section I, *supra*.   [559] *ICJ Reports 1991* 12, 34.   [560] At 161. See also 168.

... a *prima facie* showing of probable right and probable injury is all that is required. In view of the need for rapidity and the provisional nature of the order, absolutely convincing proof, such as would be necessary in forming the Court's opinion on final judgment, is not necessary.

But the now prevailing view is that the merits of the underlying claim are irrelevant and that the practice of the Court does not require a 'prima facie' case to be made out on the application for interim measures. Sztucki[561] seems to be sanguine about this result, but in fact it is by no means self-evident. It should not be in doubt that if a State were to bring an apparently hopeless—one hesitates to use the English expression 'frivolous or vexatious'—claim, it would not obtain an order for interim measures. Indeed, in the *Nuclear Tests* cases the Court said[562] that the information before the Court did not 'exclude the possibility that damage to Australia [and New Zealand] might be shown to be caused by the deposit' of fall-out from the tests. This statement answered a French contention that reports of the *Australian* National Radiation Advisory Committee from 1967 to 1972 had concluded that fall-out from the French tests did not constitute a danger to the health of the population. To put it in municipal terms, the French Government was arguing that Australian documents showed that the Applicants' case was wholly without merit, and the Court was answering that the Applicants' case was at least arguable. That of course is a very low threshold on any view.

Nor can it be in doubt that the strength of the United States claim, and the grossly unlawful acts of the Iranian Government, influenced the Court to make the extraordinary and unparalleled order in the *Diplomatic and Consular Staff* case, which, after reciting the United States allegations of outrageous conduct by the Iranian authorities, said that

continuance of the situation the subject of the present request exposes the human beings concerned to privation, hardship, anguish and even danger to life and health and thus to a serious possibility of irreparable harm.[563]

Of course, this could be said to be a finding relating only to the condition of the possibility of irreparable harm, but the context clearly shows that the Court was satisfied that Iran's conduct had been contrary to norms which were a 'fundamental prerequisite for the conduct of relations between States'. Consequently, the statement by the Court that its decision in no way prejudged any questions relating to the merits was right only in the sense that its decision was not *res judicata*.[564]

These considerations explain why the merits are so often fully argued on applications for interim measures. Thus in the *Great Belt* case Denmark

---

[561] At 123.   [562] *ICJ Reports 1973* at 105, 141.
[563] *ICJ Reports 1979* 7, at 20.
[564] See *Free Zones* case, PCIJ, *Ser. A*, 13 (Order of 19 August 1929).

argued that Finland had to show that it had a reasonable prospect of success on the merits, and that in Denmark's contention Finland did not even have a prima facie case. Finland answered that it was inappropriate for Finland to establish that it had a prima facie case, but, if it did have a duty to establish a prima facie case, it had discharged it. This is of course an entirely predictable line of reasoning. When faced with an argument that a State has no case at all, only a very brave or foolhardy adviser would rest his or her argument solely on the ground that the merits are irrelevant. Both in the international and the municipal forum the advocate must in those circumstances deal with the merits (unless, of course, there are none).

Considerations akin to these lay behind the scholarly and interesting separate opinion of Judge Shahabuddeen in that case. Relying on what is in effect the normal course of counsel's argument in the International Court (and it is no different in a national court) he suggested that to indicate interim measures without requiring the requesting State to demonstrate some arguable basis for the existence of the right sought to be protected is inconsistent with the exceptional nature of the procedure for interim protection; although it is true that the Court should not prejudge the merits, it is frequently the respondent State which raises them by denying that the applicant State has any case at all (as in that case). But he concludes, not that the applicant State must show a prima facie case on the merits, but that it should (adopting Judge Anzilotti's dissenting opinion in the *Polish Agrarian Reform and German Minority* case[565]) 'establish the possible existence of the rights sought to be protected'.[566] He added that it did not much matter whether the threshold of establishing 'the possible existence' was a prima facie test, or a test based on whether there was a serious issue to be tried. The Order of the Court itself did not address the issue directly. It noted that the right of passage itself was undisputed, and that the dispute between the parties was as to its extent. It concluded, as is indeed obvious, that a disputed right is capable of protection under Article 41.

It is, of course, impossible to prove, but it is hard to imagine that it would have made any difference to the outcome of any of the cases to date in the Permanent Court or the International Court (or any serious difference to the mode of presentation of written and oral argument) if the appropriate test had been a prima facie case on the merits. Is there a case in which interim measures have been granted in which there was not at least a prima facie case on the merits? It is true that in the *Anglo-Iranian Oil Co.* case[567] the Court indicated interim measures, and then subsequently held that it had no jurisdiction over the merits. But in that case it could not

---

[565] *PCIJ, Ser. A/B, No. 58*, 175, at 181.   [566] *ICJ Reports 1991* at p. 36.
[567] *ICJ Reports 1951* 89; *ICJ Reports 1952* 93.

be said that the United Kingdom had no prima facie case on the merits, nor (it must be said) on the jurisdiction of the Court. Judges Winiarski and Badawi Pasha, dissenting, thought that at the interim measures of protection stage the Court should satisfy itself that its jurisdiction was 'reasonably probable'. But it is noteworthy that when they arrived at the provisional conclusion that the Court would ultimately hold that it had no jurisdiction, that conclusion was said to be based upon 'a consideration, entirely summary in character' of the jurisdictional grounds relied on by the United Kingdom, but the dissenting opinion is utterly devoid of the reasons which led to that conclusion.

6. THE OBJECT OF INTERIM MEASURES

The relationship between interim measures and the merits has led to some confusion, which is based on a misreading or misunderstanding of one of the many phases of the *Chorzów Factory* case. In that case the Permanent Court had held that the expropriation of the property was contrary to international law, and had also held that it had jurisdiction to determine the level of compensation because the Geneva Convention of 1922 between Poland and Germany by necessary implication conferred jurisdiction on the Court to determine the level of reparation because (in its famous words) 'it is a principle of international law that the breach of an engagement involves an obligation to make reparation in an adequate form'.[568]

Germany then applied to the Permanent Court for an indication under Article 41 that Poland should pay as a provisional measure 30 million Reichsmarks. The application was based on the theory that the principle of compensation had been recognized by the Court and that only the higher end of the amount payable could still be in doubt, and that further damage would be occasioned by delay. The German Government made it clear to the Court that if, 'contrary to all expectation', the final sum arrived at by the Court would be less than the amount sought in the application for protective measures, the Government would refund the surplus. The Permanent Court refused to accede to the request on the ground that it had the German claims under consideration for judgment on the merits and that:

. . . the request of the German Government cannot be regarded as relating to the indication of measures of interim protection, but as designed to obtain an interim judgment in favour of a part of the claim . . .[569]

---

[568] *Ser. A, No. 9*, 4 at 21. [569] *Ser. A, No. 12*, 4 at 10.

The Court was doing nothing more, here, than deciding that Germany was in substance applying for what in English law is called interim damages (the *référé-provision* of French law), and that Article 41 could not be used as a basis for an award (however provisional) of interim damages. The Permanent Court did not decide that the mere fact that the applicant State seeks the same remedy in the interim measures phase as it seeks on the merits precludes the indication of interim measures.

It has already been seen that, in the context of jurisdiction of municipal courts, there is considerable doubt whether an order for interim damages is a provisional or protective measure under Article 24 of the Brussels Convention of 1968.[570] The reason is not that the remedy in some way parallels the final judgment sought by the plaintiff, but that it requires some form of determination on the merits: 'Il ne s'agit plus d'une mesure d'attente mais d'une mesure qui devance ce que pourra éventuellement décider le tribunal.'[571]

Frequently in municipal law an interlocutory injunction or *ordonnance de référé* parallels the final order sought. This is particularly so if the defendant has unlawfully (at least prima facie) altered the situation as between the parties, and the plaintiff seeks an interim remedy to preserve the status quo pending trial of the action. A court may grant a provisional order preventing the defendant from encroaching on the plaintiff's land, or from passing off the defendant's products as the plaintiff's, or from terminating an exclusive supply agreement. It is not necessary to give further examples, for such orders are the everyday experience of all municipal courts.

In such cases the plaintiff is under a duty to ensure that the defendant is not prejudiced if the order is granted, and if, after trial, the plaintiff is held not to have been entitled to the remedy. In English law the plaintiff has to undertake to the court (the 'cross-undertaking in damages') that, if the injunction is subsequently decided to have been unjustifiably granted, he will pay such compensation to the defendant as the court may order. Sometimes the cross-undertaking has to be reinforced by security, such as a bank guarantee. Other systems of law provide similar, although not identical, methods of protection for the defendant. In France, Germany and Italy the court may award damages to a defendant who has suffered loss through the injunction, if the plaintiff loses on the merits. Under United States federal procedure the plaintiff must post a bond to secure his liability to compensate the defendant if he is found to have been wrongfully enjoined or constrained.[572]

---

[570] *Supra*, Section III.

[571] Perrot, 'Les mesures provisoires en droit français', in *Les mesures provisoires en procédure civile* (ed. Tarzia, 1985), at p. 161.

[572] See the interesting discussion by 4 members of the United States Supreme Court in

Indeed, such is the universality of these methods of protection that in the *Passage through the Great Belt* case[573] Denmark argued that Finland should be required to furnish security to safeguard Denmark against any loss which might be suffered if the International Court were to indicate that the construction of the bridge should be halted. Denmark argued that protection against potentially unjustified provisional measures was a general principle of law. Since the Court did not indicate interim measures in that case, it did not have to consider or decide the question whether the Court would compensate (and secure the compensation for) a party for any injury suffered in complying with an interim measure should the measure be found to have been unjustified.

There can be little doubt that a principle of compensation for the unjustified grant of an injunction in private litigation is a general principle of law. Whether it is a general principle in claims in domestic courts by a State will require comparative research outside the scope of this paper. Indeed in England it was the practice until 1974 for the Government not to be required to give a cross-undertaking in damages even when it was asserting a private right.[574] But there is an obvious justice in requiring an applicant State to be responsible for damage suffered, and perhaps even to give security, as a condition for the indication of interim measures. Dumbauld suggested that the power to make the indication of interim measures dependent on the furnishing of security was implied, and in any event 'since the Court can withhold relief entirely, it may impose conditions necessary in the interest of justice'.[575]

But where the plaintiff seeks to preserve the status quo by means of provisional measures the remedy will frequently be the same remedy that will be sought on the hearing of the merits. It has been suggested above that the *Chorzów Factory* case decided nothing more than that a provisional payment of compensation is not a provisional or protective measure because Germany was merely seeking to have part of its final judgment on account. Dumbauld[576] seems to have thought that an indication in the form of an injunction was an exception to the principle, because the requesting State would be asking the Court to exercise 'police jurisdiction' to forbid a flagrant wrong. But in fact it is the *référé-provision*

Connecticut v. *Doehr*, 111 S. Ct. 2105 (1991) of the question whether due process *requires* that a plaintiff who attaches real estate must post a bond to protect a defendant.

[573] *ICJ Reports 1991* 12.

[574] *Hoffmann-La Roche & Co. AG* v. *Secretary of State for Trade and Industry* [1975] AC 295, in which it was decided that the Crown could be required to give an undertaking in damages (but not where it sought to enforce the law of the land). See now *Kirklees BC* v. *Wickes Building Supplies Ltd.* [1991] 4 All ER 240, CA, discussed *supra*, Section XIII.

[575] p. 162; see also Elkind, pp. 57, 238–241 (who also suggests that the new Article 75 (2) provides an independent basis for an indication to the requesting State that it should provide security). [576] pp. 163–164.

or interim damages order which is the exceptional remedy. It is perfectly normal for a court to order the preservation of the status quo while the plaintiff seeks to establish that it should not only be preserved pending trial, but should continue thereafter on the basis that the status quo is the lawful condition, and the change which the defendant seeks is an unlawful interference with the status quo.

Consequently, despite the protests of Judges Gros and Forster in the *Nuclear Tests* cases,[577] the fact that Australia and New Zealand sought to prevent nuclear testing in the principal claim did not debar them from seeking interim measures of protection in the same sense pending determination of that claim. Accordingly, in spite of Sztucki's misgivings,[578] the International Court was absolutely right when it said in the *Diplomatic and Consular Staff* case[579] that the *Chorzów Factory* case[580] was no impediment to its order in that case, because

. . . a request for provisional measures must by its very nature relate to the substance of the case since, as Article 41 expressly states, their object is to preserve the respective rights of either party; and . . . in the present case the purpose of the United States request appears to be not to obtain a judgment, interim or final, on the merits of its claims but to preserve the substance of the rights which it claims *pendente lite.*

There is therefore nothing exceptional or contrary to principle for a State which wishes either to preserve the status quo pending action, or to temporarily undo a violent or sudden alteration of the status quo (as happened in Tehran), to seek at the interim measures stage the same remedy that it seeks on the merits. These were the objects of the applicant States in these cases (and in the *Fisheries Jurisdiction, Military and Paramilitary Activities, Aegean Sea Continental Shelf*, and *Passage through the Great Belt* cases) and there was nothing objectionable in their pursuing these objects.

Conversely, when the interim measures are wholly unrelated to the principal claim, they will not be granted. Guinea-Bissau instituted proceedings against Senegal in respect of a dispute concerning the existence and validity of an arbitral award delimiting their maritime boundary, but it failed in its application for an indication that both parties should abstain from action in the disputed area. The object of the application was to prevent the Senegalese Navy operating in the area. Guinea-Bissau alleged that the Senegalese Navy had boarded fishing vessels and had attempted to enforce its own fishing regulations. Senegal

---

[577] *ICJ Reports 1973* 99 at 123, 113; 135 at 158.
[578] pp. 95–96.   [579] *ICJ Reports 1979* 7, at 16.
[580] The International Court incorrectly characterized the German application as intended to obtain a 'final' judgment on part of the claim.

accepted that it had done so, and relied on the presumptive validity of the arbitral award. But the International Court refused interim measures because the case was about the existence or validity of the arbitration award, and not about the respective rights of the parties in the maritime areas in question. Accordingly, the alleged rights sought to be made the subject of the provisional measures were not the subject of the proceedings before the Court on the merits of the case, and any such measures could not be subsumed by the court's judgment on the merits. A decision that the award was non-existent or null and void would in no way entail any decision that the applicant's claims in respect of the disputed maritime delimitation were well founded in whole or in part, and the dispute over those claims would not, therefore, be resolved by the Court's judgment.[581]

Judge Shahabuddeen, in his separate opinion, correctly pointed out that it was not necessary that there be a direct connection between the rights claimed in the principal claim and the remedy sought in the application for interim measures. Thus in several cases the principal claim sought only a declaration as to rights, while the application for interim measures sought a form of order similar to an injunction.[582] The appropriate test was whether the subject of the application was to protect the rights in dispute in the proceedings.[583]

---

[581] *ICJ Reports 1990* 64. Cf. the decision by the ICSID Tribunal in *Amco Asia* v. *Indonesia* (1985) 24 ILM 365, in which the Tribunal held that the power in Article 47 of the World Bank Convention to recommend provisional measures to preserve rights of the parties refers to the rights in dispute, and not other rights.

[582] *Anglo-Iranian Oil Co.* case, *ICJ Reports 1951* 89; *Fisheries Jurisdiction* case, *ICJ Reports 1972* 12.

[583] See *Polish Agrarian Reform*, PCIJ, Ser. A/B, No. 58, 175, at 177. Contrast *Aegean Sea Continental Shelf* case, *ICJ Reports 1976* 3, at p. 11.

Conclusions

It would not be useful to re-state or summarize what has gone before. But some common themes and problems have, it is hoped, emerged. There can be no doubt that the procedural power to grant provisional or protective measures reflects a general principle of law, and that principle nowadays is based on the need to prevent the judgment of the court from being prejudiced or frustrated by the actions of the parties. That general principle of law is reflected in the practice of national courts, administrative bodies, arbitral tribunals, and international courts.

The existence of a general principle of law does not mean that provisional or protective remedies are provided in the same cases and under the same conditions in every country. In particular, practice as to the relevance of the underlying merits differs. In most countries the applicant must show that he has a prima facie case on the merits, but in some countries (England and those that follow it) he must show merely that there is a serious case to be tried; and the International Court of Justice claims to pay no attention to the merits of the case when deciding on interim measures. Yet it would be wholly unrealistic to suppose that the merits are not in fact taken into account even in those systems in which, in theory, they play no part, or only a small part. No court can fail to be influenced by the plea of a litigant with all the merits on his side.

Nor is there a uniform practice with regard to the provision of security by the party in whose favour protection is granted. For it is inherent in the system of protective measures that the final decision may go against that party; and the party whose freedom of action is inhibited by temporary measures is normally given some recourse if it transpires that the measures were not justified by the merits of the case. It is to be hoped that this contribution may stimulate further research into this important, but neglected, field, especially as it has recently been the subject of inconclusive discussion in the United States Supreme Court and in the International Court of Justice.

Whether protective measures may be granted when the jurisdiction of the court on the merits of the case is not yet established is a question of general importance. National courts should have no hesitation in granting them in such circumstances, because the delay involved in resolving the issue of jurisdiction may make protective measures essential. The position in international tribunals is more delicate. For normally if the tribunal does not have jurisdiction over the merits, then no other tribunal will have jurisdiction. In such a case to grant measures of interim protection against a respondent State may have the effect of prejudging jurisdiction on the merits. But to refuse interim measures whenever a Respondent State challenged the jurisdiction might be manifestly unjust to a claimant. This tension has led to a divergence of approach, although the dominant practice, especially in the International Court of Justice (and following it, the Iran–US Claims Tribunal), has been to provide interim protection unless the lack of jurisdiction over the merits is manifest.

Where national courts or arbitral tribunals are available in more than one country, then there is no reason in principle why parties should not resort to a court for protective measures even if the court of another country, or an arbitral tribunal, has jurisdiction over the merits. There is no doubt that, exemplified by Article 24 of the Brussels and Lugano Conventions, the trend is towards the availability of interim protection in one country in aid of proceedings on the substance in another country. There is a similar trend when arbitration is pending in another country, although in the United States the courts have shown some resistance to providing interim protection if the parties have agreed to arbitration, and in England the courts have recently shown a similar resistance to act in aid of arbitration proceedings abroad. ICSID arbitration is in a special position, because the right of an investor to bring claims against a State in an ICSID tribunal may have, as its *quid pro quo*, the exclusion of the right to resort to domestic courts.

Nor can there be any doubt that protective measures may be given extra-territorial effect, provided that they do not overstep the boundaries of jurisdiction under international law. If the case has some appropriate connection with the forum, and the court does not seek to control the activities of foreigners abroad, the extension of protective measures to assets abroad is justifiable under international law. That does not mean that foreign courts will necessarily recognize those measures, although there can now be discerned an emerging trend towards recognition.

Finally, the practice of the European Court of Human Rights and the European Court of Justice shows clearly how the power of national courts to grant interim measures may be *limited* by fundamental rights, or, conversely, may be *required* in order to protect similar rights. It is a fundamental principle of law that a party should not normally be deprived of his rights without a fair hearing. All systems of law allow *ex parte* orders to be made if the case is sufficiently urgent and if irreparable harm might be suffered by the applicant if the application is notified to the opposing party. But they are now subject to the scrutiny not only of the due process clause of the United States Constitution, but also to the equally fundamental values of the European Convention on Human Rights. Two years after the European Court of Human Rights in Strasbourg subjected the English 'search and seizure' *Anton Piller* orders to scrutiny, the European Court of Justice in Luxembourg decided that the effectiveness of Community law required that national courts had a duty to set aside special rules of national law which might prevent them from granting interim relief. It is therefore apparent that one of the striking characteristics of the modern European system is the development, to which this author has endeavoured to bring attention in this contribution, of the central importance of provisional and protective measures in modern international litigation.

II

The Territorial Reach of *Mareva* Injunctions

This article explored the ramifications of those important decisions in 1988 on the extraterritorial effect of *Mareva* injunctions. Since the decisions in *Babanaft International Co. SA* v. *Bassatne* [1990] Ch. 13 (CA), *Derby & Co. Ltd.* v. *Weldon (No. 1)* [1990] Ch. 48 (CA), *(Nos. 3 & 4)* [1990] Ch. 65 (CA), and *Republic of Haiti* v. *Duvalier* [1990] 1 QB 202 (CA), many worldwide *Mareva* injunctions have been granted. In *Derby & Co. Ltd.* v. *Weldon (No. 6)* [1990] 1 WLR 1139 (CA), discussed *ante*, p. 89, the Court of Appeal decided that the *in personam* jurisdiction could be exercised not only to restrain the transfer of foreign assets, but also to order the transfer of assets from one country to another, or to order the return to England of assets held in a foreign country. The ancillary disclosure orders have in many cases led to the discovery of substantial assets hidden in such countries as Switzerland, Luxembourg, and the Cayman Islands. Indeed the article suggests that in practice it is the disclosure orders which are of more value in relation to foreign assets than the *Mareva* injunction itself. In *Bank of Crete* v. *Koskotas* [1991] 1 Lloyd's Rep. 587 (CA) the Court of Appeal accepted that the court could order a party to disclose documents held on their behalf by Swiss banks, and if the party failed to obtain custody then he could be debarred from defending the action. In that case the defendant had allegedly misappropriated more than $200 million from the Bank of Crete, and a criminal investigation into the matter was proceeding in Greece. In a subsequent decision it was held by Millett J. that the court could authorise the disclosure in Greece of bank documents obtained on discovery in the course of the English proceedings. Although the court would not normally permit documents disclosed on discovery to be used other than for the purpose of recovery of the funds, the bank would not be put in an impossible position in which it had to elect between infringing its undertakings to the English court or finding itself in breach of its duty under Greek law: 'There is a need for international co-operation between the courts of different jurisdictions in order to deal with multi-national frauds': [1992] 1 WLR 919, 925.

> . . . some situations, which are nowadays by no means uncommon, cry out—as a matter of justice to plaintiffs—for disclosure orders and *Mareva* type injunctions covering foreign assets of defendants . . .[1]

1. INTRODUCTION: THE RESTRICTIVE APPROACH

If it is mainly a matter of subjective impression that today there is a greater tendency than in the past for debtors to default, or for those in a fiduciary

From *Law Quarterly Review*, 105 (1989), 262.

[1] Kerr LJ in *Babanaft International Co.* v. *Bassatne* [1990] Ch. 13, at 33 (CA).

position to abuse their trust, it is certain that the widespread abolition of exchange controls and the growth of offshore havens for cash and securities have made it easier for defaulters involved in international business to make themselves judgment proof, and for dishonest fiduciaries to enjoy the illegal fruits of breaches of trust. This piece is intended to examine one way in which the English courts have sought to combat this problem, by extending the *Mareva* injunction to assets abroad. Such is the pace of these developments that the Court of Appeal rendered, within the space of a month or so in the summer of 1988, three separate and fully reasoned decisions (reversing its previous practice) that *Mareva* injunctions and ancillary disclosure orders could, and in some cases should, be granted in relation to assets abroad. In the course of the judgments the Court of Appeal raised, and (at least in part) decided, some fundamental questions about the jurisdiction of the English court and the enforceability of its orders abroad. The three decisions were *Babanaft International Co. SA* v. *Bassatne*,[2] *Republic of Haiti* v. *Duvalier*[3] and *Derby & Co. Ltd.* v. *Weldon* (*No. 1*).[4] In each of these cases injunctions were granted restraining the disposal of assets abroad; in the first case the injunction was granted in aid of enforcement of a judgment of the English court which had been granted against the defendants; in the second it was granted in aid of proceedings pending against the defendants in France; and in the third it was granted in aid of proceedings pending against the defendants in England.

It is not the purpose of this article to provide an exhaustive statement of the *Mareva* practice, nor to deal with all of its international implications.[5] It is merely necessary to note, by way of introduction, that since 1975 the English courts have exercised a jurisdiction to grant injunctions (which have come to be called *Mareva* injunctions, after an early decision[6]) to restrain a defendant from removing his assets from the jurisdiction pending trial. As formulated prior to the decisions discussed here, the relevant principle was that a *Mareva* injunction could be granted if the plaintiff could show that he had a good arguable case on the merits of the action, that the defendant had assets within the jurisdiction, and that there was a

---

[2] [1990] Ch. 13 (Kerr, Neill and Nicholls L JJ).

[3] [1990] 1 QB 202 (Fox, Stocker and Staughton L JJ).

[4] [1990] Ch. 48 (May, Parker and Nicholls L JJ). The important decision in *Derby & Co. Ltd.* v. *Weldon* (*Nos. 3 & 4*) [1990] Ch. 65 (CA) was rendered after this article was ready for press, but it has been possible to incorporate references to it. The court consisted of Lord Donaldson MR and Neill and Butler-Sloss L JJ.

[5] Some of them are discussed in Collins (1981) 1 Yb. Eur. L. 249; see also McLachlan (1987) 36 ICLQ 669. For the extraterritorial reach of *Anton Piller* orders (on which see n. 30, *infra*) see *Altertext Inc.* v. *Advanced Data Communications Ltd.* [1985] 1 WLR 457; cf. *Cook Industries Inc.* v. *Galliher* [1979] Ch. 439. On ancillary relief in matrimonial cases see *Hamlin* v. *Hamlin* [1986] Fam. 11 (CA).

[6] *Mareva Compania Naviera SA* v. *International Bulkcarriers SA* [1975] 2 Lloyd's Rep. 509 (CA), following *Nippon Yusen Kaisha* v. *Karageorgis* [1975] 1 WLR 1093 (CA).

real risk that a judgment in favour of the plaintiff might be unsatisfied because (for example) the defendant might remove the assets from the jurisdiction.[7]

The creation of the *Mareva* jurisdiction was not so much a step forward as the rectification of an omission or error which had stemmed from a line of authority, of which perhaps the oddest was the decision in *Lister & Co.* v. *Stubbs*,[8] to the effect that, except in proprietary claims in the strict sense, it was not possible to restrain the disposal of funds in the hands of a defendant prior to judgment. In *Lister & Co.* v. *Stubbs* a foreman had admittedly taken bribes or secret commissions from a dye-stuff supplier and invested them in land and other investments. His employers failed to obtain an interlocutory injunction restraining him from parting with them on the ground that, despite the breach of fiduciary duty, the property did not belong to the plaintiffs, who had only a monetary claim. The *Mareva* jurisdiction brought the English common law (and those jurisdictions which follow it) into line with the practice of civil law countries (the *saisie-conservatoire* and similar remedies) and of the United States (the writ of attachment), and provided a remedy where one should always have been available. It is at least understandable (though not fully justifiable) why a note of self-congratulation crept into the judgments of the Court of Appeal in the 1970s and 1980s. For example, the *Mareva* innovation is, it has been said, 'one of the most imaginative, important, and, on the whole, most beneficent of modern times'.[9]

In 1977, in *The Siskina*[10] the House of Lords gave only mild support to the *Mareva* jurisdiction in a decision to which it will be necessary to revert. What is clear from that decision is that the juridical basis of the *Mareva* injunction is the statutory power now contained in section 37(1) of the Supreme Court Act 1981 to grant an injunction 'in all cases in which it appears to the court to be just and convenient to do so.' Section 37(3) gives express statutory recognition to the *Mareva* jurisdiction by providing that the power of the court under section 37(1):

to grant an interlocutory injunction restraining a party to any proceedings from removing from the jurisdiction of the High Court, or otherwise dealing with, assets located within that jurisdiction shall be exercisable in cases where that party is, as well as cases where he is not, domiciled, resident or present within that jurisdiction.

---

[7] See especially *Rasu Maritima SA* v. *Pertamina* [1978] QB 644 (CA); *Third Chandris Shipping Corp.* v. *Unimarine SA* [1979] QB 654 (CA); *Z Ltd.* v. *A–Z* [1982] QB 558 (CA); *Ninemia Corp.* v. *Trave GmbH* [1983] 1 WLR 1412 (CA), and for the practice generally Gee and Andrews, *Mareva Injunctions: Law and Practice* (1987).

[8] (1890) 45 Ch. D. 1. See also *Mills* v. *Northern Railway of Buenos Ayres Co.* (1870) 5 Ch. App. 621; *Robinson* v. *Pickering* (1881) 16 Ch. D. 660.

[9] *Deutsche Schachtbau* v. *R'as al Khaimah National Oil Co.* [1990] 1 AC 295, at p. 317, *per* Sir John Donaldson MR, revd. on other grounds IBID. p. 329.

[10] *The Siskina* v. *Distos Compania Naviera SA* [1979] AC 210.

The reference to 'assets within that jurisdiction', i.e. in England and Wales, makes it necessary to refer to the object of section 37(3), which was to ensure that a defendant who was within the jurisdiction was not in a more favourable position than a person outside the jurisdiction. Several of the early *Mareva* cases had seemed to suggest that the injunction was available only where the defendant was outside the jurisdiction,[11] but even before section 37(3) was enacted to remove this discrimination the courts had held that the *Mareva* jurisdiction applied even to defendants within the jurisdiction.[12] It should be noted that the abolition of exchange controls in 1979 made the disposal abroad of English assets owned by English-based defendants much easier than it had been in the days of stringent (though frequently broken) exchange controls.

Two other aspects of the *Mareva* jurisdiction are relevant in the present context. First, in *Bekhor & Co.* v. *Bilton*[13] the Court of Appeal held that the court had power under what is now section 37 of the Supreme Court Act 1981 to order the defendant to provide information about his assets. As Ackner LJ put it, the court has 'power to make all such ancillary orders as appear to the court to be just and convenient to ensure that the exercise of the *Mareva* jurisdiction is effective to achieve its purpose'.[14] This power is frequently and usefully used to find (and sometimes, in the strict sense, trace) assets which might otherwise be hidden or spirited out of the jurisdiction without the knowledge of the plaintiff.

The second general point is that it has frequently been said that the *Mareva* injunction does not operate as an attachment on property, but is relief *in personam*, which restrains the owner of the assets from dealing with them.[15] In *Z Ltd.* v. *A–Z*[16] Lord Denning MR, however, suggested that the *Mareva* injunction operated *in rem* just as the arrest of a ship does, and like the old process of foreign attachment in England[17] and in the United States,[18] and like the *saisie-conservatoire* of civil law countries, it

---

[11] See, e.g., *Rasu Maritima SA* v. *Pertamina* [1978] QB 644 (CA); *The Agrabele* [1979] 2 Lloyd's Rep. 117.

[12] See *Bekhor & Co.* v. *Bilton* [1981] QB 923, at pp. 936–937 (CA), and cases cited there.

[13] [1981] QB 923 (CA).

[14] At p. 940. See also *Z Ltd.* v. *A–Z* [1982] QB 558 (CA). In a tracing claim it had been held that an order could be made against a bank to give discovery of accounts held for allegedly fraudulent defendants: *Bankers Trust Co.* v. *Shapira* [1980] 1 WLR 1274 (CA). See also *A.* v. *C.* [1981] QB 956.

[15] See, e.g., *Cretanor Maritime Co. Ltd.* v. *Irish Marine Management Ltd.* [1978] 1 WLR 966 (CA); *Iraqi Ministry of Defence* v. *Arcepey Shipping Co. SA* (*The Angel Bell*) [1981] QB 65; *Derby & Co. Ltd.* v. *Weldon* (*Nos. 3 and 4*) [1990] Ch. 65 (CA).

[16] [1982] QB 558, at p. 573 (CA).

[17] For the history of foreign attachment, which became obsolete in England by the late nineteenth century, but thrived in the United States, see the discussion by the US Supreme Court in *Ownby* v. *Morgan*, 256 US 94, at p. 104 (1921) and by Lord Denning MR in *Rasu Maritima SA* v. *Pertamina* [1978] QB 644, at pp. 657–658 (CA).

[18] But the decision of the US Supreme Court in *Shaffer* v. *Heitner*, 433 US 186 (1977) severely limited the use of what by then had become known in the United States as quasi-in

had the effect of attaching any effects of the defendant within the jurisdiction. In *Babanaft*[19] Kerr LJ recognised that Lord Denning's statements might well have gone too far, but accepted there could be no doubt that *Mareva* injunctions had a direct effect on third parties who were notified of them and who held assets comprised in the order.

The reason for the effect on third parties is the principle that a person who, knowing of an injunction, aids and abets the party enjoined in committing a breach of it, is guilty, not of a breach of the injunction, but of a contempt of court tending to obstruct the course of justice. The principle was established when one Edwin Murray was committed to prison for a month for putting on a boxing contest at 53 Fetter Lane knowing that the under-lessee had been enjoined from holding on the premises boxing contests which had been advertised under the name of meetings of the Queensberry Sports Club Ltd.[20] It was firmly applied in the context of *Mareva* injunctions to banks in *Z Ltd.* v. *A–Z,*[21] when in a judgment of enormous practical importance for the commercial community, Lord Denning MR said:[22]

. . . once a bank is given notice of a *Mareva* injunction affecting goods or money in its hands, it must not dispose of them itself, nor allow the defendant or anyone else to do so—except by the authority of the court. If the bank or any of its officers should knowingly assist in the disposal of them, it will be guilty of a contempt of court. For it is an act calculated to obstruct the course of justice . . . As soon as the bank is given notice of the *Mareva* injunction, it must freeze the defendant's bank account. It must not allow any drawings to be made on it . . . The reason is because, if it allowed any such drawings, it would be obstructing the course of justice—as prescribed by the court which granted the injunction—and it would be guilty of a contempt of court.

Throughout the early history of the *Mareva* jurisdiction it was stated to apply, or assumed to apply, to cases where the defendant had assets within the jurisdiction, and where there was a real risk that the assets might be removed abroad or otherwise dissipated.[23] This assumption underlies the reference in section 37(3) of the Supreme Court Act 1981 to the jurisdiction to grant an injunction 'restraining a party to any proceedings from removing from the jurisdiction of the High Court, or otherwise dealing with, *assets located within that jurisdiction*' (emphasis added).

rem jurisdiction, i.e. the attachment of assets to *found* the jurisdiction of the court, rather than merely to preserve assets within the jurisdiction. See also *Rush* v. *Savchuk*, 444 US 320 (1980), and the discussion in Scoles and Hay, *Conflict of Laws* (1982), pp. 236–252.

[19] [1990] Ch. at p. 25. Cf. *Att.-Gen.* v. *Newspaper Publishing plc* [1988] Ch. 333 at p. 343, 343, revd. on other grounds *ibid.*, 350.

[20] *Seaward* v. *Paterson* [1897] 1 Ch. 545; Kerr, *Injunctions* (Paterson, 6th ed., 1927), p. 675.   [21] [1982] QB 558 (CA).   [22] At pp. 573–574.

[23] See, e.g., *Third Chandris Shipping Corp.* v. *Unimarine SA* [1979] QB 645 at pp. 668–669 (CA).

The assumption also explains one aspect of the decision in *The Bhoja Trader*.[24] In that case buyers of a vessel were pursuing a claim (by arbitration in England) against sellers for breach of the sale contract. The buyers sought to prevent the sellers from calling upon, or obtaining the fruits of, a bank guarantee given by a London branch of a French bank to secure part of the price. The injunction to restrain the sellers from calling upon the bank under the guarantee was refused in conformity with the principle that the court will not normally interfere with 'the life blood of commerce' such as letters of credit and bank guarantees.[25] The court, however, would have imposed an injunction on the fruits of the guarantee, i.e. any payment actually made by the bank to the sellers, but for the fact that the guarantee provided for payment in Greece. Thus, although the obligations under the bank guarantee were situate in England (because they had been given by a bank in London) the fruits of the guarantee would have been cash situate in Greece, because 'in no real sense was the asset constituted by the right to demand payment in Greece ever within the jurisdiction'.[26] The result of *The Bhoja Trader* is commercially sound. The whole point of the seller's insistence on a bank guarantee for part of the price would have been wholly frustrated if, by alleging breach of warranty, the buyer would have been able to prevent payment of the guaranteed portion of the price. There is perhaps a confusion in the decision between the situs of the guarantee (England) and of the proceeds (Greece), but for present purposes it is sufficient to point out that the decision assumes, rather than decides, that the *Mareva* jurisdiction applies only to assets in England.

In the following years the practice developed of making disclosure orders in aid of *Mareva* injunctions, whereby the defendant was ordered to make disclosure of assets outside the jurisdiction as well as assets within it.[27] It also came to be established practice that a defendant who wished to vary a *Mareva* injunction so as to allow him ordinary living expenses had to justify the variation by (*inter alia*) making disclosure of all his assets, including overseas assets.[28] In *Bayer* v. *Winter*[29] Hoffmann J., in allowing information obtained under an Anton Piller Order[30] to be used for

---

[24] *Intraco Ltd.* v. *Notis Shipping Corp.* [1981] 2 Lloyd's Rep. 256 (CA).

[25] That this was the ratio is confirmed by *Deutsche Schachtbau* v. *R'as Al Khaimah National Oil Co.* [1990] 3 AC 295, 320 (CA), revd. on other grounds *ibid.* p. 329.

[26] [1981] 2 Lloyd's Rep. at p. 258.

[27] See, e.g., *CBS UK Ltd.* v. *Lambert* [1983] Ch. 37; *PCW (Underwriting Agencies) Ltd.* v. *Dixon* [1983] 2 All ER 158 at p. 166, and the standard form of *Mareva* order referred to in *Ashtiani* v. *Kashi* [1987] QB 888 at pp. 897–898 (CA).

[28] See, e.g., *Bekhor* v. *Bilton* [1981] QB 923 at p. 935; *Ashtiani* v. *Kashi* [1987] QB 888 at p. 901.   [29] [1986] 2 FTLR 111.

[30] See *Anton Piller KG* v. *Manufacturing Processes Ltd.* [1976] Ch. 55 (CA): this is an *ex parte* 'search and seizure' order (particularly valuable in intellectual property cases) giving the plaintiff access to the premises and documents of the defendant: for the procedure see *Supreme Court Practice* (1988) at pp. 485–488.

proceedings abroad, indicated[31] (*obiter*) that, if funds in England were inadequate to meet a plaintiff's claim, the policy of the *Mareva* injunction, to prevent disposal of assets to frustrate execution, would suggest that the court should try to make its ultimate judgment effective by assisting the plaintiff to take steps to prevent disposal in foreign jurisdictions.

The decision of the Court of Appeal in *Ashtiani* v. *Kashi*[32] represents the high-water mark of the view that the *Mareva* jurisdiction does not extend to foreign assets. This was primarily a decision about *disclosure* of assets in aid of the *Mareva* jurisdiction. All parties were Iranian citizens. The defendant brought proceedings in the United States, and succeeded in recovering a large sum of money, to part of which the plaintiffs laid claim. Subsequently, the defendant agreed to pay substantial sums of money to the plaintiffs, and on that agreement the plaintiffs sued. The defendant said that the agreement was entered into as a result of misrepresentation and under duress and without consideration. The defendant was resident in England and was served in England. The *Mareva* injunction granted by Hirst J. restrained the defendant from disposing of assets within the jurisdiction, and ordered the defendant to disclose the full value of his assets within and without the jurisdiction, identifying the nature of all such assets and their whereabouts. The defendant then disclosed the existence of bank accounts in various foreign countries, including Guernsey, Belgium and Luxembourg. The plaintiffs then obtained orders in those countries freezing the defendant's disclosed bank accounts in those countries.

The Court of Appeal, in unreserved judgments, upheld the order of Sir Neil Lawson discharging Hirst J.'s order. The court consisted of Dillon, Neill and Nicholls L JJ.[33] The leading judgment was delivered by Dillon LJ, who thought that the basis of the *Mareva* jurisdiction was 'clearly limited to assets within the jurisdiction'.[34] The limited territorial approach to the grant of *Mareva* injunctions 'as a matter of practice' was confirmed by the reference in section 37(3) of the Supreme Court Act 1981 to assets within the jurisdiction, which, he thought, clearly indicated the scope of the practice of the courts in exercising the *Mareva* jurisdiction. Neill LJ said that it was clear from the way in which the jurisdiction had been exercised since 1975 that *Mareva* injunctions were limited to restraining the dealing by a defendant with assets within the jurisdiction, and that this limitation was consistent with section 37(3) of the Supreme Court Act 1981. Nicholls LJ agreed with both judgments.

---

[31] [1986] 2 FTLR at p. 112.   [32] [1987] QB 888 (CA).

[33] The composition of the court is worthy of note, since Neill and Nicholls L JJ were members of the court in *Babanaft International SA* v. *Bassatne* [1989] 2 WLR 232 and Nicholls LJ was a member of the court in *Derby & Co. Ltd.* v. *Weldon* (*No. 1*) [1990] Ch. 48.

[34] [1987] QB at p. 899.

Dillon LJ justified the result on four grounds: first, it could very well be oppressive to the defendant that, as a result of an order of an English court, his assets everywhere should be frozen, or he should be subjected to applications for seizure orders in many other jurisdictions; secondly, it was difficult for an English court to control or police enforcement proceedings in other jurisdictions, and it was not very desirable that the English courts should attempt to control such foreign proceedings, and the difficulties were underlined where the plaintiffs were not resident within the jurisdiction of the English court; thirdly, the comment of Lord Roskill in *Home Office* v. *Harman*[35] that this involved an invasion of privacy applied with the fullest force to an order on an individual or a company to disclose all his, or its, assets throughout the world; fourthly, it had been many times laid down that the object of a *Mareva* injunction was not to give the plaintiff security for the amount of his claim in advance of judgment in the action; and, if there were an order for disclosure of foreign assets, that might lead to the plaintiff obtaining security in some foreign jurisdiction.

It cannot be said that any of these reasons is compelling. It is inherent in the nature of the *Mareva* jurisdiction that an unscrupulous plaintiff may use it to oppress the defendant. No one with any experience of its operation in practice can doubt that abuses occur.[36] But it is no objection to the provision of a remedy that *some* plaintiffs may abuse it; it is for the courts to be alert to abuses in individual cases, and to devise means to avoid them. Similarly, the whole point of obtaining a disclosure order may be to freeze the assets in foreign jurisdictions, and the fact that in some cases it may cause hardship is no ground for denying it in all cases. It is also true that it is difficult to enforce and police injunctions against foreigners relating to assets abroad. But again that is no reason for excluding the remedy altogether in cases where justice requires it. It is also true that an invasion of privacy may be involved, but it is always involved in a *Mareva* disclosure order, or in an *Anton Piller* order, or in any discovery order, but that is no reason for refusing such orders. Nor should the fact that the plaintiff may obtain security in some foreign jurisdiction be a bar to the exercise of jurisdiction. The reason of policy why the *Mareva* injunction does not give security is that otherwise it would undermine the doctrine of equality of creditors in English law. Thus in normal cases the defendant will be entitled to pay his trade creditors,[37] and even if the plaintiff succeeds in obtaining a final judgment the *Mareva* injunction will not avail him against secured creditors,[38] and he will rank equally with the other

---

[35] [1983] 1 AC 280 at p. 323.
[36] For examples see Kerr LJ in *Z Ltd.* v. *A–Z* [1982] QB 558 at p. 585 (CA).
[37] See, e.g., *Iraqi Ministry of Defence* v. *Arcepey Shipping Co. SA* (*The Angel Bell*) [1981] QB 65.
[38] *Cretanor Maritime Co. Ltd.* v. *Irish Marine Management Ltd.* [1978] 1 WLR 966 (CA).

unsecured creditors in bankruptcy. There is, however, no reason in principle why a plaintiff should be prevented from obtaining security over assets where the *lex situs* gives the creditor security.

Three further points emerge from the judgments. First, it is clear from the judgments of Dillon and Neill L JJ that their remarks are primarily directed to the ordinary type of *Mareva* case where the plaintiff's claim on the substance of the action is for debt or damages, and is not a claim to trace assets. Dillon LJ said that 'where ownership of assets, by tracing or otherwise, is in question, a different approach is warranted . . .' and that section 37(1) of the Supreme Court Act 1981 could obviously cover an injunction in respect of foreign assets where title to those assets was in question.[39] Thus where liquidators sued a director of an English company for fraud and breach of trust, the Court of Appeal upheld an order restraining him from disposing of shares in foreign companies and ordering him to disclose information about the operation of foreign companies and trusts.[40] It is not, however, clear from the report whether the claim was strictly of a proprietary nature (i.e. whether the foreign assets represented the company's property). A clearer case is *Guinness plc* v. *Saunders and Ward*,[41] where it was alleged that Ward had unlawfully received £5.2 million from Guinness and transferred it abroad. Sir Nicolas Browne-Wilkinson V.-C. made an order requiring Ward to make full disclosure of all dealings with the money, and to bring it under the control of his English solicitors.

The second general point to be made about *Ashtiani* v. *Kashi* is that, although some passages may be taken to have laid down a rule of law that there is no jurisdiction to grant *Mareva* injunctions in relation to foreign assets, there are strong indications in the judgments of Dillon and Neill L JJ that they accepted that the court had *jurisdiction* under section 37 of the Supreme Court Act 1981 to grant such injunctions, although disclosure orders relating to foreign assets would not be granted as a matter of practice or discretion except on what Dillon LJ described as 'special grounds'. One of the main objects, from the plaintiff's point of view, of a disclosure order relating to foreign assets is the opportunity it affords him of attaching those assets in the foreign jurisdiction, and this is precisely what had happened in *Ashtiani* v. *Kashi*. Dillon LJ expressed the view that:

if in a future case disclosure of foreign assets is in a proper case ordered on special grounds . . . prima facie at any rate the plaintiffs should be required to give an

---

[39] [1987] QB at pp. 899, 901. See also Neill LJ at p. 905.
[40] *Re a Company* [1985] BCLC 333.
[41] April 15, 1987, reported in *The Independent*, April 16, 1987, but not on this point. For further proceedings see [1988] 1 WLR 863 (CA).

undertaking not to use any information disclosed without the consent of the defendant or the leave of the court.[42]

2. LATER DEVELOPMENTS

The *Mareva* jurisdiction has, despite some early setbacks, been adopted widely in the Commonwealth,[43] and there have been several decisions on its territorial scope. A survey of the practice shows that the restrictive approach exemplified by *Ashtiani* v. *Kashi* has not been adopted in the Commonwealth. *Ballabil Holdings Pty. Ltd.* v. *Hospital Products Ltd.*[44] was a decision of the Court of Appeal of New South Wales, rendered before *Ashtiani* v. *Kashi*. The defendant company was being sued for damages for misrepresentation in connection with the sale of certain businesses to the plaintiff. It removed assets from New South Wales to, it seems, the United States, on the day after proceedings were commenced. On the same day a *Mareva* injunction was granted, restraining disposal of money or other assets (both in New South Wales and outside) which were the product of any of the transactions between the plaintiff and defendant. On the next day an interim receiver of the assets of the defendant company was appointed. At first instance Rogers J. held that a *Mareva* injunction could, and should, be granted, in the light of the transnational nature of international business and the ease with which the transfer of assets was daily effected, for to restrict the remedy to locally based assets would be to invite an undesirable restraint on the court's power to ensure that its orders were not stultified. In the Court of Appeal, Priestley JA agreed with Rogers J., but the majority (Street CJ and Glass JA) rested this part of the decision on the much narrower ground that the court had jurisdiction to make orders *in personam* against a defendant in relation to assets abroad, when those assets were in New South Wales when the action commenced and had since been removed. In their view it was not necessary to decide the wider question of the territorial scope of the *Mareva* jurisdiction.

It is not clear from the report of the decision in *Ballabil* whether the assets had been removed to a foreign country, or to another part of Australia, and there is no doubt that a court in a federal system might, in an appropriate case, be more prepared to make orders in relation to property in other parts of the federal state than in relation to property in politically foreign countries. Thus in *Coombs & Barei Construction Pty.*

---

[42] [1987] QB at p. 903. Both Neill and Nicholls L JJ agreed with the whole of Dillon LJ's judgment.

[43] For references to the material in Canada, Australia and New Zealand see Dicey and Morris, *Conflict of Laws* (11th ed., 1987) at p. 192.

[44] (1985) 1 NSWLR 155, affirming [1984] 2 NSWLR 662.

Ltd. v. *Dynasty Pty. Ltd.*[45] the South Australian court granted a *Mareva* injunction in relation to the defendant's assets outside South Australia, when the evidence was that the bulk of his assets was in other parts of Australia. Millhouse J. approved the approach of Rogers J. in *Ballabil* and added that it was absurd for the purposes of the *Mareva* jurisdiction that other Australian states should be regarded as foreign countries.

In *Yandil Holdings Pty. Ltd.* v. *Insurance Co. of North America*[46] plaintiffs in an insurance claim abandoned at trial what was apparently a fraudulent claim, and an order for costs was made against them. A disclosure order, requiring an affidavit as to its assets, including assets out of the jurisdiction, was made, pending taxation of costs and the levy of execution. Rogers J. thought that the reference by Dillon LJ in *Ashtiani* v. *Kashi* to 'special grounds' in which disclosure of foreign assets might be required was completely inconsistent with the tenor of the rest of Dillon LJ's judgment. But he accepted the suggestion by Dillon LJ that the person obtaining the benefit of the order should undertake not to use the information without the consent of the other parties or the leave of the court.

In Hong Kong, *Ashtiani* v. *Kashi* was not followed in *Asean Resources Ltd.* v. *Ka Wah International Merchant Finance Ltd.*,[47] where a *Mareva* injunction was granted, pending trial, restraining the disposal of shares in a Singapore company, and a receiver was appointed. Sears J. treated Dillon LJ's judgment in *Ashtiani* v. *Kashi* as deciding that there was jurisdiction to grant an order relating to foreign assets, but that in practice the order was not to be granted, and went on: 'I confess I do not understand the learned judge when he says that. If I have jurisdiction over foreign assets there must be instances where that jurisdiction will be exercised. Otherwise, the jurisdiction of the court is rendered completely powerless.'[48]

Yandil Holdings was a case of an order for disclosure in aid of a costs order following judgment. The order for costs had not yet ripened into a judgment, since taxation of costs had to be done before there was a judgment for the amount of the costs. In two cases in England orders for disclosure of foreign, as well as English, assets were made after judgment had been given against defendants. In *Interpool Ltd.* v. *Galani*[49] a judgment had been entered for over $8 million against Galani, who was

---

[45] (1986) 42 SASR 413. Cf. *Re Clunies-Ross* (1987) 72 ALR 241 (power of Federal Court in bankruptcy to restrain disposition of property in the Cocos Islands).
[46] (1987) 7 NSWLR 571.
[47] [1987] LRC (Comm.) 835. [48] At p. 840.
[49] [1988] QB 738 (CA). In *Reilly* v. *Fryer* [1988] 2 FTLR 69 (CA), a *Mareva* disclosure order in relation to foreign assets was refused, but it was wrongly conceded that *Ashtiani* v. *Kashi* applied equally after judgment as before; and the judgment creditors should have proceeded under Ord. 48.

then resident in France. When he came to England, the French judgment was registered by the judgment creditors in England under the Foreign Judgments (Reciprocal Enforcement) Act 1933.[50] Under RSC Order 48 a judgment debtor may be examined as to his assets, and the principal question was whether this power was limited to debts situate within the jurisdiction. The Court of Appeal accepted that *Ashtiani* v. *Kashi* was authority for the proposition that a *Mareva* injunction should be limited to assets within the jurisdiction and that any ancillary order for discovery should be similarly restricted. But that had no reference to the question whether a judgment debtor could be examined as to assets abroad. Accordingly the judgment debtor would be compelled to answer questions about foreign assets. In *Maclaine Watson & Co. Ltd.* v. *International Tin Council (No. 2)*[51] the plaintiffs were judgment creditors of the International Tin Council in a substantial sum. They wished to execute the judgment but had no information about the Council's assets. RSC Order 48 was held by Millett J. not to apply to an unincorporated association,[52] but he ordered disclosure of assets under the general power of section 37(1) of the Supreme Court Act 1981 to grant an injunction (including a mandatory injunction) where it was just and convenient to do so. The Court of Appeal affirmed the decision and held, applying *Interpool Ltd.* v. *Galani*, that there was no doubt that Millett J. had jurisdiction to order disclosure of the International Tin Council's assets outside the jurisdiction, as well as those within it.

It will be seen below that the approach to injunctions may be different in cases where judgment has already been given against the defendant from the position where the plaintiff has a good arguable case (or better) which has not gone to trial. In *Deutsche Schachtbau* v. *R'as Al Khaimah National Oil Co.*[53] an interlocutory injunction was granted following an order *nisi* on a foreign arbitration award under section 26 of the Arbitration Act 1950 to restrain disposal of assets of the award debtor. Sir John Donaldson MR (as he then was) suggested that, although it had been convenient to refer to the injunction as a *Mareva* injunction, it was doubtful whether it fell into that category:

The *Mareva* innovation . . . lay in giving a plaintiff some degree of protection *before* he became a judgment creditor and in anticipation that he would become one. Judgment creditors had little need of new protection since they were usually adequately protected by their right to levy execution . . . And where they were not, the court has intervened by injunction to prevent the payment to and receipt by the judgment debtor of an asset in circumstances in which it would not otherwise

---

[50] The Civil Jurisdiction and Judgments Act 1982 was not then in force.
[51] [1989] Ch. 286 (CA).   [52] [1987] 1 WLR 1711.
[53] [1990] 1 AC 295 (CA), revd. on other grounds *ibid.* p. 329.

have been available to the judgment creditor in satisfaction of the judgment debtor . . .[54]

3. *BABANAFT* AND AFTER

Such was the background in 1988 when the Court of Appeal was invited to consider the principles of the territorial scope of the *Mareva* injunction: section 37(3) of the Supreme Court Act 1981 had been enacted on the apparent understanding that the injunction was concerned with assets within the jurisdiction; there was clear authority in the Court of Appeal that it was limited to assets within the jurisdiction, at any rate prior to judgment being given against the defendant; and there was clear dissatisfaction in Commonwealth jurisdictions with that result.

The facts of each of the cases are striking. In *Babanaft International Co. SA* v. *Bassatne*[55] the judgment debtors were two Lebanese nationals; one lived mainly in Switzerland and the other mainly in Greece. After a long trial, judgment had been given against them for $15 million. They owned property in various countries (including England) through a network of companies which, in the words of Vinelott J.,[56] were 'incorporated in jurisdictions—Panama, Liberia, and the Dutch Antilles—in which it is difficult for outsiders to obtain information about their ownership, control and assets'. This is because in these countries shares in companies are generally bearer shares, whose ownership it is impossible to trace, and directors are generally nominees (such as local lawyers).

In *Republic of Haiti* v. *Duvalier*[57] the defendants were 'Baby Doc' Duvalier, who was President of Haiti from 1971 to 1986, and various members of his family. The Republic of Haiti alleged in proceedings in France that the Duvalier family had embezzled $120 million (at least) from the Republic.[58] It was found that there was a 'plain and admitted intention of the defendants to move their assets out of the reach of courts of law'. The only connection of the case with England, it seems, was that the defendants had used an English firm of solicitors to hold bank accounts and foreign securities (in each case abroad) on behalf of the defendants.

---

[54] At p. 317, citing *Bullus* v. *Bullus* (1910) 102 LT 399.
[55] [1988] 2 WLR 232 (CA).   [56] At p. 238.   [57] [1990] 1 QB 202 (CA).
[58] It is possible that in England such a claim would be contrary to public policy as being the direct enforcement by a foreign state of its rights (see Dicey and Morris, *op. cit. supra*, n. 43 at pp. 100–104, 106–109) and not merely the assertion of a 'patrimonial right' (on which see cases cited in Dicey and Morris at p. 104, n. 9). If that suggestion is right, it clearly would be arguable that interim measures in England to support such a claim would also be contrary to public policy, but the point does not seem to have been taken. The point may now be moot in view of recent political developments in Haiti.

In *Derby & Co. Ltd.* v. *Weldon (No. 1)*[59] the plaintiffs claimed that the defendants were personally responsible for the insolvency of a group of companies which had caused a loss to the second plaintiffs (of which the defendants were directors) of some £34 million. The court found that there were grounds for supposing that the defendants had acted dishonestly and that they had the ability to lock away assets in inaccessible overseas companies; and that there was a very real risk that assets in England and abroad would, by the use of foreign companies, nominee directors, bearer shares and the like, remain hidden or be spirited away, so as to render any future judgment useless.

Thus in *Babanaft* judgment had already been given; in *Republic of Haiti* proceedings on the substance of the case were pending not in England, but in France; and in *Derby & Co. Ltd.* v. *Weldon (No. 1)* proceedings were pending in England, and the restraint on disposal of assets was sought before trial. In each of the cases injunctions covering assets worldwide were granted, but subject to important conditions. In *Babanaft* the Court of Appeal made an order which was restricted to the defendants and was subject to a proviso to make it clear that third parties (such as banks) should not be affected by the order. Kerr LJ thought that it would have been more appropriate that the qualification should be that the order should not affect third parties unless and to the extent that it was enforced by the courts of the states in which any of the defendants' assets were located. In *Republic of Haiti* the Court of Appeal made a similar worldwide *Mareva*, but added a proviso in terms similar to those suggested by Kerr LJ in *Babanaft*. In *Derby & Co. Ltd.* v. *Weldon (No. 1)* the worldwide *Mareva* was also granted, in which the limitation suggested by Kerr LJ was dealt with by the plaintiffs giving to the English court an undertaking in terms which would preclude them from making any application to a foreign court to enforce the order without first obtaining leave from the English court.

The starting point for any discussion of the jurisdictional limits on *Mareva* injunctions must be section 37(1) of the Supreme Court Act 1981,[60] which gives the court power to 'grant an injunction . . . in all cases in which it appears to the court to be just and convenient to do so'. On its face this power is unlimited, and in the absence of authority there would have been grounds for arguing that once the court had *in personam* jurisdiction over the defendant, an injunction of any type might (in the discretion of the court) be granted whenever justice required it. But there is very substantial authority which puts severe limits on the jurisdiction. Not long after the passage of the Judicature Act 1873 it was held that the court had no power

---

[59] [1990] Ch. 48 (CA).
[60] For its predecessors see Judicature Act 1873, s. 25(5); Judicature Act 1925, s. 45.

to grant an interlocutory injunction except in protection of some legal or equitable right.[61] It was the application of this principle which led to the unfortunate decision in *The Siskina*,[62] where the House of Lords held that it was powerless to restrain the dissipation of a fund in England which represented the only asset of the defendant, when the proceedings on the substance of the case were pending abroad. In the *South Carolina* case[63] Lord Brandon (with whom Lord Bridge and Lord Brightman concurred) re-affirmed the principle that, although the terms of section 37(1) of the 1981 Act were very wide, the power conferred by it had been circumscribed by judicial authority dating back many years. He suggested that the power to grant injunctions was, subject to two exceptions, limited to two situations: the first was to prevent the actual or threatened invasion of a legal or equitable right; the second was to prevent behaviour (actual or threatened) which was unconscionable. The two exceptions were: first, the case where an injunction was granted to restrain the commencement or continuance of proceedings in a jurisdiction which was not the appropriate one; the second exception, given statutory recognition by section 37(1) of the Supreme Court Act 1981, may have been the *Mareva* injunction. But Lord Goff (with whom Lord Mackay agreed) said:

I am reluctant to accept the proposition that the power of the court to grant injunctions is restricted to certain exclusive categories. That power is unfettered by statute; and it is impossible for us now to foresee every circumstance in which it may be thought right to make the remedy available.[64]

What, then, are the limitations, if any, on the power to grant *Mareva* injunctions? In the first place, the defendant must be subject to the personal jurisdiction of the court. This does not mean that the defendant must be *in* England. Indeed, most of the early *Mareva* cases involved defendants who were outside England, and section 37(3) of the Supreme Court Act 1981 was enacted to confirm that the remedy was available with regard to the defendants within the jurisdiction. But if the defendant is outside the jurisdiction the case must be one in which it is open to the English court to assume jurisdiction under Order 11, e.g. because the contract on which the plaintiff sues is governed by English law.[65] The second jurisdictional limitation is that the remedy is not available, subject to one important statutory exception, where the defendant has assets in

---

[61] *North London Railway Co.* v. *Great Northern Railway Co.* (1883) 11 QBD 30. For a modern example of the principle see *Associated Newspapers Group plc.* v. *Insert Media Ltd.* [1988] 1 WLR 509.

[62] *The Siskina* v. *Distos Compania Naviera* [1979] AC 210. See Collins, *op. cit. supra*, n. 5, at pp. 254–259.

[63] *South Carolina Insurance Co.* v. *Assurantie Maatschappij 'De Zeven Provincien' NV* [1987] AC 24.   [64] [1987] AC at p. 44.   [65] Ord. 11, r. 1(1)(d).

England, but the defendant is abroad, has not submitted to the jurisdiction, and the case does not otherwise come within Order 11, rule 1(1). This is the essence of the decision in *The Siskina*,[66] where it was held that where the substance of the dispute between the parties is pending in a foreign court, the court cannot enjoin removal of English assets: the fact that an injunction is sought 'ordering the defendant to . . . refrain from doing anything within the jurisdiction' does not bring the case within what is now Order 11, rule 1(1) (*b*). But where the main proceedings are (or are to be) pending in another State which is a party to the 1968 Convention, or in the courts of another part of the United Kingdom, the court may grant a *Mareva* injunction.[67]

It has often been said that a plaintiff who seeks *Mareva* relief must give some grounds for believing 'that the defendant has assets here'.[68] But this is merely a description of the normal case, and is based on the *assumption* that the *Mareva* injunction applies solely or primarily to assets within the jurisdiction. It should not follow, for example, that if the remedy may be sought legitimately in relation solely to foreign assets the plaintiff must, as a necessary pre-condition to the obtaining of an order covering the foreign assets, also show that the defendant has assets within the jurisdiction. Such a condition would be contrary to the principle that the injunction is *in personam* and would make no sense.[69]

If the defendant is subject to the personal jurisdiction of the English court, and provided that the case has some appropriate connection with England, there is no reason in principle why an English injunction should not be granted, restraining the disposal of assets abroad. This proposition depends on the simple point that

in granting injunctions the Court operates *in personam*. The person to whom its orders are addressed must be within the reach of the Court or amenable to its jurisdiction . . . As a consequence of the rule, that in granting an injunction the Court operates *in personam*, the Court may exercise jurisdiction independently of the locality of the act to be done, provided the person against whom relief is sought is within the reach and amenable to the process of the Court. That jurisdiction is not founded upon any pretension to the exercise of judicial or administrative rights abroad, but on the circumstance of the person to whom the order is addressed being within the reach of the Court.[70]

A striking example of the exercise of this power is *Acrow* (*Automation*)

---

[66] [1979] AC 210. The law in the United States is different: see *Restatement, Second, Judgments*, s. 8(1)(*c*); Scoles and Hay, *Conflict of Laws* (1982) at p. 244.

[67] Civil Jurisdiction and Judgments Act 1982, s. 25(1).

[68] *Third Chandris Shipping Corp.* v. *Unimarine SA* [1979] QB 645 at p. 668.

[69] This is confirmed by *Derby & Co. Ltd.* v. *Weldon* (*Nos. 3 and 4*) [1990] Ch. 65 (CA), departing from the practice in *MPBXL Corp.* v. *International Banking Corp.*, unrep. 1975 (CA).

[70] Kerr, *Injunctions* (Paterson, 6th ed., 1927) p. 11.

Ltd. v. *Rex Chainbelt Inc.*[71] In that case an English company, Acrow, manufactured equipment under patent licences from a United States corporation, SI Inc. Part of the equipment consisted of a chain, which was manufactured by another United States corporation, Rex Chainbelt Inc., and sold by Rex direct to Acrow, but not on the basis of any long term contract. When disputes arose between Acrow and SI Inc., the latter directed Rex Chainbelt not to supply further chains to Acrow. In proceedings in England, SI Inc. were served outside the jurisdiction under Order 11: the licence agreement was governed by English law and contained a submission to the jurisdiction of the English courts. Rex Chainbelt were joined as defendants (probably as necessary or proper parties) and submitted to the jurisdiction by the then current procedure of entry of unconditional appearance. An injunction was granted against SI Inc., restraining them from impeding Acrow in the manufacture and sale of the equipment, but it took no part in the proceedings, and continued to urge Rex not to supply chains to Acrow. The Court of Appeal granted an interlocutory injunction restraining Rex Chainbelt Inc., and its English subsidiary, Rex Chainbelt Ltd., from obeying the directions of SI Inc. purporting to prohibit them from supplying chains to Acrow, and a mandatory injunction requiring Rex Chainbelt to use all reasonable endeavours to supply the chains to Acrow. The English connections of the case were strong, and the English court had personal jurisdiction over both sets of defendants, but the court was directing Rex, a United States company which manufactured in, and sold from, the United States to disregard the instructions of another United States company, and to use its best endeavours to make supplies from the United States to an English customer, which it was not contractually bound to make.

Thus there is no reason in principle why an English injunction should not restrain a person properly before the court from the disposal of assets abroad. The effect of *Babanaft International Co. SA* v. *Bassatne*[72] was to confirm that this general principle applied to *Mareva* injunctions. The decision in *Ashtiani* v. *Kashi*,[73] to which both Neill and Nicholls L JJ had been party, was treated as a decision on the practice in relation to the exercise of the discretion, and not as a decision on the limits of the jurisdiction of the court. As Neill LJ put it:[74]

There is abundant authority for the proposition that, where a defendant is personally subject to the jurisdiction of the court, an injunction may be granted in appropriate circumstances to control his activities abroad. Thus, for example, a party to an action may be restrained from commencing or continuing an action in a foreign court . . . The decision of this court in *Ashtiani* v. *Kashi* is authority for the

---

[71] [1971] 3 All ER 1175 (CA).   [72] [1990] Ch. 13.

[73] [1987] QB 888 (CA).

[74] [1990] Ch. at pp. 37–39. See also Nicholls LJ at pp. 41–42.

proposition that, where a *Mareva* injunction is granted before judgment, the injunction should be limited to assets within the jurisdiction of the court . . . I was a party to the decision in *Ashtiani* v. *Kashi* and I remain of the opinion that it accurately reflected the way in which the jurisdiction to grant *Mareva* injunctions had been exercised and developed in England in the period between the original decision in *Mareva Compania Naviera S.A.* v. *International Bulkcarriers S.A.* in June 1975 and June 1986. I am satisfied, however, that the court has *jurisdiction* to grant a *Mareva* injunction over foreign assets, and that in this developing branch of the law the decision in *Ashtiani* v. *Kashi* may require further consideration in a future case.

Babanaft was a case where the injunction was sought after judgment at trial, and therefore strictly any remarks on the position before judgment were *obiter*. Kerr LJ concluded that, so far as jurisdiction was concerned (although different considerations might apply in the case of the exercise of the discretion) there was jurisdiction to make the order relating to foreign assets as well before, as after, judgment. Neill LJ, while restricting most of his judgment to the position after judgment, seems to have accepted that there was no relevant difference, as regards jurisdiction, between post-judgment orders and pre-judgment orders.

Republic of Haiti v. *Duvalier*[75] was a pre-judgment case, but one of a very special kind, since the ultimate trial was to take place not in England, but in France, and the injunction was sought in aid of the French proceedings. The only connection with England was that it was alleged that the defendants used English solicitors to hold property on their behalf abroad. In the light of the decision in *Babanaft*, counsel for the defendants conceded for the purposes of argument in the Court of Appeal that the court had power to restrain a defendant who was not resident in England from dealing with assets out of the jurisdiction. But since the issue went to the jurisdiction of the court, Staughton LJ thought that it ought to be examined. Staughton LJ agreed with the view expressed in *Babanaft* that *Ashtiani* v. *Kashi* was a decision based on settled practice, rather than on any restriction on the powers of the court. He concluded that, if the point had not been conceded, he would have agreed with the views expressed *obiter* in *Babanaft* that there was jurisdiction to grant a *Mareva* injunction, pending trial, over assets worldwide. In answer to the argument for the defendants that it was wrong in principle to order persons not resident in England as to what they should or should not do out of the jurisdiction, Staughton LJ pointed to the fact that 'there have been many cases where parties out of the jurisdiction have been subjected to an injunction as to

---

[75] [1990] 1 QB 202. It was held that service of a writ claiming interim measures in aid of foreign proceedings under the Civil Jurisdiction and Judgments Act 1982, s. 25(1) is made under Ord. 11, r. 1(2) (i.e. leave is not required, but of course the court's discretion is directly involved in the making of the order for interim measures).

their conduct abroad—for example as to commencing or continuing proceedings there, or bringing children back to this country'.[76]

Derby & Co. Ltd. v. *Weldon (No. 1)*[77] was the first case to raise the question in the typical pre-judgment case. In the event, the Court of Appeal treated the question as settled by *Babanaft* and *Republic of Haiti* v. *Duvalier.* It seems to have been conceded that the court had jurisdiction, and May and Parker L JJ accepted that it had. Nicholls LJ concluded:[78]

It is now established that under Section 37 of the Supreme Court Act 1981 the English court has jurisdiction to make a *Mareva* 'restraint' order in respect of assets outside England and Wales, both before judgment [citing *Republic of Haiti*] and after judgment [citing *Babanaft*].

Subject to what is said below about the exercise of the contempt power, the grant of an injunction in relation to assets abroad cannot be said to be an exorbitant assertion of jurisdiction. It is sometimes said that an exorbitant jurisdiction is one which foreign courts will not recognise.[79] But this concept of exorbitant jurisdiction is surely too wide. Apart from cases covered by the 1968 Convention an English court will not recognise a foreign judgment unless the defendant is present in the foreign country or has submitted to its jurisdiction, but it could not reasonably be said that every other basis of jurisdiction (e.g. tort committed within the jurisdiction) was to be regarded as exorbitant. In the present context an exorbitant exercise of jurisdiction is one which, in the phrase of Nadelmann, is 'jurisdictionally improper',[80] or one which goes beyond what is internationally acceptable. The classic case is Article 14 of the French Civil Code, which allows a French national to sue any foreigner in the French court, whether or not the case has any connection with France.[81] For an English court to enjoin a person properly subject to its jurisdiction from disposing of assets abroad cannot in this sense be regarded as exorbitant. Perhaps *Republic of Haiti* v. *Duvalier* goes to the very edge of what is permissible. For the sole connection of England with that case was the presence in

---

[76] [1990] 1 QB at 216, citing *Re Liddell's Settlement Trusts* [1936] Ch. 365.

[77] [1990] Ch. 48.

[78] At p. 58. See also *Derby & Co. Ltd.* v. *Weldon (Nos. 3 and 4)* [1990] Ch. 65 (CA).

[79] This extended concept of exorbitant jurisdiction is found in *The Siskina* [1979] AC 210 at p. 254, *per* Lord Diplock; *Amin Rasheed Shipping Corp.* v. *Kuwait Insurance Co.* [1984] AC 50 at p. 65, *per* Lord Diplock; cf. *The Atlantic Star* [1974] AC 436 at p. 476, *per* Lord Kilbrandon; *Spiliada Maritime Corp.* v. *Cansulex Ltd.* [1987] AC 460 at p. 481, *per* Lord Goff.

[80] *Jurisdictionally Improper Fora*, in *Conflict of Laws: International and Interstate* (1972) at p. 222.

[81] This is treated as exorbitant by Article 3 of the 1968 Convention: cf. *Schibsby* v. *Westenholz* (1870) LR 6 QB 155; Mann, *Studies in International Law* (1973), pp. 66–69; Nadelmann, *op. cit. supra*, pp. 223–226. Cf. *Deutsche Schachtbau* v. *Shell International Petroleum Co. Ltd.* [1990] 1 AC 295, at pp. 340, 357.

England of solicitors with access to the foreign assets. The exercise of jurisdiction can be justified on the basis that the solicitors could be treated as agents of the defendants, and the relevant information was located in England.

4. EFFECT ON THIRD PARTIES

The problem of the propriety of the assumption of jurisdiction arises, as Kerr LJ recognized in *Babanaft*, if the injunction is intended to affect third parties outside the jurisdiction.[82] The effect on third parties is, as indicated earlier in this paper,[83] crucial for the effectiveness of the *Mareva* jurisdiction. For a defendant (especially a foreign defendant) may not respect the terms of the injunction, and even where the defendant is in England the threat of committal, fine or sequestration against a defendant may not be enough to deter breaches, especially where the plaintiff does not have (as he usually will not have) full knowledge of the existence and location of the relevant assets. A bank which allows the defendant to remove or dissipate assets in breach of a *Mareva* injunction is guilty of contempt, and that is invariably sufficient, in the domestic context, to freeze the money held by the bank.

But, as the facts of *Babanaft* show, serious problems of international jurisdiction arise when the *Mareva* injunction relates to property abroad. After the injunction had been granted by Vinelott J.[84] 47 entities, including numerous banks, in various countries were informed of it, and in correspondence solicitors for the judgment creditors suggested that foreign banks were bound by the English order, and that officers of a branch in London might be responsible for breaches of the injunction in foreign jurisdictions, and it was possible that these breaches might be punishable by proceedings for contempt.

It is clear that what led the Court of Appeal in *Babanaft* to exclude third parties from the operation of an order affecting foreign assets was the belief that it would be wrong for the English court to subject acts abroad to the principle that those who aid and abet a breach of an English injunction are guilty of contempt of court.[85] Kerr LJ thought that an unqualified *Mareva* injunction over foreign assets would involve an exorbitant assertion of jurisdiction over third parties outside the jurisdiction of the English court.[86] For Neill LJ

---

[82] [1990] Ch. at p. 35.   [83] Text at nn. 20–22, *supra*.

[84] The worldwide *Mareva* was originally refused by Vinelott J. but granted after an application to the Court of Appeal: see [1990] Ch. at p. 20.

[85] Under the principle in *Z Ltd.* v. *A–Z* [1982] QB 558 (CA).

[86] [1990] Ch. at p. 37.

it is wrong in principle to make an order which, though intended merely to restrain and control the actions of a person who is subject to the jurisdiction of the court, may be understood to have some coercive effect over persons who are resident abroad and who are in no sense subject to the court's jurisdiction.[87]

and Nicholls LJ said:[88]

It would be wrong for an English court, by making an order in respect of overseas assets against a defendant amenable to its jurisdiction, to impose or attempt to impose obligations on persons not before the court in respect of acts to be done by them abroad regarding property outside the jurisdiction. That, self-evidently, would be for the English court to claim an altogether exorbitant, extra-territorial jurisdiction.

There can be no doubt that for an English court to treat as punishable acts of contempt acts done abroad by a foreigner, not subject to the personal jurisdiction of the English court, would be wholly exorbitant, and contrary to the comity of nations. But it is very doubtful whether the English court would have jurisdiction, even under English law, to treat them as contempt. For it is well established that aiding and abetting the breach of an injunction is a civil contempt.[89] It is equally well established that a proceeding for civil contempt is criminal or quasi-criminal. 'A criminal contempt is one which takes place in the face of the court, or which prejudices a fair trial and so forth. A civil contempt is different. A typical case is disobedience to an order made by the court in a civil action . . . Although this is a civil contempt, it partakes of the nature of a criminal charge. The defendant is liable to be punished for it. He may be sent to prison. The rules as to criminal charges have always been applied to such a proceeding.'[90]

Nor can there be any doubt that (to quote a recent Consultation Paper of the Law Commission) 'in general, the criminal jurisdiction of the English court is limited to acts done in England'.[91] There is criminal jurisdiction to try a secondary party for aiding and abetting a crime committed in England even if the accused was abroad when he played his part, but only (it seems) if he is a British citizen.[92] But it has already been seen that the liability of a third party who assists in the breach of an injunction is not for breach of the

---

[87] [1990] Ch. at p. 40.   [88] [1990] Ch. at p. 44.

[89] See Arlidge and Eady, *The Law of Contempt* (1982) at pp. 65–68.

[90] *Comet Products (UK)* v. *Hawkex Plastics Ltd.* [1971] 2 QB 67 at p. 73, *per* Lord Denning MR; see also *Re Bramblevale* [1970] Ch. 128. But contrast *Garvin* v. *Domus Publishing Ltd.* [1988] 3 WLR 344.

[91] *Jurisdiction over Fraud Offences with a Foreign Element* (1987) at p. 1. See also Law Commission, *Report on the Territorial and Extraterritorial Extent of the Criminal Law*. Law Com. No. 91 (1978).

[92] Law Commission paper (1987) at pp. 52–53, citing *R.* v. *Jameson* [1896] 2 QB 425; *R.* v. *Robert Millar Ltd.* [1970] 2 QB 54 (CA). See the important article by Glanville Williams (1985) 81 LQR 276 at pp. 395 and 518, especially pp. 529–534.

injunction but for a contempt of court tending to obstruct the course of justice. Clearly, in the case of civil contempt the general principle of territoriality cannot be applied without qualification. Thus, a defendant who is ordered to convey foreign land, or to refrain from instituting foreign proceedings, may be punishable for acts done, or omitted to be done, abroad, if he refuses to convey the land (or conveys it to a third party), or if he institutes the foreign proceedings in breach of the injunction. The applicable principle must be that the English court has power, under English law, to punish parties to litigation or persons otherwise subject to its jurisdiction, who disobey its orders, wherever the act of disobedience takes place.

The simplest case at one end of the spectrum is that of an English defendant who is subject to an English injunction relating to acts to be done, or not done, abroad. No doubt that defendant is subject to the contempt power of the English court. At the other end is a third party who is wholly abroad and who acts wholly abroad. It should not matter whether he knows of the injunction. Thus if the House of Lords had not discharged the injunction restraining the liquidator of Laker Airways Ltd. from suing British Airways and British Caledonian in the Washington District Court,[93] the liquidator (an English accountant) would have been in contempt of court if he had continued with the United States proceedings. But it cannot seriously be suggested that Judge Greene, the United States District Judge, who was well aware of the English injunction, would have been in contempt of the English court for aiding and abetting the breach; nor, it is suggested, could the liquidator's United States lawyers have been held in contempt.[94] Thus if a worldwide *Mareva* injunction is granted, and the defendant has deposits with the Commercial Bank of Ruritania in Ruritania, and the bank has no branch in London, then, irrespective of its knowledge of the injunction, the bank and its officers will not be in contempt of the English court if they allow the defendant to remove the deposits.

The difficult case is that of the third party who is subject to the personal jurisdiction of the English court, but who acts abroad. Some examples will illustrate the point. First, a firm of English solicitors holds assets abroad on behalf of the defendant. If, knowing of the injunction, the firm allows the defendant to dispose of the assets the solicitors will be in contempt.[95]

---

[93] *British Airways Board* v. *Laker Airways Ltd.* [1985] AC 58.

[94] In *Derby & Co. Ltd.* v. *Weldon* (*Nos. 3 and 4*) [1990] Ch. 65. (CA) Lord Donaldson MR considered that where a person was wholly outside the jurisdiction, and assisted in the breach of the order, either it would not be a contempt, or it would involve an excess of jurisdiction to seek to punish him. The two ways of putting it are two sides of the same coin: it is not a contempt because there is no jurisdiction to punish for the act done wholly abroad by a person not subject to the jurisdiction.

[95] This was the situation in *Republic of Haiti* v. *Duvalier*.

Secondly, the defendant has deposits with the Cayman Islands branch of an English bank; knowing of the injunction, officers of the bank in London instruct the Cayman Islands branch to transfer the deposits to Panama. In these circumstances the London bank and its officers would be in contempt, because they have knowingly facilitated the breach of the injunction. Thirdly, the defendant has deposits with the Cayman Islands branch of an English bank, and with the Cayman Islands branch of a United States bank with a branch in London. The defendant instructs the two banks in the Cayman Islands to transfer the deposits to Switzerland, and these instructions are addressed to and acted upon by officers of the two banks in the Cayman Islands, who know of the injunction.

Thus far the Court of Appeal has not formulated a general solution to the problem of third parties resident or present in the jurisdiction who act outside it. Instead the problem has been dealt with by express limitation in the order of its effect on third parties. In *Republic of Haiti* v. *Duvalier*[96] the court adopted a distinction (which it accepted was unsatisfactory) between natural and juridical persons. The order was to apply to the acts abroad of individuals resident in England, but not to the acts abroad of corporations such as banks. The object of the order was to prevent the defendants' English solicitors from dealing with funds abroad, and its effect was to avoid putting into contempt English banks with foreign branches, or foreign banks with an English branch, in respect of movements of funds abroad. In *Derby & Co. Ltd.* v. *Weldon (Nos. 3 & 4)*[97] Lord Donaldson MR thought that the distinction between natural and juridical persons was not justifiable, and the court fashioned an order which was designed, in part, to give a justification to an English bank which might wish to support the court in its efforts to prevent the defendant from frustrating the due course of justice. The Court of Appeal gave the order extraterritorial effect as regards persons who were subject to the jurisdiction of the court, and who had been given written notice of the order at their residence or place of business within the jurisdiction, and who were 'able to prevent acts or omissions outside the jurisdiction of this court which assist in the breach of the terms of this order.' A full analysis of the effect of such an order on banks abroad would be beyond the scope of this article, but it is sufficient to point out that it could raise severe problems of international law and policy if, for example, it is to be suggested that the English head office of Lloyds Bank is 'able to prevent' payments out of its Cayman Islands or Hong Kong branch. Such an order might place greater responsibilities on the head office of Lloyds Bank in London in relation to accounts held at

---

[96] [1990] 1 QB 202, applied in *Derby & Co. Ltd.* v. *Weldon (No. 1)* [1990] Ch. 48, and criticized in *Derby & Co. Ltd.* v. *Weldon (Nos. 3 and 4)*, *supra*.

[97] [1990] Ch. 65 (CA).

those branches abroad than it would on (say) the London branch of Citibank in relation to accounts held in the very same countries.

It is suggested that where English banks, or foreign banks with branches in England, act wholly abroad (without the connivance or assistance of bank officers in London) they will not be guilty of contempt, even though they are, in principle, subject to the *in personam* jurisdiction of the English court. The reason is to be found in the distinction between personal jurisdiction and subject matter jurisdiction. In an important judgment in a different context (that of the subpoena power) Hoffmann J. showed that it did not follow from the fact that a person was within the jurisdiction that there was no territorial limit to the things which it could order a person to do: *Mackinnon* v. *Donaldson Lufkin Corp.*[98] In that case it was held that it would be an excess of jurisdiction for the English court to order the London branch of a United States bank to produce documents held at its head office in New York which were unrelated to the business of its London branch. Although that case concerned the power to subpoena documents from the New York head office of a New York bank with a branch in London, the principle applies equally to documents held in a foreign branch by an English bank. It follows from the principles of that judgment that the court should not apply the contempt power to banks in relation to business outside the jurisdiction. Consequently, it would be an exorbitant exercise of jurisdiction to apply the power to acts of banks and their officers abroad, irrespective of their knowledge of the injunction, even if they have a head office or branch in London, provided that the officers of the head office or branch in London are innocent of any complicity.[99]

5. DISCLOSURE ORDERS

Because there are severe practical limitations on the effectiveness of a restraint order over foreign assets, the valuable remedy is, in many cases, likely to be a disclosure order, ancillary to a *Mareva* injunction relating to foreign assets. If compliance with the disclosure order can be enforced, then the plaintiff can apply for an attachment in the foreign jurisdiction or for the *Mareva* injunction to be recognised or enforced in the foreign jurisdiction. As noted earlier, in *Ashtiani* v. *Kashi*[100] the Court of Appeal decided that it would normally be wrong to order disclosure of foreign assets (except for the purpose of tracing assets in proprietary claims). The

---

[98] [1986] Ch. 482.

[99] For some wider issues see Collins, 'Banking Secrecy and the Enforcement of Securities Legislation', in Goode (ed.) *Conflicts of Interest in the Changing Financial World* (1986) at p. 81.   [100] [1987] QB 888 (CA).

Court of Appeal also indicated that where on 'special grounds' disclosure might be ordered, the plaintiff should be required to give an undertaking not to use any information disclosed without the consent of the defendant or the leave of the court. The apparent reason for requiring such an undertaking was that without it it might be oppressive to the defendant that, as a result of an order of the English court, his assets abroad might be frozen, or he should be subjected to applications for seizure orders in many other jurisdictions; and, in addition, that if there were an order for disclosure of foreign assets that might lead to the plaintiff obtaining security (which was not the object or effect of a *Mareva* injunction) in some foreign jurisdiction.

After *Ashtiani* v. *Kashi*, the Court of Appeal held that in post-judgment cases it was appropriate to order disclosure of foreign assets,[101] and in neither case did the court extract an undertaking not to use the information disclosed as a basis for seeking attachments abroad. *Babanaft* was also a post-judgment case, in which oral examination of assets worldwide was ordered. There was, however, no appeal from the disclosure order. Nevertheless Kerr LJ ventured the suggestion that the view of Dillon LJ in *Ashtiani* v. *Kashi* that the court should require an undertaking not to use the information disclosed without its consent was not as a general rule correct; otherwise, Kerr LJ thought, the intended effect of Article 24 of the 1968 Convention, to allow assets to be frozen, and freezing orders to be recognised, throughout the Convention States, could be frustrated. But Neill and Nicholls L JJ adhered to the view with which they had concurred in *Ashtiani* v. *Kashi*. In particular Nicholls LJ thought that an order for disclosure, whether before or after judgment, could easily have unforeseen results which would be unjust to the defendant; one example was that the information might be used to found jurisdiction on the substance of the case (or indeed of another case) in a foreign country; and there was therefore a need for the court to control strictly the use made of the information overseas. This could be effected by the court specifying in the disclosure order the uses which could be made of the information in foreign countries; or by an undertaking not to use the information without obtaining the consent of the court.[102]

Nicholls LJ also suggested that, if the plaintiff were not resident within the jurisdiction, the court would normally need to be satisfied that it had a sufficient degree of control over the plaintiff to secure compliance with the undertaking. But in *Republic of Haiti* v. *Duvalier*[103] Staughton LJ, whilst not dissenting from the principle, thought that it would be wrong in the

---

[101] *Interpool Ltd.* v. *Galani* [1988] QB 738 (CA); *Maclaine Watson & Co. Ltd.* v. *International Tin Council (No. 2)* [1989] Ch. 286 (CA); see also *Yandil Holdings Pty. Ltd.* v. *Insurance Co. of North America* (1987) 7 NSWLR 571.
[102] [1990] Ch. at p. 47.   [103] [1990] 1 QB 202.

circumstances of the case to order the Republic of Haiti to give security. In that case an undertaking had been given to the judge not to use the information without the consent of the court, and the consent of the court had been sought and granted on a number of occasions.

The final result was reached in *Derby & Co. Ltd.* v. *Weldon (No. 1)*,[104] where the court indicated that in general plaintiffs should undertake, or it should be a condition of the order, that the decision as to whether any action should be taken abroad in respect of foreign assets should be left to the English court. In the view of Nicholls LJ, in the context of the disclosure order,

reasonable protection for the defendants is being built into the order to ensure that the information compulsorily disclosed is not misused and that it does not lead to the defendants being harassed or oppressed by having to face litigation, brought by financially more powerful parties, in overseas courts throughout the world.[105]

6. FOREIGN EFFECTS

This section will consider the effect abroad of provisional measures such as *Mareva* injunctions, particularly in the light of the 1968 Brussels Convention on Jurisdiction and the Enforcement of Judgments in Civil and Commercial Matters, which has been law in the United Kingdom since the Civil Jurisdiction and Judgments Act 1982 came into force on January 1, 1987. In his important judgment in *Babanaft* Kerr LJ agreed with Neill and Nicholls L JJ that the effect of the *Mareva* injunction should be limited in its effects on third parties. But he would have preferred a formula which restricted its effect on third parties, not absolutely, but merely 'unless and to the extent that it is enforced by the courts of the state in which the assets are situated'. Kerr LJ himself recognised that in some foreign jurisdictions there might be no practical difference between his solution and the unconditional proviso favoured by the majority. Thus some foreign courts might in any event enforce English orders in ways which would affect third parties holding assets of the defendant, and to that extent the *Babanaft* proviso might in practice prove to be nugatory. In *Republic of Haiti* v. *Duvalier* Kerr LJ's version of the proviso was adopted, although Staughton LJ doubted whether it conferred any additional benefit on the plaintiffs: until the order was enforced it would not operate on third parties, and after it was enforced the addition might well not be needed. But, he added, it might encourage the courts of other countries to enforce the English order; and if it had that effect, it would be desirable.

---

[104] [1990] Ch. 48. In *Derby & Co. Ltd.* v. *Weldon (Nos. 3 and 4)* [1990] Ch. 65 (CA), the primary object of the *Mareva* was to obtain attachments in Luxembourg and Panama.

[105] [1990] Ch. at p. 60.

Kerr LJ suggested that his formula reflected the current international approach, and was consistent with the policy behind the 1968 Convention. The key to the proper exercise of any extraterritorial jurisdiction lay in the question whether there was international reciprocity for the recognition and enforcement of a *Mareva* injunction purporting to operate on the defendant's assets abroad. In his view there was international reciprocity in the light of the 1968 Convention, which applied in most of the EEC States and was soon to be extended to EFTA States. Article 24 of the 1968 Convention allowed application to be made to the courts of a Contracting State for provisional or protective measures: this was so whether or not the main proceedings on the substance were pending in that State. But the effect of the 1968 Convention was that the courts of State A had a duty to recognise and enforce the provisional or protective orders made by a court in a State which purported to have effect in State A.

Article 24 of the 1968 Convention provides:

Application may be made to the courts of a Contracting State for such provisional measures, including protective measures, as may be available under the law of that State, even if, under this Convention, the courts of another Contracting State have jurisdiction as to the substance of the matter.

A full discussion of Article 24 and its role under the 1968 Convention[106] would be out of place in this paper, but for present purposes it is important to note two aspects. First, Article 24 authorises (but does not require) a Contracting State to grant provisional remedies even if the substance of the case is pending in another Contracting State. The accession of the United Kingdom led to a change in the law in order to provide for this power. This was necessary because of the unfortunate decision of the House of Lords in *The Siskina*[107] that a *Mareva* injunction could not be granted in order to preserve a fund in England while the substance of the matter proceeded abroad, even though freezing the fund in England was the only way in which the plaintiffs could hope to collect on their judgment. Section 25(1) of the Civil Jurisdiction and Judgments Act 1982 gives the English court power to grant interim relief where proceedings within the scope of the 1968 Convention have been, or are to be, commenced in another Contracting State or in another part of the United Kingdom. Section 25(3) allows this power to be extended by Order in Council to cases where proceedings are, or are to be, pending in other countries, but no Order in Council has yet been made. Accordingly, the English court may grant a *Mareva* injunction over persons subject to its personal jurisdiction not only where the substance of the action is pending in England, but also where it

---

[106] On this provision see Collins, *Civil Jurisdiction and Judgments Act 1982* (1983) at pp. 98–102.

[107] [1979] AC 210, on which see Collins (1981) 1 Yb. Eur. L. 249 at pp. 254–258.

is pending in another Contracting State or in another part of the United Kingdom.

The second general point is that, although the 1968 Convention is by no means unique in providing that a State may grant provisional measures when the substance of the case is assigned to another jurisdiction, it is unusual in not requiring judgments or orders to be final before they can be enforceable in other Contracting States. Thus by contrast with the bilateral Conventions concluded by the United Kingdom, the 1968 Convention provides for enforcement not only of orders which are not final, but of orders which do not merely provide for the payment of money. As a result, protective or provisional orders granted in one Contracting State may be capable of recognition and enforcement in other Contracting States.

The enforcement abroad of orders made in one Contracting State under Article 24 has been the subject of two decisions of the European Court of Justice: *De Cavel* v. *De Cavel (No. 1)*[108] and *Denilauler* v. *Couchet Frères*.[109] In the present context these cases are more important for what they did not decide than for what they did decide. In each of these cases the European Court of Justice was concerned with the enforcement in Germany of a French court order which purported to affect assets situate in Germany.

In *De Cavel* a French family court made an order in the course of French divorce proceedings. The French order purported to freeze furniture and other property in the couple's flat in Frankfurt, and also the contents of a safe hired by the wife in a Frankfurt bank, and the wife's account in a bank in Frankfurt. In *Denilauler*, in the course of proceedings in France by a French company against a German company for the purchase price of goods, the president of the court made an *ex parte* order authorising the freezing of the German company's accounts at the Société Générale Alsacienne de Banque at Frankfurt. In each of the cases the European Court held that the French order was not enforceable in Germany, but on grounds wholly unconnected with the fact that the French orders purported to reach assets in Germany. In *De Cavel* the court held that, because the 1968 Convention did not apply to questions of status and matrimonial rights in property, it equally did not apply to orders authorising provisional measures in the course of divorce proceedings. In *Denilauler* the court held that the recognition and enforcement provisions of the Convention did not

---

[108] Case 143/78 [1979] ECR 1055.

[109] Case 125/79 [1980] ECR 1553. In Case 258/83 *Calzaturificio Brennero SAS* v. *Wendel GmbH* [1984] ECR 3971 an Italian court made a protective order purporting to seize the assets of a German company (which had no assets in Italy) up to the value of the plaintiff's claim. It seems to have been assumed by the German court which was asked to enforce the order, and by the European Court, that in principle the order was enforceable in Germany.

[110] See Advocate General Warner [1979] ECR at p. 1069.

apply to *ex parte* orders which were intended to be enforced without prior service.

But in neither case did the court suggest that the French orders might not be capable of recognition and enforcement merely because they purported to apply to property in Germany. In *De Cavel* the French court appears to have exercised jurisdiction to order the putting under seal of property in Germany and the attachment of a bank account in Germany on the basis that it had jurisdiction over the divorce proceedings.[110] Observations were filed by the German and United Kingdom Governments, and by the Commission, but none of them took any point on the power of the French court in relation to assets in Germany.

In *Denilauler* the *saisie-conservatoire* was ordered by the French court under Article 48 of the French Code of Civil Procedure (ancien).[111] But under Article 48 the basis of jurisdiction is either (a) the domicile of the defendant; or (b) the situs of the property attached. The defendant was a German company, which, it seems clear, was not domiciled in France; and the property was situate in Germany, because, under French law (and the same principle applies in England) the fact that the bank was French did not affect the situs of the account, which was held at a German branch. It is therefore by no means certain that the French court had jurisdiction under French law to make an attachment of property in Germany. The question of the legitimacy of the French order, either under French law or in terms of the Convention, was not touched on in the written submissions of the Governments of the United Kingdom and Italy, or of the Commission, but it seems from the opinion of Advocate General Mayras that, during the oral hearings, the United Kingdom government expressed the view 'that under the Brussels Convention no provisional or protective measure, whether adopted *ex parte* or in adversary proceedings, can have extra-territorial effect'.[112] As indicated above, the European Court did not advert to this question, and decided that the French order was not enforceable in Germany because the enforcement provisions of the Convention did not apply to *ex parte* orders of that type. But the court also said:[113]

The courts of the place or, in any event, of the Contracting State, where the assets subject to the measures sought are located, are those best able to assess the circumstances which may lead to the grant or refusal of the measures sought or to the laying down of procedures and conditions which the plaintiff must observe in

---

[111] According to the plaintiff: [1980] ECR at p. 1557.

[112] [1980] ECR at p. 1576. See also the suggestion (in the oral procedure) by the Commission (recorded at p. 1581) that a plaintiff faced with a defendant with assets in several countries would be obliged to seek urgent measures in each.

[113] At p. 1570.

order to guarantee the provisional and protective character of the measures ordered.

The court explained that the courts where the assets are situate are those best able to lay down procedures and conditions (which in the English context would mean cross-undertakings and security) designed to guarantee the provisional and protective character of the measures. But the effect of the actual decision of the court is that measures of this kind affecting assets outside the territory of the court ordering them will be entitled to recognition and enforcement in other Contracting States provided that the orders are notified to the defendant and provided the defendant is given the opportunity *inter partes* to resist them. There is a basic inconsistency which may be capable of being explained (as is often so in the judgments of the European Court) only as the incorporation in the judgment of a minority view in the court.

There can be little doubt, however, that by implication the decisions in *De Cavel (No. 1)* and *Denilauler* accept in principle that (a) a court in a Contracting State may exercise jurisdiction under Article 24 in relation to assets abroad; (b) provided the case is within the scope of the Convention and the defendant has contested it and failed, an order made under Article 24 will be entitled to recognition and enforcement in other Contracting States.

In *Babanaft*, therefore, Kerr LJ accepted that it was implicit in the decisions of the European Court in *De Cavel* v. *De Cavel (No. 1)* and *Denilauler* v. *Couchet Frères* that extraterritorial orders akin to *Mareva* injunctions, made by the courts in one Convention State and purporting to operate on assets located in another Convention State, would be recognised and enforced by the courts of the latter State if they fell within the scope of the 1968 Convention and satisfied certain requirements designed to protect the defendant against whom the orders were made. These cases showed that a pre-judgment *Mareva* injunction granted by an English court in aid of English proceedings, freezing specific assets of a defendant located in the territory of any Convention State, was entitled to recognition and enforcement by the courts of that State if the English proceedings fell within the scope of the 1968 Convention, and did not fall within any of the exceptions, and the order was made *inter partes*, or at any rate after the defendant had had an opportunity to resist the application of the order.

The implications of these decisions, Kerr LJ thought, were that: (a) there was no reason why the English court should refrain from granting *inter partes* pre-judgment *Mareva* injunctions in cases falling within the 1968 Convention in relation to assets situated in the territories of other Convention States (and eventually in the territories of all or most of the

EFTA States; (b) there could be no question of such orders operating directly upon the foreign assets by way of attachment, or upon third parties, such as banks, holding the assets. The effectiveness of such orders for these purposes could only derive from their recognition and enforcement by the local courts, as should be made clear in the terms of the orders to avoid any misunderstanding suggesting an unwarranted assumption of extraterritorial jurisdiction. But if the orders fulfilled the requirements of the Convention, then the local courts would be bound to recognise and enforce them; apart from any EEC or EFTA connection there was no jurisdiction (as opposed to discretionary) ground which would preclude any English court from granting a pre-judgment *Mareva* injunction over assets situated anywhere outside the jurisdiction, which were owned or controlled by defendants subject to the jurisdiction of the English court, provided that the order made it clear that it was not to have any direct effect upon the assets or upon any third parties outside the jurisdiction, save to the extent that the order might be enforced by the local courts. Whether an order which was qualified in this way would be enforced by the courts of States where the defendant's assets were situated would depend on the local law. The essence of the reasoning of Kerr LJ is that the two judgments of the European Court implicitly accept that a jurisdiction to order provisional measures in foreign countries is not of itself an exorbitant jurisdiction; accordingly, the extension of the *Mareva* injunction to foreign assets is not exorbitant. Further, the fact that such orders are capable of recognition and enforcement in foreign countries provides a mechanism for simultaneously limiting their effect on third parties and providing an avenue for making them effective as against third parties in foreign countries.[114]

It cannot be regarded as finally settled that *Mareva* injunctions affecting assets abroad, even after *inter partes* hearings, are enforceable under the 1968 Convention.[115] It is clear from the report of the arguments, and from the opinions of the Advocates-General in *De Cavel (No. 1)* and *Denilauler*

---

[114] In Case 145/86 *Hoffmann* v. *Kreig* [1988] ECR 645, the European Court held that a foreign order which is capable of recognition under the 1968 Convention should, in principle, produce the same effects in the State in which enforcement was sought as it had in the State where the order was originally made. But this does not mean that the Contracting States must adopt the same remedies as English law, e.g. contempt of court. It is sufficient if they give the order the same general effect. Thus under civil law systems attachment operates like garnishment, so that the third party who pays the defendant will still remain liable to pay the plaintiff.

[115] But it is clear that, even though an English *Mareva* injunction may be capable of recognition or enforcement in the Republic of Ireland, which is a party to the 1968 Convention, it is *not* capable of recognition or enforcement in Scotland or Northern Ireland: section 18(5) of the Civil Jurisdiction and Judgments Act 1982 excludes from the operation of the intra-United Kingdom enforcement provisions so much of any judgment as is 'a provisional (including protective) measure other than an order for the making of an interim payment'.

that the legitimacy of the extraterritorial effect of provisional measures was not fully considered, or perhaps considered at all. Nor do the judgments consider the question whether it would be legitimate for the courts of State A to make orders in relation to assets in State B, when the courts of State A are not seised of the substance of the matter. In both *De Cavel (No. 1)* and *Denilauler* the French courts which made the orders were the courts which were dealing with the substance of the case.[116] In *Republic of Haiti* v. *Duvalier* the English court was not the court which was seised of the substantive proceedings. The sole connection with England was the presence of the firm of solicitors through which foreign assets were held. It is very doubtful whether such an order would be capable of recognition abroad.

7. PRACTICAL IMPLICATIONS

With varying degrees of emphasis, all three decisions indicate that *Mareva* injunctions and disclosure orders relating to foreign assets should be granted rarely or only in exceptional circumstances.[117] This may perhaps be regarded as inevitable lip-service to caution and restraint which naturally accompanies an innovation the implications of which have yet to be thought through. First, it is clear that an injunction will be more readily granted in tracing or proprietary claims, and even *Ashtiani* v. *Kashi* recognised that an order affecting foreign assets might be appropriate in such cases. Strictly, perhaps, an injunction in such a type of case should not be classified as a *Mareva* injunction. What emerges from both *Republic of Haiti* v. *Duvalier* and *Derby & Co. Ltd.* v. *Weldon (No. 1)* is that it may sometimes be difficult to determine whether the nature of the claim is proprietary. In *Republic of Haiti* the difficulty was exacerbated by the fact that the substantive proceedings were pending in France, and the Court of Appeal therefore had to consider whether the claim was proprietary in the light of the French proceedings, which in turn no doubt might have looked to Haiti law to determine whether the owner of the assets was the Republic or the Duvalier family. The court thought that the action in France was not in itself a proprietary claim; ownership of assets would be asserted only when the assets were found. In *Derby & Co. Ltd.* v. *Weldon (No. 1)* the Court of Appeal made it clear (especially in the judgment of Nicholls LJ)

---

[116] As was the Italian court in Case 258/83 *Calzaturificio Brennero SAS* v. *Wendel GmbH* [1984] ECR 3971.

[117] *Babanaft* [1990] Ch. at p. 28; *Republic of Haiti* [1990] 1 QB at p. 216; *Derby & Co. Ltd.* v. *Weldon (No. 1)* [1990] Ch. at p. 55. In *Derby & Co. Ltd.* v. *Weldon (Nos. 3 and 4)* [1990] Ch. at p. 79 Lord Donaldson MR suggested that this merely meant that the remedy ought to be granted only when it was really necessary.

that it was not the role of the court at the interlocutory stage to determine complex questions of law or fact as to whether the claim was proprietary or not. If there was a seriously arguable case that the plaintiffs had a proprietary interest under a trust the court had jurisdiction to require them to order the defendants to provide information. It should follow that in those circumstances a less exacting standard should apply in the exercise of the discretion to grant restraining and disclosure rules. In practice, this means that it will be easier to obtain the order in cases of fraud or breach of fiduciary duty, and the courts will not, it is hoped, need to resort to purely conceptual distinctions between tracing claims in the strict sense and claims for breach of fiduciary duty, which led to such unfortunate decisions as *Lister & Co.* v. *Stubbs*.[118]

Secondly, it is also very clear from the decisions that an order relating to foreign assets will more readily be granted if the order is made after judgment than before.[119] It should follow that there will be other differences in the exercise of the discretion after judgment. Thus after the plaintiff has obtained judgment, and is therefore *ex hypothesi* bound to recover if there are assets available (subject to any question of appeal), there is no reason in principle why he should have to give the usual cross-undertaking in damages, still less security for the cross-undertaking.[120] This conclusion is obvious if there is no stay of execution pending appeal, and there seems to be no reason why, if there is a stay of execution (which is only given in exceptional circumstances[121]), the judgment creditor should not be adequately and unconditionally protected. Nor, despite the view of Neill and Nicholls L JJ in *Babanaft* to the contrary, is there any reason in principle why, after judgment, a disclosure order (whether under RSC Order 48 or ancillary to the injunction) should be subject to an undertaking not to use the information without the consent of the court. The whole purpose of the order is to aid execution, and measures of execution at any rate should be permitted freely until the judgment is satisfied.

The final, and very serious, problem is the effectiveness of these orders. It is, of course, true that the court is reluctant to make orders which would

---

[118] (1890) 45 Ch. D. 1. See Goff and Jones, *Law of Restitution* (3rd ed., 1986), at pp. 656–657.

[119] See especially *Babanaft* [1990] Ch. 13; *Republic of Haiti* [1990] 1 QB 202; *Derby & Co. Ltd.* v. *Weldon* (*Nos. 3 and 4*) [1990] Ch. 65 (CA). In *Babanaft* it was held that Article 16(5) of the 1968 Convention (which gives exclusive jurisdiction to the courts of the Contracting State where judgment is to be enforced) did not preclude provisional measures affecting assets in other Contracting States as a prelude to execution in those States. This is clearly right: *cf.* Collins, *Civil Jurisdiction and Judgments Act 1982* (1983) at p. 83.

[120] Nor should a judgment debtor be entitled to '*Angel Bell*' relief (*supra*, n. 37) to pay his trade creditors out of the foreign assets.

[121] RSC Ord. 59, r. 13.

be ineffective to achieve what they set out to do.[122] But it is well established that the fear that the defendant will not obey an injunction is not a bar to its grant. In *Castanho* v. *Brown & Root (UK) Ltd.*[123] Lord Scarman, answering the point that to grant an injunction to restrain foreign proceedings would be useless, a mere *brutum fulmen*, cited with evident approval the well-known passage in *Re Liddell's Settlement Trusts*:[124]

It is not the habit of this court in considering whether or not it will make an order to contemplate the possibility that it will not be obeyed.

It would be wrong to speculate on the effectiveness of the orders made in the recent Court of Appeal decisions, because they were made in the context of litigation which is, or may be, continuing. But, in general, it cannot be said that those who are judgment debtors, or who are, on solid grounds, alleged to be in breach of fiduciary duty, are those who are most likely to obey court orders unless they are forced to obey, or have an interest in obedience. Nor are those who, on solid grounds, are alleged to have spirited assets away to, or secreted funds in, offshore companies and havens, the most likely candidates for obedience and candour in the execution of *Mareva* injunctions and ancillary disclosure orders. The problem is exacerbated when the defendant is outside the jurisdiction and is not easily amenable to the exercise of the contempt power. The mere presence of assets within the English jurisdiction which are capable of sequestration is not sufficient to secure effectiveness, for there would be no need for a worldwide *Mareva* injunction if the domestic assets were sufficient to meet the claim, and the remedy of sequestration is therefore no deterrent to a determined defendant. In practice the remedy is likely to be most effective where the defendant is an individual present within the jurisdiction (or a company with offices within the jurisdiction) or if the defendant has a real interest in defending the substance of the English action or (as the case may be) in appealing the English judgment. It is possible that these are the only cases in which the remedy will be effective, and this may be regarded as a cynical, but realistic, conclusion.

Each of the decisions shows that in appropriate cases the court may regard the remedy as one which will wholly or partially achieve its object. In *Babanaft* the court no doubt took account of the connection of the defendants with England, and of their interest in pursuing an appeal, and of the fact that they were complying with a disclosure order; in *Republic of Haiti* there were English solicitors who would be bound by the order; and in *Derby & Co. Ltd.* v. *Weldon (Nos. 1 and 3)* the defendants were

---

[122] *Att.-Gen.* v. *Guardian Newspapers Ltd.* [1987] 1 WLR 1248, at pp. 1269–1270, *per* Sir Nicolas Browne-Wilkinson V.-C., revd. (but not on the correctness of the principle) *ibid.*, 1277 (CA), 1282 (HL); see also *Att.-Gen.* v. *Guardian Newspapers Ltd. (No. 2)* [1990] 1 AC 109, at p. 223, *per* Bingham LJ.   [123] [1981] AC 557 at p. 574.

[124] [1986] Ch. 365 at p. 374, *per* Romer LJ.

connected with England and were vigorously contesting the substance of the allegations against them.[125]

In those cases where an effective order can be made, it is likely to be the disclosure order which will be the most useful in practical terms. If proper disclosure is made of assets abroad, the plaintiff will be in a position to make an application in the relevant foreign court for an attachment. If the foreign court is in a 1968 Convention Contracting State, it is likely that the courts of that State will exercise on Article 24 jurisdiction to make provisional orders in aid of proceedings in England. If the State is not a Contracting State, then the same result will follow in those countries which would allow an attachment to be made in aid of proceedings pending in other jurisdictions; it may be that the number of such countries will be very small, and that in most countries it will be necessary to start fresh, parallel proceedings on the substance and obtain security in those proceedings.

The practical consequence is that it is really the *Mareva* injunction which is ancillary to the disclosure order, rather than the traditional relationship in which it was the disclosure order which was ancillary to the *Mareva* injunction. For the disclosure order will be the main remedy in England, and the *Mareva* injunction will, in the words of Nicholls LJ in *Babanaft* be a 'holding' injunction, to give the plaintiff time to apply to the relevant foreign court for appropriate orders of attachment or the like.[126] Then an undertaking in the form required in *Derby & Co. Ltd.* v. *Weldon (No. 1)*, or a variant of it, will give the English court the power to control the plaintiff's exercise of its right to seek attachments in foreign countries, in order to prevent tactical harassment of a defendant and to limit the plaintiff's security. It is not likely to make much difference whether in the foreign country the plaintiff seeks recognition and enforcement of the English order, or makes a fresh application to the foreign court. It is only in countries which are parties to the 1968 Convention that an English interlocutory injunction would be capable of recognition and enforcement; in those countries it would depend on cost and convenience whether it would be more appropriate to seek a fresh order; in other countries the only remedy would be a fresh application.

8. SUMMARY AND CONCLUSIONS

It may be helpful to summarise the operation of the *Mareva* injunction in the international context:

---

[125] In *Derby & Co. Ltd.* v. *Weldon (Nos. 3 and 4)* [1990] Ch. at p. 81 (CA) Lord Donaldson MR pointed out that a defendant who disobeyed could have its defence struck out.
[126] [1990] Ch. at p. 41; in *Republic of Haiti* v. *Duvalier* the restraint was said to be temporary: [1990] 1 QB at p. 210.

1. A *Mareva* injunction may be granted if the plaintiff has a good arguable case on the substance of the claim, and can show that there is a real risk that the defendant will defeat execution of any ultimate judgment by disposing of, or hiding, his assets.[127]

2. The defendant must be amenable to the personal jurisdiction of the English court, and must therefore be present within the jurisdiction, or submit to the jurisdiction, or the case must come within RSC Order 11, rule 1(1) or rule 1(2).

3. A *Mareva* injunction, even in respect of assets within the jurisdiction, cannot be granted if the defendant is outside the jurisdiction, and does not submit, on the *sole* ground that a Mareva injunction is sought 'ordering the defendant to do or refrain from doing anything within the jurisdiction' (RSC Order 11, rule 1(1)(c)).[128]

4. If, however, proceedings are pending in another State which is a party to the 1968 Convention, or in another part of the United Kingdom, the English court may grant interim relief,[129] including a *Mareva* injunction, even if the substantive proceedings are not pending in England and even if the English court would have no jurisdiction over such substantive proceedings. In such a case, service outside the jurisdiction would be effected, without leave, under RSC Order 11, rule 1(2).[130]

5. The court has jurisdiction to make an order affecting assets abroad (and it may do so even if there are no assets in England[131]) but the exercise of the jurisdiction is in the discretion of the court and will be exercised with particular caution. It will be more readily exercised if the injunction is sought after final judgment has been given against the defendants, or if the claim is a proprietary claim.

6. The court may also make a disclosure order relating to assets abroad; prior to judgment it will be ancillary to a *Mareva* injunction,[132] and after judgment it will normally be made under RSC Order 48.[133]

7. The injunction will not normally be granted unless it is made clear that it is not to affect third parties (other than those subject to the jurisdiction of the English court) in respect of acts outside the jurisdiction; nor will the order (and ancillary disclosure order) normally be made unless the plaintiff undertakes that no attachment

---

[127] See, among many other examples, *Derby & Co. Ltd.* v. *Weldon (No. 1)* [1990] Ch. at p. 56 *per* Parker LJ.

[128] *The Siskina* v. *Distos Compania Naviera* [1979] AC 210.

[129] Civil Jurisdiction and Judgments Act 1982, s. 25(1).

[130] *Republic of Haiti* v. *Duvalier* [1990] 1 QB 202.

[131] *Derby & Co. Ltd.* v. *Weldon (Nos. 3 and 4)* [1990] Ch. 65 (CA).

[132] As in *Derby & Co. Ltd.* v. *Weldon (No. 1)* [1990] Ch. 48.

[133] *Interpool Ltd.* v. *Galani* [1988] QB 738 (CA).

proceedings will be taken abroad without the consent of the English court.

This paper began by indicating that the *Mareva* injunction was developed to fulfil a function which in civil law countries was affected by such remedies as the *saisie-conservatoire*, and in the United States by the remedy of attachment. The creation of the disclosure order, and the extension of the *Mareva* injunction to assets abroad, has meant that the *Mareva* injunction goes far beyond the scope of *saisie* or attachment, which are forms of execution (akin, in the case of debts, to garnishment) and are (subject to the effect of the curious French decisions considered by the European Court in *De Cavel* (*No. 1*) and *Denilauler*) strictly territorial in operation. But the extension of the *Mareva* jurisdiction to assets abroad is, it is suggested, justifiable in terms of international law and comity provided that the case has some appropriate connection with England, that the court does not purport to affect title to property abroad, and that the court does not seek to control the activities abroad of foreigners who are not subject to the personal jurisdiction of the English court.

III

Some Aspects of Service out of the Jurisdiction in English Law

When this article was written in 1972, it was widely accepted that English law did not have a general rule that the court could decline to exercise its jurisdiction on the ground that another court was the more appropriate forum. Shortly before it was published the Court of Appeal had reaffirmed that, where the court had jurisdiction as a result of the defendant having been sued in England, mere balance of convenience was not a sufficient ground for depriving a plaintiff of the advantage of prosecuting his action in an English court: to justify an application for a stay of the proceedings, the defendant had to prove that continuance of the proceedings would be oppressive or an abuse of the process: *Maharanee of Baroda* v. *Wildenstein* [1972] 2 QB 283 (CA).

The article drew attention to the fact that (by contrast with the position where the court had jurisdiction over a defendant in England) the position in cases where leave to serve out of the jurisdiction was involved was that *forum conveniens* was a decisive factor. It is now widely known that a series of decisions of the House of Lords beginning with *The Atlantic Star* [1974] AC 436 and culminating in *Spiliada Maritime Corp.* v. *Cansulex Ltd.* [1987] AC 460 established that *forum conveniens* factors applied in England not only to cases involving service out of the jurisdiction under RSC Order 11, r. 1, but also to cases where the defendant was served as of right in England.

In *Amin Rasheed Shipping Corp.* v. *Kuwait Insurance Co.* [1984] AC 50 Lord Wilberforce reaffirmed that *forum conveniens* principles applied in Order 11 cases, and in *Spiliada Maritime Corp.* v. *Cansulex Ltd.* [1987] AC 460 his approach to the exercise of the discretion was adopted, namely that the court should take into account the nature of the dispute, the legal and practical issues involved, such questions as local knowledge, availability of witnesses and their evidence, and expense. In the *Spiliada* case, Lord Goff of Chieveley indicated that in Order 11 cases the question was essentially the same as in cases involving a stay on the ground of *forum non conveniens*, i.e. to identify the forum in which the case could be suitably tried for the interests of all the parties and for the ends of justice.

Two further notes should be added. First, the House of Lords has referred to the European Court of Justice in Luxembourg the question whether *forum conveniens* principles can be applied to prevent the exercise of jurisdiction conferred by the Brussels Convention of 1968 on Jurisdiction and the Enforcement of Judgments in Civil and Commercial Matters: see *Re Harrods (Buenos Aires) Ltd.* [1991] Ch. 72 (CA); Collins (1990) 106 LQR 535. Second, the High Court of Australia rejected the developments of the *forum conveniens* doctrine in England and preferred the older test based on the defendant showing that continuance of the proceedings

From *International and Comparative Law Quarterly*, 21 (1972), 656.

would be vexatious or oppressive: but this holding was in the context of service out of the jurisdiction, and it is likely that the attention of the court was not brought to the fact that not only in England, but also in Australia, *forum conveniens* had been an important factor in such cases: *Oceanic Sun Line Special Shipping Co. Inc.* v. *Fay* (1988) 165 CLR 197; see also *Voth* v. *Manildra Flour Mills* (1990) 97 ALR 124; Collins (1989) 105 LQR 305; (1991) 107 LQR 182.

The intention of this article is twofold: firstly, to comment on some recent case law on the practice under Order 11 of the Rules of the Supreme Court or equivalent rules; and, secondly, to correct what seems to this writer an insufficient attention in the leading works on the conflict of laws in England to certain practical aspects of service out of the English jurisdiction. Three aspects will be discussed: first, the approach to the exercise of the judicial discretion and the criteria on which the discretion is exercised, with particular reference to *forum non conveniens*; second, the recent developments in the case law; and, third, the impact abroad of the procedural steps in England on the recognition of English judgments abroad. Perhaps it would be appropriate also to say by way of preface that in the view of this writer at least, Order 11 will be here for some time to come. The EEC Convention on Jurisdiction and Recognition of Judgments in Civil and Commercial Matters signed in 1968 will be in force as between the existing member States by January 1, 1973, but it may be several years before it has an impact on the enlarged Community.[1]

I

It is commonplace that the essence of the English rules on jurisdiction in actions *in personam* is the service of a writ (or other originating process) on the defendant. Service out of the jurisdiction in its modern form can be traced back to the Common Law Procedure Act 1852 which gave the power of summoning defendants residing out of the jurisdiction, provided that the cause of action arose in England. After the Judicature Act 1875, the forerunner of the modern Order 11 was made part of the rules of the Supreme Court. Those rules provided that *notice* of a writ, rather than the writ itself, should be served on the defendant abroad. The reason for this is an interesting one, particularly to public international lawyers.[2] The judges

---

[1] Discussed by Gothot and Holleaux, (1971) Clunet 747. For English text see e.g. Commerce Clearing House, *Common Market Reporter*, para. 6003.

[2] For a detailed exposition of the view that there are limits imposed by public international law on the exercise of civil jurisdiction see Mann, 'The Doctrine of Jurisdiction in International Law'. (1964) I Hague Rec. 1 at p. 73 *et seq*. See also Parry, 'The Theory of Restrictive Practices', (1958) 44 Trans. Grot. Soc. 109 at p. 118. The *Barcelona Traction Case* (*Belgium* v. *Spain* [1970] ICJ Rep. 1) contains a wealth of relevant material which will become

in 1876 apparently thought that service of the writ would be an interference with the jurisdiction of foreign countries.[3] From that date until recent times, the courts have consistently emphasised two points: first, that the exercise of the discretion to serve out of the jurisdiction has international aspects, and second, that as a result the discretion must be exercised most carefully.

In the earliest days of Order 11, the courts were concerned to ensure that the English rules of jurisdiction were not such as to tempt foreign courts similarly to put English residents to the extreme inconvenience and annoyance of travelling to some distant place to defend themselves.[4] But gradually the expression of the fear of retaliation came to be replaced by an emphasis on the views of foreign governments, on the lack of allegiance of foreigners, and on international law and comity.

In *Comber* v. *Leyland*[5] Lord Halsbury said of Order 11 that it

is a somewhat artificial provision which is apparently intended to extend the power of suit by persons in this country against persons in foreign countries. For very obvious reasons, reasons which indeed have been made very apparent by the view which foreign countries have taken of an attempt to exercise the jurisdiction of Her Majesty's courts in places beyond Her Majesty's dominions, it is provided that the action must be founded upon . . .

a breach within the jurisdiction etc. and another eminent judge, Scrutton LJ, said 'in some countries it is looked upon with great disfavour'.[6] The importance of the lack of allegiance of foreigners is of course closely linked with the notion of restraint imposed by international law and comity. As early as 1886 Lord Coleridge CJ[7] said that Order 11 was

passed after and in consequence of remonstrance as to the practice of the English courts in this matter, and to bring that practice into accordance with well-settled rules of international law, or, at all events, comity.

In 1893 Lord Esher MR said[8]

available when the pleadings are published. For reasons which are notorious, the judgment of the Court does not deal with the point, but see the separate opinion of Judge Fitzmaurice at 104.

   [3] See (1882) 74 LT 127. The powers under the 1852 Act had been granted at the instance of the Common Law Commissioners; the question had been raised whether this was allowable under international law. Willes J., one of the Commissioners, thought that it was possible for the courts of one country to have their process served in another country, but not to enforce its process by coercive measures: see (1885) 80 LT 47.
   [4] See *Cresswell* v. *Parker* (1879) 11 Ch. D. 601 at 604 (CA) *per* James LJ. The early cases on Order 11 are discussed in Piggott, *Foreign Judgments and Jurisdiction* (1908) Vol. III, pp. 183–189. See also *The Supreme Court Practice* (1970) Vol. I, pp. 70–72.
   [5] [1898] AC 524 at 527.
   [6] *Vaudrey* v. *Nathan* [1928] WN 154 at 155. See also *Re Busfield, Whaley* v. *Busfield* (1886) 32 Ch. D. 123 at 124 *per* Chitty J.   [7] *Field* v. *Bennett* (1886) 56 LJQB 89 at 91.
   [8] *Firth* v. *De las Rivas* (1893) 69 LTR 666 at 667.

formerly I tried to persuade the other judges to construe the rules relating to service of writs out of the jurisdiction so as not to break what I thought to be the comity of nations, and so as not to be guilty of any aggression by sending our bailiffs abroad to serve our writs upon foreign subjects.

In succeeding years the exercise of the jurisdiction has been described as 'a departure from the jurisdiction recognised by the comity of nations and an invasion of the sovereignty of the state within which leave to serve is granted.'[9]

The three strains are brought together in the statement of Scott LJ in *George Monro* v. *American Cyanamid*[10]

Service out of the jurisdiction at the instance of our courts is necessarily prima facie an interference with the exclusive jurisdiction of the sovereignty of the foreign country where service is to be effected. I have known many continental lawyers of different nations in the past criticize very strongly our law about service out of the jurisdiction. As a matter of international comity it seems to be important to make sure that no such service shall be allowed unless it is clearly within both the letter and the spirit of Or. 11.

As a result, the courts have consistently emphasised, in varying formulations, that the discretion to grant leave to serve out of the jurisdiction must be very sparingly exercised. To adopt some of the expressions used in the leading cases, the discretion must be exercised with considerable care,[11] extreme caution,[12] with forbearance,[13] only sparsely and in exceptional circumstances,[14] and, finally, with discrimination and scrupulous fairness.[15] In practice the case most relied upon for general statements on the exercise of the discretion is *The Hagen*,[16] where Farwell LJ expressly approved the following statement of Pearson J. in *Société Générale de Paris* v. *Dreyfus Brothers*[17]

But of course it becomes a very serious question, and ought always to be considered a very serious question, whether or not . . . it is necessary for the jurisdiction of the Court to be invoked, and whether this Court ought to put a foreigner who owes no allegiance here, to the inconvenience and annoyance of being brought to contest his

---

[9] Lord Normand in *The Brabo* [1949] AC 326 at 357, and also Lord Simonds at 347. See also Lord Radcliffe in *Vitkovice* v. *Korner* [1951] AC at 882; Lord Goddard CJ in *Malik* v. *Narodni Banka Ceskoslovenska* [1946] 2 All ER 663 at 664.

[10] [1944] KB 432 at 437. See also Diplock LJ in *The Chaparral* [1968] 2 Lloyd's Rep. 158 at 163 and in *Mackender* v. *Feldia* [1967] 2 QB 590 at 599; Winn LJ in *Aaronson Brothers* v. *Maderera del Tropica SA* [1967] 2 Lloyd's Rep. 159 at 161–162.

[11] Lord Goddard CJ in *Malik* v. *Narodni Banka Ceskoslovenska, loc. cit. supra*, n. 9.

[12] Winn LJ in *Aaronson Brothers* v. *Maderera del Tropica SA loc. cit. supra*, n. 10.

[13] Wills J. in *Massey* v. *Haynes* (1888) 21 QBD 330 at 334.

[14] Lord Birkenhead in *Dunlop Rubber Company* v. *Dunlop* [1921] 1 AC 367 at 373.

[15] du Parcq LJ in *Ocean Steamship Co. Ltd.* v. *Queensland State Wheat Board* [1941] 1 KB 402 at 417.

[16] [1908] P. 189.

[17] (1885) 29 Ch. D. 239 at 242–243, reversed on different grounds (1887) 37 Ch. D. 215.

rights in this country, and I for one say, most distinctly, that I think this Court ought to be exceedingly careful before it allows a writ to be served out of the jurisdiction.

The reason why it has been necessary to elaborate the point of the extreme care that is required before leave should be given is that the writer detects a tendency in the recent cases discussed below to be somewhat less strict than the authorities require.

What, then, are the factors which the court takes into account when deciding whether to exercise the discretion of the court to allow or refuse leave to serve notice of proceedings out of the jurisdiction? As Tucker LJ made clear in *International Corp.* v. *Besser Manufacturing Co.*[18] the way in which the discretion is exercised in one case is not much guide in another. But in every case where discretion is given to a judge, the discretion must be exercised judicially and on the correct principles. To the extent that discretion is exercised in the light of all the facts, each case does depend on its special facts. But for the practitioner as well as for the academic, the way in which it has been exercised in the past is a pointer to the arguments which can be successfully put forward in the future.

The doctrine of *forum non conveniens* in its strict sense is that a court which undoubtedly has jurisdiction may or must decline to exercise it because for reasons of convenience some other court is the appropriate forum. As the United States Supreme Court put it in *Gulf Oil Corp.* v. *Gilbert*:[19]

In all cases in which the doctrine of *forum non conveniens* comes into play, it presupposes at least two forums in which the defendant is amenable to process; the doctrine furnishes criteria for choice between them . . . The principle of *forum non conveniens* is simply that a court may resist imposition upon its jurisdiction even when jurisdiction is authorised by the letter of a general venue statute.

Although there have been suggestions that English law has a general theory of *forum non conveniens*, this writer agrees with Dr Morris[20] that English law does not have a general rule that an English court may decline to exercise jurisdiction on the ground that another court is the more convenient forum. When the English court has jurisdiction over a defendant who was present in England at the time of service of the writ, mere convenience is not enough to deprive the English court of jurisdiction.[21]

---

[18] [1950] 1 KB 488 at 492.

[19] (1947) 330 US 501 at 506–507. For the doctrine of *forum non conveniens* in the United States, see Ehrenzweig, *The Conflict of Laws* (1962) p. 121 *et seq.* and in Scotland, see Anton, *Private International Law* (1967) p. 148 *et seq.*

[20] Morris, *The Conflict of Laws* (1971) pp. 82–83 discussing, in particular, Inglis (1965) 81 LQR 380.

[21] See *Maharanee of Baroda* v. *Wildenstein* [1972] 2 QB 283, CA, in which the Court of

But in Order 11 cases the position is different and the question of the convenient forum is in practice paramount. The notion of *forum non conveniens* is not frequently invoked in terms probably because English law does not know the doctrine as such. But the grounds of the decisions on Order 11 show clearly that the underlying principle is one of convenience. More recently the *forum conveniens* factor has come to be expressed in terms by the courts. Thus in *Mauroux* v. *Pereira*[22] Megarry J. said

> . . . it is for the plaintiff to estabilsh not only that the case falls within some part of rule 1, but also that the case is otherwise a proper one for service out of the jurisdiction; and these latter words must include the issue of forum conveniens

and in *Maharanee of Baroda* v. *Wildenstein*[23] Edmund Davies LJ said: 'There are branches of our law in which the forum conveniens is a factor generally of decisive importance' and he gave as an example cases where the issue was whether leave to serve a writ out of the jurisdiction should be granted. In deciding what the convenient forum is the following factors have been relied on most frequently:

(*a*) What law governs the substance

In theory the governing law should not make much difference. It is otherwise when the main issue is whether the contract is governed by English law for the purpose of bringing the case within Order 11. But if the English court has jurisdiction to hear the action and by the English rules of the conflict of laws some foreign law governs, then evidence of the foreign law may be produced which the English court can then apply. But in practice, where there is any doubt as to whether the English court should exercise jurisdiction, the relevance of foreign law will be an important factor in the scale.[24]

Appeal reaffirmed that mere balance of convenience is not a sufficient ground for depriving a plaintiff of the advantage of prosecuting his action in an English court; to justify a stay the defendant has to prove affirmatively that it would be oppressive or an abuse of the process and that a stay would not cause injustice to the plaintiff: *St Pierre* v. *South American Stores* [1936] 1 KB 382.   [22] [1972] 1 WLR 962 at 965.

[23] [1972] 2 QB at p. 294. Another branch where convenience plays a part, although by no means a decisive one, is where there is a forum selection clause and the question arises whether the English court will give it effect. In *The Fehmarn* [1958] 1 WLR 159 at 162 Denning LJ (as he then was) thought the vital question in deciding whether a submission to the exclusive jurisdiction of a foreign court should be enforced was 'with what country is the dispute most closely concerned'. But see now *The Eleftheria* [1970] P. 94 for a different test, discussed by Collins (1971) 2 J. Mar. L. & Comm. 363 at 370.

[24] Two examples among many may be taken: in *Cresswell* v. *Parker* (1879) 11 Ch. D. 601, CA, the relief claimed was *inter alia* that the trusts of a settlement governed by Scots law be carried into execution; it was held that even if there were jurisdiction under Order 11, it would be more convenient and proper for the trust to be administered by a Scots court rather than by an English court, since *inter alia* the Scots court would know exactly what the effect of

(b) The place of the subject matter of the action

In the normal contract or tort case under Order 11 the subject matter of the action will not normally be property. Where jurisdiction is exercised under rule 1 (1) (a), (b) or (e) as affecting land or trust property in England, the fact that the property is in England is not one of the factors to be taken into account in deciding whether undoubted jurisdiction should be exercised, but a condition precedent to the exercise of the jurisdiction. But in other cases, such as where jurisdiction is exercised under rule 1 (1) (c) or (j) on the ground that the defendant is domiciled or resident in England or is a necessary or proper party, then the situation of property may be relevant though it is rarely decisive.[25]

(c) Whether there is a foreign court which has jurisdiction

If the proposed defendant seeks to argue that England is not the convenient forum he will have to show that there is a foreign court which does have jurisdiction and perhaps also, in exceptional cases, that it will exercise its jurisdiction justly.[26]

(d) Whether there are already foreign proceedings pending

This was an important consideration in *The Hagen*,[27] where there had been a collision between three ships in the Elbe, two of which were British and one of which was German. There were already pending in Germany

the Scots settlement would be. In *Mackender* v. *Feldia* [1967] 2 QB 590 the Court of Appeal relied on the fact that the law of Belgium was the presumptive proper law and that whether the contract would be void for non disclosure was therefore a matter for Belgian law. The court therefore refused leave and left the parties to their contractual choice of Belgian jurisdiction. But it must be emphasised that the mere fact that foreign law governs is not conclusive in any sense as to the exercise of the discretion. Thus there may be no dispute as to the foreign law (see *Gibbon* v. *Commerz und Creditbank AG* [1958] 2 Lloyd's Rep. 113, CA) or there may be such special circumstances as existed in *Oppenheimer* v. *Louis Rosenthal* [1937] 1 All ER 23, CA, where the background was provided by the persecution of the Jews in Germany: the plaintiff's case involved allegations of the breach in England of a contract governed by German law under which the German defendant company employed the German plaintiff to work in England. The Court of Appeal clearly thought that German law would be abused against the plaintiff in Germany and preferred that the case should be heard in England with the help of the German lawyers then refugees in London.

[25] See, e.g., *Cresswell* v. *Parker, supra*, n. 24: *Société Générale de Paris* v. *Dreyfus Brothers, supra*, n. 17.

[26] Cf. *Ellinger* v. *Guinness Mahon & Co.* [1939] 4 All ER 16: *Aaronson Brothers* v. *Maderera del Tropica SA* [1967] 2 Lloyd's Rep. 159.

[27] [1908] P. 189. But in *Société Générale de Paris* v. *Dreyfus Brothers, supra*, n. 17, the fact that proceedings were pending in France between the same parties does not appear to have been regarded as a substantial factor until the French court actually decided the dispute between the time the Order 11 question was heard by Pearson J. and the time it was before the Court of Appeal. See also *Re De Penny* [1891] 2 Ch. 63.

proceedings by the owners of the German ship against the owners of the two British ships, when the owners of one of the British ships commenced proceedings in England against, *inter alia*, the owner of the German ship. The existence of the German proceedings was a major factor in the refusal of leave under Order 11.

(*e*) Where the evidence is and where the witnesses are

This has always been regarded as a factor of general importance. Lord James in *Chemische Fab.* v. *Badische Fab.*[28] emphasised that one of the disadvantages of exercising jurisdiction over a foreigner was that he might be dragged before the English court 'without possible means of proof' and subsequent cases show the importance of the place of evidence.[29] The evidence in question may be documents, so that their presence abroad may be used to prevent the assumption of jurisdiction, just as their presence in England may justify its assumption.[30] The location of witnesses is even more important. Thus in *The Metamorphosis*[31] the plaintiffs were Dutch, the defendants were Greek and the ship was lost off Holland. Leave was not given to serve out of the jurisdiction, the most consequential factor being the inconvenience of collecting witnesses from abroad.

(*f*) The effectiveness of the court's exercise of jurisdiction

The question of the effectiveness of the English court's judgment is not often in practice raised, because it is not likely to impress an English judge if the proposed defendant indicates that he will not comply with or satisfy the English order or judgment and that it will not be enforced abroad. The effectiveness is most often raised when an injunction is the main or only relief sought.[32]

(*g*) The real object of the English proceedings

If it appears on the evidence that the plaintiff seeking leave to serve out of the jurisdiction does not have the bona fide purpose of having the dispute decided by the English court, but some other collateral purpose, leave may

---

[28] [1904–7] All ER Rep. 234; 90 LT 733.

[29] See, e.g., Slesser LJ in *Kroch* v. *Rossell, supra*, n. 23.

[30] See, e.g., *Tottenham* v. *Barry* (1879) 12 Ch. D. 797 and *Kinahan* v. *Kinahan* (1890) 45 Ch. D. 78 (assets abroad) and *Williams* v. *Cartwright* [1895] 1 QB 142 (assets in England).

[31] [1953] 1 WLR 543.

[32] See *Marshall* v. *Marshall* (1888) 38 Ch. D. 330. Cf. *Re Burland's Trade Mark* (1889) 41 Ch. D. 542.

be refused. Thus, in *The Hagen*,[33] the prime object of the plaintiffs was to embarrass the German defendants by dragging them to England.

It is not possible to catalogue every conceivable factor which may be relevant under Order 11, nor is it possible to measure precisely their relative strengths. But the factors listed above must always be considered in any difficult Order 11 situation to see whether the exercise of jurisdiction can be resisted, and if so on what grounds.

II

In this section three recent decisions will be considered to see whether they throw any light on the exercise of the jurisdiction under Order 11 and the modern approach of the courts. The first case is not in terms concerned with the discretion at all, but rather whether the matter came at all within the New South Wales equivalent of Order 11: *Distillers Co. (Biochemicals) Ltd.* v. *Thompson*. In the second case, there was no doubt that the case was within Order 11 and the only question was one of discretion: *Buttes Gas & Oil Co.* v. *Hammer*. In the third, there were two questions: whether the case was within Order 11 and, if it was, should the discretion be exercised to grant leave to serve out of the jurisdiction: *Coast Lines Ltd.* v. *Hudig & Veder Chartering*.

(*a*) Distillers Co. (Biochemicals) Ltd. *v.* Thompson[34]

In this case the Privy Council sitting as an appeal court from New South Wales was faced with the question of the jurisdiction of Australian courts over the English manufacturers of a sedative containing thalidomide. The plaintiff was the infant daughter of a woman who had taken the drug; the child was born without arms and with defective eyesight; she claimed against the English manufacturer and the Australian company for damages.

The plaintiff's case was that her birth with the disabilities was due to the fact that her mother had taken the sedative containing thalidomide during pregnancy and that thalidomide had a harmful effect on the foetus of an unborn child during early pregnancy. The limited and narrow question raised on the appeal was whether a cause of action had arisen against the English company in New South Wales under the local equivalent of Order 11. Section 18 (4) of the Common Law Procedure Act 1899 of New South Wales is to the broad effect that the court has a discretion to exercise

---

[33] [1908] P. at 189, *per* Lord Alverstone CJ. Cf. *Harris* v. *Fleming* (1879) 13 Ch. D. 208 where the party objecting to the exercise of the English jurisdiction was not acting in good faith.   [34] [1971] AC 458 (P.C.)

jurisdiction over a non-resident if 'there is a cause of action which arose within the jurisdiction'.[35] The Privy Council was asked merely whether the cause of action had arisen in New South Wales. No question therefore of the judge's discretion to authorise leave out of the jurisdiction arose on the appeal.

The facts assumed for the purpose of the appeal were broadly as follows: Distillers Co. (Biochemicals) Ltd. was an English company carrying on business in Great Britain, one of whose products was a sedative and sleep-inducing tablet marketed under the name Distival, the principal ingredient of which was thalidomide. The thalidomide had been obtained in bulk by Distillers from German manufacturers. The tablets were sold to an Australian distributor (which was a subsidiary of Distillers) which marketed and sold them through chemists in Australia with the advertising matter and in the form supplied by Distillers. The accompanying printed matter described the drug as a sedative with no side-effects.

There were no pleadings and the Privy Council was therefore forced to piece together the plaintiff's case, the main complaints of which appear to have been (i) Distillers knew or ought to have known of the harmful effects of thalidomide, and (ii) Distillers failed to warn ultimate consumers of the danger. On the assumption that those facts could be proved, where had the cause of action arisen? Where had the tort been committed?

The importance of restraint in assuming jurisdiction over foreigners under Order 11 is implicit in this important decision of the Privy Council. The court indicated three possible theories as to where the cause of action arose. The first was that 'the cause of action' meant the whole cause of action—on that basis, every ingredient of it must have occurred within the jurisdiction. The second was that it was necessary and sufficient that the ingredient which was last (in point of time) had occurred within the jurisdiction. The third was that the act on the part of the defendant which gave the plaintiff his substantial cause of complaint must have occurred within the jurisdiction.[36]

---

[35] The equivalent wording in Order 11, rule 1 (h) is 'if the action begun by the writ is founded on a tort committed within the jurisdiction'. In practice, the notion of the cause of action arising in England is used in the Order 11 cases. See, e.g., *George Munro Ltd.* v. *American Cyanamid* [1944] KB 432, at 437 *per* Scott LJ; that well-known decision is most unsatisfactory. The claim was so lacking in merit and the affidavit seeking leave of the court to serve out of the jurisdiction was so defective that it was not necessary for the Court of Appeal to consider in depth the important question raised. As a result, the unreserved judgments do not fully distinguish between the two relevant questions: first, was the tort committed in England? Second, if so, should the discretion be exercised in favour of the plaintiff?

[36] What these theories mean in practice in the case of negligence is as follows: assuming the existence of a duty, breach of duty and damage to the plaintiff, under the first theory both the breach of duty and the damage must have occurred within the jurisdiction; under the second, the damage must have occurred within the jurisdiction; and under the third, the breach of duty must have occurred within the jurisdiction. The Privy Council rejected the first because

The Privy Council adopted the third solution, that it is the place where the act which gives rise to the complaint occurs. The court said:[37]

> [T]he search is for the most appropriate court to try the action, and the degree of connection between the cause of action and the country concerned should be the determining factor . . . The right approach is, when the tort is complete, to look back over the series of events constituting it and ask the question, where in substance did this cause of action arise?

What is interesting about this formulation is that the Privy Council is in effect saying that the question of what is the convenient forum should be considered in interpreting Order 11 and equivalent rules and not only in the exercise of discretion under such rules. If the tort of negligence could be considered as having been committed *both* in the place where the careless act or omission had occurred *and* in the place where the damage was suffered, then the choice of the proper forum should in theory arise at the second stage of the inquiry: that is, assuming the tort to be within Order 11, how is the discretion of the judge to be exercised? To some extent such a method may be fairer to the plaintiff in cases where the issues are relatively narrow. Thus, if (say) the only issue is likely to be whether and to what extent damage was suffered, it would not necessarily be appropriate to insist that the plaintiff resort to the courts where the negligent act occurred.

This confusion is underlined by the characterisation of the alleged tort which is offered by the Privy Council on the assumed facts of the case. The tablets, printed matter and the package were supplied as a unit by Distillers to its Australian subsidiary in the form in which they were to reach the ultimate consumer. Yet the Privy Council was forced by its formulation of

it was inconsistent with the English decisions on the Common Law Procedure Act 1852 (especially *Jackson* v. *Spittall* (1870) LR 5 CP 542) and, more importantly, because it was too restrictive for modern times. In practice, of course, it would prevent the exercise of jurisdiction in multi-State torts by every court other than the court of the defendant's residence. The second theory was rejected, it seems, because it was too artificial and too dependent on technical rules of English pleadings. It is true that in one sense at least the tort of negligence has not been committed until damage has occurred, because damage is an essential ingredient in the cause of action. Thus, for Statute of Limitation purposes, time does not begin to run in negligence cases until damage occurs (see Winfield and Jolowicz, *Tort* (9th ed. 1971), p. 660 and cases there cited), but the Privy Council in line with authority (*George Munro* v. *American Cyanamid* [1944] KB 432) rejected such a solution as too artificial, since the place where the last ingredient occurs may be entirely fortuitous and the essence of the tort is breach of duty. See also *Cordova Land Co. Ltd.* v. *Victor Brothers Inc.* [1961] 1 WLR 793 at 798, where Winn J. preferred to look at the place where the substance of the alleged wrong occurred. This has some similarity with the approach of the Privy Council and is open to similar criticism. The general subject of the place of commission of a tort is discussed in an excellent article by Webb and North (1965) 14 ICLQ 1314. See also Ehrenzweig, *Conflict of Laws* (1962) at pp. 545–546, whose views are not, however, representative of American legal opinion and authority.

[37] [1971] AC at pp. 467–468.

the jurisdictional rule to characterise the act of negligence as the failure to give a warning that the tablets could be dangerous if taken by an expectant mother in the first three months of pregnancy. That failure, the court said, had taken place in both England and in New South Wales. Thus the tort was characterised as negligent failure to warn rather than negligent manufacture. Despite its apparent attractiveness, it is a very narrow distinction which is hard to support in logic.[38] It seems to suggest that the result might have been different if the sedative had been safe under no circumstances whatever—in such a case it would have been negligent manufacture which would have been the gist of the action, and not negligent failure to warn. The paradoxical result of such a distinction would be that the greater the negligence of the defendants, the less amenable to the jurisdiction they would be. This, from the point of view of the plaintiff, would have been an absurd result—the greater the negligence, the further she has to travel to sue? But the real weakness of the distinction arises from the fact that the issues would be the same whether the complaint were negligent manufacture or negligent failure to warn of danger—the essential issue would be the real nature of the drug and the failure to appreciate it. The real difficulty was thus avoided by the purely mechanical characterisation of the domestic rule of tortious liability. It is suggested therefore that in this decision the Privy Council did not give enough weight to the potentiality of the filtering process which the judge's discretion provides at the second stage of the enquiry.

(b) *Buttes Gas & Oil Co.* v. *Hammer*[39]

The facts of this case were very colourful. The plaintiff was a Californian oil company which had been granted an oil concession by the local sheikh, the Ruler of Sharjah, of one of the Trucial States in the Persian Gulf, which were at the relevant time under the protection of the British Government. The first Defendant was the Chairman of the second Defendant, which was another Californian oil company which had been granted an oil concession by another local sheikh, the Ruler of Umm al Qaywayn, of an adjoining Trucial State. Both oil concessions were

---

[38] For example, the tort in *Donoghue* v. *Stevenson* [1932] AC 562 may be characterised as negligent mis-statement acted upon just before the bottle is drunk instead of negligent manufacture occurring when the soft drink is manufactured. There is no logical difference between a tablet containing a dangerous drug and a bottle containing a snail labelled ginger beer. In itself neither is a dangerous object—it is what will happen to it which will make it dangerous; with an adequate warning each would be harmless. See *Hedley Byrne & Co. Ltd.* v. *Heller & Partners Ltd.* [1964] AC 465, especially at 496 *per* Lord Morris and at 508 *per* Lord Hodson. For a more cautious formulation of a similar idea see Winfield and Jolowicz, *Tort* (9th ed., 1971), p. 230.

[39] [1971] 3 All ER 1025. The writer must at this point declare an interest, as his firm was professionally engaged in this case on behalf of the defendants.

offshore concessions and between the two concession areas lay an island, Abu Musa, which was in the Sharjah concession area but was adjacent to the Umm al Qaywayn concession area. The Ruler of Sharjah issued a decree extending his territorial waters from three miles to twelve miles and laid claim to an area which the defendant company claimed was within its concession area. As a result of this dispute, the British Government prevented by force exploration work by the Defendants.[40] In June 1970 the second Defendants, Occidental Petroleum Corporation, brought two actions against the Buttes Gas & Oil Co. in the courts of California, alleging *inter alia* conspiracy between the Buttes Gas & Oil Co. and the Ruler of Sharjah to backdate the decree so as to claim 12-mile territorial waters and deprive Occidental of part of its concession. One of those actions at least had been halted by a decision of the Federal District Court that the proceedings be stayed on the ground that they involved a foreign act of State.[41]

In October 1970 the Chairman of Occidental at a press conference in London, in answer to some questions about the Persian Gulf, made allegations about Buttes similar to those which were being made in the Californian actions. Buttes issued proceedings for slander (not libel because the statements had not been repeated in any newspaper) and asked for leave to serve out of the jurisdiction. Leave was given by the Master but Mr Justice Shaw, in an unreported judgment, set aside the proceedings because he did not think it a proper case for the jurisdiction of the court to serve out of the jurisdiction to be exercised. The main arguments of the defendants were that all parties to the action were resident and/or incorporated in California; none of the parties carried on business in England; the only connection of the alleged slander with England was that the words were spoken in England; the alleged slander related to facts and events outside England; and there were already proceedings involving the same issues of fact pending in California.

This was not strictly speaking a *lis alibi pendens* case, in the sense it did not involve the question whether English or foreign proceedings should be stayed on the ground of other pending proceedings. But an analogous question was involved and it is perhaps for this reason that Lord Denning MR and Megaw LJ invoked the doctrine of *lis alibi pendens*. Lord Denning said:[42]

If the Californian actions were live actions about to come for trial, there would be something to be said for letting the issues be fought out in California. But the Californian actions are not live actions. They have been halted. In March 1971 they

---

[40] See *The Times*, June 2, 1970.
[41] See *Occidental Petroleum Corp.* v. *Buttes Gas & Oil Co.*, 331 F. Supp. 92 (DC Cal, 1971) noted at (1971) 65 AJIL 815. [42] [1971] 3 All ER at 1027.

were halted by a federal judge in California. The reason is because they involve issues about the acts of state of foreign powers. Judges of the United States will not allow the actions of foreign powers to be litigated within their courts. That decision of the federal judge is subject to appeal. I expect it will go to appeal. But goodness knows how long it will take! Even if the appeal succeeds and the actions proceed, goodness knows how long it will be before the action comes on for trial! In these circumstances, I do not think there is any room for the doctrine of lis alibi pendens. The pendency or non-pendency of those actions is not a factor in the scale.

On the issue of the convenient forum and the defendants' submission that California was the right place for the action to be tried Lord Denning thought, first, that in the matter of evidence England was no less convenient because witnesses would have to come also from the Persian Gulf and England as well as from California, and, second, that the dispute was international in character and not really Californian.

Megaw LJ added that Mr Justice Shaw was wrong to have treated *The Hagen*[43] as authority for the proposition that, in the exercise of the discretion, if there was any doubt at all, it ought to be resolved in favour of the foreigner. He thought that all that Farwell LJ had in mind in the relevant dictum was a doubt on the construction of Order 11, that is, a doubt as to whether the case fell within any of the sub-heads of jurisdiction.

Lord Denning's formulation is a helpful one for future cases: where does convenience lie and is this a dispute which properly belongs to another court? If there is any basic criticism to make of the approach of the Court of Appeal it is that one detects that the court is placing the burden on those who seek to have the proceedings set aside of proving that England is not the convenient forum. The strictness of the older authorities would, it suggested, lead to the inescapable conclusion that it is for the applicants under Order 11 to show that the case is within the letter and the spirit of Order 11.

(c) *Coast Lines Ltd.* v. *Hudig & Veder Chartering NV*[44]

This case involved two questions: first, whether a charterparty was governed by English law for the purpose of Order 11, and, second, if the charterparty was governed by English law, how the discretion to authorise service should be exercised.

This is not the place for a detailed discussion of the proper law aspects of this case, but a summary is indispensable for the understanding of the basic

---

[43] [1908] P. 189.

[44] [1972] 2 QB 34. See Bissett-Johnson (1972) 21 ICLQ 530, who overlooks the fact that, in many cases of this kind, the defendant who fails to set aside service under Order 11 will go on to defend the action and thereby submit to the jurisdiction.

point (and its importance for the modern approach to Order 11)—namely, that the Court of Appeal allowed service out of the jurisdiction in a case where (a) the contract was only doubtfully governed by English law and (b) the result of the dispute would depend on whether it was heard in England or in the competing forum, Holland.

The plaintiffs were an English company who chartered their ship to the defendants, the Dutch company, on a voyage charter. The charterparty was for carriage of cargo on an English ship from Rotterdam in the Netherlands to the Republic of Ireland. It was drawn up in Rotterdam and signed there on behalf of both parties, after negotiations conducted over the telephone between the charterers in Rotterdam and the shipowners' brokers in Cardiff. The document was in English (in the Gencon form of charterparty used throughout European shipping trade) and the freight and demurrage were expressed in sterling.

The issue arose in the following way: the charterparty contained the usual exemption whereby the shipowners were relieved from liability for unseaworthiness, unless due to the personal negligence of the owners or their managers; the bills of lading were issued in Rotterdam and made the owners liable to the cargo-owners to exercise due diligence to make the ship seaworthy. Therefore, as between the shipowners and the charterers, the shipowners were not liable in the ordinary way for unseaworthiness; but, as between the shipowners and the cargo-owners, the shipowners were liable. Under English law where the charterers have responsibility for presentation of the bills of lading and thereby impose on the shipowners a greater liability than that provided for in the charterparty, they are bound to indemnify the shipowners against their liability to the cargo-owners.[45] By English law the exemption in the charterparty was valid,[46] but by Dutch law the exception clause must be disregarded, because the Dutch Commercial Code at the relevant time prohibited such an exception by applying the Hague Rules even to charterparties. The uncontested evidence on Dutch law was that the Commercial Code applied the relevant provisions to all cases of carriage of goods by sea from the Netherlands, even though the contract of carriage was expressed to be governed by some other law, or was more closely connected with some other law, or the parties provided for the exclusive jurisdiction of some court outside the Netherlands.

The English shipowners were claiming an indemnity from the Dutch charterers and sought leave to serve their writ out of the jurisdiction. From the point of view of the plaintiffs, it was not a mere question of convenience—the probability was that they would succeed if the case were

---

[45] See *Scrutton on Charterparties* (17th ed. 1964), p. 65.

[46] Because the prohibition in the Carriage of Goods by Sea Act 1924 does not apply to charterparties.

fought in England, and would lose if they had to seek their remedy in Holland. Lord Denning MR and Megaw LJ held that the charterparty was governed by English law and that leave to serve out of the jurisdiction should be given. Stephenson LJ had doubts about the proper law question, but he was not prepared to dissent and agreed on the discretion point.

The modern English law on the proper law of the contract is that in the absence of an express choice of law and in the absence of surrounding circumstances from which a choice can be inferred, a contract will be regarded as being governed by the system of law with which the transaction has its closest and most real connection. In practice it is difficult to draw a clear distinction between the choice inferred from the circumstances on the one hand and the close connection test on the other,[47] and it may in fact be a distinction without a difference, or a difference only of language and not of law.[48]

Rules and presumptions are nowadays of very little weight in this area and yet Lord Denning's judgment has a curiously nineteenth-century air about it. In applying the closest and most real connection test, he thought the fact that the contract was made in Rotterdam by Dutch charterers for shipment at Rotterdam pointed to Dutch law, but that the contract was for carriage in an English ship owned by English owners for carriage on the high seas pointed to English law. He went on:

Put those two into the scales, one on one side, the other on the other. You will find they are equal; other circumstances point one way, then another. There is nothing to choose. So, as a last resort, you take the law of the flag, which is English law.[49]

For Lord Denning the other decisive factor was the invalidity of the clause under Dutch law. Again applying the nineteenth-century presumption, he regarded that as a pointer to English law because it could not be assumed that the Dutch charterers would put their signature to a contract which they did not intend to honour.[50]

Megaw LJ's approach was somewhat different, although the result of his reasoning was precisely the same. He thought that the illegality under Dutch law was only relevant as negativing an inferred intention that Dutch law should govern. He approached the question from the point of view of the substance of the transaction rather than the form of the contract. He concluded:

---

[47] See, e.g., Lord Morris in *Compagnie d'Armement Maritime SA* v. *Compagnie Tunisienne de Navigation SA* [1971] AC 572 at 587 and Lord Dilhorne in *James Miller & Partners Ltd.* v. *Whitworth Street Estates (Manchester) Ltd.* [1970] AC 583 at 611.

[48] See Collins, *op. cit., supra*, n. 23 at pp. 364–365 and 378.

[49] [1972] 2 QB at 44.

[50] For another recent example of the application of this presumption, see *Sayers* v. *International Drilling* [1971] 3 All ER 163, criticised by Collins (1972) 21 ICLQ 320 (post, p. 393).

the fact that the subject-matter of the charterparty was an English ship and that the whole of the transaction contemplated by the contract concerned the activities of that English ship, in loading, carrying and discharging the cargo, produces the result that the transaction, viewed as a whole and weighing all the relevant factors, has a closer and more real connection with English law than with the law of the Netherlands.[51]

Stephenson LJ was inclined to the view that the balance tipped, if at all, in favour of Dutch law but deferred to the views of Roskill J. (the commercial judge) and the other members of the Court of Appeal as being more experienced in such matters than he.

It will be clear from the above summary that the question of the proper law in this case is not free from doubt and that only Megaw LJ seemed to have any confidence in the conclusion that English law governed. The court was clearly very sympathetic to the plaintiffs and was unwilling to leave them to their fate in the Dutch courts. Yet the trend of the authorities under Order 11 is that extreme caution must be exercised before granting leave to serve out of the jurisdiction. But it is hard to avoid the conclusion in this case that the contract was found to be governed by English law in order to bring the case within Order 11 and that the Court of Appeal's distaste for the Dutch law impelled them to uphold the judge's exercise of his discretion to allow service out of the jurisdiction. Indeed, both Lord Denning and Megaw LJ treated Dutch law as the main reason why the plaintiffs should be allowed to sue in England. In Lord Denning's words:

Once it is held that the charterparty is by implication governed by English law, the next question is whether leave should be given to serve the writ out of the jurisdiction. This is a very serious question. The charterers are a Netherlands company. They owe no allegiance here. They have no place of business here. They have, as yet, no assets here. It is a strong thing to force them to come to England to contest a case against them. So we must be exceedingly careful before doing so. That was pointed out long ago: *The Hagen*. If the Netherlands courts were free to apply the proper law of the contract (*i.e.*, English law), I would not be disposed to grant leave to serve out of the jurisdiction. But the Netherlands courts are not free. They are compelled by the Netherlands law to apply a special law of the Netherlands (*i.e.*, Art, 517d), which is not the proper law of the contract and which is set out of line with the maritime law of all other countries. The Netherlands courts are compelled to apply a law which is contrary to the general understanding of commercial men. In these circumstances, I do not think we should send the English shipowners to the Netherlands courts. We should retain the case in these courts where we can and will apply English law, which is the proper law of the contract.[52]

---

[51] [1972] 2 QB at 47.

[52] *Ibid*. at 45. See also Megaw LJ at 49.

It is suggested that it is not a proper use of the power to serve out of the jurisdiction to bring a foreigner before the English court in a doubtful case and deprive him of the benefit of the law of his own country. The emphasis is on the doubtful aspect of the case. In *The Hagen*[53] Farwell LJ said that doubts on the construction of Order II should be resolved in favour of the foreigner. Megaw LJ in *Buttes Gas & Oil Co.* v. *Hammer*[54] said that the statement of Farwell LJ was limited to doubts in construction and could not be interpreted as meaning that any doubt as to the exercise of the discretion should be resolved in favour of the foreigner. Stephenson LJ in the *Coast Lines* case said: 'It is tempting to say, as Farwell LJ indicated in *The Hagen*, that the court's discretion ought to be exercised only in plain cases to which the rule clearly applies but not in doubtful or borderline cases like the present.'[55] And yet curiously he goes on to resist that temptation and to conclude, 'that the discretion given by the rule is unfettered except by comity, convenience and the justice of the case'.

It is submitted that the discretion *is* limited and should not be exercised against a foreigner in doubtful cases, since Order II, rule 4, makes it clear that leave shall not be granted 'unless it shall be made sufficiently to appear to the Court that the case is a proper one for service out of the jurisdiction'. In particular, the Court's distaste for the law which the foreign court will apply should not be determining.

III

In December 1971 the United States Court of Appeals for the Third Circuit gave judgment in an appeal which is of considerable practical and academic relevance to the English confict of laws. In *Somportex Ltd.* v. *Philadelphia Chewing Gum Corp.*[56] the American court enforced an English judgment which had been rendered in default of defence against a foreign defendant. The interest of the decision lies both in the light it throws on the effect abroad of familiar English procedural steps and also in the contrast it offers to the received English thinking on the recognition of foreign judgments.

In order that the procedural steps taken in England may be readily understood, it may be helpful if the principal steps in an Order II proceeding are summarised here:

(i) An application for the grant of leave is made by affidavit and by Order II, rule 4 (2), it is provided that 'no such leave shall be granted unless it

---

[53] [1908] P. 189 at 201.   [54] [1971] 3 All ER 1025.

[55] [1972] 2 QB at 51.

[56] 318 F. Supp. 161 (ED Pa. 1970), aff'd. 453 F. 2d (3rd Cir. 1971), cert. den. 92 S. Ct. 1294 (1972).

shall be made sufficiently to appear to the Court that the case is a proper one for service out of the jurisdiction'.[57]

(ii) Once the order has been made (usually by a master or, in the Commercial Court, by a judge) notice of the writ will be served abroad by the plaintiff on the defendant (Order 11, rule 5).

(iii) If the defendant takes no further steps the plaintiff will be entitled to enter judgment against the defendant in default of appearance (Order 13).

(iv) If the defendant enters an unconditional appearance he will be regarded by the English court (and by most foreign courts) as having submitted to the jurisdiction of the English court and if he wishes to avoid such a submission and to contest the jurisdiction he will be well advised not to enter an unconditional appearance.

(v) If the defendant wishes to contest the jurisdiction of the English court he may avail himself of Order 12, rule 8 (1), which provides:

A defendant to an action may at any time before entering an appearance therein, or, if he has entered a conditional appearance, within fourteen days after entering the appearance, apply to the Court for an order setting aside the writ of service of the writ, or notice of the writ, on him, or declaring that the writ or notice has not been duly served on him or discharging any order giving leave to serve the writ or notice on him out of the jurisdiction.

The application is normally made by summons supported by affidavit.

(vi) The rule just quoted clearly envisages that a defendant may apply to the court to contest its jurisdiction before entering any kind of appearance.[58] The entry of appearance is a technical step which involves nothing more than filling in a form in duplicate and lodging the completed form at the High Court. But because failure to take this step can result in a judgment being entered against a defendant by default, the normal practice where the jurisdiction is contested is for the defendant to enter what is called a 'conditional appearance'. By Order 12, rule 7, it is provided:

A conditional appearance . . . is to be treated for all purposes as an unconditional appearance unless the Court otherwise orders or the defendant applies to the Court within the time limited for the purpose, for an order under rule 8 [i.e. an order that the writ or service be set aside] and the Court makes an order thereunder.

Therefore if the defendant enters a conditional appearance but fails to object to the jurisdiction by a subsequent application, or is unsuccessful in such an application, he is treated by English procedural law as having entered an unconditional appearance.

---

[57] See *Mauroux* v. *Pereira* [1972] 1 WLR 962 for a decision of Megarry J. to the effect that the plaintiff has a dual burden: first to show that the case is within Order 11 and second to persuade the court that the discretion should be exercised in his favour.

[58] See *Boyle* v. *Sacker* (1888) 39 Ch. D. 241.

(vii) In order to complete the procedural picture for the present purpose, by Order 21, rule 1, it is provided, 'A party who had entered an appearance in an action may withdraw the appearance at any time with the leave of the Court.' But leave to withdraw an appearance is not normally given unless the appearance has been entered by accident or mistake.

The normal practice for a defendant who contests the jurisdiction is to enter a conditional appearance and then take steps to set aside the writ and service of the notice of the proceedings. But as indicated above it is possible, although not common practice, for the jurisdiction to be contested before entry of appearance. One of the reasons why it is not common is that if no appearance of any kind is entered it is possible for the plaintiff to enter judgment in default of appearance. If, however, the plaintiff did so enter judgment in the knowledge that the jurisdiction was to be contested by the defendant, the judgment would undoubtedly be set aside and in all probability the plaintiff would be ordered to pay the costs of the setting aside.

The practical reason why a defendant may not wish to enter even a conditional appearance is that if he fails on the jurisdiction point the conditional appearance will be converted into an unconditional appearance and a *foreign* court may regard such an appearance as a voluntary appearance. This raises a problem which is familiar when the effect of an appearance under protest to a foreign court is being considered in the context of the English recognition of foreign judgments. What makes *Somportex* so interesting is that the problem is raised in the court of the original judgment and not, as so often, in the court which is being asked to enforce it.

When an English court is asked to enforce a foreign judgment rendered against a defendant who has merely appeared to object to the jurisdiction of the foreign court, the better view is that such an appearance is not to be regarded as a submission to the jurisdiction of the foreign court for the purposes of enforcement of foreign judgments[59] and that the decision to the contrary in *Harris* v. *Taylor*[60] is probably wrong. This is not the place for a detailed discussion of that case—a judicial discussion can be found in a recent decision of Megaw J.[61] when he referred to a well-known passage from the case of *Re Dulles' Settlement*[62] in which Denning LJ (as he then was) said:

I cannot see how anyone can fairly say that a man has voluntarily submitted to the jurisdiction of a court, when he has all the time been vigorously protesting that it

---

[59] See *Re Dulles' Settlement (No. 2)* [1951] Ch. 842, *Daarnhouwer & Co.* v. *Boulos* [1968] 2 Lloyd's Rep. 259; Dicey and Morris, *The Conflict of Laws* (8th ed. 1967), pp. 976–978.
[60] [1915] 2 KB 580.
[61] *Daarnhouwer & Co.* v. *Boulos* [1968] 2 Lloyd's Rep. 259 at 265–269.
[62] [1951] Ch. 842 at 850.

has no jurisdiction. If he does nothing and lets judgment go against him in default of appearance, he clearly does not submit to the jurisdiction. What difference in principle does it make, if he does not merely do nothing, but actually goes to the court and protests that it has no jurisdiction? I can see no distinction at all . . .

That an appearance to contest the jurisdiction should not be regarded as a voluntary submission is recognised by many treaties. Thus, for example, Article 4, para. 1 (b), of the Anglo-French Treaty for the Reciprocal Enforcement of Judgments 1934 provides (following in this respect the Foreign Judgments (Reciprocal Enforcement) Act 1933, s. 4):

It is understood that the expression 'voluntarily appearing in the proceedings' does not include an appearance merely for the purpose of protecting property situated within the jurisdiction of the original court from seizure, or of obtaining the release of property seized or for the purpose of contesting the jurisdiction of the original court.

Similarly, Article 18 of the EEC Convention on Jurisdiction and Enforcement of Judgments provides that an appearance solely to challenge jurisdiction is not to be regarded as a submission.

The uncertainty which in many systems of law surrounds the question of the effect of an appearance to contest the jurisdiction may explain the procedural steps which the defendants took.

The plaintiff in *Somportex* was an English company which commenced proceedings in the English court in 1967 for breach of contract against a Pennsylvania corporation. The defendant did not do business in England and the plaintiff accordingly applied under Order 11, rule 1 (f), of the Rules of the Supreme Court for leave to serve notice of the writ out of the jurisdiction. Leave was granted by the Master and notice of the writ was served in Pennsylvania. English solicitors then, in accordance with the usual practice, entered a conditional appearance on behalf of the defendants pending a decision whether to take steps to set aside the proceedings on the ground that the case was not within Order 11.

As explained above, in the normal case where the defendant wishes to contest the jurisdiction of the English court, a summons is issued to set aside service of the notice of writ and all subsequent proceedings on the ground that the court should not in its discretion have given leave to serve out of the jurisdiction. In this case a summons was issued but the defendant did not pursue this summons. Instead it applied for leave to withdraw the conditional appearance under the Order 21 rule quoted above. The Master and the Judge in Chambers held that the defendants were entitled to withdraw their appearance, but the Court of Appeal reversed and held that leave should not be given for the withdrawal: *Somportex* v. *Philadelphia Chewing Gum.*[63] The Court of Appeal thought that the conditional

[63] [1968] 3 All ER 26 (CA).

appearance had been entered after competent legal advice and that the American company should not be entitled to go back on the election it had made, since the plaintiffs had continued the English action on the basis of the entry of appearance. Accordingly it was held that leave would not be given for the appearance to be withdrawn. As Lord Denning MR put it:

I think that one has to put oneself in the position of the American company and their advisers when faced with this notice of the writ. They could have not entered an appearance at all, in which case by the law of Pennsylvania they would not be bound by any judgment. Instead of doing that, however, after consultation with a distinguished firm of lawyers in the city of London they decided to enter a conditional appearance. That was a very important step for them to take (especially if they had assets in England or were likely to bring assets into England) because it was an essential way of defending their own position. After all, if they did not enter an appearance at all, and in consequence the English courts have judgment against them in default of appearance, that judgment could be executed against them in England in respect of assets in England. In order to guard against that eventuality, they had first to enter a conditional appearance here, then argue whether it was within the jurisdiction of the court or not. If it was outside the jurisdiction, all well and good. The writ would be set aside. They would go away free. If it was within the jurisdiction, however, their appearance became unconditional and they could fight out the case on the merits. In these circumstances it seems to me that they were very wise to enter a conditional appearance. It was a step which would be advised by any competent lawyer if there was a likelihood that assets would then or afterwards come into England.[64]

He concluded that the defendants having decided on the latter course, the plaintiffs had altered their position.

Salmon LJ added (in apparent disregard of the principle behind the decision of the Court of Appeal—which included Denning LJ—in *Re Dulles' Settlement*[65]):

. . . if the summons to set aside the writ failed, the conditional appearance then becoming unconditional, it would in law amount to a submission to the jurisdiction of the English courts. This would enable the English company to execute any judgment which they might obtain against the American company in the U.S.A.[66]

The basic fallacy behind the reasoning of Salmon LJ is that it is for the foreign court to decide whether there has been a submission (in the sense that notion is understood by the foreign court) and not for the procedural law of the court which rendered the judgment which is sought to be enforced. Under English procedural law, if a conditional appearance has been entered and if the defendant does not succeed in having the proceedings set aside, the appearance automatically becomes an unconditional one. The defendant has not actually voluntarily submitted—he is merely deemed to have done so for local procedural purposes.

[64] *Ibid.* at 29.   [65] [1951] Ch. 842.   [66] [1968] 3 All ER at 31.

In the light of the subsequent American proceedings, it appears that the conversion of the appearance from a conditional one to an unconditional one did not have a substantial effect on the enforceability of the English judgment in the United States. But the defendants clearly thought (like Salmon LJ) that an English judgment would be enforceable if the appearance stood. To put it another way, they thought that the relevant American law was the same as *Harris* v. *Taylor*,[67] that is, a submission to contest the jurisdiction may become, for the purpose of enforcement of foreign judgments, a voluntary submission. No doubt it was for this reason that the defendants sought to withdraw their appearance. It is indeed curious that the Court of Appeal presided over by Lord Denning MR in the *Somportex* case did not take the opportunity to further the policy expressed in *Re Dulles' Settlement*, namely, that individuals should be given an opportunity of contesting the jurisdiction without submitting to it. There were two ways open to the Court of Appeal to allow withdrawal of the appearance. In the first place, although this does not appear to have been argued, by Order 12, rule 7, a conditional appearance is to be treated as unconditional *unless the court otherwise orders* or unless the defendant applies to set aside service and obtains an order to that effect. The court clearly had the power to order the appearance not to stand as unconditional. In the second place, there is nothing in the wording of Order 21, rule 1 (which allows the court to give leave for the withdrawal of an appearance), to suggest that it must be limited to the normal case of accident or mistake. No doubt the Court of Appeal did not find the conduct of the defendants in seeking to withdraw from the English courts very meritorious, but in international cases English courts should be mindful of what they themselves would do if the situation were reversed. Suppose the Pennsylvania court were to take jurisdiction over an English defendant in a similar case, e.g., on the ground that the contract was made in Pennsylvania. Suppose also that the English defendant entered a special or conditional appearance in the Pennsylvania court and contested the jurisdiction of the Pennsylvania court, but unsuccessfully. If the Pennsylvania court were later to give judgment in favour of the plaintiff, the defendant having taken no further part in the proceedings, would the judgment be enforceable in England? The answer on the authorities is probably that the judgment would not be enforced. In the first place, the fact that English courts take jurisdiction in similar cases by virtue of Order 11 is without relevance, since reciprocity plays no part in the English rules on the enforcement of foreign judgments.[68] In the second place, as

---

[67] [1915] 2 KB 580.

[68] A Pennsylvania judgment will only be recognised in England if the defendant was resident or carried on business in Pennsylvania at the commencement of the proceedings or voluntarily submitted to the jurisdiction. Reciprocity plays no part: see *Re Trepca Mines*

explained above, the appearance to contest the jurisdiction of the foreign court will not be regarded by the English court as a voluntary submission to the jurisdiction of the foreign court, even if the foreign court so regards it.

The defendants were given an opportunity by the Court of Appeal to proceed with their application to set aside service of the writ, but they did not take it. They withdrew from the case and after service of the statement of claim on them or their solicitors, judgment was entered in favour of the plaintiffs in default of defence for a very substantial sum. The plaintiffs then sought to enforce the English judgment in the Pennsylvania federal court. It has already been seen that if the situation had been reversed and it had been a question of the enforcement of a Pennsylvanian judgment in England, the judgment would not have been enforced. But the current United States standards for the enforcement of foreign judgments are much less strict and the modern tendency is to recognise foreign judgments if the foreign procedure was fair and if there were sufficient contacts with the foreign country.[69]

When the matter came before the Federal District Court[70] in Pennsylvania, the court held that the English default judgment was enforceable because the English court had personal jurisdiction over the defendants because of the appearance which had become unconditional; even though the purpose of the appearance was to contest the jurisdiction of the Egnlish court, the defendants had made a conscious choice to enter an appearance which by virtue of English law became unconditional. Thus the American court, at first instance, followed an approach like that of the English court in *Harris* v. *Taylor* and did what Salmon LJ in the English proceedings had predicted it would do. But when the case came before the Federal Court of Appeals for the Third Circuit, the appeal court did not apply that line of reasoning (although it did not expressly reject it) and put its decision on broader grounds.

In the American court the defendants resisted enforcement of the judgment on four main grounds. The first was that the facts were such that the case was not in truth within Order 11 and that the English court therefore lacked jurisdiction. The Federal court rejected this argument, as an English court would have done;[71] the reason was that the facts and law relative to the question of the English court's jurisdiction were issues which could have, and should have been, litigated in the English court. The second

---

[1960] 1 WLR 1273 (CA): *Soc. Co-op. Sidmetal* v. *Titan International* [1966] 1 QB 828 (Widgery J.); Dicey and Morris, pp. 985–986.

[69] The decisions, which are by no means uniform, are very fully discussed by Peterson, 'Foreign Country Judgments and the Second Restatement of Conflict of Laws' (1972) 72 Col. L. Rev. 220.   [70] 318 F. Supp. 161 (ED Pa. 1970).

[71] See, e.g., *Pemberton* v. *Hughes* [1899] 1 Ch. 781 (CA) and Dicey and Morris, pp. 1004–1006.

was an attack on the English practice whereby a conditional appearance attacking jurisdiction may be converted into an unconditional one; but the court held that procedure was not contrary to its own notions, since the English practice in that respect was identical to the United States Federal practice and to the Pennsylvania rules of procedure. The third ground of attack was that the English judgment included a sum of damages of loss of goodwill and also a sum by way of lawyers' fees, neither of which items is recoverable according to Pennsylvania law. The court held that to enforce such a judgment was not contrary to public policy.[72] The final argument was a suggestion that as the defendants did not carry on business in England there were not sufficient contacts to meet constitutional standards of due process. That argument was rejected on the ground that the negotiation conducted by the defendants through the alleged agents was an activity sufficient to provide the necessary connection. The authorities on the recognition of inter-State judgments do not lay down a strict test. Indeed all that appears to be necessary is that the defendants have certain minimum contacts with the foreign State such that the maintenance of the action does not offend traditional notions of fair play and substantial justice.[73] The governing standard followed by the Federal court was that laid down more than seventy years ago in the famous case of *Hilton* v. *Guyot* by the Supreme Court, in language which is deserving of quotation:

Where there has been opportunity for a full and fair trial abroad before a court of competent jurisdiction, conducting the trial upon regular proceedings, after due citation or voluntary appearance of the defendant, and under a system of jurisprudence likely to secure an impartial administration of justice between the citizens of its own country and those of other countries, and there is nothing to show either prejudice in the court, or in the system of laws under which it was sitting, or fraud in procuring the judgment, or any other special reason why the comity of this nation should not allow it full effect, the merits of the case should not, in an action brought in this country upon the judgment, be tried afresh as on a new trial or an appeal upon the mere assertion of the party that the judgment was erroneous in law or in fact.[74]

What is not clear from the judgment of the American court is whether the English judgment entered in default of defence would have been any less effective if it had been a judgment entered in default of appearance. In other words, would the judgment have been recognised if the defendants

---

[72] An English court would almost certainly have reached a similar conclusion: Dicey and Morris, pp. 1012–1013.

[73] See, e.g., *McGee* v. *International Life Ins. Co.* (1957) 355 US 220, Supreme Court.

[74] (1895) 159 US 113 at 202–203. The Supreme Court in that case thought that reciprocity by the foreign country was a condition precedent to recognition. But that is now largely obsolete. See *Restatement Second, Conflict of Laws* (1971) s. 98, comment e, but compare Peterson *op. cit. supra* n. 69 at 233–236.

had taken absolutely no part in the English proceedings? In the English proceedings Lord Denning MR and Salmon LJ clearly thought that the English judgment would not have been recognised in such circumstances. It would appear, however, that such a judgment would have been recognised because the guiding principle acted on by the American court was one of comity which 'should be withheld only when its acceptance would be contrary or prejudicial to the interest of the nation called upon to give it effect'.[75]

The litigation discussed in this section is not only of interest for the contrast it shows between American and English notions of the enforcement of foreign judgments. It also has considerable practical interest for American and English private international lawyers. If leave is given by the English court to serve a foreign defendant out of the jurisdiction, in practice the defendant has four choices:

1. First, he may enter an unconditional appearance. If he defends the action and loses, or fails to defend the action with the result that judgment in default of defence is entered against him, then the judgment will be enforceable in most foreign countries because of the submission to the English jurisdiction.

2. Second, he may ignore service of notice of the writ. If he does this, judgment may be entered against him in default of appearance and the judgment will be enforceable against any assets which he has, or may subsequently bring into, England. Whether it is enforceable abroad will depend on whether the very liberal principles of the American court or the stricter continental standards are applicable.

3. Third, he may enter a conditional appearance and seek to set aside the proceedings. If he succeeds, that is an end of the matter. If he fails, the conditional appearance will stand as unconditional and he must defend the action or risk judgment being entered in default of defence. Whether a default judgment will be enforceable abroad will depend on whether the foreign court regards that appearance as equivalent to a submission (as the English court did in *Harris* v. *Taylor*) or whether it applies an altogether different test (as the American court did in the case discussed in this section).

4. Fourth, he may enter no appearance of any kind, but merely apply by summons or motion to set aside the proceedings. This is not a common procedure and there is a danger that the plaintiff will enter judgment in default of appearance. But a true understanding of the decision in the *Somportex* case may lead to an increased use of this procedure.

In practice, the steps to be taken in the English court cannot be divorced

---

[75] 453 F. 2d. at 440.

from the consequences which will flow from those steps in the State where the defendant has his assets and where the plaintiffs will seek to enforce the judgment. The choice between the second and third courses of action may be a difficult one and cannot normally be made without knowledge of the effect of an English judgment under the foreign law.

IV

Forum Selection and an
Anglo-American Conflict

The history of the litigation discussed in these notes underlines the importance of jurisdiction clauses in international contracts. The Supreme Court's decision in *M/S Bremen* v. *Zapata Off-Shore Co.*, 407 US 1 (1972) established that a forum selection agreement in an international contract would generally be upheld. The jurisdiction agreement in that case was a negotiated compromise (providing for English jurisdiction) in an international towage contract between an American rig owner and a German tug owner. The Supreme Court subsequently upheld a jurisdiction agreement contained in a standard form contract of passage for a cruise beginning and ending in Los Angeles, California: *Carnival Cruise Lines, Inc.* v. *Shute*, 111 S. Ct. 1522 (1991). In England the decision of Brandon J. in *The Eleftheria* [1970] P. 94 was approved in the Court of Appeal by Brandon LJ in *The El Amria* [1981] 2 Lloyd's Rep. 119, 123–124 (CA) and in the House of Lords by Lord Brandon in *The Sennar* (*No. 2*) [1985] 1 WLR 490, 500 (HL).

Today a frequent focus is on the application of jurisdiction clauses in cases covered by the Brussels and Lugano Conventions. Where they apply (subject to special rules for consumer contracts and employment contracts) the court has no discretion to override a jurisdiction clause. A most important practical question is that of so-called 'non-exclusive' jurisdiction clauses, i.e. clauses which confer jurisdiction on a court, but without prejudice to the right of one or other of the parties to proceed in another court. An 'exclusive' jurisdiction clause obliges the parties to resort to the relevant jurisdiction: on the distinction see Dicey and Morris, *Conflict of Laws* (11th ed. 1987), p. 404 n. 93, approved in *Sohio Supply Co.* v. *Gatoil (USA) Inc.* [1989] 1 Lloyd's Rep. 588 (CA). In *Kurz* v. *Stella Musical GmbH* [1992] Ch. 196 an agreement for joint ventures in the staging of musicals contained a non-exclusive submission to the jurisdiction of the English court. The German defendant company objected to the jurisdiction of the English court on the ground that the clause was ineffective because Article 17 of the 1968 Convention contemplated only jurisdiction agreements whose effect would be to confer exclusive jurisdiction. It was held that Article 17 did not prevent the parties from providing for the jurisdiction of more than one court. The provision in Article 17 that the chosen court or courts shall have exclusive jurisdiction had the effect of excluding the jurisdictions which would otherwise be imposed on the parties by other provisions of the 1968 Convention, but did not preclude a non-exclusive jurisdiction clause.

From *International and Comparative Law Quarterly*, 20 (1971), 550, and 22 (1973), 332.

A recent series of litigation in England and the United States has taken a course which must give rise to serious misgivings among private international lawyers—for in this litigation the federal courts of the United States have arrogated to themselves jurisdiction and indicated they would apply American law in a case where two parties, at arm's length and with equal bargaining power, chose English jurisdiction and avoided a choice of American law.[1]

The facts

The principal parties to the litigation were two corporations, one American and the other German. The former, Zapata Off-shore Company, was a Delaware corporation with its principal place of business in Houston, Texas, and which carried on business in the operation of oil rigs. The latter, Unterweser Reederei GmbH, was a towage contractor. Zapata owned the oil rig *Chaparral* and Unterweser owned the tug *Bremen*.

In 1967 Zapata, which wished the *Chaparral* to be transported from Louisiana to Italy, solicited bids from various towage contractors, among them Unterweser. It appears that Unterweser normally stipulates in its towage contracts for German jurisdiction and German law but on this occasion, and after the parties had been in negotiation over various clauses in the contract, English jurisdiction was agreed upon as a reasonable compromise.[2] It was in these circumstances that in November 1967 Unterweser entered into a contract with Zapata to tow the *Chaparral* from Venice, Louisiana, to Ravenna, Italy. The contract contained a choice of English jurisdiction in the following language: 'Any dispute arising must be treated before the London Court of Justice.' The only other provision of the contract which need be specifically referred to here was the provision for limitation of the tugowners' liability, which was broadly to the effect that Unterweser, its masters and crew were not to be responsible for defaults or errors in navigation and that any damage caused to the *Chaparral* was to be for the account of its owners.[3]

---

[1] In England: *Unterweser Reederei GmbH* v. *Zapata Off-Shore Company*; *The Chaparral* [1968] 2 Lloyd's Rep. 158 (Karminski J. and CA).

In the United States: *Zapata Off-Shore Company* v. *Unterweser Reederei GmbH* [1970] AMC 1241; [1971] 1 Lloyd's Rep. 122 (5th Cir. 1970).

[2] See [1968] 1 Lloyd's Rep. at 159, *per* Karminski J. It would appear that the suggestion by the dissenting judge in the American court ([1971] 1 Lloyd's Rep. at 128) that the contract contained an express choice of English law is in error. However, the parties' advisers would have known that at that time the English courts would treat an express choice of English jurisdiction as an implied choice of law. That inference will not so easily be drawn since *Compagnie d'Armement Maritime SA* v. *Compagnie Tunisienne de Navigation SA* [1970] 3 WLR 389 (HL).   [3] See [1971] 1 Lloyd's Rep. at 127 for the text.

The voyage commenced early in January 1968, but a few days later, on January 9, the rig suffered a casualty in international waters in the Gulf of Mexico. On the instructions of Zapata, the *Bremen* made for Tampa, Florida, with the *Chaparral*. On arrival the *Bremen* was arrested by a US marshal as a result of the prior institution of a suit for $3,500,000 damages by Zapata. This was the beginning of the first round in the litigation between Zapata and Unterweser. Each blamed the other for the disaster—Unterweser alleged that the *Chaparral* was not seaworthy and Zapata alleged that the *Bremen* was unseaworthy and had been negligently navigated.

It is not clear whether Zapata commenced litigation in the United States with full knowledge of the advantages that course offered for it, but the battle which follows will not be readily comprehensible unless it is borne in mind that the exemption from liability contained in the contract would be given effect to in England if the contract is governed by English or German law, but not, it appears, in the federal courts of the United States.[4]

The *Bremen* was released from custody at the end of January 1968 after Unterweser had furnished an appropriate letter of undertaking in the sum of $3,500,000. Shortly afterwards Unterweser filed a motion in the Federal District Court in Florida applying to the court (i) to dismiss Zapata's claim for want of jurisdiction, (ii) to decline jurisdiction on the ground of *forum non conveniens*, and (iii) to stay further prosecution of the action. In addition, Unterweser was forced (because of time limits imposed by American law) to commence separate proceedings for exoneration or limitation of their liability—in these limitation proceedings Zapata filed a further claim asserting the same cause of action as in its first suit and Unterweser counterclaimed. But Unterweser's limitation action, which was commenced in July 1968 solely, it appears, in order to preserve its rights should it have been unsuccessful in contesting the jurisdiction of the American courts, postdated the institution of proceedings in England.

The English proceedings

On February 21, 1968, Unterwester sought and subsequently obtained (*ex parte*) leave to serve notice of an English writ on Zapata in the United States. Unterweser's claim in the English court was for moneys due under the towage contract and for damages for breach of contract. Zapata sought to have service of the writ set aside on the ground (*inter alia*) that the English court in its discretion ought not to have granted leave to serve out of the jurisdiction. When the matter came before Karminski J. the judge

---

[4] There is a very strong policy in the United States against the exemption of tugowners from liability for negligence: see, e.g., *Dixilyn Drilling Corp.* v. *Crescent Towing & Salvage Co.*, 372 US 697 (1963).

refused to set aside service and Zapata appealed to the Court of Appeal.

Under Order 11, r. 2, of the Rules of the Supreme Court, the English court may assume jurisdiction if the action begun by the writ is in respect of a contract which contains a term to the effect that the English court shall have jurisdiction to hear and determine any action in respect of the contract. The exercise of jurisdiction is discretionary and the existence of proceedings abroad is only one of the several factors which the English court will take into account.[5]

When the matter came before the English Court of Appeal the position in the United States proceedings was that Unterweser had just commenced its limitation proceedings in the federal court in order to preserve its rights. Before the English Court of Appeal, Zapata argued that service of the English proceedings be set aside in view of the American proceedings and in particular because the effect of the US proceedings was that Zapata could not put forward a counterclaim in the English proceedings and, in any event, Unterweser would have to assert their counterclaim in the US proceedings. The Court of Appeal firmly rejected these arguments in language which deserves quotation. Willmer LJ said:[6]

It is always open to parties to stipulate (as they did in this case) that a particular Court shall have jurisdiction over any dispute arising out of their contract . . . *Prima facie* it is the policy of the court to hold parties to the bargain into which they have entered . . . [T]he Court has a discretion, but it is a discretion which, in the ordinary way and in the absence of strong reason to the contrary, will be exercised in favour of holding parties to their bargain.

Diplock LJ said:[7]

[Order 11, r. 2] authorizes service out of the jurisdiction where the contract contains a term to the effect that the High Court has jurisdiction to hear and determine any action in respect of the contract. This does not raise any question of conflict with ordinary comity because, so far as I know, it is the policy of the Courts of most countries, if it be reasonable at any rate to do so, to see that parties keep their word.

And Widgery LJ put it thus:[8]

The parties here have quite deliberately chosen that their dispute shall be decided in the Courts of this country, and it would need strong grounds in my view to deprive either party who sought to take advantage of that course from receiving the advantage which he expects from it.

On the facts that decision was clearly right. The argument that there would

---

[5] Any account of the nature of this discretion must begin with *The Hagen* [1908] P. 189. For recent cases on Ord. 11, see *Mackender* v. *Feldia* [1967] 2 QB 590 and *Cordova Land Co. Ltd.* v. *Victor Bros. Inc.* [1966] 1 WLR 793.   [6] [1968] 1 Lloyd's Rep. at 162–163.
[7] *Ibid.* at 163.   [8] *Ibid.* at 164.

be duplication of proceedings did not lie easily in the mouth of Zapata, which had agreed to the exclusive jurisdiction of the English court but had nevertheless resorted at the earliest possible opportunity to the American courts.

The American proceedings

Diplock LJ, in noting that it was the policy of most countries to keep parties to a jurisdiction selection to their word, suggested tentatively that the papers before him indicated that the federal and state Courts in the United States took the same view. The subsequent proceedings did not, unfortunately, bear out that suggestion.

There is no uniform practice in the United States with regard to the efficacy of exclusive submissions to the jurisdiction of foreign courts. But the modern tendency has been towards recognising their validity and giving them effect provided that they are reasonable.[9] In the words of the *Second Restatement of the Conflict of Laws*[10] '. . . the parties' agreement as to the place of the action cannot oust a state of judicial jurisdiction, but such an agreement will be given effect unless it is unfair or unreasonable'.

But even the *Restatement* recognises that such a provision may be disregarded 'if the forum chosen by the parties would be a seriously inconvenient one for the trial of the particular action'.[11] On this approach, as in England, the American courts would have a discretion. Judicial formulation of the principles on which the courts will act is sufficiently vague to make it difficult to predict the outcome of any particular case. But with this approach, which closely follows the current English approach, one thing at least is clear and that is that the party which seeks to sue in breach of a submission clause has the burden of showing why the submission to the exclusive jurisdiction of a foreign court should not be given full effect. The present state of the English authorities is such that there would be little doubt that, if the fact situation had been reversed and an English court had been faced with a submission to the exclusive jurisdiction of an American court, the English court would have declined to exercise jurisdiction.[12]

---

[9] See, e.g., Reese, 'The Contractual Forum: Situation in the United States' (1964) 13 AJCL 187; Lenhoff, 'The Parties' Choice of a Forum: Prorogation Agreements' (1961) 15 Rutgers L. Rev. 414: Ehrenzweig, *Conflict of Laws*, pp. 48–53 (1962); Leflar, *American Conflicts Law*, pp. 114–116 (1968). The position in the United States is complicated by the frequent use of forum-selection clauses in contracts of adhesion. These usually arise in the interstate contexts. By their nature they are not so likely to arise in the international context. Cf. *National Equipment Rental Ltd.* v. *Szukhent*, 375 US 311 (1964).

[10] s. 80, *Restatement Second, Conflict of Laws* (1971).   [11] *Ibid.* comment.

[12] The most recent authority is *The Eleftheria* [1970] P. 94; [1969] 1 Lloyd's Rep. 237; [1969] 2 All ER 641, where Brandon J. reaffirmed the principles on which the English court will act where plaintiffs sue in England in breach of an agreement to refer disputes to a foreign

But it was fortunate for Zapata that the casualty occurred in the Gulf of Mexico at the beginning of the voyage and that the *Bremen* could therefore be persuaded to put in at a port within the Fifth Federal Circuit's jurisdiction. For the Court of Appeals for the Fifth Circuit had previously shown a marked hostility to exclusive submissions to foreign courts. In 1958 that court had swept aside a clause in bills of lading designating Genoa, Italy, as the exclusive forum with the following language:

In essence, the motion [to decline jurisdiction] was based upon [the forum selection clause] as buttressed by the doctrine of *forum non conveniens*. Any consideration of such a question starts with the universally accepted rule that agreements in advance of controversy whose object is to oust the jurisdiction of the Courts are contrary to public policy and will not be enforced.

—*Carbon Black Export Inc.* v. *SS Monrosa*.[13]

The precise grounds of the *Carbon Black* decision are a matter of controversy[14] but at its narrowest it certainly places the burden of proof, not on the party attempting to avoid the clause, but on the party seeking to uphold it—he must show that the selected forum is more convenient than the forum in which the suit is brought. That approach is diametrically opposed to the approach of other US federal courts[15] and to that of the English courts.

Thus it was that a majority of the Court of Appeals (Circuit Judges Gewin and Ainsworth) refused in the case of *The Chaparral* to give effect to the exclusive submission to the English courts. The court upheld the lower court's injunction against proceedings elsewhere and upheld the exercise of the lower court's discretion to assume jurisdiction, on the

court and the defendants apply for a stay: the discretion of the court should be exercised by granting a stay unless strong cause for not doing so is shown and the burden of proving such strong cause is on the plaintiff. See Collins, Note (1971) 2 J. Mar. L. & Comm. 370; Bissett-Johnson, 'The Efficacy of Choice of Jurisdiction Clauses in International Contracts in English and Australian Law' (1970) 19 ICLQ 541. The case represents a welcome departure from a tendency exhibited, for example, in *The Fehmarn* [1958] 1 WLR 159 (CA) to assume jurisdiction despite a submission to a foreign court merely because the balance of convenience (especially in the matter of evidence) is with England. *The Eleftheria* itself bears useful comparison with the decision of the Court of Appeals for the Fifth Circuit in *The Chaparral*. In *The Eleftheria* the judge recognised that the bulk of the factual evidence was in England but he gave effect to the choice of Greek jurisdiction because Greek law governed and was different in relevant respects from English law.

[13] 254 F. 2d 297 (5th Cir. 1958), cert. dismissed 359 US 180 (1959).

[14] See, e.g., Reese, *op. cit. supra*, n. 9, at pp. 191–192; Note (1960) 45 Corn. LQ 364.

[15] See, e.g., *Wm. H. Muller & Co.* v. *Swedish American Lines Ltd.*, 224 F. 2d 806 (2d Cir. 1955), cert. den. 350 US 903 (1955). But see *Indussa Corp.* v. *SS Ranborg*, 377 F. 2d 200 (2d Cir. 1967), treated by the majority in *The Chaparral* as having overruled *Muller: sed quaere*. There is little doubt, however, that the *Indussa* decision, although not expressly dissenting from the general principle of the *Muller* decision, does exhibit some dissatisfaction with it. For a case (interstate rather than international) applying the *Muller* approach, see *Central Contracting Co.* v. *Maryland Casualty Co.*, 367 F. 2d 341 (3rd Cir. 1966).

following grounds: (i) the court had the power to restrain parties from proceeding in foreign courts where the foreign litigation would frustrate a policy of the forum or would be vexatious or oppressive or threaten the forum's jurisdiction or where there are other equitable considerations; (ii) the *Carbon Black* decision compelled the conclusion that the forum selection clause could not be taken into account; and (iii) even if the clause should be taken into account, the convenient forum was the United States court since the casualty occurred near to its jurisdiction, a considerable number of potential witnesses lived in the area, the preparations for the voyage had taken place in the area and the testimony of the German witnesses was available from depositions already taken.

Circuit Judge Wisdom, in a learned and powerful dissenting judgment, challenged the majority on the law and on the facts. For him, the *Carbon Black* rule was erroneous both historically and analytically; the *Second Restatement* approach should be adopted and the burden should be on the party denying the efficacy of the submission to show a significant balance of greater inconvenience in litigating in the designated forum. On the facts, he emphasised that the agreement had been entered into freely, the English courts would provide an adequate remedy and most of Unterweser's witnesses were in Europe. There is no doubt that the dissent reads better to a private international lawyer than the majority opinion, but the decision would not be of such significance if it had merely stopped at what had gone before. There would have been ground for criticism but not perhaps for complaint. But in a passage truly remarkable for narrow nationalism the majority held:[16]

The only other nation having significant contacts with, or interest in, the controversy is Germany. England's only relationship is the designation of her Courts in the forum clause. Zapata, the only claimant in the limitation action, is a United States citizen. The discretion of the District Court to remand the case to a foreign forum was consequently limited. This is especially true since, as the Court noted, there are indications that Zapata's substantive rights will be materially affected if the dispute is litigated in an English Court. The towage contract contained . . . exculpatory provisions . . . These provisions are apparently contrary to public policy and unenforceable in American Courts. However, according to the affidavit of . . . Zapata's English maritime law expert, these clauses would be held prima facie valid and enforceable by an English Court. The District Court was entitled to consider that remanding Zapata to a foreign forum, with no practical contact with the controversy, could raise a bar to recovery by a United States citizen which its own convenient Courts would not countenance.

These words speak for themselves. The court, in effect and in substance, said that it would take jurisdiction in order to protect an American

---

[16] [1971] 1 Lloyd's Rep. at 127.

company from the legal consequences of a contract which it had freely entered into and would take jurisdiction in a case with considerable international implications in order to defeat the reasonable expectations of the foreign party. There can be little doubt that the policy expressed by the court would even have overridden an express choice of English or German law. American courts are eager to protect their citizens against their own follies. Granted that there may be good and cogent grounds for protecting the weak, especially those who enter into contracts of adhesion,[17] nevertheless the American courts have gone to quite remarkable lengths in disregarding the realities of international commerce.[18]

The implications

To sum up

1. A genuine international contract was entered into between an American company and a German company, in which the parties deliberately and freely negotiated the choice of English jurisdiction.

2. A casualty occurred on the high seas, near the beginning of the voyage, and the American court took jurisdiction when the German ship arrived in port, the American company, in breach of contractual provision, having commenced proceedings in the United States court, and had the German ship arrested.

3. The German company commenced proceedings in the English courts but was forced, because of time-limits imposed by American law, to commence limitation proceedings in the United States. The American court in the limitation proceedings enjoined the parties from proceeding in any other court. The German company applied for a stay of the limitation proceedings and for a lifting of the injunction pending the outcome of the English proceedings. The application was refused, the American court taking jurisdiction on the ground (*inter alia*) that American domestic law should be available for the benefit of the American party.

A mere recitation of these essential facts must cause disquiet. The federal court exhibited a very real and profound lack of understanding of international commercial transactions. It did not appear to have any knowledge of the fact that the business men who enter into contracts of this kind know their law and they know their courts. If a particular law or a particular forum is chosen certain consequences flow. In this case, the

---

[17] See, e.g., *Ocean Steam Navigation Co.* v. *Corcoran*, 9 F. 2d 724 (2d Cir. 1925) and other cases cited by Ehrenzweig, *op. cit. supra*, n. 9, at pp. 534–536.

[18] For a striking example, see *Chemical Carriers Inc.* v. *L. Smit & Co.*, 154 F. Supp. 886 (SDNY 1957), where the court refused to give effect to a choice of Dutch law and jurisdiction in favour of a Liberian company which was apparently deserving of the court's protection because it was really American in all but form.

English courts were chosen as a reasonable compromise. The German company must be taken to have known that the exculpatory clauses would be given effect in England and must have made insurance arrangements accordingly. Similarly it can hardly be doubted that the American company made insurance arrangements on the basis of the efficacy of the contract. As the dissenting judge pointed out, the allocation of responsibility may have been reflected in the contract price. Nor was the choice of English jurisdiction fortuitous and to be lightly regarded. As Salmon LJ has pointed out:[19]

. . . it is not uncommon in the shipping world to find foreign shipowners in their contracts agreeing that any dispute between them shall be decided by the English commercial court according to English law.

The same judge said in a recent case concerning an arbitration:[20]

It is perhaps worth noting that this contract is a typical example of contracts commonly entered into by foreign merchants all over the world. These contracts have nothing to do with this country but nevertheless provide for arbitration in London because of the confidence which the merchants repose in the integrity, expertise and comparative expedition with which arbitrations are conducted and justice is administered in the United Kingdom.

The American federal court entirely failed to appreciate that choice of jurisdiction in an international commercial transaction is not a minor clause relating to machinery but very often a vital factor in negotiations. Every practitioner must know of cases where contracts would never have been entered into but for the choice of some particular law or jurisdiction. If such choices are to be so freely disregarded the whole point of having a rational system of private international law will have disappeared.

2. CHOICE OF FORUM AND THE EXERCISE OF JUDICIAL DISCRETION—
THE RESOLUTION OF AN ANGLO-AMERICAN CONFLICT

The Supreme Court of the United States has recently rendered a decision which should make a significant contribution to international commercial life and which has brought about a resolution of what the present writer described as a conflict of Anglo-American jurisdiction: *M/S Bremen and Unterweser Reederei GmbH* v. *Zapata Off-Shore Co.*[21] The object of this

---

[19] *Tzortzis* v. *Monark Line A/B* [1968] 1 All ER 949 at 952.
[20] *Pagnan & Fratelli* v. *Corbisa Industrial Agropacuaria Ltda.* [1971] 1 All ER 165 at 166.
[21] 407 US 1 (1972) reversing the majority decision of the Court of Appeals for the Fifth Circuit, 428 F. 2d 888 (1970), which had been affirmed (also by a majority decision) after rehearing by the full Court of Appeals, 446 F. 2d 907 (1971). The judgments of the Court of

note is to comment on one aspect of judicial discretion in the law of international jurisdiction—where the parties have submitted to the exclusive jurisdiction of the courts of a particular country—and to compare the recent developments in the law of England and of the United States.

Judge Jerome Frank may not have had the law of international jurisdiction in mind when he wrote over forty years ago that 'many have feared that discretionary element in justice, and even when they come to see that it is unavoidable, treat it as something to be deplored and not altogether *comme il faut*'.[22] But like Judge Frank, every private international lawyer is conscious of the need for strict rules of law to be tempered by justice, public policy and discretion. This is perhaps nowhere in civil law more so than in the exercise of judicial jurisdiction. In English law, discretion plays a vital role in three areas which are not always fully distinguished from the primary subject of this note: first, the English court is always called upon to exercise its discretion before permitting service abroad on a foreign defendant of process originating in English proceedings;[23] secondly, the court has a discretion to enjoin the continuance of foreign proceedings in cases of vexation;[24] thirdly, the court has a discretion to stay proceedings which have been commenced in England, which it will exercise most sparingly and only in cases of clear oppression of the defendant.[25] Forum selection clauses provide a fourth category (or perhaps an illustration of all three categories). Where a contract contains an exclusive submission to the jurisdiction of some selected court, any one of the following questions may arise in connection with the exercise of discretion: should the selected court always take jurisdiction, even over a foreigner? Should another court defer to the jurisdiction of the selected court? Does either court have the power to enjoin the parties from proceeding in the other court?

Forum selection clauses in England

The position in English law may be summarised shortly as follows:

1. The problem discussed in this note does not arise if the clause on its true

---

Appeals and of the Supreme Court will be more accessible to British readers at [1971] 1 Lloyd's Rep. 122 and [1972] 2 Lloyd's Rep. 315, respectively.

[22] Frank, *Law and the Modern Mind* (1930), Anchor ed. 1963, p. 149.

[23] See, e.g., *The Hagen* [1908] P. 189 and the more recent cases discussed in Collins, 'Some Aspects of Service Out of the Jurisdiction in English Law' (1972) 21 ICLQ 656 (ante, p. 226).

[24] This discretion is more sparingly exercised, see Dicey & Morris, *The Conflict of Laws* (8th ed. 1967), pp. 1081 *et seq*. For a recent refusal to enjoin foreign proceedings, see *Settlement Corporation* v. *Hochschild* [1966] Ch. 10.

[25] See Dicey & Morris, pp. 1083 *et seq*. For recent cases, see *Maharanee of Baroda* v. *Wildenstein* [1972] 2 QB 283 AND *The Atlantic Star* [1972] 3 All ER 705.

construction does not bind the parties to the exclusive jurisdiction of a particular court. If the non-exclusive jurisdiction of the English court is selected, then the English court may grant leave to serve proceedings outside the jurisdiction under Order 11, rule 2, of the Rules of the Supreme Court[26] if the contract in question does not provide for a method of service within the jurisdiction. If the non-exclusive jurisdiction of a foreign court is selected and one of the parties sues in England, the forum selection clause may be one of the factors upon which the other party could rely in order to set aside or stay the English proceedings. Whether the clause in question confers exclusive or non-exclusive jurisdiction is a question of construction which, on general principles, ought to be decided according to the law which governs the contract.[27]

2. Where the contract contains a submission to the exclusive jurisdiction of the courts of a particular country, the general policy of the English court is to hold the parties to their bargain. They do so in three principal ways:

(i) if the court selected is the English court and the proposed defendant is outside the jurisdiction, the Rules of the Supreme Court provide that the English court may grant leave to serve the proceedings out of the jurisdiction;[28]

(ii) if there is a submission to the jurisdiction of a foreign court, but the plaintiff applies to the English court for leave to serve out of the jurisdiction under Order 11 (on the ground, for example, that the contract was made in England or breaches have occurred in England), the English court will, at any rate if the defendant objects, refuse leave to serve out of the jurisdiction or set aside such service unless there are exceptional circumstances.[29] In such cases there is an even heavier burden on the plaintiff who wishes to bring the defendant within the jurisdiction than in

---

[26] Which provides that service out of the jurisdiction may be authorised by the court where the contract between the parties contains a term to the effect that the High Court has jurisdiction to hear and determine any action in respect of the contract. If the contract also contains a prescribed method of service *within* the jurisdiction, service in that manner is effective and the leave of the court is not required. But if the contract does not presribe a method of service at all, or prescribes a method of service outside the jurisdiction, the leave of the court under Order 11 is required, see Order 10, rule 3, and Order 11, rule 2.

[27] This is suggested by *Hoerter* v. *Hanover etc. Telegraph Works* (1893) 10 TLR 22 and 103 and by *YTC Universal Ltd.* v. *Trans Europa etc. SA* (reported only, but not on this point, at (1968) 112 SJ 842); see Kerr J. and Sachs LJ in *Evans Marshall & Co. Ltd.* v. *Bertola SA* [1973] 1 WLR 349. See also *Austrian Lloyd Steamship Co.* v. *Gresham Life Assurance Society Ltd.* [1903] 1 KB 249; *Re United Railways of Havana & Regla Warehouses Ltd.* [1961] AC 1007 at 1082.

[28] Under Order 11, rule 2. This was the basis of jurisdiction in the English proceedings in *The Chaparral* [1968] 2 Lloyd's Rep. 158 (Karminski J. and CA).

[29] See, e.g., *Hoerter* v. *Hanover etc. Telegraph Works, supra,* n. 27; *Re Schintz* [1926] Ch. 710; *Ellinger* v. *Guinness, Mahon & Co.* [1939] 4 All ER 16: *Mackender* v. *Feldia AG* [1967] 2 QB 590; *Evans Marshall & Co. Ltd.* v. *Bertola SA* [1973] 1 WLR 349.

cases of applications to stay actions which have been instituted in England against a defendant in England;[30] and

(iii) if the court selected is a foreign court, and a plaintiff invokes the jurisdiction of the English court (e.g., by arrest of a ship or by service within England) the defendant in the English proceedings may apply to the court for a stay of those proceedings.

3. The majority of the reported English decisions on forum selection clauses have been concerned with cases where the English court had undoubted jurisdiction (e.g., by arrest of a ship or by service on the defendant in England) but where the proceedings had been commenced in breach of a submission to the exclusive jurisdiction of a foreign court. In some of those cases the defendants have suggested that the English court did not have jurisdiction at all and have therefore sought to have the proceedings set aside, but it is now well established that in such cases the English court has jurisdiction, but that it has a discretion to stay the proceedings to enable the dispute to be litigated in the foreign court.[31]

4. The plaintiff must show 'some good cause'[32] why the English proceedings should continue, or 'a strong case' why the proceedings should not be stayed.[33] It is not merely a matter of the 'balance of convenience', but if the plaintiff is to be allowed to continue his proceedings in England one of the factors will be whether the essential issue between the parties is one of fact and all, or almost all, of the evidence is situate in England. In such cases the inconvenience and expense of a trial abroad may be so great as to cause real and avoidable hardship to the plaintiff in the English proceedings.[34]

5. The overriding point is that, in all such cases, the English court has a discretion, and matters of discretion are not really suitable for hard and fast rules. Guidance may be sought in the recent decisions, particularly those of *The Fehmarn*,[35] *The Eleftheria*,[36] and *Evans Marshall & Co. Ltd. v. Bertola SA*.[37] If and in so far as there is any conflict between these

---

[30] This follows from principle (and in particular from the extreme care with which the jurisdiction must be exercised under Order 11) and was recognised in *The Eleftheria* [1970] P. 94 at 103–104 *per* Brandon J. It was conceded by the plaintiffs in *Evans Marshall & Co. Ltd. v. Bertola SA* (see judgment of Kerr J.), and accepted by Edmund Davies LJ: [1973] 1 WLR 349. In practice, however, cases on Order 11 are freely cited in stay cases, and vice versa.

[31] See, e.g., *The Fehmarn* [1957] 1 WLR 815 (Willmer J.). The defendants did not appeal on this point: [1958] 1 WLR 159. Similarly in *The Eleftheria* [1970] P. 94 the defendants did not pursue their application for the proceedings to be set aside.

[32] *Kirchner* v. *Gruban* [1909] 1 Ch. 413.

[33] See, e.g., Willmer J. in *The Fehmarn, supra*, n. 31.

[34] *The Eleftheria* [1970] P. 94.

[35] [1958] 1 WLR 159.

[36] [1970] P. 97.

[37] [1973] 1 WLR 349. This important decision was rendered after this Note was substantially completed.

decisions, it is that the judgment of Lord Denning in *The Fehmarn* lays down a test which is rather different from that found in the other reported cases. He thought the true test was whether the dispute was a matter which properly belonged to the courts of England.[38] It may be that there is no real conflict between this approach and the other decisions and that all that it indicates is that Lord Denning is, perhaps, prepared to apply a less stringent test in deciding whether actions brought in breach of such sanction should be allowed to continue. As Brandon J. said in *The Eleftheria*, 'I think that the Court must be careful not just to pay lip service to the principle involved and then fail to give effect to it because of a mere balance of convenience.'[39]

The law of the United States and the proceedings in the *Chaparral/Bremen* litigation

The litigation arose out of a casualty which occurred on the high seas in the Gulf of Mexico when the oil rig *Chaparral* was being towed by the tug *Bremen* en route from Louisiana to Italy. The tug was owned by a German company and the rig by a Delaware corporation with its principal place of business in Texas. The ensuing litigation has been described in some detail[40] and therefore the facts need not be explored again. What lay behind the procedural battle was that the contract, in addition to providing for English jurisdiction, contained an exemption clause which would have excluded the German company's liability for defaults or errors in navigation. The parties assumed that such a clause would be upheld by the English courts but that the United States courts would strike it down as a matter of public policy. It was therefore to the advantage of the rig-owners for the circumstances of the casualty to be litigated in the United States and to the advantage of the tugowners for them to be litigated in England. In proceedings brought by the German company in England, the English courts upheld the contractual submission to their jurisdiction.[41]

But in parallel proceedings brought in the United States by the American company the Court of Appeals for the Fifth Circuit (by a majority of two to one, Circuit Judge Wisdom dissenting) refused to give effect to the submission to the jurisdiction of the English courts on the ground that to enforce such submissions was contrary to public policy. In a narrow and nationalistic decision, it sought to protect the American litigant by allowing it to pursue its remedy in the United States courts and thus

---

[38] [1958] 1 WLR at 162. See also Edmund Davies LJ in *Evans Marshall & Co. Ltd.* v. *Bertola SA*, *supra*, n. 30.

[39] [1970] P. at 103.

[40] See Collins, (1971) 20 I.C.L.Q. 550 (ante, p. 253) and J. D. Becker, *supra*.

[41] See *The Chaparral* [1968] 2 Lloyd's Rep. 158.

avoid the exclusion clause in the contract.[42] It upheld a lower court's decision refusing the stay of the American proceedings and even enjoining the continuance of the English proceedings.

The case was reheard by the full Court of Appeals, with 14 judges sitting, when again by the narrowest of majorities (eight to six) the United States court refused to give effect to the submission clause. The majority merely adopted its earlier judgment but Circuit Judge Wisdom, again dissenting (but this time with the support of five other judges), added to his earlier opinion by concluding:

the decision of the majority is a backward step by a forward-looking court. It has no place in a shrinking world where international commercial transactions are becoming increasingly commonplace. The safeguard against abuse of the forum clause is the local court's power to determine the reasonableness of enforcing the clause. But the burden of proving unreasonableness should fall on the party seeking to escape from the obligation he contracted to undertake. Zapata [the American company] has failed to show any good reason for backing out of its bargain.[43]

The German company then petitioned the Supreme Court of the United States for a writ of certiorari, which was granted, to enable the Supreme Court to pronounce upon the standards to be applied in determining the reasonableness of international forum provisions.[44]

The basic issue for the Supreme Court was a simple one: was it to accept the federal decisions which denied force to submission provisions on the ground that they were ousters of jurisdiction and so contrary to public policy[45] or those other decisions which held that they were prima facie enforceable if reasonable.[46] By a majority of eight to one, the Supreme Court held that the decision of the Circuit Court of Appeals was wrong. In so doing, it exhibited a broad approach where the lower courts had been narrow and was internationalist where the lower courts had been nationalist.

The judgment of the Supreme Court was delivered by Chief Justice Burger. On the facts he emphasised the following: (i) the parties had negotiated the contract and made changes, but not to the forum-selection clause or to the exclusion clause; (ii) the agreement was unaffected by fraud, undue influence or overweening bargaining power; (iii) the rig could have been damaged at any point along its extensive route and the

---

[42] 428 F. 2d 888 (1970); also at [1971] 1 Lloyd's Rep. 122.

[43] 446 F. 2d 907 at 911 (1971).

[44] The written briefs of the parties on the appeal are helpfully reproduced at (1972) 11 Int. Leg. Mat. 599.

[45] The leading case in that line was the decision of the Court of Appeals for the Fifth Circuit in *Carbon Black Export Inc.* v. *The SS Monrosa*, 254 F. 2d 297 (1958), cert. dismissed, 359 US 180 (1959).

[46] See, e.g., *Wm. H. Muller & Co.* v. *Swedish American Line Ltd.*, 224 F. 2d 806 (2d Cir. 1955), cert. denied, 350 US 903 (1955).

facts that the casualty had occurred in the Gulf of Mexico and that the tug had been towed to Florida were fortuitous; (iv) there was strong evidence that the forum-selection clause was a vital part of the agreement; and (v) it was unrealistic to think that the parties did not conduct their negotiations, including the price, with the consequences of the forum clause (that is, the application of English law[47]) figuring in their calculations.

The rule which the Court approved was that forum-selection clauses 'are prima facie valid and should be enforced unless enforcement is shown by the resisting party to be "unreasonable" under the circumstances'.[48] The reasons for the rule were elaborated at considerable length by the Court, perhaps in reaction to the narrow and nationalist attitude of the Court of Appeals. The enforceability of such clauses accorded 'with ancient concepts of freedom of contract' and reflected 'with appreciation of the expanding horizons of American contractors who seek business in all parts of the world'.[49]

The Court's viewpoint is that of the self-interested internationalist. United States commerce abroad would be hampered if its courts did not adopt an internationalist approach. As the Court put it, 'The expansion of American business and industry will hardly be encouraged if, notwithstanding solemn contracts, we insist on a parochial concept that all disputes must be resolved under our law and in our courts.'[50]

The Court was aware that businessmen preferred their own courts:

Not surprisingly foreign businessmen prefer, as do we, to have disputes resolved in their own courts, but if that choice is not available, then a neutral forum with expertise in the subject matter. Plainly the courts of England meet the standards of neutrality and long experience in admiralty litigation. The choice of that forum was made in an arms-length negotiation by experienced and sophisticated businessmen and absent some compelling and countervailing reason it should be honoured by the parties and enforced by the courts.[51]

---

[47] There was no express choice of English law (as distinct from choice of English jurisdiction) in the contract. The law as generally understood in England at the time the contract was entered into was that a choice of English jurisdiction was for all practical purposes a choice of English law (see, e.g., *Tzortzis* v. *Monark Line A/B* [1968] 1 All ER 949) but subsequently the House of Lords has held that a choice of jurisdiction may well lead to an inference that the parties intended the law of that jurisdiction to govern but that it is not a necessary or inevitable inference: *Compagnie d'Armement Maritime SA* v. *Compagnie Tunisienne de Navigation SA* [1971] AC 572. On this, see Collins, Note (1971) 2 J. Mar. L. & Comm. 363 at 376–381.

[48] 407 US at 10. Justice Byron White concurred in the result but thought that the factual issues on reasonableness should be left for the lower court. Justice Douglas dissented on the ground that the exemption clause was contrary to US public policy and therefore the forum-selection clause should be overridden because it was in effect part and parcel of the exemption clause. The approach of the majority owes much to the American Law Institute *Restatement (Second) Conflict of Laws*, s. 80. See Reese, 'The Contractual Forum: Situation in the United States' (1964) 13 AJCL 187.

[49] 407 US at 12.

[50] *Ibid.* at 8.

[51] *Ibid.* at 12.

Factors which may displace the choice of forum

It may be helpful to suggest some of those factors which may support an argument against the efficacy of a particular selection of jurisdiction. These are all subject to two overriding considerations: the first is that it will be for the party denying the efficacy of the forum selection clause to show cause why it should not be enforced; the second is that, in cases where it is the discretion of the court which is the prime element, each case will depend on its own fact and on the impression that these facts make on the judge. The following factors are derived from the judgment of the Supreme Court discussed above and from the English decisions:

1. _Inequality_

The Supreme Court in the _Bremen/Chaparral_ case was confining its observations to agreements which were 'freely negotiated', unaffected by 'overweening bargaining power', 'freely bargained for' and not 'an adhesive contract'.[52] In the law of the United States, unlike that of England, specific distinctions are drawn between freely negotiated contracts, on the one hand, and contracts of adhesion on the other.[53] In this context, the question is not whether the agreement is, as a matter of law, vitiated by the lack of equality, but rather whether justice requires that a distinction be drawn between freely negotiated contracts and standard form contracts, particularly where there is a lack of equality. Although an English court would not draw quite the same distinction, it is likely that it would take into account such matters, as indeed Karminski J. did in the _Chaparral_ litigation.[54]

2. _Invalidity_

The Supreme Court indicated that the result would be different if the contract were affected by fraud or undue influence.[55] Unless this is to be taken just as a very general matter going to the discretion, the court did not recognise that a difficult question of conflict of laws is presented by such a case. If the contract is governed by some foreign law, is it for the American courts to deny efficacy to a forum selection contained in such a contract because it is void by American Federal or State law? Even if the contract is invalid, does it necessarily follow that the forum selection clause is invalid? The point arose in England in the case of _Mackender_ v. _Feldia AG_.[56] The

---

[52] _Ibid._ at 12.

[53] See, e.g., Kessler, 'Contracts of Adhesion—Some Thoughts about Freedom of Contract' (1943) 43 Colum. L. Rev. 629; Wilson, 'Freedom of Contract and Adhesion Contracts' (1965) 14 ICLQ 172; Cheshire & Fifoot, _Law of Contract_ (8th ed. 1972), pp. 22–23.

[54] When he emphasised that the contract had been 'freely entered into': [1968] 2 Lloyd's Rep. 158 at 159.   [55] 407 US at 12.   [56] [1967] 2 QB 590.

plaintiffs were underwriters who had insured foreign diamond merchants against loss of jewels and stones. When the diamond merchants claimed in respect of a theft, the underwriters alleged that the merchants had engaged in smuggling activities and that the non-disclosure of these activities rendered the contract of insurance void. The policy provided that it should be governed by Belgian law and that any dispute should be subject exclusively to Belgian jurisdiction. The underwriters nevertheless sought a declaration from the English court that the policy was void and applied for leave to serve out of the jurisdiction on the ground that the contract was made in England. The diamond merchants objected to the exercise of the jurisdiction on the ground of the jurisdiction clause. The underwriters replied that because of the alleged non-disclosure there was no contract and therefore the foreign jurisdiction clause was invalid. The Court of Appeal rejected the latter argument and set aside the English proceedings.

The judgments (which were unreserved) give rise to a number of difficulties and the grounds for the decision are by no means clear.[57] The principal ground was that on the facts the plea of the underwriters did not amount to a plea that there had been no contract or no agreement (in which event it might have been arguable that there had been no effective jurisdiction or choice of law clause) but that the contract was voidable or unenforceable. Therefore the dispute as to non-disclosure or illegality was a dispute arising within the foreign jurisdiction clause. The Court of Appeal accordingly set aside service of notice of the writ.

The Court of Appeal thus avoided the really difficult question raised when the contract is alleged to be void. As a matter of English law, it is clear on principle that the fact that the contract has been brought to an end by acceptance of a repudiation is not sufficient to displace such a clause.[58] Nor is it sufficient to plead either that the contract is voidable for misrepresentation or unenforceable by reason of illegality.[59] But if the allegation is that there is no agreement because of mistake or because of some other factor which makes a contract void (rather than voidable), then more difficult questions arise. The better view is that the law which should govern this question is the 'putative proper law', that is, the law which by the English conflict of laws rule would govern the contract, assuming there were a contract.[60] For this purpose an express choice of law would be disregarded and the test of the proper law would be what system of law it is with which the alleged contract has its closest and most real connection.

---

[57] Cf. Morris, *The Conflict of Laws* (1971), pp. 239–240 with Cheshire, *Private International Law* (8th ed. 1970). pp. 217–218.

[58] See *Heyman* v. *Darwins Ltd.* [1942] AC 356, HL, which decides that whether acceptance of repudiation has had that effect is a matter for the arbitrators.

[59] *Mackender* v. *Feldia* [1967] 2 QB 590.

[60] Cf. *Re Bonacina* [1912] 2 Ch. 394; but see Diplock LJ in *Mackender* v. *Feldia* [1967] 2 QB at 602.

But the question remains open in England and unnoticed in the United States.

3. *Public policy*

The Supreme Court indicated that a contractual choice of forum might not be enforceable if enforcement would contravene 'a strong public policy' of the forum in which the action is brought.[61] What in substance the court was saying was that there might be circumstances which would justify the result which the plaintiffs in the American proceedings were seeking, namely the application of the substantive law of the contractual forum. In the result, public policy did not affect the case because the policy against exemption clauses in towage contracts was held by the Supreme Court to rest upon considerations with respect to the towage business strictly in American waters, which considerations were not controlling in an international commercial agreement.[62] No doubt a similar attitude might prevail in the English court, although it appears not to have been the subject of a decision precisely in point. Recently, however, the English court has assumed jurisdiction under Order 11 on the ground the contract was governed by English law in order that the case not be heard in Holland, since Dutch courts would apply Dutch law whatever the proper law of the contract.[63]

4. *Injustice*

The Supreme Court emphasised that the courts of England met 'the standards of neutrality and long experience in admiralty litigation';[64] to put it another way, there was no suggestion that the parties would not get a fair trial in England. It is clear that in English law if there is evidence that the plaintiffs will not get a fair trial in the foreign court, that will be good reason for the clause to be overridden. Thus, in one case, *Ellinger* v. *Guinness Mahon & Co.*,[65] service out of the jurisdiction was allowed despite an exclusive submission to the jurisdiction of the German courts and a choice of German law, because the plaintiff was a Jew who was unlikely to obtain justice in Nazi Germany.

5. *Remedies*

The English cases suggest that, if there is a remedy, such as an injunction, which is available in English law but not under the foreign law, the English

---

[61] 407 US at 15.

[62] See, e.g., *Bisso* v. *Inland Waterways Corp.*, 349 US 85 (1955); *Dixilyn Drilling Corp.* v. *Crescent Towing & Salvage Co.*, 372 US 697 (1963).

[63] *Coast Lines Ltd.* v. *Hudig & Veder Chartering NV* [1972] 2 QB 34, discussed in Collins, *op. cit. supra*, n. 23 at 669–672 (ante, pp. 239–243).

[64] 407 US at 12.

[65] [1939] 4 All ER 16.

court may be more inclined to take jurisdiction in order to grant the remedy.[66] Similarly, it has been suggested that the English court might take jurisdiction if the plaintiffs would be faced with a time bar in the foreign court which was not applicable in England.[67] Such considerations are evidence perhaps of the vestiges of judicial hostility to forum selection clauses.

6. *Governing law*

If foreign law applies and is materially different from English law, the English court is more likely to defer to the foreign court.[68] But if the foreign law does not differ materially from English law, or if there is no issue as to foreign law, or if any such issue is a comparatively small part of the case, then an English court would be more likey to take jurisdiction and allow the English proceedings to continue.[69]

7. *Inconvenience*

This is the ground which, in practice, is most commonly relied upon by the plaintiff who wishes to sue in breach of a submission to the exclusive jurisdiction of a foreign court and it is the attitude of the courts to this plea which will determine the general efficacy of such clauses. The American Supreme Court put it very highly and suggested that the degree of inconvenience would have to be such that trial in the contractual forum would have to be so gravely difficult and inconvenient that the party suing in breach of the forum selection clause would for all practical purposes be deprived of its day in court. As the Supreme Court put it:

Courts have also suggested that a forum clause, even though it is freely bargained for and contravenes no important public policy of the forum, may nevertheless be 'unreasonable' and unenforceable if the chosen forum is *seriously* inconvenient for the trial of the action. Of course, where it can be said with reasonable assurance that at the time they entered the contract, the parties to a freely negotiated private international commercial agreement contemplated the claimed inconvenience, it is difficult to see why any such claim of inconvenience should be heard to render the forum clause unenforceable.[70]

---

[66] See *Law* v. *Garrett* (1878) 8 Ch. D. 26; *Kirchner* v. *Gruban* [1909] 1 Ch. 413; Kerr J., Sachs LJ and Cairns LJ in *Evans Marshall & Co. Ltd.* v. *Bertola SA*, *supra*, n. 30.

[67] *The Eleftheria* [1970] P. at 100. But cf. *The Media* (1931) 41 Ll. LR 80.

[68] *The Eleftheria* [1970] P. at 150; *The Cap Blanco* [1913] P. 130; *Kirchner* v. *Gruban* [1909] 1 Ch. 413.

[69] See, e.g., *The Fehmarn*, *supra*, n. 31; *Evans Marshall & Co. Ltd.* v. *Bertola SA*, *supra*, n. 30. So far as the United States is concerned, it is perhaps worthy of note that the Supreme Court had been made aware in the written pleadings of all parties that Salmon LJ had said in *Tzortzis* v. *Monark Line A/B* [1968] 1 All ER 949 at 952: '. . . it is not uncommon in the shipping world to find foreign shipowners in their contracts agreeing that any dispute between them shall be decided by the English commercial court according to English law.' Cf. *Pagnan & Fratelli* v. *Corbisa Industrial Agropacuaria Ltd.* [1971] 1 All ER 165, 166.

[70] 407 US at 16–17.

The Court recognised that different considerations might apply if two Americans had agreed to resolve their essentially local disputes in a remote alien forum. Such a case might indicate that the contract was one of adhesion, or that the inconvenience was not foreseeable, or that the choice was designed to circumvent an important public policy. But that was not so in the case of a freely negotiated international commercial transaction between a German and an American corporation for towage of a vessel from the Gulf of Mexico to the Adriatic Sea.

In England, as indicated above, the test is somewhat less stringent and the way it has been put recently is that an important factor is whether the essential issue between the parties is one of fact and all (or almost all) of the evidence is situate in England.[71] If the inconvenience and expense so caused of a trial abroad would be so great as to cause real and avoidable hardship to the plaintiff in the English proceedings, then an exclusive jurisdiction clause may be overridden. In other cases, however, there has been a tendency to rely on what appears to have been a mere balance of convenience, especially with regard to the presence or absence of witnesses.[72]

8. *Conduct of the parties*

In a sense, in every judicial decision this is a vital factor, because judges are always influenced, and rightly so, by the merits of a case. In all such cases, the judge will really ask himself the following questions: Why have plaintiffs brought this action in my court in breach of the clause? Why do the defendants wish the action to be brought in the foreign court?

It is therefore appropriate to conclude with special emphasis on one of the factors listed by Brandon J. in *The Eleftheria*,[73] and that is whether the defendants genuinely desire trial in the foreign country, or only seek procedural advantages. If the defendant behaves properly and does not attempt to play procedural or tactical games, then the chances are that he will obtain a stay of the English proceedings. Despite the different judicial formulations of the governing principle to be found in *The Fehmarn*,[74] the real point in that case was that the defendants had already indicated that they would not object to a submission of the dispute to private arbitration but had refused the plaintiffs' request for security. When they later objected to the proceedings in England and insisted on the dispute being

---

[71] *The Eleftheria* [1970] P. at 100.
[72] Especially in *The Fehmarn, supra,* n. 31; *The Athenée* (1922) 11 Ll. LR 6; *The Vestris* (1932) 43 Ll. LR 86. See now *Evans Marshall & Co. Ltd.* v. *Bertola SA, supra,* n. 30.
[73] [1970] P. 94 at 100.
[74] [1958] 1 All ER 333.

heard in the USSR (as the contract provided), their application for a stay lacked all merit. As Denning LJ said:[75]

The correspondence leaves in my mind, just as it did in the learned judge's mind, the impression that the German owners did not object to the dispute being decided in this country but wished to avoid the giving of security.

Where the court has a discretion, the applicant must come with clean procedural hands. If he does so come, then the court is more likely to uphold the parties' bargain.

To put it another way, although the cases require the plaintiff to show good reason why the clause should be overridden, in practice the court will want to know what advantage the defendant obtains from the foreign forum and whether that is a proper advantage. If he seeks merely to inconvenience the plaintiff or to delay the proceedings, he is unlikely to receive much sympathy from the court.

---

[75] *Ibid.* at 336. In *Evans Marshall & Co. Ltd.* v. *Bertola SA, supra,* n. 30, the defendants had precipitated proceedings in England by appointing new distributors for their products in the United Kingdom in alleged breach of contract. The facts of the *Bremen/Chaparral* litigation show that the American rigowners persuaded the German tugowners to put in at a US port and then promptly commenced proceedings in violation of the forum selection clause.

V

The *Marc Rich* Case and Actions for Negative Declarations

As the postscript originally published with this piece shows, the essential question which it raises has been referred to the European Court by the Court of Appeal: now reported *sub nom. The Maciej Rataj* [1992] 2 Lloyd's Rep. 552 (CA). That question is whether the *lis pendens* principles of the Brussels Convention allow a party to pre-empt the natural forum by bringing an action for a negative declaration in a less appropriate forum (but one with jurisdiction under the Convention). In the Court of Appeal Neill LJ expressed concern that the European Court might decline to answer the question, no doubt on the basis that the case was already covered by the decision in Case 144/86 *Gubisch* v. *Palumbo* [1987] ECR 4861. But the article endeavours to show that the case may be different where the action for a negative declaration is brought first, as in *The Maciej Rataj*, rather than second, as in *Gubisch* v. *Palumbo*.

> . . . claims for negative declarations are a novel type of pre-emptive forum-shopping with novel implications . . . Claims for declarations, and in particular negative declarations, must be viewed with great caution in all situations involving possible conflicts of jurisdictions, since they obviously lend themselves to improper attempts at forum shopping.[1]

It is a customary (although not the invariable) practice, for a contribution to a collection of essays in honour of a friend to explain the relevance of the contribution. In the case of this piece it is doubly necessary for these reasons. The first is that, among Jacques Grossen's many interests, the one which for this contributor stands out is his interest in international arbitration. The second is that this contributor believes that the best form of tribute is to present some material, or some ideas, which may stimulate some thought or further research. Accordingly, examination of an important decision of the European Court of Justice in the field of international arbitration has led the writer into a related area of international jurisdiction, which has not previously been the subject of sustained treatment, and which, it is hoped, will be a starting point for future research, particularly of a comparative nature.

From *Mélanges Grossen* (1992), 385.

[1] *The Volvox Hollandia* [1988] 2 Lloyd's Rep. 361, 364, 371, *per* Kerr LJ (CA).

I

The regrettable history of the *Marc Rich* litigation began with a series of telexes in January 1987, in the course of which Marc Rich & Co. AG agreed to purchase a cargo of Iranian crude oil from Soc. Italiana Impianti. One of the telexes from Marc Rich to Impianti set out the terms of the contract, but also contained a provision for English law and London arbitration. Impianti did not reply to that telex but the ship which Marc Rich then nominated loaded the cargo. Marc Rich complained that the cargo was contaminated and claimed that it was entitled to substantial compensation.

Early in 1988 Marc Rich notified Impianti that it would refer the dispute to arbitration under the contract. Impianti then commenced proceedings in the court of Genoa for a declaration that it was not under any obligation to pay damages to Marc Rich. A few days later Marc Rich gave notice to Impianti of appointment of its arbitrator and called upon Impianti to appoint its arbitrator. When Impianti took no steps in the arbitration, Marc Rich applied to the English court to appoint an arbitrator on Impianti's behalf under the Arbitration Act 1950.

In the English proceedings, Impianti objected to the jurisdiction of the English court on the basis that because Impianti was domiciled in Italy and the case had no relevant connection with England, the Brussels Convention of 1968 required it to be sued in Italy. Marc Rich's contention was that the English court had jurisdiction to appoint an arbitrator, and that the proceedings in England were outside the scope of the Brussels Convention because they fell within the arbitration exclusion in Article 1(4). In January 1989 the English Court of Appeal asked the European Court whether the arbitration exclusion applied to litigation where the initial existence of the arbitration agreement was in issue.[2] Not until 18 months later did the European Court answer the question in Marc Rich's favour. It held that the exclusion of arbitration in Article 1(4) extended to litigation pending before a national court concerning the appointment of an arbitrator, even if the existence or validity of an arbitration agreement was a preliminary issue in that litigation.[3]

Meanwhile, in the Italian proceedings, Marc Rich objected to the jurisdiction of the Genoa court and petitioned the Corte di Cassazione for a declaration that the Italian courts lacked jurisdiction. The Corte di Cassazione refused to adjourn its decision until the European Court had given judgment, and it ruled in January 1991 that the Italian court had

---

[2] *Marc Rich & Co. AG* v. *Soc. Italiana Impianti PA, The Atlantic Emperor* [1989] 1 Lloyd's Rep. 548 (CA).
[3] Case C-190/89, July 25, 1991, text in (1991) 7 Arb. Int. 251.

jurisdiction because, under Italian law, Impianti had not agreed to the arbitration clause. Following this decision, in order to prevent judgment being given against them by default in Italy, Marc Rich lodged a defence on the merits.

Marc Rich subsequently sought from the English court an injunction restraining Impianti from proceeding with the Italian action, but it was refused by Hobhouse J. and the Court of Appeal[4] on the ground (*inter alia*) that Marc Rich had by its procedural steps in Italy voluntarily submitted to the jurisdiction of the Italian court. The consequence of all of the procedural efforts is that the English court is bound to recognise the decision of the Italian court that there is no arbitration agreement.

The litigation raises some important issues, not least the effect of the enormous delays in the European Court on the position of the parties, but the purpose of this paper is to pick up one, so far neglected, aspect of the case, namely the fact that the Italian proceedings were for a negative declaration.

II

The action for a negative declaration is for a declaration by the court that the defendant has no valid claim or right against the plaintiff, and the classic work of Professor Borchard shows that such an action is available in the common law countries and also in many civil law systems.[5] When deciding that the federal courts had jurisdiction to hear a claim for a declaration by an insurer that it was not liable to the insured, the United States Supreme Court said:[6]

. . . the character of the controversy and of the issue to be determined is essentially the same whether it is presented by the insured or the insurer . . . It is the nature of the controversy not the method of its presentation or the particular party who presents it, that is determinative.

In England there has been some hostility to actions for negative declarations. There is no doubt that the court has jurisdiction to grant them, but it has been said that 'a declaration that a person is not liable in an existing or possible action is one that will hardly ever be made, but that in practically every case the person asking it will be left to set up his defence in the action when it is brought'.[7]

---

[4] *Financial Times*, January 24, 1992 (CA).

[5] Borchard, *Declaratory Judgments*, 2nd ed. 1941, Chap. III. See also the important work of Zamir, *The Declaratory Judgment*, 1962, pp. 207 *et seq.* on the modern English authorities.

[6] *Aetna Life Insurance Co.* v. *Haworth*, 300 US 227, 244 (1937).

[7] *Guaranty Trust Co. of New York* v. *Hannay & Co.* [1915] 2 KB 536, 564–5, *per* Pickford LJ (CA). See also *Re Clay* [1919] 1 Ch. 66 (CA); *Midland Bank plc* v. *Laker Airways Ltd.* [1986] QB 689 (CA); *Booker* v. *Bell* [1989] 1 Lloyd's Rep. 516.

Recently, film producers who wished to distribute in the United States a film featuring the character Sherlock Holmes brought an action against the daughter of Sir Arthur Conan Doyle (the creator of the character) in England, seeking a declaration that she had no right under United States law to prevent the distribution. The action was struck out for the reason (*inter alia*) that it would be futile, because there was no evidence that the English judgment would be recognised in the United States.[8] That was a case in which the United States courts would have had jurisdiction had Conan Doyle's daughter wished to sue the distributors. But they would have had no jurisdiction to grant a negative declaration against her because she had no relevant connection with the United States. Accordingly, no question of concurrent jurisdiction or concurrent proceedings arose in that case.

The impact of concurrent jurisdiction in the context of negative declarations has arisen in two different situations in England: the first is where the plaintiff A seeks a declaration in England that it is under no liability to the defendant B, and B is suing (or can sue) A in a foreign country. The second situation is where the plaintiff A is suing (or can sue) the defendant B for debt or damages in England, and B is claiming a declaration in foreign proceedings that it is under no liability to A.

III

Sometimes a plaintiff has sought a negative declaration in the English court in order to support a claim for an injunction to restrain the foreign proceedings.[9] When British Airways and British Caledonian Airways brought proceedings in the English courts to restrain the liquidator of Laker Airways Ltd. from pursuing an anti-trust conspiracy claim against them in the United States courts, they added a claim for a declaration that they were not liable to Laker Airways. They did this in case the English court would hold that a claim for an injunction to restrain foreign proceedings could not be made except in the course of an action for some relief in addition to the claim for an injunction. The claim for an injunction was ultimately rejected by the House of Lords[10] and it was not necessary in that case to decide whether the claim for a negative declaration was essential or even appropriate. But in *Midland Bank plc* v. *Laker Airways Ltd.*[11] Midland Bank were granted an injunction restraining the liquidator from joining them in the United States conspiracy action, but the Court of

---

[8] *Tyburn Productions Ltd.* v. *Conan Doyle* [1991] Ch. 75.
[9] See, e.g., *Smith Kline and French Laboratories Ltd.* v. *Bloch* [1983] 2 All ER 72 (CA); cf. *Metall und Rohstoff AG* v. *ACLI Metals (London) Ltd.* [1984] 1 Lloyd's Rep. 598 (CA).
[10] [1985] AC 58.   [11] [1986] QB 689 (CA).

Appeal struck out their claim for a declaration that they were not liable under English law for, or in connection with, the collapse of Laker Airways, on the ground that the liquidator had never suggested they were.

Indeed, it is well established that a claim for an injunction restraining foreign proceedings does not need to be supported by a declaration that the plaintiff is not liable to the defendant. As early as 1915 it was said that 'a person can be restrained from instituting or continuing proceedings in a foreign court if a proper case of injustice be made out without any declaration of right'.[12] This is because injunctions of this kind are:

> most commonly sought by defendants who are not seeking to assert any independent cause of action but simply a right not to be sued in the foreign court.[13]

Nor can an action for a negative declaration against a defendant subject to the English jurisdiction make England the *forum conveniens* where the appropriate forum is in a foreign country. In Camilla Cotton Oil Co. v. *Granadex SA*[14] the defendants, Granadex and Tracomin, were Swiss buyers of peanuts from the defendants, Camilla. Granadex and Tracomin had brought proceedings in Geneva claiming that Camilla was liable for the defaults of Camilla's agent. Camilla brought proceedings in England for a declaration that it was not liable. The House of Lords held that (even though the Swiss companies had apparently not contested the jurisdiction of the English court) the claim would be struck out because it would serve no useful purpose in the Swiss proceedings.

A clearer case of forum-shopping was *First National Bank of Boston* v. *Union Bank of Switzerland*.[15] The plaintiffs were an American bank which had branches in London and Geneva. The defendants were the leading Swiss bank with many branches, including one in London. Both banks were the victims of a fraud, perpetrated (in part) by an employee of the American bank's London branch. UBS alleged in Swiss proceedings that FNBB was bound to reimburse them $5 million which they had paid out on the instructions of FNBB's fraudulent employee, and in those proceedings attached $5 million by a sequestration order against FNBB. FNBB then issued proceedings in England against UBS claiming that they were not liable to UBS. In those proceedings FNBB added as defendants the alleged conspirators. The Court of Appeal decided that the claim against UBS would be stayed because it would serve no useful purpose, since all the issues raised by it were already properly before the Swiss courts. Sir Michael Kerr said:[16]

---

[12] *Guaranty Trust Co. of New York* v. *Hannay & Co.* [1915] 2 KB 536, 556 (CA).

[13] *Associated Newspapers plc* v. *Insert Media Ltd.* [1988] 1 WLR 509, 514, *per* Hoffmann, J. See also *South Carolina Insurance Co.* v. *'De Zeven Provincien' NV* [1987] AC 24.

[14] [1976] 2 Lloyd's Rep. 10 (HL).

[15] [1990] 1 Lloyd's Rep. 32 (CA).   [16] [1990] 1 Lloyd's Rep. at 38.

The expression 'forum shopping' is commonly used to describe the institution of proceedings whereby plaintiffs seek to compel defendants to litigate issues in one jurisdiction when these are already being or about to be litigated in another jurisdiction which is suitable for their resolution. It also frequently involves an attempt to persuade the Courts of one country to arrogate to themselves a jurisdiction which belongs more properly to the Courts of another country; so that the grant of the plaintiff's application in one jurisdiction may involve a breach of comity towards the Courts of another country. In my view, the present case is a blatant example of such an attempt. To allow FNBB's claim for a declaration of non-liability to proceed against UBS would be contrary to the spirit of comity between our courts and the Swiss Courts. In all the circumstances I have no hesitation in concluding that it is an abuse of the process of our Courts.'

Each of these cases was one in which the English court had *in personam* jurisdiction: in the *Camilla* case because, it seems, the defendants in the English action had entered an appearance, in the *First National Bank of Boston* case because UBS had a branch in London. But where the English court is asked to exercise jurisdiction over a person outside the jurisdiction, the claim for a negative declaration will be treated with even greater suspicion. Where the Brussels Convention and the Lugano Convention do not apply, the plaintiff must seek leave from the court under Order 11 of the Rules of the Supreme Court to serve the proceedings outside the jurisdiction on a foreign defendant.

In *Insurance Company of Ireland* v. *Strombus International Insurance Co.*[17] the defendants were a Bermudian insurance company which had insured a Ghanaian company against business interruption caused by interruption of electrical power. The defendants and the insured were both subsidiaries of a Californian company. The risk was reinsured with the plaintiffs in the London market. When a claim was made on the policy, the reinsurers denied liability and commenced an action in England claiming a declaration that the reinsurance was void for non-disclosure and that in any event it did not cover the claims. After the writ was issued and served, the insured commenced proceedings in California claiming payment under the primary cover and the insurers joined the reinsurers in the Californian action. The English proceedings for a negative declaration were set aside by the Court of Appeal because the continuance of the English proceedings would cause great inconvenience. Whether or not it was proper to allow service abroad of proceedings for a negative declaration which were intended as a pre-emptive strike, the court had to be careful not to bring a foreigner as defendant where no positive relief was claimed against him, unless it could be shown that a solid practical benefit would ensue.

Stronger language, already quoted,[18] was used in *The Volvox Hollandia*,[19]

---

[17] [1985] 2 Lloyd's Rep. 138 (CA).   [18] Text at note 1 above.
[19] [1988] 2 Lloyd's Rep. 361 (CA).

where there were proceedings in the Netherlands for limitation of liability arising out of the damage caused to a pipeline in the North Sea by a dredger owned by the defendants (a Dutch company) in the English proceedings. The defendants had been employed to dig a trench and lay a pipeline by Saipem Spa, the well-known Italian contractors, who in turn had undertaken to Conoco (UK) Ltd., an oil company in a large American group, to complete the work. All relevant contracts were governed by English law and contained submissions to the jurisdiction of the English courts.

Accordingly, the English court had jurisdiction under Order 11 to authorise service out of the jurisdiction on the Dutch defendants in relation to the contractual claims.[20] Conoco and Saipem commenced proceedings against the Dutch shipowners for (*inter alia*) a declaration that they were not entitled to limit their liability. The English Court of Appeal held (by a majority) that limitation of liability was an internationally recognised defence afforded to shipowners, and the practice was to allow a shipowner to choose the court of its domicile as the forum in which to set up the limitation fund and establish the right to limit its liability. The claims for negative declarations were, according to Kerr LJ, a blatant example of 'forum shopping'; they distorted the settled law and practice governing the rights of shipowners to seek to limit their liability. They involved an exorbitant assumption of jurisdiction by the English court without regard for the implications of the relevant international conventions. They involved an attempt at forum shopping in the face of proceedings already properly instituted in the Netherlands, so that 'a race for judgment' would be likely to result.[21] This judgment was somewhat harsh on the plaintiffs. The lower court had placed great emphasis on the fact that all four parties to the English litigation had expressly agreed (though not in all cases with each other) that disputes would be determined in England and by English law.[22]

This survey would suggest that there are few cases involving litigation in more than one country where a party is likely to gain an advantage by claiming a negative declaration in England. In *Meadows Indemnity Co. Ltd.* v. *Insurance Corp. of Ireland plc*[23] Meadows (a Guernsey company which was the subsidiary of an American company) was the reinsurer of financial guarantee insurance placed with the Insurance Corp. of Ireland, an Irish insurance company (ICI), by ICB, an English bank. When there was a default on a loan covered by the guarantee, ICB called on ICI to pay on the insurance. When ICI refused to pay, ICB commenced proceedings

---

[20] The Brussels Convention was not at that time in force for the United Kingdom.

[21] [1988] 2 Lloyd's Rep. at 364. See also *Finnish Marine Insurance Co. Ltd.* v. *Protective National Insurance Co.* [1990] 1 QB 1078.

[22] [1987] 2 Lloyd's Rep. 520, 529.   [23] [1989] 2 Lloyd's Rep. 298 (CA).

against ICI in the Irish courts for payment. Those proceedings were defended by ICI on the ground of (*inter alia*) non-disclosure and misrepresentation. Meanwhile Meadows commenced proceedings in England for a declaration that it was not liable to ICI under the reinsurance contract, and also for a declaration against ICB that ICI was not bound under the contract of insurance. The Court of Appeal in England struck out Meadows' claim for a declaration that ICI was not liable to ICB, because the jurisdiction to grant declarations could not be exercised when there was no contested issue between Meadows and ICB; but the court allowed the continuance of Meadows' action against ICI for a declaration of non-liability and of ICI's third party proceedings against ICB for a declaration of non-liability. Subsequently, the Irish Supreme Court confirmed that Meadows could be joined in the Irish proceedings.[24] Therefore the consequence of the decision of the Court of Appeal was to allow precisely parallel proceedings in two jurisdictions, when the Irish court had already suggested that the purpose of Meadows in starting the English proceedings was to avoid being joined in the Irish litigation. In refusing a stay of the English proceedings, Hirst J. had relied on the fact that England was the only forum in which all three parties were involved in one single action.[25] It is suggested that, when refusing to interfere with the exercise of the judge's discretion, the Court of Appeal erred in not taking account of the change in circumstances, for by then the Irish court had held it had jurisdiction over Meadows.

In *Booker* v. *Bell*[26] a declaration of non-liability was made in favour of insurers against a defendant who did not appear and was not represented. The full facts do not appear from the report, but it seems that the defendant was being sued in California for fraud and that he had claimed that English underwriters were bound to indemnify him in respect of the claim in the Californian action. The declaration of non-liability was made by Gatehouse J. because he was satisfied that under fundamental principles of English insurance law, quite apart from the express exclusions in the policies, the underwriters would not be liable to indemnify the defendant in respect of the claims in California; it was right to grant the declaration because the underwriters needed to know whether they were under an obligation to support the defence in the Californian case.

IV

The preceding section was concerned with cases in which the negative declaration was being sought in the court which was considering whether to

---

[24] *International Commercial Bank plc* v. *Insurance Corp. of Ireland plc* [1989] IR 453. The Brussels Convention was not in force when the proceedings were commenced.
[25] [1989] 1 Lloyd's Rep. 181.   [26] [1989] 1 Lloyd's Rep. 516.

exercise its jurisdiction. It has already been seen that the Irish court was not much impressed, when deciding to join a party to Irish proceedings, with the fact that the party had commenced an action for a negative declaration in England.[27]

The English courts are equally unimpressed by the existence of foreign proceedings for declarations of non-liability. Thus in *Du Pont de Nemours* v. *Agnew*[28] there were proceedings against the well-known drug company in Chicago by an individual, who claimed that, as a result of the drug company's negligence, both of his legs had had to be amputated. He was awarded huge punitive damages by the jury, and Du Pont sued its insurers in London claiming to be indemnified against its liability. Most of the defendants then sued Du Pont in Illinois seeking a declaration that they were not bound to indemnify Du Pont, and seeking an injunction to restrain the English proceedings.

Those insurers who were carrying on business in London applied to have the English action stayed on the ground of *forum non conveniens*; the foreign insurers applied to set aside service of the writs on them outside the jurisdiction. Both sets of applications failed, because (it was held) England was the appropriate forum: the most important factor was that English law governed the policies, and it was English public policy which would decide whether an insured was entitled to be indemnified in respect of punitive damages. The Court of Appeal did not think that the existence of the American proceedings was a significant factor in the exercise of either the discretion to stay the proceedings as against the English defendants or to set aside the proceedings as against the foreign defendants. It noted that the purpose of the American proceedings was to rely on an alleged rule of public policy in Illinois that a defendant should not escape the punishment inherent in punitive damages by obtaining indemnity from his insurers. But the Court of Appeal was careful not to categorise the American proceedings for a declaration of non-liability as artificial or contrived.[29]

More recently, however, Potter J. suggested that proceedings brought in New York by reinsurers claiming a declaration that they were not liable to insurers were in the nature of a pre-emptive strike in the knowledge that the insurers were contemplating proceedings in England. As a result, he would not have regarded the New York proceedings as conclusive, or even

---

[27] *International Commercial Bank plc* v. *Insurance Corp. of Ireland plc* [1989] IR 453, 463.

[28] (*No. 1*) [1987] 2 Lloyd's Rep. 585 (CA). But an injunction to restrain the Illinois proceedings was subsequently refused by the Court of Appeal: (*No. 2*) [1988] 2 Lloyd's Rep. 240.

[29] Similarly in *The Stolt Marmaro* [1985] 2 Lloyd's Rep. 428 (CA) proceedings pending in Italy for a negative declaration were not a significant factor in the decision that England was the *forum conveniens* for Ord. 11 purposes.

as of great weight, in deciding whether to stay the English proceedings.[30]

The foreign proceedings for a negative declaration may be regarded by the English court as so artificial as to justify the grant of an injunction by the English court to restrain them. In *Sohio Supply Co.* v. *Gatoil (USA) Inc.*[31] a contract for the sale of crude oil governed by English law called for the buyers to open a letter of credit in favour of the sellers. When the buyers failed to open a letter of credit, the sellers terminated the contract. The buyers commenced proceedings in Texas for a declaration that they were not liable to the sellers. The English court assumed jurisdiction over the buyers under RSC Ord. 11 and granted an injunction against the buyers restraining the continuance of the Texas proceedings. Staughton LJ said:[32]

[. . .] the Texas action is an action for a negative declaration, commenced by the buyers when, as is quite plain, they were apprehensive that proceedings might be commenced against them in England. I would not do anything to encourage that sort of proceeding.

V

The preceding sections have shown, it is hoped, that actions for negative declarations are frequently purely tactical in nature, and are capable of being abused for the purpose of forum shopping. It will also have been seen that the cases have involved conflicts of jurisdiction not only between England and the United States (the largest group), but have also involved Ireland, Italy, the Netherlands and Switzerland, all of which are, or will be, parties to the Brussels Convention or the Lugano Convention.

As the Marc Rich case, with which this contribution began, shows, actions for negative declarations in such countries inevitably have a Convention dimension. Article 21 of each Convention provides that where proceedings involving 'the same cause of action' are brought in the courts of different Contracting States, any court other than the court first seised shall of its own motion decline jurisdiction in favour of that court.

Can a defendant who expects to be sued for damages or debt in one State make a pre-emptive strike by suing in another State for a negative declaration? In *Gubisch Maschinenfabrik* v. *Palumbo*[33] an Italian citizen

---

[30] *Arkwright Mutual Insurance Co.* v. *Bryanston Insurance Co. Ltd.* [1990] 1 QB 649, where it was held that the court had no jurisdiction to stay if the defendant was domiciled in England: this aspect of the decision was overruled in *Re Harrods (Buenos Aires) Ltd.* [1991] 2 WLR 397 (CA).   [31] [1989] 1 Lloyd's Rep. 588 (CA).

[32] At 593. Contrast *Du Pont de Nemours* v. *Agnew (No. 2)* [1988] 2 Lloyd's Rep. 240 (CA), where an injunction was refused, because, according to Dillon LJ, it was not open to the court to grant an injunction merely because England, rather than Illinois, was the appropriate forum, or, according to Neill LJ, because the application had been made too late.

[33] Case 144/86 [1987] ECR 4861.

had ordered machine tools from a German manufacturer. The German company commenced proceedings in Germany against the Italian for payment of the price. The Italian then commenced proceedings in Italy for a declaration that the order was inoperative because he had revoked it before the German company had accepted it; alternatively, he asked for the sales contract to be rescinded for lack of consent or because the tools had not been delivered in time. The Italian Corte di Cassazione asked the European Court whether the case fell within Article 21 where, in relation to the same contract, one party applies to a court in a Contracting State for a declaration that the contract is inoperative (or in any event for its discharge) whilst the other institutes proceedings before the courts of another Contracting State for its enforcement.

It is important to emphasize that in *Gubisch* v. *Palumbo* the Italian proceedings for a negative declaration were not a pre-emptive strike. The German proceedings were commenced first, and therefore if Article 21 applied it was to be the Italian proceedings which were to be stayed. Therefore the Italian Government argued that the two claims did not involve 'the same cause of action'; the German Government (supported by the Commission) urged a broad interpretation of the expression, so that the German proceedings would have priority. But Advocate General Mancini clearly realised the consequence of the latter view should the position be reversed and the claim for a negative declaration be brought in the court first seised. He pointed out that if Article 21 applied to such a case, it would be sufficient to challenge the validity of a contract in order to paralyse, by raising an objection of *lis pendens*, any subsequent action brought on the basis of that contract before the courts of another State. That, he thought, was not the objective of Article 21. But the Court disagreed. Influenced perhaps by the merits of the case (which undoubtedly required that the Italian proceedings not be permitted to complicate the affair) it held:[34]

[. . .] in a case such as this, involving the international sale of tangible moveable property, it is apparent that the action to enforce the contract is aimed at giving effect to it, and that the action for its rescission or discharge is aimed precisely at depriving it of any effect. The question whether the contract is binding therefore lies at the heart of the two actions. If it is the action for rescission or discharge of the contract that is brought subsequently, it may even be regarded as simply a defence against the first action, brought in the form of independent proceedings before a court in another Contracting State. In those procedural circumstances it must be held that the two actions have the same subject-matter, for that concept cannot be restricted so as to mean two claims which are entirely identical [. . .] [T]he concept of *lis pendens* pursuant to Article 21 [. . .] covers a case where a

---

[34] At 4876.

party brings an action before a court in a Contracting State for the rescission or discharge of an international sales contract whilst an action by the other party to enforce the same contract is pending before a court in another Contracting State.

Since that decision it has been assumed that Article 21 applies fully where the claim in the competing jurisdiction is for a negative declaration. Thus in *Overseas Union Insurance Ltd.* v. *New Hampshire Insurance Co.*[35] the plaintiffs were reinsurers of insurance placed with New Hampshire in connection with the repair or replacement of electrical appliances sold with a five-year warranty by a French company. New Hampshire commenced proceedings against the reinsurers in the French courts. Subsequently, the reinsurers brought an action against New Hampshire in the English court seeking a declaration that they had lawfully avoided their obligations under the reinsurance policies, because of non-disclosure and/or misrepresentation. The English Court of Appeal referred a number of questions to the European Court on the operation of Article 21, in particular whether it applied even if the defendant was not domiciled in a Contracting State.

For present purposes, it is sufficient to point out (a) that the European Court held that Article 21 applied irrespective of the domicile of the parties to the two sets of proceedings; and (b) that, as the opinion of Advocate General Van Gerven makes clear, there was no dispute that the two sets of proceedings involved 'the same cause of action' in view of *Gubisch* v. *Palumbo*. The *Overseas Union* case was also one where the claim for a negative declaration was brought *after* the main proceedings had been commenced in another Contracting State.

The Combined effect of (a) the failure to re-open the question of the applicability of Article 21 to actions for negative declarations and (b) the holding that Article 21 applies where the defendant to one of the sets of proceedings is not domiciled in the Contracting States is to widen considerably the scope for forum-shopping. Article 4 of the Brussels Convention and the Lugano Convention permit 'exorbitant' heads of jurisdiction to be exercised against such defendants. Therefore, if an American insurer reinsures in the London market with a French reinsurer, the French reinsurer may claim a negative declaration in the French courts, and pre-empt English proceedings, even if the obligation of the reinsurer is to pay in England.

The defendant in the proceedings for a negative declaration in such a case is not wholly without a remedy. In the first place, a court in a Contracting State is of course not bound to exercise its jurisdiction to grant a negative declaration. There is no reason why it should not apply its own procedural rules (e.g. that the plaintiff must have a legitimate interest in

---

[35] Case C-351/89 [1992] QB 434; see also *Kloeckner & Co. AG* v. *Gatoil Overseas Inc.* [1990] 1 Lloyd's Rep. 177.

the claim for a declaration) in order to determine whether the action should proceed.[36]

Secondly, the bold decision of Sheen J. in *The Maciej Rataj*[37] suggests that Article 21 may not apply if the claim for a negative declaration amounts to such a misuse of the Brussels Convention that it cannot be said to amount to the 'same cause of action'. In that case cargo-owners complained that a cargo of soya bean oil discharged in Rotterdam and Hamburg had been contaminated with diesel oil. The cargo owners proceeded in England *in rem* against the ship which had carried the cargo and against a sister ship in the same ownership. But before those proceedings had commenced the shipowners brought proceedings in Rotterdam claiming a declaration that they were not liable for the alleged contamination. The shipowners sought a stay of the English proceedings under Article 21 on the basis that the Dutch courts had been first seised. This, therefore, unlike *Gubisch* v. *Palumbo* or *Overseas Union* v. *New Hampshire*, was a case which directly raised the problem which Advocate General Mancini had foreseen.

Sheen J. expressed the view that:[38]

In Rotterdam the shipowners are not claiming a 'remedy' against any of the owners of cargo; they merely ask the Court to say that the owners of cargo are not entitled to the remedy of damages against them. There is no issue between the parties which the shipowners need to have decided. The shipowners have not suffered injury by reason of the conduct of the cargo-owners. They have no claim against the cargo-owners. The shipowners would not be aggrieved if neither party pursued this litigation.

The Rotterdam proceedings presuppose that a claim will be brought by the owners of cargo. They are solely a pre-emptive strike designed to give the shipowners the choice of forum by a misuse of the Convention and contrary to the spirit of the Convention.

He held that *Gubisch* v. *Palumbo* (and the other cases referred to above in which it was assumed that Article 21 applied to claims for negative declarations) did not require a stay of the proceedings:

In each of these three cases there was a useful purpose in seeking declaratory relief, which was to declare or define the existence or extent of the substantive legal rights vested in or obligations assumed by the party seeking the declaration. That is very different from the declaration sought by the shipowners in the Rotterdam proceedings, which is no more than a declaration that they are not liable in damages to the cargo-owners. [. . .] If in fact the shipowners have performed the contract of carriage they will have a defence to any action brought against them by the owners of cargo, but it is a complete misuse of language to say that the shipowners have a cause of action. They have no cause to commence an action. Of

---

[36] Case C-365/88 *Kongress Agentur Hagen GmbH* v. *Zeehaghe BV* [1990] ECR I-1845.
[37] [1991] 2 Lloyd's Rep. 458. [38] At 463.

course a defence relates to the same contract and involves the same subject-matter, but that is not to the point.

VI

Where the Brussels Convention and the Lugano Convention do not apply it is clear from the practice of the English courts at least that the claim for a negative declaration is not likely to be of much assistance to a party who uses it for purely tactical purposes. If the claim for a negative declaration is made in England, the cases suggest that it is only very rarely that the English court would exercise jurisdiction if another court is the *forum conveniens* or if proceedings are pending in another country. The underlying reason is simple: the most appropriate reason for bringing a claim for a negative declaration is so that the plaintiff can know where he stands if, for some reason, the defendant will not or cannot take action against him. It is not possible to anticipate all the cases in which that might be appropriate, but obvious examples are where an insurer needs to know if he is under a duty to indemnify the insured for liability in proceedings brought or to be brought by a third party; or where the defendant has asserted a claim which may affect, for example, the plaintiff's ability to sell a property and yet the defendant refuses to bring proceedings to vindicate his right.

But in most of the cases discussed in this piece the party seeking a negative declaration was not doing so because of the other party's inability or unwillingness to bring proceedings. On the contrary, the claim for a negative declaration was brought because the other party had brought, or was going to bring, proceedings, but in another jurisdiction. Most of them were therefore forum shopping cases.

When the Brussels Convention and the Lugano Convention apply, no doubt the decision in *Gubisch* v. *Palumbo* will prevent forum shopping in those cases where the claim for a negative declaration is brought in the court which is *not* the court first seised. But where it is brought first, then, while that decision stands, it will be the responsibility of that court to strike out the proceedings if they are not brought *bona fide*. It is clear that the English courts will not allow the negative declaration to be used as an artificial basis of jurisdiction. There is nothing in the Convention system to prevent them from doing so, and it is to be hoped that the courts of other Contracting States will exercise similar restraint.

POSTSCRIPT

The decision of Sheen J. in *The Maciej Rataj* [1991] 2 Lloyd's Rep. 458, in

Section V above, has been the subject of an appeal to the Court of Appeal, *sub nom. The Tatry* 5 June and 19 July 1992, discussed by Collins in *Law Quarterly Review* 109 (1992), 545. The Court of Appeal thought that Sheen J. was wrong to hold that the case was not covered by the decision in *Gubisch* v. *Palumbo*, but referred a number of questions to the European Court, including a question the effect of which is whether the decision in *Gubisch* v. *Palumbo* applies to a case where the action for a negative declaration is brought in one Contracting State before an action for damages is brought in another Contracting State.

VI

The Hague Evidence Convention and Discovery: A Serious Misunderstanding?

The thesis of this article is that the controversy in the United States on the question whether use of the Hague Evidence Convention for discovery *inter partes* was mandatory in relation to foreign parties, or merely permissive, was based on a misconception. The Hague Evidence Convention was not intended to apply, and did not apply, at all to discovery *inter partes*. This argument was not raised in the Supreme Court. All of its members held that the Convention was not the exclusive means for taking discovery involving parties from countries which are signatories to the Convention. Five members held that there was no rule that first resort should be made to the Convention; instead, the court in such a case should balance the factors (including the sovereign interests involved and the effectiveness of resort to Convention procedures) in deciding whether resort should be had to the Convention. A minority of four thought that there should be a general presumption of first resort to the Convention, because (among other reasons) the use of discovery methods other than the Convention impinged upon the sovereignty of foreign states: see *Société Nationale Industrielle Aérospatiale* v. *US District Court*, 482 US 522 (1987).

Accordingly, neither the majority nor the minority in the *Aérospatiale* case addressed the question whether the Convention applied to discovery *inter partes*, and both assumed that 'evidence' and 'discovery' were co-terminous. They were no doubt influenced by the briefs submitted by the foreign governments, which to a greater or lesser extent supported the view that comity required consideration to be given to the Hague Evidence Convention procedures even as regards discovery between the parties. For example, the brief of the French Government suggested that France, the United States and other signatory states to the Hague Convention intended to provide a mechanism to define and ease discovery among parties engaged in international commercial activities. Even more astonishingly, the French brief suggested that 'to a lesser extent' the Hague Convention also harmonised conflicting notions of discovery in various common law countries.

Although the Supreme Court accepted that US-style discovery *inter partes* was within the scope of the Convention, the effect of the majority's balancing test has been to make the Convention applicable in only a minority of cases. There are isolated cases in which the plaintiff was forced to resort to the Convention procedures (e.g. *Hudson* v. *Hermann Pfauter GmbH*, 117 FRD 33 (NDNY 1987); *Re Perrier Bottled Water Litigation*, 148 FRD 348 (D. Conn. 1991)), but in the great majority of cases the effect of the Supreme Court decision was the same as if it had decided that the Hague Convention applied only to evidence in the strict sense and not to discovery *inter partes*: see e.g. *Haynes* v. *Kleinewefers GmbH*, 119 FRD 335 (EDNY 1988); *Doster* v. *Carl Schenk AG*, 141 FRD 50 (MDNC 1991).

From *International and Comparative Law Quarterly*, 35 (1986), 765.

A change was proposed to Rule 26(a) of the Federal Rules of Civil Procedure to provide that 'discovery at a place within a country having a treaty with the United States applicable to such discovery shall be conducted by methods authorised by the treaty unless the court determines that those methods are inadequate or inequitable and authorises other discovery methods not prohibited by the treaty'. The Advisory Committee Notes correctly pointed out that 'the rule of comity stated [in the proposed rule] does not apply to discovery of documents and things from parties who are subject to the court's personal jurisdiction, and who may be required to produce such materials at the place of trial'. This is, of course, very similar to the conclusion of the lower courts in the *Aérospatiale* case that the Hague Convention simply did not apply to discovery sought from a foreign litigant who was subject to the personal jurisdiction of the United States court. The revision to the Federal Rules was strongly opposed, and the opposition included a diplomatic note from the British Government, which expressed the fear that a US court might, in breach of international law and comity, order discovery to take place in a foreign country even if doing so were in violation of that country's law or policy. It is in fact doubtful whether a US court would so order. On the other hand, the US Department of Justice considered that the change unnecessarily restricted discovery from foreign litigants and urged that the revised Rule not contain any language relating to foreign discovery. That view prevailed, and in September 1992 the Standing Committee on the Federal Rules of Practice and Procedure proposed rules which contained no provision for foreign discovery.

It is likely that the confusion between evidence and discovery also lies behind the extraordinary decision of the Court of Appeals for the Second Circuit in *Malev Hungarian Airlines* v. *United Technologies International Inc.*, 964 F. 2d 97 (2d Cir. 1992). In this case Pratt & Whitney, the well-known engine manufacturer, filed an action in the Municipal Court of Budapest, Hungary, against Malev, the Hungarian national airline. In its action Pratt & Whitney sought specific performance of an alleged multi-million dollar contract for Malev to purchase a number of jet engines from Pratt & Whitney in connection with the modernisation of its fleet of aircraft. Some two months later, four days after Malev filed its answer in the Hungarian court, Malev initiatied an action in the United States District Court for the District of Connecticut, in which it requested the district Court enter an order pursuant to 28 USC, section 1782, permitting discovery of Pratt & Whitney by Malev in the United States. It sought to depose a number of individuals located in Connecticut who held various positions with Pratt & Whitney and to obtain documents purportedly relevant to the litigation in Hungary. Malev requested discovery of, among other things, every document in Pratt & Whitney's files concerning (*a*) any engine contract it had with the national airlines of Yugoslavia and Romania; (*b*) Pratt & Whitney's efforts to sell engines to the airlines of Poland, Czechoslovakia and the Soviet Union; and (*c*) Pratt & Whitney's development of its jet engine for all of Eastern Europe.

Section 1782(a) provides:

> The district court of the district in which a person resides or is found may order him to give his testimony or statement, or to produce a document or other thing for use in a proceeding in a foreign or international tribunal. The order may be made pursuant to a letter rogatory issued, or request made, by a foreign or

international tribunal, or *upon the application of any interested person* . . . (emphasis added)

The current form of the section was introduced in 1963, and one of the changes had been the insertion of the phrase 'upon the application of any interested person'. The Court of Appeals for the Second Circuit held that there was nothing in the section which required the party seeking discovery to resort first to the foreign tribunal for discovery: to require an interested person first to seek discovery from the foreign court was at odds with the purposes of the section as articulated in the legislative history. It would undermine the policy of improving procedures for assistance to foreign and international tribunals by imposing an additional burden on persons seeking assistance from the federal courts for matters relating to international litigation. Additionally, it would undermine the policy of prompting foreign courts to act similarly based on the generous example of the United States.

The dissenting opinion of Judge Feinberg is highly persuasive. He pointed out that the indications were clear that this was all out discovery warfare, which would require significant supervision by the District Court, and that Malev sought information in the United States which, if appropriately sought, could have been obtained through the Hungarian court, but Malev never sought it there. He reasoned that there was no indication, either in the text or in the legislative history of s. 1782, that Congress intended the statute to be used for anything other than to provide information necessary to foreign litigation but beyond the power of the foreign court. Malev sought to use the section to engage in United States style discovery against its opponent in the foreign litigation, where the parties and all the information sought were subject to the process of the foreign court.

Judge Feinberg's opinion can be supported on another ground, namely that s. 1782 has nothing to do with discovery at all. It is true that there is some evidence from reported cases that it has been used for this purpose: see *John Deere Ltd* v. *Sperry Corp.*, 754 F. 2d 132 (3d Cir. 1985); *Re Application of Asta Medica*, 794 F. Supp. 442 (D. Me 1992); contrast *Re Court of the Commr. of Patents of South Africa*, 88 FRD 75 (ED Pa. 1980). It is also true that the House of Lords refused to restrain a Dutch defendant from seeking discovery under s. 1782 from US witnesses (not, it should be noted, from the parties to the litigation) in support of proceedings in England: *South Carolina* case [1987] AC 24.

But s. 1782 says nothing about discovery, and (as Judge Feinberg pointed out) it is used mainly for evidence-gathering in criminal cases. Section 1782 has its origin in 1855—not long before the equivalent United Kingdom legislation, the Foreign Tribunals Evidence Act 1856. Since the nineteenth century that statute (and its successor, the Evidence (Proceedings in Other Jurisdictions) Act 1975) has been held not to apply to discovery, but only to evidence in the strict sense.

It is suggested, therefore, that (just as in the Hague Convention controversy which culminated in *Aérospatiale*) the key lies in the distinction between evidence and discovery. If s. 1782 does not apply to discovery *inter partes* at all, then the question of the export of US-style discovery to every foreign litigation in which there is a US party will simply not arise. But, so long as the *Malev* decision stands, every US litigant abroad (and perhaps also any foreign litigant abroad who also has a presence in the United States) will be potentially subject to US-style discovery.

I. INTRODUCTION

In 1982 a helicopter manufactured by Messerschmitt, leading German manufacturers, crashed in Texas. In the same year a helicopter manufactured by Société Nationale Industrielle Aérospatiale, leading French manufacturers, crashed in Alaska. Relatives of those killed in the crashes sued the manufacturers in the relevant federal courts in Texas and Alaska, alleging negligent design or manufacture. The defendants conceded the jurisdiction of the federal courts. As part of the normal United States discovery procedure, the plaintiffs sought orders for production of documents by the defendants and production of the defendants' employees for oral deposition. The defendants resisted imposition of the orders on the ground that, since their documents and their employees were located abroad, in Germany in the case of Messerschmitt, and in France in the case of Aérospatiale, the plaintiffs could only obtain the discovery by proceeding in Germany and France under the Hague Convention on the Taking of Evidence Abroad 1970, to which Germany, France and the United States are all parties. In each case the Federal Circuit Court of Appeals held that discovery had to be given in accordance with the Federal Rules of Civil Procedure, and that the plaintiffs did not have to seek discovery through the mechanism of the Hague Evidence Convention.[1]

The conclusion in the *Messerschmitt* case that an American plaintiff in American proceedings against a foreign defendant is not normally obliged to resort to the assistance of a foreign court to secure discovery 'because the proceedings are in a United States court, involve only parties subject to that court's jurisdiction, and ultimately concern only matters that are to occur in this court's jurisdiction, not abroad',[2] is so plainly correct that it comes as a matter of considerable surprise to find that the Supreme Court had agreed to review this decision,[3] and also the decision of the Court of Appeals for the Eighth Circuit in a similar case involving the crash in Iowa of an aircraft manufactured in France by Aérospatiale.[4] No doubt this review was prompted by the considerable divergence of approach (although not usually of result) in the many cases[5] decided in federal and

---

[1] *Re Messerschmitt Bolkow Blohm GmbH*, 757 F. 2d 729 (5th Cir. 1985); *Re Société Nationale Industrielle Aérospatiale*, 788 F. 2d 1408 (9th Cir. 1986).

[2] 757 F. 2d 729, 731.

[3] The grant of certiorari was subsequently vacated when the appeal became moot.

[4] *Re Société Nationale Industrielle Aérospatiale*, 782 F. 2d 120 (8th Cir. 1986).

[5] The decisions mainly concern the question whether the US court *must* resort to the Hague Evidence Convention to secure discovery, i.e. whether the Convention procedures are exclusive; or, if not, whether international comity requires that consideration be given to resort to the Convention procedures in the first instance. The decisions are fully reviewed in

state courts on this question since the California Court of Appeal held in 1981 and 1982 that the Hague Evidence Convention was capable of applying to *inter partes* discovery in United States proceedings.[6]

It is not the object of this article to review all the American cases or to pre-empt the Supreme Court's task. Rather its object is to suggest that some serious misconceptions about the purpose and nature of the Hague Evidence Convention have crept into the discussion of the subject in the United States, and that those misconceptions have become entrenched by repetition and have influenced the reasoning, if not the result, in many of the cases. The United States courts have correctly identified the purposes of the Hague Evidence Convention as including that of bridging the gap between civil law and common law systems in the provision of evidence in an admissible form, and that of alleviating concerns in civil law countries about the perceived intrusion on their sovereignty by evidence-gathering conducted by foreign lawyers, while at the same time taking account of the needs of litigants to collect evidence in those countries.[7] But it is suggested that they have seriously misunderstood the Convention, and overlooked or misinterpreted its history, when they have expressed the views that the Convention was designed to provide a 'uniform system of discovery in foreign countries',[8] or 'an orderly system of foreign discovery',[9] or that the Convention was designed to deal with the problems caused by the fact that discovery was 'a judicial function in civil law countries to be accomplished by courts'[10]—for there is no discovery in civil law countries. Still less was the Convention intended 'to reconcile the markedly different discovery procedures that exist in common law countries, such as the United States, and civil law countries, such as West Germany'.[11] Nor does the history of the Convention support the proposition that 'the principal purpose of the

---

the Circuit Court of Appeals decisions referred to above, and in the US Government's briefs to the Supreme Court in two cases which the Supreme Court did not in the event review: (1984) XXIII ILM 412, 1332.

[6] *Volkswagenwerk AG* v. *Superior Court*, 123 Cal. App. 3d 840 (1981); *Pierburg GmbH & Co. KG* v. *Superior Court*, 137 Cal. App. 3d 238 (1982). See also *Volkswagenwerk AG* v. *Superior Court*, 33 Cal. App. 3d 503 (1973), which was not a Hague Evidence Convention case.

[7] See e.g. *Re Société Nationale Industrielle Aérospatiale*, 782 F. 2d 120, 124 (8th Cir. 1986); *Re Société Nationale Industrielle Aérospatiale*, 788 F. 2d 1408, 1411 (9th Cir. 1986); *Graco Inc.* v. *Kremlin Inc.*, 101 FRD 503, 519–520 (ND Ill. 1984); *Adidas (Canada) Ltd.* v. *SS Seatrain Bennington*, slip opinion (SDNY 1984); *International Society for Krishna Consciousness, Inc.* v. *Lee*, 105 FRD 435, 439 (SDNY 1984); *COFACE* v. *Phillips Petroleum Co.*, 105 FRD 16, 26 (SDNY 1984); *Gebr. Eickhoff Maschinenfabrik* v. *Starcher*, 328 SE 2d 491, 496 (W. Va. 1985).

[8] *Re Société Nationale Industrielle Aérospatiale*, 788 F. 2d 1408, 1410; *Re Messerschmitt Bolkow Blohm GmbH*, 757 F. 2d. 729, 730 (5th Cir. 1985).

[9] *Philadelphia Gear Corp.* v. *American Pfauter Corp.*, 100 FRD 58, 60 (ED Pa. 1983).

[10] *Re Société Nationale Industrielle Aérospatiale*, 782 F. 2d 120, 123.

[11] *Philadelphia Gear Corp.* v. *American Pfauter Corp.*, 100 FRD 58, 59.

Convention was to alleviate difficulties encountered by litigants in common law countries who were seeking to obtain discovery in civil law countries', or the claim that there are 'repeated statements found both in the body of the Convention and in the commentaries of its drafters that it was intended to supplement or improve available methods of discovery and not to limit them'.[12]

In addition to the misconception by United States courts that the Hague Evidence Convention was designed to further the processes of discovery, there also grew up a misconception, fostered by subsequent discussions at the Hague Conference on Private International Law, that the reservations made by the United Kingdom and other signatories, excluding pre-trial discovery of documents from the ambit of the Convention, were 'limited', and did not extend to discovery by way of oral depositions or to discovery of specified documents. So far has this reaction gone that one district court felt able to come to the astonishing conclusion that, notwithstanding that West Germany had made an express reservation, deliberately permitted by the Convention, declaring that it would not execute letters of request issued for purposes of pre-trial document discovery, the effect of the Convention was 'that German courts should seek to implement in good faith any legitimate discovery procedure that may be requested' by the United States court.[13]

2. EVIDENCE AND THE ANGLO-AMERICAN DIVERGENCE IN DISCOVERY PRACTICE

In order that the background and development of the Hague Evidence Convention be understood, it is important to bear in mind, first, an important difference between the civil law approach and the common law approach to evidence and its discovery, and, second, two major differences between modern English discovery practice and modern American discovery practice.

In civil law countries there is nothing equivalent to discovery, whether of the type known to English law, or the more extensive system of discovery in the United States. The Anglo-American concept of discovery is the eliciting by the parties (under the supervision of the court) of material which, although not admissible at trial for the purpose of proving or disproving facts in issue, may lead to the discovery of admissible evidence. In civil law systems the evidence-gathering is done by the court, and not by the parties, and the court orders the taking of evidence *stricto sensu*, i.e.

---

[12] *International Society for Krishna Consciousness, Inc.* v. *Lee, supra* n. 7, at pp. 442–443. See also *Pierburg GmbH & Co. KG* v. *Superior Court*, 137 Cal. App. 3d 238, 244 (1982).

[13] *Philadelphia Gear Corp.* v. *American Pfauter Corp.*, 100 FRD 58, 61.

material to prove or disprove facts in issue, and not material which may lead to the discovery of evidence.[14] There is no question in civil law countries of the interlocutory compulsory production of documents for discovery purposes or the compulsory taking of oral testimony, whether from the parties or from third parties, which may lead to the discovery of evidence.

There are, moreover, two important differences between English and American discovery procedure. The first difference is that the discovery procedure in England is limited largely to the discovery of *documents*.[15] Each party, once the pleadings are finalised, has a duty to disclose to the other all relevant unprivileged documents in its possession relating to the issues. The Rules of the Supreme Court 1965, which were in force at the time of the negotiation and conclusion of the Hague Convention and still regulate discovery in England, provide that after the close of pleadings in an action there shall be discovery by the parties to the action of the documents which are or have been in their possession, custody or power relating to matters in question in the action; within 14 days of the close of pleadings each party must serve a list of the documents which are or have been in his possession, custody or power relating to any matter in question in the action; the court may limit discovery of documents to specified documents or to specified issues; if a party does not voluntarily comply with the duty to disclose, the court may order him to serve a list of documents, and the court may order a party to swear an affidavit stating whether any document specified or described in the application or any class of document so specified or described is or has at any time been in his possession, custody or power.[16] It is well established that the duty to disclose documents is not limited to those which would be admissible in evidence, but extends to any document which 'contains information which may enable the party either to advance his own case or to damage that of his adversary, if it is a document which may fairly lead him to a train of enquiry which may have either of these two consequences'.[17]

But the American discovery practice of oral examination before trial (which had its historical origin in the English Chancery method of fact discovery) never developed in England. As the leading authority on federal practice puts it, modern United States discovery procedure can result in 'excessively costly and time-consuming activities',[18] and Justice Powell has pointed out that the discovery rules have not infrequently been

---

[14] See Cohn, *Manual of German Law* (2nd ed. 1971), Vol. 2, pp. 219–229; Herzog, *Civil Procedure in France* (1967), Chap. 5.

[15] The other form of discovery in English law is that of interrogatories (RSC Ord. 26) but this has become rare.

[16] RSC Ord. 24, rr. 1, 2(1) and (5), 3, 7(1).

[17] *Compagnie Financière du Pacifique* v. *Peruvian Guano Co.* (1882) 11 QBD 55, 62–63.

[18] Moore, *Federal Practice* (1984), Vol. 4, para. 26–52.

exploited to the disadvantage of justice.[19] Today English lawyers tend to view with hostility the expensive, time-consuming, dilatory and wasteful aspects of American pre-trial oral depositions for discovery purposes.[20] In modern practice there is a fundamental difference, therefore, between the English and American systems, and the use of the word 'discovery' to describe both systems frequently leads to confusion.

A further source of potential confusion is that it is not always sufficiently recognised outside the United States that the examination for discovery purposes serves a dual purpose, 'the ordinary purpose of discovery with the wide line of enquiry which that permits and also the purpose of obtaining in the form of a deposition evidence from the witness which will be admissible at the trial in the event of the witness not being called in person'.[21] Since evidence obtained in the discovery stage may be tendered at the trial, it is not every United States 'discovery' request or examination which would be characterised as discovery outside the United States.

The second major difference between English and United States practice is that it is only in two exceptional cases[22] that discovery may be obtained against a third party in English proceedings, whereas third party discovery is freely permitted under United States law. It has been established since 1890[23] that, in the words of Lord Brandon almost 100 years later,[24] 'there is no way in which a party to an action in the High Court in England can compel pre-trial discovery as against a person who is not a party to such action, either by way of the disclosure and inspection of documents in his possession or power, or by way of giving oral or written testimony'.

In three important decisions before the 1968 Hague Conference, two of them involving United States litigation, it was held that the English courts would not allow foreign letters regatory to be used to obtain discovery, either by way of document discovery or oral depositions, from third parties. In the first, *Burchard* v. *Macfarlane*,[25] there was litigation pending in Scotland relating to the sale of a ship by the defendants to the plaintiffs, and the parties sought to take evidence in England on commission under the Evidence by Commission Act 1843, which made provision for compelling the attendance of witnesses and the production of documents before commissions to take evidence issued in one part of the United

---

[19] *Herbert* v. *Lando*, 441 US 153, 179 (1979).

[20] See Collins (1979) 13 Int. L. 27, 28–29.

[21] *Re Westinghouse Uranium Contract* [1978] AC 547, 635 (*per* Lord Diplock); see also *Application of Forsyth* [1984] 2 NSWLR 327, 331–332.

[22] An action seeking the identity of a wrongdoer: *Norwich Pharmacal Co.* v. *Commissioners of Customs & Excise* [1974] AC 133; or an action for personal injuries: Administration of Justice Act 1970, s. 34(2), and RSC Ord. 24, r. 7A.

[23] *Elder* v. *Carter* (1890) 15 QBD 194.

[24] *South Carolina Insurance Co.* v. *Assurantie Maatschappij 'de Zeven Provincien' NV* [1986] 3 WLR 398, 404 (HL).   [25] [1891] 2 QB 241 (CA).

Kingdom to be executed in another part. The commission granted by the Scottish court was that the Chairman and Secretary of Lloyd's Register of British and Foreign Shipping should appear before a commissioner in London to produce documents under their control, including correspondence passing between the defendants and Lloyd's Register relating to the condition of the vessel, and other documentary material relating to the condition of the ship, among them the reports between Lloyd's and its agents. It was held that the 1843 Act was intended to relate exclusively to the production of documents ancillary to the examination of a witness, and was not allowed to be used for discovery against persons not parties to the action. Discovery could not be obtained under the Act where it could not be ordered in England, and it was irrelevant that it could have been obtained under the law of the requesting court.

In *Radio Corporation of America* v. *Rauland Corporation*[26] there was an action proceeding in Illinois in which RCA claimed infringement of patents. The defendants in the litigation alleged a conspiracy over many years between RCA and other American and foreign companies to violate the American antitrust laws by an arrangement to pool patents connected with the electronics industry and by means of licensing and cross-licensing agreements to parcel out among the alleged conspirators exclusive trading rights in various parts of the world. In 1955 the defendants obtained from the Illinois court letters rogatory addressed to the judicial authorities in England seeking evidence from two English companies, English Electric Co. Ltd. and EMI Ltd. The letters rogatory asked the English court to take evidence from the English companies and to order their officers to produce documents and answer oral interrogatories. The application in England was made under the Foreign Tribunals Evidence Act 1856, which provided that an English court, where a foreign court was desirous of obtaining testimony in relation to a pending civil or commercial matter, could order the examination on oath, on interrogatories or otherwise, of the witness and could order the attendance of the witness for examination or the production of any writings or other documents. It was held that, where the order related to oral testimony or documents, all that could be obtained under the Act was 'direct' material immediately relevant to the issue in dispute and such as might be used at the trial and not 'indirect' material by way of discovery and testimony for that purpose.

Devlin J. said:

The essential principles of discovery in the United States do not seem to be very different from the principles in this country; that is to say, discovery is not merely limited to the obtaining, by means of disclosure, of such material as may be strictly relevant to the issues in the action such as might be admissible on the hearing of the

---

[26] [1956] 1 QB 618, applied in *Application of Forsyth* [1984] 2 NSWR 327.

action, but it covers also the obtaining of material which might lead to a line of enquiry which would itself disclose relevant material . . . [I]t is plain that that principle has been carried very much further in the United States of America than it has been carried in this country. In the United States of America it is not restricted merely to obtaining a disclosure of documents from the other party to the suit, but there is a procedure, which might be called a pre-trial procedure, in the courts of the United States which allows interrogation not merely of the parties to the suit but also of parties who may be witnesses in the suit, or whom it may be thought may be witnesses in the suit, and which requires them to answer questions and produce documents. The questions would not necessarily be restricted to matters which were relevant in the suit, nor would the production be necessarily restricted to admissible evidence, but they might be such as would lead to a train of enquiry which might itself lead to relevant material.[27]

He said that *Burchard* v. *Macfarlane* was authority for the view that there was a distinction between discovery or 'indirect' material on the one hand and proof or 'direct' material on the other hand and that was the distinction with which it was necessary to approach the expression 'testimony' in the Act. Testimony which was in the nature of proof for the purpose of the trial was permissible, but testimony, if it could be called 'testimony', which consisted of mere answers to questions in the discovery proceeding designed to lead to a train of enquiry was not permissible. Whether the evidence was relevant or not would depend upon the rules of evidence which were appropriate in the foreign court, but whether it was relevant testimony within the meaning of the section depended on whether it was testimony that was relevant to an issue in the matter and not whether it was testimony which was merely material which might lead to a train of enquiry which would in fact disclose the testimony. Lord Goddard CJ thought that the application was 'merely an attempt to get evidence in the course of discovery proceedings which are known to the American courts—and are also known to the Canadian courts—which are a sort of pre-trial before the main trial. It is an endeavour to get in evidence by examining people who may be able to put the parties in the way of getting evidence. That is mainly what we should call a "fishing" proceeding which is never allowed in the English courts . . .'[28]

Finally, in *American Express Warehousing Co.* v. *Doe*,[29] proceedings were pending in New York against a number of Lloyd's underwriters arising out of a claim by the plaintiff for indemnity under policies alleged to cover a series of frauds in connection with the well-known vegetable oil scandal. The underwriters sought to avoid the policies on the ground of misrepresentation and/or non-disclosure. The plaintiffs in the American

---

[27] *Idem*, pp. 643–644.   [28] *Idem*, p. 649.
[29] [1967] 1 Lloyd's Rep. 222 (CA). See also *Penn-Texas Corp.* v. *Murat Anstalt* (*No. 1*) [1964] 1 QB 40 (CA); (*No. 2*) [1964] 2 QB 647 (CA).

action sought evidence in England under the Foreign Tribunals Evidence Act 1856 from Lloyd's brokers, who were not parties to the American action, as to similar insurance placed with Lloyd's underwriters because under New York law the defence of misrepresentation and/or non-disclosure was only available if the misrepresentation or non-disclosure was material, and the New York courts looked to the effect on the mind of the particular insurer. Accordingly, the warehouse company wished to find evidence of similar risks which were undertaken by the Lloyd's underwriters. It was held that the application related to evidence, and not discovery, and was therefore admissible. Lord Denning MR indicated that where documents were sufficiently specified there was no objection to an order being made to give testimony and produce supporting documents ancillary to the testimony. It was not a mere application for discovery and the documents were sufficiently specified.[30]

These differences between the civil law and common law systems and between the English and American systems have been emphasised because they form the essential background to the negotiations which led to the Hague Evidence Convention. It is suggested that the negotiations and the Convention cannot properly be understood without an appreciation of the facts (a) that discovery is not known in civil law countries; (b) that the English courts had firmly set their faces against their being used for discovery in aid of foreign proceedings; and (c) that there was a growing hostility abroad, especially in England, to American-style discovery.

3. THE HAGUE EVIDENCE CONVENTION[31]

The Hague Evidence Convention was entered into as a result of an initiative of the United States, which had submitted to the Hague Conference that the existing system of letters rogatory had a number of limitations.[32] In particular, the United States had suggested that preparation of letters could be burdensome and expensive, especially when required to be translated, even though the witness abroad might speak the language of the forum; the judge before whom an examination was made might know nothing about the case, and questioning might well be founded on principles of the law of the foreign forum, and, if the examination was

---

[30] *Idem*, p. 225.
[31] Hague Convention on the Taking of Evidence Abroad in Civil or Commercial Matters 1970, Cmnd. 6727. For proceedings of the Hague Conference, see (a) Actes et documents de la Onzième Session, 1968 ('1968 Documents'); (b) Actes et documents de la Quatorzième Session, 1980 ('1980 Documents'); (c) Report on the second meeting of the Special Commission on the operation of the Convention, 1985, reprinted in (1985) XXIV ILM 1668.
[32] See Memorandum of the United States with respect to the revision of Chapter II of the 1954 Convention on Civil Procedure, 1968 *Documents*, p. 15.

made in the country whose procedures did not provide for a verbatim record, the judge's memorandum and summary might contain ambiguities or engender misunderstandings; the memorandum and summary might be difficult to use in the requesting court because of these ambiguities with the result that letters rogatory obtained after the expenditure of considerable time and money might be of little or no practical value in the actual litigation; in those jurisdictions in which the examination of the witness was by the judge, the device of permitting counsel to suggest supplementary questions to be proposed at the end of the judge's initial examination had not always adequately met the evidentiary needs of the party who had submitted the letters rogatory. Many of these problems were resolved by the Hague Evidence Convention: letters of request can now be in English or French, unless the Contracting State to whom the letter is addressed has made an appropriate reservation; the judicial authority which executes a letter of request should follow a request from the authority in which the action is pending that a special method or procedure be followed; commissioners may be appointed to take evidence, in the manner provided by the law of the court in which the action is pending.

It is apparent that neither these criticisms, nor the solutions in the Convention, expressly mention discovery. A careful study of the conference materials will show that the United States delegation did not, in the proceedings in 1968 which led to the Convention, suggest that the United States was primarily concerned with the conduct of discovery abroad. The suggestion that the United States was asking for improvements in the system of letters rogatory in order to deal with third party discovery or *inter partes* discovery is entirely lacking in the following documents where one might otherwise expect to see it: the United States memorandum to the Netherlands State Commission and the Permanent Bureau of the Hague Conference; the answers by the United States to the questionnaire prepared by the Secretariat; the report of the Special Commission of Experts, whose chairman was Mr Philip Amram of the United States, who played a major role in the negotiation of the Convention; and the explanatory report by Mr Amram on the Convention.[33] Nor, it is submitted, is there any such indication in the detailed minutes of the Conference. Nor is there any reference to the use of the Convention for discovery purposes in the 1969 Report of the United States delegation,[34] or in the documents submitted to the Senate when its advice and consent was sought in 1972, namely the message from the President, the Secretary of State's letter of transmittal, and Mr Amram's explanatory report.[35] The whole emphasis of these documents is on what is described as 'the

---

[33] 1968 Documents, pp. 15, 27, 55, 202.   [34] (1969) VII ILM 785, 804–820.
[35] (1973) XII ILM 323.

elimination of formal and technical obstacles to securing evidence abroad in a form that is usable in the court where the action is pending'.[36] There are, it is true, occasional references to evidence from parties,[37] but the whole tenor of the documents indicates that what the United States was proposing, and what the delegates were discussing, was the obtaining of evidence in the strict sense, and not discovery. Indeed, the explanation of Article 23, in the report by Mr Amram, appears deliberately to understate the possible role of discovery requests in the Convention scheme, by noting that 'some States may be quite prepared to accept Letters for this purpose while other States may refuse them'.[38]

There is no evidence whatsoever for the view put forward by one recent commentator that 'the quintessential effect of the Convention is to require Contracting States to execute US-style discovery requests that would not have been possible in the past under the domestic laws of civil law countries',[39] or that the limitations in the Convention 'cannot restrict the execution of reasonable requests for US-style discovery',[40] and the authorities[41] cited as support for these propositions quite simply do not bear them out. Nor is there anything in the history or wording of Article 9(2), which provides that the court requested shall follow a request that a special method or procedure be followed, to justify the suggestion[42] that it requires effect to be given to discovery requests.

It is at this point necessary to pick up the history of what ultimately became Article 23 of the Convention, and to show how discovery did come to play a role in the conference, and how the discussion developed in a way which has led to some confusion. The confusion seems to have come about because the United Kingdom, fearing that the Convention might be used to seek third party discovery, sought to limit its use for that purpose.[43] In so doing, the United Kingdom rightly ignored the possibility of *inter partes* discovery being relevant for Convention purposes, but (perhaps over-influenced by English discovery practice) concentrated exclusively on third

---

[36] Secretary of State's transmittal letter (1973) XII ILM 326: cf. Report of US Delegation (1969) VII ILM 785, 820. [37] e.g. 1968 Documents, pp. 16, 28, 41.

[38] 1968 Documents, p. 204; (1973) XII ILM 327, 329.

[39] Heck (1986) 24 Col. J. Trans. L. 231, 232; see also *idem*, p. 237.

[40] *Idem*, p. 237.

[41] Amram (1973) 67 AJIL 104, 106; US Delegation Report (1969) VII ILM 810–811.

[42] *Philadelphia Gear Corp. v. American Pfauter Corp.*, 100 FRD 58, 61; cf. Heck, *op. cit. supra*, n. 39, at pp. 236–237.

[43] This attitude has also no doubt been influenced by a lingering suspicion on the part of the United Kingdom and others (see 1968 Documents (*supra* n. 31), p. 94. Working Document No. 10) that United States discovery could be obtained for contemplated proceedings as well as existing proceedings. This is not a valid objection (see 1980 Documents, p. 420); but insufficient attention has been directed to the point that the United States system of pleading allows a complaint to make only the barest allegations, and the discovery system allows the plaintiff to take discovery to find whether or not he has a case: see Collins (1979) 13 Int. L. 27–28.

party documentary discovery and ignored the prospect of the Convention being used for oral discovery depositions. In summary, what happened was that during the negotiations there was discussion of the possibility of expanding the expression 'evidence' in Article 1 of the draft Convention (in the French text, '*tout acte d'instruction*') by adding the words 'including the taking of statements of witnesses, parties or experts and the production or examination of documents or other objects or [of?] property'. That suggestion was eventually abandoned in favour of reliance on the legislative history of the French text, but not before the United Kingdom delegation had raised in the context of Article 1 the fear that the Convention might be used to obtain discovery of documents and the concern that foreign courts were not properly equipped to execute letters rogatory requesting discovery of documents.[44]

What ultimately emerged from these discussions was Article 23, which was proposed by the United Kingdom delegation and adopted in October 1968.[45] By Article 23:

A Contracting State may, at the time of signature, ratification or accession, declare that it will not execute Letters of Request issued for the purpose of obtaining pre-trial discovery of documents as known in Common Law countries.

Mr Amram's final report on the Convention contains the following passage on Article 23:

Finally, article 23, adopted at the request of the United Kingdom delegation, permits a State to declare that it will not execute a Letter of Request if it has been issued for the purpose of obtaining pre-trial discovery of documents as known in Common Law countries. This refers to a procedure by which one of the Parties to an action may obtain access, before trial, to documents in the possession of his adversary, to aid him in the preparation of his pleadings or in preparation for trial. The procedure varies widely among the various States and is not even uniform in all Common Law jurisdictions. Accordingly, some States may be quite prepared to accept Letters for this purpose while other States may refuse them. Article 23 provides the machinery for the exercise of this option.[46]

The April 1969 report by the United States delegation to the Eleventh Session of the Hague Conference[47] mentions Article 23 without explaining its purpose. The 1971 letter of transmittal from Secretary of State Rogers did not refer to Article 23 at all except to say that it was one of those provisions which constituted the general clauses of the convention, most of

---

[44] 1968 Documents, pp. 157–158.
[45] *Idem*, pp. 171, 177. Those in favour included Canada and Ireland, who have not signed or ratified the Convention. See also Ristau, *International Judicial Assistance* (1984), p. 226.
[46] 1968 Documents (*supra* n. 31), p. 204; (1973) XII ILM 327, 329.
[47] (1969) VII ILM 785, 804 *et seq.*

which were said to be customary provisions for administration of the Convention, and the accompanying explanatory report by Mr Amram contained a passage about Article 23 which is identical to that in his Hague Conference report.[48]

It is a reasonable inference from (a) the history of the English case law on the use of letters rogatory for discovery and (b) the then recent experience in England in the *RCA* and *American Express* cases, that the essential concern of the United Kingdom delegation was to prevent the use of the Convention for third party discovery. Because in those cases the oral depositions were intended to elicit the discovery of documents, the British concern was understandably concentrated on the documentary aspect.

No common law countries except the United Kingdom and the United States were original signatories to the Convention.[49] The representatives of the civil law countries can hardly have intended the expression 'evidence' to mean anything other than evidence in the strict sense, i.e. material to prove or disprove facts in issue, and it is unlikely in the extreme that the expression in the French text, *tout acte d'instruction*, was intended to comprehend discovery, since it is not known in any civil law or French-speaking country. Similarly the representatives of the United Kingdom could not have intended 'evidence' to include discovery, since it was well established in the English case law that 'evidence' or 'testimony' is material in the nature of proof for the trial,[50] and it is impossible to believe that the United Kingdom intended to reverse a consistent line of authority extending almost 80 years in a Convention which was designed primarily to overcome certain procedural obstacles in the obtaining of evidence abroad.

It is true that Mr D. M. Edwards, who was a member of the British delegation, in a short note on the Convention,[51] makes the passing remark that 'as a consequence of the inclusion of "other judicial acts" within the terms of the Convention, orders for discovery will now no doubt be included'. This remark, which is the only contemporaneous suggestion[52] that discovery was to be included within the Convention scheme, is not borne out by the discussion of the expression '*d'autres actes judiciaires*' in the conference reports: examples discussed were securing copies of birth certificates, obtaining extracts from public records, appointing receivers

---

[48] (1973) XII ILM 324.

[49] Subsequently Barbados, Cyprus, Israel and Singapore acceded to the Convention. Of those States Barbados and Israel have made no reservation under Art. 23. Cyprus and Singapore made reservations in similar form to that of the United Kingdom.

[50] *Radio Corporation of America* v. *Rauland Corporation* [1956] 1 QB 618, 646; for a later re-affirmation of the point, see *Re Westinghouse Uranium Contract* [1978] AC 547, 608–609, 642.

[51] (1969) 18 ICLQ 646, 650.

[52] Amram (1969) 55 ABAJ 651 does not mention discovery.

and requiring security, and 'there was unanimous agreement that the broad and all-inclusive term "other judicial acts" must be restricted'.[53]

The position, therefore, when the Convention was concluded in 1970 and came into force in 1972 was, it is suggested, as follows:

1. There had been no public suggestion by the United States, the prime mover of the Convention, that it was intended for use for discovery purposes *inter partes*, and there was no discussion at the conference of its positive use for that purpose.

2. It is unlikely that the majority of the delegates at the conference thought that the expression 'evidence' bore any meaning other than its normal meaning, i.e. material to prove or disprove facts.

3. The United Kingdom delegation, however, feared that the Convention might be used to obtain discovery of documents in United States proceedings from third parties, and accordingly sought and obtained the insertion of Article 23.

4. DEVELOPMENTS AFTER 1970: THE THEORY OF THE 'LIMITED' RESERVATION

In 1970 the Convention was signed by five States (the Federal Republic of Germany, Norway, Portugal, the United Kingdom and the United States); in 1972 it entered into force after three States (Denmark, Norway and the United States) had ratified it; in 1975 the United Kingdom enacted the Evidence (Proceedings in Other Jurisdictions) Act 1975 which was intended, *inter alia*, to give effect in the United Kingdom to the Hague Convention, and which came into force in May 1976[54] shortly before the United Kingdom ratified the Convention and made a reservation under Article 23.[55]

The Evidence (Proceedings in Other Jurisdictions) Act 1975 contains no specific reference to the Hague Convention, but it was designed to implement the Convention.[56] It provides that the United Kingdom court may give effect to a request for evidence by a foreign court for the purposes of civil proceedings which have been instituted or are about to be instituted. The order for obtaining evidence may make provision, *inter*

---

[53] 1968 Documents (*supra* n. 31), p. 203; (1973) XII ILM 327, 329. See also Ristau, *op. cit. supra* n. 45, at pp. 185–186. In 1980 Documents, the United States response (p. 400) to the question on the practical operation of the phrase 'other judicial acts' does not suggest a wide meaning. See also the United Kingdom response at p. 411.

[54] SI 1976 No. 429.

[55] All States which have ratified the Convention, except the United States, Barbados, Israel and Czechoslovakia, have made a reservation under Art. 23.

[56] See *Re Westinghouse Uranium Contract* [1978] AC 547, 608; *Re Asbestos Insurance Coverage Cases* [1985] 1 WLR 331, 335 (HL).

alia, '(a) for the examination of witnesses, either orally or in writing; (b) for the production of documents'.[57] But the order is not to 'require any particular steps to be taken unless they are steps which can be required to be taken by way of obtaining evidence for the purposes of civil proceedings in the court making the order'.[58] This very obscure phrase was held by the House of Lords in the *Westinghouse* case[59] to enshrine the distinction between direct evidence (which can be obtained under the Act) and indirect material (which cannot).

By section 2(4) it is provided that the order of the court

shall not require a person—

(a) to state what documents relevant to the proceedings to which the application for the order relates are or have been in his possession, custody or power; or
(b) to produce any documents other than particular documents specified in the order as being documents appearing to the court making the order to be, or to be likely to be, in his possession, custody or power.

The reservation made by the United Kingdom under Article 23 declared that the United Kingdom would not execute letters of request issued for the purpose of obtaining pre-trial discovery of documents. The reservation went on to declare that the United Kingdom understood letters of request issued for that purpose to include any letter of request which required a person '(a) to state what documents relevant to the proceedings to which the letters of request are, or have been, in his possession, custody or power; or (b) to produce any documents other than particular documents specified in the letter of request as being documents appearing to the requested court to be, or to be likely to be, in his possession, custody or power'. This wording is almost identical to that in the 1975 Act, and both appear to have been intended to reflect the English concept of discovery set out in Order 24 of the Rules of the Supreme Court 1965 discussed above: (a) follows closely Order 24, rule 2(1), which requires each party to serve a list of documents 'which are or have been in his possession, custody or power relating to any matter in question between them in the action', and (b) is inspired by Order 24, rule 11,[60] which allows the court to order production of documents on the basis of evidence 'specifying or describing the documents of which inspection is sought and stating the belief of the deponent that they are in the possession, custody or power of the other party and that they relate to a matter in question in the cause or matter'.

---

[57] S. 2(2).
[58] S. 2(3).
[59] [1978] AC 547, 634 (*per* Lord Diplock); cf. pp. 609 (Lord Wilberforce), 653 (Lord Keith). Oxman (1983) 37 U. Miami L. Rev. 733, 775, who is a proponent of the 'limited' reservation theory, minimises the importance of this provision.
[60] And perhaps also by statements in the *American Express* case [1967] 1 Lloyd's Rep. 222, 225.

The other original ratifying States which made a reservation under Article 23 (Denmark, Finland, France, Norway, Portugal and Sweden) merely declared that they would not execute letters of request for the purpose of obtaining pre-trial discovery of documents as known in common law countries. It is not clear why the United Kingdom decided to amplify its reservation by declaring what it understood discovery of documents to 'include'. But in the period after the Convention came into force the theory developed that the explanation of what discovery 'included' in the United Kingdom reservation amounted to a more limited form of reservation than that made by the civil law countries which had not included any such explanation. The Special Commission on the Convention reported in 1978 that 'it seemed that the reservation had been sought essentially for the purpose of countering requests for evidence which lack specificity in that they do not describe precisely enough the documents to be obtained or examined' and that 'in making the reservation the United Kingdom had restricted its scope'.[61]

That the theory of a 'limited' United Kingdom reservation is a myth is supported by three factors. First, in any event the reservation only indicates matters which are 'included' in pre-trial discovery of documents. Second, the reservation is clearly intended to provide a description of discovery as understood by English lawyers, and only differs from the English discovery rules in that it does not include orders for the production of specific documents as part of the discovery process. Third, the suggestion that the United Kingdom reservation is intended to allow the production of specific documents for discovery purposes (as distinct from evidentiary purposes) is dispelled by the fact that the decision of the House of Lords in the *Westinghouse* case indicates that the effect of section 2(3) and (4) of the 1975 Act was to confirm that evidence meant evidence in the strict sense, and that the Act could not be used for discovery, even in relation to specific documents.[62] As Lord Diplock put it:

> The request for the production of documentary evidence . . . must not only satisfy the requirements of subsection (3) which exclude fishing discovery, but also the stricter requirements of subsection (4),[63]

and it is clear from the other speeches that the combined effect of subsections (3) and (4) is that neither (a) a request for *discovery* of *specified* documents, nor (b) a request for unparticularised documents for evidentiary purposes, is admissible.

The myth has also developed that the power of reservation under Article

---

[61] 1980 Documents (*supra* n. 31), p. 420; (1978) XVII ILM 1425, 1428. This view is apparently shared by senior officials of the Hague Conference: Droz and Dyer (1981) 3 Northwestern J. Int. L. Bus. 155, 166–167. See also Comment (1984) 132 U. Pa. L. Rev. 1461, 1469.   [62] [1978] AC 547, 610–611, 619, 642.   [63] *Idem*, p. 645.

23 for pre-trial discovery of *documents* means that the Contracting States are bound to execute letters rogatory from the United States (for no other Contracting State has the system of discovery by oral deposition) seeking *oral* depositions for discovery purposes.[64] But in *Westinghouse* the House of Lords held clearly that the 1975 Act and the Hague Convention do not require the execution of letters rogatory for oral discovery purposes.[65] There is no difference in principle between documentary and oral discovery in this respect. Lord Diplock pointed out:[66]

Subsection (3) applies to both oral and documentary evidence. It is this provision which prohibits the making of an order for the examination of a witness not a party to the action for the purpose of seeking information which, though inadmissible at the trial, appears to be reasonably calculated to lead to the discovery of admissible evidence. This is permitted by rule 26 of the United States Federal Rules of Civil Procedure. Under the procedure of the High Court in England depositions of witnesses, either at home or abroad, may be taken before examiners for use at the trial, but the subject matter of such depositions is restricted to the evidence admissible at the trial. So the evidence requested in the letters rogatory can only be ordered to the extent that it is confined to evidence which will be admissible at the trial of the action in Virginia.

Accordingly, as Woolf J. put it in *Re International Power Industries NV*,[67] it is quite clear from the *Westinghouse* case 'that pre-trial discovery, as it is known in the United States, is not an exercise which this court should order to be performed pursuant to letters rogatory, that pre-trial discovery is distinct from the obtaining of evidence for the trial and that the approach of this court must be to allow letters rogatory only in so far as they are confined to obtaining evidence and are not requiring the exercise of pre-trial discovery'.

It is, of course, true that the practice of the English courts under the 1975 Act is not conclusive evidence of the meaning of the 1970 Convention. But it confirms that the English courts and the United Kingdom legislature have treated the practice before and after the 1970 Convention as being the

[64] Cf. Ristau, *op cit. supra* n. 45, at p. 233; in its brief in the *Club Méditerranée* case the US Government suggested that 'the precise import of Article 23 is highly uncertain': (1984) XXIII ILM 1332, 1338.

[65] See [1978] AC 547, 610, 611, 634–635.

[66] *Idem*, p. 634, and cf. p. 654 (*per* Lord Keith). See also *Re Asbestos Insurance Coverage Cases* [1985] 1 WLR 331 (HL); *Re State of Norway's Application, In Re Anders Jahre* [1987] QB 433 (CA); *SEC* v. *Certain Unknown Purchasers of the Common Stock etc. of Santa Fe International Corporation* (1984) XXIII ILM 511 (Drake J.). Each of these cases concerned material required for trial, but which was alleged by the witness to be of a 'fishing' character.

[67] [1985] Butterworths Company Law Cases 128, 137. In *J. Barber & Sons* v. *Lloyd's Underwriters* [1987] QB 103 oral depositions of parties were allowed, but Evans J. indicated that they could only involve questions which were relevant to the issues, and not questions which were likely to lead to discovery of evidence.

same. It is not realistic to suppose that the British delegation at the Hague Conference thought otherwise.

Nevertheless, perhaps as part of an effort to extend the scope of the Convention, and a result of the discussions in the Special Commission in 1978, the United States persuaded Denmark, Finland, Norway and Sweden to bring their declarations into line with that of the United Kingdom, and when the Netherlands acceded in 1981 it made a similar declaration.[68] The Report of the Special Commission does not make it clear why the United States was so concerned about this question, but the report of the US delegation[69] reveals that the United States delegate had enquired about the reasons for these declarations and stressed that unless American litigants could obtain assistance from the Contracting States during the pre-trial stage of a civil suit in the United States, the Convention would turn into a one way street as far as the United States was concerned. It is apparent from this document that the United States was seeking to have the reservations under Article 23 withdrawn or modified. Mr Ristau, the United States delegate, conceded that there had been abuses in the discovery system but argued that efforts were under way to prevent or minimise the abuse.[70]

By the time of the meeting of the Special Commission in 1985,[71] most of the experts were said to favour a limited reservation either along the lines of the statement by the United Kingdom or the reservation contained in Article 16 of the additional protocol of the inter-American convention on the taking of evidence abroad adopted in 1984. The Special Commission concluded that the discussions had clearly shown the necessity for a substantial number of States of a reservation in order to avoid abuses which could arise in connection with pre-trial discovery of documents; but the adoption of an unqualified reservation as permitted by Article 23 would seem to be excessive and detrimental to the proper operation of the Convention; the tendency which had appeared since 1978 and which had led a number of States to limit their reservations had gained ground, and the majority of States were now prepared to frame, or to the extent that they had not yet done so, to limit, their reservations along the lines of the reservation formulated by the United Kingdom or the similar reservation contained in the protocol drawn up under the auspices of the Organisation of American States.[72]

---

[68] Some of these declarations may be read as exhaustive definitions of pre-trial discovery of documents: see Oxman, *op. cit. supra* n. 59, at pp. 775–776, and Ristau, *op. cit. supra* n. 45, Vol. 1, Appendix C.   [69] (1978) XVII ILM 1417.

[70] *Idem*, p. 1421.   [71] (1985) XXIV ILM 1668.

[72] See also McClean and McLachlan, *The Hague Convention on the Taking of Evidence Abroad: Explanatory Documentation prepared for Commonwealth Jurisdictions* (Commonwealth Secretariat, 1985), pp. 12–14.

It would seem that the United States, which had been conspicuously silent before the conclusion of the Convention in 1970 about its use for discovery purposes, had, from 1978 onwards, engaged in a campaign, at least partially successful, to encourage the use of the Convention for third party discovery purposes. In the period between 1976 and 1985 the prevailing orthodoxy in the discussions at the Hague Conference came to be that the United Kingdom reservation was 'limited',[73] and that it would be desirable if other States brought their reservations into line with that of the United Kingdom. In fact the United Kingdom reservation could only be regarded as a limited description of pre-trial discovery of documents by ignoring the word 'including'; even if it were an exhaustive definition of document discovery it encompassed all document discovery except discovery of particular specified documents. But the House of Lords had in any event made it clear that the 1975 Act could not be used for any form of discovery, and it is surprising that the reports of the proceedings in the Hague Conference do not give any hint that the United Kingdom legislature and courts had set their faces against any use of the Convention for discovery purposes.

5. CONCLUSIONS

This analysis leads to the following conclusions. First, the Hague Evidence Convention was intended primarily to apply to 'evidence' in the sense of material required to prove or disprove allegations at trial. It was not intended to apply to discovery in the sense of the search for material which might lead to the discovery of admissible evidence. Second, there was some concern at the Hague Conference that United States litigants might endeavour to use the Convention for third party discovery, and Article 23 was inserted as an attempt (perhaps only partially successful in drafting terms) to make it clear that there was no obligation on Contracting States to allow the Convention to be used for third party discovery. This is so whether the discovery is of documents or by way of oral deposition. Third, there is no reason whatsoever to believe that the Convention was ever intended to apply to normal *inter partes* discovery, and not even the attempts of successive US delegations from 1978 onwards to encourage the use of the Convention for discovery appear to have envisaged anything other than third party discovery.

This does not mean that the Convention can never be used in connection with what would be regarded as third party discovery in the United States.

---

[73] In *Boreri* v. *Fiat SpA*, 763 F. 2d 17, 19 (1st Cir. 1985), the court contrasted a general reservation by Italy under Art. 23 with 'some restrictions' imposed by other States.

In the first place, it has been shown above that some at least of what is described as discovery in the United States is in reality intended for trial.[74] Secondly, it is clear that the requested court cannot undertake a minute examination of whether the material is required as evidence *stricto sensu*. As Lord Keith put it in the *Westinghouse* case,[75] 'the court of request should not be astute to examine the issues in the action and the circumstances of the case with excessive particularity for the purpose of determining in advance whether the evidence of that person will be relevant and admissible'. Thirdly, although there is no obligation on States which are party to the Convention to execute a request for discovery (and *a fortiori* if they have made reservations under Article 23), there is no reason why in appropriate cases they should not do so without obligation.[76]

If this analysis is right then the following propositions which can be derived from the United States cases are correct: the Hague Evidence Convention has a role to play in the collection of evidence abroad from third parties who are not subject to the *in personam* jurisdiction of the United States courts;[77] but the Convention was not intended to shield foreign litigants from the normal burdens of litigation in American courts, and, in particular, from pre-trial discovery;[78] and where the United States court has jurisdiction over a foreign litigant the Convention does not apply to the production in the United States of evidence in that litigant's possession, even though the documents or information sought may physically be located in the territory of a foreign signatory.[79]

But these conclusions do not mean that the Hague Evidence Convention *never* has a role to play in the production of evidence by parties. Thus, a foreign co-defendant may not appear, and its evidence may be necessary to prove the case against its co-defendants. Or there may be cases in which for other reasons it may be essential for evidentiary steps to be taken in the foreign country. Thus an order for on-site inspection of the defendant's plant abroad may perhaps be thought to be an intrusion of sovereignty,[80]

---

[74] See *supra* text at n. 21. This was recognised by the Munich Court of Appeal in the Siemens aspect of the *Corning* case: (1981) XX ILM 1025, 1039.

[75] [1978] AC 547, 654.

[76] The decision of the Bavarian Ministry of Justice to allow oral depositions in the *Corning* case ((1981) XX ILM 1047) may be regarded in this sense, or, alternatively, as a legal view that the bar on discovery related only to documentary discovery.

[77] *Re Anschuetz & Co. GmbH*, 754 F. 2d 602, 609–610, 615 (5th Cir. 1985); *Graco Inc.* v. *Kremlin, Inc.*, 101 FRD 503, 519–520 (ND Ill. 1984).

[78] *Re Anschuetz & Co. GmbH*, 754 F. 2d 602, 611; *Re Société Nationale Industrielle Aérospatiale*, 788 F. 2d 1408, 1411 (9th Cir. 1986); *Graco Inc.* v. *Kremlin, Inc.*, 101 FRD 503, 519–520.

[79] *Re Anschuetz & Co. GmbH*, 754 F. 2d 602, 611, 615; *Re Messerschmitt Bolkow Blohm GmbH,* 757 F. 2d 729, 731 (5th Cir. 1986); *Re Société Nationale Industrielle Aérospatiale*, 782 F. 2d 120, 125 (8th Cir. 1986).

[80] *Volkswagenwerk AG* v. *Superior Court*, 123 Cal. App. 3d 840 (1981).

although this must be regarded as doubtful.[81] In such cases the use of the Convention would resolve any doubt. But in the normal case, it is suggested, the Convention has no part to play in discovery between the parties.

Once the United States court has personal jurisdiction over the defendant, then the rules of civil procedure of the forum apply. If the case is in a federal court, the Federal Rules of Civil Procedure govern and, if the defendant is unwilling or unable to comply with its discovery obligations, then the court may apply the normal range of sanctions available to it under Rule 37:[82] they include orders that the matters regarding which the order was made or any other designated factors shall be taken to be established for the purposes of the action; or an order striking out pleadings; or an order treating as a contempt of court failure to obey the orders. Thus in *Insurance Corp. of Ireland Ltd.* v. *Compagnie des Bauxites de Guinée*[83] the Supreme Court held that a federal court could treat a foreign defendant as subject to the jurisdiction for failure to comply with discovery ordered in connection with its objection to the jurisdiction.

This result can certainly involve a conflict with foreign jurisdictions. As Professor Oxman[84] has shown clearly, the assumption of *in personam* jurisdiction on the basis of 'minimum contacts'[85] (often perceived abroad as *minimal* contacts) can lead to what is regarded in foreign countries as an excess of jurisdiction, not only in relation to the application of adjudicatory jurisdiction to the merits, but also to an extension of discovery, which becomes in practice, if not in law, extraterritorial. In turn, this can lead to the application or extension of blocking legislation of the French type. Thus any French defendant to an action in the United States is prohibited from complying with United States discovery rules, or orders, in so far as they involve disclosure of 'information of an economic, commercial, industrial, financial or technical nature to be used as evidence in foreign judicial or administrative proceedings'.[86]

The problem is caused, not by the discovery obligations of foreign parties, but by the consequences of the assumption of wide rules of *in personam* jurisdiction. This writer has suggested that in ordinary litigation

[81] See e.g. *Re Anschuetz & Co. GmbH*, 754 F. 2d 602, 606 (5th Cir. 1985); cf. *Graco Inc.* v. *Kremlin Inc.*, 101 FRD 503, 518 (ND Ill. 1984).

[82] *Société Internationale* v. *Rogers*, 357 US 197 (1958), applied in *Re Société Nationale Industrielle Aérospatiale*, 782 F. 2d 120 (8th Cir. 1986). The mere fact that a court has *in personam* jurisdiction to compel production by subpoena from a third party does not necessarily mean that it should always exercise that power; see e.g. *Laker Airways Ltd.* v. *Pan American World Airways*, 607 F. Supp. 324 (SDNY 1985); *Mackinnon* v. *Donaldson Lufkin Jenrette Securities Corp.* [1986] 2 WLR 453.   [83] 456 US 694 (1982).

[84] (1983) 37 U. Miami L. Rev. 733, 740–742.

[85] See especially *World-Wide Volkswagen Corp.* v. *Woodson*, 444 US 286 (1980). The cases are fully discussed by Hay (1986) 35 ICLQ 32.

[86] Law of 16 July 1980, inserting section I bis to Law of 26 July 1968.

there is no reason why a foreign party should not have to give discovery of documents which are relevant to the case merely because they are abroad.[87] The problem arises when the assumption of adjudicatory or legislative jurisdiction is exorbitant, and when that excess of jurisdiction is compounded by the exercise of enforcement jurisdiction to compel the production of material abroad.[88]

The answer to this problem does not lie in the Hague Evidence Convention for two reasons. The first reason is the technical one that most countries will not allow the use of the Convention for discovery. Accordingly, it is no solution to Aérospatiale's dilemma, caused by the French blocking statute, to ask the parties to resort to the Hague Evidence Convention: France is a country which has made a full reservation under Article 23. The second reason is that the underlying problem is not one of discovery and evidence, but of *in personam* jurisdiction over the merits. For many years foreign manufacturers whose products are sold in the United States (and their insurers) have been well aware that they do business of this kind at a price, and one of the elements of that price is the wide jurisdiction which United States courts exercise in personal injury cases, and the heavy damages which United States juries award in those cases. It is easy to understand why defendants in these cases would wish to put plaintiffs to the expense and difficulty of seeking discovery in foreign countries. But the Hague Evidence Convention, as originally envisaged and now constituted, is not the answer to a much wider question. To tinker with the problem by an unjustified and unworkable interpretation of the Convention will only serve to make matters worse.

Postscript

Since this article was written, the briefs submitted to the Supreme Court by the governments of France, Germany, Switzerland and the United Kingdom have become available. All the briefs (but for differing reasons) support reversal on the basis that resort to the Hague Convention should be considered. The belated conversion of European governments to the merits of the use of the Hague Convention for discovery purposes raises wider questions, comment on which must be deferred. For present purposes it is sufficient to say that there is nothing in the briefs to affect the thesis of this article.

---

[87] Collins, 'International Law Aspects of Obtaining Evidence Abroad', in *Extraterritorial Application of Laws and Responses Thereto* (Olmstead (ed.), 1984), p. 186.

[88] See Jennings (1957) 33 BYIL 146, 171; Jennings and Mann, International Law Association, 52nd Conference Proceedings (1966), p. 112.

VII

Harris v. *Taylor* Revived

The decision in *Henry* v. *Geoprosco International Ltd.* [1976] QB 726 (CA) revived the long-discredited decision in *Harris* v. *Taylor* [1915] 2 KB 580 (CA). The criticism which followed led to considerable pressure for reversal of the effect of these decisions, and this was effected by section 33 of the Civil Jurisdiction and Judgments Act 1982. Section 33 provides that a judgment debtor shall not be regarded as having submitted by reason only of the fact that he appeared (conditionally or otherwise) in the foreign proceedings (*a*) to contest the jurisdiction of the court; (*b*) to ask the court to dismiss or stay the proceedings on the ground that the dispute in question should be submitted to arbitration or to the determination of the courts of another country; or (*c*) to protect, or obtain the release of, property seized or threatened with seizure in the proceedings. In Case 150/80 *Elefanten Schuh GmbH* v. *Jacqmain* [1981] ECR 1671 the European Court held, in the context of Article 18 of the 1968 Convention, that pleading to the merits as an alternative to an objection to the jurisdiction would not be a submission. The House of Lords has held, in the context of submission to the jurisdiction of the English court, that a step in the proceedings only amounts to a submission when the defendant has taken some step which is only necessary or only useful if the objection to the jurisdiction has been waived: *Williams & Glyn's Bank* v. *Astro Dinamico* [1984] 1 WLR 438 (HL).

The point of principle raised by *Harris* v. *Taylor* and *Henry* v. *Geoprosco International Ltd.* has, therefore, been generally answered in a sense contrary to those decisions. In Australia the Standing Committee of the Attorneys General has recommended legislation similar to the 1982 Act, and such legislation has been enacted in several states: Sykes and Pryles, *Private International Law* (3rd. ed. 1991), 115; Nygh, *Conflict of Laws* (5th ed. 1991), 119. The position in Canada is unclear in the sense that although some authorities support *Harris* v. *Taylor*, the commentators are satisfied that common sense will ultimately prevail and that it will not be followed: Castel, *Canadian Conflict of Laws* (2nd ed. 1986), 243, McLeod, *Conflict of Laws* (1983), 589.

In the United States it was held that a special appearance for the purpose of contesting jurisdiction was sufficient to give the court jurisdiction over the defendant if the law of the forum so provided: *York* v. *Texas*, 137 US 15 (1890). But today legislation in the states provides that a special appearance does not amount to a submission, and the effect on the modern rules of civil procedure in the Federal courts and many state courts is that an objection to jurisdiction would not amount to a submission if the obligation fails: Scoles and Hay, *Conflict of Laws* (2nd ed. 1992), 277–278.

From *Law Quarterly Review*, 92 (1976), 268.

I. INTRODUCTION

When a 60-year old decision had been variously described by textwriters as 'unfortunate'[1] and 'revolting to commonsense',[2] when it had (or so one thought) been distinguished almost out of existence by appellate judges of the calibre of Lord Evershed MR and Denning LJ,[3] when it had not been followed by so eminent a commercial lawyer as Megaw J.,[4] one might have reasonably assumed that it was a case which could be consigned 'into the limbo of lost causes'.[5]

Such was the position of *Harris* v. *Taylor*[6] until March 1975, when the Court of Appeal, speaking through Roskill LJ, reasserted the authority of *Harris* v. *Taylor* and dealt with the textwriters in the following words: '. . . however distinguished the authors and editors of these textbooks, the law must be taken to be as laid down by the courts, however much their decisions may be criticised by writers of such great distinction.'[7]

In *Harris* v. *Taylor* the plaintiff sought to enforce an Isle of Man judgment in the English court. The defendant had appeared conditionally in the Isle of Man court to set aside the proceedings on certain jurisdictional grounds, of which more later. The Isle of Man court had dismissed the application to set aside the proceedings, the defendant had taken no further part, and judgment was entered in default. When the plaintiff brought his judgment to England, a unanimous Court of Appeal held that the judgment was enforceable in England because the defendant had submitted to the jurisdiction of the Isle of Man court. In *Henry* v. *Geoprosco* the plaintiff sought to enforce in England an Alberta judgment for damages for breach of a contract of employment. The defendants had applied to the Alberta court, unsuccessfully, for an order setting aside service on jurisdictional grounds (to be developed below) and for a stay of the proceedings by reason of the arbitration clause in the contract. The Alberta court refused the defendants' motion and they took no further part in the proceedings. When the plaintiff brought his default judgment to England, the Court of Appeal, following *Harris* v. *Taylor*, held that the

---

[1] Wolff, *Private International Law* (2nd ed., 1950), p. 259.

[2] Dicey and Morris, *Conflict of Laws* (9th ed., 1973), p. 996.

[3] *Re Dulles' Settlement (No. 2)* [1951] Ch. 842.

[4] *Daarnhouwer* v. *Boulos* [1968] 2 Lloyd's Rep. 259.

[5] The phrase is that of Sellers LJ in *Matthews* v. *Kuwait Bechtel Corporation* [1959] 2 QB 57, 69, in relation to another case.　　　　　　　　　　　　[6] [1915] 2 KB 580.

[7] *Henry* v. *Geoprosco International Ltd.* [1976] QB 726, at p. 746. As for the judiciary, and the intervening decisions, the Court of Appeal, in relation to Lord Evershed MR and Denning LJ 'ventured the view that the suggested distinction of *Harris* v. *Taylor* on the ground of *res judicata* is not supportable in principle' (p. 745) and, so far as Megaw J. was concerned, 'he was not entitled to take the course which he did' (p. 746).

defendants had voluntarily submitted to the jurisdiction of the Alberta courts and that the judgment was accordingly enforceable in England.

It is not the intention of this writer to repeat all of the criticisms which have been made by the textwriters of *Harris* v. *Taylor*. His intention is a little more modest. It is to suggest first that, irrespective of the question whether it was rightly decided, the decision in *Harris* v. *Taylor* should be limited to a very specific factual situation, namely, where the protest to the jurisdiction of the foreign court takes the form of a procedure which is very closely similar to the conditional appearance in English law. This is because it will be suggested that the Court of Appeal in *Harris* v. *Taylor* was influenced, in deciding what was a submission to the jurisdiction of a foreign court, by the rules relating to appearance in domestic English procedural law. This is not the place for a theoretical discussion of characterisation, but there is perhaps an analogy between the way the Court of Appeal in *Ogden* v. *Ogden*[8] characterised a foreign rule by analogy with an English rule and the way in which the Court of Appeal in *Harris* v. *Taylor* only a few years later applied a purely domestic procedural notion of submission to a case involving the question whether there had been a submission in the international sense. Secondly, it will be suggested that the Court of Appeal in *Henry* v. *Geoprosco* was mistaken in drawing the conclusion from *Harris* v. *Taylor* that there is an essential distinction between a protest against the *existence* of jurisdiction and its *exercise*. It is therefore proposed to consider:

(a) the English procedural rules relating to appearances;
(b) the decision of the Court of Appeal in *Harris* v. *Taylor* in the light of these rules and its relationship with other decisions; and
(c) the implications of the decision in *Henry* v. *Geoprosco*.

2. ENGLISH PROCEDURAL LAW

Where leave to serve out of the jurisdiction is granted and the defendant is served abroad, if the defendant wishes to challenge the jurisdiction of the English court or its exercise, he has an option. He may either enter a conditional appearance and contest the jurisdiction by summons or motion or, alternatively, he may protest against the jurisdiction by summons or motion without entering any form of appearance. The usual procedure is the first.

Order 12, r. 7, deals with conditional appearances and is to the following effect:

[8] [1908] P. 46.

(1) A defendant to an action may with the leave of the Court enter a conditional appearance in the action.

(2) A conditional appearance . . . is to be treated for all purposes as an unconditional appearance unless the Court otherwise orders or the defendant applies to the Court, within the time limited for the purpose, for an order under Rule 8 and the Court makes an order thereunder.

As the notes to the *Supreme Court Practice 1976* point out[9] the effect of this rule is to enable the defendant to prevent a judgment in default being entered against him, while at the same time remaining entitled to object to the jurisdiction of the court. If the defendant fails to apply within the time limit to set aside the proceedings, the appearance automatically becomes an unconditional one. If he applies to set aside the proceedings and succeeds, the action then comes to an end. If he applies to set aside the proceedings and fails, then the appearance becomes unconditional.

The procedure was described by Lord Denning MR in *Somportex* v. *Philadelphia Chewing Gum Corporation*[10] in the following words, in relation to an American company which had entered a conditional appearance after being served in the United States:

That was a very important step for them to take (especially if they had assets in England or were likely to bring assets into England) because it was an essential way of defending their own position. After all, if they did not enter an appearance at all, and in consequence the English courts gave judgment against them in default of appearance, that judgment could be executed against them in England in respect of assets in England. In order to guard against that eventuality, they had first to enter a conditional appearance here, then argue whether it was within the jurisdiction of the court or not. If it was outside the jurisdiction, all well and good. The writ would be set aside. They would go away free. If it was within the jurisdiction, however, their appearance became unconditional and they could fight out the case on the merits. In these circumstances it seems to me that they were very wise to enter a conditional appearance.

It is, however, possible to contest the jurisdiction of the English courts without entering a form of appearance, although this is rare. It is clear that it is not necessary to enter an appearance from the wording of Order 12, r. 8 (1), which is to the following effect:

A defendant to an action may at any time before entering an appearance therein, or, if he has entered a conditional appearance, within fourteen days after entering the appearance, apply to the Court for an order setting aside the writ or service of the writ, or notice of the writ, on him, or declaring that the writ or notice had not been duly served on him or discharging any order giving leave to serve the writ or notice on him out of the jurisdiction.

[9] Note 12/7/1, p. 109.
[10] [1968] 3 All ER 26, 29. See Collins, (1972) 21 ICLQ 656, 673–681 (ante, pp. 243–252).

This procedure is comparatively rare, perhaps because of the fear of advisers of defendants that judgment in default of appearance might be entered.[11]

3. PROCEDURAL ASPECTS OF THE DECISION IN *HARRIS V. TAYLOR*

The judgment of the Court of Appeal was on appeal from a decision of Bray J.[12] The plaintiff was a domiciled Manxman who sued the defendant (who was an Englishman) for damages for loss of consortium and for criminal conversation with the plaintiff's wife, which was alleged to have taken place both in the Isle of Man and England. The claim for damages for loss of consortium was subsequently not pursued by the plaintiff. After the defendant had left the Isle of Man, the plaintiff applied for and obtained an order for service out of the jurisdiction of the writ, and the writ was subsequently served on the defendant in England. The defendant obtained leave to enter and entered a 'conditional' appearance to the action in the Isle of Man court and filed a motion to set aside service of the writ. The motion was based on the following grounds:

(i) the rules of the High Court of Justice 1884 of the Isle of Man did not contemplate or authorise service out of the jurisdiction;

(ii) no cause of action arose or existed within the jurisdiction of the Isle of Man courts;

(iii) the defendant was domiciled in England and had never had a domicile in the Isle of Man.

After considering the evidence filed and hearing argument on both sides, the Isle of Man court dismissed the motion and adjudged the writ to have been duly served. Subsequently two judgments were entered in the Isle of Man against the defendant. The first was an interlocutory judgment, whereby it was adjudged that the defendant should pay damages to be assessed. That interlocutory judgment recited that the defendant had failed to appear or enter an appearance to the writ of summons which had been duly served on him. After a jury had assessed the damages for criminal conversation at £800 judgment was entered against the defendant for that sum in a final judgment which contained a recital that the defendant had not filed or delivered a defence or appeared in the action.

At that point, therefore, it would seem that the defendant had appeared

[11] A case where no appearance of any kind was entered but only a summons was issued to set aside the proceedings was *Black-Clawson International* v. *Papierwerke Waldhof-Aschaffenberg AG* [1975] AC 91.

[12] Reported at (1914) 111 LT 564, which contains a full report of the proceedings in the Manx court.

conditionally and that when he had failed in his protest against the jurisdiction, judgment had been entered both in default of appearance and in default of defence. Had there been no further evidence, it would appear that even by Isle of Man law the defendant had not submitted to the jurisdiction (i.e., the conditional appearance had not automatically been converted into an unconditional appearance), since one of the grounds of the two judgments against him was that he had failed to enter an appearance. The arguments as reported do not take the matter any further. It appears that evidence of the law of the Isle of Man was called before Bray J. by each side. He referred to the defendant's application for leave to enter a conditional appearance and noted that appearance in the Isle of Man was not formally entered, but on the day named the defendant would appear in court in person or by solicitor, and the judge would take note of his appearance in his book. In this case the note of the judge of the Isle of Man stated that 'Mr. Cruickshank appears conditionally to set aside writ. The defendant to file a motion to set aside writ'.

Bray J. posed the question as whether 'the conditional appearance here was a voluntary appearance' and went on as follows:

> I had the evidence of two advocates practising in the Isle of Man on each side. They did not throw much light on this point. The word 'conditional' used in reference to appearance has no recognised meaning in the High Court of the Isle of Man. It is not often used. There are no rules authorising or dealing with 'conditional appearances'. I have no doubt that it was used because of its use in the English courts, and I think, therefore, that I ought to give it the meaning it has in our courts. I think the court in giving leave must have intended that the entry of conditional appearance should have the same effect as it has in our courts . . . (p. 568)

The English practice which Bray J. went on to describe is substantially the same today. As shown above, the current rule is Order 12, r. 7, which provides that a conditional appearance is to be treated for all purposes as an unconditional appearance unless the court otherwise orders or the defendant applies to the court, within the time limited for the purpose, for an order under Rule 8 and the court makes an order thereunder. Rule 8 allows a defendant to apply to the court for an order setting aside the writ or service of a writ.

Bray J. was right to formulate the question as whether the conditional appearance was a voluntary appearance. But he was quite wrong to rely on the evidence of the Isle of Man lawyers on the point. The question was not whether there had been a voluntary appearance in the sense recognised by the Isle of Man. The true question was whether there had been a voluntary appearance within the meaning of that expression in the English rules of private international law relating to international jurisdiction of courts.

But having found the evidence of the Isle of Man law unsatisfactory on this point, he compounded the error by testing the position according to the domestic rules of procedure in England, namely, whether a conditional appearance in England becomes a voluntary appearance if the attack on the court's jurisdiction is unsuccessful. It is not clear why he relied so much on the domestic English practice. Perhaps in view of the unsatisfactory nature of the evidence of Isle of Man law, he was applying the presumption that Isle of Man law be deemed to be the same as English law. Or perhaps he was merely being influenced by the English procedure. The former explanation is more likely. In any event, after referring to the English practice, he concluded

It is a complete appearance to the action for all purposes subject only to the right reserved by the defendant to apply to set aside the writ or service. If it is an appearance, and I think it is so, it is clearly a voluntary appearance: (see *Boissière* v. *Brockner*, sup.). As pointed out by Cave J., in that case, the defendant by the course he has taken has set up one answer to the claim and has taken his chance of winning on this ground. He has clearly submitted to the jurisdiction of the court upon this point. In my opinion the defendant has voluntarily submitted himself to the jurisdiction of the court . . . (p. 568)

When the case came before the Court of Appeal the plaintiff stressed that under Isle of Man law there was no such thing as judgment in default of appearance. It was argued that the only case in which the rules of the Isle of Man court provided for a judgment in default was where there had been default in delivery of defence. It would appear that the main point of this argument was to get over the recital in the judgments issued by the Isle of Man court that there had been no appearance. The Court of Appeal did not deal satisfactorily with the recitals in the two Isle of Man judgments. Buckley LJ[13] suggested that the words in the interlocutory judgment 'having failed to appear or enter an appearance' referred to the failure of the defendant to appear in the court and to his failure to enter a formal appearance. In this way, Buckley LJ suggested, the interlocutory judgment could be made consistent with the practice of the Isle of Man court and with the final judgment, although he indicated that the point was not an important one because the Isle of Man court was entitled to treat the appearance of the defendant on his motion to set aside service as an appearance in the action for all purposes. But he does not deal with the reference in the final judgment to a failure of appearance. Pickford LJ said it was not quite clear what the practice of the Isle of Man court was in the matter, and that it was certainly somewhat curious that if there was no power to sign judgment in default of appearance the practice book should contain such a form of judgment. But he did not think the point was of

[13] [1915] 2 KB at p. 588.

much importance, since the time for delivering a defence had expired and there had been a default. Although he was inclined to think that the court treated the defendant's appearance of his motion as in the nature of a conditional appearance, the point was not of any great importance because the evidence showed that if the appearance was only intended as a conditional appearance the court had power to treat it as a full appearance. That, in his view, was enough to amount to a submission. That reasoning is curious; it seems to suggest that even if the local court does not in fact treat the conditional appearance as being transformed into a full appearance, nevertheless the English court would so consider it. Bankes LJ did not deal with the technical point.

Thus the Court of Appeal did not deal adequately with the suggestion that the Isle of Man court itself did not treat the case as one in which the defendant had appeared. Buckley LJ was constrained to interpret the interlocutory judgment in a way so as to make it consistent with the final judgment, by a process of reasoning which is not only obscure but also ignores the fact that even the final judgment referred to the failure of appearance. Pickford LJ apparently took the view that even where the court does not treat the conditional appearance as a full appearance if the motion against the jurisdiction fails, nevertheless, if it has power to do so it will in some sense be regarded as having exercised that power even if it has not. But for both Buckley LJ and Pickford LJ the appearance under the local law was crucial. The essence of the judgment of Buckley LJ is in the following passage:

He went to the Court and contended that the Court had no jurisdiction over him. The Court, however, decided against this contention and held that the defendant was amenable to its jurisdiction. In my opinion there was a voluntary appearance by the defendant in the Isle of Man Court and a submission by him to jurisdiction of that Court . . . If it can be regarded as a qualified appearance, it was an appearance for the purpose of getting a decision of the Court on the question whether the defendant was bound by the jurisdiction of the Court. The decision was against him, and thereafter it was not open to the defendant to say that he was not bound. The doctrine applicable to these cases is that if the defendant has placed himself in such a position that it has become his duty to obey the judgment of the foreign Court, then the judgment is enforceable against him in this country.[14]

Pickford LJ concluded:

if a defendant applies to a Court to set aside the service of a writ under which judgment could be obtained against him, and the Court is one which has power to treat that application as constituting an appearance to the action, that in my opinion amounts to such a submission on the part of the defendant to the jurisdiction of the Court as renders him liable to obey the judgment of the Court.[15]

[14] Pp. 587–588.   [15] At p. 590.

Bankes LJ put his judgment on a broader ground, finding that if a defendant applied to a court for the exercise of its protection he will be under an obligation to obey the ultimate judgment of the court.

Neither the decision of Bray J. nor any of the judgments of the Court of Appeal supports any suggestion that an important basis of *Harris* v. *Taylor* was the fact that the defendant sought to persuade the Isle of Man court in its *discretion* not to exercise a jurisdiction which it undoubtedly had. The defendant contested the jurisdiction on three grounds: the first was that service out of the jurisdiction was not available under Manx law—that was clearly an argument that the court had no jurisdiction; the second was that no cause of action arose or existed in the Isle of Man—that may have been an assertion that the case was not within the Manx equivalent of Order 11 or a reason for its not exercising its discretion; and precisely the same considerations apply to the third ground, that the defendant was not domiciled in the Isle of Man. One simply does not know what the Isle of Man rules were and the judgments are of no assistance.

It is suggested, therefore, first, that a crucial part of the judgments of Buckley and Pickford L JJ in *Harris* v. *Taylor* relates to the demonstration that the Isle of Man judgment was in default of defence rather than in default of appearance and that the ratio is that where a defendant appears conditionally to contest the jurisdiction of the foreign court, and fails, the conversion of the conditional appearance to an unconditional appearance amounts to a voluntary submission; secondly, that none of the judgments in the case draws the distinction, which in *Henry* v. *Geoprosco International* was said to be so crucial to the decision in *Harris* v. *Taylor*, between a protest against the *existence* of jurisdiction and its *exercise*.

It may be helpful at this point to put *Harris* v. *Taylor* in the context of related earlier decisions. The older authorities may be summarised as follows:

1. Before an *arbitrator* a party may both protest against the jurisdiction and defend the case on the merits without submitting.[16]

2. If the defendant defends a foreign action on the merits because he fears that his property will be seized in execution it does not make his submission any the less 'voluntary'.[17]

3. Although there is no decision directly in point, there are *obiter* statements in a number of cases that an appearance to save or protect

---

[16] *Ringland* v. *Lowndes* (1864) 17 CB (NS) 514; *Davies* v. *Price* (1864) 34 LJQB 8; *Hamlyn* v. *Betteley* (1880) 6 QBD 63; *Westminster Chemicals & Produce Ltd.* v. *Eichholz & Loeser* [1954] 1 Lloyd's Rep. 99, 105; *Henry* v. *Geoprosco International Ltd.* [1976] QB at p. 747.
[17] *De Cosse Brissac* v. *Rathbone* (1861) 6 H. & N. 301; *Voinet* v. *Barrett* (1885) 55 LJQB 39; *Guiard* v. *De Clermont* [1914] 3 KB 145.

goods which have been seized by the foreign court before judgment as a foundation of jurisdiction is not a voluntary submission.[18]

The only support for *Harris* v. *Taylor* in the older authorities comes from two converging sources.

There are several statements, although not in the context of a protest to the jurisdiction, that a defendant who appears before the foreign court and takes the chance of a judgment in his favour, but loses, is bound.[19] Those statements related to the defendant who took a chance on the merits but in *Boissière* v. *Brockner*[20] Cave J. seems to have gone a little further. That was a case where the defendants appeared before the French court, objected to the jurisdiction of the court, and failing success on that plea asked for judgment on the merits; the French court overruled the plea on jurisdiction but decided in favour of the defendants on the merits; both parties then appealed to the Court of Appeal at Caen, the defendants again objecting to the jurisdiction but asking the Court of Appeal to affirm the judgment on the merits if the plea on jurisdiction should be overruled; the Court of Appeal affirmed the decision of the lower court both on jurisdiction and on the merits; the Cour de Cassation, on a further appeal, set aside the judgment in favour of the defendants and remitted the case to the Court of Appeal at Rouen; the defendants maintained the plea to the jurisdiction but lost on the merits and after the defendants refused to attend a further hearing for the taking of accounts judgment for approximately £2,000 was entered against them. The plaintiffs sought to recover on the judgment by action at common law in England and the defendants pleaded (*inter alia*) that the French court had no jurisdiction and that they had only appeared before the French court under protest. It was a case in which the defendants had both protested the jurisdiction *and* defended the case on the merits. But Cave J. used language which though apt to cover the actual case could be taken to cover a case where there is only a protest. Heavily influenced by the statements about the defendant 'taking his chance', he referred to the 'man who appears without duress, and therefore voluntarily in one sense, but who accompanies his appearance with a protest and appears, not because he is impelled to do so,

---

[18] *Voinet* v. *Barrett* (1885) 55 LJQB 39, 41–42; *Guiard* v. *De Clermont* [1914] 3 KB at p. 155; cf. *Schibsby* v. *Westenholz* (1870) LR 6 QB 155, 162. It is suggested in Dicey and Morris (p. 997) that *Re Low* [1894] 1 Ch. 147 is authority against this view. But that was a case where the Scots court had seized property to found its jurisdiction and the defendant had subsequently defended the whole case on its merits. It was not a case where the appearance was limited to preserving or saving goods from seizure. That may happen, for example, where the defendant denies that he has goods within the jurisdiction or where he challenges the constitutionality of the attachment (as is possible in the United States: see *Mitchell* v. *W. T. Grant Co.* (1974) 416 US 600).

[19] *Schibsby* v. *Westenholz* (1870) LR 6 QB 155, 162; *Voinet* v. *Barrett* (1885) 55 LJQB 39, 41, 42. On the older cases see Clarence Smith, 'Personal Jurisdiction' (1953) 2 ICLQ 510, 514–522.   [20] (1889) 6 TLR 85.

but because he judges it to be for his interest to do so. That is, he intends to take all the advantage he hopes to gain by appearing and by a protest to relieve himself from the disadvantage. He wishes to have the benefit without the burden'. He concluded, on this aspect

In fact, the defendants in this case submitted the very question of jurisdiction to the Court, and took their chance of a decision in their favour on that ground; and if that objection failed they asked the foreign Court to decide in their favour on the merits of the case . . . I am of opinion that the appearance of the defendants was voluntary within the meaning of that term, as laid down in *Voinet* v. *Barrett*.[21]

Thus the decision appears to rest not only on the appearance to protest the jurisdiction but also on the fact that the defendant also defended the case on the merits.[22]

Re Dulles' Settlement (No.2)[23] was not a case of submission to the jurisdiction of a foreign court. The only relevant question was whether a father, resident in the United States, had submitted to the jurisdiction of the High Court for the purpose of an order for maintenance under the Guardianship of Infants Acts 1886 to 1925. Although he had also contested the issue of custody of the child, on the application for maintenance he had protested against the jurisdiction and no other question on that issue had been canvassed. The Court of Appeal (Evershed MR and Denning LJ) decided that there had been no submission.

Since no question of a foreign judgment arose, *Harris* v. *Taylor* was not really in point. That can be illustrated by assuming a simpler case. If in *England* a defendant enters a conditional appearance, protests against the jurisdiction and loses, his conditional appearance becomes unconditional by virtue of the Rules of the Supreme Court. If he takes no further part in the proceedings, judgment will be entered in default of *defence* and there will be a valid English judgment. If he protests against the jurisdiction without entering an appearance, loses, and takes no further part, judgment will be entered against him in default of *appearance*. In neither case is *Harris* v. *Taylor* relevant. Nor, it is suggested, is the case relevant in the more obscure procedure relating to custody and maintenance. Quite

---

[21] At pp. 85–86.
[22] There are Canadian decisions to the same effect: *McFadden* v. *Colville Ranching Co.* (1915) 8 WWR 163; *Richardson* v. *Allen* (1916) 28 DLR 134—in each of these cases the defendant had conditionally appeared in the Ontario court and delivered a defence without prejudice to his right to contest the jurisdiction. The other Canadian decisions are of little assistance: two hold that an application to set aside a default judgment is not a submission (*Esdale* v. *Bank of Ottawa* (1920) 51 DLR 485; *McLean* v. *Shields* (1885) 9 OR 699) although the only English authority is to the contrary (*Guiard* v. *De Clermont, supra*). *Harris* v. *Taylor* was followed in *Kennedy* v. *Trites* (1916) 10 WWR 412 on apparently similar facts, but it is not reported in full. See also Castel, *Private International Law* (1960), pp. 264–265.
[23] [1951] Ch. 842.

different rules apply to submission to English courts. Provided the court has jurisdiction by English law[24] whether there has been a submission is a question of fact and degree. Thus a defendant will be regarded as having submitted if he enters an unconditional appearance;[25] or if he takes out a summons to set aside a default judgment and asks for an order that the plaintiff serve a statement of claim[26] or fights an injunction on the merits even without entering a formal appearance.[27] But even before *Re Dulles*, in relation to the old rules on the settlement of the property of a respondent wife in divorce proceedings, Lord Merrivale P. said:[28]

I am not persuaded that an appearance to such a petition as the present, qualified at all stages of the case by a distinct and reasoned denial of the existence of jurisdiction, could with any propriety be regarded as a submission to the exercise of the jurisdiction so denied.

As the cases mentioned above suggest, submission is normally relevant in a domestic context when the defendant, who has taken certain steps, wishes to ventilate the question of the court's jurisdiction. If the prior steps have amounted to a voluntary submission, he will not be allowed to contest the jurisdiction. But if he limits himself to questioning the jurisdiction, the issue of jurisdiction will of course be decided. If he wins, that is an end of the matter. If he loses, the question of jurisdiction will have been decided against him and he will not be allowed to reopen it. But no English court could decide a disputed issue of its jurisdiction by holding that it had jurisdiction *merely* because the defendant had contested the jurisdiction— that indeed would be a proposition revolting to common sense.

As Lord Evershed MR pointed out in *Re Dulles (No. 1)*[29] the question whether there has been a submission is one of inference from all the facts. It may well be, as the Court of Appeal suggested in *Henry* v. *Geoprosco*,[30] that it is difficult to see how in *Re Dulles* the father had not submitted on the question of maintenance by defending wardship and custody proceedings on the merits. But in any event it was not really necessary to involve or distinguish *Harris* v. *Taylor* because that case dealt with a quite different question. Nevertheless, Denning LJ clearly did think that for general purposes *Harris* v. *Taylor* was in conflict with the general proposition that a defendant does not voluntarily submit to the jurisdiction of a court 'when he has all the time been vigorously protesting that it has no jurisdiction'.[31] He therefore purported to distinguish it. First, he commented that because

---

[24] Or the jurisdictional rules can be waived: see *Moore* v. *Gamgee* (1890) 25 QBD 244 but this is not always possible: see Dicey and Morris, p. 377.

[25] Cf. *Tozier* v. *Hawkins* (1885) 15 QBD 680.

[26] *Fry* v. *Moore* (1889) 23 QBD 395.   [27] *Boyle* v. *Sacker* (1888) 39 Ch. D 249.

[28] *Tallack* v. *Tallack* [1927] P. 211, 222.   [29] [1951] Ch. 265, 276.

[30] [1976] QB at 746.

[31] *Re Dulles (No. 2)* [1951] Ch. at p. 850.

the Isle of Man rules were similar to Order 11, the Isle of Man judgment should be recognised on a basis of reciprocity. As the Court of Appeal in *Henry* v. *Geoprosco* pointed out that was not a correct statement of the law.[32] Denning LJ then distinguished *Harris* v. *Taylor* in these words:[33]

> *Harris* v. *Taylor* is an authority on res judicata in that the defendant was not allowed in our courts to contest the service on him out of Manx jurisdiction; because that was a point that he had raised unsuccessfully in the Manx court, and he had not appealed against it. To that extent he had submitted to the jurisdiction of the Manx court and was not allowed to go back on it. But the case is no authority on what constitutes a submission to jurisdiction generally.

Lord Evershed MR indicated[34] that he agreed with Denning LJ that *Harris* v. *Taylor* could only be regarded as deciding that the matter of jurisdiction had become *res judicata*; even on that basis, he suggested that it might be open to reconsideration by the House of Lords on the ground that the question of a foreign court's jurisdiction (in the international sense) should be open to consideration of the English court.[35]

4. *HENRY* V. *GEOPROSCO INTERNATIONAL LIMITED*[36]

(a) The facts and issues

The plaintiff was a resident of Alberta, Canada. The defendants were a Jersey company with their head office in London. By an agreement made in Alberta in 1970 the defendants agreed to employ the plaintiff as a member of an 'oil well workover party' in the Trucial States. The contract provided for arbitration, although no place for the holding of any

---

[32] [1976] QB at p. 744. See *Re Trepca Mines* [1960] 1 WLR 1273.
[33] [1951] Ch. at p. 851.   [34] [1951] Ch. at p. 849.
[35] In *Daarnhouwer & Co.* v. *Boulos* [1968] 2 Lloyd's Rep. 259 the plaintiffs obtained a consent judgment in the Sudan against a firm. The defendant applied to the Sudanese court for the judgment to be set aside on the ground that the judgment had been obtained by fraud, that he had not been a partner in the alleged partnership and that he had not been properly served or sued. The Sudanese courts rejected the application and held that the summons made to the defendant's Sudanese lawyer was good service. Counsel for the plaintiffs, in the English proceedings to enforce the judgment, conceded that the defendant had not raised the merits in the Sudanese court and had been concerned solely with jurisdiction. Megaw J. distinguished *Harris* v. *Taylor* on the ground that the defendant had put the *facts* in issue in the Isle of Man, and that the facts had not been put before the Sudanese court for determination; even if he were wrong in the interpretation of *Harris* v. *Taylor*, it was in conflict with *Re Dulles*, and he preferred the later authority. He added also that *Harris* v. *Taylor* was distinguishable on two further grounds; first, that there had been actual service in that case on the defendant—why this is a relevant distinction is not clear; second, that in *Harris* v. *Taylor* the Manx court's exercise of jurisdiction was not inconsistent with English notions under Order 11—but as indicated above, reciprocity plays no part.
[36] [1976] QB 726. The judgment of Willis J. is at [1974] 2 Lloyd's Rep. 536.

arbitration was named. There is some suggestion in the report that the arbitrator was to be appointed by the President for the time being of the Institute of Arbitrators in London, although London was not expressly referred to in the contract. The plaintiff took up his appointment and went to the Trucial States but in September 1970 the defendants dismissed him. The plaintiff started proceedings for wrongful dismissal in the Supreme Court of Alberta. By Alberta law, the Alberta court had jurisdiction because the contract was entered into in Alberta and the Supreme Court gave leave to serve the statement of claim on the defendants outside the jurisdiction. Service was effected in Jersey.

In 1971 the defendants invited the plaintiff to discontinue the proceedings because of the arbitration clause. In 1972 the defendants served a notice of motion on the plaintiff in the Alberta court seeking an order setting aside the service of the statement of claim on the ground (*inter alia*) that the plaintiff's affidavit seeking leave to serve out of the jurisdiction was defective and, significantly, that the Supreme Court of Alberta was not the *forum conveniens*. They further sought a stay of proceedings by reason of the arbitration clause. The Alberta court refused the defendants' motion and they took no further part in the proceedings.

In effect, therefore, the defendants sought to say that in its discretion the Alberta court should not exercise its undoubted jurisdiction because (a) Alberta was not the *forum conveniens* and (b) because the arbitration clause was a so-called *Scott* v. *Avery* clause, namely, a clause which made going to arbitration a condition precedent to liability—although the Court of Appeal stated that as a matter of English law that last submission was plainly untenable upon the true construction of the clause.

By Alberta law, it is not necessary to enter an appearance of any kind before applying for a stay under the Arbitration Act there, although the position is different in England. In 1973 judgment was entered for the plaintiff in default of defence or appearance. The plaintiff sought to enforce the judgment in England by action at common law, since the 1920 and 1933 Acts do not apply to Alberta judgments. The defendants argued that the judgment was not enforceable in England because they had not submitted to the jurisdiction of the Alberta courts.

It was ultimately conceded that the only question for the English court was whether, as a matter of English law, the defendants had submitted to the jurisdiction of the Supreme Court of Alberta, although the parties had earlier sought to adduce evidence of what as a matter of the law of Alberta amounts to a voluntary submission.

The defendants accepted that in effect they had invited the Supreme Court of Alberta to divest itself of the jurisdiction which they accepted it possessed under the law of Alberta and had invited the Alberta court not to accept jurisdiction by reason of the arbitration clause in the service agreement and their invocation of the Alberta Arbitration Act, but argued that none of those grounds constituted a voluntary submission. They suggested that nothing short of a submission of 'the merits' of the dispute would amount to such a voluntary submission.

(b) The decision of the court

The Court of Appeal drew attention to the following points in relation to the decision in *Harris* v. *Taylor*:[36]

. . . first, that the Isle of Man High Court had by its own local law jurisdiction over the defendant; secondly, that that court had a discretion whether or not to exercise that jurisdiction over the defendant; thirdly, that that court having heard a plea by the defendant that it could not and should not do so decided both that it could and should exercise that jurisdiction; fourthly, that it was not argued in the English action that that decision was in any way wrong by the local law, and fifthly, that the defendant, having voluntarily invited the Isle of Man High Court, by the appearance which he made, to adjudicate on his submission that that jurisdiction of that court could not and should not be exercised over him and having lost, had voluntarily submitted to the jurisdiction of that court so that thereafter the defendant could not be heard to say that that court did not have jurisdiction to adjudicate on the entirety of the dispute between him and the plaintiff.[37]

The court then discussed four of the nineteenth century cases, of which two relate only to general questions of international jurisdiction and have nothing to do with the specific problem of submission;[38] the other two[39] are both cases where the defendant defended the foreign case on the merits, albeit in the alternative in the latter case. The Court of Appeal drew specific attention to the emphasis placed in the former case on the defendant 'taking a chance' of a judgment in his favour. As for *Re Dulles*, the Court of Appeal pointed out that it was not a decision on the enforcement of foreign judgments and that for that reason alone it was a little surprising that in such a case the Court of Appeal as constituted in *Re Dulles* should have thought itself able to disregard *Harris* v. *Taylor*, which was a decision directly on that subject; that Denning LJ was wrong to distinguish *Harris* v. *Taylor* as a decision on *res judicata* relating to the factual question whether the cause of action had arisen in the Isle of Man, since that question was not decided on the facts; that Denning LJ was wrong to suggest that recognition of foreign judgments rested on reciprocity;[40] that *Harris* v. *Taylor* could not be distinguished on the ground that it was solely a decision on *res judicata*—that was because the

---

[36] *Supra*, n. 6.   [37] [1976] QB at pp. 738–739.
[38] *Buchanan* v. *Rucker* (1808) 9 East 192; *Pemberton* v. *Hughes* [1899] 1 Ch. 781.
[39] *Voinet* v. *Barrett*, and *supra*, *Boissière* v. *Brockner*, *supra*.
[40] See *Re Trepca Mines* [1960] 1 WLR 1273, with which the court agreed.

decision could only be *res judicata* if the defendant was bound by it; that in any event the statements in *Re Dulles* were *obiter* and unnecessary for the decision of the case, and were pronounced by the court in an interlocutory appeal consisting of only two members.[41] The court in *Henry* v. *Geoprosco* was clearly of the view that even on its facts *Re Dulles* was wrongly decided, but in any event the decision in *Re Dulles* (whether right or wrong on its facts) 'leaves the authority of *Harris* v. *Taylor* wholly unshaken'. The court went on[42]

It can fairly be said that *Harris* v. *Taylor* is not a decision the underlying principles of which should be extended. That we unhesitatingly accept. But in our judgment, only the House of Lords is free, if their Lordships thought fit so to do, to say that *Harris* v. *Taylor* was wrongly decided and unless and until their Lordships do so, it binds this court for what, as we think, it so clearly decides. It follows that we find ourselves unable to agree with the statement by Denning L.J. that *Harris* v. *Taylor* is not an authority on what constitutes a submission to the jurisdiction. So far as this court is concerned it is a binding authority on that subject.

It follows from what we have already said that we also find ourselves, again with the most profound respect, unable to agree with the decision of Megaw J. in the *Boulos* case [1968] 2 Lloyd's Rep. 259. We do not think that the judge sitting at first instance was free, any more than we in this court are free, to choose between *Harris* v. *Taylor* and *In re Dulles' Settlement* (*No. 2*). We think the judge was bound by *Harris* v. *Taylor* and that he was not entitled to take the course which he did, as set out at [1968] 2 Lloyd's Rep. 259, 268.

We need hardly say that we have considered with the utmost care and respect the views expressed by the editors of *Dicey's Conflict of Laws* in successive editions of that work, by way of criticism of *Harris* v. *Taylor*, culminating in the views expressed in the 9th ed. (1973) to which we have already referred, as well as the views of Professor Cheshire in various editions of *Cheshire's Private International Law*. But however distinguished the authors and editors of these textbooks, the law must be taken to be as laid down by the courts, however much their decisions may be criticised by writers of such great distinction.

On that view of the authorities the Court of Appeal indicated that so far as they bound the Court of Appeal they justified the following propositions:

1. The English courts will not enforce a judgment of a foreign court against a defendant who does not reside within the jurisdiction of that court, has no assets within that jurisdiction and does not appear before that court, even though that court by its own local law has jurisdiction over him.

This is well established, and in modern times only dicta in *Re Dulles* in Denning LJ (disapproved in *Re Trepca Mines*) cast any doubt on this proposition.

---

[41] Cf. *Boys* v. *Chaplin* [1968] 2 QB 1, 23–24, 30, 35–36.
[42] [1976] QB at p. 746.

2. English courts will not enforce a judgment of a foreign court against a defendant who, though he does not reside in the jurisdiction of that court, has assets within that jurisdiction and appears before that court solely to preserve those assets which have been seized by that court.

There is no actual decision to this effect. But there are sufficient dicta to give this proposition weighty support, and this decision adds to them.

3. The English courts will enforce the judgment of a foreign court against a defendant over whom that court has jurisdiction by its own local law (even though it does not possess such jurisdiction according to the English rules of conflict of laws) if that defendant voluntarily appears before that foreign court to invite that court in its discretion not to exercise the jurisdiction which it has under its own local law. The court added that it was not necessary to decide whether, where a defendant appears in a foreign court solely to protest against the jurisdiction of that court (whether or not by its own local law that court possesses such jurisdiction) and such protest fails, such appearance under protest amounts to a voluntary submission. The court did say, however, that it was not deciding that an appearance *solely* to protest against the jurisdiction is, without more, a voluntary submission but 'the authorities compel this court to say that if such a protest (for example) takes the form of or is coupled with what in England would be a conditional appearance and an application to set aside an order for service out of the jurisdiction and that application then fails, the entry of that conditional appearance (which then becomes unconditional) is a voluntary submission to the jurisdiction of the foreign court'.

Thus the court wavers in its appreciation of the *ratio decidendi* of *Harris v. Taylor*. The main holding is that it is authority for the proposition that if a defendant invites the foreign court not to exercise, as a matter of discretion, the jurisdiction which it possesses under foreign law then there will be a submission. But, as shown above, there is no distinction drawn in *Harris v. Taylor* between a challenge to the *existence* of jurisdiction, on the one hand and to the *exercise* of jurisdiction, on the other. Perhaps for this reason the court added that, whether the challenge is to the existence or exercise of jurisdiction, there will be a submission if the challenge is accompanied by what in England would be described as a conditional appearance.

The court then went on to consider the distinction between a submission on the merits and a protest to the jurisdiction. A submission 'on the merits' did not mean the merits of the entire dispute[43] but occurred 'where any issues arise for decision at any stage of the proceedings in the foreign court

[43] Although it was used in this sense by Viscount Dilhorne and Lord Wilberforce in *Black-Clawson International* v. *Papierwerke Waldhof-Aschaffenburg AG* [1975] AC 591 at 626 and 631.

and that court is invited by the defendants as well as by the plaintiff to decide those issues'.[44] This rather obscure formulation is certainly designed to include the submission of a preliminary issue of fact or law, but how much further it goes is not clear. The Court of Appeal applied it to hold that the application for a stay under the Arbitration Act of Alberta, coupled with the argument that the arbitration clause in the service agreement was a *Scott* v. *Avery* clause, amounted to a submission. This was because the argument on the *Scott* v. *Avery* point was designed to show that as a matter of construction no cause of action had accrued because arbitration had not been resorted to, and therefore 'the defendants would be voluntarily asking the court to adjudicate on the merits of that part of their defence'.

But the court made it clear that although the case could have been decided solely on the ground that the application for a stay under the arbitration clause was a submission, it was also being decided on the ground that the application to the Alberta court not to exercise its jurisdiction in its discretion was a submission; the defendants 'took their chance'; *Harris* v. *Taylor* and the cases on which it was based were indistinguishable.[45]

(*c*) Conclusion

The importance to the Court of Appeal of the distinction between the existence and exercise of jurisdiction is underlined by the fact that at the outset of its judgment, the court referred to a concession made by counsel for the defendants, that the present case was not a case of a party sought to be brought before a foreign court contesting that that court had no jurisdiction to entertain a claim against him. Rather it was a case where the defendants invited the Alberta court to divest itself of the jurisdiction which the defendants accepted that the Alberta court possessed under

---

[44] [1976] QB at p. 749.

[45] The court also considered the argument based on section 4 (2) (*a*) (i) of the Foreign Judgments (Reciprocal Enforcement) Act 1933 which appears to adopt a rule different from that in *Harris* v. *Taylor* by providing that a foreign court shall be deemed to have jurisdiction if the judgment debtor submitted to the jurisdiction of the foreign court 'by voluntarily appearing in the proceedings otherwise than for the purpose of protecting, or obtaining the release of, property seized, or threatened with seizure, in the proceedings or *of contesting the jurisdiction* of that court' (emphasis added). The Court of Appeal held that the common law was as stated in *Harris* v. *Taylor* and that it was wrong to argue backwards from the Act. There can be little doubt that foreign countries which have entered into treaties with the United Kingdom under that Act have proceeded on the basis that a submission to contest jurisdiction does not confer a jurisdiction on a court which it does not otherwise have: see, e.g., United Kingdom–France Treaty, Article 4 (1) (*b*). Article 18 of the EEC Convention on Jurisdiction and Enforcement of Civil and Commercial Judgments of 1968 (to which the United Kingdom is not yet a party) provides that appearance confers jurisdiction unless it was entered 'solely to contest the jurisdiction'.

Alberta law. As indicated above, the distinction finds no place in the earlier authorities. But it is suggested that in any event it is not a realistic distinction. Even in the case of a protest against the English jurisdiction, there is no clear distinction between the existence and exercise of jurisdiction. In the first place, an application to set aside service under Order 11 is often made in the alternative: namely, that the case is not within Order 11 at all or, if it is, it is not a proper case for service out of the jurisdiction in the discretion of the court. Secondly, the approach of the court to applications to set aside under Order 11 shows that the courts themselves do not draw any rigid distinction: thus, for example, it is well established that a case must not only be within the letter of Order 11 but also within its substance.[46] Thirdly, the result of a successful application to set aside under Order 11, whether it is made on the basis that the case is not within Order 11 at all or on the basis that the court should in its discretion not exercise its discretion, results in the complete setting aside of the proceedings, not merely in a stay of proceedings. The position is similar in many common law countries, such as the Provinces of Canada and the States of Australia. In the United States the so-called 'long-arm statutes' (the local equivalent of Order 11) give wide bases of jurisdiction, but the doctrine of *forum non conveniens* is sufficient to prevent their oppressive exercise. In civil law countries the question of the existence of jurisdiction is all important—once jurisdiction is established, there is usually no question of the exercise of a discretion.

To summarise:

1. The actual decision in *Harris* v. *Taylor* does not support any distinction between a challenge to the existence of jurisdiction and a challenge to its exercise.

2. The true basis of the decision in *Harris* v. *Taylor* is that the defendant was treated as having entered a conditional appearance in the foreign court which became unconditional when his challenge to its jurisdiction failed, and that such an unconditional appearance is a submission.

3. That reasoning is fallacious, because in deciding what is a submission in the international sense the English court should not be influenced by what amounts to an appearance in domestic English procedural law. In any event, it seems unlikely that the defendant did in fact enter a conditional appearance in the Isle of Man.

4. If the defendant enters a conditional appearance and that appearance becomes unconditional after a protest to the jurisdiction (whether to its existence or exercise) both *Harris* v. *Taylor* and *Henry* v. *Geoprosco International* require the judgment to be recognised.

5. If the defendant does not enter any kind of formal appearance but

---

[46] See, e.g., *GAF Corporation* v. *Amchem Products Inc.* [1975] 1 Lloyd's Rep. 601.

nevertheless contests the jurisdiction of the foreign court and loses, neither *Harris* v. *Taylor* nor *Henry* v. *Geoprosco International* requires recognition of the judgment, except that the latter requires it if the protest is against the *exercise* of jurisdiction.

6. The distinction between the existence and exercise of jurisdiction is blurred in English law and unknown in many systems and does not provide a rational basis for a rule of private international law.

7. Nothing short of a submission of some or all of the merits (i.e. something other than a procedural question) should amount to a submission. It is to be hoped that in a subsequent case both *Harris* v. *Taylor* and *Henry* v. *Geoprosco International* will be reconsidered by the House of Lords.[47] Until then, the only safe course for a defendant who has no assets in the foreign country and no desire to have assets there in the future, is to ignore the foreign proceedings altogether.

---

[47] Perhaps by an appeal from a judge at first instance direct to the House of Lords under the 'leap-frog' provisions of the Administration of Justice Act 1969.

VIII

Blocking and Clawback Statutes: The United Kingdom Approach

The extraterritorial effect of United States legislation still continues to disturb UK–US relations. The principal areas of controversy relate to anti-trust, securities regulation and export control. In the field of anti-trust, the United States courts have moderated the 'effects' doctrine by devising an *ad hoc* interest-balancing test to determine whether jurisdiction should be exercised, based on whether the interests of, and links to, the United States are sufficiently strong *vis-à-vis* those of other nations to justify an assertion of extraterritorial authority: *Timberlane Lumber Co.* v. *Bank of America*, 549 F. 2d 597 (9th Cir. 1976) and 749 F. 2d 1378 (9th Cir. 1984). But it is notorious that the balance almost always tips in favour of the United States. Most recently in *Re Insurance Antitrust Litigation*, 938 F. 2d 919 (9th Cir. 1991) the Court of Appeals for the Ninth Circuit held that the balance was in favour of the United States in relation to an alleged conspiracy between British reinsurers and US insurance companies, because the effects were felt largely in the United States and the defendants foreseeably intended that their conduct would have effect there, even though it was lawful under English law. In its *amicus* brief to the United States Supreme Court (where an appeal is pending) the United Kingdom government argued that international law and comity required that the US courts should not exercise jurisdiction over those antitrust claims in the case which was directed against business activity conducted in London by the British insurance and reinsurance industry for a legitimate business purpose in a manner consistent with the British regulatory and competition regime: see also (1990) 61 BYIL 569 and (1991) 62 BYIL 623 (protests in relation to *Transnor (Bermuda) Ltd.* v. *BP North American Petroleum*, 738 F. Supp. 1472 (SDNY 1990)). The United Kingdom continued to argue for a restrictive approach to the exercise of antitrust jurisdiction under EEC law in the *Wood Pulp* case ((1988) 59 BYIL 506–507), although on the facts it supported the Commission's exercise of jurisdiction. It is likely that the actual decision in the case goes beyond the position expressed by the United Kingdom as the permissible limits of jurisdiction, but falls short of American ideas of those limits: Cases 89/85 etc. *Ahlstrom Oy* v. *Commission* [1988] ECR 5193. It has already been seen (Chap. I, *ante*, pp. 101–107) that the United Kingdom Government has also objected to the application of the US securities laws to transactions abroad. In the area of export control, the United Kingdom Government has described claims by the United States Government to control the export of goods from the United Kingdom by subsidiaries of US companies as 'extravagant' and 'unwarranted encroachments on UK jurisdiction . . . contrary to international law': see Collins and McLachlan, United Kingdom Report, in *International Law of Export Control* (ed. Meessen, 1992), 160.

From *Journal of Business Law* (1986), 372, 452.

Most of the orders and directions made under the Protection of Trading Interests Act 1980 were made in the aftermath of (*a*) the United States regulation of export controls in relation to the West Siberian pipeline and (*b*) the Laker affair: see the list given in a parliamentary reply in (1987) 58 BYIL 589–590. In the *Aérospatiale* case (Chapter VI, *ante*, pp. 289–312) one of the issues before the US Supreme Court was whether the United States court could order discovery from a French party, which that party was prevented from producing under the French blocking statute. The United Kingdom filed an *amicus* brief in which it said that the United Kingdom Government issued orders and directions under the 1980 Act only after determining that vital UK interests in maintaining its territorial sovereignty were seriously threatened by an exercise of foreign jurisdiction, and after carefully weighing the potential effect on relations with the country concerned. It pointed out that the United Kingdom was entitled to exercise its sovereign power within its jurisdiction, and it was entitled to protect that exercise by the sovereign act of promulgating defensive legislation. It therefore urged the Supreme Court to take into account considerations of comity in deciding whether a foreign party should be ordered to give discovery, and that one of those considerations should be that a US court should not lightly disregard foreign states' enactments of defensive laws: see (1986) 57 BYIL 576–577. The US Supreme Court decided that the French blocking statute was irrelevant. Applying *Société Internationale, etc. SA* v. *Rogers*, 357 US 197 (1958) it confirmed that such laws do not deprive an American court of the power to order a party subject to its jurisdiction to produce evidence even though the act of production may violate foreign law. Nor could the enactment of such a statute by a foreign nation require American courts to engraft a rule of first resort on to the Hague Convention, or otherwise to provide the nationals of such a country with a preferred status in US courts. The blocking statute was relevant to the court's particularized comity analysis only to the extent that its terms and its enforcement identify the nature of the sovereign interests in non-disclosure of specific kinds of material: 482 US at 544.

THE BACKGROUND

It was not the United Kingdom which took the lead in enacting blocking statutes designed to counteract United States antitrust measures. In the immediate aftermath of the landmark post-war decision in *US* v. *Alcoa*[1] on the extraterritorial reach of the antitrust laws a grand jury was empanelled

---

[1] 148 F. 2d 416 (2d Cir. 1945). The literature on the subject covered by this paper is enormous. See in particular Jennings, *Extraterritorial Jurisdiction and the United States Antitrust Laws* (1957) 33 BYIL 146; Mann, *Doctrine of Jurisdiction in International Law* (1964–I) 111 Hague Rec. 9 and *Studies in International Law* (1973), p. 1; Mann, *Doctrine of International Jurisdiction Revisited after Twenty Years* (1984) 186 Hague Rec. 9; Rosenthal and Knighton, *National Laws and International Commerce: The Problem of Extraterritoriality* (1982); Lowe, *Extraterritorial Jurisdiction* (1983); *Perspectives on the Extraterritorial Application of U.S. Antitrust and Other Laws* (ed. Griffin 1979); *Extra-territorial Application of Laws and Responses Thereto* (ed. Olmstead 1984).

in 1947 to investigate the supply and distribution of newsprint in the United States. Subpoenas were issued against more than 50 Canadian newsprint companies. This procedure was described by the Prime Minister of Ontario as implying

the right of the Government of the United States to invade the territorial integrity of Canada without application to the Canadian Government, to any provincial government, to any Canadian court, or to any established channel of international representation in regard to international business.[2]

Ontario then enacted the Business Records Protection Act,[3] the first of the modern blocking statutes.

The first major United Kingdom involvement in the problem was a grand jury investigation of the petroleum industry in 1952.[4] Subpoenas were served on foreign companies, including the Anglo-Iranian Oil Company (now British Petroleum), and the British Minister of Fuel and Power wrote a letter, in the form of a directive, to Anglo-Iranian, in which he said:

Her Majesty's Government consider it contrary to international comity that you or your officers should be required, in answer to a subpoena couched in the widest terms, to produce documents which are not only not in the United States of America, but which do not even relate to business in that country.

Sir Anthony Eden, the then Foreign Secretary, subsequently certified that this letter was a directive issued with the official approval and under the full authority of Her Majesty's Government and 'embraced a claim of sovereignty'. The District Court in Washington quashed the subpoena on the curious ground that these documents amounted to an assertion of sovereign immunity for Anglo-Iranian which the court upheld.

In the same year Judge Ryan in the New York Southern District found that ICI had been party, with Du Pont and others, to a conspiracy to restrain trade by dividing world markets. He ordered ICI to re-convey certain patents to Du Pont. British Nylon Spinners, who were licensees of ICI, obtained an order in England restraining the re-transfer. Evershed MR said that it was 'an assertion of an extra-territorial jurisdiction which we do not recognise for the American courts to make orders which would destroy or qualify those statutory rights belonging to an English national who is not subject to the jurisdiction of the American courts'.[5] Denning LJ noted that the effect of the English jurisdiction would be that ICI would not have to obey the order of the US court because the order of Judge

---

[2] International Law Association, 51st Report, 1964, p. 567.

[3] For text see Whiteman, *Digest of International Law*, Vol. 6, p. 168. See *Hirshhorn* v. *Hirshhorn et al.*, 105 NYS 2d 628 (1951), where the plaintiff failed to obtain discovery of documents in Canada because of the Ontario statute.

[4] See 13 FRD 280, 19 ILR 197 (DC Cir. 1952).   [5] [1953] Ch. 19, 26 (CA).

Ryan provided that it was not to operate against ICI for action taken in compliance with the law of any foreign government to which ICI was subject.

The problem came to a head with the grand jury investigation of the shipping industry in 1960 and the Federal Maritime Commission investigation of 1960 and 1961.[6] By this time it is possible to see three elements of objection in the governmental protests. The first element is concern at the exercise of substantive jurisdiction in relation to acts abroad. Thus in June 1960, in relation to the filing orders of the Federal Maritime Board, the British Government said that the orders covered contracts made and executed wholly outside the United States and that 'Her Majesty's Government consider such acts of United Kingdom companies performed outside the United States to be beyond the legitimate limits of United States jurisdiction'.[7] The second element is concern at the demand for documents outside the United States which relate to matters occurring outside the United States. In 1962 the Minister of Transport wrote to British shipping companies requiring them not to produce or make available to the Federal Maritime Commission 'certain documents located outside the United States and relating to transactions which were effected wholly within the United Kingdom and were not within the substantive jurisdiction of the United States'.[8] The third concern relates to the general nature of procedure in the United States, and especially to the extensiveness of discovery procedures. As the British Government put it in 1960, the Federal Maritime Board order 'seems to involve a "fishing expedition" into the affairs of the companies and for this reason it would not seem to be in accordance with the spirit of justice as normally administered in the United States and the United Kingdom and, if persisted in, could not fail to be damaging to mutual trading relations'.[9]

An important factor by the early 1960s had been the development in the United States throughout the previous decade of the recognition of the role of foreign government compulsion, both with regard to conduct of foreign corporations and foreign countries and to the production of documents and records situate abroad. As regards conduct abroad, it came to be recognised that United States law *could* be applied to conduct mandated by a foreign government, but that there was a discretion to be exercised by balancing the interests of the States concerned.[10] In particular many of the early orders by the United States contained an exception for conduct

---

[6] Contrast *Re Grand Jury Investigation of the Shipping Industry*, 186 F. Supp. 298 (DC 1960) with *Montship Lines Ltd.* v. *Federal Maritime Board*, 295 F. 2d 147 (DC Cir. 1961).

[7] *Op. cit.* n. 2, p. 579.

[8] *British Practice in International Law*, 1962, I, p. 17.

[9] *Op. cit.* n. 2, p. 579.

[10] *Restatement Second, Foreign Relations Law*, 1965, Section 40.

required by foreign law.[11] As the Governments of Australia, Canada, France and the United Kingdom have put it recently:[12]

. . . the foreign sovereign compulsion and act of state doctrines require a U.S. court to consider and give conclusive effect to the statement of a friendly foreign sovereign that it mandated private conduct. It would be illogical to reach such a result, but then to hold that such conduct may nevertheless constitute or be a feature of conspiracy under U.S. antitrust law. Such a holding could lead to the very exacerbation of international conflict that the foreign sovereign compulsion and act of state doctrines are designed to avoid. Attempts by U.S. courts to hold that conduct mandated by a foreign sovereign constituted a feature of conspiracy under U.S. anti-trust law would, in many instances, be resisted by foreign governments as a matter of national sovereignty. This could lead to further foreign governmental measures to counteract what many nations view as assertions of U.S. jurisdiction that are inconsistent with international law.

The position with regard to disclosure of documents rests on the leading case of *Société Internationale* v. *Rogers*,[13] which requires no discussion. It is sufficient to say that whilst by the mid-1960s the case-law was perceived as indicating a way in which conflicts between US law and foreign law could be resolved, it no longer provides such a resolution. The positions have become entrenched. The balancing required by the cases (and reflected in the new Draft Restatement[14]) has come down heavily in favour of US law.[15] The recognition of the Ontario blocking statute by US courts in the 1950s[16] has been replaced by a hostility to blocking and secrecy laws. In many cases, of course, this is the result of unmeritorious defendants (often common criminals) seeking to hide behind banking secrecy laws, but in the antitrust field it has also become the dominant philosophy, to the extent that in *Re Uranium Antitrust Litigation*[17] the court even refused to put the foreign national interests in the balance.[18]

---

[11] e.g. the decree in the *ICI–Du Pont* case referred to above, and *US* v. *General Electric*, 115 F. Supp. 835 (NJ 1953). For subsequent developments see *Continental Ore Co.* v. *Union Carbide*, 370 US 690 (1962); *Mannington Mills Inc.* v. *Congoleum Corp.*, 595 F. 2d 1287 (3d Cir. 1979); *Timberlane Lumber Co.* v. *Bank of America*, 549 F. 2d 597 (9th Cir. 1976); *Linseman* v. *World Hockey Association*, 439 F. Supp. 1315 (Conn. 1977); *Interamerica Refining Corp.* v. *Texaco Maracaibo Inc.*, 307 F. Supp. 1291 (Del. 1970).

[12] Brief on petition for certiorari to the United States Supreme Court in *Matsushita Electrical Industrial Co.* v. *Zenith Radio Corp.* (1985), pp. 11–12.

[13] 357 US 197 (1958).

[14] See Rosenthal and Yale-Loehr (1984) 16 NYUJ Int. L. & Pol. 1075.

[15] In *Mackinnon* v. *Donaldson, Lufkin and Jenrette Securities Corp.* [1986] Ch. 482, 499. Hoffmann, J. pointed out that US and foreign observers had not failed to notice that the balance invariably came down in favour of the interests of the United States.

[16] *Supra* n. 3.   [17] 480 F. Supp. 1138 (ND Ill. 1979).

[18] The banking secrecy cases raise somewhat different issues: see, e.g., *SEC* v. *Banca della Svizzera*, 92 FRD 111 (SDNY 1981); *US* v. *Vetco*, 644 F. 2d 1234 (9th Cir. 1981); *US* v. *Bank of Nova Scotia*, 691 F. 2d 1384 (11th Cir. 1982), cert. den. 462 US 1119 (1983); *Re Grand Jury Proceedings Bank of Nova Scotia*, 740 F. 2d 817 (11th Cir. 1984), cert. den. 105 S. Ct. 778 (1985); *US* v. *Davis*, 767 F. 2d 1025 (2nd Cir. 1985).

The third concern, the nature of the discovery process, is well illustrated by *RCA* v. *Rauland*.[19] That case arose, like the *Westinghouse* case more than a decade later, out of proceedings in which one of the parties defended on the ground that there had been a conspiracy (in this case, by the plaintiff and others) in violation of the antitrust laws. The defendants obtained from the Illinois District court letters rogatory addressed to the courts of England (and of three other countries) for the examination of witnesses and the production of documents in their possession. In England the named witnesses included EMI, English Electric and the Marconi Co. The English court refused to allow the examination, not on the ground that the US proceedings raised issues outside the jurisdiction of the United States court, but because the then prevailing United Kingdom legislation relating to execution of letters rogatory of foreign courts allowed the procedure to be used only for gathering *evidence*, and not for discovery. Devlin J. said:[20]

[I]t is plain that that principle [discovery of documents may be obtained because they may fairly lead to a line of inquiry] has been carried very much further in the United States of America than it has been carried in this country. In the United States of America it is not restricted merely to obtaining a disclosure of documents from the other party to the suit, but there is a procedure, which might be called a pre-trial procedure, in the courts of the United States which allows interrogation not merely of the parties to the suit but also of persons who may be witnesses in the suit, or whom it may be thought may be witnesses in the suit, and which requires them to answer questions and produce documents. The questions would not necessarily be restricted to matters which were relevant in the suit, nor would the production be necessarily restricted to admissible evidence, but they might be such as would lead to a train of inquiry which may of itself lead to relevant material. It is that pre-trial procedure, the obtaining of depositions from witnesses with a view to discovery, which the District Court at Illinois is at present engaged upon . . .

Lord Goddard CJ said:[21]

[I]t seems to me perfectly clear . . . that this is merely an attempt to get evidence in the course of discovery proceedings which are known to the American courts—and are also known to the Canadian courts—which are a sort of pre-trial before the main trial. It is an endeavour to get in evidence by examining people who may be able to put the parties in the way of getting evidence. That is mainly what we should call a 'fishing' proceeding which is never allowed in the English courts . . .

One aspect which was not emphasised in the early stages of the dispute was the treble damages remedy in United States antitrust law. At first the treble damaged remedy was used by the United Kingdom as evidence that

---

[19] [1956] 1 QB 618 (Div. Ct.).
[20] At pp. 643–644.   [21] At pp. 649.

the extraterritorial application of US antitrust law was an exercise of penal jurisdiction, and not an exercise of civil jurisdiction. As Professor Jennings put it in his 1957 article,[22] the action for treble damages was 'punitive and coercive'. The United Kingdom Government said[23] in 1979 during the exchanges with the United States Government over what became the Protection of Trading Interests Act 1980:

Her Majesty's Government's main objections to the private treble damage action which is . . . a crucial aspect of U.S. Anti-Trust enforcement, are that it has been adopted as a complement to Government enforcement, that it provides an incentive to private parties to act as 'private Attorneys-General', but such a system of enforcement is inappropriate and in many respects objectionable in its application to international trade. Her Majesty's Government believe that two basically undesirable consequences flow from the enforcement of public law in this field by private remedies. First, the usual discretion of a public authority to enforce laws in a way which has regard to the interests of society is replaced by a motive on the part of the plaintiff to pursue defendants for private gain thus excluding international considerations of a public nature. Secondly, where criminal and civil penalties co-exist, those engaged in international trade are exposed to double jeopardy.

Matters came to a head in relation to the *Westinghouse* litigation, and was dealt with in the Protection of Trading Interests Act 1980, which served as the model for the 'Clawback' statutes in other jurisdictions, by restricting the enforceability of foreign judgments for multiple damages in the United Kingdom, and by allowing to defendants who had been forced to pay multiple damages awards on limited right of recourse against the successful plaintiffs.

The rest of this paper will deal with the attitude of the United Kingdom legislature, executive and judiciary, to these four problems: the substantive exercise of jurisdiction; the attempts to obtain documents situate outside the United States; the nature of US discovery; and the civil penal treble damages remedy. The relevant legislation is the Shipping Contracts and Commercial Documents Act 1964, the Evidence (Proceedings in Other Jurisdictions) Act 1975, and the Protection of Trading Interests Act 1980. The main judicial decisions are those in *Re Westinghouse Uranium Contract Litigation*[24] and *British Airways Board and British Caledonian Airways Limited* v. *Laker Airways Limited.*[25]

---

[22] (1957) 33 BYIL 146 at 148.

[23] British Embassy, Washington, to United States Department of State (1979) 50 BYIL at 364; see also (1980) 51 BYIL at 446.

[24] [1978] AC 547.

[25] [1985] AC 58. Among the many US decisions in this litigation see, especially, *Laker Airways* v. *Sabena*, 731 F. 2d 909 (DC Cir. 1984).

2. SUBSTANTIVE EXERCISE OF JURISDICTION

One of the purposes of the Shipping Contracts and Commercial Documents Act 1964 was to provide British shipowners with a 'foreign compulsion' defence in United States courts. During its passage through Parliament, the Government confirmed that the Act was intended to allow 'the shipowner who is charged in America with an offence to say that this is British law and he is subject to British penalties and the American court ought not in those circumstances to impose a fine'.[26] Section 1 of the 1964 Act gave the Minister of Transport power to give directions to any person in the United Kingdom to prohibit compliance with foreign measures where (*inter alia*) (*i*) the measures constituted 'an infringement of the jurisdiction which, under international law, belongs to the United Kingdom' and (*ii*) the directions prohibiting compliance with any foreign measure were 'proper for maintaining the jurisdiction of the United Kingdom'.

The approach of the Protection of Trading Interests Act 1980 (which supersedes the 1964 Act) is similar, but in one respect significantly different. By section 1(1) of the 1980 *Act*:

If it appears to the Secretary of State—

(*a*) that measures have been or are proposed to be taken by or under the law of any overseas country for regulating or controlling international trade; and

(*b*) that those measures, in so far as they apply or would apply to things done or to be done outside the territorial jurisdiction of that country by persons carrying on business in the United Kingdom, are damaging or threaten to damage the trading interests of the United Kingdom,

the Secretary of State may by order direct that this section shall apply to those measures either generally or in their application to such cases as may be specified in the order.

The significant change is that there is no longer a direct reference to infringement of the jurisdiction which under international law belongs to the United Kingdom. The ambit of the 1980 Act is wider than that of the 1964 Act. It applies to measures which are damaging or threaten to damage the trading interests of the United Kingdom. Once the Secretary of State has made that determination he may, by section 1(3), give to any person in the United Kingdom who carries on business there directions for prohibiting compliance with any such requirement or prohibition as 'he considers appropriate for avoiding damage to the trading interests of the United Kingdom' and by section 3 a person who without reasonable excuse contravenes any such directions is guilty of an offence.

[26] Quoted in Lowe, *Extraterritorial Jurisdiction* (1983) p. 140.

The powers under the 1980 Act have not been used only in the antitrust sphere. An order was made in 1982 citing certain provisions of the US Export Administration Regulations as measures which were damaging to the trading interests of the United Kingdom. This order was made in the context of the United States export embargo affecting companies in the United Kingdom which had contracts in respect of the Siberian pipeline. As the British Government put it in a note from the British Embassy to the United States Department of State:

HMG's views on claims made by courts or other authorities of overseas countries to jurisdiction over persons and activities located in the United Kingdom have been made clear to successive United States Administrations. Successive United Kingdom Governments have had cause to object both when U.S. courts have exerted jurisdiction over activities conducted outside the territorial jurisdiction of the United States, and when authorities in the United States have purported to extend their regulatory activities under U.S. law so as to compel or prohibit certain conduct by persons in the United Kingdom . . . as the United States Government is aware, the Parliament of the United Kingdom enacted a Protection of Trading Interests Act 1980 in order to provide essential safeguards for persons in the United Kingdom where overseas countries took measures, or decisions were made under certain of their laws, which were damaging the trading interests of the United Kingdom. It has been made clear from the foregoing that HMG will not accept actions against persons in the United Kingdom by authorities of other countries whose jurisdiction does not extend to such persons.[27]

It hardly needs saying that the essence of the British Government's position in antitrust cases is that in the context of the application of the US antitrust laws to conduct outside the United States by non-US citizens the 'effects' test is inconsistent with international law, and this applies to civil antitrust treble damages cases because they are 'penal' actions for the purposes of international law.[28]

In its aide-memoire to the Commission of the European Communities in the *Dyestuffs* case in 1969 the British Government said:[29]

. . . the United Kingdom Government have for their part consistently objected to the assumption of extraterritorial jurisdiction in antitrust matters by the courts or authorities of a foreign state when that jurisdiction is based upon what is termed the 'effects doctrine'—that is to say, the doctrine that territorial jurisdiction over conduct which has occurred wholly outside the territory of the State claiming jurisdiction may be justified because of the resulting economic 'effects' of such conduct within the territory of that State. This doctrine becomes even more open to objection when, on the basis of the alleged 'effects' within the State claiming jurisdiction of the conduct of foreign corporations abroad (that is to say, conduct

---

[27] (1982) 53 BYIL at 454.
[28] See (1979) 50 BYIL 354 and the Attorney-General's submission in *Re Westinghouse Uranium Contract Litigation* [1978] AC 547 at pp. 589–595.   [29] Lowe, p. 144.

pursued outside the territory of that state), such corporations are actually made subject to penal sanctions.

The aide-memoire went on to say that substantive jurisdiction in antitrust matters could only be taken on the basis of either the territorial principle or the nationality principle, and

[t]he territorial principle justifies proceedings against foreigners and foreign companies only in respect of conduct which consists in whole or in part of some activity by them in the territory of the State claiming jurisdiction. A State should not exercise jurisdiction against a foreigner who or a foreign company which has committed no act within its territory. In the case of conspiracies the assumption of jurisdiction is justified: (a) if the entire conspiracy takes place within the territory of the State claiming jurisdiction; or (b) if the formation of the conspiracy takes place within the territory of the State claiming jurisdiction even if things are done in pursuance of it outside its territory; or (c) if the formation of the conspiracy takes place outside the territory of the State claiming jurisdiction, but the persons against whom the proceedings are brought has done things within its territory in pursuance of the conspiracy.

The *Westinghouse* case[30] needs no detailed account. One point which has been much overlooked is that the British Government and the House of Lords treated the case as one of the exercise of extraterritorial jurisdiction by the United States over RTZ and other English companies, notwithstanding that in its Illinois action Westinghouse had alleged that some of the meetings at which the conspiracy was entered into took place in the United States. This indicates that it is not sufficient for a plaintiff in a treble damages suit, or the United States Government, merely to *allege* that relevant conduct has taken place in the United States.[31]

The main argument put by the British Government in the Laker case related, not to the 'effects' doctrine, but to the point that the exercise of United States antitrust jurisdiction over airlines flying transatlantic routes was contrary to the international arrangements between the United Kingdom and the United States. As is by now well known, British Airways and British Caledonian were among the defendants in the treble damages action brought by the liquidator of Laker Airways in Washington. British Airways and British Caledonian (and some other defendants) sought injunctions in the English courts to restrain the liquidator from pursuing the antitrust action in Washington. After Parker J. had refused the injunctions the British Government made an order under the Protection of Trading Interests Act 1980[32] applying section 1 of the 1980 Act to the Sherman Act and the Clayton Act in their application to agreements or discussions to which a UK designated airline was party, and any act done

---

[30] [1978] AC 547.
[31] It was noticed, but not developed, in *FTC* v. *St Gobain* 636 F. 2d 1300 (DC Cir. 1980).
[32] SI 1983 No. 900.

by UK designated airlines concerning tariffs or otherwise relating to the operation by it of an air service authorised pursuant to the inter-governmental agreements. Shortly afterwards the Secretary of State made a general direction under the Act directing that no person in the United Kingdom who carried on business there should comply, or cause or permit compliance, with any requirement or prohibition imposed on that person pursuant to the Sherman Act or the Clayton Act in so far as the requirement or prohibition related to or arose out of any of such agreements, discussions or acts. In the Court of Appeal it was held that that direction (and the direction to be discussed in the next section prohibiting the production of documents in the United Kingdom) had the effect of rendering the issues raised untriable and it would be a denial of justice to the airlines to allow Laker Airways to continue with the United States claims. In the House of Lords it was held that these considerations did not support the grant of an injunction because the order and directions, if they made any difference, would operate to the disadvantage of Laker Airways in the US proceedings rather than that of British Airways and British Caledonian since, it was said, the Secretary of State was 'on their side' and would consent to disclosure of documents.[33]

In the subsequent decision in *Midland Bank plc* v. *Laker Airways Ltd.*[34] the Court of Appeal granted an injunction restraining the liquidator of Laker Airways from joining Midland Bank and its subsidiary in the United States proceedings. The liquidator alleged that Midland Bank had joined in a conspiracy to sabotage a financial rescue plan for Laker Airways. The Court of Appeal distinguished the British Airways case on the basis that the lack of connection of Midland Bank with the United States (at least as regards its relevant activities) made it unconscionable for an English liquidator to seek to apply US law on it, and, particularly, *per* Dillon LJ, because the exercise of jurisdiction by the United States courts in such circumstances would be extraterritorial. The liquidator was seeking to make the bank liable for acts done in England and subject to English law.

3. PRODUCTION OF DOCUMENTS

One of the main purposes of the power to prohibit the production of documents both under the 1964 Act and under the 1980 Act was to enable United Kingdom companies to take advantage in the United States of a 'foreign compulsion' defence. The 1964 Act entitled a Minister to give directions to a person prohibiting him from complying with a requirement to produce or furnish to any court, tribunal or authority of a foreign

---

[33] See [1985] AC at p. 94. See also *Laker Airways* v. *Sabena*, n. 25, *ante*.
[34] [1986] QB 441.

country any commercial documents or commercial information if the following conditions were fulfilled: (*a*) the commercial document was not within the territorial jurisdiction of the foreign country, or the commercial information was to be compiled from documents not within that jurisdiction, and (*b*) the requirement constituted or would constitute an infringement of the jurisdiction which, under international law, belonged to the United Kingdom.[35] The 1980 Act is wider. Section 2(1) of the 1980 Act applies to 'any commercial document which is not within the territorial jurisdiction' of the foreign country, but it applies also to 'any commercial information' without reference to its source. The Secretary of State may give directions for prohibiting compliance with a foreign requirement for production of documents or supply of information if it is inadmissible on one of four grounds: (*a*) that it infringes the jurisdiction of the United Kingdom or is otherwise prejudicial to the sovereignty of the United Kingdom; (*b*) if compliance with the requirement would be prejudicial to the security of the United Kingdom or to the relations of the government of the United Kingdom with a government of any other country; (*c*) if it is made otherwise than for the purposes of civil or criminal proceedings which have been instituted in the overseas country; (*d*) if it requires a person to state what documents relevant to any such proceedings are or have been in his possession, custody or power or to produce for the purposes of any such proceedings any documents other than the particular documents specified in the requirement. Conditions (*c*) and (*d*) are designed to deal with problems which arose in the *Westinghouse* case, which will be dealt with more fully in the next section on discovery. The 1964 Act and the 1980 Act confirm that it is not the mere location of documents abroad which is a ground for an objection to an order for their production, but both require some additional element before the order of a US court can be regarded as objectionable, either as a matter of public international law or for some other reason. It is clear that the grounds given in the 1980 Act are not co-extensive with an infringement of international jurisdiction, and that is particularly clear from conditions (*c*) and (*d*), which reflect objections to investigatory procedures carried on outside the ambit of civil or criminal proceedings and pre-trial and discovery procedures within the scope of existing proceedings. The United Kingdom Government's view is that the order for production of documents by a foreign court is only an infringement of United Kingdom jurisdiction in relation to documents situate in the United Kingdom if either (*a*) the proceedings are penal or (*b*) the foreign court does not have international jurisdiction over the substance of the case. The present writer has argued that a demand for such documents compounds the breach of the rules relating to the exercise

---

[35] Section 2(1).

of prescriptive jurisdiction and trespasses on the area of unlawful enforcement action.[36] The British Government, in the exchanges over what became the 1980 Act, said that this power 'embodies the principle that demands for compulsory production in one state of documents or information situated outside that state raise issues for other states which may lead these latter states to take such steps as they consider appropriate, within the limits of their proper jurisdiction, to limit or exclude such compulsory production'.[37]

The directions given to British Airways and British Caledonian not to produce documents in relation to the actions in the US proceedings by Laker Airways did not assist them in the House of Lords. In reversing the Court of Appeal's finding that it would be unjust to allow the US proceedings to continue because it would prevent British Airways and British Caledonian from giving discovery of information and documents that would assist their defence in the United States proceeding, Lord Diplock said:[38]

to this the short and realistic answer is that if the two companies think . . . that disclosure of particular documents or information would help their own defence rather than hinder Laker's ability to establish its complaint in the American action when it comes to trial, the direction enables them to apply to the Secretary of State for his consent to such disclosure, and since, to put it colloquially, the Secretary of State is 'on their side', such consent would appear more likely than not to be forthcoming. So the Order and directions, if they make any difference, operate to the disadvantage of Laker in the American action rather than that of [British Airways] and [British Caledonian], who, to the extent that they do not seek or are refused the Secretary of State's consent to disclosure of particular information or documents, will be saved the irrecoverable costs of pre-trial discovery on the American pattern of documents in their possession or control in the United Kingdom and of information known to their officers and employees in the United Kingdom who do not pay regular visits to the United States.[39]

4. DISCOVERY PROBLEMS

It has already been seen above that in a consistent line of cases, even before the Hague Convention of 1970 on the taking of evidence abroad,

---

[36] See Collins, *International Law Aspects of Obtaining Evidence Abroad, in Extraterritorial Application of Laws and Responses Thereto* (ed. Olmstead 1984), pp. 188–189.
[37] (1982) 21 *International Legal Materials* 840 at 848.   [38] [1985] AC at 94.
[39] It should be noted also that the question of foreign compulsion in relation to documents will not arise necessarily from legislation such as the protection of Trading Interests Act 1980. It may also arise from the ordinary common law rules relating to bank secrecy. Thus, in one of the cases arising out of the Marc Rich affair, *X AG v. A Bank* [1983] 2 All ER 464, the Commercial Court enjoined a US bank with a branch in London from disclosing records kept in its London branch.

English courts were not prepared to allow the letters rogatory procedure to be used to enable parties to foreign litigation (in practice United States litigation) to obtain discovery in England, and one of the leading cases was a case involving antitrust issues, *RCA* v. *Rauland*.[40] Article 23 of the Hague Convention empowers contracting states to make a reservation to the Convention to the effect that they will not execute letters of request issued 'for the purpose of obtaining pre-trial discovery of documents as known in common law countries'. The British Government made a reservation to the effect that it would not execute letters of request for the purposes of obtaining pre-trial discovery of documents, and understood letters which required a person (*a*) to state what documents relevant to the proceedings to which the letters of request related were or had been in his possession, custody or power, or (*b*) to produce any documents, other than particular documents specified in the letter of request, as being documents appearing to the requested court to be or to be likely to be in his possession, custody or power, to be letters of request issued for the purpose of obtaining pre-trial discovery of documents. The Evidence (Proceedings in Other Jurisdictions) Act 1975 was passed in part in order to give effect to the 1970 Convention, and it provided[41] that an order giving effect to a foreign application for assistance could not require a person (*a*) to state what documents relevant to the proceedings to which the application for the order related were or had been in his possession, custody or power, or (*b*) to produce any documents other than particular documents specified in the order as being documents appearing to the court making the order to be, or to be likely to be, in his possession, custody or power.

In the House of Lords, Westinghouse failed to obtain an order for the examination of witnesses in England for the purposes of the Virginia proceedings for a variety of reasons, the most important of which was that the evidence was in reality sought by the United States Department of Justice, and that it was sought for the purpose of investigation activities outside the United States of British companies and individuals who were not subject to United States jurisdiction, in respect of alleged infringement of United States antitrust laws. This constituted an abuse of the sovereignty of the United Kingdom. Lord Wilberforce said:[42]

> . . . I think that there is no doubt that, in deciding whether to give effect to letters rogatory, the courts are entitled to have regard to any possible prejudice to the sovereignty of the United Kingdom . . . Equally, that in a matter affecting the sovereignty of the United Kingdom, the courts are entitled to take account of the declared policy of Her Majesty's Government is in my opinion beyond doubt . . . The intervention of Her Majesty's Attorney-General establishes that quite apart

---

[40] [1956] I QB 618.   [41] Section 2(4).   [42] [1978] AC at pp. 616–617.

from the present case, over a number of years and in a number of cases, the policy of Her Majesty's Government has been against recognition of United States investigatory jurisdiction extraterritorially against United Kingdom companies. The courts should in such matters speak with the same voice as the executive . . .; they have, as I have stated, no difficulty in doing so.

Lord Dilhorne said:[43]

For many years now the United States has sought to exercise jurisdiction over foreigners in respect of acts done outside the jurisdiction of that country. This is not in accordance with international law and has led to legislation on the part of other states, including the United Kingdom, designed to protect their nationals from criminal proceedings in foreign courts where the claims to jurisdiction by those courts are excessive and constitute an invasion of sovereignty.

Section 4 of the Protection of Trading Interests Act 1980 reinforced the decision in the *Westinghouse* case by providing that a United Kingdom court should not make an order under section 2 of the Evidence (Proceedings in Other Jurisdictions) Act 1975 in relation to foreign letters rogatory 'if it is shown that the request infringes the jurisdiction of the United Kingdom or is otherwise prejudicial to the sovereignty of the United Kingdom', and a certificate signed by or on behalf of the Secretary of State to the effect that it infringes that jurisdiction or is so prejudicial shall be conclusive evidence.

5. PENAL DAMAGES AND THE CLAWBACK

In *Jones* v. *Jones*[44] Lord Coleridge, referring to an action for pound-breach and rescue of chattels distrained for non-payment of tithe rent-charge in which the plaintiff claimed treble damages under eighteenth century legislation said:

His claim is, however, not for £40 but for £120, that is for £80 more than is due, and he claims the £120 as 'treble damages' under a statute which gives 'treble damages' to a 'person grieved' by pound breach and rescue against the 'offender'. 'Treble damages' cannot possibly be compensation to the person grieved, and are plainly inflicted on the offender as a punishment. In other words they are a penalty. The plaintiff is as much suing for a penalty as if he sued for a penalty eo nomine . . . It was a fixed principle of procedure in equity to refuse a bill of discovery in aid of a penal action . . . in the exercise of the jurisdiction the rules of equity, though not absolutely binding, were accepted by the courts of common law as their guide.

Ninety years later the Attorney-General in a very different context in the *Westinghouse* case said:[45]

---

[43] At p. 631. See also Lord Diplock at p. 639 and Lord Fraser at p. 650.
[44] (1889) 22 QBD 425 at 427.   [45] [1978] AC at 594.

The penal sanctions attaching to violations of United States anti-trust legislation include severe criminal penalties and penal damages. In this respect no valid distinction can be drawn between the proceedings brought by the state and those brought by private individuals to enforce a monetary penalty.

The Protection of Trading Interests Act 1980 contains two sections dealing with foreign judgments for multiple damages. In one, section 5, the United Kingdom Parliament prohibits the enforcement in the United Kingdom of foreign judgments for multiple damages. In the other, section 6, the legislature gives a limited right for a judgment debtor who has satisfied a foreign judgment for multiple damages to recover the non-compensatory amount from the judgment creditor.

As regards the enforcement of United States treble damages awards in the United Kingdom, the position before the 1980 Act was that such judgments would have been enforceable, if at all, only at common law, since neither the Administration of Justice Act 1920 (which applies mainly to Commonwealth countries) nor the Foreign Judgments (Reciprocal Enforcement) Act 1933 (which applies, in the main, to countries with which the United Kingdom has a treaty for the reciprocal enforcement of judgments) applied to United States judgments. At common law a United States judgment would be enforceable in England if either (a) the judgment debtor was present (e.g. through a fixed place of business) in the relevant state of the United States at the time of commencement of the proceedings, or (b) the judgment debtor had submitted to the jurisdiction of the United States court by appearance or by contract. In any event a foreign judgment which was 'penal' was not enforceable either at common law or under the statutes. But the case law suggested that a penalty in this context normally meant a sum payable to the state, and not a private plaintiff, so that an award of punitive or exemplary damages was not penal.[46] It is possible that an award of multiple damages in an antitrust action might nevertheless have been regarded as penal at common law, but in effect the point is put beyond doubt by section 5 of the Protection of Trading Interests Act 1980.

The effect of that section is that certain foreign judgments are not to be enforceable under the 1920 Act or the 1933 Act or at common law. The judgments to which the section applies include (a) a judgment for multiple damages, or (b) a judgment based on foreign restrictive practices law designated by the Secretary of State. A judgment for multiple damages means 'a judgment for an amount arrived at by doubling, trebling or otherwise multiplying a sum assessed as compensation for the loss or damage sustained by the person in whose favour the judgment is given'.[47]

---

[46] See Dicey & Morris, *Conflict of Laws*, 10th ed. 1980, p. 1094; cf. *SA Consortium General Textiles* v. *Sun and Sand Agencies Ltd.* [1978] QB 279, 309.   [47] s. 5(3).

The effect of this definition is that the *whole* of the foreign judgment for multiple damages is unenforceable in the United Kingdom, and not merely that part of it which is not compensatory. The types of foreign restrictive practices rules which the Secretary of State may designate for the purpose of the section are 'any provision or rule of law which appears to him to be concerned with the prohibition or regulation of agreements, arrangements or practices designed to restrain, distort or restrict competition in the carrying on of business of any description or to be otherwise concerned with the promotion of such competition as aforesaid'.[48] The effect of this is that even a judgment purely for compensation, but based on a foreign antitrust rule, would be unenforceable in the United Kingdom.

The 'clawback' provision is section 6. This allows certain persons connected with the United Kingdom against whom multiple damages awards have been made abroad, and who have discharged the award in whole or in part, to recover the non-compensatory part from the judgment creditor. The section applies to judgments for multiple damages as defined above. The judgment debtor who can seek to recover money paid under such judgment must be (normally, with special provisions for British colonies and territories for whose international relations HMG is responsible) (*a*) a British citizen; or (*b*) a corporation incorporated in the United Kingdom; or (*c*) a person carrying on business in the United Kingdom. The person against whom the claim is made, the judgment creditor, does not have to be present within the United Kingdom. If the judgment creditor is not within the jurisdiction then, under the present Rules of the Supreme Court, the judgment debtor who seeks to recover under this Section will have to obtain leave to serve out of the jurisdiction under Order 11, Rule 1(1). When the pending amendments to the Rules of the Supreme Court come into force service will be without leave under Order 11, Rule 1(2).

The judgment debtor may recover where damages have been paid either to the party in whose favour the judgment was given or to another party who was entitled as against the judgment debtor to contribution in respect of the damages.[49] An amount is deemed to be paid where an amount is obtained by execution against the judgment debtor's property or against the property of a company which (directly or indirectly) is wholly owned by the judgment debtor. The amount which the judgment debtor may recover is so much of the amount paid as exceeds the part attributable to compensation (and if only part of the judgment has been paid by the judgment debtor, a proportionate part).[50]

Recovery under this section is not available where the judgment debtor is an individual who was ordinarily resident in the foreign country when the proceedings in which the judgment was given were instituted, or a body

---

[48] s. 5(4).   [49] s. 6(1).   [50] s. 6(2).

corporate which had its principal place of business there at that time. Nor does it apply where the judgment debtor carried on business in the foreign country and the proceedings in which the judgment was given were concerned with activities exclusively carried on in that country.

The approach of the 1980 Act may be compared usefully with that of similar legislation in other countries. As regards the enforcement of foreign judgments, the South Africa Protection of Businesses Act 1978, as amended in 1984, provides that no relevant judgment for multiple or punitive damages shall be recognised or enforced in South Africa; but the restriction applies only to that part of the amount awarded as damages which exceeds the amount determined as compensation for the damage or loss actually sustained by the judgment creditor. Both the Canadian Foreign Extraterritorial Measures Act 1984 and the Australian Foreign Proceedings (Excess of Jurisdiction) Act 1984[51] give the Attorney-General power to determine which part of a foreign antitrust judgment is capable of enforcement. The clawback provisions of the other statutes deserve a little more attention, because their provisions are somewhat more effective than the United Kingdom statute. The essential defect of the United Kingdom provisions is that the remedy is only effective if the judgment creditor who has obtained a foreign award for the multiple damages and been satisfied in whole or in part by the judgment debtor has assets in the United Kingdom which could satisfy any judgment given under the clawback section. It is essential that the judgment be capable of enforcement in the United Kingdom because (except for limited reciprocal arrangements between the countries most affected) a clawback judgment in the United Kingdom is not likely to be recognised abroad. Thus, unless the American judgment creditor has a branch or a subsidiary or other assets in the United Kingdom the clawback judgment is unlikely to be of any real assistance to the judgment debtor. Under section 1B(4) of the South African legislation not only is the original judgment creditor liable to the judgment debtor but also, where the judgment creditor is a company, as it usually will be, 'any other company which is the controlling company or a controlled company' of the judgment creditor or 'is a company which is controlled by the same controlling company as controls' it, those companies shall be liable, jointly and severally together with the judgment creditor. Similarly, section 9 of the Canadian legislation provides that a court which renders a clawback judgment may order the seizure and sale of shares of any corporation incorporated by or under a law of Canada or a Province in which the person against whom the judgment is rendered has 'a direct or indirect beneficial interest, whether the share certificates are located inside or

---

[51] See also the earlier Australian Foreign Antitrust Judgments (Restriction of Enforcement) Act 1979.

outside Canada'. Under Section 10(5) of the Australian legislation 'any corporation that is related'[52] to the judgment creditor is jointly and severally liable with it to pay the amount of a clawback judgment.

The 1980 Act did not emerge without forceful criticism from the United States.[53] The US Government urged on the British government the view that the provisions for non-enforceability of antitrust judgments and the clawback provisions were inflexible and provided no procedure for giving due weight to United States concerns. In particular it regarded the clawback provision as being contrary to international law and comity.[54]

CONCLUSION

Formal conclusions are not necessary. But it may be helpful to end with some of the questions which blocking and clawback statutes raise: first, are their objectives clearly identified? Second, are those objectives effected? A tentative conclusion only is suggested. There are three objectives: one is to express governmental attitudes to the encroachment of United States legislation on their sovereignty; another is to afford a foreign governmental compulsion defence to orders in United States courts; a third objective is to provide a form of retaliation against United States judgments. The first objective has been achieved; the second clearly has some effect; but there is little evidence that the third objective has been, or can be, achieved.

---

[52] Which is widely defined by the Australian companies legislation to include parents, subsidiaries and affiliates.

[53] See Lowenfeld (1981) 75 AJIL 629. See also Lowe (1981) 75 AJIL 237.

[54] See (1982) 21 *International Legal Materials* 840.

IX

Interaction between Contract and Tort in the Conflict of Laws

This article originated as a thesis at Columbia University Law School under the supervision of Professor Maurice Rosenberg. The relationship between contract and tort in international transactions remains a matter of considerable difficulty, particularly in the field of employment law, which is dealt with in Chapter XI. The distinction between contractual and tortious claims may make a vital difference in cases covered by the Brussels and Lugano Conventions on jurisdiction and the enforcement of judgments, since the jurisdictional rules for contract in Article 5(1) and for tort in Article 5(3) may lead to different jurisdictions. The European Court has held that the expressions 'matters relating to a contract' and 'matters relating to tort, delict or quasi-delict' are to be given autonomous interpretations. The consequence is that a claim connected with a contract cannot be treated as a tortious claim for jurisdictional purposes, even if it is so classified by the law of a member state: Case 189/87 *Kalfelis* v. *Schroder, Munchmeyer, Hengst & Co.* [1988] ECR 5565. Most recently, in Case C-26/91 *Jacob Handte & Co.* v. *TMCS*, 17 June 1992, the European Court held that a claim by an ultimate purchaser against a manufacturer in the French courts was to be regarded as tortious in nature, even though under French Law it was classified as a claim on an implied contract. Consequently, the French court did not have jurisdiction in a product liability claim.

I. INTRODUCTION: CONTRACT OR TORT?

A glance at any text on the conflict of laws will reveal that different chapters are assigned, sometimes under the general heading of 'obligations', to the fields of contract and tort. The reasons seem obvious enough. Contract and tort represent the twin pillars of civil obligation in the common law. They are distinguishable, if not in detail then at least in outline, in historical growth in a system where characteristically the right followed the remedy.[1] While they operated municipally in different spheres it was natural to separate and apply different rules to them in cases involving a foreign element.

The modern law of tort reflects the need to protect an increasing number

From *International and Comparative Law Quarterly*, 16 (1967), 103.

[1] See Winfield, *The Province of the Law of Tort* (1931) pp. 40–91; Winfield, *Tort* (6th ed., 1954) pp. 800–813 (this section has been omitted from the current 7th ed., 1963); Guest, 'Tort or Contract?' (1961) 3 *U. Malaya L. Rev.* 191.

of social interests, the need to regulate varying standards of conduct, and, above all, the need to adjust these interests and standards in an effort to apportion the risks in modern industrial and mechanised society. The prime policy of the law of contracts has been to protect the interest in the performance of promises. But it is a commonplace that with the growth of economic power the *laissez-faire* basis of its rules in fact allows it to become the instrument of change from status to contract and back again to status, this being the familiar paradox of liberty. The increasing standardisation of contracts has moved the emphasis of the law of contract away from the primacy of promise.[2] For the benefit of weaker parties the law has implied many terms into contracts which perform similar functions to those rules governing tortious liability.[3]

Since the adjustment of universal risks has become a major policy of both the law of contract and of tort, it is not surprising that the rules which govern them have moved closer together. Whatever the historical reasons for the divergence, it is clear that the forms of action have left the law a legacy of contradiction and confusion. Duties co-exist in some areas but not in others. When they do co-exist they do not necessarily reflect uniform standards of desired conduct. Their historical origins have left a number of technical rules which separate them and may make it necessary to choose between them. This area has been called the 'borderland of contract and tort' by Prosser.[4] For example, in a contract of carriage the duty to take care arises both by the terms of the contract, express or implied, and also by the general law of negligence.[5] Such concurrent liability gives rise, in the municipal context, to a number of questions: which breaches of contract and what types of contract create alternative liability in tort?[6] For what purposes should the distinction be made?[7]

---

[2] See generally Kessler, 'Contracts of Adhesion—Some Thoughts About Freedom of Contract' (1943) 43 Colum. L. Rev. 629; Prausnitz, *The Standardization of Commercial Contracts in English and Continental Law* (1937); Wilson, 'Freedom of Contract and Adhesion Contracts' (1965) 14 ICLQ 172.

[3] See Goodhart, 'A Master's Liability for Defective Tools' (1958) 74 LQR 397, 406.

[4] Prosser, 'The Borderland of Contract and Tort', in *Selected Topics on the Law of Torts* (1954) p. 380.

[5] See, e.g., *Kelley v. Metropolitan Ry.* [1895] 1 QB 944 (CA). But see, e.g., *Williamson v. Pacific Greyhound Lines* (1945) 67 Cal. App. 2d 250, 153 P. 2d 990, which speaks of 'gravamen' or 'essential facts or grievance' as the test for determining whether an action is in contract or in tort (for jurisdictional purposes).

[6] See Prosser, *Torts* (3rd ed., 1964) pp. 635–639. A common problem is that of professional negligence. In the United States attorneys have been held liable to their clients in tort: see, e.g., *O'Neil v. Gray* (1929) 30 F. 2d 776 (2d Cir.) (statute of limitation). In England, the duty owed by a solicitor to his client apparently sounds only in contract: *Groom v. Crocker* [1939] 1 KB 194 (CA) (measure of damages). This is so even after the decision in *Hedley Byrne & Co. Ltd. v. Heller & Partners Ltd.* [1964] AC 485 (HL): see *Clark v. Kirby-Smith* [1964] Ch. 506 and *Cook v. S.* [1966] 1 All ER 248 (measure of damages). For convincing criticism see Jolowicz [1965] Camb. LJ 27.

[7] The purposes include limitation of actions (*Bagot v. Stevens Scanlon* [1966] 1 QB 197),

A duty which may exist in tort may be increased, modified or negated by the terms of a contract. It is for the law to determine how far limitations of liability, especially with the increase of standardisation and inequalities of bargaining positions, must be cut down to prevent total negation of liability. Solutions vary from regulation by treaty and statute[8] in restricted fields and by doctrines of public policy and reasonableness[9] to near-complete tolerance of limitations of liability.[10]

Put all this in the context of the conflict of laws and it is easy to see that all the difficulties will be multiplied. In England and, until recently, in the United States the rules of the conflict of laws reflected a strict separation of contract and tort. But as the domestic history of contract and tort reveals a coalescence of their functions and thereby also a trend towards unity of rules, so also there are movements to undermine the dichotomy in the conflict of laws. In domestic law contract and tort inter-react so that contract comes to fulfil the functions of tort while tort borrows many of its standards from the field of contract. But the conflict of laws lags behind, only slowly coming to terms with the changes that have taken place in domestic law.

Where different systems reveal a concurrence of rights to action in one fact situation a court will have to decide whether to give primacy to one or the other, or to neither. Where a contract varies, adds to, or diminishes an obligation in tort, then a court may have to decide the vital policy question of whether to give primacy to the interests protected by the law of tort or those protected by the law of contract.

In cases of possible concurrence of action the inquiry must be directed to the methods by which a system of law divines whether such concurrence exists, to the extent to which the courts give freedom to the parties to frame their causes of action and their defences. Characterisation is a hoary weapon in the armoury of the conflict of laws. Is its use in this area of the relation of contract and tort any different from its use in other areas of the law? Is it a useful or necessary tool?

Where duties that would otherwise exist in tort are altered by the terms of a contract, one State may uphold the freedom of the parties to vary their rights and duties, another may prevent such contracting out. How is such a

---

measure of damages (cases *supra*, note 6) and the jurisdiction of courts (*Jarvis* v. *Moy, Davies, Smith, Vandervell & Co.* [1936] 1 KB 399 (CA)).

[8] See, e.g., Carriage of Goods By Sea Act, 49 Stat. 1207 (1936), 46 USCA, ss. 1300–1315.

[9] See, e.g., *Liverpool & Great Western Steam Co.* v. *Phenix Ins. Co.* (1889) 129 US 397, 441.

[10] Despite legislative inroads, this is still the general rule in England. The House of Lords has affirmed the general rule by holding that the doctrine of fundamental breach is nothing more than a rule of construction: *Suisse Atlantique, etc.* v. *NV Rotterdamsche Kolen Centrale* [1967] 1 AC 361.

conflict to be resolved? Will it depend on whether an action is based on contract or tort? Will the notions of the forum prevail?

Where questions of the conflict of laws arise, the courts, as might be expected, have gone off in all directions, and the character of the action as tort or contract has become entangled with other rules.[11]

2. CONCURRENCE AND EXCLUSION IN THE ENGLISH CONFLICT OF LAWS

It is trite law that a single act of negligence may give rise to a claim either in tort or for breach of a term express or implied in the contract.[12]

A foreman millwright was injured when he fell into a trench in an attempt to avoid a load, swinging from a crane, which was coming towards him. All of this took place in Kuwait. His contract of employment was signed in England, and provided that it should be construed and have effect in accordance with English law. His employers were resident in Panama. The question which arose for the Court of Appeal was whether service out of the jurisdiction could be effected on the defendants. This in turn depended on whether the action was to be regarded as one of tort or of contract. For under the Rules of the Supreme Court[13] service was permissible if the action was one of the contract made in England or to be governed by English law. The court held that the duties of an employer to his servant arise both in contract and in tort, and therefore gave leave for service out of the jurisdiction.[14] Lord Justice Sellers pointed out:

[T]he difference between a claim in tort and a claim in contract . . . is very rarely one which calls for any consideration at all . . . The issue for consideration now is whether this action can *for the purposes of this rule* be framed in contract.[15]

What law would be applied in such a case once personal jurisdiction is established? It is a commonplace that in cases of contract English courts

---

[11] Prosser, *supra*, note 4, at 449.

[12] *Lister* v. *Romford Ice & Cold Storage Co. Ltd.* [1957] AC 555, 573, *per* Lord Simonds.

[13] Now RSC, Ord. 11, r. 1 (*f*).

[14] *Matthews* v. *Kuwait Bechtel Corp.* [1959] 2 QB 57 (CA). There had been some suggestions, notably by Denning LJ (dissenting) in *Romford Ice & Cold Storage Co. Ltd.* v. *Lister* [1956] 2 QB 180, 188–189 (CA) and in *Davie* v. *New Merton Board Mills Ltd.* [1959] AC 604 (HL) by Lord Simonds, at 619, and Lord Reid, at 642, that the master's duty to his servants should be regarded as part of the law of tort. But in *Lister* v. *Romford Ice & Cold Storage Co. Ltd.* [1957] AC 555 (HL) Lord Simonds, at 573, and Lord Tucker, at 594, treated the liability as both contractual and tortious. See also Jolowicz, Note [1959] Camb. LJ 163; Webber, Note (1959) 22 Modern L. Rev. 521; Kahn-Freund, 'Notes on the Conflict of Laws in Relation to Employment in English and Scottish Law' (1960) 3 *Riv. Dir. Internazionale e comparato del Lavoro* 307.

[15] [1959] 2 QB at 64 (emphasis added).

apply the 'proper law of the contract'. In the absence of an express choice by the parties, the courts will apply, in varying formulations, the law intended by the parties, the law to which they may be presumed to have submitted themselves, or the law with which the contract has its most substantial connection.[16] The doctrine of the proper law is flexible, to say the least, and states the conclusion itself rather than the criteria on which it must be based. Perhaps its chief virtue is that a court can determine the governing law in the context of the specific issue before it.[17] Although the courts have never committed themselves to such a view, on this approach different aspects of a contract might be governed by different laws.[18]

The source and classic formulation of the English conflict rule for torts is the famous judgment of Willes J. in *Phillips* v. *Eyre*. He laid down two 'rules' for the actionability of a tort committed abroad, both of which have been a continuing source of difficulty and confusion.[19] The effect is a distinct 'homeward trend', because the act, say the cases, *must* be a tort by English law, and *need not* in some circumstances be a tort by the relevant foreign law. It is not difficult to see a contrast with the internationalist approach for contracts.

Much ink has been spilled on the concept of characterisation,[20] most of it divorced from the actual workings of the judicial process. English courts have only rarely talked the language of characterisation, and the reason may lie in the peculiar workings of the adversarial process.

Whether the proceeds from land are immovables for purposes of succession,[21] or whether a foreign statute of limitations goes to the

---

[16] Recent formulations of the rule are to be found in *Tomkinson* v. *First Pennsylvania Banking & Trust Co.* [1961] AC 1007 (HL) at 1068 (by Lord Denning) and 1081 (by Lord Morris) applying the test suggested in *Bonython* v. *Commonwealth of Australia* [1951] AC 201 219 (PC): 'The system of law by reference to which the contract was made or that with which the transaction has its closest and most real connection.' See also *Rossano* v. *Manufacturers' Life Ins. Co* [1963] 2 QB 352, 360, *per* McNair J.

[17] See Morris, 'The Proper Law of a Tort' (1951) 64 Harv. L. Rev. 881, 882.

[18] Cf. *Re Helbert Wagg* [1956] Ch. 323, 340; *Zivnostenska Banka* v. *Frankman* [1950] AC 57, 83 (HL); *Kahler* v. *Midland Bank* [1950] AC 24, 42 (HL); *Re United Railways* [1960] Ch. 52, 92 (CA), *rev'd in part sub nom. Tomkinson* v. *First Pennsylvania Banking & Trust Co., supra*, note 16. These cases all contain views that a contract may be 'split', that not all aspects need be governed by the law of a single country.

[19] 'First, the wrong must be of such a character that it would have been actionable if committed in England . . . Secondly, the act must not have been justifiable by the law of the place where it was done' (1870) LR 6 QB 1, 28–29 (Ex. Ch.). The effect of the first branch, as usually understood, is that the act must be a tort under the domestic law of the forum, although *The Halley* (1868) LR 2 PC 193 is the only English decision which directly supports it. The second branch has been interpreted to mean that it is enough that the act is not innocent by the *lex loci*, i.e., it does not have to give rise to tortious liability under the *lex loci;* see *Machado* v. *Fontes* [1897] 2 QB 231, 233, 235 (CA).

[20] See generally Lorenzen, *Selected Articles on the Conflict of Laws* (1947) pp. 80–135; Falconbridge, *Conflict of Laws* (2nd ed., 1954) pp. 50–123; Dicey, *Conflict of Laws* (7th ed., 1958) pp. 41–56 [hereinafter cited as *Dicey*].

[21] See *Re Hoyles* [1911] 1 Ch. 179 (CA).

substance of a right,[22] these relate to the interpretation of *rules*. What they have in common with the elusive distinction between contract and tort is that what is concerned is a choice between different sets of rules. But when the choice is between causes of action it will usually be unnecessary for the court to decide whether the action is in contract or in tort. Provided that the plaintiff has a sufficient cause of action in one, it is no business of the court to force him on to the other. In this sense, the choice of the relevant rule will depend more on the plaintiff than on the judge.

Robertson[23] talks of characterisation 'going by default'[24] in cases which he feels ought to be concerned with the distinction between contract and tort. But in citing two such cases[25] he fails to clarify the role of the court in a case involving concurrent causes of action. It is surely not its role, if the plaintiff has a cause of action in one, to suggest that it should be framed in the other. He poses the problem of the action for breach of promise to marry brought in England, which is treated as tortious by one jurisdiction (where the breach occurred) and as contractual by another (the proper law of the contract). Concluding that, if under the law of the contract, the breach is actionable without proof of damage, while under the law governing the tort proof of damage is required, *the English court will characterise the action as contractual*,[26] he ignores the consideration that tort will not get in the act, as it were, if the plaintiff pleads breach of contract.

The role of the *lex fori* in the framing of the cause of action is illustrated by the recent case of *Phrantzes* v. *Argenti*.[27] The plaintiff sued her father in an English court claiming that under Greek law she was entitled to be provided with a dowry. The plaintiff failed, not because English domestic law did not give any analogous right, nor because it was against English public policy to enforce the right, but because English law, the *lex fori*, did not provide a cause of action and relief appropriate to the foreign right. It could not provide the remedy of an order directing that a contract be entered into and it could not order a payment of money without thereby effecting a material alteration of the rights given by Greek law. But if the remedies given by English law had been appropriate, Lord Parker emphasised that 'it matters not what label is given to the right'.[28] By this he meant that it was for English law to provide the type of action and remedy to effectuate the foreign right. In that case there were no systems of law

---

[22] See *Huber* v. *Steiner* (1835) 2 Bing. NC 202; 132 ER 80.

[23] Robertson, *Characterization in the Conflict of Laws* (1940).   [24] *Ibid*, at 183.

[25] *Rauton* v. *Pullman* (1937) 183 SC 495, 191 SE 416; *Conklin* v. *Canadian Colonial Rys.* (1935) 266 NY 244, 194 NE 692.

[26] Robertson, *op. cit.*, *supra*, n. 23, at pp. 76–78, 177–179. He also talks, at p. 178, of the proper law of the contract as being capable of being the law of a jurisdiction which does not recognise contractual liability of this type, but it is difficult to see how this is possible.

[27] [1960] 2 QB 19.   [28] *Ibid*. at 34.

competing for primacy. It was Greek law or nothing which was to be applied, and the plaintiff failed to find an appropriate cause of action under English law through which, so to speak, her rights under Greek law could be channelled.

(*a*) Concurrent causes of action

[W]hen the breach of duty alleged arises out of a liability independently of the personal obligation undertaken by contract, it is tort; and it may be tort even though there may happen to be a contract between the parties; if the duty in fact arises independently of that contract. Breach of contract occurs where that which is complained of is a breach of duty arising out of the obligations undertaken by the contract.[29]

It has been suggested[30] that this test, proposed for very limited municipal purposes,[31] is a suitable one for conflict of laws purposes also. It may appear that it will be workable in a system untrammelled by technical conflicts rules distinguishing between contract and tort. But it is doubtful whether any separate test is required for conflicts purposes in a system like the English one, where the plaintiff will frame his cause of action in accordance with the most advantageous theory. It will therefore depend on whether the domestic law recognises concurrent causes of action, or restricts the plaintiff to one of the categories. It would be exceptional if what was a breach of contract for domestic purposes would, say, be tested by the rule in *Phillips* v. *Eyre* for conflicts purposes.

Typical examples of possible concurrence are contracts of carriage and contracts of employment. There is no English case directly in point. Dicey[32] suggests that the courts are inclined to characterise the liability of a carrier for the safety of his passengers as delictual and so apply the conflicts rules relating to torts. The sole authorities relied upon for this generalisation are Scottish decisions. In *Naftalin* v. *LMS Ry.*[33] the deceased, a Scotsman, bought a round-trip ticket for a journey from Glasgow to London on the defendants' railway. He was killed in England on the return trip. His widow sued for *solatium* under Scots law. Her claim was denied on the ground that the facts revealed a delictual relation; therefore it was necessary to show that a similar right was given by the *lex loci delicti* under the second branch of the rule in *Phillips* v. *Eyre*, and since English law had no concept of *solatium*, there could be no recovery. In answer to a claim based on the contract of carriage, the reasoning[34] was that the widow was not a party to the contract of carriage, and that the rights under the

---

[29] Greer LJ in *Jarvis* v. *Moy, Davies, Smith, Vandervell & Co.* [1936] 1 KB 399, 405 (CA).
[30] Stromholm, *Torts in the Conflict of Laws* (1961) p. 161.
[31] That of county court jurisdiction.
[32] Dicey, pp. 831–832.   [33] 1933 SC 259.
[34] *Ibid.* at 264 (Lord Hunter), at 269 (Lord Anderson), and at 272 (Lord Murray).

contract were purely personal, giving no rights to personal represent-atives.[35] It seems that a legitimate deduction from this decision would be that the injured party, or his personal representatives under a survival statute, could sue on the contract, but that a claim under the Fatal Accidents Acts would be regarded as one in tort.[36] Although the Canadian case[37] which the editors of Dicey cite for the proposition that the proper law of the contract may be relied on by the plaintiff is not in point, there are cases involving carriage of goods in which the action is said to be in contract.[38] Moreover, it is well settled in English domestic law that an action in either contract or tort will lie for an injury done to a passenger on a railway,[39] and there would appear to be no reason not to apply the law of the contract of carriage in appropriate circumstances where the Inter-national Conventions[40] are not applicable.

It was not until *Matthews* v. *Kuwait Bechtel*[41] that it was authoritatively decided that a claim against an employer for breach of his obligation to supply a safe system of work would lie in contract. An early Canadian case[42] had referred to the *lex fori*, as the law governing the contract, an action against an employer, although the injury occurred in a jurisdiction where there would have been no recovery. But the majority of the Canadian lower courts regarded the obligation as one imposed by the law of tort,[43] although the point has been left open by the Supreme Court of

---

[35] Similar reasoning was applied in the decision of the New York Court of Appeals in *Kilberg* v. *Northeast Airlines* (1961) 9 NY 2d 34, 172 NE 2d 526, and it is noteworthy that the lower court in *Naftalin* v. *LMS*, *supra*, note 33, treated the measure of damages as a procedural matter to be governed by the *lex fori*, which was the approach of the New York Court of Appeals. But see *Davenport* v. *Webb* (1962) 11 NY 2d 392, 183 NE 2d 902. The result of the rule in *Phillips* v. *Eyre* as interpreted in England by *Machado* v. *Fontes*, *supra*, note 19, is that, since it is not necessary that there be civil liability by the *lex loci delicti*, the question of damages will be referred to English law.

[36]See also *Goodman* v. *L. & NWR* (1877) 14 SLT 449, for the denial of a claim of *solatium*, although it does not appear where the ticket was bought.

[37] *Scott* v. *American Airlines Inc.* [1944] 3 DLR 27 (Ont. High Ct.), which concerned the effect of a release on a claim which was said to be in tort.

[38] See, e.g., *Re Missouri Steamship Co.* (1889) 42 Ch. D. 321 (CA), a claim for damages for the wreck of goods on their way from Massachusetts to England, where Lord Halsbury noted, at 335, that in substance it was an action on a contract. An early Scots case, *Horn* v. *North British Ry.* (1878) 5 R. 1055, allowed recovery for *solatium* based on the contract of carriage, but was overruled in *McElroy* v. *McAllister*, 1949 SC 110, in so far as it treated questions of damages as procedural, and so its authority is doubtful. There is little authority on the proper law of a contract of carriage, and what there is dates from the days of the rigid application of the *lex loci contractus*. See *P&O Co.* v. *Shand* (1865) 3 Moo. PC (NS) 272. See also *Cohen* v. *SE Ry* (1877) 2 Ex. D. 253, 261, 262. See also Dicey, pp. 830–831.

[39] See, e.g., *Kelley* v. *Metropolitan Ry.*, *supra*, note 5.

[40] See Warsaw Convention, 1929 (air transport), and the International Conventions on the Carriage of Goods By Rail, and on the Carriage of Passengers and Luggage By Rail, 1952.

[41] *Supra*, note 14.

[42] *Dupont* v. *Quebec Steamship Co.* (1897) 11 SC 188, 203 (Quebec Ct. of Review).

[43] See *Lee* v. *Logan* (1906) 31 SC 469, 474 (Quebec Ct. of Review); *Grand Trunk Ry* v. *Marleau* (1911) 21 KB 269, *affirming* (1910) 38 SC 394.

Canada.[44] The significance of the Canadian decisions is that all they decide is whether the domestic law of the forum allows an action in contract in employment cases and so they reinforce the view that it is primarily for the plaintiff to frame his cause of action in such a way as to reflect the most advantageous law.

Motor-accident insurance has given rise to a number of conflict of laws problems involving the relation of contract and tort. It is to avoid fraudulent claims against insurance companies that some jurisdictions do not allow actions by a gratuitous passenger against his driver, or require a showing of more than ordinary negligence. Is there any method under traditional[45] conflicts principles by which the forum can allow an action by a guest passenger when the place of injury denies it? Two Canadian decisions show how such principles can be manipulated to allow recovery, and raise the question, to be considered below, of the efficacy and usefulness of artificial escape routes from the *lex loci delicti* as a substitute for, and circuitous abandonment of, the strict principle. In *Key* v. *Key*[46] the court suggested that an action against the driver could be based on an implied contract of reasonable care, to avoid the requirements of the *lex loci delicti*. This reasoning was applied in a Quebec case[47] to allow recovery for an Ontario accident. But in *McLean* v. *Pettigrew*[48] the Supreme Court rejected this view. Basing itself on a large number of French cases, in the absence of sufficient Quebec authority, it held that there was no contract between a driver and a gratuitous passenger.[49] But it then proceeded, by even more artificial reasoning, to hold that the defendant's acts were 'not justifiable' by Ontario law, under the second branch of the rule in *Phillips* v. *Eyre*, on the ground that the defendant was criminally liable under Ontario law, even though he had been acquitted. Once again, it depended on the domestic law of the forum whether the action could be based on a contract.

Another problem which raises a similar question, and which has much exercised American courts, is that of the direct action statute, which allows the person injured to sue an insurance company directly without first establishing the liability of the insured.[50] On the assumption that the acts of the insured were negligent, the question whether the insurer is directly

---

[44] *Logan* v. *Lee* (1907) 39 SCR 311 (Sup. Ct. of Canada).

[45] The leading case of *Babcock* v. *Jackson* (1963) 12 NY 2d 473, 191 NE 2d 279, which involved this very question of guest statutes in the conflict of laws, marked the first large step in the modification of the traditional rules. It is noteworthy that the dissenting judge in the Appellate Division, Halpern J., suggested the contract characterisation to avoid the application of Ontario law: (1962) 17 App. Div. 2d 694, 230 NYS 2d 114. 123–124.

[46] (1930) 65 Ont. LR 232 (Ont. App. Div.).

[47] *Assad* v. *Latendresse* (1941) 79 SC 286.

[48] [1945] 2 DLR 65 (Sup. Ct. of Canada).

[49] *Ibid.* at 67.   [50] See Third Parties (Rights Against Insurers) Act 1930.

liable could be referred to the *lex delicti* as a matter of procedure, to the *lex loci delicti* as a matter of tortious liability,[51] to the proper law of the contract as a matter of contractual liability, or to a combination of these. The solution advocated by the editors of Dicey is that the plaintiff must prove that the act of the insured would have been actionable if done in England and not justifiable by the *lex loci delicti*, and then that the proper law of the contract of insurance allows direct recovery against the insurer.[52] This appears to involve an incorporation of the rule in *Phillips* v. *Eyre* into a contract of insurance, but at least mitigates the severity of that rule by relaxing the dual requirement with regard to the insurer's liability. A recent Australian case, *Plozza* v. *South Australian Insurance Co.*,[53] apparently the only Commonwealth decision on the subject, comes to a similar conclusion. The victim was injured in Victoria, which has no direct action statute. The insurance policy was issued in South Australia, which has such a statute, and where the action was brought. The insurance company argued that since it was not directly liable under Victorian law, the *lex loci delicti*, the second branch of the rule in *Phillips* v. *Eyre* applied. The court held that the plaintiff must establish the negligence of the insured, with reference to the law of Victoria, but that the direct action was an action *sui generis*, in the nature of a statutory extension to contractual liability. Therefore it was the proper law of the contract by which the liability of the insurer was to be gauged.[54]

All of these examples show how the severity of the English conflict of laws rules for tort liability can be mitigated. But they equally raise the question of the value of that rule if it can be avoided, artificially or not, by invoking the rules for contracts. Liability in contract and tort is not based on principles so different as to justify such divergent results. A rule which can be avoided by the invocation of domestic rules on causes of action is just the sort of rule which discredits a system of conflict of laws.

(*b*) Exclusion of liability

If the traditional scheme makes an artificial distinction between contractual and tortious duty, then it is easy to see that further conflicts rules must be proffered to cope with conflicts between conflicts rules. The interplay of remedies and defences has led to the difficulties considered under the general problem of 'releases in the conflict of laws'.[55] There is little

---

[51] Rabel, *Conflict of Laws*, Vol. 2 (2nd ed., 1960) p. 263, states dogmatically that this question is to be determined by the *lex loci delicti*. See also Batiffol, *Traité Élémentaire de Droit International Privé* (3rd ed., 1959) p. 673.   [52] Dicey, p. 959.

[53] [1963] SASR 122 (South Australia Sup. Ct.).

[54] It may well be that the court was influenced by the fact that it was applying the *lex fori* as well as the *lex contractus*.

[55] See Note, 'Releases in the Conflict of Laws' (1960) 60 Col. L. Rev. 522.

authority in England and discussions in the literature are brief.[56] Two fact situations are regularly mooted: the first is where a defence is based on a contractual term excluding liability which is valid by the proper law of the contract but which is not recognised by the *lex loci delicti*. The second is where the defence would be recognised by the *lex loci delicti*, but is invalid by the law governing the contract. Both problems raise difficult questions of the interpretation of the rule in *Phillips* v. *Eyre* and of the scope of the law of the place of the tort.

The suggestion in Dicey[57] is that if a defence is based on a contractual term valid by the proper law of the contract, but invalid by the *lex loci delicti*, then it may be pleaded as a defence to an action based on the foreign tort. In practice what would happen is that the plaintiff would sue on the tort, to be met with a defence invoking an exculpatory clause in the contract. The sole authority[58] cited in Dicey did not deal with this fact situation, but with a case where a defence valid by the *lex loci delicti* would not have aided the defendant under the domestic law of the forum.

Clearly the action would not be justifiable by the *lex loci delicti* within the second branch of the rule in *Phillips* v. *Eyre*. But whether the action would lie might depend on the scope of the first branch, that is, would it have been 'actionable if committed in England'? English law recognises certain defences based on *foreign contracts* to torts alleged to have been committed in England. In *Kahler* v. *Midland Bank*[59] the plaintiff claimed share certificates in a London bank. The shares had been deposited on his behalf by his Czech bank. To leave Czechoslovakia in 1939, he was forced to transfer his account to another Czech bank. After the war the English bank refused to hand over the certificates because Czechoslovakian exchange control regulations did not permit the Czech bank to instruct the Midland Bank to hand over the shares. The House of Lords held that the claim in detinue was defeated by the defence based on the foreign exchange control regulations, under the proper law of the contract, Czech law. In a similar though simpler case,[60] Sellers J. held that a claim of trespass against some sailors for remaining on their ship was defeated by their contract of employment, as it depended on Greek law, the proper law of that contract, whether they were entitled still to remain. Both of these cases are concerned with rights in the nature of property rights, where the right of the plaintiff to sue in tort depended on the relevance of a foreign contract. But there seems no reason why, say, a claim based on negligence should not be defeated by an exculpatory clause in a foreign contract. The

---

[56] See Dicey, pp. 960–961; Hancock, *Torts in the Conflict of Laws* (1942) pp. 201–202, 207–208; Rabel, *op. cit., supra*, note 51, at 293–294.   [57] Dicey, p. 960.

[58] *Canadian Pacific Ry.* v. *Parent* [1917] AC 195 (PC).   [59] [1950] AC 24 (HL).

[60] *Galaxios SS Co.* v. *Panagos Christofis* (1948) 81 Ll. LR 499.

[61] [1944] 3 DLR 27 (Ont. High Ct.).

plaintiff could hardly argue that, though a valid English contract would afford a defence, a valid foreign contract would not do so. In *Scott* v. *American Airlines*[61] the deceased was killed on a flight from Detroit to Buffalo when the plane crashed in Ontario. His wife accepted compensation in Michigan, and then proceeded to sue in Ontario. The Michigan compensation agreement was set up as a defence. The court held that the validity and construction of the contract were to be determined by the law of Michigan, and found that by accepting compensation the plaintiff had waived her common law remedy to sue in tort either in Michigan or in Ontario.

It is a legitimate deduction from these cases and from principle that an exculpatory clause valid by the proper law of the contract in which it is contained will be a defence to a tort committed in England. It does not follow, however, that in all cases the efficacy of such a defence necessarily depends upon a cumulation of the *lex loci delicti* and the proper law. This merely happens to be true when England is both the forum and the place of the tort, since English law is generally lenient to exculpatory clauses. But it is not clear how the editors of Dicey arrive at the conclusion that in an action based on a foreign tort a contractual defence will be allowed even if not recognised by the *lex loci delicti*. Perhaps what they have in mind is an extension of the first branch of the rule in *Phillips* v. *Eyre*. Under this approach the court would visualise the tort as having been committed in England, and then, by noting that foreign contracts normally provide defences to English torts, could conclude that it would not have been actionable if committed in England. But since the editors of Dicey have criticised the first branch of the rule and said that 'little can be adduced in its favour from the point of view of justice or convenience',[62] it is worth wondering why they seek to extend it in the foregoing way, if that is the basis of their conclusion that a contractual term will be a defence 'although . . . according to the *lex loci delicti* the term is void, or if valid, not available as a defence to a delictual action'.[63] If, instead, they are announcing a rule for the resolution of conflicts between the *lex contractus* and the *lex loci delicti*, they do not do so clearly.

In similar vein, they suggest that if by the proper law of the contract the exemption clause is void, then it cannot provide a defence to an action in tort even though it may have been valid by the *lex loci delicti*.[64] But this seems to be inconsistent with the second branch of the rule in *Phillips* v. *Eyre*, under which there can be no suit in England on a foreign tort which is 'justifiable' under the *lex loci delicti*. If the plaintiff sues on a foreign tort, he is met by a defence that liability is excluded under the *lex loci delicti*. It may depend on the scope and form of the rule of the *lex loci* regarding

---

[62] Dicey, p. 943.   [63] *Ibid.* 960.   [64] *Ibid.* 961.

exculpatory clauses. If its rule is that one *may* exclude liability, then it could be argued that there is no exemption because the contractual term is invalid by its law. It must be for the *lex fori* to determine the validity of the contractual exemption according to its proper law. It would be an unnecessary extension of the *renvoi* principle to delegate this function to the *lex loci delicti*. But if the defence is framed in the nature of *volenti non fit injuria* it would appear that, if the *lex loci delicti* admits such a defence irrespective of the validity of the contract, the act would be 'justifiable' by the *lex loci delicti*. In *Canadian Pacific Ry.* v. *Parent*[65] the deceased had travelled on the defendant's railway at less than full fare, in consideration of which he waived any claim for personal injuries. The journey was from Manitoba to Quebec. The accident occurred in Ontario, and suit was brought by his widow in Quebec. By Quebec domestic law the signing of a pass releasing them from liability would not have aided the defendants. The Privy Council, *inter alia*, found that the pass was a defence under the *lex loci delicti*, and failed to consider the relevance of the contract of carriage, the proper law of which was either Manitoba or Quebec law. The lower courts[66] had treated the contract as governed by Manitoba law (which was presumed to be the same as Quebec law) and found the release ineffective. Thus the case may be authority for the view that certainly the *lex fori* and possibly the *lex contractus* is irrelevant if the *lex loci delicti* recognises a defence of *volenti*.

Essentially the problem in this type of case is for the plaintiff to allege and prove a breach of contract, and thus make the defences given by the place of injury irrelevant. Differing approaches are illustrated by three Canadian decisions.[67] In *Dupont* v. *Quebec Steamship Co.*[68] the deceased met his fate on a British ship in Trinidad. He was employed under a contract made in Quebec. The defence of common employment was recognised under English and Trinidad law, but not in Quebec law. The court allowed recovery on a contract theory by characterising the defence as contractual, and by holding that the parties intended their relationship to be governed by the law of Quebec. In *Logan* v. *Lee*[69] the same result was reached by a different line of reasoning. The trial judge held that the responsibility was a contractual one, but the Court of Review treated the responsibility of a master as delictual. However, it held that even if recognised as a defence by New Brunswick law, the *lex loci delicti*, it could be invoked only by virtue of a Quebec contract, which did not recognise

---

[65] [1917] AC 195 (PC).

[66] (1915) 51 SCR 234; (1914) 24 KB 193; (1914) SC 319.

[67] See Johnson, *Conflict of Laws* (2nd ed., 1962) pp. 677–691, for a discussion of the Quebec decisions.　　　　　　　　　　　　　　　　　　　　[68] (1897) 11 SC 188.

[69] (1907) 13 RL (NS) 543, *aff'd* (1907) 31 SC 469, *aff'd* (1907) 39 SCR 311. See also *Albouze* v. *Temiscaming Navigation Co. Ltd.* (1910) 38 SC 279.

the defence. This would seem to be a kind of *renvoi*, in which the court determined the scope of the foreign tort law. The Supreme Court of Canada affirmed, but did not decide the choice of law question, since it found that there was a right of action under the New Brunswick Workmen's Compensation Act. But in *Marleau* v. *Grand Trunk Ry. Co.*[70] Quebec courts firmly rejected a contract approach in deciding that the issue of contributory negligence must be referred to the *lex loci delicti*, Ontario. They proceeded on the purely conceptual reasoning that the duties arising between master and servant are delictual.

Since concurrent liability is recognised now in England in employment cases, the plaintiff will be able to rely on the contract and thus make any defences under the *lex loci delicti* irrelevant, except in so far as they are incorporated into the contract.

3. THE RELATION OF CONTRACT AND TORT IN THE TRADITIONAL UNITED STATES CONFLICTS LAW

The preceding section began with a discussion of the English case involving the millwright injured in Kuwait. The facts of that case are reminiscent of those in the decision of the Court of Appeals for the Second Circuit, *Walton* v. *Arabian American Oil Co.*,[71] which has become internationally known for its vigorous criticism of the traditional tort choice of law rules.

The plaintiff was a resident of Arkansas who was injured, while temporarily in Saudi Arabia, in an accident involving a truck driven by an employee of the defendants, a well-known oil company incorporated in Delaware. There was, apparently, no contractual relationship between the plaintiff and the defendant company. The plaintiff had a good case in negligence under New York law. But his claim was dismissed. The reason why he failed lies in the differences between the English and American rules of conflict of laws. If the case had arisen in England the plaintiff would have made out his case by showing actionability under English law. The onus would then have been on the defendant to show that its acts were 'justifiable' by Saudi Arabian law.

Instead, Judge Jerome Frank, obliged to follow the New York conflicts rules,[72] concluded with some reluctance that the substantive law applicable was that of the place where the alleged tort occurred. Under the federal rules it was an abuse of the discretion of the court for it to note that law

---

[70] (1910) 38 SC 394, *aff'd* (1911) 21 KB 269.

[71] 233 F. 2d 541 (2d Cir.), *cert. denied* (1956) 352 US 872.

[72] Under the decision in *Klaxon Co.* v. *Stentor Electric Mfg. Co.* (1941) 313 US 487 requiring federal courts in diversity of citizenship cases to follow the conflicts rules of the state in which they sit.

judicially without adequate proof of its contents. He was fully aware of the injustice of this result; both the parties were Americans, and the plaintiff was a transient in Saudi Arabia and so in a much worse position than the defendant to obtain information concerning Saudi Arabian law.

The result reflects more than a difference in systems of pleading between English and American law. It goes to the philosophical basis of the two systems of conflict of laws. In *Phillips* v. *Eyre* Willes J. said that

The civil liability arising out of a wrong derives its birth from the law of the place, and its character is determined by that law.[73]

This is a characteristic statement of the notorious vested rights theory, but the formulation of the rule for torts enunciated by that case, especially in the light of later interpretations in subsequent cases, shows that only lip-service has been paid to it in English law. First, the plaintiff only has to prove actionability by the *lex fori*, and, second, it is not necessary that the act be a tort by the *lex loci delicti*, provided at least that it is not 'justifiable'. Even if the decisions equating 'justifiability' with 'innocence' are not acceptable, it is clear that English law does not regard the foreign law as an indispensable part of the cause of action, and in the rules regarding tortious conduct does not indulge in presumptions about the foreign law being identical with the forum law. In tort claims foreign law operates only as a defence.[74]

As it operated in the United States the vested rights theory made any claim 'arising' in a foreign jurisdiction the 'creation' of that jurisdiction. Its basic philosophical premise was the territoriality of law; only a state with jurisdiction could create a right, and that right appeared to operate of its own accord.

The result was that 'the general and almost universal rule is that the character of an act as lawful or unlawful must be determined wholly by the law of the country where the act is done'.[75] It was early recognised[76] that the right cannot arise of its own accord, and that the forum itself must have a rule pointing to the relevant foreign jurisdiction. There was no super-law which determined what the place of a tort was. So the efforts of Cook and Lorenzen were directed at the ambiguity of such phrases as 'place of the

[73] (1870) LR 6 QB 1, 28.   [74] Compare Dicey, p. 935.

[75] *American Banana Co.* v. *United Fruit Co.* (1909) 213 US 347, 356. *per* Holmes J. But see Learned Hand J. in *Guinness* v. *Miller* (1923) 291 F. 768, 770 (SDNY), *aff'd* (1924) 299 F. 538 (2d Cir.), *aff'd* (1925) 269 US 71.

[76] The leading criticisms of the vested rights theory are those of Cook and Lorenzen. See, e.g., Cook, *Legal and Logical Bases of the Conflict of Laws* (1942) pp. 314–324; Lorenzen, *Selected Articles on the Conflict of Laws* (1947) pp. 1–18, 279–288, 362–364; Cheatham, 'American Theories of Conflict of Laws: Their Role and Utility' (1945) 58 Harv. L. Rev. 361, 379–385; Cheatham, 'Problems and Methods in the Conflict of Laws' (1960) 99 *Hague Recueil* 233, 278–291. For the more positivist, and jurisprudentially sounder, views of Judge Learned Hand see Cavers, 'The Two "Local Law" Theories' (1950) 63 Harv. L. Rev. 822.

tort' or 'place of contracting' as demonstrating the fallacy of the vested rights theory. But the borderland between contract and tort provided an even better example of the shortcomings of that theory. Even if the place of the tort and place of contracting were suitable rules for decision, when a choice between them was necessary, only the forum could make that choice. In 1935 the Supreme Court held that at least two states had the constitutional power to legislate on workmen's compensation, the state of the employment contract and the state of the tort, without denial of due process.[77] Since both states could 'create' rights, a choice between them could not be compelled by any notion of vested rights.

Perhaps the sole virtue of the vested rights theory was that it did not require actionability by the domestic law of the forum. But it left a legacy of inflexible and artificial rules for the resolution of inter-state conflicts. In contract law, it provided the dogmatic place of contracting rule espoused by the *Restatement*[78] for the validity of contracts, and a justification for denying autonomy to the parties in the section of the governing law. But it is doubtful whether the strict rules for contracts deduced from the theory ever represented the law.[79] The English rule of the proper law, the law intended by the parties or the law with which the transaction had its closest connection, was as far removed from the *Restatement* as it was close to the actual trend of the decisions. But it was not until 1945 that the various rules on the place of contracting, the place of performance, and the law which the contracting parties may be presumed to have in contemplation were rationalised into a rule providing for the application of the 'law of that state with which the facts are in most intimate contact'.[80] In 1954, in *Auten* v. *Auten*,[81] the New York Court of Appeals laid down a test of 'grouping of contacts' and 'center of gravity' which has been generally approved, not least by the authors of the *Second Restatement* with their formula that a contract is governed by 'the state with which the contract has its most significant relationship'.[82]

Whereas in contracts the vested rights theories and the first *Restatement* were faced with a mass of cases which were irreconcilable with their theories, in torts these same theorists were instrumental in creating the law. The decisions survived the theories. 'If a cause of action in tort is created at the place of wrong, a cause of action will be recognised in other states. If no cause of action is created at the place of wrong, no recovery in

---

[77] See *Alaska Packers Assn.* v. *Industrial Accident Commn.* (1935) 294 US 532.

[78] s. 332.

[79] See Nussbaum, 'Conflict Theories of Contracts: Cases Versus Restatement' (1942) 51 Yale LJ 893.

[80] *WH Barber Co.* v. *Hughes* (1945) 223 Ind. 570, 586, 63 NE 2d 417, 433.

[81] (1954) 308 NY 155, 124 NE 2d 99.

[82] *Restatement (Second), Conflict of Laws*, Tentative Draft No. 6 (1960) s. 332b.

tort can be had in any other state.'[83] It was such a rule that led to the decision in *Walton* v. *Arabian American Oil Co.*[84] Although the injustice in that case concerned the burden of proof put on a transient plaintiff, Judge Frank showed himself highly sympathetic to criticisms of the traditional rule, which was in his opinion unduly influenced by notions derived from Hobbesian sovereignty. There was increasing clamour for a revision of the rule to avoid the arbitrary and unjust results to which the rule could lead, and to the eventual adoption of a more flexible rule by the proposed *Second Restatement*,[85] and especially by a number of decisions fully articulating the reasons for the rejection of the old rule and the adoption of a new one.

A relationship of master and servant, carrier and passenger, or vendor and vendee may provide a basis for the contention that a case should be characterized as one of contract rather than tort.

These are the words not, as one might expect, of a traditionalist, but as a comment to the proposed *Second Restatement*.[86] It goes on to suggest that under its proposed rules the same result may be reached however the problem is characterised. But it is noteworthy that the terminology of characterisation is still employed at a time when it is coming under increasing attack.[87]

Just as in domestic law there are frequently advantages in suing in contract rather than tort, or vice versa, for example, because of differing measures of damages or differing statutes of limitation, so in conflicts it is often more advantageous to rely on a contract theory for questions of damages,[88] statutes of limitation[89] or burden of proof.[90]

As in English law, there are areas of regular concurrence in American law. Employment contracts are an obvious example. The doctrine of common employment was normally pigeon-holed in the tort category. For example, in *Alabama Great Southern RR Co.* v. *Carroll*,[91] the plaintiff was injured in Mississippi in the course of his employment. He sued in Alabama, where the contract of employment was made arguing that the

---

[83] *Restatement, Conflict of Laws* (1934), s. 384.   [84] *Supra*, note 71.

[85] See *Restatement (Second) Conflict of Laws*, Tentative Draft No. 9 (1964) s. 379, proposing the law of the state with 'the most significant relationship'. The pioneering work was Morris, 'The Proper Law of a Tort' (1951) 64 Harv. L. Rev. 881.

[86] s. 379, *comment g.*

[87] See, e.g., Ehrenzweig, 'Characterization in the Conflict of Laws: An Unwelcome Addition to American Doctrine', in *XXth Century Comparative and Conflicts Law* (1961) pp. 395–408.

[88] See, e.g., *Kilberg* v. *Northeast Airlines* (1961) 9 NY 2d 34, 172 NE 2d 526; *Maynard* v. *Eastern Airlines* (1949) 178 F. 2d 139 (2d Cir.).

[89] See, e.g., *Williams* v. *Illinois Central RR Co.* (1950) 229 SW 2d 1 (Mo.).

[90] See, e.g., *Hollinquest* v. *Kansas City So. Ry.* (1950) 88 F. Supp. 905 (WD La.).

[91] (1892) 97 Ala. 126, 11 So. 803.

Alabama statute making employers liable became a term of the contract. The court held that not only did the statute not apply on the facts, applying only to accidents in Alabama, but also that the duties involved in the cause of action rested not on contract but on tort. The opposite view was taken in North Carolina.[92] In general, however, in workmen's compensation cases 'American courts have attempted to solve conflict problems by the choice of jurisdiction rather than by the choice of law'.[93] The Supreme Court has allowed jurisdiction, *inter alia*, to the state where the accident occurred[94] and to the state where the contract of employment is centred.[95] In *Lauritzen* v. *Larsen*[96] the Supreme Court, indicating that a Jones Act suit was one for a Maritime *tort*, said that the law of the contract was not a substantial influence in the choice between competing laws to govern a Maritime tort.

Fact situations involving inter-state carriage have given rise to more frequent problems. An early case adopting a strict view that only the *lex loci delicti* was relevant is *Pittsburgh CC & St. L. Ry.* v. *Grom*.[97] In that case a round-trip ticket was bought in Kentucky for a journey to Atlantic City. It was held that the negligence must be measured by the law of Pennsylvania, which had no *res ipsa loquitur*. In enunciating a strict vested rights approach, the court said that rights given under the *lex loci delicti* can only be taken away by that law. However, the better view is that such actions sound in both contract and tort, and so railway passengers have been able to take advantage of more favourable standards of proof[98] and longer statutes of limitation[99] by being allowed to frame their causes of action in contract. But if the accident results in death, it appears from the decisions that the plaintiff suing under a wrongful death statute was unable to escape any limitations on the right of recovery imposed under the *lex loci delicti* by suing on the contract of carriage. In *Maynard* v. *Eastern Airlines*[100] the deceased bought a ticket in New York for a trip to Boston. He was killed in Connecticut, where recovery was limited to 20,000 dollars. Suit was brought in a federal court in New York. The plaintiff, to avoid the Connecticut limitation, sought to rely on a contract theory since the contract of carriage was made in New York and there was a good case that

---

[92] See *Williams* v. *Southern R. Co.* (1901) 128 NC 286, 38 SE 893.

[93] Ehrenzweig, *Conflict of Laws* (1962) p. 604.

[94] See *Pacific Employers Assn.* v. *Industrial Accident Commn.* (1939) 306 US 493; *Carroll* v. *Lanza* (1955) 349 US 408.

[95] See *Alaska Packers Assn.* v. *Industrial Accident Commn.*, *supra*, note 77.

[96] (1953) 345 US 571, 588–589.

[97] (1911) 133 SW 977 (Ky. Ct. of App.).

[98] *Hollinquest* v. *Kansas City So. Ry.*, *supra*, note 90.

[99] *Williams* v. *Illinois Central RR Co.*, *supra*, note 89. See also *Sawyer* v. *El Paso & NE Ry.* (1908) 108 SW 718 (Tex.). But see *Rauton* v. *Pullman* (1937) 183 SC 495, 191 SE 416.

[100] (1949) 178 F. 2d 139 (2d Cir.).

New York law governed the contract of carriage. The Second Circuit held that no action would lie on an implied contract. The reason was that the 'gravamen' of the action was in tort. This spurious characterisation technique was rejected in the unorthodox case of *Kilberg* v. *Northeast Airlines*.[101] The deceased was a New York domiciliary who bought a ticket in New York for a journey to Massachusetts. He was killed in Massachusetts. The Massachusetts wrongful death statute limited recovery to a maximum of 15,000 dollars. The administrator of the deceased sued both under the Massachusetts statute and for breach of the contract of carriage. The New York Court of Appeals affirmed the dismissal of the contract action by the lower court. The reasoning was not that of *Maynard* v. *Eastern Airlines* and its 'gravamen' theory, but that wrongful death actions are unknown to the common law and derive from statute only; moreover, the statute which governs is that of the place of injury. The court did recognise, however, that if the alleged contract breach had caused injuries not resulting in death, a contract suit based on New York law would be available.[102]

But that was not the end of the matter. For the court then went on to suggest that the Massachusetts limitation should be disregarded on two grounds: first, that such a limitation was contrary to New York public policy as expressed in its Constitution; secondly, it adopted a view of damages which though close to some English views[103] was a novel one in the American law, and found little subsequent support.[104] It held that the measure of damages was a procedural or remedial (treated as synonymous) question to be governed by the law of the forum, New York. The constitutionality of the reasoning was subsequently upheld.[105]

In *Kilberg* v. *Northeast Airlines* the device used to avoid the harshness of the *lex loci delicti* rule as applied to a New York domiciliary on a journey to begin and end in New York was no less artificial than the rule itself. To call the question of whether a plaintiff is to receive 15,000 or 150,000 dollars a procedural matter is to call into question the usefulness of any technique of characterisation except as a device of the last resort to avoid accepted but harsh rules. The claim in contract was only important as a device for avoiding the Massachusetts limitation. What was clear was that if the court could have adopted a contract approach it would not have hesitated

---

[101] (1961) 9 NY 2d 34, 172 NE 2d 526.

[102] See *Dyke* v. *Erie Ry.* (1871) 45 NY 113; *Fish* v. *Delaware, L. & WR Co.* (1914) 211 NY 374, 105 NE 661, *appeal dismissed* (1917) 245 US 675.

[103] See Dicey, pp. 962–965.

[104] See *Davenport* v. *Webb* (1962) 11 NY 2d 392, 183 NE 2d 902, holding that the law of the state of injury governs the question of prejudgment interest. Compare *Berner* v. *British Commonwealth Pacific Airlines Ltd.* (1964) 230 F. Supp. 240 (SDNY).

[105] See *Pearson* v. *Northeast Airlines* (1962) 309 F. 2d 553 (2d Cir.), *cert. denied* 374 US 913. See also *Gore* v. *Northeast Airlines* (1963) 222 F. Supp. 50 (SDNY).

to do so. In *Maynard* v. *Eastern Airlines* the reasoning was purely conceptualistic.[106]

It was the attempt to avoid the harshness of the place of the wrong rule that inspired the reasoning behind what is also an exceptional decision, the Connecticut case of *Levy* v. *Daniels' U-Drive Auto Renting Co.*[107] A Connecticut company rented a car in that state to a resident of the state. Levy was a passenger when he was injured in Massachusetts through the negligence of the driver. A Connecticut statute purported to make any person renting a motor-vehicle liable for any damage caused by its operation. Massachusetts had no such statute. The statute was interpreted to mean 'liable for tortious damage', but its provision for liability was held to be incorporated into every contract of hiring in Connecticut. So, according to the court, the plaintiff had to prove the driver's tortious conduct by Massachusetts law, but once this was proved, it was not necessary to show that the defendant was liable under Massachusetts law, for 'the right of the plaintiff as a beneficiary of this contract to maintain this action is no longer an open question in this state'.[108]

In this way somewhat formalistic reasoning was employed to give effect to the policy of the Connecticut statute, which was to protect the safety of traffic by inducing companies to rent only to competent and careful drivers. Vicarious liability is a category that does not fit well with the vested rights theory, and the courts have been reluctant to refer all problems of vicarious liability to the *lex loci delicti*. There is no problem under the traditional theories if both the actor and his principal are within the same state, but if the defendant sought to be made vicariously liable is outside, the courts have usually required that the defendant have some connection with the *locus delicti*.[109] If the *lex loci delicti* imposed no vicarious liability, the escape route under the traditional law was the contractual approach, but this has found little support.[110]

Carried to extreme lengths the use of a contractual approach could have all but destroyed the primacy of the *lex loci delicti*. It has already been seen that the Supreme Court of Canada[111] rejected the notion of implied contract in an effort by the plaintiff to avoid Ontario's guest statute. When the important case *Babcock* v. *Jackson*[112] was before the New York

---

[106] See Ehrenzweig, *supra*, note 87, at 397–398. See also *Herman* v. *Northeast Airlines* (1957) 149 F. Supp. 417, 420 (EDNY).   [107] (1928) 108 Conn. 333, 143 A. 163.

[108] *Ibid.*, at 339, 143 A. at 165. See also *Graham* v. *Wilkins* (1958) 145 Conn. 34, 138 A. 2d 705.

[109] See Reese & Flesch, 'Agency and Vicarious Liability in the Conflict of Laws' (1960) 60 Col. L. Rev. 764; *Restatement (Second), Conflict of Laws*, Tentative Draft No. 6 (1960) s. 390 (f). But see Ehrenzweig, 'Vicarious Liability in the Conflict of Laws' (1960) 69 Yale LJ 978.

[110] See *Hansemann* v. *Hamilton* (1959) 176 F. Supp. 371 (DC Col.).

[111] *McLean* v. *Pettigrew, supra*, note 48.

[112] (1963) 12 NY 2d 473, 191 NE 2d 279, *reversing* (1962) 17 App. Div. 2d 694, 230 NYS 2d 114.

Appellate Division (which applied the place of injury rule to deny recovery to a New York guest from a New York host because the accident occurred in Ontario), Judge Halpern, in a vigorous dissent, suggested five ways of avoiding a strictly territorial result.[113] One of these was the contractual argument:

[T]he implied promise by the defendant to drive the automobile with care, even though gratuitous in origin, would become an enforceable one, once the plaintiff had become a passenger in the defendant's automobile in reliance upon the defendant's promise. The defendant would then be liable for any injury suffered by the plaintiff by the reason of the defendant's breach of his voluntary promise . . . The law of New York would be the governing law of the contract, either under the traditional choice-of-law rule in contracts or under the 'center of gravity' rule of *Auten* v. *Auten*.[114]

The eventual disposition of the case shows the reason for this argument. In almost no case is purely conceptual analysis used to distinguish contract and tort. *Maynard* v. *Eastern Airlines* is a notable exception. What the courts appear to do is to apply forum law by a contractual characterisation if they can. If, however, they are faced with a line of precedents against such a course, as in *Kilberg*, another way out has to be found. If the situation is novel, it will depend on the timidity of the court whether it comes out like the lower courts in *Babcock* or adopts an unorthodox approach like that of *Levy* v. *Daniels' U-Drive*.

A pressing problem of automobile liability in the conflict of laws is that of the 'direct action' statute. State X has a statute which provides that if an accident occurs within its borders the injured person may sue the insurer directly without first establishing the liability of the insured in a prior suit. The insurance policy is issued in State Y with a provision that no action may be maintained against the insurer until the liability of the insured is first established. It has been seen that the analytic approach of Dicey and a recent Australian case requires the court first to determine that the conduct is tortious by the conflicts rules of the forum and then that the contract of insurance allows a direct action. Similar suggestions have been made in the American literature,[115] but the cases are on the whole not reconcilable with any such approach. The Supreme Court has held that a state may subject an out-of-state insurance company to direct action if the accident occurs in the state, even if the policy prohibits direct action.[116] Louisiana's statute overrides such no-action clauses, even if valid under the law governing the contract.[117] Wisconsin decisions have given effect to no-

---

[113] They were (1) public policy, (2) 'center of gravity' theory, (3) characterisation as contract, (4) the English choice of law rule as applied in Canada, (5) *renvoi*, a reference to the whole law of Ontario, asking whether the Ontario guest statute applied in such a situation.

[114] 230 NYS 2d at 123.   [115] See, e.g., Note (1960) 74 Harv. L. Rev. 357, 375.

[116] *Watson* v. *Employers Liability Assurance Corp. Ltd.* (1954) 348 US 66.

[117] As in the *Watson* case, *supra*.

action clauses under the old direct-action statute, which has, however, been amended to override these clauses.[118]

The statutes have not fared very well in third states. A variety of techniques has been used to avoid the application. A right of direct action has been held contrary to public policy in Illinois[119] and, until recently, in New York,[120] as prejudicial to the jury for notice of possible insurance coverage. Statutes giving such rights have been held procedural in Texas,[121] Illinois[122] and Mississippi[123] with the result that they are considered purely local and not to be enforced in other states. There is no uniformity and no attempt at systematic analysis. In this area the borderland of contract and tort can only lead to chaos. If states have the power to overide contractual terms for this purpose, then other states are capable of recognising that power. But the difficulty of finding a compromise between the expectations of the parties as expressed in the contract of insurance and the interest of the state of injury in providing more effective tort remedies has not led to rules similar to those on vicarious liability, an analogous area, but instead to a philosophy of 'give-it-up'.

The direct-action statute problem shows that in mixed contract-tort situations the courts have eschewed a formal approach and have shown no inclination to attribute primacy to either the contractual or tortious elements in the situation. Instead it is the public policy of the forum which dominates this area. A similar conclusion holds good for pre-tort and post-tort releases.[124] For example, it was said in *Siegelman* v. *Cunard White Star*,[125] discussing an earlier decision,[126]

> It is true that in that case there was no defense, as there is here, based on a contract . . . but we do not think that should change the result. That might be a ground for judging the claim [based on a maritime tort] and the defense by different laws.

There can be no logical answer to the question of how to resolve a conflict

---

[118] WSA 260.11. For cases giving effect to 'no action' clauses, see, e.g., *Kranig* v. *State Farm Mutual Ins.* (1960) 9 Wis. 2d 214, 101 NW 2d 117; *Orn* v. *Universal Automobile Assn.* (1961) 198 F. Supp. 377 (ED Wis.).

[119] See *Mutual Service Casualty* v. *Providence Mutual Casualty* (1960) 25 Ill. App. 2d 429, 166 NE 2d 316.

[120] See *Morton* v. *Maryland Casualty* (1955) 1 App. Div. 2d 892, 148 NYS 2d 524, aff'd (1957) 4 NY 2d. 488, 151 NE 2d 881. But see, for an opposite conclusion, *Collins* v. *American Automobile Assurance Co.* (1956) 230 F. 2d 416 (2d Cir.). See Note (1957) 57 Col. L. Rev. 256. See also *Oltarsh* v. *Aetna Insurance Co.* (1965) 15 NY 2d 111, 204 NE 2d 622.

[121] See *Penny* v. *Powell* (1961) 162 Tex. 497, 347 SW 2d 601.

[122] *Supra*, note 119.

[123] *Cook* v. *State Farm Mutual* (1961) 128 So. 2d 363 (Miss.).

[124] See Note (1960) 60 Col. L. Rev. 522; Annot. (1953) 30 ALR 2d 1398; Sinclair, 'Conflict of Laws Problems in Admiralty—The Passenger Ticket' (1963) 17 SWLJ 521.

[125] (1955) 221 F. 2d 189 at 193 (2d Cir.).

[126] *Jansson* v. *Swedish American Line* (1950) 185 F. 2d 212 (1st Cir.).

between the *lex loci delicti* and the *lex contractus* if their attitudes to limitations of liability differ. The place of injury may forbid limitation and the law governing the contract may allow it. If the place of injury is also the forum, then an easy answer is to deny the defence on the ground of public policy.[127] In one case[128] the forum was a federal court in California, the place where the contract was entered into was Florida, and the injury to the plaintiff occurred in Kansas. The plaintiff was a trapeze artist employed by the defendants under a contract with sweeping exceptions. The court determined their scope and validity by the *lex contractus*, but was also careful to point out that they were valid by Kansas law, the *lex loci delicti*.

When limitations have been valid by the *lex loci delicti* but invalid by the *lex contractus*, courts have been willing to adopt the argument of the plaintiff that the action is founded on the contract. In a New York case,[129] the court tested the limitation by Michigan law as the law of the contract even though the injury occurred in New York. In *Conklin* v. *Canadian Colonial Airways*[130] the deceased bought a ticket in New York for a flight to Newark. The contract stipulated that the carrier should not be liable for more than 5,000 dollars. The court held that its validity was to be determined by the law of New York, where such a limitation was forbidden,[131] though the crash took place in New Jersey.

The effect of post-tort releases has generally been assigned to the law of the state which is held to govern the original tort. Often the process has been entirely mechanical. In *Bittner* v. *Little*[132] the Third Circuit was faced with a contract which, according to the plaintiff, was a covenant not to sue under New York law. The defendants claimed that it was a release and therefore to be governed by the law of the place of injury. The court decided the conflict by the mechanical application of the *Restatement* rule that 'a liability to pay damages for a tort can be discharged or modified by the law of the state which created it'.[133] In *Daily* v. *Somberg*,[134] however, the Supreme Court of New Jersey, though it eventually applied the same

---

[127] See, e.g., *Lake Shore & MSR Co.* v. *Teeters* (1906) 166 Ind. 335, 77 NE 599.

[128] *Ringling Bros. & Barnum & Bailey* v. *Olvera* (1941) 119 F. 2d 584 (9th Cir.). See also *Al G. Barnes* v. *Olvera* (1946) 154 F. 2d 497 (9th Cir.). Compare *Duskin* v. *Pennsylvania Central Airlines Corp.*, 167 F. 2d 727 (6th Cir.), *cert. denied* (1948) 335 US 829.

[129] See *Fish* v. *Delaware, L. & WR Co.*, *supra*, note 102. See also *Clark* v. *Southern R. Co.* (1918) 69 Ind. App. 697, 119 NE 539. But see *Smith* v. *Aitchison, T. & SFR Co.* (1912) 194 F. 79 (8th Cir.).

[130] (1935) 266 NY 244, 194 NE 692. See also *Dyke* v. *Erie Ry.* (1871) 45 NY 113.

[131] This result is not easy to reconcile with the decision in *Kilberg* v. *Northeast Airlines*, *supra*, note 101, unless the difference be between statutory and contractual limitation. It does not appear whether there was any claim under a wrongful death statute in *Conklin*. See also *Whitford* v. *Panama R. Co.* (1861) 23 NY 465.

[132] (1959) 270 F. 2d 286 (3d Cir.). See also *De Bono* v. *Bittner*, 13 Misc. 2d 333, 178 NYS 2d 419, *appeal dismissed* (1959) 8 AD 2d 796, 190 NYS 2d 323.

[133] s. 389.   [134] (1958) 28 NJ 372, 146 A. 2d 676.

rule, at least did so with some articulation of policy. The plaintiff was injured in an accident in Ohio, and negligently treated in New Jersey. A release was executed in New Jersey which by Ohio law would have released not only the original claim which arose in Ohio but also any claim against the doctors for subsequent negligence. The court held that the tort claims should be separated:

The release of his Ohio tort claim . . . may be governed by Ohio law . . . but its effect on the New Jersey claim must in the light of the pertinent interests and policy considerations, be governed by the law of New Jersey.[135]

The pertinent interests were 'the reasonable expectations of the parties' and the 'protective rights of the plaintiff'.

The articulation of the policy interests at stake foreshadows later developments. But what should be clear from the foregoing is that a stage had been reached where the borderland of contract and tort had evolved into a network of chaos and confusion. While the rules relating to contracts had been evolving into a more liberal and flexible standard, the rules governing out-of-state torts had evolved into stringent, inflexible and often unjust territoriality. Where both sets of rules overlapped, the result was confusion.

4. THE NEW APPROACH

(*a*) How significant is a contact?

George H. Hambrecht was killed when a DC-8 in which he was a passenger crashed on landing at one of its scheduled stops. Mr. Hambrecht was a domiciliary of Pennsylvania. He was on his way from Philadelphia to Phoenix, Arizona. His round-trip ticket was bought in Philadelphia from United Air Lines, a Delaware corporation with its principal place of business in Chicago, Illinois. The crash occurred in Denver, Colorado.

The will was probated in Pennsylvania. His executors commenced an action in Pennsylvania courts under the local survival statute alleging that his death had been caused by the negligence of the defendant airline operators.

Five states have already been mentioned. In the event the conflict centred around the application of the laws of only two of those states, Pennsylvania and Colorado. What makes *Griffith* v. *United Air Lines Inc.*[136] so significant is the way it eschews the traditional choice of law rule, and the way it refuses to find an escape route either in surreptitious characterisation or in the technicalities of the forms of pleading.

The conflict arose because of the differing measures of damage supplied by Pennsylvania and Colorado law. Under the Pennsylvania survival

---

[135] *Ibid.* at 381–382, 146 A. 2d at 682.   [136] (1964) 417 Pa. 3, 203 A. 2d 796.

statute recovery could be had for loss of prospective earnings. The Colorado statute, however, provided:

> . . . in tort actions based upon personal injury, the damages recoverable . . . shall be limited to loss of earnings and expenses sustained or incurred prior to death, and shall not include . . . prospective profits or earnings after date of death.[137]

All of the relevant Pennsylvania decisions proclaimed the primacy of the place of the wrong, many of them relying on the first *Restatement*. But the time had come for a reconsideration of that rule. Quite apart from the jurisprudential inadequacies of the vested rights theory, it was being increasingly recognised that the rule pointing to the place of the wrong was inadequate from the point of view of social policy. It took no account of the many differing interests that are served by the law of torts, punitive, admonitory, compensatory, and the rest. Moreover, it failed to separate the issues involved. Was there any reason why standards of conduct, damages, survival of actions, interspousal immunity, and other issues should be subjected to one and the same jurisdiction? Should a rule formulated when movement across state boundaries was less frequent and more deliberate apply equally at a time of quick and easy mass transportation and effective communication?

What approaches could the Pennsylvania court in the *Griffith* case have taken? In the early stages of the revolt against the place of the wrong rule the techniques had been creative statutory construction and evasive characterisation. In *Schmidt* v. *Driscoll Hotel Inc.*[138] the Supreme Court of Minnesota imposed liability under its 'dram shop' statute upon a seller of alcohol for injury caused by an intoxicated person even though the injury was caused in Wisconsin. All of the parties involved were residents of Minnesota. In *Haumschild* v. *Continental Casualty*[139] the Supreme Court of Wisconsin held that incapacity to sue for negligence because of marital status is a matter of family law rather than tort law. Therefore the wife was allowed to sue in Wisconsin, the state of domicile, although California, the place of the injury, forbade such suit.

Both of the foregoing paid lip-service to the traditional rule. The court in *Griffith* v. *United Air Lines* was faced with a problem of a survival statute and its applicability to questions of damages. In the course of the growing disenchantment with the traditional rule, both of these questions had been characterised as procedural and referred to the law of the forum. Another characterisation technique, treating the action as one of contract, had been

---

[137] Colo. Rev. Stat. Ann., s. 152–1–9 (Supp.) (1960).
[138] (1957) 249 Minn. 376, 82 NW 2d 365.
[139] (1959) 7 Wis. 2 d 130, 95 NW 2d 814. See also *Thompson* v. *Thompson* (1963) 105 NH 86, 193 A. 2d 439.

attempted but without success. Was the Pennsylvania court willing to try its hand at any of these?

The court was at pains to avoid spurious and facile characterisation. It was not willing to adopt the approach of Judge Traynor in *Grant* v. *McAuliffe*[140] and use the fact that a survival statute was in issue as an excuse to characterise the question as one of administration of estates and therefore referable to forum law. It was equally unwilling to apply forum law under the approach of *Kilberg* v. *Northeast Airlines*,[141] which would have involved treating the question of damages as procedural.

It was the question whether the action should be decided on contract choice of law principles that most exercised the court in the *Griffith* case. In *Kilberg* the court had decided that no action in contract would lie for wrongful death, although it would have lain for injuries not resulting in death. In *Griffith* the plaintiff executor alleged that the airline had contracted to transport the decedent safely and that in breach of this contract had negligently operated the airplane. The court found first that there was no contract of 'safe carriage', for the carrier is not an insurer. But this did not prevent the plaintiff from asserting a breach of contract of non-negligent carriage. In the absence of any Pennsylvania decision allowing the plaintiff to elect between actions in *assumpsit* and in trespass for personal injuries caused by the negligence of carriers, the court looked to decisions in New York, Maine and England in reaching its conclusion that there were concurrent causes of action.

If an action in contract was possible, what was to be the next step? The Colorado survival statute read that '*in tort actions* . . . damages . . . shall not include . . . prospective profits of earnings'. The court could have treated this at its face value as not affecting contract actions. Or it could have treated the Colorado statute as entirely irrelevant in a Pennsylvania contract action. Instead, it eschewed any such escape route:

To so dispose of the issue would be to ignore the realities of the situation. Counsel for plaintiff admitted that this action was brought in *assumpsit* in order to avoid the effect of the Colorado limitation. Yet the recovery sought is clearly a tort recovery—damages to decedent's estate as a result of decedent's negligently caused death. The principles which will govern defendant's liability are principles of negligence, not of contract, since the action is for negligent breach, not simple breach, of contract.[142]

Thus, since negligence was the gist of the action,

The essentials of this case remain the same regardless of its label. Mere technicalities of pleading should not blind us to the true nature of the action. The choice of law will be the same whether the action is labeled trespass or *assumpsit*.[143]

---

[140] (1953) 41 Cal. 2d 859, 264 P. 2d 944. See Traynor, 'Is This Conflict Really Necessary?' (1959) 37 Tex. L. Rev. 657, for the afterthought of the judge who decided it.
[141] *Supra*, note 101. [142] 203 A. 2d at 800. [143] *Ibid.*

Naturally the next question for the court was the appropriate choice of law rule. Having abandoned any conceptual distinction between contract and tort for the purpose of the action, it was obvious that it would bring the tort choice of law rule into line with the more flexible one for contract. This does not necessitate the conclusion that the distinction would be eliminated for conflicts of laws purposes. What it does mean is that where the policies served by concurrent causes of action are the same whether the label be contract or tort, then a unifying choice of law principle must be found to accommodate those policies.

By now there will be few who do not know the outcome of the weekend trip which Miss Georgia Babcock took with Mr and Mrs Jackson to Canada. The leading case of *Babcock* v. *Jackson*[144] has been followed in some other jurisdictions, but by a quirk of the judicial system has for some reason not been given full rein in the state which gave it birth, New York.

In *Babcock* the New York Court of Appeals firmly rejected the place of the wrong rule as invariably governing all aspects of an action based on a tort committed out of state. It criticised the vested rights theory for ignoring the interest of jurisdictions other than that of the place of the wrong in the resolution of specific issues, and noted the trend of a few courts to reject, by whatever means they could, the inevitable application of the rigid rule and so apply the law with 'a more compelling interest'.

Throughout the decision runs a concern for the policies involved. The basic question is, what reason is there for applying Ontario's statute giving immunity to a host for injuries caused to his guest? Why should the Ontario rule affect the outcome of litigation between New York residents?

The opinion quotes the proposal of the *Second Restatement* Rule that the governing law is the law of the state with 'the most significant relationship with the occurrence' in the light of the *issues* and the *purposes* of the tort rules involved.[145] It then goes on to find that the interests of New York are greater and more direct. The policy of the Ontario statute is to prevent fraudulent claims by residents of Ontario against Ontario defendants and their insurers. The court does not find it relevant to inquire whether the Ontario statute applies by Ontario law to New Yorkers casually present in Ontario. All it is concerned with is how to accommodate the interests of New York in compensating its residents and the interests of Ontario in protecting its insurance companies. Fortunately for the court the fact-pattern is a very tidy one. The sole contact with Ontario is that the accident happened there. There is no Canadian involved, either as tortfeasor or as insurer. There is no suggestion that the defendant acted in reliance on Ontario law. There is no question of standard of conduct involved. 'The

---

[144] (1963) 12 NY 2d 473, 191 NE 2d 279.
[145] *Restatement (Second), Conflict of Laws*, Tentative Draft No. 8 (1963) s. 379. The most recent draft is No. 9 (1964).

issue . . . is . . . whether the plaintiff, because she was a guest in the defendant's automobile, is barred from recovering damages *for a wrong concededly committed*.'[146]

If there is any single approach in *Babcock* it is a compromise between the weighing of the interests of the states in the furtherance of their own policies, with a nod towards the expectations of the parties. Although the publicists have been very influential in the formation of new and policy-oriented choice of law rules, they differ so much in their basic philosophies that the courts feel themselves obliged to take account of every approach while adopting none. The leading cases in the new conflict of laws, *Babcock, Griffith*, and *Wilcox* v. *Wilcox*,[147] are all obviously influenced by the writers, but also find it unnecessary to adopt any particular approach. They all apply the law of the forum and they all reject the law of the place of the accident. To this extent they reflect the predominance of the law of the forum in much of the new jurisprudence.

What the vested rights theory provided was a comparatively simple and predictable method for choosing the governing law. What the local law theory left unanswered was the way in which courts should incorporate into the local law rights and defences based on some foreign laws. The problem of an alternative method in the solution of conflicts of interest has been a continuing source of controversy. The writers are virtually unanimous in rejecting the notion that in any given legal category, such as contract or tort, there is an all-embracing 'governing law'. The late Professor Currie was best known for his 'governmental interest' theory.[148] What is especially significant is the emphasis it gives to forum law, and the way in which the role of the forum is to determine if there is any conflict, and if there is any then to apply its own law. The basic approach has been several times repeated. The court when asked to apply foreign law should assume prima facie that forum law is applicable. It should then determine the governmental policy expressed in the law of the forum; then do the same for the foreign law. If only one is found to have a legitimate basis for the assertion of an interest in the application of that policy, then that rule will be applied. If both, then forum law should be applied.[149]

Ehrenzweig is in sympathy with Currie's approach, but he de-emphasises the primacy of the forum law whenever it can claim any interest. Instead the basic law is that of the forum, but pragmatic analysis, with considerable emphasis on the expectations of the parties, will show generally recognised

---

[146] 191 NE 2d at 284.   [147] (1965) 133 NW 2d 408 (Wisc.).

[148] Most of the relevant articles are collected in Currie, *Selected Essays on the Conflict of Laws* (1963). See also Currie, 'Comment on *Babcock* v. *Jackson*' (1963) 63 Col. L. Rev. 1333; Currie, 'The Disinterested Third State' (1963) 28 *Law & Contemp. Prob.* 754.

[149] See Currie, *Selected Essays* at 48, 74–76, 183–184, 367–368; Comment, 63 Col. L. Rev. at 1242–1243.

exceptions.[150] In short, for him conficts law is private law. His approach leads to some eccentric choice of law rules, such as that the law where the automobile is garaged governs questions involving guest–host immunity.[151] In particular he is opposed to the question-begging nature of the 'significant relationship' formula of the *Second Restatement*.[152] The basic philosophy of that *Restatement* is that the courts must be given a free rein to consider and accommodate a large number of interests: respect for the interests of foreign States, the policies of the rules in supposed conflict, the value of predictability and certainty, the expectations of the parties, and not least the dictates of justice.[153] Cavers[154] adds the warning that the choice of law must not be hardened into 'jurisdiction-selecting rules', which make a State the object of the choice without regard to the content of the law that is chosen or its effect on the issue before the court.

After analysing the respective interests of Ontario and New York in the outcome of litigation between New York domiciliaries over an accident that occurred in Ontario, Judge Fuld in *Babcock* concluded that it was New York that had the dominant contacts and the superior claim for application of its rule. But he employed language which Cavers warned might be used as a 'jurisdiction-selecting rule':[155]

[I]t is New York, the place where the parties resided, where their guest–host relationship arose and where the trip began and was to end, rather than Ontario . . . which has the dominant contacts . . . [T]he rights and liabilities of the parties which stem from their guest–host relationship should remain constant and not vary and shift as the automobile proceeds from place to place.[156]

Cavers' view was that if this part of the judgment were interpreted to mean that the law of the common residence determines guest–host immunity, it would ignore the interest of New York if the law-fact pattern were reversed. It would not necessarily follow, say, that a New York court should deny recovery to an Ontario guest injured by an Ontario host for an accident in New York. For that would ignore the interest of New York in inducing care on the roads and of preventing victims becoming financial burdens on the state. However, in *White* v. *Motor Vehicle Accident Indem.*

---

[150] See, e.g., Ehrenzweig, 'Choice of Law: Current Doctrine and "The Rules" ' (1961) 49 Calif. L. Rev. 240, 245; Ehrenzweig, 'The Lex Fori—Basic Rule in the Conflict of Laws' (1960) 58 Mich. L. Rev. 637.

[151] See Ehrenzweig, 'Guest Statutes in the Conflict of Laws' (1960) 69 Yale LJ 595, 603.

[152] See Ehrenzweig, 'The Most Significant Relationship in the Conflicts Law of Torts' (1963) 28 *Law & Contemp. Prob.* 700.

[153] See Reese, 'Conflict of Laws and the Restatement (Second)' (1963) 28 *Law & Contemp. Prob.* 679, 682–687.

[154] See Cavers, 'Re-Restating the Conflict of Laws: The Chapter on Contracts', in *XXth Century Comparative and Conflicts Law* (1961) pp. 349, 350.

[155] See Cavers, Comment (1963) 63 Col. L. Rev. 1219, 1222–1223.

[156] 191 NE 2d at 284–285.

Corp.[157] a lower court interpreted *Babcock* as an inflexible jurisdiction-selecting rule. It held that an Ontario resident, when proceeding on the basis of injuries received as a guest of an Ontario motorist who was involved in an accident in New York, was not a 'qualified person' entitled to proceed against the MVAIC.

But the decision has been abused in other ways. In *Dym* v. *Gordon*[158] both parties were residents of New York who had come separately to Colorado. The plaintiff was injured by the negligence of the defendant while a guest in his car. The Appellate Division held the defendant not liable under the Colorado guest statute. Colorado was the place with the dominant contacts because the parties were temporarily resident there, the guest–host relationship arose there, and the trip began and was to end in Colorado. New York's interest in providing remedies for its residents went unexamined. There was no evidence that the defendant relied on the Colorado rule. The purposes of the Colorado statute were similarly ignored. But this case is of little significance when compared with the later decision, by a bare majority, of the Appellate Division, in *Macey* v. *Rozbicki*.[159] The plaintiff and defendant were residents of Buffalo, New York. The plaintiff was a guest, for one week, of the defendant at her summer house in Ontario, near the New York border. One day on a trip to church they were involved in an accident. The vehicle was licensed, garaged and insured in New York. What was the distinction between these facts and those in *Babcock*? Clearly, the place of the accident was not quite as fortuitous as that in *Babcock*. The visit to Canada was longer by a few days. The parties had not gone to Canada together. The similarities were that both were residents of New York; Ontario had little more interest in the outcome than it had before; New York's concern was just as great; there would have been no more injustice to the parties for the court to have imposed liability. Instead, *Babcock* was treated, in effect, as laying down a rule on these lines:

Where a guest is injured by his host their rights and liabilities depend on the law of the state where the particular trip is to begin and end.

If the ratio of *Babcock* is that rights depend on the law of the state where the trip begins and ends, then presumably *Macey* v. *Rozbicki* could be limited just as well to lady drivers. Clearly, both these cases represent a revolt against new doctrine.

The Court of Appeals in *Dym* v. *Gordon*[160] did not take quite such a

---

[157] (1963) 39 Misc. 2d 678, 241 NYS 2d 566.
[158] (1964) 22 AD 2d 702, 253 NYS 2d 802, *aff'd.* (1965) 16 NY 2d 120, 209 NE 2d 792.
[159] (1965) 23 Misc. 2d 532, 256 NYS 2d 202. See also *Leonard* v. *O'Mara* (1964) 22 AD 2d 835, 253 NYS 2d 826.
[160] (1965) 16 NY 2d 120, 209 NE 2d 272.

restrictive view of *Babcock* as had the Appellate Division. Nevertheless it gave effect to the Colorado guest statute on the theory that

Colorado has such significant contacts with the *relationship* itself and the *basis of its formation* the application of its law and underlying policy are clearly warranted.[161]

Judge Fuld, the author of the opinions in *Auten* and *Babcock*, dissented. He felt that the court in taking such a narrow approach by treating the place where the relationship arose as decisive was frustrating the liberal purpose of *Babcock*.

Babcock v. *Jackson* has thus had a checkered career in New York courts, both state[162] and federal,[163] but its liberalising influence, despite these setbacks, continues to grow.[164] But so far it is the only case in New York of any authority which reached a result which would have been different under the *lex loci delicti* rule.

Mr and Mrs Wilcox were returning to Wisconsin, their home, from a vacation in Nebraska. On their way home, an accident occurred in Nebraska, and Nebraska had a guest statute making the liability of the host dependent on a showing of gross negligence. Wisconsin has no such statute. In a suit brought in Wisconsin the trial judge held that the *lex loci delicti* governed and that therefore gross negligence must be proved. The Supreme Court of Wisconsin reversed: *Wilcox* v. *Wilcox*.[165] The case contains a more elaborate discussion of case law and theory than does *Babcock* but as before there is a mixture of jurisdiction-selecting tendencies and analyses of governmental interests and of the policies expressed in the competing laws.

There appears to be no reason why the duty of the host to the guest should vary on the basis of factors . . . not . . . related to the public policy of the state most intimately concerned or associated with a changed relationship between the parties.[166]

This formulation, very similar to that in *Babcock*, at first sight is the kind of choice of law rule that the same court applied in the *Haumschild* case to

---

[161] *Ibid.* at 125, 209 NE 2d at 794.

[162] See *Fornaro* v. *Jill Bros.* (1964) 22 AD 2d 695, 253 NYS 2d 771; *Ardieta* v. *Young* (1965) 22 AD 2d 349, 256 NYS 2d 199. See also *Keller* v. *Greyhound Corp.* (1963) 41 Misc. 2d 255, 244 NYS 2d 882; *Manning* v. *Hyland* (1964) 42 Misc. 2d 381, 249 NYS 2d 381; *Blum* v. *American Hostels* (1964) 21 AD 2d 683, 250 NYS 2d 522; *In Re O'Connor's Estate* (1964) 21 AD 2d 333, 250 NYS 2d 696; *Brewi* v. *Handrich* (1965) 45 Misc. 2d 121, 256 NYS 2d 171; *Murphy* v. *Barron* (1965) 45 Misc. 2d 940, 258 NYS 2d 139.

[163] See *King* v. *Hildebrandt* (1964) 331 F. 2d 476 (2d Cir.); *Flexitized Inc.* v. *National Flexitized Corp.* (1964) 335 F. 2d 774 (2d Cir.); *Mertens* v. *Flying Tiger Line* (1964) 341 F. 2d 851, 858 (2d Cir.); *Skahill* v. *Capital Airlines Inc.* (1964) 234 F. Supp. 906 (SDNY); *Pallen* v. *Allied Van Lines Inc.* (1963) 223 F. Supp. 394 (SDNY).

[164] See, e.g., *Oltarsh* v. *Aetna Insurance Co.* (1965) 15 NY 2d 111, 204 NE 2d 622, holding a foreign direct-action statute enforceable in New York.

[165] (1965) 133 NW 2d 408 (Wisc.).   [166] *Ibid.* at 415.

relegate interspousal immunity to the law of the domicile. But the court's analysis of the policy interests is more explicit than that in *Babcock*, and it would seem that *Wilcox* has insulated itself from the danger of being abused in the way that *Babcock* has been in New York. The Wisconsin court first noted the contacts with its own state: the parties were residents, the trip was to begin and end there, the insurance policy was issued by a Wisconsin company, and the car was licensed and garaged in Wisconsin. Wisconsin's policy is to provide compensation for a person negligently injured, for a variety of reasons, including the prevention of the burden falling on the injured person or the state authorities and the deterrence of negligent conduct. Nebraska's policy was said to be the prevention of ingratitude of a guest against his kindly host and the prevention of collusive law-suits against insurance companies. But, the court said, Nebraska's policy was directed at Nebraska parties and Nebraska insurance companies.

This was a very similar analysis to that in *Babcock*, but the court went on to lay greater stress on the expectations of the parties. The occurrence outside the state with which the parties were familiar was quite fortuitous. With a nod toward the views of Ehrenzweig, the court noted that the insurance policy was issued in Wisconsin and that it was the law of Wisconsin that was anticipated and insured against.

The basic approach of the court was summed up as follows:

[I]f the forum state is concerned it will not favor the application of a rule repugnant to its own policies, and . . . the law of the forum should presumptively apply unless it becomes clear that nonforum contacts are of the greater significance.[167]

Thus the clear trend of the decisions is away from the *lex loci delicti*, relegated by *Wilcox* to the 'nether world of jurisprudence'. Less fully articulated decisions have been rendered by the Supreme Court of Iowa in *Fabricius* v. *Horgen*,[168] and by the Court of Appeals for the Seventh Circuit in *Watts* v. *Pioneer Corn Co. Inc.*,[169] both decided in recent months. But we are still without a decision of a court of authority which admits an exception to the *lex loci* rule and applies some law other than its own. It is facile to say that the new approach encourages forum-shopping without asking why it is that forum-shopping is to be deprecated. Traditional conflicts law has placed great emphasis on the premise that the result of litigation should not depend on the choice of the forum. With the extension of bases of jurisdiction and with the use of techniques of characterisation more and more has come to depend on the choice of forum. The policy underlying the announced need to avoid forum-shopping is clearly the interests of the defendant. It is that the legitimate

---

[167] *Ibid.* at 416. [168] (1965) 132 NW 2d 410 (Iowa).
[169] (1965) 342 F. 2d 617 (7th Cir.). See also *Gianni* v. *Fort Wayne Air Service Inc.* (1965) 342 F. 2d 621 (7th Cir.).

expectations of the parties should be respected and that the defendant should not be caught by an unexpected law. Justified action in reliance on one law should be protected in other states.

But what are 'legitimate' expectations? What action is 'justified'? How 'unexpected' can a law be? There is an unavoidable tendency for a court to apply its own law. This tendency will be reinforced if it is to consider how its policies are going to be furthered in situations where previously it would have applied the *lex loci*. The 'counting-up' of contacts without reference to the policies involved is frequently warned against. But at least such a process places greater emphasis on what the parties are likley to expect. The greatest virtue of the Ehrenzweig approach is the emphasis that is laid on the factor of insurance. The weakness of the governmental interests theory is the tendency to treat conflicts questions as those of public rather than private law. For under the public law approach the interests of the forum will be given primacy over the interests of the parties. It was in reaction against such a trend that Judge Burke, speaking for a majority of the New York Court of Appeals in *Dym* v. *Gordon*, castigated the approach

which blithely applies the public policy of the forum under the denomination of 'governmental interests'.[170]

(b) Contract or tort: revisited

The preceding sections began with the facts of *Griffith* v. *United Air Lines*, and went on to consider the approaches which it rejected, and to describe the milieu in which it was decided. The question, it will be recalled, was whether the Colorado rule on measure of damages was to apply, Colorado being the place of injury, or whether greater recovery would be granted under the law of Pennsylvania, where the decedent was domiciled, bought his ticket, and where his estate was being administered.

The opinion, reflecting all the usual influences, attempts an analysis of the policy factors at stake. Under this analysis the state where the injury occurred has little interest in the amount of damages recoverable unless the defendant acted in reliance on that state's rule. This appears to run together the arguments of governmental interest and those giving primacy to the expectations of the parties. A very speculative analysis of the policies of the Colorado statute excluding prospective earnings was then made. The court felt that the Colorado statute was intended to prevent Colorado courts from engaging in speculative computation of expected earnings; or perhaps it was based on purely local procedural considerations; or perhaps it was intended to protect Colorado defendants from large

---

[170] 16 NY 2d at 126, 209 NE 2d at 795.

judgments. None of these militated against a judgment by a Pennsylvania court against a defendant not domiciled in Colorado in favour of a Pennsylvania resident. Moreover, like New York in *Kilberg*, Pennsylvania had a strong public policy against limitation of liability, expressed in its Constitution.[171]

United could reasonably anticipate that it might be subject to the laws of such states (as do not limit recovery) and could financially protect itself against such eventuality. The element of surprise is lacking.[172]

It is suggested that such an approach is preferable to largely speculative consideration of the policies involved in the laws of other states.

What of the breakdown of the distinction between contract and tort that is the nub of the *Griffith* decision? 'Mere technicalities of pleading' were not to affect the result. While it is true that many terms implied by the courts into contracts fulfil the same purposes as most tort rules, it does not follow that the borderland had disappeared in the conflict of laws. Just as the contract-tort dichotomy shows one of the weaknesses in the vested rights approach of the first *Restatement*, so it emphasises exactly how tentative are the tentative drafts of the *Second Restatement*.

Perhaps the *Second Restatement* is a little too cautious in suggesting that in some cases the application of the rule of most significant relationship expressed for both contracts and torts may lead to the same result whether a problem is characterised as one of tort or contract.[173] Two extremes are possible: on the one hand, there is the tendency in *Griffith* to assimilate the two, though perhaps only for the limited purpose of determining the principle to be applied in negligent breach of contract resulting in personal injury; on the other are the lists of contacts suggested in the *Second Restatement* which might lead to the conclusion that never the twain shall meet.

The forum will consider in determining with which state a contract has its most significant relationship, or so the *Restatement* hopes, the following factors: place of contracting, negotiation or performance, the *situs* of the subject-matter and the domicile or place of business of the parties.[174] Naturally the order is only a guide, none of the factors is conclusive, and the list is not exhaustive. But it is noteworthy that when one turns to the corresponding list for torts,[175] one finds that the court is directed to the place of injury, conduct, domicile or place of business of the parties, and lastly to the place where the relationship, if any, between the parties is

---

[171] *Kilberg* and *Griffith* were treated as decisions on public policy in *Wiener* v. *United Air Lines* (1964) 237 F. Supp. 90, 95 (SD Cal.).   [172] 203 A. 2d at 807.

[173] *Restatement (Second), Conflict of Laws*, Tentative draft No. 9 (1964) s. 379, comment g.

[174] *Ibid.*, Tentative Draft No. 6 (1960) s. 332 (b) (1).

[175] s. 379 (2) (a)–(d).

centred. The factors might intercept each other at the place of performance if the injury occurs there, but it is only when one reaches the last category under the tort factors that they really meet. No guide is given to the court as to how it is to accommodate the policies respectively served by the law of contract and of tort.

Two years before the *Griffith* case a federal court in Pennsylvania had adopted a similar approach with regard to the relationship of contract and tort. In *Getty Oil Co.* v. *Mills*[176] the question was whether the defendant was liable for one and a half million dollars' worth of damage allegedly caused through negligent inspection of a pipeline which was later used by the plaintiff as part of a pipeline to transport oil to the Persian Gulf. The court held that there was no evidence to support a recovery in contract on the basis of agency or third-party beneficiary. But it pointed out the facts relied upon to support such a recovery would be the same as those alleged to constitute negligence. The real issue, said the court, was whether the inspection was negligent.

But this is by no means a self-evident proposition. Though in certain circumstances if the sole issue is whether the defendant is negligent the contracts may lead to one law, a conflict is likely to arise if a business relationship is centred in a jurisdiction which requires a showing of negligence and the place of injury imposes strict liability, or vice versa. There might be a very real conflict between the policies expressed in the law of contract to protect justified expectations of the parties and in the law of tort to distribute the risks of modern industrialised society. Moreover, it is not clear that a conceptual analysis can entirely be abandoned.

The still relevant borderland of contract and tort is illustrated by litigation in New York federal courts over an airplane crash which occurred in Florida. A DC-7C was manufactured and sold in California by Douglas Aircraft Co. to Braniff Airways. The sale took place in 1957, and the plane crashed in Florida in 1958. The plaintiffs, members of crew, sued the Douglas Aircraft Co. in New York in 1963 for injuries sustained: *George* v. *Douglas Aircraft Co. Inc.*[177] The then New York statute of limitation allowed a six-year period for an action to recover damages for personal injury, except for an action for personal injury resulting from negligence, for which there was a three-year period.

An earlier case[178] in the Southern District of New York had pointed out that

The New York cases discussing a cause of action for personal injuries based on a breach of implied warranty defy characterization within the classical framework of

---

[176] (1962) 204 F. Supp. 179 (D. Pa.). See also *Ruberoid Co.* v. *Roy* (1965) 240 F. Supp. 7 (ED La.).   [177] 332 F. 2d 73 (2d Cir.) *cert. denied* (1964) 379 US 904.
[178] *Public Administrator* v. *Curtiss-Wright Corp.* (1963) 224 F. Supp. 236 (SDNY).

'contract' or 'tort' liability . . . However, the conflict of laws rules of the forum eliminate the need for strict classification of the cause of action before us. In *Babcock* v. *Jackson* . . . the New York Court of Appeals applied essentially the same conflict of late rule to a tort cause of action as it had previously applied to a contract cause of action in *Auten* v. *Auten*.[179]

But the court, while noting the similarity of approach between *Babcock* and *Auten*, did not realise that they do not necessarily stand for the same *rule*, if they stand for any rule at all. The approach may lead to the same results, but the issues must be closely related before that can happen.

The question at issue in the *Douglas Aircraft* case was which statute of limitations applied, that of Florida, where the accident occurred, or that of California, where the plane was manufactured and delivered. Calfornia had a one-year statute of limitations for actions based on personal injury, which applied to both contract and tort, so that if it was applicable the plaintiffs would be out of court. Florida, on the other hand, had a five-year period for contract and a four-year period for tort. The New York 'borrowing statute' incorporated the statute of limitation of any state where '*the cause of action arose*'.

The Second Circuit proceeded to draw a distinction between questions of choice of law and questions of the applicability of statutes of limitation. On the choice of law point, which was not before the court at this stage, it concluded that the law of Florida would probably govern. For as the place of injury, it had the interest in maintaining the 'general security', in Pound's phraseology, by imposing strict liability on a manufacturer; it would also be likely to incur the burden of caring for those injured within its borders; the manufacturer could provide against such liability by procuring insurance.

But the action was barred by the California one-year statute of limitations. For the purpose of the New York borrowing statute was to protect a defendant from the prolonging of liability because of his absence from a jurisdiction where there was no reason to expect him to be present. The court recognised that a major aspect of the *Babcock* decision was that it envisaged that the choice of law would depend on the particular issue involved. In this way the court reconciled the interests of the plaintiffs and the reasonable expectations of the defendant.

Having concluded that the California statute applied, the court then went on to consider, in case a New York state court might consider the action as arising in Florida, whether the five-year or the four-year Florida limitation would apply. The plaintiffs could succeed on this ground if their action were founded on a contract, which under Florida law was allowed for five years. But for the five-year period to apply the contract had to be in

---

[179] *Ibid.* at 238–239.

writing, for a three-year period applied to unwritten contracts. The difficulty was that the only written contract was between Douglas Aircraft and Braniff Airways, the operators. Florida decisions on products liability spoke in terms of 'implied warranty', but would not regard the plaintiffs as third party beneficiaries of the contract of sale. The Second Circuit felt that Florida courts would characterise the action either as in tort or on a contract implied by law. The court warned that it was

simply confusing to consider an obligation which the law imposes irrespective of the intention of the parties or even in direct contravention of their expressions as in the same category as a contractual warranty, express or fairly implied.[180]

What these cases indicate is that the courts are applying similar principles to actions based on negligence, whether considered as contract or tort, and are showing a similar tendency in cases of strict liability based on implied warranty. But it may be that if the court 'feels' that it is faced with a contract situation it may pay more attention to the expectation of the parties than it would if it had a tendency to characterise as tort. It can be said that formal characterisation has no meaning in this area; but it does not follow that age-old conceptions will no longer be influential in determining whether to further state interests at the expense of business expectations. It has been suggested that if the injured party's relation to the supplier is viewed as contractual, the state of purchase, as opposed to the state of injury, might apply its own more lenient law of liability in the interests of contractual certainty.[181]

The difficulty of what law to apply to cases of pre- and post-tort releases was largely conceptual and was confounded by the vested rights approach. The new approach will lead to more rational results. In *Bowles* v. *Zimmer Mfg. Co.*[182] the Seventh Circuit used a grouping of contracts to determine the effect of a release executed in favour of a driver who had negligently injured the plaintiff. The question was whether the release operated as a defence in favour of the manufacturer of a defective surgical pin used in treating the plaintiff after the injury. Though the action was brought in Indiana, the pin was manufactured and sold in Indiana, the court applied the law of Michigan, where the release was executed and where the plaintiff was treated. Recently, the New York Appellate Division, in *Ardieta* v. *Young*,[183] has used the *Babcock* approach to determine the effect of a release and so apply the law of Ontario.

The picture is completed by the recent liberal decision of the New York Court of Appeals in *Oltarsh* v. *Aetna Insurance Co.*[184] applying a foreign

---

[180] 332 F. 2d at 79.
[181] See Note, 'Products Liability and the Choice of Law' (1965) 78 Harv. L. Rev. 1452, 1462.   [182] (1960) 277 F. 2d 868 (7th Cir.).
[183] (1965) 22 AD 2d 349, 256 NYS 2d 199.   [184] *Supra*, note 164.

direct-action statute. The plaintiffs were New York residents who were injured in a Puerto Rican building, through the fault, it was alleged, of the owners, a Puerto Rican corporation. The Puerto Rican company carried insurance with the defendants, a Connecticut corporation. Puerto Rican law provided a right of direct action against the insurance company. The court, considering the argument that the statute was merely procedural and so the question should be governed by the law of the forum which had no similar statute, held that the statute went beyond providing a procedural short-cut, and created a new right of action in favour of injured persons. It is noteworthy that though the court realised that the procedural-substantive categories were 'traditional rubrics', it could not avoid using them to arrive at its result. But the court, speaking through Judge Fuld, also employed the modern terminology in finding that it was Puerto Rico which had the 'most significant relationship and contact with respect to the matter in dispute'. It was not against the policy of New York to have insurance companies as defendants in original suits against them. The rule preceding disclosure of insurance was not absolute. Further, Puerto Rico had a legitimate interest in protecting the rights of persons injured there.

CONCLUSIONS

An examination of what little English material there is on the vague area between contract and tort in the conflict of laws reveals some inconsistency and much uncertainty. The rule in *Phillips* v. *Eyre* is rigid and forum oriented, whereas the proper law of the contract approach is flexible and internationalist in outlook. If the rigid rule of torts can be avoided by framing the cause of action on a contract, then doubt cannot but be thrown on the continuing usefulness of the rule in *Phillips* v. *Eyre*. A proper law of the tort approach would at least remove the need to shop around for an action on a contract and prevent the result of the action from depending on a technicality of English domestic law. For the differences between contract and torts are largely historical and have little modern social purpose. That differences remain should be no excuse for perpetuating the distinction in the conflict of laws.

But at least in English law the tort rule will normally operate in favour of the plaintiff, as foreign law appears to be relevant only as a defence. In the traditional American law, however, the law of the place where the alleged tort was committed was supposed in some mystical sense to be the source of the right of action. That this was a curious view of the sources of law did not escape the commentators. Its formal weakness was further demonstrated by those situations where the *lex fori* had to choose between competing causes of action.

It is apparent that it is for the forum to provide the machinery of action and in a sense to allow the plaintiff to seek his own way to the connecting factor, tort or contract. It is in this way that the plaintiff himself, so to speak, characterises the action. The only difficulty will be where he seeks to take a contractual line in a field traditionally reserved to tort, as the plaintiffs in *Matthews* v. *Kuwait Bechtel* and *Levy* v. *Daniels' U-Drive* were successful in doing.

Characterisation is becoming increasingly out of favour in conflict of laws theory. This is a reaction to the older view that it was a scientific method of deciding fundamental problems that the conflict of laws tended to throw up with monotonous regularity, for example, whether a right was substantive or procedural, whether a rule related to marriage or to property, and so on. The real answers to these questions were not to be found in a jurisprudence of concepts, but in decisions which consciously weighed the policies and results involved in choosing one category or another.

The *Second Restatement* retains the language of characterisation for the area between contract and tort. But characterisation in this area presents special problems. If the sole question is whether the forum allows an action in contract in a case which would at first glance suggest tort, then the forum must decide, with its attention fully on the consequences, whether it is to allow an action in contract and so frustrate the policy of the law that would otherwise govern the tort. The artifical characterisation used in *Levy* v. *Daniels' U-Drive* to avoid the application of the law of the place of injury is preferable to the conceptual analysis of the 'gravamen' of the action in *Maynard* v. *Eastern Airlines* precisely because it was effected with the policy interests of the forum state in contemplation. That the method used to achieve the result was untidy was the fault of the rigid place of the injury rule for torts.

The pseudo-scientific method has proved inadequate for mixed contract-tort situations. The treatment that the courts have given to the not dissimilar problems of releases and direct-action statutes shows that in these areas there cannot be any facile analytic answers. In the former the courts are required to make a conscious choice between the obligations which are imposed by the relevant tort law and their variation by the contract in cases where two systems conflict. In the latter the result must depend on the view which the forum takes of the insurance law and its connection with the parties. In both the final decision will be influenced by the public policy of the forum state.

Although the cases indicate that the courts are now looking to the substance of the action and are thereby applying similar principles of actions based on negligence or strict liability whatever the technical designation, be it contract, tort, or warranty, it is premature to conclude that for choice of law purposes the differences between contract and tort have been erased. Characteristically, the law of contract is concerned with business expectations, and the courts will be more likely to weigh the expectations of the parties more heavily in cases involving a contract. But this is probably becoming equally so in tort cases as insurance tends to cover the losses, industrial and commercial, with which the law of tort is so concerned.

The Supreme Court of Pennsylvania in *Griffith* v. *United Air Lines* made a brave attempt to discard characterisation as a tool for the solution of conflicts problems. But both the *Oltarsh* v. *Aetna Insurance Co.* case and the *Second Restatement* show that it is by no means dead in modern conflicts law. There still remains a difference in modern domestic law between contract and tort, and this difference must be reflected in the conflict of laws. Characterisation is concerned with the use of legal language, and there are still issues which can only be resolved by categorising them in the technicalities of the law. In *George* v. *Douglas Aircraft* the issue was the applicable statute of limitations. The Second Circuit interpreted the phase 'where the cause of action arose' in the light of the specific issue before it. So long as a court is willing, as the court was in that case, to characterise a claim in a manner which is directed to the determination of a specific issue, there is a place for characterisation in the modern law.

The courts and the writers are not agreed on the proper approach which must be taken for the future. In the field of the relation between contract and tort the fundamental difficulty is to resolve the conflict between the expectations of the parties as expressed in their contract and the interests of the state in the enforcement of its tort remedies. It is noteworthy that the recent decision of the New York Court of Appeals in *Dym* v. *Gordon* emphasises the law of the place where the relationship between the parties is centred and deprecates the use of the public policy of the forum in the guise of the application of 'governmental interests'.

But standardisation of contracts and increasing inequalities of bargaining power have made business expectations somewhat one-sided. With this reservation, however, the approach which the New York Court of Appeals articulates in *Dym* v. *Gordon* could be a workable one, provided that it is not used without relating the relationship to the specific issue involved. For the facts of that case show that it was a regression from *Babcock* v. *Jackson* in so far as the court failed to relate the relationship involved to the issue before the court.

In cases where contract and tort overlap it is not enough to point to the undoubted fact that the courts are now tending to use similar formulae for the contract and tort situations. Where there is a mixed contract-tort situation the 'relationship' will usually be the contract between the parties.

It is this factor, however, that the *Second Restatement* places last in its suggested list of factors which determine the 'significant relationship'. It is the law of the contract on which the parties can plan their insurance. It is the law of the contract which most effectively reflects their expectations.

X

Exemption Clauses, Employment Contracts and the Conflict of Laws

Although the questions of principle raised in *Sayers* v. *International Drilling Co.* [1971] 1 WLR 1176 (CA) remain live ones, the actual decision in the case would now be different because the exception clause in such circumstances would be invalidated by the Unfair Contract Terms Act 1977. That Act was part of a general development to restrict the application of foreign law in order to protect the weaker party. The EEC Conventions on jurisdiction and on contractual liability also contain special provisions in favour of employees. The Brussels Convention (as amended in 1989) and the Lugano Convention contain similar (but not identical) provisions, the substance of which is that in matters relating to individual contracts of employment, the place of performance of the obligation in question will be the place where the employee habitually carries out his work, or if the employee does not habitually carry out his work in one country, the employer may also be sued in the courts of the place where the business which engaged the employee was or is situated: Article 5(1). The effect of Article 17 (as amended) of the Brussels Convention and Article 17 of the Lugano Convention is that, as against the employee, a jurisdiction agreement is to be effective only if it is entered into after the dispute has arisen.

The EEC Convention on the Law Applicable to Contractual Obligations ('the Rome Convention') is given effect in the United Kingdom by the Contracts (Applicable Law) Act 1990. The substance of Article 6 of the Rome Convention is that an express choice of law in an employment contract is not to have the effect of depriving the employee of the protection afforded to him by the mandatory rules of the law which would be applicable in the absence of an express choice; and that, in the absence of a choice of law, a contract of employment is to be governed by the law of the country in which the employee habitually works, or, if he does not habitually work in one country, by the law of the country in which the place of business through which he was engaged is situated, unless it appears from the circumstances as a whole that the contract is more closely connected with another country.

In *Johnson* v. *Coventry Churchill International Ltd.* [1992] 3 All ER 14 a deputy judge held that the plaintiff's personal injury claim against his English employer for failure to provide a safe system of work was governed by English law, even though he was employed to work in Germany and was injured there. English law was applied on the basis of the exception to the double actionability rule: justice dictated that English law should be applied to the particular issue (namely, whether the plaintiff had to show negligence or whether, as under German law, he had to prove wilful breach of duty) since English law had the most significant relationship

From *International and Comparative Law Quarterly*, 21 (1972), 320.

with the issue and the parties. The same result could have been reached more simply, by applying English law on the applicable law of contract, but breach of an implied term of the contract of employment was not pleaded.

INTRODUCTION

The effect of contractual defences on tort claims is a subject on which the conflict of laws provides meagre authority. It is therefore a matter of some regret that a recent decision of the Court of Appeal,[1] in a case which raised major questions of public policy and of the conflict of laws in relation to employment contracts, has largely ignored the difficulties inherent in the subject.

When an action is brought in England based on a tort committed abroad, the defence may be that liability has been excluded or modified by a contract between the parties. A serious question arises if the contract is governed by a system of law other than that of the place where the tort was committed. The defence may be valid by the proper law of the contract but invalid by the *lex loci delicti*; or it may be invalid by the proper law of the contract but recognised as a defence by the *lex loci delicti*.

The problems arise from the interplay of contract and tort in the conflict of laws.[2] Questions of contract are normally governed by the proper law of the contract and questions of tort are normally governed by a combination of English law and the *lex loci delicti*. If the proper law of the contract and the *lex loci delicti* are themselves in conflict, the solution at first sight is far from clear.

The key question is whether the plaintiff's claim is based on contract or on tort. The English rules of pleading are sufficiently flexible, if the law provides concurrent remedies, to allow the plaintiff to choose whether his claim is in contract or in tort. Whether there are concurrent remedies must itself be a question of English laws as the *lex fori*. Thus, a claim by a client against his solicitor is based on contract only in English law and therefore the measure of damages in contract and not in tort applies,[3] whereas the liability of carriers and employers lies both in contract and in tort.[4] Thus, in the international context, a claim by an employee against his foreign employer for failing to provide a safe system of work may come within the separate heads of Order 11 which allow service out of the jurisdiction in

---

[1] *Sayers* v. *International Drilling Co.* [1971] 1 WLR 1176; [1971] 3 All ER 163.

[2] On this problem generally, see Collins, 'Interaction between Contract and Tort in the Conflict of Laws' (1967) 16 ICLQ 103 (ante, p. 352); Kahn-Freund, 'Delictual Liability and the Conflict of Laws' (1968–II) 124 Hague Rec. 1 at 129–157. The latter is a major work the whole of which deserves and rewards careful reading.

[3] *Clark* v. *Kirby-Smith* [1964] Ch. 506.

[4] See Lord Simonds in *Lister* v. *Romford Ice & Cold Storage Co. Ltd.* [1957] AC 555 at 579.

contract and tort cases: *Matthews* v. *Kuwait Bechtel*.[5] Therefore, for example, if the employee is injured in England as a result of his foreign employer's negligence, he may obtain leave to serve his employer out of the jurisdiction on the basis that a tort has been committed in England; conversely, if he is injured abroad as a result of his foreign employer's negligence, he may obtain leave to sue his employer under Order 11 if the contract of employment was made in England or governed by English law.

If the claim is based on contract and the exemption clause is valid by the proper law of the contract, then the clause will, subject to any question of public policy or applicable legislation, be given effect in England.[6] If the exemption clause is invalid by the proper law of the contract, then the clause will not be given effect. In the event of the claim being based on tort, more difficult problems arise. When a tort is committed in England, English law normally applies[7] and English law will give effect, subject to any statutory provision, to an exemption clause in a valid contract between the parties. The reason for this is, not some rule regulating the relationship between tort claims and contractual defences in the conflict of laws, but that English domestic law recognises contractual defences to tort claims.[8]

But where the tort is committed abroad the 'bewildering variety of individual reasons'[9] given by the House of Lords in *Boys* v. *Chaplin*[10] leads to uncertainty and confusion. Prior to that decision, the main controversy in the English conflict of laws rule for torts was whether it was necessary for the act complained of to be a tort by the *lex loci delicti* as well as by English law. That controversy involved the interpretation of the second branch of the rule in *Phillips* v. *Eyre*[11] as applied in *Machado* v. *Fontes*.[12] While *Machado* v. *Fontes* stood, a plaintiff would succeed in England if the

---

[5] [1959] 2 QB 57 (CA).

[6] See, e.g., *Vita Food Products Inc.* v. *Unus Shipping* [1939] AC 277 (PC).

[7] *Szalatnay-Stacho* v. *Fink* [1947] KB 1 (CA) is frequently cited as conclusive authority that, where a tort is committed in England, English law and only English law is relevant. But this case must be open to reconsideration in the light of *Boys* v. *Chaplin* [1971] AC 356, if only for the simple reason that the English rules of private international law relating to torts cannot apply only to torts committed abroad, any more than the choice of law rules relating to contracts apply only to contracts made abroad.

[8] This is an application of the *volenti non fit injuria* principle.

[9] The phrase is North's, in Cheshire, *Private International Law* (8th ed., 1970 by Cheshire and North), p. vi. For a truly remarkable recent example, see *Albert* v. *Motor Insurers' Bureau* [1972] AC 301, where Lord Diplock expressly concurred in the views of the Lords Donovan and Pearson, which he did not share, in order to form a majority against views which he did share, at least in part.

[10] [1971] AC 356, affirming [1968] 2 QB 1. See Graveson, 'Towards a Modern Applicable Law in Tort' (1969) 85 LQR 505; McGregor, 'The International Accident Problem' (1970) 33 MLR 1; Shapira, 'A Transatlantic Inspiration: The "Proper Law of the Tort" ' (1970) 33 MLR 27; North and Webb, 'The Effect of *Chaplin* v. *Boys*' (1970) 19 ICLQ 24; Karsten, '*Chaplin* v. *Boys*: Another Analysis' (1970) 19 ICLQ 35.   [11] (1870) LR 6 QB 1.

[12] [1897] 2 QB 231 (CA). See Dicey and Morris, *Conflict of Laws* (8th ed., 1967) (hereinafter cited as *Dicey and Morris*), pp. 922–926.

act complained of would have been a tort if it had been committed in England and if the defendant were unable to show that his act was innocent by the *lex loci delicti*.[13] In other words, for the plaintiff to succeed in England he did not have to show that the act was a tort by the *lex loci delicti* as well as by English law. It would be hard to imagine a more forum-based rule in the conflict of laws and the rule in *Phillips* v. *Eyre* as applied in *Machado* v. *Fontes* did little credit to the English rules of the conflict of laws.

This is not the place for a detailed discussion of *Boys* v. *Chaplin*, and the following summary of the reasoning of their Lordships cannot be taken as exhaustive of the nuances and of the difficulties of some of the formulations:

(a) For both Lord Hodson and Lord Wilberforce, the basic rule was that for the plaintiff to succeed the act complained of should both be a tort by English law and also civilly actionable by the *lex loci delicti*. But the rule was not an invariable one. Lord Hodson thought there should be some latitude in cases where it would be against public policy to admit or exclude claims; he would therefore in cases where such a policy existed adopt the American Law Institute's *Restatement, Conflict of Laws* (*Second*) rule that the system of law with the most significant connection with the occurrence and the parties should apply. Lord Wilberforce also thought there should be a qualification to the general rule along the lines of the *Restatement* (*Second*) where justice required the application of a foreign or English rule to a particular issue.

(b) Lord Guest also thought that double actionability was required, but rejected the proper law of the tort approach because it produced uncertainty.

(c) Lord Donovan and Lord Pearson preferred the traditional approach of *Phillips* v. *Eyre* as applied in *Machado* v. *Fontes*. They would therefore apply English law, provided the act was not innocent under the *lex loci delicti*. Double actionability was therefore not necessary, but there was a residual discretion in the court to reject claims in order to prevent forum-shopping.

Thus three of their Lordships would overrule *Machado* v. *Fontes* and require, as a basic rule, double actionability (Lords Hodson, Wilberforce and Guest) although two of them would be prepared to relax it in the interests of justice in an exceptional case to apply (or not to apply) a foreign rule (in Lord Wilberforce's formulation) or to admit or exclude certain claims (in Lord Hodson's formulation); three of their Lordships are opposed to a proper law doctrine (Lords Guest, Donovan and Pearson)

---

[13] The principle is put in this way because the better view is that it is for the defendant to plead and prove justifiability and not for the plaintiff to make out an affirmative case for the absence of justifiability by the *lex loci delicti*.

although two of them prefer a rule which the majority rejects. What for lower courts will be the *ratio* of the case is a matter for speculation, although it may be confidently asserted that it is not that only the *lex loci delicti* is relevant.[14]

2. EXEMPTION CLAUSES AND *SAYERS* V. *INTERNATIONAL DRILLING CO.*[15]

What, then, would be the position if there were a defence to a foreign tort based on an exemption clause in a contract? If the *lex loci delicti* recognised the contract as excluding or limiting liability, it is reasonably safe to assume that, public policy considerations apart, all of the speeches in *Boys* v. *Chaplin* would lead to the conclusion that the defence would be recognised. But if the *lex loci delicti* does not recognise the defence, more difficult questions arise.

It is suggested in *Dicey and Morris*[16] that the contractual exemption can be successfully pleaded as a defence to an action based on a foreign tort, even though the exemption is void or not otherwise available as a defence by the *lex loci delicti*. The present writer has submitted[17] that the suggestion involves an unwarranted extension of the first branch of the rule in *Phillips* v. *Eyre*. The act would clearly not be justifiable under the *lex loci delicti* and therefore the reasoning must be derived from the notion that since contractual exemptions are normally recognised as defences to English torts the act would not normally have been actionable in England had it been committed there. But, as will appear, it is not always the case that contractual exemptions are recognised in English law and in any event there is no authority for such an extension of the rule in *Phillips* v. *Eyre*.[18]

If the claim is in tort, the question, it is submitted, should be analysed by reference to the speeches in *Boys* v. *Chaplin*. On the present state of the

---

[14] The fallacy in McGregor, *op. cit.*, *supra*, n. 10 at 14, is that he rejects every possible *ratio* but the least likely one by finding a majority against them, but does not apply the same test to the least likely *ratio*, i.e., application only of the *lex loci delicti*. Karsten, *op. cit.*, *supra*, n. 10 at 37–38, uses a similar technique to find that the *ratio* is the exception to the *Phillips* v. *Eyre* rule formulated by Lords Hodson and Wilberforce. The true position is probably that there is no *ratio* which is of sufficiently wide scope as to cover any case but one involving precisely the same issues as *Boys* v. *Chaplin*. But the question will continue to trouble lower courts. It will be difficult for judges of first instance to do more than apply *Phillips* v. *Eyre* (but without *Machado* v. *Fontes*). The Court of Appeal is free to take its own view of the *ratio* of *Boys* v. *Chaplin* and there are already signs in practice that the Court of Appeal takes the same somewhat cynical view of *Boys* v. *Chaplin* as the Court of Criminal Appeal used to take of *DPP* v. *Smith* [1961] AC 290.   [15] [1971] 1 WLR 1176; [1971] 3 All ER 163.

[16] At p. 941.   [17] Collins, *op. cit.*, *supra*, n. 2 at 112–116 (ante, pp. 361–365).

[18] The views expressed in *Dicey and Morris* should perhaps be read in the light of the present author's criticism. See Kahn-Freund, *op. cit.*, *supra*, n. 2 at 144 and Morris, *The Conflict of Laws* (1971), p. 275.

authorities, a contractual defence should not be recognised in England as a defence to a foreign tort unless it is recognised by the *lex loci delicti* or when there are compelling public policy grounds for recognising the defence.

In *Sayers* v. *International Drilling Co.* the plaintiff was an English oil rig worker. The defendant was a Dutch oil drilling company, which was a subsidiary of a major American oil drilling company. The plaintiff was employed by the defendant company to work on a rig off the coast of Nigeria. The contract was made in England through an English representative of the Dutch company who was based in the London office of a UK subsidiary of the same US parent. The contract (which was a standard form contract in English providing for payment in sterling) contained an exemption clause which was at the heart of the issue in the case. By clause 8 of the contract the employee agreed to accept benefits under the defendants' compensation programme in lieu of any rights under English law. The plaintiff went to Nigeria and two weeks later he was injured while working on the oil rig as a result of what he alleged was the negligence of his fellow-workmen. It was common ground that the compensation payable under the defendants' programme was less than the damages recoverable at common law for negligence.

It was also common ground that the clause limiting the plaintiff's rights would have been void if the contract had been governed by English law. By section 1 (3) of the Law Reform (Personal Injuries) Act 1948:

Any provision contained in a contract of service . . . shall be void insofar as it would have the effect of excluding or limiting any liability of the employer in respect of personal injuries caused to the person employed . . . by the negligence of persons in common employment with him.

It appears that the contractual limitation was pleaded as a defence on the basis that it formed part of a Dutch international contract and that the plaintiff by way of reply claimed that the contract did not avail the company and that he would rely on section 1 (3) of the Law Reform (Personal Injuries) Act 1948. He also claimed that the contract of employment was governed by English law. What is not clear is whether the reply was put in the alternative or whether it was suggested only that the contract did not avail the company *because* of section 1 (3) of the 1948 Act—the distinction is far from academic, as will appear.

It was ordered (on whose application, it is not clear) that the issues raised in relation to the contract and the proper law should be tried as a preliminary issue in the action. Bean J., in an unreported judgment, held that the proper law of the contract was Dutch and that the limitation clause afforded a defence. The uncontested expert evidence on Dutch law called by the company was to the effect that such a clause is valid under Dutch law, provided it is contained in what is called an international contract.[19] The plaintiff appealed, and the grounds appear to have been solely that the judge had been wrong in holding that the proper law of the contract was Dutch and that he should have held that it was English law which governed the contract. It will be shown below that, if such was the way in which the case was presented, then the issues were put in too narrow and simple a fashion to take proper account of the very difficult question which arose. This probably accounts for the unsatisfactory nature of the decision of the Court of Appeal and for the fact that only Lord Denning MR appears to have appreciated the real nature of the issue in the case.

There were two divergent judicial attitudes in the case. The majority, Salmon LJ and Stamp LJ, adopted what may be called the proper law of the contract approach—both dealt with the case on the footing that the only relevant question was whether the proper law of the contract was Dutch or English. Lord Denning MR adopted what may be called the proper law of the issue approach—for him the real question was what law should determine the issue raised in the case. The two approaches will be considered in turn, first in the light of the judgments in the case and then in the light of English public policy.

(*a*) The proper law of the contract approach

For Salmon LJ and Stamp LJ there was only one question: what was the proper law of the contract? They accepted that if the contract were governed by English law, then section 1 (3) of the Law Reform (Personal Injuries) Act 1948 would render the exemption clause void; but they also thought that if the contract were governed by Dutch law, the exemption clause would be a valid defence to the action.

It is now well-settled law that in the absence of an express choice of law and in the absence of circumstances from which a choice of law can be inferred, a contract is governed by the system of law with which it has the closest and most real connection.[20] The application of that formula in this

---

[19] Although the presumption against the application of the doctrine of *renvoi* is usually put in a way which suggests that none of the rules of private international law of the chosen law are to apply (see *Re United Railways of Havana etc. Ltd.* [1960] Ch. 52, 96–97, CA) such a formulation is too wide. In the broad sense, the rules of Dutch law about international contracts would be part of Dutch private international law. But the presumption against *renvoi* is in truth a presumption against the application of those conflicts rules of the applicable law which lead to another legal system. This question is not raised in the Court of Appeal decision here discussed.

[20] For recent formulations, see *James Miller & Partners Ltd.* v. *Whitworth Street Estates (Manchester) Ltd.* [1970] AC 583 at 663–664 (Lord Reid), 605–606 (Lord Hodson), 611 (Viscount Dilhorne) and 614 (Lord Wilberforce); and *Compagnie d'Armement Maritime SA* v. *Compagnie Tunisienne de Navigation SA* [1971] AC 572 at 583 (Lord Reid), 587 (Lord Morris) and 603 (Lord Diplock). Only the latter of these cases was cited in *Sayers* v.

case has an air of artificiality, since the form of the contract (which was in English) was somewhat American-influenced. The factors which pointed to English law included the following: (i) one of the parties, the employee, was English; (ii) the language of the contract was English; (iii) the contract was made in England by a London-based representative of the defendant company; and (iv) the salary was to be paid in sterling. The only significant connection with Holland was that the employer was a Dutch company—it appears that the group of which the company is a member uses the Dutch company for operations in places such as Nigeria, but uses the English subsidiary for North Sea operations. In these circumstances both Salmon LJ and Stamp LJ held that the system of law with which the contract had its closest connection was that of Holland. Their reasons may be summarised shortly as follows:[21]

(1) the contract was of a standard form used for employees of various nationalities and it would give such contracts business efficacy for them to be governed by a single law, that of the employer, and

(2) the fact that the contract expressly excluded the employee's rights under English law indicated, or gave recognition to, the fact that the law of the country of origin of the employee was not to be applicable.

In addition, Salmon LJ invoked 'the rule of validation'[22] so as to apply the system of law (Dutch) which upheld the clause rather than the system which made it void (English). It will be submitted below that this was not a legitimate case for the application of the maxim *ut res magis valeat quam pereat*. Stamp LJ also placed considerable reliance on the fact that the employer was Dutch, that the business belonged to a Dutch corporation, that the owner was subject to the law of the Netherlands and within the jurisdiction of the courts of that state—but these are four different ways of making the same point and it would be a novel doctrine that the law of the employer were deemed to govern.[23]

In borderline cases such as this it is no easy question to decide what law governs a contract and it is therefore not surprising that Lord Denning MR

International Drilling Co. (in argument and in the judgment of Lord Denning MR) but the issues in the former decision were far more germane to the point in SAYERS.

[21] See [1971] 1 WLR at 1184 and 1186.

[22] The phrase, if not the concept, is Ehrenzweig's. See, e.g., Ehrenzweig, *Private International Law* (1967), p. 45. See *Dicey and Morris*, p. 708, for a discussion of the limits of the doctrine in England. For another surprising application of it, see *Coast Lines Ltd.* v. *Hudig & Veder Chartering NV* [1972] 2 QB 34.

[23] See Kahn-Freund, 'Notes on the Conflict of Laws in Relation to Employment in English and Scottish Law' (1960) 3 *Riv. Dir. Internazionale e Comparato del Lavoro* 307 for a short but very perceptive analysis of the proper law of employment contracts and for the conclusion that 'Whereas both the employer's centre of control and management and the employee's place of performance are relevant factors in determining the proper law, neither of them can be allowed to become a "fetish" ' (at 311).

came to an opposite conclusion. For him the connections with England led to the conclusion that the proper law of the contract was English—these outweighed the fact that the employer was Dutch, especially since the employment contract was administered in London.[24]

(b) The proper law of the issue approach

The reasoning of Lord Denning MR put shortly was as follows: (i) the claim of the plaintiff was founded in tort and the applicable law in the case of a claim in tort was the proper law of the tort, that is, the law of the country with which the parties and the acts done had the most significant connection; (ii) the defence of the company was based on contract, and in considering that defence the court must apply the proper law of the contract, that is, the system of law with which the contract had its closest and most real connection; (iii) it was not two systems of law which were to be applied, but one, and that was the system of law with which the *issues* had their closest connection; and (iv) on the facts the proper law of the tort was Dutch and the proper law of the contract was (*semble*) English, but because the action was founded on tort the issue of liability should be determined by Dutch law.

The judgment of Lord Denning MR is of very considerable interest, but although the proper law of the issue is a notion which has much to commend it, the reasoning of his judgment is open to certain fundamental criticisms:

1. In suggesting that the law governing tort liability should be the proper law of the tort, Lord Denning MR repeated the formulation made by him in *Boys* v. *Chaplin* in the Court of Appeal that the applicable law was 'the law of the country with which the parties and the act done have the most significant connection'.[25] In *Sayers* v. *International Drilling Co.* he indicated that that view was confirmed by Lord Wilberforce in the House of Lords. But, as has been shown above, the way that both Lord Hodson and Lord Wilberforce put the 'most significant connection' test was that it was a particular exception to the general rule of *Phillips* v. *Eyre*, to be applied where public policy or justice required the admission or exclusion of claims that would otherwise be excluded or admitted. The generalised proper law of the tort theory found no favour in the House of Lords.

---

[24] As in many cases where the proper law of the contract is in doubt, the whole discussion in this case has a somewhat unreal air. It is a legitimate inference from the judgments that the form of the contract was devised by the American parent company for worldwide use. If the company had intended to ensure that the rights under the contract would be governed by the law of incorporation of whichever group company happened to be the employer, it would have been a simple matter for it to have inserted an express choice of law.

[25] [1968] 2 QB at 26.

2. The proper law of the tort, according to Lord Denning, was Dutch because Nigerian law (the *lex loci delicti*) was inapplicable in view of the fact that Nigerians had nothing to do with the rig. Dutch law was applicable because the only common bond between the employees was that they were employed by the Dutch company. But what is truly remarkable about this conclusion is that, notwithstanding his view that the Dutch nationality of the common employer was decisive in determining the proper law of the tort, nonetheless it was also his view that the proper law of the *contract* of employment was English. It surely cannot be that, where a foreign company employs employees of different nationalities, the liability in tort of the company to an English employee employed under an English contract is governed by the law of incorporation of the employer.

3. After stating that in his view the proper law of the contract would be English, Lord Denning suggests that the clause in the contract excluding the employee's rights under English law 'turns the scale against English law'.[26] It is not clear whether this is meant to qualify his conclusion on the proper law of the contract or to indicate that English law is not the proper law of the issue. Whichever it is, the *petitio principi* is clear. If the contract, apart from the clause, is governed by English law, then section 1 (3) of the 1948 Act must operate to make the clause void. It would indeed be an odd application of the rule of validation to use it to save the one clause in the contract which English law specifically made void.

4. To have placed reliance, as Lord Denning did, on Mr Sayers' intention to put his faith in the company's compensation programme, as expressed to the trial judge, was to ignore the fact that the English legislature had decided as a matter of policy that such agreements were void. Indeed, if there is a common criticism of the judgments of all three members of the Court of Appeal in this case, it is that they did not pay sufficient attention to the public policy factors involved.

3. PUBLIC POLICY AND THE PROPER FORMULATION OF THE ISSUES

The clear purpose and effect of section 1 of the Law Reform (Personal Injuries) Act 1948 is to abolish the defence of common employment and to make void any provision in a contract of employment which excludes or limits the liability of the employer for the negligence of fellow-employees.

The Act has no choice of law provision, but on general principles, there must be some limitation to its application. Which, if any, of the following connections with England bring the section into play? That the contract of employment is made in England, or that it is governed by English law, or

---

[26] [1971] 1 WLR at 1181.

that the work is to be done in England, or that the accident occurs in England? In cases where the act does not strictly apply, can it yield a principle of public policy such that the courts would refuse to enforce contractual clauses which offend the spirit of the Act but are not caught by it?

The presumption that an Act of Parliament is not to be taken as having extra-territorial effect is well-settled.[27] In practice, when applied to statutes dealing with contracts or contractual provisions, that presumption means that the Act is to be taken prima facie as affecting only contracts governed by English law.[28] The presumption is not easily rebutted, but it is, unfortunately, extremely difficult (if not impossible) to derive any clear principle from the authorities as to the circumstances in which an Act of Parliament may be given extra-territorial effect.[29]

Section 1 (3) of the Law Reform (Personal Injuries) Act 1948 is clearly intended to protect the employee against the superior bargaining power and expertise of the employer. The section is mandatory in the sense that no agreement can oust it, but there are no penal sanctions for infringement of this policy and no contract caught by the section is illegal in any sense.[30] The section clearly applies to all contracts of employment governed by English law. The place where the work is done and the place of the accident must be irrelevant, because the section strikes at clauses in employment contracts *ab initio* and the place of employment, and *a fortiori* the place of the accident, may be matters only for speculation when the contract is made. The mere fact that the contract is made in England should not itself be of decisive weight, not only because the place of contracting is often fortuitous but also because there must be many cases in practice of employment contracts made in England by international concerns which have little or no connection with England. The authorities which give primacy to the place of contracting are obsolete[31] and the

---

[27] See, e.g., Mann, 'The Doctrine of Jurisdiction in International Law' (1964–I) III Hague Rec. 1, 64–69; and, for a recent example of the principle, *Treacy* v. *DPP* [1971] AC 537.

[28] See, e.g., Kahn-Freund, 'Reflections on Public Policy in the English Conflict of Laws' (1952) 39 Trans. Grot. Soc. 39, 61–62, and authorities cited there. The number of authorities which establish this proposition in terms is surprisingly small, and indeed many of the earlier cases apply the presumption to limit an Act to contracts *made* in England. There are, of course, many authorities which establish that foreign legislation affects only contracts governed by the relevant foreign law.

[29] Thus in the case of accidents which occurred outside England but in the course of an employment governed by English law, the Workmen's Compensation Acts have been held not to apply (*Tomalin* v. *Pearson* [1909] 2 KB 61) but the Fatal Accidents Acts have been held to apply (*Davidsson* v. *Hill* [1901] 2 KB 606). See *Dicey and Morris*, p. 732 for other examples.

[30] There is, therefore, no room for the application of the decision in *Boissevain* v. *Weil* [1950] AC 327, whereby a penal statute given extra-territorial effect was held to render illegal a contract not governed by English law. For criticism, see Mann, *op. cit., supra*, n. 27, 124–125.   [31] See *Dicey and Morris*, p. 756.

modern Scottish case which applied Scottish hire purchase legislation to a contract made in Scotland but governed by English law is not sufficiently reasoned to provide much guidance.[32] The Commonwealth authorities are not flexible enough to allow the approach of those American courts which apply local statutes to cases involving foreign elements where the transaction has a sufficient connection with the interests of the enacting state,[33] or of those courts which balance the conflicting policies of the competing laws.[34]

The conclusion must be that the section does not apply to contracts governed by foreign law[35] and that in particular the fact that the employment contract was made in England does not bring the section into play. Can the section, then, yield a principle of public policy? The flexibility of the English rules for choice of law is such that the policy of the section could not be given effect unless it applied, for example, to accidents occuring in England in the course of an employment governed by English law.

Suppose, for example, that a foreign manufacturing company sets up a branch in England rather than an English subsidiary. It employs numerous English workmen under a standard form of contract which (a) expressly provides that the law of the country of origin of the employer is to apply and (b) limits the employer's liability for the negligence of fellow-employees. If the limitation is valid by the proper law, the English court will not, in the absence of very compelling reasons to the contrary, treat the choice of law as other than bona fide and legal, since the connection with the foreign law is sufficiently established by the nationality of the employer. But it is difficult to conceive that the English court would not apply the section in these circumstances in an action by an employee of that company. But the justification could, on this hypothesis, only be one of public policy. There are, it is true, obstacles in the way of such a step. The English courts are notoriously unwilling to derive a public policy from a statute, and the doctrine of common employment attacked by the 1948 Act was a judicial doctrine which dated from 1837[36] and which was still active until the Act. But the Act was the product of a government of a social and political persuasion very different from that of the judges who produced

---

[32] *English* v. *Donnelly*, 1958 SC 494.

[33] Cf. *Alaska Packers Assocn.* v. *Industrial Accident Commn.* (1935) 294 US 532 and *Lauritzen* v. *Larsen* (1953) 345 US 571, and many other cases.

[34] Cf. *Richards* v. *US*, 369 US 1 (1962).

[35] The choice of law must be bona fide and legal under the *Vita Food* case, *supra*, n. 6, and any choice designed solely to avoid legislation will be subject to attack. See *Kay's Leasing Corp.* v. *Fletcher* [1956] ALR 673.

[36] *Priestly* v. *Fowler* (1837) 3 M. & W. 1. For a short account, see Clerk and Lindsell, *Torts* (13th ed., 1969), p. 147.

the doctrine of common employment in the nineteenth century. In the words of Denning LJ (as he then was)[37]

The doctrine of common employment was an irrational exception to the liability of an employer . . . It has now been abolished by statute, and should be disregarded in the same way as if it had never been enunciated. Statute law and common law should be integrated as one law.

If there can be overriding economic considerations for not enforcing a foreign contract[38] then nearly 25 years after the legislature has abolished the doctrine of common employment there may be overriding social reasons for deriving a policy from an Act which, to adopt words used of another statute,[39] 'is a piece of social legislation designed for the protection of certain persons'. It is therefore tentatively[40] suggested that a cautious and sparing use of the public policy doctrine is appropriate where the application of English law would not violate the interests of any other state or the legitimate expectations of any party and where justice demands it. To afford the protection of the section to Mr Sayers in the circumstances of the case offends against no principle of justice or reason. The curious feature of the case is that the Court of Appeal (it seems) would in all likelihood have held the contract to have been governed by English law but for the very clause the validity of which was in issue. In the light of the social purpose of the statute, what is surely inadmissible is the application of the presumption that the contract should, in cases of doubt, be held to be governed by the law of the country which upholds the offending clause. Whatever validity that theory may have when the parties are of equal bargaining power, it cannot reasonably be applicable when one of the competing systems (especially when it is the *lex fori*) intends to protect the weak against one-sided or standard form contracts.

Even if the 1948 Act does not yield an affirmative principle of public policy, the decision in *Sayers* v. *International Drilling Co.* is open to numerous other criticisms, and it is suggested that the issues and the decision could have been formulated along the following lines:

(1) The plaintiff's claim against his employer could be based on tort or contract, at his option: *Matthews* v. *Kuwait Bechtel*.[41] Since, as will appear, a claim in tort was more likely to succeed, Lord Denning MR was right in treating the claim as one in tort.

---

[37] In *Broom* v. *Morgan* [1953] 1 QB 597 at 608–609.

[38] See Denning LJ in *Boissevain* v. *Weil* [1949] 1 KB 482 at 491, affirmed on different grounds [1950] AC 327.

[39] Lord President Clyde in *English* v. *Donnelly*, 1958 SC 494, 499.

[40] A further obstacle to the application of the public policy doctrine is that the House of Lords in *Imperial Chemical Industries Ltd.* v. *Shatwell* [1965] AC 656 did not take the opportunity to remove the doctrine of *volenti non fit injuria* from the sphere of employment relations. See Brodetsky, Note (1964) 27 MLR 733.　　　[41] [1959] 2 QB 57.

(2) That being so, the rules of the conflict of laws relating to foreign torts were applicable. Those rules are in a considerable state of flux, and the following arguments could have been derived from the speeches of the House of Lords in *Boys* v. *Chaplin*:

(i) on the traditional approach, the act of negligence in Nigeria would have been actionable had it occurred in England and was not proved to have been either justifiable or innocent under Nigerian law, and there having been no evidence of Nigerian law, the act must be presumed to have been actionable under Nigerian law. In particular since there was no evidence that the exemption clause would be given effect to in Nigeria, English law must be applied; or

(ii) on the approach of Lords Hodson and Wilberforce there was no reason to depart from the double actionability rule on the facts, since the claim was not against public policy and justice would not be effected by excluding it.

Therefore on any view of *Boys* v. *Chaplin* the claim was prima facie admissible and the contractual defence was not admissible.

(3) Even if the contractual defence had been relevant, the exemption clause and its invalidity under English law should not have been a factor in the decision against English law and for Dutch law as the proper law.[42]

(4) Even if the rule in *Phillips* v. *Eyre* should be jettisoned altogether, as Lord Denning seems to suggest, and the sole test should be the proper law of the tort or of the issue, then the issues and the policies should have been carefully segregated in the light of the facts and of public policy. Following the approach of Lord Wilberforce in *Boys* v. *Chaplin* the issue should therefore have been whether one Britsh subject, resident in the United Kingdom, should be prevented from recovering damages, in accordance with English law, against a Dutch company which engaged him in England under a standard form contract governed by Dutch law and where, on the evidence, the damages must be presumed to be recoverable by the *lex loci delicti*; or whether the Dutch company can rely in an English court on an exemption clause that would be invalid by Dutch domestic law were it not contained in an international contract, that would be invalid by English law were the contract governed by English law or (semble) had the accident occurred in England and which must be presumed to have been invalid by the *lex loci delicti*. Put in this way, the conclusion that the proper law of the issue was not Dutch private international law seems obvious.

---

[42] In the event of Dutch law being held applicable, consideration should have been given to the question whether it was ordinary Dutch domestic law (under which the clause would have been invalid) or the Dutch rules of private international law (under which it was assumed the clause was valid) which was applicable.

4.CONCLUSIONS

The problems discussed in this article admit of no very easy answer. The conflict of laws is an area of the law where highly technical concepts are often used mechanically to solve legal problems without much regard to justice. As Professor Kahn-Freund has very wisely put it:[43]

Whenever a technical legal argument becomes intellectually and academically very attractive there is an (admittedly rebuttable but nevertheless strong) presumption that something is wrong with the law.

But, conversely, it is suggested that when a solution is intellectually and academically *unattractive* there is an equally strong presumption to the same effect, which can be rebutted normally only by showing that the unattractiveness is due to a conscious and rational rejection of older authority and learning.

Is there, then, any rule which is likely to serve the often conflicting policies of certainty and justice? Is there any rule which represents contemporary English private international law? Any discussion is bound to be clouded by the uncertainties and difficulties engendered by the decision of the House of Lords in *Boys* v. *Chaplin*. On the more traditional approach of *Phillips* v. *Eyre* (simpliciter or even with the now overruled *Machado* v. *Fontes*), it is submitted that the contractual defence is irrelevant unless it would be recognised by English domestic law to prevent actionability under the first branch of the rule or unless it is recognised by the *lex loci delicti* as negativing liability under the second branch of the rule. If to admit or exclude the defence would do injustice then the question of the law with the more significant connection would be derived from the speeches of Lords Hodson and Wilberforce, and particularly from the carefully considered views of the latter. The question is what law should govern the particular issue. As Lord Wilberforce said:[44]

I think that the necessary flexibility can be obtained from that principle which represents at least a common denominator of the United States decisions, namely, through segregation of the relevant issue and consideration whether, in relation to that issue, the relevant foreign rule ought, as a matter of policy or as Westlake said of science, to be applied. For this purpose it is necessary to identify the policy of the rule, to inquire to what situations, with what contacts, it was intended to apply; whether not to apply it, in the circumstances of the instant case, would serve any interest which the rule was devised to meet.

Therefore the search is likely to be for the law with the most significant relationship with the issue. *Boys* v. *Chaplin* apart and subject to overriding

---

[43] *Op. cit., supra*, n. 2 at 148.   [44] [1971] AC at 391.

consideration of public policy, it is submitted that the admissibility of a contractual defence depends on the law with the most significant relationship with the tort. That law, where the relationship of the parties derives from a contract, will usually (but, as *Sayers* v. *International Drilling Co.* shows, not invariably) be the same as the law governing the contract.

XI

Contractual Obligations—The EEC Preliminary Draft Convention on Private International Law

On 1 April 1991 the Contracts (Applicable Law) Act 1990 came into force and gave effect to the Rome Convention on the Law Applicable to Contractual Obligations. This article considered the 1972 draft, which was concerned not only with contractual obligations, but also with non-contractual obligations. In part because of the uncertainty over the continued membership of the United Kingdom in the European Communities (which was resolved by the 1975 referendum), little progress was made on the Covention until 1978, when it was decided (at the request of the United Kingdom delegation) to limit the Convention to contractual obligations, and to return to non-contractual obligations at a later stage. In 1979 a draft Convention was completed, and the Convention was finalised at a special meeting in Rome of the Council of the European Communities in June 1980, and opened for signature on 19 June 1980, when it was signed by the six original Member States and Ireland. It did not come into force until 1991 because of the need to make arrangements for the European Court to have jurisdiction to give rulings on its interpretation. In December 1988 two Protocols on the interpretation of the Rome Convention by the European Court were finalized, but they are not yet in force. Even before it came into force it had been incorporated in the laws of some of the EEC Member States (Denmark, Luxembourg, Belgium and Germany), had been applied by courts in the Netherlands and France, had been relied on by an English court (*Libyan Arab Foreign Bank* v. *Bankers Trust Co.* [1989] QB 728, 747), and had even inspired a decision of the European Court in jurisdiction in relation to disputes arising out of employment contracts (Case 133/ 81 *Ivenel* v. *Schwab* [1982] ECR 1891). When the European Commission accepted the Benelux proposal which ultimately resulted in the Rome Convention, Mr Vogelaar, the Director-General for the Internal Market and Approximation of Legislation, emphasized that unified rules would (*inter alia*) strengthen confidence in the stability of legal relationships and facilitate agreements on jursdiction according to the applicable law. The Giuliano-Lagarde Report said that the effect of the Brussels Convention of 1968 was to give a choice to litigants between the courts of several countries, and that to prevent 'forum-shopping', to increase legal certainty, and to anticipate more easily the law which would be applied, it would be advisable to unify conflict of laws rules in fields of particular economic importance, so that the same substantive law would be applied irrespective of where the proceedings were brought. Whether there was a need to prevent 'forum-shopping', or, if there was, whether the Rome Convention satisfies it, has been doubted. In

From *International and Comparative Law Quarterly*, 25 (1976), 35.

England, in paricular, there was some scepticism. Lord Wilberforce expressed the hope that 'no one will mention the name of Mr. Vogelaar of Brussels' and said that the common law rules constituted 'an excellent body of law built up by judges over the years' which had not been criticized, and for the reform of which there had been no demand: HL Deb. 515, col. 1476, 15 February 1990.

Although there are some differences between the 1972 draft and the 1980 Convention, the points of principle raised in this article continue to arise under the final version, especially the relationship between the basic rule that a contract is governed by the law of the country of closest connection, on the one hand, and the presumptions based on the place of residence or business of the party who is to effect the characteristic performance, on the other. This article was not alone in criticising Article 7(1). It provides that, when the law of a country is applicable under the Convention, effect may be given to the mandatory rules of the law of another country with which the situation has a close connection, if, and in so far as, under the law of the latter country, those rules must be applied whatever the law applicable to the contract. In considering whether to give effect to mandatory rules of this kind, regard is to be had to their nature and purpose to the consequences of their application or non-application. This controversial provision is based on a theory which originated in Germany and was accepted by the Dutch Supreme Court in 1966 (the *ALNATI* case, 1967 Rev. Crit. 522), and in the Hague Convention on the Law Applicable to Agency. Its historical origin probably lies with the German theory that foreign public laws (especially exchange control and import or export restrictions) should apply if the interests of the forum or of a third country are not unduly violated. The operation of Article 7(1) may be illustrated by the effect abroad of United States legislation enacted in order to impose sanctions on foreign countries. In the celebrated *Sensor* decision in the Netherlands ((1983) 23 ILM 66) an embargo, directed against the Soviet Union, had been placed by the United States on the export by American companies (defined to include European subsidiaries) of equipment for the trans-Siberian pipeline. A Dutch subsidiary of an American company which had agreed to sell equipment to a French company for the pipeline refused to supply the equipment on the ground that it was bound by the export embargo. The Dutch court held that the contract of sale was governed by Dutch law because, in the absence of an express choice of law, the contract of sale had its closest connection with the Netherlands: the Dutch seller's obligation was characteristic of the contract. Notwithstanding that the contract was governed by Dutch law and did not involve performance in the United States, the Dutch court held that it was bound to accord priority over Dutch law to the application of mandatory provisions of foreign law if the contract had a sufficient connection with the foreign country concerned. Without indicating what connection would be sufficient, it was held that this condition was not fulfilled, and accordingly the contract was enforceable. In England, United States sanctions intended to block accounts held by Libya in London branches of United States banks were held inapplicable because the deposits were governed by English law and did not require performance in the United States. There was no room for the application of any other connecting factor: *Libyan Arab Foreign Bank* v. *Bankers Trust Co.* [1989] QB 728; *Libyan Arab Foreign Bank* v. *Manufacturers Hanover Trust Co. (No. 2)* [1989] 1 Lloyd's Rep. 608.

There was opposition in the United Kingdom to the idea of a formula whereby mandatory rules of a foreign country which were neither part of the *lex contractus* nor the *lex loci solutionis* might be given effect because 'the situation' had a close connection with that country. Accordingly, Article 7(1) was opposed by the United Kingdom delegation, because it was 'a recipe for confusion, . . . for uncertainty . . . for expense . . . and for delay . . .' (North, *Contract Conflicts* (1982), 19–20). Because of this opposition, Contracting States were given a right of reservation in relation to Article 7(1). The United Kingdom (as did Germany, Ireland and Luxembourg) made a reservation to Article 7(1), and consequently it is not in force in the United Kingdom, and section 2(2) of the 1990 Act so provides.

I. INTRODUCTION

The search for unification of private international law through international conventions has been a long and only partially successful one.[1] The European Communities have entered the lists with what is described as a 'preliminary draft Convention on the law applicable to contractual and non-contractual obligations'.[2] This preliminary draft was completed in June 1972 by a group of legal experts (the Brussels Working Group) nominated by the governments of the founder member States of the European Communities.

In principle, of course, the harmonisation and improvement of the rules of private international law must be welcomed, provided at any rate that the rules codified or developed by any convention are broadly acceptable and do not represent a step backwards in relation to any significant system which they replace. The report of the Brussels Working Group indicates that:

the object of this proposal [by the Benelux countries, to effect a unification of private international law] was to abolish the drawbacks arising from diversity of rules of conflict, notably in the law on contract[3]

---

[1] See Nadelmann, 'Multilateral Conventions in the Conflicts Field: An Historical Sketch' (1972) 19 *Neths Int. L. Rev.* 107, and *Conflict of Laws: International and Inter-State* (1972) pp. 86–165.

[2] The draft Convention was accompanied by a report (XIV/408/72), the bulk of which, in so far as it related to contractual obligations, was prepared by Professor Giuliano, of the University of Milan. In August 1974 the Law Commission and the Scottish Law Commission issued a consultative document, prepared by their joint working group, which was circulated to interested persons in the United Kingdom. The views expressed in the consultative document are the tentative views of the joint working group and do not represent the views of the Law Commissioners. The document contains a useful summary of the report of the Brussels working group and some very helpful comments upon, and criticisms of, the preliminary draft Convention. In the notes to this article it will be referred to as '*Law Com. Consultative Doc.*'.

and quotes Mr Vogelaar, the European Commission Director-General for the Internal Market and Approximation of Legislation, who had referred (*inter alia*) to the need to forestall 'forum shopping'. But is there really this need? There is less diversity in the conflict of laws rules relating to obligations (at any rate contractual obligations) than in most areas of private international law. In principle, in most countries parties may freely choose the law to govern their contract. It is true that there are differences of emphasis: in some countries the choice is less free than in others, and in some countries and in some cases the choice may be overridden. But those are all exceptional cases and it is unlikely that the flow of international trade is impeded by any divergencies in practice. It must therefore be doubted whether the divergencies, which undoubtedly exist, create any practical difficulties.

From the English standpoint at any rate, although it must be more a matter of impression than of scientific proof, it is likely that the true causes of forum shopping are to be found elsewhere than in the divergencies of the rules of private international law. The plaintiff usually shops in the forum with which he is most familiar or in which he gains the greatest procedural advantage or puts the defendant to the greatest procedural disadvantage. Thus in *The Atlantic Star*[4] the action in the English Admiralty Court was between two Dutch companies; the action in England was stayed in the light of the already pending proceedings in Belgium. The action was brought in England in good faith, apparently because a court-appointed surveyor's report had been produced in the Belgian proceedings which was favourable to the defendants and there was evidence that the Belgian court would usually accept the opinion arrived at by the surveyor. That therefore was a case where the rules of evidence in England were more favourable to the plaintiff.[5]

Nor should it be thought that a convention on a subject as specialised as the private international law relating to contracts would not have serious and far-reaching effects on the domestic law of the United Kingdom. It will

---

[4] [1974] AC 436.

[5] On the other hand, in *Coast Lines Ltd.* v. *Hudig and Veder Chartering NV* [1972] 2 QB 34, English shipowners sued Dutch charterers in England and were granted leave to issue and serve their writ out of the jurisdiction on the basis that the charterparty was governed by English law. One of the factors which influenced the Court of Appeal in allowing service out of the jurisdiction was that if the action were brought in Holland an exemption clause in the charterparty would have to be disregarded because the Dutch commercial code applied its provisions to all cases of carriage of good by sea from the Netherlands, even though the contract of carriage was governed by some other law. That, therefore, is a case which supports Mr Vogelaar's view that differences in private international law rules may affect the choice of forum. But it is possible that the real reason the plaintiffs sued in England was that they were an English company and that it was only later that they realised the advantages which they would obtain from suing in England. It should be added that it is by no means clear that the draft Convention would prevent there being different results in such a case in the two possible countries in which a suit could be brought: see *infra* on Art. 7.

be seen below in greater detail that the draft Convention provides (as does the law of the United Kingdom) for the primacy of the proper law of the contract, subject to certain, but not very well defined, exceptions. If adopted, it will apply without any condition of reciprocity and even if the applicable law is not that of a contracting state. Thus the member States of the EEC will be adopting a code of private international law not only for their relations *inter se* but also in relation to other states. As regards the United Kingdom, therefore, the common law rules will cease to apply even in relation to other countries and in particular to Commonwealth countries which have adopted the common law.

More important, however, is the limitation which the Convention would place on the power of each contracting State to legislate in its domestic law. The effect of the Convention would be to impose an international obligation on the contracting States to refrain from legislating in relation to legal relationships which the Convention provides are to be governed by some other system of law. Thus the loose rules of private international law become strict rules of public international law.

An example may be the implied terms imposed by the Consumer Credit Act 1974. It is unlikely at present that its application would be restricted to contracts subject to English law and undesirable that it should be so restricted.[6] If a foreign country enters into a hire purchase contract with an individual resident in England, the choice of foreign law may be perfectly bona fide and legal, but an important policy of English law would be defeated if the Consumer Credit Act 1974 were interpreted so as not to be applicable to such a contract. While it is true that, in the absence of 'a choice of law clause', an Act of Parliament affecting contracts will normally be construed so as to apply to contracts governed by English law, that is not an inflexible rule and acts of a social nature have been held to apply to contracts executed or performed in the United Kingdom, irrespective of their proper law.[7]

It is possible that private international lawyers are not the persons best qualified to isolate and recommend those areas where, as a matter of domestic law, the normal rules of the conflict of laws should be overridden. An obvious and much discussed example is the area of employment contracts and, perhaps for the very reason that it is so frequently discussed, the draft Convention does make special provision in the case of employment contracts. Article 2 provides an exception to the general rule that a contract should be governed by the law chosen by the parties, namely, that, in relations between employer and employee, the choice of law made by the parties should in no case prejudice the operation of

---

[6] See Dicey and Morris, *Conflict of Laws* (9th edn., 1973) p. 756.

[7] See, e.g. cases cited at *Dicey & Morris*, pp. 755–756, but cf. *Sayers* v. *International Drilling* [1971] 1 WLR 1176.

manadatory rules for the protection of the employee which are in force in the country in which he habitually carries out his work. So far as the other types of contract are concerned, the draft Convention merely provides (in a provision—Art. 7—to be discussed in greater detail below) that where a contract is also connected with a country other than the country whose law is the proper law and the law of that other country contains mandatory rules which govern the matter in such a way as to exclude the application of every other law, those rules should be 'taken into account to the extent that the exclusion is justifiable by the special nature and purpose of the rules', and that the application of any law may be refused if it is manifestly incompatible with public policy (Art. 22).

The draft Convention provisionally excludes insurance contracts from its ambit and, as mentioned above, special provision is made for employment contracts. But contracts of hire purchase, moneylending contracts and other consumer credit contracts would fall within its scope. Would it really be the intention of the member States to give up their power to legislate in these areas to the extent that the draft Convention makes their laws inapplicable (except under the rather uncertain public policy exception) to such contracts or at any rate applicable only on the very limited terms of Article 7? By section 16 (5) (c) of the Consumer Credit Act 1974 the Secretary of State may by order provide that the Act shall not regulate consumer credit agreements where 'an agreement has a connection with a country outside the United Kingdom'. If a consumer credit agreement were entered into in the United Kingdom but (because of the nationality of one of the parties to the agreement) were expressed to be governed by some foreign law, the effect of the draft Convention would be that the Consumer Credit Act could not be applied to it, except 'to the extent that the exclusion is justifiable by the special nature and purpose' of mandatory rules governing the matter in such a way as to exclude the application of every other law, or if the application of the foreign law is manifestly incompatible with public policy.

It would of course be subversive of a rational system of private international law to allow too significant a scope to the legislator of a country which was not the country whose law was the proper law of the contract. Thus English and other courts do not normally apply the foreign *lex loci contractus*.[8] But the principle that the legislation of the forum must be given effect even if it overrides the ordinary principles of private international law is a salutary one, for private international law is not a system which gives substantive answers and the overriding statutory rule, if it is rarely invoked, provides a less subversive safety valve than the unbridled rules of public policy.

[8] But see *The Torni* [1932] P. 78.

2. SCHEME OF DRAFT CONVENTION

It may be helpful at this point to indicate in outline the main provisions of the draft Convention relating to the law applicable to contracts, and then to discuss them in greater detail. They will not be discussed in the same order in which they appear in the Convention and drafting points will be kept to a minimum, in view of the provisional nature of the draft. The basic provisions are as follows:

1. The proposed rules apply 'in situations of an international character only' (Art. 1).

2. They do not apply to certain classes of agreement, including negotiable instruments, arbitration agreements and agreements on the choice of court, (provisionally) insurance contracts, and to the formation, internal organisation or dissolution of companies or other similar entities (Art. 1).

3. The basic rule is that a contract is to be governed by the law chosen by the parties (Art. 2). Such choice may, it appears, be express or implied (Art. 4) and may be made at the time of the making of the contract or afterwards (Art. 3).

4. In the absence of an express or implied choice, the contract is to be governed by the law of the country with which it is most closely connected and normally that country is to be the country of residence or place of business of the person 'who is to effect the performance which is characteristic of the contract' unless it is clear that the contract is more closely connected with another country (Art. 4).

5. The law governing the obligation determines the conditions of performance, the consequences of non-performance and the ways in which the obligation may be extinguished (Art. 15). As regards the manner of performance, the law of the country in which performance takes place must be taken into account (Art. 15). Where the contract is connected with some other country and the law of that country contains mandatory rules which govern the matter in such a way as to exclude the application of every other law, those rules shall be taken into account to the extent that the exclusion is justifiable by the special nature and purpose of the rules (Art. 7).

6. The draft Convention does not apply to the status or capacity of individuals (Art. 1) but it provides that no natural person may invoke his capacity against a person who, in good faith and without acting imprudently, considered him to have capacity under the law of the place where the act was executed (Art. 20).

7. The draft Convention contains alternative solutions for the effect of silence of a party on a proposal as to the choice of applicable law (Art. 2)

and also on the effect of silence on the conclusion of a contract (Art. 8). The validity of consent as to the applicable law (Art. 2) as to the contract (Art. 8) is governed by the law applicable to the contract.

8. A document will be formally valid if valid either by the law applicable to the contract or by the law of the place of contracting (Art. 18) and provision is also made for the mode of proof of documents (Art. 19). The existence and force of presumptions of law and the burden of proof are to be determined by the law applicable to the contract (Art. 19).

9. There are special provisions for employment contracts (Art. 2 and Art. 5), for contracts dealing with immovable property (Art. 6) and for assignment of choses in action (Art. 16 and Art. 17).

10. Miscellaneous provisions include the following:

(i) The draft Convention does not apply to the transfer of ownership or to the effects of a contract on other rights *in rem* (Art. 9).

(ii) Renvoi is excluded (Art. 21).

(iii) Provision is made for the exclusion of the otherwise applicable law if it is manifestly incompatible with public policy (Art. 22).

3. SPHERE OF APPLICATION OF CONVENTION

It is notoriously difficult to delimit the area of the conflict of laws. It would not be considered very useful if one defined the area of the law of tort as the area concerned with torts, but such a definition would be a harmless tautology. If the limitation of the rules of the draft Convention to 'situations of an international character' were understood in this sense as meaning no more than a statement of the obvious, namely that conflict of laws rules deal with cases with an international element, then no further discussion would be required. The limitation, however, raises an important theoretical question, which has received greater attention abroad than in England, namely, whether the rules of private international law relate only to 'international contracts'. Take for example a contract for the sale of goods between two Italians which contains a choice of English law. Is the effectiveness of the choice of law to be tested by reference to the rules in the draft Convention or is this a situation which is not of an international character? In 1939 Lord Wright pointed out that those familiar with international business were aware how frequent it was to provide for the choice of English law or English arbitration even where the parties were not English and the transactions were carried on completely outside England.[9] More recently Salmon LJ (as he then was) said '. . . it is not uncommon in the shipping world to find foreign shipowners in their

---

[9] *Vita Food Products Inc.* v. *Unus Shipping Co.* [1939] AC 277 at p. 290.

contracts agreeing that any dispute between them shall be decided by the English commercial court according to English law.'[10] But these were both cases where the law chosen was that of the forum, and the forum is hardly likely to reject the choice of its own law.[11]

There is weighty academic support in England for a view which has been expressed frequently in other countries,[12] that the freedom of choice by law exists only in relation to 'international contracts'. The very choice of a foreign law may make a situation have a foreign element, even though without that choice it might be a wholly domestic transaction. Provided that such a case comes within the concept of a situation of an international character no harm could be done by the inclusion of that formula. It would merely be a statement of the truism that matters of the conflict of laws are concerned with cases with a foreign element. If it is to have a narrower meaning, it could result in there being in a sense two systems of the conflict of laws, one for situations of an international character as that expression is used in the draft Convention and another for situations containing a foreign element but not being 'situations of an international character'. This is particularly so in cases of a choice of English law, because of the importance of London as a commercial centre. Even in cases which do not involve trade across national frontiers, arbitration may take place in London between non-English parties. If such a case does not involve an international situation within the meaning of the Convention, then it would seem that the common law rules of the conflict of laws should remain in full effect in relation to the case.

The matters excluded from the scope of the Convention call for little comment. Article 1 excludes (*inter alia*) matters which one would not expect to find dealt with in a convention dealing with obligations (whether contractual or tortious) such as rules governing rights in property between husband and wives, wills, intestate succession and gifts, and the formation, internal organisation or dissolution of companies or other similar entities. Negotiable instruments are also excluded and that is understandable in

---

[10] *Tzortzis* v. *Monark Line A/B* [1968] 1All ER 949 at p. 954. In *Pagnan and Fratelli* v. *Corbisa Industrial Agropacuaria* [1971] 1 All ER 165 at p. 166, he referred to contracts commonly entered into by foreign merchants all over the world providing for arbitration in London although the contracts had nothing to do with England.

[11] See Wolff, *Private International Law* (2nd ed., 1950) pp. 421–422. The same result can always be reached by the parties not pleading foreign law.

[12] See *Dicey & Morris*, pp. 729–732; Lipstein, 'Conflict of Laws 1921–1971—The Way Ahead' [1972] CLJ 66 at pp. 109–110; Batiffol, *Droit Internationale Privé* (5th ed., 1971) Vol. 2, p. 221; Loussouarn and Bredin, *Droit du Commerce International* (1969) pp. 593–594; cf. cases at *Clunet* (1972), p. 843 n. Oppetit; *Clunet* (1972), p. 390 n. Oppetit; *Rev. Crit.* (1974), p. 82 n. Level; *Enc. Dalloz, Rép. de Droit Int.* (1968) Vol. I, pp. 563–564 (Batiffol); *J. Cl. Droit Int. Fasc.* 552-B, paras. 10–15 (Dayant). It should be noted that the Hague Conventions on the Sale of Goods apply to sales '*à caractère internationale*'.

view of their specialised nature and the existence of other international conventions dealing with them.

Insurance contracts have been provisionally excluded. It is not clear why special rules of the conflict of laws should apply to insurance contracts. It is true that they are subject to a greater degree of social regulation[13] than many other types of contract. Their exclusion may be a pointer to the fact that a convention dealing with the conflict of laws has more significant consequences in internal law than might at first sight appear.

The exclusion of arbitration agreements and agreements on the choice of law by the same Article is odd. There is no reason in theory why certain aspects of arbitration and forum selection clauses should not be left to the law governing the contract.[14]

4. CHOICE OF LAW

The draft Convention adopts the almost universal rule that the parties are free to choose the law governing their contract. In some countries it is said that the rule only applies if the contract is one having an international charcter, as in Belgium, the Netherlands, France, possibly Germany, but not Italy.[15] In England there is the famous statement of Lord Wright in the *Vita Food* case[16] that

where there is an express statement by the parties of their intention to select the law of the contract, it is difficult to see what qualifications are possible, provided the intention expressed is bona fide and legal, and provided there is no reason for avoiding the choice on the ground of public policy.

But as indicated above, there are many cases where contracts having no connection whatsoever with England are subjected expressly to English law because of the confidence which foreign merchants have in English law and English justice. As Lord Wright said, 'Connection with English law is not as a matter of principle essential.'

The draft Convention (quite rightly, it is suggested) contains no exception to this principle to the effect that the choice of the governing law must be 'genuine' or 'bona fide'. It is true that the second paragraph of Article 2 provides that 'conditions governing the validity of the consent of the parties as to the applicable law shall be determined by that law' but that rather critical provision, to be considered below, relates only to defects in

---

[13] For the United Kingdom, see Insurance Companies Act 1974.

[14] Thus, in England, matters relating to the construction of a forum selection clause are left to the proper law of the contract: *Evans Marshall & Company Limited* v. *Bertola* [1973] 1 WLR 349 and *The Sindh* [1975] 1 Lloyd's Rep. 372.

[15] See *Brussels Working Group Report*, pp. 23–24. See *Law Com. Consultative Doc.*, p. 15, for criticism of the formulation of this exclusion.   [16] [1939] AC at p. 290.

the consent of the parties as to the designation of the applicable law and is probably not intended to deal with the question of genuineness.

The draft Convention does not state in terms that the choice of law may be express or implied. But that is clearly intended as appears from Article 4 which speaks of 'the absence of an express or implied choice of law'.[17] Like English law and other systems the Convention draws a distinction between an implied choice and an objectively determined applicable law in the absence of an express or implied choice. In practice, however, such a distinction is very difficult to draw and may not be very meaningful. Thus, many of the cases discussed in *Dicey and Morris*[18] as being examples of an inferred intention may also be regarded as cases where the contract was held to be governed by a system of law with which the transaction had its closest and most real connection. For example, in *Whitworth Street Estates (Manchester) Limited* v. *James Miller and Partners Limited*[19] the House of Lords considered (as a subsidiary question, since the main question was the procedural law which governed an arbitration in Scotland) the question of the proper law of an RIBA standard form building contract (in the English form) for the conversion of premises in Scotland. The contract contained no choice of law clause and the majority held that the use of the English form showed 'the intention of the parties to be bound by English law'[20] or that both parties 'intended that the contract should be governed by the law of England'.[21] The minority, particularly Lord Wilberforce, approached the matter from the point of view of the other test, namely, the objective one in relation to the system of law with the most substantial connection.

The case also decided that events taking place after the time of the contract could not be taken into account as evidence of the intention of the parties at the time of the contract. This is a rule relating to construction of contracts in general.[22] The general rule on the continent is different and there the courts may take subsequent conduct into consideration.[23] This difference will therefore have to be clarified in the draft Convention. In Article 3 the Convention deals with a different, but related, point, when it provides that the choice of the applicable law may be made by the parties either at the time of conclusion of the contract or at a later date, and that the choice may be varied at any time by agreement between the parties.[24] These provisions may, however, have unintended and undesirable results. Both on general principles and according to the term of the draft

---

[17] See *Law Com. Consultative Doc.*, p. 21 for the sensible recommendation that this should be made clear in Article 2.   [18] At p. 735–739.   [19] [1970] AC 583.

[20] Lord Hodson at p. 606.   [21] Lord Dilhorne at p. 611.

[22] *Wickman Tools v. Shuler AG* [1974] AC 235.

[23] See Mann, Note (1973) 89 LQR 464.

[24] See Tomaszewski, 'La désignation, postérieure à la conclusion du contrat, de la loi qui le régit', *Rev. Crit.* (1972), p. 567.

Convention, at the time of the making of the contract it must be governed by some law (the law of State X). The law of State X must contain mandatory rules governing the contract. It is difficult to see how legal policy can be furthered by allowing the parties to agree at a later date that the law of State X should not govern the contract and that the law of State Y should govern it, quite irrespective of whether the law of State X allows the parties to remove themselves from its control. It is one thing to allow subsequent conduct to be evidence of the choice of law, it is quite another to allow changes in the choice of law during the currency of an agreement. In England, of course, the parties can in effect do this if the original choice is a foreign law by not pleading the foreign law in the course of proceedings. But take the following example. Provisions in a hire purchase agreement are invalidated by the law of State X, which is also the law originally chosen by the contract. One of the parties, after learning of this illegality, persuades the other party to change the applicable law to the law of State Y which validates the clause. It is suggested that in such a case the clause should be invalid and not validated by the purported change in the applicable law. The only qualification in the draft Convention is that any variation in the choice of the applicable law which is made after the conclusion of the contract is to be without prejudice to the rights of third parties. But it is not easy to see in what circumstances such a variation could affect the rights of third parties.

Article 4 deals with the question of the governing law in the absence of an express or implied choice, and introduces the notion of 'characteristic performance'. Article 4 has the same basic principles as English law, namely, that the contract is to be governed, in the absence of an express or implied choice, by the law of the country with which it is most clearly connected, but its method for isolating that system of law is radically different. It is sufficiently important to merit quotation in full:

In the absence of an express or implied choice of law, the contract shall be governed by the law of the country with which it is most closely connected. That country shall be:

(a) the country in which the party who is to effect the performance which is characteristic of the contract has his habitual residence at the time of conclusion of the contract;
(b) the country in which that party has his principal establishment at the time of conclusion of the contract, if the characteristic performance is to be effected under a contract concluded in the court of a business activity;
(c) the country in which the party's subsidiary establishment is situated, if it follows from the terms of the contract that the characteristic performance is to be effected by that establishment.

The preceding paragraph shall not apply if either the characteristic performance, the habitual residence or the establishment cannot be determined or if from the circumstances as a whole it is clear that the contract is more closely connected with another country.

Given that the basic aim is the same, are these criteria better than the very loose ones adopted by the English courts, in that (a) they will be easier for lawyers and judges to apply and (b) they will be more likely to lead to the appropriate law? In the view of this writer, the answer is no on both counts. In the first place, it adds several alternative and vague tests to one (admittedly vague) test. In the second place, it is suggested that those additional tests do not necessarily lead to the appropriate governing law.

Article 4 applies only in the absence of an implied or express choice of law. The basic provision is that the contract shall be governed by the law of the *country* with which it is most closely connected. The English test speaks of 'the system of law' with which the transaction has its closest and more real connection, rather than the country, although there are conflicting dicta.[25] If one looks to the system of law with which the contract is most closely connected, there is a greater tendency to place the emphasis on the form and language of the contract rather than the place or places with which the negotiation and, especially, the performance of the contract has a connection. Another aspect of the 'system of law' formulation is that it is more adequate to cater for countries such as the United Kingdom which has several 'law districts'.

Subject, then, to the reservation about the use of the expression 'country', the basic rule of Article 4 is almost identical with the rule in English law. But the succeeding elaboration of the basic rule is most unsatisfactory. The basic rule is elaborated by providing that the law of the country with which the contract is to be treated as being most closely connected is the country of residence or business establishment of the party who is to effect the performance which is characteristic of the contract. In the case of an individual it is to be the country of his habitual residence at the time of the conclusion of the contract; in the case of an enterprise it is to be the country of the principal establishment of that enterprise at the conclusion of the contract unless the characteristic performance is to be effected by a subsidiary establishment, in which case it is to be the country in which the subsidiary establishment is situated at the time of the conclusion of the contract.

There are two main objections to the elaboration of the basic rule in the preceding ways. In the first place, there must be some doubt as to whether residence or place of business is the proper connecting factor in the case of

---

[25] See cases cited in *Dicey & Morris* at p. 744. This is not a purely verbal question, as is shown by the result in *Whitworth Street Estates (Manchester) Limited* v. *James Miller & Partners Limited, supra,* n. 19. See also *Coast Lines Ltd.* v. *Hudig and Veder Chartering, supra,* n. 5 and Carter, Note, BYIL, 1972–73, p. 432.

commercial contracts, which represent the vast bulk of contracts containing a foreign element; in the second place, the concept of 'characteristic performance' as a test does not, rightly, find much favour among the EEC countries. The combination of these tests does not, it is submitted, lead to an appropriate law. To put it in terms of English law, it amounts at the very least to a resurrection of the presumption in favour of the law of the place of performance: most recently, such presumptions have been deprecated by the Court of Appeal in *Coast Lines Limited* v. *Hudig and Veder Chartering NV*.[26]

Article 4 links this retrograde step to a 'rule' of residence or place of business which is only really workable when the place of residence or business and the place of performance are the same. If they are not the same, it would lead to the odd result that if, for example, in an agency contract the agent was a resident of State X who was to perform all his duties in State Y it would be the law of State X which would govern the contract. In commercial matters, where individuals are concerned, the state of residence is not a suitable or appropriate connecting factor. Nor is the test of the principal or subsidiary establishment a suitable test in the case of contracts concluded by companies. Take for example a distribution agreement entered into between a producer in State X and a multinational corporation whose principal establishment is in State Y, providing for the world wide distribution of the former's products by the latter. Apart from the difficulty of determining the party who is to effect the characteristic performance (which will be considered below) and assuming that it is the multinational distributor corporation, Article 4 would lead to the law of State Y—although on the facts there is no reason to believe that the law of State Y is any more connected with the contract than the law of State X or (say) the place where the parties anticipate that most of the distribution will take place. Nor, it is suggested, is it very sensible to have a specific provision providing for the governing law to be that of the country where the relevant party's subsidiary establishment is situated, if it follows from the terms of the contract that the characteristic performance is to be effected by that establishment. International commercial contracts do not usually provide which 'subsidiary establishment' or branch is to effect the performance of the contract. To vary the previous example, if the producer in State X appoints the multinational corporation in State Y to distribute the former's products in State Z, where the latter has a branch, the contract would not normally provide that the branch would effect the distribution and the corporation in State Y would probably not wish to be so limited. The contracting party is the company and not the branch. It is

---

[26] [1972] 2 QB 34 at pp. 44, 47 and 50. For a similar view see *Law Com. Consultative Doc.*, p. 31.

suggested, therefore, that the residence and establishment tests are quite unsuitable for international commercial contracts.

What, then, of the place of 'characteristic performance'? If this were the governing presumption (entirely without reference to residence or place of business establishment) it would not do very much more than represent a revival of the presumption that the law of the place of performance is to govern the contract, merely refining that presumption by making it the performance not of both parties but of one party only. What is the 'characteristic performance'? The use of the concept is limited to cases where each of the parties is to perform in a different country. In such a case there is more than one place of performance. The concept seeks to isolate the place of performance by one of the parties, by identifying the performance of that party as more 'characteristic' of the contract as a whole. As the Brussels Working Group points out, the problem does not really arise in 'unilateral' contracts.[27] The notion of 'characteristic performance' has developed mainly in Switzerland although it is not unknown in other countries.[28]

In the majority of cases the use of the concept of 'characteristic performance' will not lead to any different result than the notion of performance *simpliciter* and would be subject to the same objections. Thus, in the case of sale of goods, the place of performance (where ownership is transferred or where delivery takes place) may have little connection with the system of law with which the transaction as a whole (particularly if it is part of a string of contracts) has it closest connection. In the case of agency, it is normally the agent who performs most of the positive functions under the contract and whether one calls the place where the agent performs the place of performance *simpliciter* or the place of characteristic performance does not matter. Does the notion of 'characteristic performance' in fact add anything at all? For example, in a typical distribution agreement, the producer will have an obligation to produce and maintain the quality of the goods and the distributor will have the duty

---

[27] According to the *Brussels Working Group Report* (p. 37) there is no problem in identifying the characteristic performance in the case of unilateral contract. According to the Group, in bilateral or synallagmatic contracts, where the parties undertake to deliver reciprocal performances, the obligation of one of the parties will normally be limited to the payment of money. It goes on to indicate that the payment of money would not be in such a circumstance a characteristic performance and it would therefore be the performance of those obligations for which payment is due (e.g. transfer of ownership or the supply of a service) which would constitute the 'centre of gravity and socio-economic function of the contractual transformation'. The distinction between unilateral and bilateral contracts is discussed at some length by Diplock LJ (as he then was) in *United Dominions Trust (Commercial) Limited* v. *Eagle Aircraft Services Limited* [1968] 1 All ER 104 at pp. 108–110. For further criticism, see *Law Com. Consultative Doc.*, p. 30.

[28] See Batiffol, *op. cit.*, *supra*, n. 12, at pp. 232–233. Cf. *Rev. Crit.* (1955), p. 330; Drobnig, *German Private International Law* (2nd ed., 1972), p. 233.

to use best or reasonable endeavours to promote the sale of the goods. If production is in State X and distribution is in State Y it is suggested that it is not really meaningful to talk of 'the characteristic performance' as being that of the distributor. Both sets of obligations are equally characteristic and yet most lawyers will incline to the view, that all things being equal, the place of distribution was more likely to be the place of the governing law.[29] Another difficult example, but a very common one, would be an international loan agreement. Occasionally the parties do not agree on an express choice of law. The contract might be between a group of international banks centred in London providing for loans to a company in South America to be raised in the European Eurodollar Market, but where technically payments are made through New York. Why is the provision of the money any more characteristic of such a contract than its repayment?[30]

To deal with these difficulties and also with the very real possibility that the place of characteristic performance will not in fact lead to the properly applicable law, the draft Convention provides that the specific rules of residence/principal establishment of the party to perform the characteristic obligation will not apply if (a) the characteristic performance cannot be determined, (b) the habitual residence or the establishment cannot be determined, or (c) from the circumstances as a whole it is clear that the contract is more closely connected with another country. The first exception deals with the difficulty mentioned above, namely, that in the more complicated types of agreement it will not be possible to determine which party is performing the characteristic obligations of the contract. The second exception deals with a more mundane situation where the habitual residence or establishment cannot be determined, but the third exception, of course, brings the matter full circle so there is a three stage operation which ends where it begins. The search initially is for the law of the country with which the contract is most closely connected. Article 4 contains a rule of habitual residence/principal establishment/characteristic performance indicating which country 'shall be' the country with which the contract is most closely connected. And yet there is an overriding rule that the characteristic performance rule does not apply if from the circumstances as a whole it is clear that the contract is more closely connected with another country. Why then have a complicated rule which is in effect deprived of meaning by the overriding provision that in any event the search is for the country with which the contract is most closely connected? It would surely be better, if a close connection rule is to be elaborated, to

---

[29] Although for a case where the contract was impliedly governed by Spanish law, the law of the producer, in view of its form and in view of a submission to the jurisdiction of the Spanish courts, see *Evans Marshall & Company Limited* v. *Bertola SA* [1973] 1 WLR 349.

[30] See also *Law Com. Consultative Doc.*, p. 30 for other examples.

indicate what are the factors (place of performance/residence/place of contracting/form of contract/language of contract, etc.) by way of example rather than have a dubious rule subject to an exception which may deprive it of all meaning.

5. SCOPE OF APPLICABLE LAW AND APPLICATION OF MANDATORY RULES

The draft Convention provides in Article 15 that the applicable laws determined in accordance with the principles outlined above determines the conditions of performance, the consequences of non-performance and the ways in which the obligation may be extinguished. That is broadly similar to English law. It would appear (although it is not clear) that the law governing the contract is to determine whether specific performance is available, in contrast to the rule prevailing in England.[31] Article 15 also provides that as regards the manner of performance the law of the country in which performance takes place must be taken into account. This is similar to the rule in English law[32] that the mode of performing a contract (as distinct from substance of the obligation) is governed by the law of the place at which the obligation is to be performed.

In English law there are exceptions to the primacy of the proper law of the contract. They include the application of English Acts of Parliament which, expressly or impliedly, override the proper law,[33] the overriding nature of public policy, and (perhaps most important in practice) the unenforceability of a contract whose performance is unlawful by the law of the country where the contract is to be performed.[34] The draft Convention contains a provision relating to exceptions to the law chosen by the parties and the other laws specifically applicable under the draft Convention in the following terms (Article 7):

Where the contract is also connected with a country other than the country whose law is applicable under [certain specific articles of the convention] and the law of that country contains mandatory rules which govern the matter in such a way as to exclude the application of every other law, these rules shall be taken into account to the extent that the exclusion is justifiable by the special nature and purpose of the rules.

This is a most unfortunate provision. Legal security is not advanced by it and, far from contributing to certainty in the law, it is likely to create the

---

[31] See *Baschet* v. *London Illustrated Standard* [1890] 1 Ch. 73.
[32] *Dicey & Morris*, p. 792.   [33] *Boissevain* v. *Weil* [1950] AC 327.
[34] The scope of this last exception is uncertain and it may be limited to contracts governed by English law. See *Dicey & Morris*, pp. 781–788.

greatest uncertainty. It envisages a situation where *ex hypothesi* the contract is governed by a particular applicable law. For some other law to be taken into account the following conditions must be present:

(a) the contract must be connected with some other country
(b) the law of that other country must contain mandatory rules
(c) those mandatory rules must purport to exclude the application of every other law
(d) the exclusion of the application of every other law must be justifiable by the special nature and purpose of those mandatory rules.

Thus if a provision is valid by the law chosen by the parties, it is not that law which will determine whether other mandatory rules invalidate the clause, but the law of some other country and that other country is to be not the country which is most closely connected with the contract (for that country already supplies the governing law of the contract) but merely some country which is 'also connected' and it is for the law of that other country to decide whether the normally applicable law is excluded. What is the lawyer to advise or the Judge to decide in such a circumstance? The only guidance the Convention gives him is that he is to take those other mandatory rules into account 'to the extent that the exclusion is justifiable by the special nature and purpose of the rule.'[35] It is suggested that the generality and vagueness of this rule is such as to create immense difficulties in practice for commercial men, lawyers and judges. Certainty and simplicity are not the exclusive aims of the law of contract, but they are very important ones and commercial men should, otherwise than in exceptional cases, need to take advice only on one system of law before entering into their contracts. The draft Convention is clearly not the place for a resolution of the very difficult problems which arise from, or are connected with, what Professor Lipstein has described as 'the interplay between the application of ordinary rules of the conflict of laws and self-limiting choice of law rules concerning the application of domestic public law'.[36] Nor is this article the place for a discussion of these problems, which have been exhaustively treated by Dr F. A. Mann in a recent article.[37] All

---

[35] The *Brussels Working Group Report* (p. 45) understates the position when it says that a proposed rule is 'sufficiently flexible to allow the judge some discretion' and that it confers on the judge 'a delicate task'. See also *Law Com. Consultative Doc.*, pp. 38–43 for criticism, in particular that Art. 7 is too indefinite and gives inadequate guidance.

[36] *Op. cit.*, *supra*, n. 12, p. 73.

[37] Mann, 'Statutes and the Conflict of Laws', BYIL, 1972–73, p. 117. See also, for recent treatment of this difficult question, Francescakis, 'Quelques précisions sur les "lois d'application immédiate" et leurs rapports avec le règles de conflits de lois', *Rev. Crit.* (1966), p. 16; Wengler, 'Immunité législative des contrats multinationaux', *Rev. Crit.* (1971), p. 637.

that should be pointed out in connection with Article 7 is that, first, it treats this enormously complex and practical problem with less than the attention it deserves, and, second, it enlarges the problem in the following way: the normal conflict is between the ordinary rules of private international law of State X, the State of the forum, which leads to the application of the law of State Y, on the one hand, and the public law of State X, which insists on the application of the internal law of State X. Article 7 enlarges this problem (perhaps in order to avoid charges of encouragement of forum shopping) by allowing the possible application not only of the public law of the forum but also of any of the public law of any State with which the contract is 'connected'.

6. STATUS AND CAPACITY

Article 1 of the draft Convention expressly excludes from its scope questions of the status or capacity of natural persons and questions relating to the formation, internal organisation or dissolution of companies or other legal persons or associations of natural or legal persons. That exclusion is subject to Article 20, which provides that no natural person may invoke his incapacity against a person, who in relation to a juristic act, in good faith and without acting imprudently, considered him to have capacity under the law of the place where the act was executed. This is a curious provision. Presumably it should follow (although the Article does not say so) that if an individual does actually have capacity under the law of the place where the act was executed, he may not invoke his incapacity (under the proper law of the contract or under his domicile) irrespective of the prudence or otherwise of the other party to the contract. If this interpretation is correct (and it cannot be said that the provision is clear) then the Article tends towards the primacy of the law of the place of contracting, which in modern commercial relations is a retrograde step.

In the English conflict of laws, questions of capacity are controversial. The law in relation to individuals is uncertain[38] and in relation to corporations difficult to apply.[39] The practitioner needs to take a very broad view of capacity in international commercial transactions, otherwise he would have to advise his clients to take advice on the laws of several different countries. It would be helpful to have a uniform rule on the capacity both in relation to individuals and corporations and if there is to be a convention it is to be hoped that a uniform provision can be introduced, preferably referring this question to the system of law with which the contract is most closely connected.

[38] *Dicey & Morris*, p. 765.　　　[39] *Dicey & Morris*, pp. 706–707.

7. QUESTIONS OF CONSENT

The second paragraph of Article 2 provides that conditions governing the validity of the consent of the parties as to the applicable law shall be determined by that law. This is apparently intended to deal only with defects in the consent of the parties to the designation of the applicable law and is said to be modelled on Article 2 (3) of the Hague Convention of 1955 on the law applicable to international sales of goods.[40] This type of provision poses no problem if the law chosen by the parties upholds that consent. But if under that law the parties have not made any effective choice, what then? Is the ineffective choice not to be taken into account as one of the factors pointing to the law with the closest connection with the contract? In *Compagnie d'Armement Maritime* v. *Compagnie Tunisienne de Navigation*,[41] Lord Diplock used an ineffective choice of law to rebut the inference of an implied choice of law from an arbitration clause providing for arbitration in England. But Lord Wilberforce (with whom Lord Dilhorne agreed) thought that such an argument was 'too subtle and ingenious'. To test the validity of a choice of law by reference to the law chosen comes perilously close to renvoi. But, more important, it is suggested that there is no need to have a provision dealing with the validity of consent as to the applicable law. If there is a contract at all, it is difficult to see how the choice of law would not be the subject of consent.

The annex to the draft Convention contains alternative provisions on another problem which, it is suggested, does not really arise. These alternative provisions deal with the effect of the silence of a party on a proposal as to the applicable law. There was no agreement in the Brussels Working Group on this point, neither as to whether there should be a provision at all, nor as to the rule to be adopted if there was to be a provision. The first variant provides that the effect of silence as to the applicable law shall be determined in accordance with the law of the place of habitual residence of the silent party, subject to exceptions if there has been a previous course of dealing between the parties or if the parties were or should have been aware of international trade usages. The second variant provides that agreement on the choice of applicable law may be deduced from the silence of one of the parties only if that interpretation follows from a previous course of dealing between the parties or form international trade usages; but if the contract has already been concluded, the law which governs it shall determine whether the silence implies a choice of applicable law.

It does not seem that this is a real problem at all. If *ex hypothesi* there is a

---

[40] *Report of Brussels Working Group*, p. 26.   [41] [1971] AC 572.

contract containing a choice of law clause, there seems no reason at all why the contract as a whole (including the choice of law clause) should not be fully binding. This is not the same problem as silence as to the conclusion of a contract (which relates to the formation of the contract)—that problem arises in the context of the contract concluded (or not concluded) by correspondence and is dealt with in the following pararaph. It is suggested therefore that there should be no rule on this topic. The first variant has in addition the defect of a reference to residence, which is not a satisfactory connecting factor in commercial matters and the second variant, which refers the effect of silence on a choice of applicable law to the law governing the contract, has elements both of tautology and of renvoi.

Article 8 (1) provides that conditions governing the validity of the consent of the parties to the contract are to be determined according to the law applicable under the preceding articles, namely, the law chosen by the parties or in the absence of a choice the law with the closest connection. In England the better view is that the formation of the contract is governed by the law which would be the proper law of the contract if the contract were validly concluded, possibly not taking account for this purpose of any express choice of law.[42] The Brussels Working Group was divided on the question whether the general principle also applied to the effect of one party's silence on the formation of the contract and as a result the annex to the draft Convention contains two alternative provisions dealing with silence. The first variant provides that the effect of the silence of a party on the conclusion of a contract shall be determined in accordance with the law of the place of habitual residence of that party, subject to the possibility of consent being inferred (whatever the law of the place of habitual residence may say) from a previous course of dealing between the parties. The second variant provides that the conclusion of a contract may not be inferred from the silence of a party unless it follows from a previous course of dealing between the parties or from international trade usages.[43] It is suggested that the general rule on the formulation of a contract is adequate to cope with the problem of offer and acceptance, which is only a species of the more general problem. No special provision, therefore, is required for this problem.

8. FORMAL VALIDITY

The relevant provisions call for little comment. Article 18 provides for the formal validity of a 'juristic act' if it is done in accordance with the

---

[42] *Dicey & Morris*, pp. 763–765, and cf. *Mackender* v. *Feldia* [1967] 2 QB 590.

[43] The first alternative is similar to that suggested by Wolff, *op. cit.*, *supra*, n. 11, p. 439, and criticised in *Dicey & Morris* at p. 764.

conditions prescribed either by the law which governs the material validity of the act or which governed its material validity at the time when it was done, or by the law of the place where it was done. By Article 19 (2), the law of the forum shall determine the admissibility of the modes of proof of juristic acts. But a party may also rely on a mode of proof which is admissible under any law referred to in Article 18 under which the act is formally valid, provided that the use of such mode of proof is not incompatible with the law of the forum. Article 19 (3) provides that the law which in accordance with Article 18 governs the formal validity of the act shall determine both how far an informally executed document which establishes obligations on the part of its signatory or signatories shall be sufficient proof of these obligations and also what modes of proof shall be admissible to add to or contradict the contents of the document. Where the document has probative value both according to the law governing the material validity of the act and according to the law of the place where it was executed, only the former of these two laws shall apply.

The provision on formal validity is unobjectionable and follows closely the rule which, it is probable, would be adopted in England.[44] It is possible that difficult problems of characterisation will arise since it is by no means clear in some cases whether a matter is one of form or of substance.[45] A consideration of the draft rules concerning presumption and method of proof is outside the scope of this paper, but perhaps it is worth pointing out that to extract certain procedural matters from the *lex fori* (but not other heads) and subject them to the *lex causae* may lead to unjust results, since procedural rules cannot be seen in isolation and ought to be viewed against a whole procedural system—to take one or two rules out of such system and put them into another system may deprive one or both of the parties of other safeguards which the former system provides.

9. SPECIFIC TYPES OF CONTRACT

The draft Convention deals specifically with employment contracts. Article 2 (3) provides that, in relations between employer and employee, the choice of law made by the parties shall in no case prejudice the operation of mandatory rules for the protection of the employee which are in force in the country in which he habitually carries out his work. Article 5 provides that in the absence of an express or implied choice of law, contracts of employment shall be governed by the law of the country (a) in which the employee habitually carries out his work or (b) in which the establishment

---

[44] *Dicey & Morris*, p. 771.
[45] Cf. French cases, cf. *Rev. Crit.* (1973), p. 58 and *Rev. Crit.* (1974), p. 498.

which engaged the employee is situated, if the employee does not habitually carry out his work in any one country, unless from circumstances as a whole it is clear that the contract of employment is more closely connected with another country.

The former provision is a specific example of what the draft Convention deals with in more general terms in Article 7, namely the mandatory effect of contracts other than the law chosen by the parties or the law with which the contract has its closest connection. Article 2 (3) mentions in this connection only mandatory rules in force in the country in which the employee habitually carries out his work. This is perhaps another example of the criticism which was directed above at Article 7, namely, that a most difficult problem is dealt with superficially. Other laws whose rules may have an equally immediate claim to recognition may be the law of the country in which the employer is situated or the law of the country in which the employment is actually taking place (which may not necessarily be the same as the country in which the employee habitually carries out his work). Thus in *Sayers* v. *International Drilling Company*,[46] the plaintiff was an English oil rig worker employed by a Dutch oil drilling company to work on a rig off the coast of Nigeria. The Court of Appeal held that the contract of employment was governed by Dutch law and that therefore the Law Reform (Personal Injuries) Act 1948, section 1 (3) did not apply. Article 2 (3) would lead to the same result since English law was neither the proper law nor was England the place in which the plaintiff could be said habitually to carry out his work.

The problems which arise from this type of situation cannot easily be resolved by the application of rules of private international law, and it is suggested that Article 2 (3) does not really assist their resolution.

Although Article 5 quite properly draws attention to two important factors in deciding on the applicable law of a contract of employment, it may be doubted whether it is appropriate to make the rules so definite. Once again, the place of habitual employment is not a very satisfactory test—if the place of employment is likely to be paramount (which it probably ought to be) surely a better test would be the law of the place where the parties contemplate that the employment will take place. This may of course be the place where the employee habitually carries out his work, but not necessarily so.[47]

The other references to specific types of contract call for little comment. Article 6, in relation to contracts whose subject matter is immovable

---

[46] [1971] 1 WLR 1176. See Collins (1972) 21 ICLQ 320 (ante, p. 393).

[47] On employment contracts generally, see, e.g., Kahn-Freund, 'Delictual Liability and the Conflict of Laws', (1968–II) *Hague Rec.* 1 at pp. 138–141; *J. Cl. de Droit International*, Fasc. 573 (Lyon-Caen); *International Encyclopedia of Comparative Law*, Vol. III, Private International Law (ed. Lipstein), Part 28, Labour Contracts (Gamillscheg).

property, provides that in the absence of an express or implied choice of law the contract shall be governed by the law of the place where the immovable property is situated, unless from the circumstances as a whole it is clear that the contract is more closely connected with another country. This is the same as the rule in English law. Articles 16 and 17 deal with the vexed question of the assignment of choses in action. The solution adopted in Article 16 is broadly in accordance with the views now prevailing in England, namely, that obligations as between the assignor and the assignee are governed by the proper law of the assignment and the law governing the chose in action determines its assignability, the relationship between the assignee and the debtor, and questions of priority. Article 17 provides that the transfer of a claim by operation of law is to be governed by the law of the juridical institution for the purposes of which that transfer was provided, but the law governing the original claim determines the assignability as well as the rights and obligations of the debtor.

10. CONCLUSIONS

This article has dealt with the provisions of the draft Convention dealing with contract, and not with those relating to quasi-contract and tort. In so far as it relates to contractual obligations, it is a first step in the right direction, subject to the following qualifications:

1. There must be some doubt whether the practical need for unification of this area justifies its being given priority, and this writer would welcome evidence of the difficulties to which the present situation in practice gives rise.

2. The unification of the rules of private international law by a treaty taking effect in public international law may limit the powers of domestic legislators more than is generally recognised, and more consideration has to be given to policy questions of internal law (especially, but by no means exclusively, in the field of employment contracts) than private international lawyers are equipped to give.

3. The draft Covention reaches results which are generally in line with international business practices, but at least two provisions seem to this writer to be defective: Article 4, on the method to be applied in isolating the system of law with which the contract is most closely connected, and Article 7, on the application of laws (other than the governing law) which have a connection with the contract.

XII

Floating Charges, Receivers and Managers and the Conflict of Laws

Interest in the topics dealt with in this article was stimulated by professional involvement in the insolvency of the Rolls-Royce aero-engine company in 1971, the forerunner of many modern international insolvencies. The analysis and conclusions in this article have been generally adopted: see Wood, *Law and Practice of International Finance* (1980), Chap. 15; Picarda, *Law Relating to Receivers, Managers and Administrative Receivers* (2nd ed., 1990), Chap. 40. Since it was written, the Insolvency Act 1986 has established the mutual recognition of receivers appointed in different parts of the United Kingdom. An important development was the introduction by the same legislation of the 'administrative receiver'. The administrative receiver is a receiver or manager of a company's property appointed by or on behalf of debenture holders under a charge. This status expands the powers of a purely contractual receiver, for example to obtain information about the affairs of the company from third parties.

In *Re International Bulk Commodities Ltd.* [1992] 3 WLR 328 a Liberian company traded in England, but did not register as a foreign company. It granted fixed and floating charges in favour of the London branch of a Swiss bank. The charges were created under an English-form debenture. When the company failed to repay loans, receivers were appointed. It was held that the receivers were to be regarded as administrative receivers under the 1986 Act, notwithstanding that the company was not formed and registered under the Companies Act 1985. That foreign element was not relevant where the company had granted a debenture secured by a floating charge in English form; where it had engaged in activities both in England and abroad; and was liable to be wound up by the English court. Accordingly, and this was the practical point in the case, the receivers were to be regarded as administrative receivers and therefore 'office holders' who were entitled to require information from the directors about the location of the company's accounts and assets.

The English court has recognised the receiver and manager of an Irish company appointed under an Irish debenture, and held that the receiver was entitled to funds held in a bank in London in priority to the rights of unsecured creditors who had obtained a *Mareva* injunction: *Cretanor Maritime Co. Ltd.* v. *Irish Marine Management Ltd.* [1978] 1 WLR 966 (CA). See also *Re Sorrel Resources Ltd.* (1987) 11 BCLR (2d) 184 (recognition of Alberta receiver and manager in British Columbia).

After more than 20 years it may be helpful to recall the Rolls-Royce case. By 1971 Rolls-Royce Limited was in financial difficulties as a result of its long-term

From *International and Comparative Law Quarterly*, 27 (1978), 691.

commitments to produce RB 211 engines for the Lockheed Tristar, and the board asked the trustees for the debenture stockholders to appoint a receiver and manager. The effect of the appointment of the receiver was to crystallize the floating charge contained in the debenture stock trust deeds, so that the whole of the assets of Rolls-Royce became subject to a fixed charge in favour of the debenture stockholders. At the time of the announcement, there was pending in the Commercial Court an action by two Californian companies against Rolls-Royce Limited for damages for repudiation of an alleged contract for the delivery of nickel by the Californian companies to Rolls-Royce. At the time of the announcement Rolls-Royce was a company in receivership with only faint prospects of unsecured creditors receiving any substantial dividend. In these circumstances, the receiver and the plaintiffs entered into negotiations for the settlement of the claim; the negotiations were concluded in February 1971, by the entry of a consent judgment in favour of the plaintiffs. A judgment debt against a company in receivership cannot be enforced in England against assets subject to a crystallized floating charge. A few weeks later the receiver learned that the judgment creditors (or their assignee) had commenced proceedings in New York, New Jersey, Delaware, California, France and Germany, to enforce the judgment. In each jurisdiction, assets of substantial value were attached by the judgment creditors.

An unsuccessful attempt was made to set aside the English judgment on the ground that one of the judgment creditors had ceased to exist prior to the entry of the judgment and that the judgment was therefore a nullity: *Mercer Alloys Corp.* v. *Rolls-Royce Ltd.* [1972] 1 All ER 211 (CA). The judgment creditors pressed ahead with the French proceedings in the hope of confirming registration of the English judgment in France and obtaining payment in full by execution against the French assets, which were debts due from French customers to Rolls-Royce. Under the Anglo-French Treaty for the Reciprocal Enforcement of Judgments of 1934 (now for almost all practical purposes superseded by the Brussels Convention of 1968), a certified copy of a judgment was deemed to be a judgment which was capable of execution in England as of the date of the certificate. In the French proceedings the judgment creditors had produced certificates of a Master of the Supreme Court certifying the original consent judgment. Rolls-Royce applied to the English court for an order setting aside the certificate, and obtained an *ex parte* order from the commercial judge that the judgment creditors be restrained from producing, relying or continuing to rely in the French proceedings on the Master's certificate. The parties agreed to use their best efforts to persuade the French court not to deliver judgment until the summons had been heard by the English judge and his decision indicated to the French court. But the summons was never heard and the French court never gave judgment because the parties entered into negotiations for the withdrawal of the attachment proceedings, and eventually entered into such an agreement. The judgment creditors eventually received payment in full, as did all other creditors of Rolls-Royce, in the liquidation.

It is likely that the French court would have decided in favour of the judgment creditors. This conclusion is supported by a subsequent decision of the French Cour de Cassation which, it seems, has received little attention outside France: *Soc. Interciné* v. *Davis*, French Cour de Cassation, 19 October 1977, noted Lagarde, 1977 Rev. Crit. 126 and 1978 Rev. Crit. 370, and Schapira, 1978 Clunet 617. In this case a Swiss company obtained an English judgment against its debtor, an English company; subsequently another creditor appointed a receiver over the English company, which had the effect of preventing any form of execution against property in England. The Swiss company then sought to enforce the English judgment in France. The receiver resisted on the ground that the judgment had been deprived of executory force in England following the crystallization of the floating charge. The French court held that the certificate of the English judgment showed that the judgment was enforceable and, accordingly, the judgment had to be enforced in France. In France this judgment has been taken to mean that an English floating charge will not be given effect by the French courts.

The increasing internationalisation of finance and business, coupled with the effects of economic recession, has made international insolvency law of great practical importance. In particular it has made the peculiarly English institution of the receiver and manager under a floating charge an international figure, both in his native guise and in the similar forms in the Commonwealth, and in particular in Canada and Australia. It is the purpose of this contribution to indicate some of the problems to which the institution of the floating charge and the position of a receiver and manager appointed under such a charge give rise in international transactions.[1]

I. THE FLOATING CHARGE AND THE RECEIVER AND MANAGER

A common method of securing the repayment of loans to companies in England, and those countries which have adopted the English system, is for the borrower to grant a floating charge over all its undertaking and assets. The essential characteristic of a 'floating' charge is that the company which grants it remains free to carry on its business and use its assets in the normal course of its business until the lender intervenes, by appointing a receiver or in certain other ways, to enforce his security. When the lender intervenes to appoint a receiver, the floating charge 'crystallises' and becomes a fixed charge on all the property and assets of the company at the time of the appointment of the receiver. As Lord Macnaghten said in *Governments Stock and Other Securities Investment Co. Ltd.* v. *Manila Railway Co. Ltd.*:

A floating security is an equitable charge on the assets for the time being of a going concern. It attaches to the subject charge in the varying condition in which it happens to be from time to time. It is of the essence of such a charge that it remains dormant until the undertaking charged ceases to be a going concern, or until the person in whose favour the charge is created intervenes. His right to intervene may

---

[1] *Kerr on Receivers* (15th ed., Walton, 1978) contains a short piece, at pp. 339–348, by Mr Muir Hunter, QC, on certain aspects of the extra-territorial effects of floating charges, which appeared after this article was substantially completed.

of course be suspended by agreement. But if there is no agreement for suspension, he may exercise his right whenever he pleases after default . . . During the period of grace, or until there is a winding up, the company are to be free to carry on their business; they are to carry it on as of right. When that period comes to an end, the charge will have its ordinary effect.[2]

In the vivid words of Lord Macnaghten in *Illingworth* v. *Houldsworth*[3] a floating charge is 'ambulatory and shifting in its nature, hovering over and so to speak floating with the property which it is intended to affect until some event occurs or some act is done which causes it to settle and fasten on the subject of the charge within its reach and grasp'.[4] The floating charge is a present charge (albeit not fixed) of property belonging to the company at the date of the creation of the debenture, and also a future charge of, or contract to grant a charge over, after-acquired property. In the case of book debts or accounts receivable, the charge operates by way of equitable assignment to the debenture-holder.[5]

When the creditors seek to enforce their security the normal method they use is to appoint a receiver and manager to act in substance on their behalf but in law as an agent for the company over whose assets the charge exists. In the normal case, the receiver and manager is not a court official. As Jenkins LJ put it in *Re B. Johnson & Co. (Builders) Ltd.*:

. . . a receiver and manager for debenture holders is a person appointed by the debenture holders to whom the company has given powers of management pursuant to the contract of loan constituted by the debenture, and, as a condition of obtaining the loan, to enable him to preserve and realise the assets comprised in the security for the benefit of the debenture holders. The company gets the loan on terms that the lenders shall be entitled, for the purpose of making their security effective, to appoint a receiver with powers of sale and of management pending sale, and with full discretion as to the exercise and mode of exercising those powers. The primary duty of the receiver is to the debenture holders and not to the company. He is receiver and manager of the property of the company for the debenture holders, not manager of the company.[6]

---

[2] [1897] AC 81 at p. 86.   [3] [1904] AC 355.
[4] At p. 358. See also *Evans* v. *Rival Granite Quarries Ltd.* [1910] 2 KB 979 at pp. 999–1001; Gore-Browne, *Companies* (43rd ed., 1977, para. 18–3). On the historical aspects, see Pennington, 'The Genesis of the Floating Charge' (1960) 23 MLR 630. See also Farrar, 'The Crystallisation of a Floating Charge' (1976) 40 Conv. (NS) 397.
[5] See, e.g., *Robbie* v. *Witney Warehouse Co. Ltd.* [1963] 1 WLR 1324 at p. 1337, *per* Russell LJ; *George Barker (Transport) Ltd.* v. *Eynon* [1974] 1 WLR 462 at p. 467, *per* Edmund-Davies LJ; *BCL* v. *Anglo-African Leasing Ltd.* [1977] 2 All ER 741 at p. 745, *per* Templeman J.
[6] [1955] Ch. 634 at pp. 661–662. On the distinction between receivers and managers who are court-appointed and those who are not, see *Kerr on Receivers, op. cit., supra,* n. 1 at p. 279. See also the judgment in the *Barcelona Traction* case (*Belgium* v. *Spain*) [1970] ICJ Rep. at p. 41, where the International Court of Justice said: 'In the present case, Barcelona Traction is in receivership in the country of incorporation. Far from implying the demise of

The function of the receiver and manager is to receive or recover the assets of the company and, in his capacity as manager, to carry on the business of the company with a view to realisation of the security. The assets may be saleable at a better price as a 'going-concern' business, and the receiver and manager may therefore carry on the business with the ultimate purpose of selling the business and its goodwill as well as the physical assets comprised in the charge. This operation may be financed by the debenture holders, or by the receiver himself (who is personally liable for any debts contracted by himself as receiver, and who may recoup himself out of the proceeds of sale).[7]

What, therefore, happens in practice is that when a substantial undertaking gets into financial difficulties the mortgage or debenture holders appoint a receiver and manager to manage the business, and collect its assets, often with a view to the sale of the business and undertaking for the benefit of the secured creditors. Because in law the crystallisation of the charge operates as the immediate creation of a fixed charge on the assets, unsecured creditors are not able to enforce their rights against the property of the company. Therefore under English law an unsecured creditor who obtains a judgment against the company cannot take steps to attach by judicial process a debt due to the company, because they have been assigned to the debenture holder,[8] nor levy execution on the goods of the company, because they have become subject to a fixed charge.[9]

The floating charge has, therefore, both a contractual and a proprietary aspect. The property comprised in the charge will normally consist of *all* of the property of the company, both present and future. That means that it will cover not only the property which the company has at the time of the creation of the charge (i.e. when the debenture is executed) but also all of the property which the company subsequently acquires. In practice, the

---

the entity or of its rights, this much rather denotes that those rights are preserved for so long as no liquidation has ensued. Though in receivership, the company continues to exist . . . In brief, a manager was appointed in order to safeguard the company's rights; he has been in a position directly or indirectly to uphold them. Thus, even if the company is limited in its activity after being placed in receivership, there can be no doubt that it has retained its legal capacity and that the power to exercise it is vested in the manager appointed by the Canadian courts.'

[7] See Companies Act 1948, s. 369. His rights of management may be effectively removed if the company goes into liquidation: *Gosling* v. *Gaskell* [1897] AC 575; *Sowman* v. *David Samuel Trust* [1978] 1 WLR 22.

[8] *Norton* v. *Yates* [1906] 1 KB 112; *Cairney* v. *Back* [1906] 2 KB 746. The precise effect of the assignment can give rise to practical difficulties with regard to the availability of set off: see cases cited *supra* in n. 4, and also *Handley Page Ltd.* v. *Customs and Excise Commissioners* [1970] 2 Lloyd's Rep. 459; *Rother Iron Works* v. *Canterbury Precision Engineers Ltd.* [1974] QB 1.

[9] *Davey & Co.* v. *Williamson & Son* [1898] 2 QB 194; *Geisse* v. *Taylor* [1905] 2 KB 658.

effect is that when the debenture holder enforces the charge, and it crystallises and becomes a fixed charge, the charge will fasten on all the property of the company at the date of crystallisation of the charge.

The property over which the floating charge will 'hover' and, if it is enforced, on which it will crystallise may consist of all, or most, of the following species of property: land and buildings, stock in trade, book debts or accounts receivable, industrial property (such as patents, trade marks, copyright), and other incorporeal property such as the goodwill of the business and the benefit of pending contracts. In conflict of laws terms the property may be immovable or movable, and, if movable, tangible or intangible. The property may all be in the State in which the company has its principal place of business, or if the company has any export or import business, both inside and outside the State of the centre of its activities.

The importance of the proprietary effect of a floating charge in the international context is illustrated by *The Cretan Harmony*.[10] In that case a Cypriot company sought and obtained a 'Mareva' injunction[11] against an Irish company, whereby the Irish company was restrained from removing or disposing of any assets out of the jurisdiction up to $700,000 pending arbitration between the parties, who were respectively owners and charterers of a ship. After the injunction had been granted, the dispute was settled and the charterers (the defendants) agreed to pay the owners $375,000 by instalments. The charterers, however, then defaulted in the payment of the instalments, and the owners obtained judgment against the charterers for the balance, but before the owners were able to execute their judgment on assets within the jurisdiction a receiver was appointed over the Irish company, pursuant to a power given in a debenture executed by it in 1974 granting a floating charge in favour of the Ulster Bank Ltd. to secure all moneys due or to become due to the bank. The charterers' only asset within the English jurisdiction was a sum of approximately £70,000 on deposit with the First National Bank. The receiver sought to have the Mareva injunction discharged so that he could recover the sum on deposit for the benefit of the debenture holder.

The Court of Appeal held that the debenture holder was entitled to the money. The Mareva injunction did not operate as an attachment or assignment; it was relief *in personam* and did not effect a seizure of the asset. It merely restrained the owner from dealing with the asset in certain ways. The receiver in his capacity as agent of the company was bound by

---

[10] *Sub nom. Cretanor Maritime Co. Ltd.* v. *Irish Marine Management Ltd.* [1978] 1 WLR 966 (CA).

[11] That is, an injunction restraining the defendants from removing or disposing of assets out of the jurisdiction pending resolution by the English court of the plaintiffs' claim against the defendants: see the review of this practice by the House of Lords in *The Siskina* [1979] AC 210.

the injunction, but the debenture holder was not so bound. The court assumed that the law of the Irish Republic relating to floating charges was the same as English law; that therefore the debenture created an immediate equitable charge over the assets of the charterers, wherever situated, subject to a power in the charterers, so long as the charge continued to float, to deal with their assets in the course of business as though the charge did not exist; while the charge continued to float, third parties dealing with the charterers in the course of their business could ignore it; but the appointment of the receiver crystallised the charge, that is, it put an end to the power under which, until that time, the charterers were able to deal with their assets in the course of their business as if no charge existed; the equitable assignment thereupon took complete and unqualified effect; the debenture holder became entitled to a fixed charge on the deposited fund in the English bank; the debenture holder was an equitable assignee, the injunction gave the owners no present right against the fund, and the rights of the owners as execution creditors would have to give way to the prior rights of the debenture holder.

The dual character, contractual and proprietary, of the floating charge is pervasive in the international context. Among the questions which arise are these: What law governs capacity to grant a floating charge? What is the governing law of the charge? To what property does it extend? What recognition will it be given abroad? Will the status of the receiver and manager be recognised abroad? It is the intention of this piece at least to draw attention to some possible answers to these difficult questions.

2. CAPACITY TO CREATE A FLOATING CHARGE

What law governs the capacity of a company to create a floating charge? A floating charge may be created by a company incorporated in a country whose law does not know the institution of the floating charge (such as France or Spain) or whose law is positively hostile to it, such as Scotland before 1961,[12] and the charge may extend to assets in a country which does recognise the floating charge.[13]

The answer to the question of capacity may depend on how the question

---

[12] See *Ballachulish Slate Quarries Co.* v. *Bruce* (1908) 16 SLT 48; *Carse* v. *Coppen*, 1951 SC 233; but see now Companies (Floating Charges and Receivers) (Scotland) Act 1972.

[13] The converse situation, the creation of a floating charge by a company whose country of incorporation does recognise the charge, over assets situate in a country which does not recognise it, does not raise a question of capacity. Thus in *Re Anchor Line (Henderson Brothers) Ltd.* [1937] Ch. 483, the question was whether effect should be given, in an English liquidation, to a floating charge executed in Scotland by an English company, in so far as the proceeds of sale of the company's property in the hands of the liquidator represented Scots property. It was held that effect should be given to the charge.

is framed. Is it a question of capacity to contract? Or of capacity to contract to grant a mortgage? Or of capacity to contract to grant a particular type of mortgage, i.e. a floating charge?

In *Carse* v. *Coppen*[14] a company registered in Scotland with a place of business and assets in England borrowed pursuant to a debenture executed in Scotland but in English form. The debenture created a floating charge over all its assets, i.e. it applied not only to its English assets but also to its Scots assets. The floating charge was 'utterly repugnant' to the principles of Scots law, and was not recognised as creating a security at all in Scotland, where the term 'equitable security' was meaningless.[15] It was therefore conceded that the debenture could not create a security over assets in Scotland, but the liquidator asked the Scots court whether the debenture had created a valid and effectual floating charge over other assets of the company in England.

The Court of Session held, by a majority (Lord Keith dissenting), that the company had not created a valid charge over the English assets. The court accepted that the judge at first instance, Lord Birnam, had been wrong in treating *Re Anchor Line (Henderson Brothers) Ltd.*[16] as authority for the proposition that the validity of such a floating charge depended on the law of incorporation, but held nevertheless that such a proposition represented the law of Scotland.

Lord President Cooper noted that a study of such authorities as Dicey, Foote, Cheshire and Westlake indicated that the theoretical problem was one of some difficulty, and that generalisation was 'now totally impracticable'; that distinctions were drawn in the literature between (i) universal or general assignments and (ii) specific or particular assignments, between assignments of corporeal and incorporeal property, between assignments of different types of incorporeal property, between different solutions for different types of question; that it was possible 'amid each and all of these bewildering permutations and combinations' to find good authority for the *lex domicilii*, the *lex situs* and the *lex actus*. He preferred to particularise the problem narrowly. The question arose in the liquidation of a Scots company and before a Scots court, and 'as granted, the floating charge was a universal or general assignment, and not limited to English assets nor to any specific or particular subjects, and it is as a universal assignment that its efficacy must be judged'.[17] He thought it of special significance that the company was a Scots company (and not a foreign company) because the Companies Act 1948, which applied both to England and Scotland, contained a number of special provisions relating to floating charges and receivers which were limited to English companies. He went on:

[14] 1951 SC 233. [15] 1951 SC at p. 239.
[16] [1937] Ch. 483. [17] At p. 241.

That all this protective machinery, contained in a statute applicable to both Scotland and England, should have been expressly confined to companies registered in England seems to me to be unthinkable except upon the view that companies registered in Scotland and subject to Scots law could not create floating charges. The law which determines the nature and extent of the powers of any corporation is the law of the country in which it is incorporated—in this case, Scots law . . .[18]

The answer given by Scots law, in colourful terms, was plain: the whole method of creating a floating charge was foreign to Scots law, and amounted to 'bungled conveyancing which has not successfully created any right of security in any part of the property, either in the uncalled capital or in anything else'.[19] The Lord President concluded:

I am accordingly prepared to affirm that, when the Scottish courts are asked by the liquidator of a Scottish company to state what effect he is to give to a universal assignment of the company's undertaking, property and assets by way of a floating charge, the answer is 'None'. The law of Scotland does not empower Scottish corporations to create securities by such methods, which, in the words of Lord Dunedin, are to us 'absolutely unmeaning'. The matter is dealt with on similar lines in Graham Stewart on *Diligence* with reference to 'universal assignments', to which I equate a floating charge. Moreover the Scottish courts, or a liquidator acting under their direction, have no means of applying English equity *in personam* for the enforcement of an 'equitable charge'.[20]

In *Carse* v. *Coppen* the floating charge extended to all of the property of the Scots company in both Scotland and England, but the Lord President considered, *obiter*, what the position would have been had the floating charge been limited, in terms, to property in England, and concluded that his line of reasoning would have led to the same result, 'upon the view that Scottish companies cannot create floating charges'. On this question, Lord Carmont suggested that, if there appeared in the memorandum of the company a general power to charge the company's assets in England, this power might be held to justify the execution in England of a floating charge over assets in England. But Lord Carmont did not commit himself to such a view, and Lord Russell reserved his opinion on the validity and effect of a charge limited to assets outside Scotland.

Lord Keith dissented on the ground that the validity of the charge depended on English law. The reasoning which led to that conclusion was as follows:

1. The debentures were not universal assignments. They were acknowledgements of debt with an undertaking to pay principal and interest and containing a charge of the whole of the company's assets

---

[18] *Ibid.*
[19] Lord Kinnear in *Ballachulish Slate Quarries Co.* v. *Bruce* (1908) 16 SLT 48 at pp. 51–52.
[20] At p. 242.

by way of security. These were not universal assignments, of which examples were sequestration or transmission by death, but the creation of a charge, albeit over all the assets of the company.

2. The debentures were executed in Scotland and complied with all the formalities of execution in Scotland.

3. There was nothing in the memorandum of the company which made the documents *ultra vires*.

4. Whether the debenture holder obtained a title to assert his rights over the assets of the company in England depended on the law of England where the assets were situated.

5. The omission of any reference in the sections of the Companies Act 1948 dealing with floating charges and receivers to companies registered in Scotland could yield no inference that the legislature intended that a floating charge could not be created by a Scots company over assets situated in a country where the law recognised that type of security.

It is plain from the judgments of Lord President Cooper and Lord Keith that the essential difference between them was whether the floating charge was a type of universal assignment. If it is so regarded then it is much easier to reach the conclusion that its validity depends on the law of domicile, by analogy with the rules relating to bankruptcy and liquidation.[21] But it suggested that the Scots court was over-influenced by the concept of universal succession which is derived by Scots law from Roman law. The essence of the idea of universal succession is that the successor steps into the shoes of the predecessor. Lord Keith of Avonholm, in *National Bank of Greece and Athens SA* v. *Metliss*,[22] described the conception of universal succession as being common to legal systems which have borrowed from Roman law, and went on:

Used generally with reference to an heir who takes up a succession on death, it carries with it a liability on the heir to the deceased's creditors for the deceased's debts. From this aspect he represents the deceased. The *persona* of the deceased is regarded as continued in the heir, or, as it is otherwise expressed, he is *eadem persona cum defuncto* . . . The term 'universal successor' may be foreign to English law but it cannot be regarded as strange in this House for the doctrine is part of the common law of Scotland, though now affected by statute, and till within the last hundred years had important consequences to the heir in a succession . . . I would quote only one short passage from Stair, III. 4.23: 'Heirs in law are called universal successors, *quia succedunt in universum jus quod defunctus habuit*, they do wholly

---

[21] See Dicey and Morris, *Conflict of Laws* (9th ed., 1973), pp. 691 and 716.

[22] [1958] AC 509 at p. 530. See also Denning LJ and Parker LJ in the Court of Appeal [1957] 2 QB 33 at pp. 42–43 and 51–52. On universal succession in the conflict of laws see also Cheatham, 'The Statutory Successor, the Receiver and the Executor in Conflict of Laws' (1944) 44 Col. L. Rev. 549.

represent the defunct, and are as one person with him, and so they do both succeed to him active, in all the rights belonging to him, and passive, in all the obligations and debts due by him'.

Even if a trustee in bankruptcy may be regarded for certain purposes as a successor, a receiver or debenture holder is, it is submitted, not a successor. From the time of the creation of the charge until its crystallisation, the company still has full rights to deal with its property and manage its business. In the normal case, the charge will not crystallise and the company will repay its debts. Even where it defaults, and the charge crystallises, and even where the company is hopelessly insolvent, the company retains its equity of redemption, and is theoretically entitled to receive the proceeds of sale after satisfaction of the amounts owed to the debenture holder.[23]

A floating charge, even when it has crystallised, is no more than a peculiarly sophisticated form of mortgage, and should not be regarded as a universal assignment.

It is suggested that, although the capacity of a corporation is determined by the law of incorporation, it does not follow that the law of incorporation must know (or even recognise) the concept of the floating charge. Thus, Spanish law may not have any institution resembling the floating charge in its law, and yet Spanish companies have power to enter into contracts and give mortgages over their assets. It should follow, therefore, that a Spanish company may validly contract under English law to grant a floating charge over its English assets. The proper approach, therefore, should be to consider whether the company has power to contract to grant a mortgage under the law of its incorporation ,and then to test the validity and effect of any exercise of that power by reference to the *lex situs*.[24]

3. THE GOVERNING LAW OF THE CHARGE

By the expression 'the governing law of the charge' is meant the law which governs its contractual aspects. By the English rules of the conflict of laws, the contractual aspects of a mortgage are governed by the proper law of the contract of mortgage and not by the *lex situs* of the property. Thus if a contract of mortgage is governed by English law, the English court will enforce it *in personam* even if it is not an effective charge by the *lex situs*.[25]

---

[23] On the position of the directors after a receiver and manager is appointed see *Newhart Developments Ltd.* v. *Co-operative Commercial Bank Ltd.* [1978] QB 814 (CA).

[24] It is now possible for a Scots company to create a floating charge, which since 1961 has been recognised in Scots law (see Companies (Floating Charges and Receivers) (Scotland) Act 1972) but *Carse* v. *Coppen* remains an authority in Scotland on the common law position. See also Anton, *Private International Law* (1967), pp. 256–257.

[25] *British South Africa Co.* v. *De Beers Consolidated Gold Mines Ltd.* [1910] 2 Ch. 502; [1912] AC 52; *Re Smith* [1916] 2 Ch. 206.

Increasingly the modern practice has been to include express choices of law in debentures, and it would require very unusual circumstances for an express choice of law not to be effective. If there is no express choice of law, then the proper law will be the system of law with which the contract has its closest and most real connection.[26] In the case of a floating charge given by an English company over all its undertaking and assets, in the usual English form, it will be difficult to resist the conclusion that the proper law is English law.

In *Re Anchor Line (Henderson Brothers) Ltd.*[27] a shipping company, registered in England, had its head office in Glasgow, Scotland, where a considerable part of its business was carried on. When it got into financial difficulties, the company granted, by a document executed in Scotland, a floating charge in favour of the Union Bank of Scotland. The charge was in English form and was registered in the Companies Registry in London. Luxmoore J. held:

In form the charge is substantially an English debenture with the usual floating charge. Such a charge is unknown to the law of Scotland. It was given by an English company and although it was executed in Scotland it must I think be construed according to English law.[28]

4. THE SCOPE OF THE CHARGE

An important question which is likely to arise in an international context is whether the charge or mortgage is intended to, and does, apply to property outside the State in which the borrower has its principal place of business, say, England. This question must be distinguished sharply from the question whether other countries would recognise the charge as having extra-territorial effect. If, by its terms, or by implication, the charge is not intended to have extra-territorial effect, then the latter question is hardly likely to arise.

Although it is quite possible for an English debenture to be limited to property in England, usually the floating charge covers the property and assets of the borrower, both present and future, and wherever situate. It is well settled in English law that such a change extends to property and assets of the company abroad. In *British South Africa Co.* v. *De Beers Consolidated Mines Ltd.*[29] Swinfen Eady J. held that an English debenture purporting to charge by way of floating security all the property and assets of an English company amounted, where the English company possessed land abroad, to an agreement to charge that land, which was a valid

---

[26] See Dicey and Morris, *op. cit.*, *supra*, n. 20, at p. 742.   [27] [1937] Ch. 483.
[28] At p. 487.
[29] [1910] 1 Ch. 353 at p. 387 (reversed on other grounds [1912] AC 52).

equitable security by English law. That decision was followed in *Re Anchor Line (Henderson Brothers) Ltd.*[30] by Luxmoore J. in a decision which illustrates strikingly the distinction between the question whether by English law a charge extends to property abroad, and the question whether the foreign country in which the property is situate will recognise the charge. It has already been seen[31] that in that case an English shipping company which owned property in Scotland executed a floating charge in Scotland in favour of a Scots bank over all its undertaking and property and assets. The charge was registered in England, but at that time Scots law did not recognise a floating charge, which was unknown to the law of Scotland and repugnant to it. The company went into liquidation, its assets were sold and the proceeds of sale were left in the hands of the liquidator in England. The question before the court was whether in the distribution of the assets of the company effect should be given to the floating charge executed in Scotland in so far as the proceeds of sale represented property in Scotland. It was held, as shown in the preceding section, that the charge was governed by English law because in form it was substantially an English debenture with the usual floating charge and was given by an English company. The judge further held:

When an English company possesses land abroad and purports to charge it by way of floating charge, the charge, putting it at its lowest, amounts to an agreement to charge that land, and is a valid equitable security according to English law.[32]

Luxmoore J. held, therefore, that the proceeds of sale of the property of the company expressed to be subject to the floating charge, including the proceeds of sale of property in Scotland, were payable to the mortgage holder.[33]

5. FOREIGN EFFECTS OF THE FLOATING CHARGE

In the preceding section it was shown that in general an English floating charge of the property and assets of an English company, wherever situate, will be effective under English law to grant a charge of property situate abroad. But it does not follow that the charge will be entitled to or obtain recognition abroad. The notion of the floating charge may be repugnant to

[30] [1937] Ch. 483.   [31] *Supra*, text at n. 25.   [32] At pp. 487–488.
[33] But see Lord Keith in *Carse* v. *Coppen*, 1951 SC 233 at pp. 247–248 for the view that Luxmoore J. in *Re Anchor Line* had failed to give effect to the then s. 270 of the Companies Act 1929 (now s. 327 of the Companies Act 1948). Cf. *Re Commonwealth Agricultural Services Engineers Ltd.* [1928] SASR 343. In that case a South Australian company executed a floating charge over all its assets, some of which were situate in Queensland where the charge was not effective because not registered. The charge was held to apply to funds in South Australia representing the proceeds of Queensland assets.

the law of the place where the assets of the company are situate. Thus it was conceded by the parties in *Carse* v. *Coppen*[34] and accepted by all the judges that because the floating charge was at that time repugnant to Scots law the charge could not in any event be effective as regards Scots property. The present position appears to be, although the matter is not free from doubt, that the appointment of a receiver under a floating charge granted by an English company operates as an attachment on Scots property.[35]

A frequent case in practice is where the *lex situs* of property included in the charge requires registration. Under English law, a floating charge is void against the liquidator and any creditor of the company unless it has been registered at the Companies Registry pursuant to section 95 (2) (*f*) of the Companies Act 1948. Is further registration in every country in which the company is likely to have assets necessary if the charge is to be fully effective? Many systems of law require registration of a charge over local assets, or at any rate over assets of a company which carries on business within the relevant jurisdiction, notwithstanding that the charge might have been registered in the country of incorporation of the company granting it. Gower, therefore, rightly warns[36] that floating charges on the assets of English companies with property abroad should comply with the registration requirements of foreign countries where the assets are situate, and section 95 (4) of the Companies Act 1948 envisages that in the case of charges created and registered in the United Kingdom 'further proceedings may be necessary to make the charge valid or effectual according to the law of the country in which the property is situate'. Whether registration will be necessary will depend upon what domestic registration requirements, if any, apply to cases with a foreign element, and, if so, what conflict of laws rules are applicable. In England the only floating charges which have to be registered are those by companies incorporated in England, or those which are charges on property in England created by, or acquired by, a company incorporated outside England which has an established place of business in England.[37]

In the United States, the Uniform Commercial Code, in its revised form (adopted in a number of States, including New York), contains complex provisions dealing with the perfection of security interests in multiple State transactions. At the risk of over-simplification, section 9–102 of the Code may be summarised as follows:

---

[34] 1951 SC 233. See also Anton, *op. cit. supra*, n. 22, at pp. 406–407.

[35] See *Gordon Anderson (Plant) Ltd.* v. *Campsie Construction Ltd.*, 1977 SLT 7, noted in [1977] JBL 160; s. 7 of the Administration of Justice Act 1977.

[36] Gower, *Modern Company Law* (3rd edn., 1969), pp. 426–427.

[37] Companies Act 1948, s. 106.

1. Perfection of security interests in goods (other than mobile goods such as motor vehicles and construction machinery) depends on the place where the goods were when 'the last event occurs on which is based the assertion that the security interest is perfected or unperfected'.

2. Perfection of security interests in debts and mobile goods depends on the law (including the conflict of laws rules) of the jurisdiction in which the debtor (that is, the mortgagor) is located. If the debtor is located in a jurisdiction which is not a part of the United States, and which does not provide for perfection of the security interest by registration in that jurisdiction, the law of the jurisdiction in the United States in which the debtor has its major executive office in the United States governs the effect of perfection or non-perfection through registration. Alternatively, if the debtor is located in a jurisdiction which is not a part of the United States or Canada and the security is accounts receivable, the security interest may be perfected by notification to the account debtor.

The effect of these complex provisions appears to be that if a floating charge is granted by, say, an English company or a Canadian company and is registered in England or Canada, as the case may be, then no further registration or filing is necessary to make it effective as against intangible property such as book debts situate in New York.[38]

Although as a matter of general principle the proprietary effects of a charge are governed by the *lex situs* of the property at the time when the charge is created the mandatory provisions of the law of the State where the charge comes to be enforced must be complied with. The latter may well be the same as the law of the State where the property is situate at the time of creation of the charge, but the property may move to another State at a later stage. This is what happened in *Luckins* v. *Highway Motel (Caernarvon) Pty. Ltd.*[39] In that case, a company incorporated in Victoria gave a floating charge over the whole of its undertaking, property and assets whatsoever and wheresoever, both present and future. The charge was registered in Victoria, but not in Western Australia. The company had no office or place of business in Western Australia, but it operated tourist passenger buses, some of which travelled through Western Australia, although none of the tours started or finished in Western Australia. But when its bus tours passed through Western Australia, the company incurred debts in Western Australia for food, accommodation and camping

---

[38] *Kerr on Receivers, op. cit. supra*, n. 1, at p. 341, states that UK floating charges not registered in the United States will be invalid as against creditors claiming assets situate in the United States, but appears to have overlooked ss. 9–10.

[39] (1975) 133 CLR 164.

fees. The debenture holder appointed a receiver and manager of the undertaking and assets of the company, and the question arose in the Western Australian courts as to whether the receiver was entitled to take possession of a bus owned by the company which was then situate in Western Australia or whether another unsecured creditor who had obtained judgment against the company could take it in execution. The case was complicated by the fact that there was no evidence as to whether the bus was present in Western Australia (or some other place) either at the date of the creation of the charge in 1973 or at the date of the crystallisation of the charge in 1974.

The High Court of Australia, on appeal from the Western Australian courts, held that the charge was ineffective in Western Australia. Gibbs J. said, in relation to the argument of the receiver and manager, that if a charge over the bus was lawfully created in 1973 in the place where the bus was then situate, the charge ought to be recognised in Western Australia:

It may be accepted, although there is not a great deal of authority on the point, that in general the validity of a charge on chattels is to be determined in accordance with the law of the place where the chattels are situated when the charge is created . . .—although perhaps it could be suggested that the validity of a floating charge should be determined by the laws of the place where the assets were situated when the charge crystallizes. It may also be accepted that if the bus had been validly subjected to a charge in Victoria, the debenture holder in whose favour the charge was given would not lose his rights simply because the bus was moved from Victoria to Western Australia . . .[40]

But the question of the *situs* of the property was not sufficient to dispose of the matter, even if the evidence as to its *situs* had been clear, since the effect of the Western Australian companies legislation was that certain charges had to be registered in Western Australia. In default of registration they were void, and the relevant legislation applied to a foreign company which had a place of businesss or was 'carrying on business within' Western Australia. By a majority, the High Court of Australia held that the company was carrying on business in Western Australia because of the debts it incurred there for food, accommodation and camping fees in connection with the bus tours which it was conducting. The court further held that, although the legislation did not apply to a charge on property outside Western Australia, it did apply to the bus in question, although the members of the court differed on their reasons for this conclusion, some taking the position that the question whether the charge was on property outside the State depended on the terms of the charge, and others that it depended on the actual location of the relevant assets at any time.

Thus, even if the charge was valid by the law of the place where the property originally was, the mandatory provisions of the place where the

[40] At pp. 174 to 175.

charge was sought to be enforced had to be complied with. As Gibbs J. put
it:

> . . . it is within the competence of the legislature of Western Australia to enact that
> a charge on goods within the State, even if valid elsewhere, shall be void unless the
> requirements laid down by that legislature have been complied with . . . [T]he case
> depends on whether . . . the Act, on its proper construction, made the registration
> of the charge in Western Australia essential to its validity as a security over chattels
> in Western Australia.[41]

Stephen J. put the policy behind the decision that the Western Australia
legislation applied to render the charge void as follows:

> A contrary view would distort the operation of the [legislation]; in the case of a
> floating charge, the [legislation] would then afford no protection in the perhaps not
> uncommon situation of credit dealings being had in State A with a foreign company
> which, having originally only assets in State B, at that time charged its assets
> wherever situate, and has thereafter extended its business into State A and
> acquired assets there. Floating charges are by no means uncommon, whether to
> secure bank overdraft accommodation or for other purposes, and were [the
> legislation] to be given other than an ambulatory interpretation it would constitute
> a trap rather than a safeguard; a search within State A of the register of such a
> registered foreign company would disclose no charges although in fact all its assets
> in State A were subject to a floating charge . . . It is not unreasonable that a
> mortgagee, relying for his security on a floating charge over moveables or over
> assets to be acquired by the mortgagor in the future, should ensure that, whatever
> State in the future those assets move to or be located in, his charge is there
> registered so that those who may deal with the mortgagor can ascertain its true
> position as to encumbrances over assets.[42]

6. PROCEEDINGS BY UNSECURED CREDITORS IN FOREIGN COUNTRIES

Unsecured creditors may seek to enforce their claims abroad against the
property of a company which has charged all its assets to a debenture
holder in the hope that they may defeat the rights of debenture holders in a
country, which for one reason or another, does not recognise the rights of
the debenture holders.[43] The *lex situs* may not recognise the rights of the

---

[41] At p. 175.

[42] At pp. 184–186. For a similar result see *Hockey* v. *Mother O'Gold Consolidated Mines Ltd.* (1903) 29 VLR 196; *Re Australian Life and General Assurance Co. Ltd.* [1931] VLR 317. Cf. *Re Interview Ltd.* [1975] IR 382.

[43] *Kerr on Receivers, op. cit. supra*, n. 1, at pp. 343–347, contains an account of the litigation in the Rolls-Royce receivership in 1971 which involved such an attempt. Since both the author of that section of Kerr and the writer of this article were involved professionally in that litigation, it would not be appropriate to say more than that this writer disagrees in a number of details with the account given there. Cf. *Mercer Alloys Corporation* v. *Rolls-Royce Ltd.* [1972] 1 All ER 211.

debenture holders for a variety of reasons. Thus in *Luckins* v. *Highway Motel* (*Caernarvon*) *Pty. Ltd.*[44] the charge, even though it may have been valid by the *lex situs* at the time the charge was created, or at any rate crystallised, was void because it was not registered under the law of the place where the property came to be and where unsecured creditors sought execution. Or the *lex fori*/*lex situs* may not recognise the existence of the charge. Thus until 1961, the law of Scotland not only did not know the concept of the floating charge in its domestic law, but also refused to give any effect in relation to property in Scotland to a form of floating charge executed in England and governed by English law.[45]

If the debenture holder is unable to persuade the court that, even if the floating charge is unknown to its law, its real nature is that of an agreement to charge property which only becomes fully effective on crystallisation, and therefore the conflict rules relevant to assignments and mortgages are applicable, is there anything that the security holder can do to prevent unsecured creditors from exercising their rights of execution against the property situate abroad? A similar problem arises in company liquidations. When a company goes into liquidation, English law provides that no action or proceeding shall be proceeded with or commenced against the company except by leave of the court.[46] The orderly distribution of assets can be interfered with if creditors seek to commence proceedings in foreign countries in the hope that they can obtain judgment and execute against foreign assets in priority to other creditors. In the context of liquidation, it has been held that provisions such as these do not apply in principle to proceedings in foreign courts,[47] although the court will restrain proceedings in Scotland or Northern Ireland[48] and there is equitable jurisdiction *in personam* over a foreigner under which proceedings in a foreign court may be restrained in exceptional circumstances.[49]

In *Re Maudslay, Sons & Field*,[50] an English company had given a floating charge over all its undertaking and property, and receivers were appointed by the English court upon the application of the debenture holders. Among the assets of the company were moneys due to them from a French company. An English creditor of the company, the holder of a dishonoured acceptance, sought to attach in France the debt due from the

---

[44] (1975) 133 CLR 164.

[45] See *Carse* v. *Coppen*, 1951 SC 233, and § II *supra*.

[46] See s. 231 of the Companies Act 1948.

[47] See *Re Oriental Inland Steam Co.* (1874) 9 Ch. App. 557; *Re Vocalion* (*Foreign*) *Ltd.* [1932] 2 Ch. 196.

[48] See *Re International Pulp and Paper Co.* (1876) 3 Ch. D. 549; *Re Dynamics Corporation of America* [1972] 3 All ER 1046.

[49] See *Re Vocalion* (*Foreign*) *Ltd.* [1932] 2 Ch. 196 at p. 209. The creditor may be put to his election between proving in the liquidation and continuing with his foreign proceedings.

[50] [1900] 1 Ch. 602.

French company to the company in receivership. The debenture holders sought, in the English court, to restrain the English creditor from attaching or otherwise attempting to obtain payment of the moneys due to the company in receivership from the French company. The question for Cozens-Hardy J. was whether the English court could interfere with the rights of creditors, English or otherwise, from pursuing any remedies available to them in foreign courts. The uncontested evidence of French law was that the debt could have been assigned or charged, but that to be effective as against third parties (including creditors) the assignment or charge had to be in writing, the charge had to be registered in France, and that formal notice in writing of the assignment or charge after such registration should have been served on the debtor (namely the French company) by an officer of the French court. No such registration or notice had been effected. Cozens-Hardy J. started with the proposition that it was plain, according to English law, that the debenture holders had, by contract with the company, a charge upon all its assets, including the French debt, and put the main question as follows:

Does the existence of this charge, which is undoubtedly valid according to English law, entitle the debenture-holders to prevent the claimants, who are unsecured creditors and not debenture-holders, from asserting and enforcing the rights that are given to them by French law against this French debt?[51]

He held that the answer was in the negative, following *Liverpool Marine Credit Co.* v. *Hunter*[52] where it was held that the mortgagees of a ship were not entitled, by proceedings in England, to prevent an English unsecured creditor of the ship owner from arresting the ship at New Orleans, the law of Louisiana declining to recognise the mortgage. It followed, therefore, that the attachment of the French debt by the unsecured creditors prevailed over the assignment under English law to the debenture holders following the crystallisation of the charge, because the debt was situate in France and the *lex situs* did not recognise the assignment pursuant to the crystallisation, in view of the lack of registration and notice. The appointment of the receiver did not affect the position. The receiver was not put in possession of the foreign property by the mere order of the court since something else had to be done and until that had been done in accordance with the foreign law, no person who took proceedings in the foreign country was guilty of a contempt either on the ground of interfering with the receiver's possession or otherwise. The judge concluded that it could not be reasonable that he should deprive English creditors of a right against French assets which French creditors undoubtedly enjoyed. The principle of this case is that, at any rate if the charge is not valid by foreign

---

[51] At p. 609.   [52] (1867) LR 4 Eq. 62; (1868) 3 Ch. App. 479.

law, then the debenture holders cannot restrain, by proceedings in the English courts, an unsecured creditor from pursuing whatever remedies may be available to him in the foreign court.

As his name implies, the receiver and manager has a dual status. As receiver, his duty is to get in the assets of the company in receivership, and as manager to manage its affairs and business with a view, in a favourable case, to turning the business around and making it profitable and solvent again, or, in the more usual case, with a view to its ultimate sale, as a going concern. A receiver and manager appointed out of court by the debenture holders is usually (as a result of express provision in the debenture) deemed to be the agent of the company and his powers supersede those of the Board. Actions to recover the property of the company are brought by the receiver acting in the name of the company.[53]

The status of a receiver and manager is complicated in foreign countries by two factors. Firstly, in some countries the status of a receiver and manager will be so foreign as to be difficult for the local courts to comprehend and, secondly, in others the expression 'receiver' will bear a connotation different from that of the English receiver and manager. If the true character of the English receiver and manager is given full effect, namely, that in substance he is an officer of the company, his powers and capacity to act should depend on the law of the State of incorporation, e.g. England.[54] This was the effect of the decision of the High Court in Ontario in *Re C. A. Kennedy & Co. Ltd.*[55] although the reasoning in that decision leaves something to be desired.

In that case company A, an English company, gave an English bank a floating charge over all its assets. One of its assets was a debt due from company B, a company incorporated in Ontario. Company C, incorporated under the laws of the Dominion of Canada and with its principal place of business in Quebec, was a creditor of company A which, after obtaining judgment against company A in Ontario, sought to attach the debt due from company B to company A. The question for the Ontario divisional court was whether the receiver on behalf of the bank, or company C, took precedence in relation to the debt due to company A from company B. There was no question as to the proper registration of the floating charge,

---

[53] *M. Wheeler & Co.* v. *Warren* [1928] 1 Ch. 840; *Gough's Garages* v. *Pugsley* [1930] 1 KB 615; *Newhart Developments Ltd.* v. *Co-operative Commercial Bank Ltd.* [1978] 2 WLR 636.
[54] See *Kerr on Receivers, op. cit. supra,* n. 1, at p. 411, for the recommendations regarding recognition of receivers of the Advisory Committee on the EEC draft Bankruptcy Convention.   [55] (1976) 14 OR (2d) 439.

since it was accepted there was no statutory provision in Ontario for registration of the floating charge executed in England. The only question was whether the Ontario courts should recognise and give effect to the priority which the bank, through the receiver, had in England in relation to the debt due from company B. The court accepted evidence that under English law the benefit of that debt was assigned in equity to the debenture holder upon crystallisation of the floating charge. It was accepted that the relative right of competing claimants to a debt were to be determined in priority in accordance with *lex situs* of the debt.

The court went on to hold that the Ontario courts would recognise the appointment of a receiver in a foreign jurisdiction. The precedents relied on[56] were essentially bankruptcy cases, and not cases of a receiver and manager appointed out of court under a debenture, but the court relied on them to reject the argument of the local unsecured creditor that the Ontario courts should follow the approach of the American courts, namely, that they would not enforce a voluntary assignment to the prejudice of their own citizens who may have demands against the assignor.[57] The Ontario court said:

The position taken by various American courts in regard to the rights of a foreign receiver seems parochial in the extreme. It means that in a contest between a receiver appointed in Detroit, Hull or Winnipeg and an Ontario creditor as to which should have priority in regard to an Ontario asset of an insolvent, the receiver might lose, while if the same contest were between a receiver appointed in Windsor, Ottawa or Kenora the receiver might win. No precedent has been brought to our attention that would force us to adopt the American approach. In the absence of such precedent we choose to follow what we consider to be the English rule that complete recognition be given to an assignment to a receiver made in a foreign jurisdiction.[58]

There is no doubt that English-style receivers and managers find it hard to convince American lawyers and courts that their powers should be recognised. This is, firstly, because of the unusual character of a receiver and manager under English law and the consequent confusion by the American legal system of the English institution with a court-appointed receiver in a bankruptcy proceeding. Secondly, even in the case of court-appointed receivers, a foreign receiver is only permitted to maintain an action in most American courts if such an action does not prejudice the interests of local creditors.[59]

[56] *Re ITT* (1975) 58 DLR (3d) 55; *Macaulay* v. *Guaranty Trust Co. of New York* (1927) 44 TLR 99; *Dulaney* v. *Merry & Son* [1901] 1 KB 536; *Re Anderson* [1911] 1 KB 896; *Williams* v. *Rice and Rice Knitting Mills Limited* [1926] 2 WLR 192.

[57] On recognition by United States courts of foreign liquidators and trustees in bankruptcy see Leflar, *American Conflicts Law* (3rd ed. 1977) pp. 433–441; *Clarkson Co. Ltd.* v. *Shaheen*, 544 F. 2d 624 (2nd circuit, 1976).   [58] At pp. 447–448.

[59] See *Restatement Second, Conflict of Laws*, para. 406, comment (a).

A more liberal approach has recently been exhibited by a federal court in California in *Clarkson Co. Ltd. and Rapid Data Corporation* v. *Rockwell International Corporation.*[60] The facts were as follows. In 1973 Rapid Data Corporation, a Canadian company, borrowed a substantial sum from the Bank of Montreal and the First National City Bank of New York and granted the Bank of Montreal a floating charge over all its property and assets to secure both loans; in January 1974 an unsecured creditor filed a bankruptcy petition against Rapid Data and Clarkson were appointed interim receiver in bankruptcy, but the petition was subsequently withdrawn. Meanwhile the Bank of Montreal appointed Clarkson as receiver and manager under the debenture.

Rapid Data had a claim against the defendants, Rockwell, for damages for alleged breach of a contract to supply calculator components, and in 1976 Clarkson, as receiver, and Rapid Data commenced proceedings against Rockwell in the California court. Rockwell contested the capacity of each of the plaintiffs to sue. First, as regards Rapid Data, it was argued that the appointment of a receiver and manager with full authority to run the business as well as plenary power over the mortgaged property, i.e. all Rapid Data's property, deprived Rapid Data of capacity to sue. Although the court recognised that the appointment of the receiver and manager paralysed the company's power to deal with the property and carry on its business, the company was both a proper and necessary party because it was in any event entitled to any recovery in excess of the amount owed to the banks, and its right to sue had not been terminated by the appointment of a receiver.

As regards the capacity of Clarkson, the receiver and manager, to sue, the court held that the question of capacity of any entity acting as representative is governed by the law of the State in which the court presides but seemed in fact to look primarily to Canadian law to hold as follows:

1. The assignment by Rapid Data to the bank·contained in the floating charge was by way of security.
2. It was inconceivable that the assignment of a claim as security for a debt could deprive the secured party of the right, recognised by Canadian law, to pursue the claim through a privately-appointed receiver.
3. There was no showing that the assignment deprived Clarkson of capacity under Canadian law.
4. The private receiver was a legal status unknown in the United States.
5. Receivers appointed by foreign courts were generally permitted to sue in California as a matter of comity, provided that the rights of

[60] 441 F. Supp. 792 (ND Cal. 1977).

local creditors were not prejudiced and there was no conflict with the public policy of California.

6. Although Clarkson, as private receiver, were appointed by private parties pursuant to contract, they nevertheless asserted a status created by the laws of a foreign jurisdiction, and recognition of such entities for purposes of suit in Californian courts must also be a matter of comity.

7. There was no prejudice to local creditors and the fact that bankruptcy proceedings in California might afford (Canadian) creditors greater protection than a receivership under Canadian law did not justify a refusal to countenance an action on grounds of public policy 'unless enforcement of the foreign right would be prejudicial to recognised standards of morality or to the general interests of California citizens'. The differences between United States and Canadian law were hardly sufficient to warrant dismissal on any ground of public policy.[61]

In effect, therefore, the Californian court proceeded by way of Californian law as the *lex fori* governing procedural matters (that is, who could sue in a representative capacity) to the law of incorporation in order to find who was the appropriate representative under the law governing the status of the company in receivership. Provided that the first step is essentially formal, this approach seems unobjectionable and is in line with the submission made earlier that the powers of the receiver and manager *quo* officer of the company depend upon the law of incorporation.

---

[61] The court was troubled by the fact that the banks, holders of the debenture, were not parties, but accepted letters from the banks, ratifying the action and agreeing to be bound by the result, as sufficient.

INDEX